Communicating at Work

Principles and Practices for Business and the Professions

Ninth Edition

Ronald B. Adler
Santa Barbara City College

Jeanne Marquardt Elmhorst
Central New Mexico Community College

Boston Burr Ridge, IL Dubuque, IA Madison, WI New York San Francisco St. Louis
Bangkok Bogotá Caracas Kuala Lumpur Lisbon London Madrid Mexico City
Milan Montreal New Delhi Santiago Seoul Singapore Sydney Taipei Toronto

Higher Education

COMMUNICATING AT WORK: PRINCIPLES AND PRACTICES FOR BUSINESS AND THE PROFESSIONS

Published by McGraw-Hill, a business unit of The McGraw-Hill Companies, Inc., 1221 Avenue of the Americas, New York, NY, 10020.

This book is printed on acid-free paper.

3 4 5 6 7 8 9 0 CCI/CCI 0 9 8 7

ISBN: 978-0-07-351188-7
MHID: 0-07-351188-9

Vice President and Editor-in-Chief: *Emily Barrosse*
Publisher: *Phillip A. Butcher*
Sponsoring Editor: *Suzanne S. Earth*
Senior Developmental Editor: *Jennie Katsaros*
Editorial Assistant: *Erika Lake*
Senior Marketing Manager: *Leslie Oberhuber*
Managing Editor: *Jean Dal Porto*
Senior Project Manager: *Becky Komro*
Art Director: *Jeanne Schreiber*
Art Editor: *Emma C. Ghiselli*
Designer: *Marianna Kinigakis*
Interior Design: *Amanda Kavanagh*
Senior Photo Research Coordinator: *Alexandra Ambrose*
Photo Research: *Sherri Adler*
Cover Image and Interior Design Element: © *Julie Karabenick, www.karabenick-art.net,* Composition *42, acrylic on canvas, 28 × 28", 2004.*
Media Producer: *Nancy Garcia Hernandez*
Senior Production Supervisor: *Janean A. Utley*
Composition: *10.5/12 Goudy, by Techbooks*
Printing: *45# New Era Matte, Courier, Kendallville*

Credits: The credits section for this book begins on page 560 and is considered an extension of the copyright page.

Library of Congress Cataloging-in-Publication Data

Adler, Ronald B. (Ronald Brian), 1946-
Communicating at work : principles and practices for business and the professions / Ronald B. Adler, Jeanne Marquardt Elmhorst.—9th ed.
p. cm.
ISBN-13: 978-0-07-351188-7 (pbk. : alk. paper)
ISBN-10: 0-07-351188-9 (pbk. : alk. paper)
1. Business communication. 2. Interpersonal communication. I. Elmhorst, Jeanne Marquardt. II. Title.
HF5718.A33 2008
658.4′5—dc22

2006046798

www.mhhe.com

about the authors

Ronald B. Adler is on the faculty of Santa Barbara City College, where he specializes in organizational and interpersonal communication. He is the author of *Confidence in Communication: A Guide to Assertive and Social Skills* and coauthor of *Understanding Human Communication*, *Interplay: The Process of Interpersonal Communication* as well as the widely used text *Looking Out/Looking In*. Professor Adler is a consultant for a number of corporate, professional, and government clients and leads workshops in such areas as conflict resolution, presentational speaking, team building, and interviewing.

Jeanne Marquardt Elmhorst is an instructor in communication studies at Central New Mexico Community College in Albuquerque, New Mexico. Her courses reflect the variety in the communication discipline: business and professional, public speaking, listening, intercultural, and interpersonal. Jeanne lived and taught in Asia for three years and continues to find opportunities to travel, study, and volunteer in other countries. She enjoys designing and presenting communication training for business and not-for-profit clients.

preface

How important is communicating at work? Virtually anyone with on-the-job experience will affirm that good communication skills are an essential ingredient of success for both organizational and personal goals. *Communicating at Work* provides a practical introduction to the principles and skills of effective communication in business and professional settings.

Based on theory and research that are confirmed by real-world experience, *Communicating at Work* is crafted to help all career-minded readers. Novices to the business world will be introduced to skills they will need for on-the-job success. Readers who have ample job experience but recognize that there is always potential for communicating more effectively will also find useful tips and tools. While *Communicating at Work* is clearly a college-level textbook, it contains information that can help all career-minded readers.

What's Familiar

This edition of *Communicating at Work* retains the approach that has been so well received in the past: A practical, real-world focus, in which every page contains useful advice and examples about how to communicate effectively. A focus on communications technology offers tips on when and how to use e-mail, instant messaging, videoconferencing, presentation software, and other technologies. Strong coverage of workplace diversity helps readers communicate with others from different backgrounds and choose approaches that work for everyone involved. Finally, an emphasis on ethical communication discusses how communicators can achieve their goals in a way that doesn't compromise moral integrity. All of this material is packaged in a design that aims to capture the sophistication of today's workplace.

What's New

This edition builds on the time-tested approach described above in several important ways:

New Chapter Lineup

The coverage of presentational speaking offers more useful information without adding length. A separate chapter (14) now focuses exclusively on persuasive presentations, reflecting the importance of influencing others in the world of business and the professions. Longtime users will recognize that situational analysis and organization now are combined in a single chapter (10), so students can learn these key concepts most quickly.

New and Expanded Coverage

Throughout this edition, readers will find coverage of new topics and expansion of other important concepts. These include theories of organizational cultures (Chapter 2), an expanded explanation of how misunderstandings are grounded in the symbolic nature of language (Chapter 4), tips on cultivating personal networks (Chapter 1), the benefits and dangers of using specialized business terms (Chapter 4), the nature of more- and less-powerful speech (Chapter 4), improving nonverbal effectiveness (Chapter 4), sources of on-the-job conflict (Chapter 5), how to use informational interviews for career advancement (Chapter 7), and stages in group problem solving (Chapter 8).

New Pedagogy

- *On Your Feet* activities in every chapter get students speaking comfortably from the very beginning of the course. These activities offer an easy-to-follow framework for organizing and presenting brief (often just one minute) talks on a variety of interesting topics that reinforce concepts from the text. Examples include describing one's "dream team" of co-workers, reporting on a communication experiment from their own lives, telling a story to make a point, and recalling a unique organizational culture.
- *Self-Assessments* in every chapter give readers a chance to assess how well they are applying concepts. For example, readers can inventory their personal communication networks, diagnose their cultural intelligence, assess their personal conflict style, and assess the way they present themselves nonverbally.
- New *Career Tip* boxes give practical advice on a diverse array of topics including careers in communication, how to apologize without groveling, playing the devil's advocate in groups headed for potentially bad decisions, finding visual aids online, and the use of video feedback to improve delivery in presentations.
- New *Ethical Challenges* explore ways of incorporating ethical considerations in day-to-day work contexts.
- New *In Print* Resources (from popular press and scholarly works) and updated, expanded *On the Web* recommendations provide a wealth of resources for exploring topics covered in the book in more detail.
- Streamlined *chapter objectives* give students a clear picture of exactly what they need to learn to succeed in the course—and in their careers.

Resources for Instructors and Students

An array of resources makes teaching and learning both more efficient and effective.

- ***Communicating at Work* Web site, the Online Learning Center** at **www.mhhe.com/adler9** The Web site provides instructors with downloadable supplements and provides students with learning tools to help them master course concepts.
- An **updated Instructor's Manual, Resource Integrator, and Test Bank** by Carolyn Clark provide a wealth of teaching strategies, classroom activities, resources for professors and students, and examination questions. The Chapter Integrator section breaks each chapter down by course objectives and identifies instructional resources relevant to each objective. EZ test makes it easy to create examinations from the bank of existing questions, as well as allowing instructors to add new ones of their own.
- **PowerPoint** slides of key information from the book allow instructors to present lecture material in computer-generated format.
- **The Student Side of the Online Learning Center** contains learning tools to help students comprehend and review course concepts. These tools are fully integrated with the text through the use of icons in the text margins that notify students which tool to use. The Web site contains self-quizzes, videos, business document templates, outline tutor, PowerPoint tutor, and glossary flash cards.

- ***Communication Concepts* video** provides scenarios of common types of business and professional interaction for analysis. The video is available in VHS format and on the Online Learning Center Web site.
- **PageOut: The Course Web site Development Center** All online content for this text is supported by WebCT, eCollege.com, Blackboard, and other course management systems. PageOut was designed for novice instructors who are just beginning to explore Web options. Even the novice computer user can create a course Web site with a template provided by McGraw-Hill. To learn more about PageOut, ask your McGraw-Hill representative for details, or fill out the form at **www.mhhe.com/pageout**.

acknowledgments

We are indebted to the professionals whose reviews told us what to retain and what to change in this edition: Kathleen Capuano, Rider University; Michael Cavanaugh, East Carolina University; Carolyn Clark, Salt Lake Community College; Carrie Cropley, Santa Barbara City College; Lina Cruz-Evans, Phoenix Community College; Peggy J. Huey, University of Tampa; Christine Kelly, Otterbein College; Gordon Morrell, Yardi Systems; David Roach, Texas-Tech University; Molly Steen, University of California, Santa Barbara; and Robert Zetocha, Southeast Community College.

We continue to appreciate the advice of reviewers from previous editions:

Allen Bean, Southeast Community College
Fritzi Bodenheimer, Montgomery College
Ellen Bonaguro, Northern Illinois University
Suzanne Buck, University of Houston
Thomas J. Costello, University of Illinois–Urbana
Anne Cunningham, Bergen Community College
John W. Haas, The University of Tennessee
Mary J. Hale, University of Colorado–Boulder
Martha J. Haun, University of Houston
Dolores Jones, Charleston Southern University
Shirley Jones, Salt Lake Community College
Art Kanehara, Salt Lake Community College
Jeffrey Kellogg, University of Mississippi
Roselyn Kirk, Salt Lake Community College
Mary L. Kish, Ithaca College
Reed Markham, Salt Lake Community College
Leonard A. McCormick, Tarrant County Junior College
Christina Michura, Central Texas College
Lisa M. Millhouse, West Chester University
Josef D. Moorehead, California State University–Sacramento
James Quisenberry, Moorhead State University
George Rodman, City University of New York
Ted Spencer, Eastern Washington University
Francine Sulinski, University of Maine–Orono
Terry Swan, University of Mississippi
L. Marianne Taylor, Tri-County Technical College
Loretta Walker, Salt Lake Community College
Edgar B. Wycoff, University of Central Florida

We are grateful to Carolyn Clark for crafting the Instructor's Manual and new end-of-chapter activities, as well as for many other insightful suggestions. A project of this magnitude can only succeed when a group of dedicated professionals work together. We want to express our gratitude to the editorial, marketing, and production teams at McGraw-Hill: Phil Butcher, Suzanne Earth, Jennie Katsaros, Becky Komro, Leslie Oberhuber, Marianna Kinigakis, Janean Utley, and Nancy Hernandez.

A talented group of freelance professionals also contributed to the book you are holding. Jessica Bodie Richards' software talents made manuscript preparation a breeze. Photographs chosen by Sherri Adler contribute to the engaging design.

Ronald B. Adler
Jeanne Marquardt Elmhorst

A Practical, Real-World Focus

career tip

Minimizing Interruptions

Interrupting someone who expects to be listened to will usually annoy that person—whether a co-worker, customer, or supervisor. Although some interruptions are signs of involvement and interest ("Really?" "That's great!") and others are genuine requests for information ("Hold on: Did you say Jane or Joan?"), interruptions are rarely appreciated. When you cut others off, speakers may think that you don't care about their ideas or that you believe your ideas are better than theirs. You can be perceived as rude, egocentric, and controlling—someone who believes that what you have to say is more important than others' ideas.

You can cut back on interrupting by using several strategies:

- Count to three after the speaker seems to be finished. You may be surprised by how much more the other person has to say.
- Concentrate on what the speaker is saying and then paraphrase it back when s/he is finished.
- When you catch yourself interrupting, apologize and ask the speaker to continue.
- Ask a co-worker to count the number of times you interrupt in a day. You and your colleague might even agree on a subtle signal (e.g., a cough) to alert you about interruptions.

Source: Adapted from L. Barker and K. Watson, *Listen Up* (New York: St. Martin's Press, 2000), p. 88.

Career Tips

Career Tip boxes give practical advice on how to be more successful in work-related situations. New topics include careers in communication, getting a job overseas, getting recognized by your bosses, and the use of video feedback to improve delivery in presentations.

Presentations

Coverage includes basic steps for organizing business presentations and preparing PowerPoint presentations.

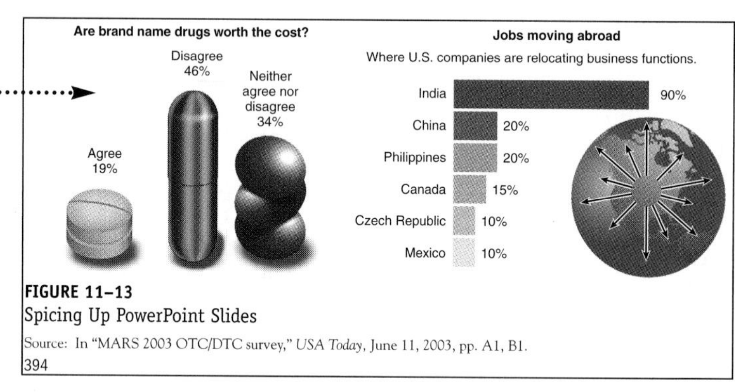

FIGURE 11–13
Spicing Up PowerPoint Slides

Source: In "MARS 2003 OTC/DTC survey," *USA Today*, June 11, 2003, pp. A1, B1.

394

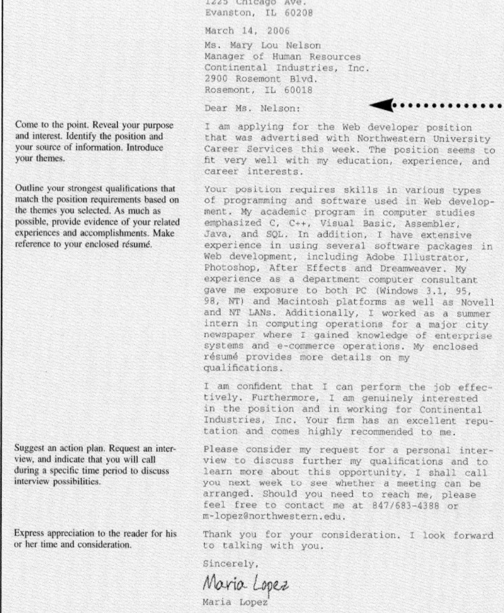

1225 Chicago Ave.
Evanston, IL 60208

March 14, 2006

Ms. Mary Lou Nelson
Manager of Human Resources
Continental Industries, Inc.
2900 Rosemont Blvd.
Rosemont, IL 60018

Dear Ms. Nelson:

Come to the point. Reveal your purpose and interest. Identify the position and your source of information. Introduce your themes.

I am applying for the Web developer position that was advertised with Northwestern University Career Services this week. The position seems to fit very well with my education, experience, and career interests.

Outline your strongest qualifications that match the position requirements based on the themes you selected. As much as possible, provide evidence of your related experiences and accomplishments. Make reference to your enclosed résumé.

Your position requires skills in various types of programming and software used in Web development. My academic program in computer studies emphasized C, C++, Visual Basic, Assembler, Java, and SQL. In addition, I have extensive experience in using several software packages in Web development, including Adobe Illustrator, Photoshop, After Effects and Dreamweaver. My experience as a department computer consultant gave me exposure to both PC (Windows 3.1, 95, 98, NT) and Macintosh platforms as well as Novell and NT LANs. Additionally, I worked as a summer intern in computing operations for a major city newspaper where I gained knowledge of enterprise systems and e-commerce operations. My enclosed résumé provides more details on my qualifications.

I am confident that I can perform the job effectively. Furthermore, I am genuinely interested in the position and in working for Continental Industries, Inc. Your firm has an excellent reputation and comes highly recommended to me.

Suggest an action plan. Request an interview, and indicate that you will call during a specific time period to discuss interview possibilities.

Please consider my request for a personal interview to discuss further my qualifications and to learn more about this opportunity. I shall call you next week to see whether a meeting can be arranged. Should you need to reach me, please feel free to contact me at 847/683-4388 or m-lopez@northwestern.edu.

Express appreciation to the reader for his or her time and consideration.

Thank you for your consideration. I look forward to talking with you.

Sincerely,

Maria Lopez

Maria Lopez

Business Writing

Expanded coverage of business writing includes information on choosing the best format for résumés and job applications, via traditional and electronic formats. Business document templates on the book's Web site provide additional templates so students can create cover letters, résumés, agendas, and memos.

career tip

Working in Virtual Teams

1. *Strive for some "face time," especially during the group's formation*. Virtual teams are most cohesive, trusting, and successful when members have had a chance to spend time together in person, especially during the group's development.
2. *Be mindful of time zone differences*. When members of a virtual team are dispersed across time zones, it's especially important to schedule meetings so no members are inconvenienced. Time differences can be especially challenging when groups span several continents. For example, if some members are in California and others in India are time shifted by a half day, the only times that may work for people with normal schedules are early morning and early evening. Remember Asia is a day *ahead* of the United States; Europe is a half to a full day *behind*.
3. *Use time zones to your advantage*. Consider handing off tasks that members in other time zones can tackle while you are off work. For example, a member in Seattle can request information at the end of the workday, and teammates in Florida can respond at the start of their next workday, so an answer will be in the sender's in-box when s/he logs on 3 hours later.
4. *Keep a personal touch*. Express some of the same emotions and personal thoughts that you would in face-to-face communication. Doing so can build camaraderie and the human feeling that virtual teams may lack without face-to-face communication.
5. *Consider using "back channels."* Use telephone, personal e-mail, and instant messaging to confer directly with one or more team members when you need to deal with issues and relationships personally in a way that will save the group time and effort.
6. *Do a trial run of technology*. Make sure in advance of meetings that all the technology upon which your team relies is working. It can be frustrating and discouraging to waste meeting time dealing with glitches.
7. *Seek input from all team members*. Sometimes members who are more comfortable with the technology of the virtual team will "speak" more than those who have more expertise in the team area, but not with the technology being used.
8. *Be aware of cultural differences in communication style*. These exist in cyberspace as well as in face-to-face communication. Remind yourself of style differences in high- and low-context cultures, expectations of leaders and team members, preferences for direct and indirect means of expression. Learn to read between the lines of those who may not directly criticize your ideas or offer advice.

Sources: Kathleen Melymuka, "Tips for Teams," *Computerworld* 31 (April 28, 1997), p. 72; and J. Dan Rothwell, *In Mixed Company: Communicating in Small Groups and Teams*, 9th ed. (Belmont, CA: Wadsworth, 2007), pp. 386–387.

Technology

Technology in the Workplace

Communicating at Work covers the latest developments and offers guidelines and advice for using the new technologies. Topics include instant messaging, videoconferencing, and presentation software. On the Web recommendations provide a wealth of resources.

Ethics

Ethical Considerations

Throughout the text, and in Ethical Challenge boxes, students are invited to consider ways of incorporating ethical considerations into day-to-day work contexts.

ethical challenge

Golden and Platinum Rules

The Golden Rule tells us to treat others the way we would like to be treated, and the "Platinum Rule" is to treat others the way *they* would like to be treated. The best way to honor the Platinum Rule is to listen to others, discovering what they want. On the other hand, realists acknowledge that it is impossible to give equal attention to every message and still accomplish the multitude of tasks that occupy every workday.

How can you, as a busy worker, respond to nonessential messages without alienating the people who deliver them?

FIGURE 2–1 Racial and Ethnic Composition of the United States, 1999 and 2025

Note: White, black and Asian/other categories exclude Hispanics, who may be of any race. The Asian/other category includes American Indians, Eskimos, Aleuts, and Pacific Islanders. Totals may not add to 100 due to rounding.

Source: "The Changing American Pie, 1999 and 2025," Population Research Bureau, Washington, DC, 2000.

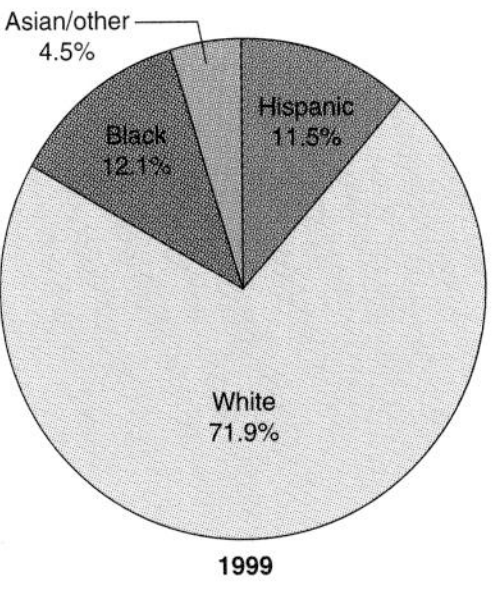

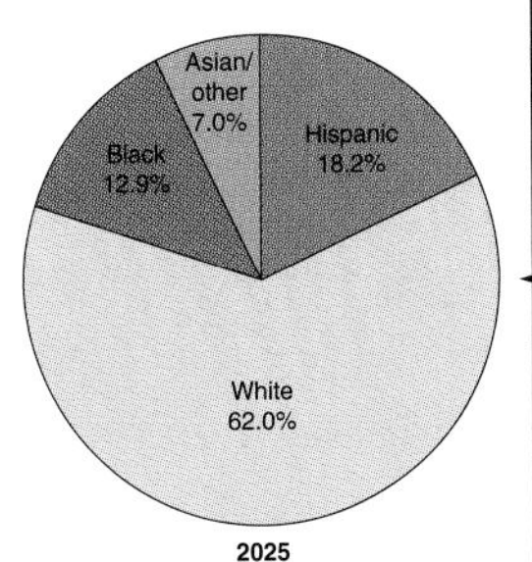

companies also have many U.S. sites. Immigrants accounted for over half of the growth in the U.S. labor force at the turn of the 21st century.[6] By 2016, experts predict that 2 million foreign-born workers will be moving to the United States every year.[7]

While overseas companies are part of the North American economy, Americans are moving abroad in growing numbers. Over 8 million were working overseas in 2003,[8] many for the 3,000 U.S. firms with global operations and others for over 36,000 foreign companies in more than 180 countries.[9] Among Fortune 500 corporations, the average U.S. multinational corporation has operations in about 17 countries, not to mention major interests in a number of affiliates worldwide.[10]

Diversity

Focus on Diversity

Working with people from different backgrounds is more important and more common than ever. *Communicating at Work* encourages cultural understanding by exploring issues of diversity throughout the text.

New Pedagogy

On Your Feet

This new feature provides activities to get students speaking comfortably from the very beginning of the course. Examples include describing one's "dream team" of co-workers and recalling a unique organizational culture.

on your feet

Best and Worst Communication Climates

Be prepared to describe to your group two organizations to which you have belonged:

- One with the most positive, confirming climate
- One with the most negative, disconfirming climate

The organizations you describe may be a work group, team, class, volunteer group, or any other group of people formed with the purpose of accomplishing a task.

Make sure your account of each group includes

- A description of how the communication qualities listed on pages 139–143 (or the absence of these qualities) helped create the climate you are describing.
- One or more specific examples that captures the kinds of communication that created the positive or negative climate.
- The lessons you've learned about communication from the experiences you have described.

Self-Assessment

Self-Assessments encourage students to assess how well they are applying concepts. For example, they can diagnose their cultural intelligence, assess their personal conflict style, and assess the way they present themselves nonverbally.

Self-Assessment **Diagnosing Your Cultural Intelligence**

These statements reflect different facets of cultural intelligence. For each set, add up your scores and divide by four to produce an average. Our work with large groups of managers shows that for purposes of your own development, it is most useful to think about your three scores in comparison to one another. Generally, an average of less than 3 would indicate an area calling for improvement, while an average of greater than 4–5 reflects a true CQ strength.

Rate the extent to which you agree with each statement, using the scale:
1 = strongly disagree, 2 = disagree, 3 = neutral, 4 = agree, 5 = strongly agree.

_____ Before I interact with people from a new culture, I ask myself what I hope to achieve.

_____ If I encounter something unexpected while working in a new culture, I use this experience to figure out new ways to approach *other* cultures in the future.

_____ I plan how I'm going to relate to people from a different culture before I meet them.

\+ _____ When I come into a new cultural situation, I can immediately sense whether something is going well or something is wrong.

Total _____ ÷ 4 = _____ Cognitive CQ

Quick Guide to *Communicating at Work*

This handy reference tool offers a step-by-step guide for planning the most common types of business and professional presentations: meetings, interviews, and problem-solving negotiations.

Media Resources for Students and Instructors

OLC icon 

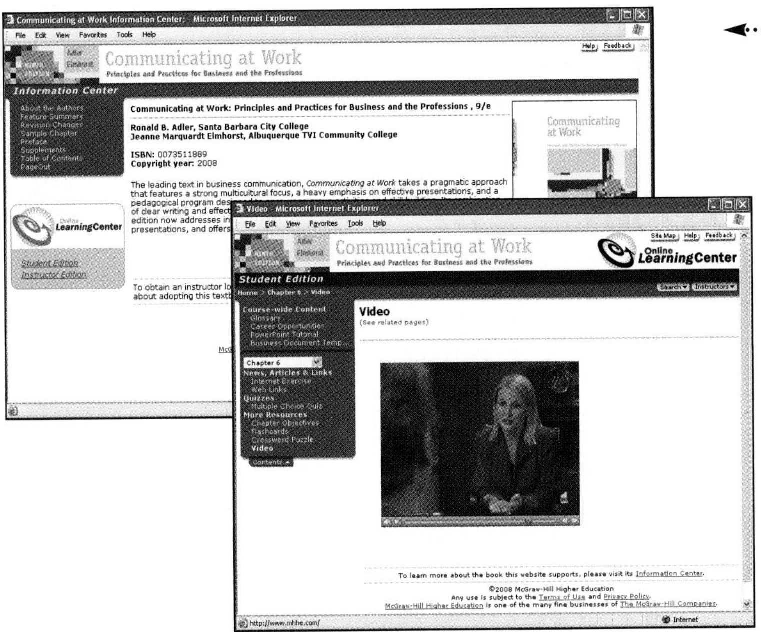

The Online Learning Center at www.mhhe.com/adler9 provides a variety of resources to help students review key course content. Icons in the text prompt students to use corresponding features on the Web site.

Self-Quizzes—Self-scoring quizzes with feedback allow students to assess their understanding of chapter concepts.

Videos—Six 5-minute segments illustrate key points found in the text:

1. Defensive/Supportive Communication
2. Aggressive/Assertive Communication
3. The Job Interview
4. Small-Group Communication
5. Presentation Techniques
6. Nonverbal Messages

Business Document Templates—Provide templates for résumés, cover letters, agendas, and memos.

PowerPoint Tutorial—Presents the basic steps for creating and using a PowerPoint presentation.

Glossary Flash Cards—Provide a review of key terms.

Instructors can download the Instructor's Manual Resource Integrator and PowerPoint slides from the Online Learning Center.

brief contents

table of contents

part one

part two

Personal Skills

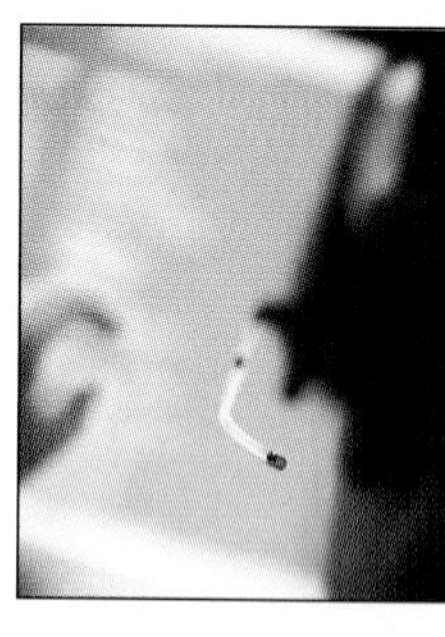

part three

Interviewing

part four

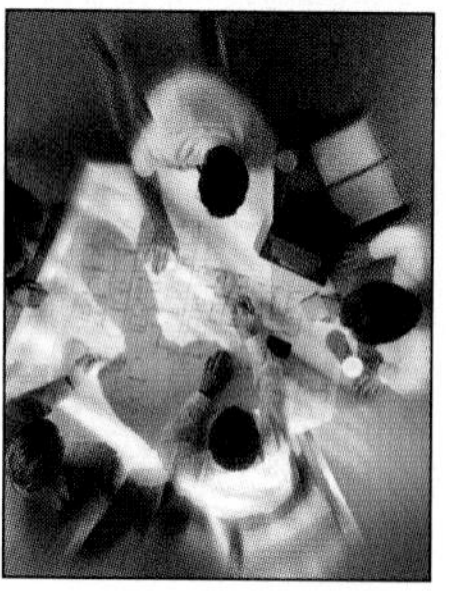

part five

Making Effective Presentations
Strategic Case: Fresh Air Sports 322

10 Developing and Organizing the Presentation 324

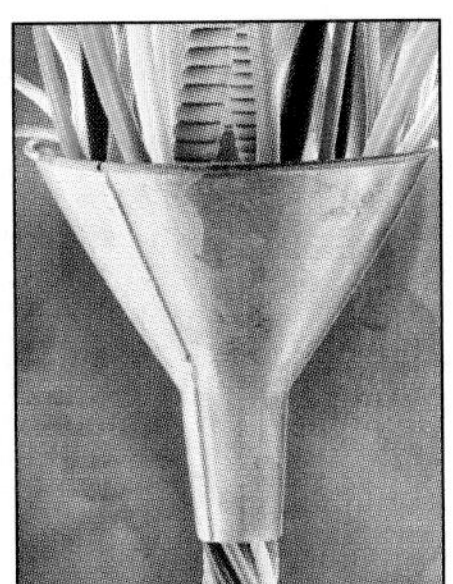

11 Verbal and Visual Support in Presentations 370

12 Delivering the Presentation 404

14 Persuasive Presentations 468

Communicating at Work

Principles and Practices for Business and the Professions

part one: strategic case

Sundown Bakery

When Carol Teinchek and Bruce Marshall first started Sundown Bakery, the business was fairly simple. Carol ran the shop up front, while Bruce ran the bakery and ordered supplies. When the business began to grow, Carol hired two part-time clerks to help out in the shop. Marina had moved to the country 2 years ago from El Salvador, and Kim was a newly arrived Korean who was working his way through college. Bruce hired Maurice, a French Canadian, as an assistant.

The ovens were soon running 24 hours a day, supervised by Maurice, who was now master baker, and two assistants on each of three shifts. Marina and Kim supervised the shop, since Carol was usually too busy managing general sales distribution to spend much time with customers. Bruce still spent 3 or 4 hours a day in the bakery whenever he could get out of his office, but he spent most of that time coordinating production and solving problems with Maurice.

Within the next year, Sundown expanded from its original location, adding two new shops as well as two kiosks in local malls. Carol and Bruce hired a new operations manager, Hans Mikelson, who had formerly been regional manager of a national chain of coffee shops. Mikelson had plenty of new ideas about how to operate an expanding business: He had a Web site created, added an extensive range of drinks and meal items to the menu, and instituted two dress codes—one for all counter help and another for kitchen employees. He also put together an employee manual to save time orienting new employees. All of these changes were announced by memos from Mikelson, which were distributed to employees by the store managers.

The expanding size of Sundown led to a change in the company. The family feeling that was strong when Sundown was a small operation was less noticeable. The new employees barely knew Bruce and Carol, and, as a result, there was less give-and-take of ideas between the owners and workers.

Mikelson's memos on the dress code and the employee manual created a crisis. Old-time employees were furious about receiving orders from "the bureaucrats," as management came to be called. Bruce and Carol recognized the problem and wanted to keep the lines of communication open, but they weren't sure how to do so. "I'm just a baker," Bruce confessed in exasperation. "I don't know how to run a big company."

Another set of challenges grew out of the changing character of the employees. In the original location alone, Sundown now employed workers from seven different countries. José, who was born in Brazil, confessed to Bruce that he felt uncomfortable being managed by Carol. "It's nothing personal," he said, "but where I come from, a man doesn't take orders from a woman." The Sundown employee profile was different in other ways. Two of the assistant bakers were openly gay; one of the sales clerks got around by wheelchair.

Carol, Bruce, and Hans know that good products alone aren't enough to guarantee the continuing success of Sundown Bakeries. They need to improve the quality of communication among the growing team who make and sell their products.

As you read the chapters in this unit, consider the following questions:

Chapter 1

1. Analyze the likely causes of the resentment over the employee manual and uniforms by considering the impact of the sender, message, decoding, feedback, context, and probable sources of noise. Describe how the problems you identified could have been minimized by different communication strategies.
2. Identify the changes in communication channels between employees and management as Sundown has grown. What channels can be used to make communication about changes in the business most productive?
3. Consider the relational messages employees seem to have received from management as Sundown's business grew.
4. How have Sundown's formal and informal communication networks changed as the company

expanded? In what ways have both the formal and informal networks contributed to Sundown's growing pains? In what ways can these networks be used to improve the relationships between management and employees?

Chapter 2

1. How do changes in the demographic makeup of Sundown Bakeries reflect transformation of the larger workforce? Consider the following dimensions of culture as you describe the impact of culture on communication within the company: high- and low-context styles, individualism and collectivism, and power distance.
2. How would you describe the early organizational culture of Sundown? How has the culture changed as the company grew? Consider the issues listed on pages 64–65 as you answer this question.
3. What advice would you give to Sundown's management team about how to maintain the most effective culture in the face of the company's growth?

1 Communicating at Work

Chapter Outline

Chapter Objectives

After reading this chapter you should be able to

1 Explain the role of communication in career success, providing examples to support your claims.

2 Apply the basic elements, the process, and key principles of communication to a specific situation, showing how each one affects the outcome of the interaction.

3 Apply the concepts of ethical communication discussed here to one or more ethically challenging situations.

4 Describe how formal and informal communication networks operate in a given situation, and how you can use the most effective channels to accomplish your goals within an organization.

5 Analyze the advantages and disadvantages of various face-to-face and electronic communication channels and choose the most appropriate and effective one for a given situation.

The Importance of Communication

Virtually everyone communicates at work. No matter what the field, and no matter how much you know about your job, specialized knowledge alone isn't enough to guarantee success; communication skills are also vital. Table 1–1 summarizes the results of one survey in which employers list the skills and qualities for their ideal candidate. Communication skills always top the list.[1]

Additional research validates the importance of communication-related skills, including working on teams, teaching others, serving customers, leading, negotiating, working with cultural diversity, interviewing, listening, conducting meetings, and resolving conflicts.[2] This fact explains why almost 90 percent of U.S. companies provide some type of communication skills training.[3]

Subscribers to the *Harvard Business Review* rated "the ability to communicate" the most important factor in making an executive "promotable," more important than ambition, education, and capacity for hard work.[4] Research spanning several decades has consistently ranked communication skills as crucial for managers.[5] One 20-year study that followed the progress of Stanford University MBAs revealed that the most successful graduates (as measured by both career advancement and salary) shared personality traits that distinguish good communicators: a desire to persuade, an interest in talking and working with other people, and an outgoing, ascendant personality. As students, these achievers developed their communication skills by choosing courses in areas such as persuasion, selling ideas, negotiation, and other forms of speaking.[6]

Table 1–1 Top Ten Qualities/Skills Employers Want

1. Communication skills
2. Honesty/integrity
3. Interpersonal skills (relate well to others)
4. Strong work ethic
5. Teamwork skills (work well with others)
6. Analytical skills
7. Motivation/initiative
8. Flexibility/adaptability
9. Computer skills
10. Detail oriented

Source: *Job Outlook 2005* (Bethlehem, PA: National Association of Colleges and Employers), accessed from **www.jobweb.com/joboutlook/2005outlook/3a.htm** with permission of the National Association of Colleges and Employers.

The need for communication skills is important in virtually every career, not just those that are traditionally regarded as people-oriented. Practitioners in Big Six accounting firms spend 80 percent of their work time communicating with others, individually and in groups.[7] Likewise, engineers spend most of their professional lives speaking and listening, mostly in one-to-one and small group settings.[8] Technical people with good communication skills earn more, and those who are weak communicators suffer.[9] William Schaffer, international business development manager for computer giant Sun Microsystems, made the point emphatically: "If there's one skill that's required for success in this industry, it's communication skills."[10] Writing in *The Scientist*, author Jim Richman echoes this sentiment: "If I give any advice, it is that you can never do enough training around your overall communication skills."[11] Other high-tech experts back up this claim. Over 90 percent of the personnel officials at 500 U.S. businesses stated that increased communication skills are needed for success in the 21st century.[12]

On-the-job communication skills can even make the difference between life and death. The Los Angeles Police Department cited "bad communication" among the most common reasons for errors in shooting by its officers.[13] Researchers discovered that "poor communication" was the root of over 60 percent of reported medical errors—including death, serious physical injury, and psychological trauma.[14] Research published in the *Journal of the American Medical Association* revealed a significant difference between the communication skills of physicians who had no malpractice claims against them and doctors with previous claims.[15]

Most successful people recognize the role communication skills have played in their career. In one survey of over 1,000 adult workers, 87 percent of the respondents rated communication skills as being "very important" for performing their jobs.[16] When college graduates in a wide variety of fields were asked what abilities were vital to their success, most respondents identified communication. In fact, the majority said that communication skills were more important than the major subject they had studied in college.[17] MBA graduates rated the ability to communicate effectively as the single most useful skill in their careers.[18] In one

career tip

Careers in Communication

While communication plays an important role in every job, it is the focus of many careers. The National Communication Association (**www.natcom.org**) publishes a list of communication-related fields and some typical specialties within them. While a degree in communication may not be mandatory for jobs like these, academic study of the field is excellent preparation.

- **Advertising/marketing:** market researcher, copy writer, account executive, sales manager, media planner, media buyer, creative director, media sales representative.
- **Electronic media/radio-television/broadcasting:** archivist/librarian, community relations director, unit manager, video editor, news director, writer, technical director, advertising sales coordinator, traffic/continuity specialist, media buyer, announcer, disc jockey, newscaster, public relations manager, casting director, producer, business manager, account executive, floor manager, talk show host, director of broadcasting.
- **Journalism/publishing:** reporter, editor, author, writer, project manager, publisher, news service researcher, technical writer.
- **Public information/development:** public information officer, press agent, development officer, fund raiser, membership recruiter, media analyst/planner, creative director, public opinion researcher.
- **Organizational affairs:** human resources specialist or manager, director of organizational communication, industrial and labor relations representative, negotiator, ombudsman, customer service representative, newsletter editor, trainer, human resources manager.
- **Government/political affairs:** public information officer, speech writer, legislative assistant, campaign staffer/director, research specialist, lobbyist, press secretary.

survey of business school alumni, oral communication skills were judged as "mandatory" or "very important" by 100 percent of the respondents—every person who replied.[19]

The importance of communication is not surprising when you consider the staggering amount of time people spend communicating on the job. One study based on responses from over 1,000 employees at Fortune 1000 companies found that workers send and receive an average of 178 messages each day via telephone, e-mail, faxes, pagers, and face-to-face communication.[20] Some experts have estimated that the average business executive spends 75 to 80 percent of the time communicating—about 45 minutes of every hour.[21]

The importance of communicating effectively on the job is clear. But this discussion so far hasn't even addressed the fact that communication skills often make the difference between being hired and being rejected in the first place. When almost 250 employers were asked "What skills are most important for college graduates?" their overwhelming response was oral communication and interpersonal skills, followed by teamwork and analytical abilities.[22] In another survey, 1,000 managers rated the abilities to speak and listen effectively as the two most important factors in helping college graduates find jobs in a competitive workplace, placing them ahead of attributes like technical competence, work experience, and specific degree earned.[23] When 400 employers were asked to identify the top characteristic they seek in job candidates, the leading answer was "communication skills."[24] Finally, when 170 well-known business and industrial firms were asked to list the most common reasons for *not* offering jobs to applicants, the most frequent replies were "inability to communicate" and "poor communication skills."[25]

The Nature of Communication

Understanding the importance of communication isn't the same thing as understanding how the process works. A close look at what happens when people try to communicate can offer clues about why some attempts succeed and others fail.

The Process of Communication

No matter what the setting or the number of people involved, all communication consists of the same elements. Although the process of communication is more than the total of these parts, understanding them can help explain what happens when one person tries to express an idea to others.

A Model of Communication The communication process begins with a **sender,** the person who transmits a **message.** Some messages are deliberate, while others (such as sighs and yawns) may be unintentional. The sender must choose certain words or nonverbal methods to send an intentional message. This activity is called **encoding.** The **channel** (sometimes called the *medium*) is the method used to deliver a message. As a business communicator, you can often choose to write a letter or memo, send a fax or e-mail, or deliver the message orally over the phone or in person.

Even if a message does get to its intended receiver intact, there's no guarantee that it will be understood as the sender intended it to be. The **receiver** must still **decode** it, attaching meaning to the words or symbols. Receivers don't just absorb messages like sponges; they respond to them. The discernible response of a receiver to a sender's message is called **feedback.** Some feedback is nonverbal—smiles, sighs, and so on. Sometimes it is oral, as when you react to a colleague's ideas with questions or comments. Feedback can also be written, as when you respond by writing your co-worker a memo. In many cases, no message can be a type of feedback. Failure to answer a letter or to return a phone call can suggest how the noncommunicative person feels about the sender. When we add the element of feedback to our communication model, we begin to recognize that in face-to-face settings people are simultaneously senders and receivers of information. This explains why these two roles are superimposed in the communication model pictured in Figure 1–1.

One of the greatest sources of communication problems is **noise**—the term communication scholars use for factors that interfere with the exchange of messages. The most obvious type of noise is *external* (also called *physical*) *noise*. This includes sounds that distract communicators—such as the babble of voices in the next room or the annoying ring of someone's cell phone in a meeting—an overcrowded room, or a smelly cigar. A second kind of noise is *physiological:* hearing disorders, illnesses, disabilities, and other factors make it difficult to send or receive messages. To appreciate the importance of physiological noise, recall how hard it is to pay attention

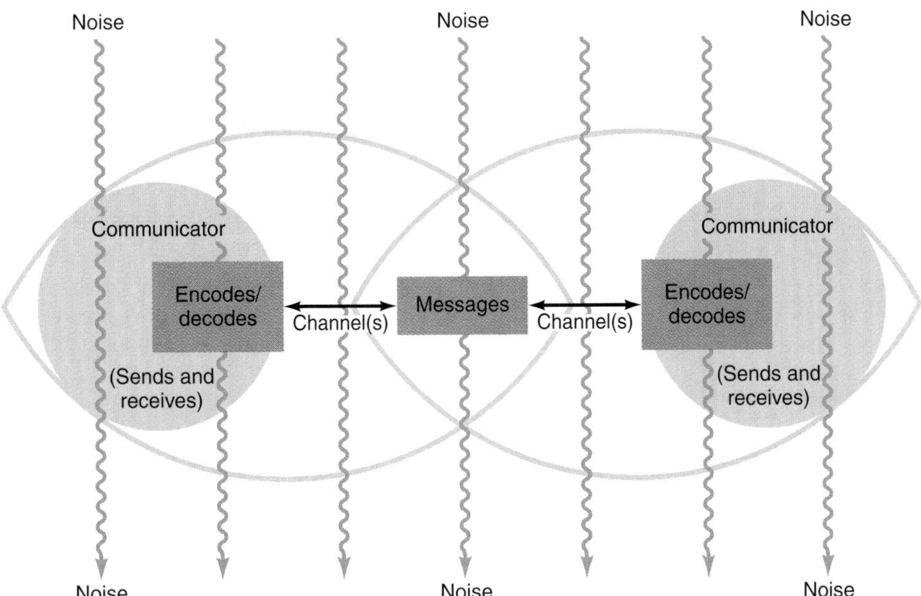

FIGURE 1–1 Communication Model

when you are recovering from a late-night study session or have the flu. The third type of noise is *psychological*—forces within the sender or receiver that interfere with understanding, such as egotism, defensiveness, assumptions, stereotypes, biases, prejudices, hostility, preoccupation, and fear.

Communication Contexts Communication always takes place in some setting, and the **context** in which it occurs can have a powerful effect on what happens. For example, the *physical context* can influence the content and quality of interaction. Imagine how discussing a problem with your boss or asking for a raise might be received differently depending on whether the conversation took place in your boss's office or over lunch at a local restaurant.

The *social context* refers to the nature of the relationship between the communicators, as well as others whose presence may affect the nature of communication. Imagine, for instance, the difference in asking a manager for a raise if you had a long history of friendship versus one of animosity, or if your ages were close or radically different. An interesting application of how changing the social context can shape interaction occurred during a round of secret negotiations in the 1990s between Israel and the Palestine Liberation Organization. The hosts, the Norwegian foreign minister and his wife, invited the negotiators to their home, where they played on the floor with the hosts' 4-year-old child. After changing the context, impasses were broken and a groundbreaking Mideast peace accord was hammered out.[26]

The *chronological context* refers to the ways in which time influences interaction. A sample of time-related considerations shows the importance of adapting to the chronological context: time of day (e.g., first appointment in the morning or last in the afternoon) or the time of year (e.g., holiday season, tax time). You can boost your chances for success by paying attention to chronological factors. When calling someone or requesting a person's help, consider asking, "Is this a good time?" or "Do you have time now, or would another time be more convenient?"

The *cultural context* of communication includes both the organizational and the ethnic and/or national backgrounds of the persons communicating. Chapter 2 discusses the role of culture in detail. For now, you can get a sense of the importance of culture by imagining how just a few differences in backgrounds might influence communication between people from differing backgrounds such as: baby boomers and generation X-ers or Y-ers, Euro-Americans and Hispanics, New Yorkers and Californians, or Americans and Chinese.

Communication Principles

The communication model pictured in Figure 1–1 is not yet complete. It is like a still picture of a live event: All the elements are present except action. Several characteristics describe the dynamic nature of the communication process.

Communication Is Unavoidable A fundamental axiom of communication is "One cannot not communicate." As you will learn in Chapter 4, facial expression, posture, gesture, clothing, and a host of other behaviors offer cues about our attitudes. The impossibility of not communicating means that we send messages even by our absence. Failing to show up at an event or leaving the room suggests meanings to others. Because communication is unavoidable, it is essential to consider the unintentional messages you send.

Communication Operates on Two Levels Every time two or more people communicate, they exchange two kinds of messages. The most obvious ones are **content messages**—information about the topic under discussion. But at a less apparent level, the communicators also exchange **relational messages**—signals indicating how they feel about one another.[27] Relational messages indicate a variety of attitudes. An important one is *affinity*—the degree to which a communicator likes the other person in general or a particular message that is being sent. Another kind of relational message deals with *control*—the amount of influence in that situation. Communication theorists sometimes talk about three self-explanatory distributions of control that can exist between communicators: "one up," "one down," and "straight across." A third type of relational message can reflect a communicator's degree of *respect* for the other person or people. Note that respect and affinity aren't always identical: It is possible to like others without respecting them and to respect them without liking them.

Communication Is Irreversible At one time or another, we have all wished we could take back words we regretted uttering. Unfortunately, this isn't possible. Our words and deeds are recorded in others' memories, and we can't erase them. As the old saying goes, people may forgive, but they don't forget. In fact, often the more vigorously you try to erase an act, the more vividly it stands out.

Communication Is a Process It isn't really accurate to talk about an "act" of communication as if sending or receiving a message were an isolated event.

Rather, every communication event needs to be examined as part of its communication context. Suppose, for example, your boss responds to your request for a raise by saying, "I was going to ask you to take a *cut* in pay!" How would you react? The answer probably depends on several factors: Is your boss a joker or a serious person? How does the comment fit into the history of your relationship—have your boss's remarks been critical or supportive in the past? How does the message fit with ones you have received from other people? What mood are you in today? All these questions show that the meaning of a message depends in part on what has happened before. Each message is part of a process: It doesn't occur in isolation.

Communication Is Not a Panacea Although communication can smooth out the bumps and straighten the road to success, it won't always get you what you want. Misunderstandings and ill feelings can increase when people communicate badly. This helps explain why some problems grow worse the longer they are discussed. Even effective communication won't solve all problems: There are some situations in which the parties understand one another perfectly and still disagree. These limitations are important to understand as you begin to study communication on the job. Boosting your communication skills can increase your effectiveness, but it isn't a cure-all.

Ethical Dimensions of Communication

One writer observed, "The trouble with business ethics is that many people think the phrase is an oxymoron. They hear it, giggle, and say things like, 'You mean like military intelligence, eh?'"[28] Despite this cynical attitude, there is a growing recognition that behaving ethically is an essential part of being an effective, promotable employee. Scandalous business practices led to the downfall of major corporations like Enron and WorldCom and have cost others millions of dollars. As a result of these ethical lapses, sensitivity to communicating in a principled way has grown, and several hundred corporations and organizations now include an ethics officer in their organizational chart who reports directly to the chairman.[29] Employees share this concern for ethics. One survey of 800 recent MBA graduates revealed that virtually all were willing to forgo some money to work for an organization with a better reputation for corporate social responsibility and ethics.[30]

Doing the ethical thing isn't always easy. On a personal level, you are likely to face conflicts between what you believe is right and what is practical. For instance, you might have to deal with a customer or colleague whose business or approval you want, but who is behaving badly—perhaps making sexist or racist remarks. After a trip together, co-workers turn in inflated expenses and expect you to do the same. Your team is under pressure to finish a project, but you recognize potential safety issues being shortcut. Besides personal challenges, sooner or later you are likely to experience situations like these where others in your organization behave in ethically questionable ways. Do you speak up when a colleague makes promises to clients that you know the company can't keep? Should you challenge your boss when he or she treats other employees unfairly or illegally?

ethical challenge

Ethical Communication Choices

See the bottom of this page for descriptions of five guidelines for judging ethical communication:

- The Categorical Imperative
- The Golden Rule
- The Utilitarian Rule
- The Professional Ethic
- The Publicity Test

Outline the range of ways you could handle each situation below. Use one or more of the ethical guidelines to decide on a course of action that is both principled and realistic. Justify your decision.

1. A co-worker tells you he's about to buy an expensive car that will strain his budget to the maximum. You recently learned that he is slated to be laid off at the end of the month but were told to keep this information in strictest confidence. What do you do?
2. Your friend is applying for a job and has given you as a reference. A questionnaire sent by the employer asks if there is any reason you cannot recommend the applicant. You know that your friend is struggling with an alcohol problem, which led to dismissal from a previous job. Do you mention this problem on the reference form? If so, how?
3. Your boss calls you into her office and praises you for doing excellent work on a recent project. She suggests that this level of performance is likely to earn you a promotion and raise. In truth, a colleague made a far greater contribution to the project. How do you respond to your boss's praise?
4. You and two co-workers will each be presenting competing proposals to a steering committee on Monday. At a party over the weekend you run into a very influential member of the committee. You know that talking up your idea could give you an advantage over the other two proposals, but you wonder if it is right to let a personal relationship give you an edge over your co-workers. What do you do?
5. While you are entertaining a customer, he makes a blatantly offensive joke. How do you respond?

Source: Some of the scenarios above are adapted from the quiz "How Ethical Are You?" in John E. Richardson, ed., *Business Ethics 03/04*, 15th ed. (Guilford, CT: McGraw-Hill/Dushkin, 2003), p. 200.

It has been said that ethics centers on a sense of responsibility for someone other than yourself.[31] A blanket obligation to communicate ethically can be too vague to be helpful in specific situations. Three philosophical principles offer standards that can help you decide how to behave in a principled manner:[32]

The Categorical Imperative: Could our society continue to function if everyone acted in this fashion?

The Utilitarian Rule: Does this action do the most good for the most people over the greatest period of time?

The Golden Rule: Is this the way in which I would want to be treated by others?

Two additional guidelines can help you evaluate whether you are behaving ethically:

The Professional Ethic: How would this action be judged by an impartial jury of your professional peers?

The Publicity Test: Would you be comfortable having the public learn about your behavior in the broadcast or print media?[33]

Using Communication Networks

The story of Sundown Bakery (pages 2–3) shows that, as organizations grow, a system for managing the flow of communication has to develop. The regular patterns of communication between people are called **communication networks.**[34] Two kinds of networks exist: formal and informal.

Formal Communication Networks

Formal communication networks are systems designed by management to dictate who should talk to whom to get a job done.[35] In a small organization, networks are so simple that they may hardly be noticeable; in a larger organization, they become more intricate. The most common way of describing formal communication networks is with **organizational charts** like the one in Figure 1–2. Organizational charts are more than a bureaucrat's toy; they provide a clear guideline of who is responsible for a given task and which employees are responsible for others' performance. Figure 1–2 is a typical organizational chart. It shows that Henry Muller reports to his boss, Herman Flores, while Terri Kwan reports to Bill North. Organizational charts show that communication can flow in several directions: upward, downward, and horizontally.

Downward Communication **Downward communication** occurs whenever superiors initiate messages to their subordinates. As Table 1–2 shows, there are several types of downward communication:

- *Job instructions:* "When you restock the shelves, put the new merchandise behind the old stock."
- *Job rationale*: "We rotate the stock like that so the customers won't wind up with stale merchandise."
- *Procedures and practices*: "Don't try to argue with unhappy customers. If you can't handle them yourself, call the manager."
- *Feedback:* "You're really catching on fast. If you keep up the good work, you'll be an assistant manager by the end of the year."

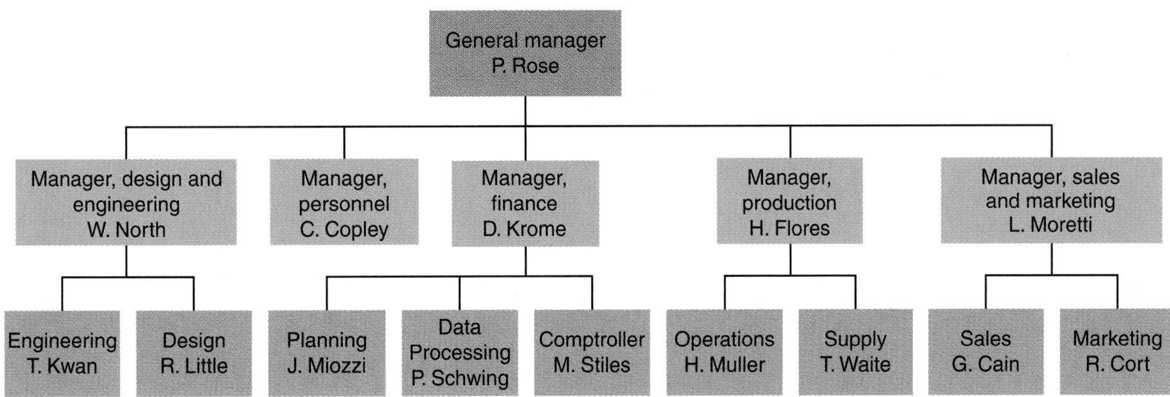

FIGURE 1–2
Dynacom System, Inc., Organizational Chart

Table 1–2 Types of Formal Communication in Organizations

	Downward Communication	Upward Communication	Horizontal (Lateral) Communication
Definition	Superior to subordinate	Subordinate to superior	Between co-workers with different areas of responsibility
Types	Job instructions Rationale for job Organizational procedure and practices Feedback to subordinates Indoctrination to organization culture	What subordinates are doing Unsolved work problems Suggestions for improvement Subordinates' feelings about job and co-workers	Coordinate tasks Solve problems Share information Manage conflicts Build rapport
Potential Benefits	Prevention/correction of employee errors Greater job satisfaction Improved morale	Prevention of new problems and solution of old ones Increased acceptance of management decisions	Increased cooperation among employees with different duties Greater understanding of organization's mission
Potential Problems	Insufficient or unclear messages Message overload Message distorted as it passes through one or more intermediaries	Superiors may discourage, disregard, or downplay importance of subordinates' messages Supervisors may unfairly blame subordinates for unpleasant news	Rivalry may occur between employees from different areas Specialization makes understanding difficult Information overload discourages contacts Physical barriers discourage contact Lack of motivation

- *Indoctrination*: "People can buy the stuff we sell at other places, but we can bring them in here by giving them what they want quickly and pleasantly. If we do that, we'll all come out ahead."

Most managers would agree—at least in principle—that downward communication is important. It's hard to argue with the need for giving instructions, explaining rationale, describing procedures, and so on. Like their bosses, employees recognize the importance of downward communication. A study at General Electric (GE) revealed that "clear communication between boss and worker" was the most important factor in job satisfaction for most people. GE was so impressed with the findings of this study that it launched a program to encourage managers to communicate more, and more directly, with their employees, including holding informal meetings to encourage interaction.[36]

The desire for feedback is probably so strong among most employees because supervisors rarely provide enough of it. As two researchers in the field, Daniel Katz and Robert Kahn, put it: "The frequent complaint . . . by the individual is that he does not know where he stands with his superiors."[37] Many companies do take a

career tip

Getting Recognized by Your Bosses

According to Muriel Solomon, "The big secret to getting recognized is to give creative thinking a priority." She advises that you can showcase your talent, create interest in your work, and display your potential in several ways:

- **Present proposals to your boss.** Learn the history of a challenge, develop a specific plan that shows creativity and understanding of the company's needs. Don't wait for someone to recognize you or choose you for a prime assignment.
- **Volunteer for committees, to chair a committee, or to sponsor a workshop, hearing, or sports event.** Create opportunities to enlarge your working relationships with people at many levels of your organization. Prepare concise summaries and submit reports to your boss.
- **Get your thoughts printed.** Contribute quality writing in the company magazines, department newsletters, or association or professional journals. Distribute copies to your boss, bulletin boards, intranets.
- **Use thoughtful gestures to build bridges.** Devote 5 minutes a day to raising your visibility by thanking people who worked on your project, calling or sending notes of thanks to the supervisors of those who helped you (with a blind copy to the one whose help you received), and feeding your gratitude into the grapevine.

Source: Muriel Solomon, *Getting Praised, Raised and Recognized* (Englewood Cliffs, NJ: Prentice Hall, 1993).

more enlightened approach to feedback. Ed Carlson, former president of United Airlines, is generally credited with turning the company from a loser into a winner during his tenure. Part of his success was due to keeping United's employees—all of them—aware of how the company was doing. "Nothing is worse for morale than a lack of information down in the ranks," he said. "I call it NETMA—Nobody Ever Tells Me Anything—and I have tried hard to minimize that problem."[38] True to his word, Carlson passed along to the field staff information on United's operations that was previously considered too important to circulate.

Upward Communication Messages flowing from subordinates to superiors are labeled **upward communication.** Virtually every organization *claims* to seek out upward messages, but many aren't as open to employee opinions as they claim. In some organizations, questioning the boss can be a recipe for professional suicide. "The disconnect between rhetoric and reality is why Scott Adams [creator of the 'Dilbert' comic strip] is a millionaire," says management expert Warren Bennis.[39]

Businesses that really are open to upward communication can profit from the opinions of employees.[40] Sam Walton, founder of Wal-Mart, the largest retailer in the United States, claimed that "our best ideas come from clerks and stockboys."[41] Industry observers credit the dramatic turnaround of Mattel Corporation to the openness to employee suggestions of its CEO, John Aberman.[42] Upward communication can convey four types of messages:[43]

- *What subordinates are doing:* "We'll have that job done by closing time today."
- *Unsolved work problems:* "We're still having trouble with the air conditioner in the accounting office."

- *Suggestions for improvement:* "I think I've figured a way to give people the vacation schedules they want and still keep our staffing up." As the Career Tip on page 15 suggests, getting recognized by your boss can pave the way to career advancement.
- *How subordinates feel about each other and the job:* "I'm having a hard time working with Louie. He seems to think I'm mad at him." Or, "I'm getting frustrated. I've been in the same job for over a year now, and I'm itching for more responsibility."

These messages can benefit both subordinates and superiors, and this explains why the most satisfied employees feel free to express dissent to their bosses.[44] Bennis emphasizes the critical role upward communication plays in the success of an organization:

> *[T]he longer I study effective leaders, the more I am convinced of the under-appreciated importance of effective followers. What makes a good follower? The single most important characteristic may well be a willingness to tell the truth. In a world of growing complexity, leaders are increasingly dependent on their subordinates for good information, whether the leaders want to or not. Followers who tell the truth, and leaders who listen, are an unbeatable combination.*[45]

Upward communication is especially important for women. Females who engage in more interactions with their supervisors advance in the organizational hierarchy faster than those who do not spend as much time communicating upward.[46] A probable explanation for this fact is that women have fewer informal connections with powerful

Dilbert: © Scott Adams/Dist. by United Feature Syndicate, Inc. Reprinted by permission.

decision-makers in some organizations. Given this absence of connections, it makes sense that women would rely on official contacts to work efficiently and effectively.

Despite the importance of upward communication, employees find participation in upward communication extremely difficult. Table 1–2 suggests some reasons why. Being frank with superiors can be risky, especially when the news isn't what the boss wants to hear.[47] Busy superiors can also be too isolated, busy, or certain of their expertise to pay attention to employees. Some organizations have developed systems to promote upward communication in the face of challenges like these. Pillsbury Corporation employees can voice their messages on an anonymous voice mail system. An independent company creates transcripts of all calls and forwards them to Pillsbury's CEO.[48]

Most of the responsibility for improving upward communication rests with managers. They can begin the process by announcing their willingness to hear from subordinates. A number of vehicles facilitate upward messages: an open-door policy, grievance procedures, periodic interviews, group meetings, and the suggestion box, to name a few. Formal channels aren't the only way to promote upward messages. Informal contacts can often be most effective; chats during breaks, in the elevator, or at social gatherings can sometimes tell more than planned sessions. But no method will be effective unless a manager is sincerely interested in hearing from subordinates and genuinely values their ideas. Just talking about this isn't enough. Employees have to see evidence of a willingness to hear upward messages—both good and bad—before they will really open up.

Horizontal Communication A third type of organizational interaction is **horizontal communication** (sometimes called **lateral communication**). It consists of messages between members of an organization with equal power.[49] The most obvious type of horizontal communication goes on between members of the same division of an organization: office workers in the same department, co-workers on a construction project, and so on. In other cases, lateral communication occurs between people from different areas: accounting calls maintenance to get a machine repaired, hospital admissions calls intensive care to reserve a bed, and so on. Horizontal communication serves five purposes:[50]

- *Task coordination:* "Let's get together this afternoon and set up a production schedule."
- *Problem solving:* "It takes 3 days for my department to get reports from yours. How can we speed things up?"
- *Sharing information:* "I just found out that a big convention is coming to town next week, so we ought to get ready for lots of business."
- *Conflict resolution:* "I've heard that you were complaining about my work to the boss. If you're not happy, I wish you'd tell me first."
- *Building rapport:* "I appreciate the way you got that rush job done on time. I'd like to say thanks by buying you lunch when it's convenient."

Research suggests that people in most organizations communicate horizontally, but the reasons for doing so in high-performing groups are different from those in less effective ones.[51] Low-performing groups are likely to reach out to different parts of the organization to get information on how to follow existing procedures. For example, an engineer might contact the purchasing department to check on the status of an equipment order. By contrast, lateral contacts in high-performing organizations are used to get the information needed to solve complex and difficult work problems. For instance, before starting design work on a new product, the same engineer might contact the sales manager to find out what features customers want most. Top-performing organizations encourage people from different areas to get together and share ideas. At Hewlett-Packard, Worldwide Personnel Manager Barbara Waugh and her colleagues spent 5 years improving horizontal communication. "My role is to create mirrors that show the whole what the parts are doing—through coffee talks and small meetings, through building a network, through bringing people together who have similar or complementary ideas."[52]

Despite the importance of good horizontal communication, several forces work to discourage communication between peers.[53] *Rivalry* is one. People who feel threatened by one another aren't likely to be cooperative. The threat can come from competition for a promotion, raise, or other scarce resource. Sometimes rivalry occurs over an informal role. For example, two office comedians might feel threatened each time the other gets a laugh; that could inhibit their cooperation. Another challenge is the *specialization* that makes it hard for people with different technical specialties to understand one another. *Information overload* can also discourage employees from reaching out to others in different areas, and a simple *lack of motivation* is another problem. Finally, *physical barriers* can interfere with horizontal connections.

Informal Communication Networks

So far, we have focused on networks within organizations that are created by management. Alongside the formal networks, every organization also has **informal communication networks**—patterns of interaction based on friendships, shared personal or career interests, and proximity. One business writer described the value of informal networks:

> *A firm's organizational chart will tell you about authority. It doesn't always show how things get done or created. You know the rules, but you don't know the ropes. For that, you need a map to the network, the corresponding informal structure that is usually invisible.*[54]

Informal relationships within organizations operate in ways that have little to do with the formal relationships laid out in organizational charts.[55] Figure 1–3 shows the difference between the formal structure and the actual flow of information in one division of a hypothetical petroleum firm. And beyond any sort of organizational connection, people are connected with one another through informal personal networks—with friends, neighbors, family members, and all sorts of other relationships.

Some informal networks arise because of personal interests. Two colleagues who are avid basketball fans or share a fascination with rare books are more likely to swap information on work than co-workers who have no such bonds. Personal friendships also create connections that can lead to increased communication. Finally, physical proximity increases the chances for interaction. Shared office space or frequent meetings around the copying machine make it likely that people will exchange information. Even sharing restrooms can lead to networking, as public relations executive James E. Lukaszewski observes in describing what happens during breaks in predominantly male business meetings:

> *This may sound facetious, even silly, but when these meetings break, where are the women and where are the men? The guys go to the porcelain in that little room with M-E-N on the door. . . . The guys are standing there, facing the wall, talking and deciding things. It's a critical opportunity for important verbal communication to take place during times of decision making.*[56]

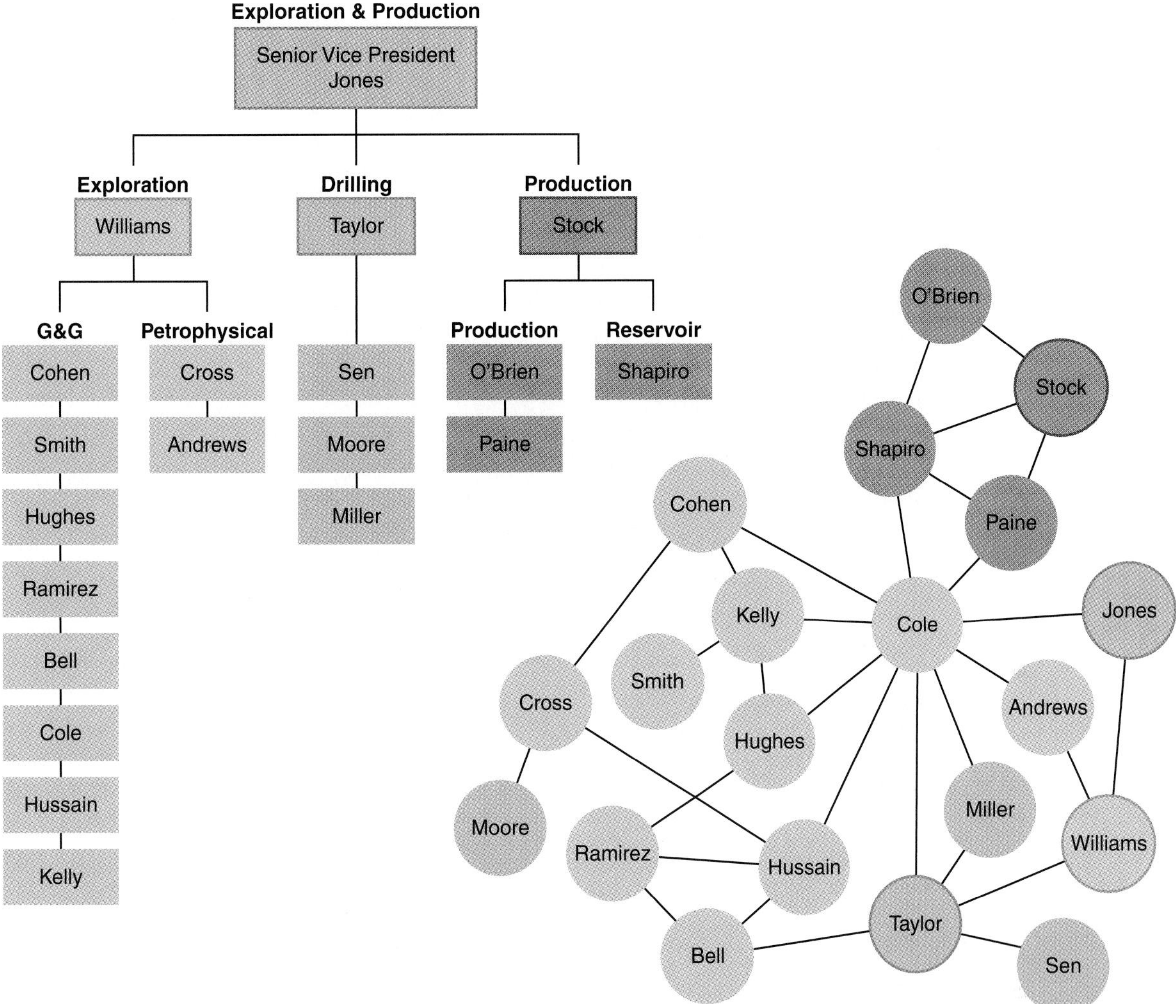

FIGURE 1–3
Formal versus Informal Communication Networks

Source: R. Cross et al., "Knowing What We Know: Supporting Knowledge Creation and Sharing in Social Networks," *Organizational Dynamics* 30, no. 2 (2001), pp. 100–120. Reprinted with permission from Elsevier Science.

Functions of Informal Networks within Organizations As the following examples show, not all informal messages are idle rumors. Informal communication can serve several useful functions.

- *Confirming formal messages:* "The boss is really serious this time about cutting down on overnight travel. I heard him yelling about it when I walked past his office."
- *Expanding on formal messages:* "The invitation to the office party says 'casual dress,' but don't make it too informal."
- *Expediting official messages:* You might learn about openings within an organization from people in your network long before the vacancies are published.

- *Contradicting official messages:* You might learn from a friend in accounting that the deadline for purchases on this year's budget isn't as firm as it sounded in the comptroller's recent memo.
- *Circumventing formal channels:* Your tennis partner who works in duplicating might sneak in an occasional rush job for you instead of putting it at the end of the line.

Many companies elevate informal communication to an official policy by encouraging open, unstructured contacts between people from various parts of the organization. For example, Hewlett-Packard's approach to problem solving has been termed MBWA, "management by wandering around."

Some observers consider informal contacts to be the primary means of communication within an organization. In one survey, 57 percent of the respondents said that the grapevine is "the only way to find out what's really happening" in their organizations.[57] A decade of research shows that engineers and scientists were five times more likely to turn to a person for information than to impersonal sources like the databases or files.[58] Two well-known analysts flatly assert that as much as 90 percent of what goes on in a company has nothing to do with formal events.[59] Writing in the *Harvard Business Review,* David Krackhardt and Jeffrey Hanson capture the difference between formal and informal networks: "If the formal organization is the skeleton of a company, the informal is the central nervous system."[60]

Like the human nervous system, informal networks are faster, and often more dependable, than formal channels.[61] They also provide a shortcut (and sometimes a way around) for the slower and more cumbersome formal channels, making innovation easier.[62] This fact helps explain why organizational decision-makers tend to rely on verbal information from trusted associates.[63] Smart communicators don't just rely on informal contacts with peers for information; they take advantage of sources throughout the organization. One study revealed that general managers spent a great deal of time with people who were not direct subordinates, superiors, or peers—people with whom, according to the official chain of command, they had no need to deal. Although many of these people—secretaries, lower-level subordinates, and supervisors with little power—seemed relatively unimportant to outsiders, successful managers all seemed to cultivate such contacts.[64]

Enlightened organizations do everything possible to encourage constructive, informal interaction. Siemens Corp. leaves overhead projectors and empty pads of paper in its factory lunchrooms to facilitate informal meetings.[65] Corning Glass deliberately installed escalators in its new engineering building to boost the kind of face-to-face contacts that are less likely in elevators. 3M sponsors clubs for any group of employees who request them, realizing that this sort of employee interaction is likely to encourage new ideas that will help the company. Other firms mingle workers from different departments in the same office, convinced that people who rub elbows will swap ideas and see themselves as part of a companywide team.

Informal networks don't just operate within organizations. Friends, neighbors, and community members increase their effectiveness by sharing information. In some cities, chambers of commerce host networking events to encourage these ties among community businesses. Even without these organized contacts, most people are surprised to realize just how many people they know who can offer useful information. Consider all the networks to which you already belong: family members, friends, neighbors, social acquaintances, fellow workers, members of your religious community, professionals (doctors, dentists, accountants, attorneys, etc.), school contacts (faculty, fellow students, counselors, etc.).

Cultivating Personal Networks Everyone is part of informal networks. As one writer put it, "Shared information is the foundation upon which civilization has been built. . . . We always networked. We just called it being "neighborly.'"[66] While all of us have personal contacts, **networking,** as the term is usually used, has a strategic dimension that goes beyond being sociable. It is the process of deliberately meeting people and maintaining contacts to get career information, advice, and leads—and in turn to help others. As you explore and expand your network, keep the following tips in mind.[67]

View everyone as a networking prospect The Self-Assessment tool on page 22 will help you identify many people in your personal networks who can help you achieve your goals. Beyond the people you already know, almost everyone you meet has the potential to be a source of useful information. The passenger seated next to you on a plane or train might be acquainted with people who can help you. The neighbor who you chat with at a block party might have the knowledge or skill to help you solve a problem. Within an organization, the best informants are often people you might overlook. Administrative assistants are exposed to most of the information addressed to their bosses, and they usually serve as gatekeepers who can give or deny access to them. Custodial and maintenance people travel around the building and, in their rounds, see and hear many interesting things. Of course, treating everyone you deal with respectfully is ethical as well as smart.

Self-Assessment Communication Network Inventory

Complete the table below to get a sense of some key people who are already members of your personal networks and who can help you be more successful in your career. After completing the inventory, develop an action plan by choosing which contacts you can pursue. Keep yourself on target by setting deadlines for contacting the people you have identified.

	Name	Type of Information This Person Could Provide	Questions I Could Ask This Person	Best Channel to Contact This Person	Help You Might Offer This Person
Family members					
Friends*					
Neighbors*					
Social acquaintances*					
Fellow workers and bosses*					
Members of religious and charitable community*					
Professionals (doctors, dentists, accountants, etc.)*					
School contacts (faculty, students, etc.)*					

**Past and present.*

Treat your contacts with gratitude and respect Don't make the mistake of equating networking with being dishonest or exploitive. As long as you express a genuine desire for information openly, there's nothing to be ashamed of. Furthermore, seeking information doesn't mean you have to stop enjoying others' company for social reasons.

When others do give you information, be sure to express your appreciation. At the very least, a "thank you" is in order. Even better, let your networking contacts know exactly *how* the information they gave you was helpful.

Help others Don't just be an information-seeker. Whenever possible, make an effort to put people who will benefit from contact in touch with one another: "You're looking for a new bookkeeper? I know someone who might be right for you!" Besides being the right thing to do, helping others will earn you a reputation for generosity that can serve you well.[68] The Self-Assessment on page 22 offers a tool for noting ways that you can use your personal networks to help meet others' needs.

Get referrals to secondary sources The benefits of personal networks don't stop with your personal acquaintances. Each of the people you know has his or her own connections, some of whom could be useful to you. Social scientists have demonstrated the "small world" phenomenon: Research on the "six degrees of separation" hypothesis involving over 45,000 messages and over 150 countries has demonstrated that the average number of links separating any two people in the world is indeed a half-dozen.[69] You can apply this principle to your own information by only seeking people removed from your personal network by one degree: If you ask 10 people for referrals and each of them knows 10 others who might be able to help, you have the potential of support from 100 information-givers. For example, you may not know anyone who can recommend the best accounting software program or who is plugged into the job market in Oklahoma City, but there's a good chance someone in your network can refer you to a person who can help you find the answer you're seeking.

Secondary sources are so valuable that some networking groups and Web sites exist to help users find the contacts they need. See the list of Web sites on pages 36–37 for tips about how to find these groups. Having a network of people who can refer you to others can be especially helpful in today's workforce, where people often stay in a job for only a year or two.

Seek a mentor A mentor is a person who acts as a guide, trainer, coach, and counselor; who teaches you the informal rules of an organization or a field; and who imparts the kinds of wisdom that come from firsthand experience. Many organizations have formal programs that match new employees with experienced ones. Other mentor-protégé relationships develop informally and unofficially. However you find one, a mentor can be invaluable. This is especially true for women, minorities, and people trying to break into nontraditional fields where "good old boy" networks can be hard to penetrate.[70]

A successful mentoring relationship isn't a one-time affair. Instead, it passes through several stages.[71] In the initial phase, the parties get to know one another and gain confidence in each other's commitment to the relationship. After the initial stage, a period of cultivation occurs in which the mentor guides his or her protégé through a series of conversations and tasks with the goal of buiding knowledge, confidence, and skill. By the third phase of the relationship, the protégé can function mostly on his or her own, with occasional guidance from the mentor. Finally, the fourth stage involves either separation or a redefinition of the relationship as one of peers. Not all mentoring relationships are this involved or long-lasting; but whether they are relatively brief or ongoing, they can provide great value and satisfaction for both the mentor and protégé.

Whatever the relationship, some rules guide mentoring relationships.[72] Look for someone with a position in a field that interests you. Don't be bashful about aiming high: You may be surprised by the willingness of successful people to give back by helping aspiring newcomers. Approach your mentor professionally, showing that you are serious about growing in your career. See "The Career Research Interview" in Chapter 7 for guidelines on how to handle this process.

Once you have found a mentor, show respect for his or her time by keeping most of your contacts to regularly scheduled times. Be sure to follow up on your mentor's suggestions about reading, checking Web sites, and attending activities.

Your Elevator Speech

Often the chance to present yourself and your ideas lasts less than a minute. You meet a prospective customer at a party. You run into your boss on the street. You are introduced to a potential employer in a hallway. Whether encounters like these turn out well or badly may depend on your foresight and preparation.

When the opportunity arises, you can make a good impression by delivering what has been called an "elevator speech." (This type of communication gets its name because it should be brief enough to deliver in the length of an elevator ride.) Elevator speeches can accomplish a variety of goals. Besides serving as introductions, they can be a tool for seeking help, establishing a relationship, gaining visibility, marketing yourself or your organization, getting feedback, expanding your personal network, and doing an end-run around someone who is blocking your progress.

Practice your skill at presenting yourself briefly and effectively by planning and delivering an elevator speech to your classmates. Your speech should contain four parts and take less than a minute to deliver.

1. State your name and your current job title or position.

   "Hi. I'm Claire Yoder. I'm a senior, graduating in December."

2. Describe some personal strengths or distinguishing information.

   "I'm completing my accounting major this semester with a 3.8 GPA and I've developed additional skills in tax preparation through volunteer work with Tax-Help USA."

3. Depending on your audience, state either what you can do for others *or* ask for their help:

   "If you or someone you know needs help with tax preparation, I can help," *or* "If you know of any openings in accounting, I'd like to hear about them."

4. Indicate how the person can get in touch with you:

   "Here's my card with my e-mail address. I'd like to hear from you."

While modesty is a virtue, don't be bashful about presenting yourself as an interesting and competent person. Whether or not you want to, you are always presenting yourself to others. Brevity and sincerity are the keys to an elevator speech. Don't overwhelm your audience with information; present enough to make sure you create a positive impression and ideally to be asked for more information.

For more help planning your elevator speech, see **http://www.saleslinks.com/sideline/99c/11v1.htm**.

Source: After Marie Wallace, "The Elevator Speech—It's There for You," retrieved June 21, 2006, from Law Library Resource Exchange at **http://www.llrx.com/columns/guide18.htm**.

Realize that a mentoring relationship should be primarily professional. If you have serious personal problems, turn to a counselor. A mentor may be able to help you with some personal problems as they affect your work life, but a mentor should not become an emotional crutch. Remember that any personal insights shared by mentors and protégés should be kept confidential. Finally, don't expect a mentor to grant you special favors, intervene on your behalf with your boss, or boost your chances for promotion. The advice you receive should be reward enough.

Face-to-Face and Electronic Communication Channels

As a business communicator, you often can choose how to deliver a message. Deciding which communication channel to use isn't a trivial matter; communication researchers have studied extensively the factors that lead to good channel choice.[73] Sometimes a written message succeeds where an oral one fails; at other times, talking to the recipient will produce results that the printed word can't match. An understanding of these two channels will help you make the best choice about how to deliver your important messages.

Face-to-Face Communication

Talking to others in person has several apparent advantages:

- *Richness.*[74] In person, a wide array of nonverbal cues help you better understand another person. Is the customer in a hurry? Is your boss angry? Is a colleague joking or serious? Seeing and hearing others can help you answer questions like these.
- *Speed.* Once you make contact with your audience, there's no time lag between the transmission of a message and its reception. If you need a price or have to have the funds in an account released *now,* putting your request in a letter or memo won't be much help.
- *Control.*[75] You might spend hours drafting a memo, letter, or report only to have the recipient scan it superficially or not read it at all. In a personal contact, however, you have much more command over the receiver's attention. Another enormous advantage of face-to-face communication is that it permits *instantaneous feedback.* When you speak directly to one or more listeners, you can respond to questions as soon as they arise. You can rephrase or elaborate when your listeners seem confused, and you can speed up if details aren't necessary.
- *Personal quality.* Face-to-face contact has the potential to create personal bonds that are more difficult in other types of communication. A corporate manager, whose company spends over $4 million annually on employee travel, makes the case for face-to-face contact: "Nothing takes the place of a handshake, going to lunch, seeing their eyes."[76]

Although it has many advantages, face-to-face communication isn't always the best approach. The biggest drawback of personal contacts is the difficulty in arranging them. Even when communicators are in the same building, scheduling a meeting can be difficult and frustrating. When the people who need to meet are separated by greater distances, personal contact is expensive and time-consuming. Even a crosstown trip for a half-hour meeting can take most of the morning or afternoon. A personal encounter might also be unproductive if the contact antagonizes one or more of the participants. If the personalities or the subject is likely to make someone angry or defensive, then less confrontational forms of communication might be better.

Teleconferencing

Face-to-face meetings may be desirable, but distance often makes them impractical. **Teleconferencing** is billed by its promoters as the next best thing to meeting in person. This technology allows participants in two or more locations to see and speak with each other. For example, retailers like Wal-Mart and Kmart use teleconferencing to keep headquarters-based merchandisers in touch with far-flung store managers.[77] Chapter 9 offers tips on how to set up and communicate effectively in teleconferences.

career tip

Cell Phone Do's and Don'ts

Like most technologies, cell phones have created some problems while solving others. The following guidelines will help you use this communication tool in the best way.

- Know your company's policy regarding personal cell phone calls in the office. Also, be sensitive to the informal rules about cell phone use in your work group.
- Avoid using your cell phone where others will be forced to overhear you, such as in restaurants, at performances, and on public transportation. If you must receive calls, use the phone's vibrating ringer to alert you and move to a more private place to talk.
- Don't interrupt an ongoing face-to-face conversation to speak on the phone. It gives the impression that those you are talking with are not as important as the caller. If you know you will be receiving a business-related call that you must take, forewarn the others and take only that call, not other calls. If you must respond to a caller, excuse yourself and make it short—less than 30 seconds.
- Avoid using annoying rings like "take me out to the ballgame." If possible, use the vibrate function or a plain ring.

Telephone and Voice Mail

The telephone lets you contact a receiver who would be impossible to reach in person. You can touch base with someone halfway around the world in less time than it takes to catch an elevator to the next floor. The phone can even help you get through to busy people who are nearby. A phone conversation does lack the visual feedback that often reveals how your message is getting across, although vocal cues—tone of voice, pauses, interruptions, pitch, and rate—can give you a good idea of the other person's reaction to your message.

Despite its advantages, telephoning has drawbacks. Even when you are able to "reach out and touch someone" with the phone, making contact can be problematic if you reach the caller at a bad time. Your chances of having a successful conversation will drop if the other person is hurried, angry, or distracted. For this reason, it's smart to ask, "Is this a good time?" before launching into your conversation.

Real-time communication isn't the only type of telephone communication. **Voice mail** is a high-tech version of the answering machine. Many communicators hate voice mail, often with justification. Some voice mail menus and submenus can take forever, and "clever" greetings can be annoying. But voice mail does have its advantages. It allows you to leave a message at any time of the day or night. You can feel confident that the recipient will actually receive the message in your own voice, just as you spoke it, without the omissions and distortions that come when an intermediary transcribes your message.

Even at their best, voice mail messages might seem inferior to speaking in person to the other party. Sometimes, though, a voice mail message can be even better than personal contact. Leaving a recorded message can save time and make it easier for you to deliver potentially awkward messages. With voice mail you can decline an invitation, express just the right amount of irritation, or offer an excuse. You can use voice mail most effectively if you follow the suggestions in the Career Tip box on page 27.

career tip

Guidelines for Using Voice Mail

Voice mail can be a useful tool or an annoyance to the receiver, depending on how you use it. The following tips will help you get your message across most effectively when you begin speaking after the beep.

1. Know the schedule of the person you're trying to reach. Doing so can boost the odds of reaching the person you're seeking (or not reaching him/her in person, if that is your goal). Some people are most likely to be near their phones in the early morning or late afternoon. Others are likely to be in (or out) during lunch. Be aware of time zone differences.
2. Leave the name of the person for whom the message is directed if the mailbox is shared by more than one person. Don't make the recipient guess who you're trying to reach.
3. Identify your name and phone number at the beginning of the message. Doing so will save the recipient from having to replay the whole message. Unless the recipient knows you well, leave your first and last name. You may not be the only John, Kim, Lizzie, or Gus in the receiver's circle of acquaintances. If there's any possibility of misunderstanding, spell your last name. Remember that your name and number are as familiar to you as your own face, but the receiver needs to understand them clearly.
4. Organize your message in advance. Don't confuse the recipient by leaving a rambling message that makes you sound muddle-headed and is likely to annoy the recipient.
5. Keep the message as short as possible. A long message—even if it is well organized—may contain too much information for the listener to digest. If you have a great deal to say, consider alerting your receiver to the main points, and then send the details via fax, memo, or e-mail.
6. Speak slowly and clearly. The vocal fidelity of some voice mail systems is poor, and you don't want your message to be misunderstood. Also, the recipient may not be able to write as quickly as you normally speak.

Despite its advantages, oral communication isn't a perfect medium. Possibly the greatest disadvantage of speech is its *transience*. All communication is fragile, but the spoken word is especially prone to being forgotten or misunderstood. Listeners quickly forget much of what they hear—half of a message almost immediately and half of the remainder 2 days later. Thus, a customer might forget three of the five product features you mentioned, or your boss might forget exactly *why* you need more staff support and only recall the dollar amount you requested.

Even if they remember an oral message, listeners are likely to *distort* it. Some details drop out with each telling of a story. Facts and figures change. The farther the message travels in space and time from its original sender, the greater the chance of distortion.

Written Communication

Written communication comes in a variety of forms. Letters, memos, bulletins, and reports are familiar fixtures in almost everybody's career.

Written messages have a set of advantages and drawbacks different from their spoken counterparts. Unlike speech, written communication is *permanent*. Once your words are down on paper, they are saved for future reference—either to your delight or to your undying embarrassment and chagrin. While people may have trouble accurately recalling what you said a few hours ago, they can refer to your written remarks years later. Even if the receiver has lost or forgotten your message, you can always supply a copy from your files.

Along with its permanence, written communication can be *easier to understand* than speech. Readers can study complex passages as many times as necessary, a luxury they do not have when the same message is delivered orally. They can take a break if their interest wanes and, after a cup of coffee or a quick stretch, come back to what they were reading refreshed and ready to go on.

Perhaps the greatest advantage of written communication is that you can *compose it in advance*. You can take as much time as necessary to shape a message just as you want it, pondering every word if necessary. You can try out several versions on test readers to anticipate the reactions of your real audience, and you can make changes until you get the desired response.

Finally, written messages are *less prone to errors*. Even the best-rehearsed oral presentations can go awry. You can misplace an important set of papers or forget to mention a key idea. Furthermore, the spontaneity that makes spoken communication so effective can backfire. Your attempt to improvise might sound confusing or lame, and the joke you thought would make the perfect ice-breaker might fall flat. Every speaker has thought, hours after a conversation, "If only I'd said . . . " When you communicate in writing, you have time to choose exactly the right words.

Electronic mail (or **e-mail**) allows communicators to send and respond to one another's written messages via computer. In high-tech societies, e-mail has become the most-used communication tool on the job. According to one survey, 71 percent of managers use e-mail as their primary form of communication. By comparison, only 13 percent of managers polled use the telephone most often and just 14 percent rely on face-to-face meetings.[78] Like the telephone and faxes, e-mail is virtually instantaneous: Once you click on the "send" icon on your computer, the message will be delivered to the addressee in a matter of minutes. Along with being a tool for external communication, e-mail is used as an alternative to telephones and personal contacts within an office, where it is often labeled as part of an **intranet**—an infrastructure that allows people within an organization to exchange information in digital form.[79]

career tip

Instant Messaging at Work

Instant Messaging (IM) is less intrusive than a phone call and more immediate than e-mail. It can be a business blessing or curse, depending on its use. Follow these guidelines for respectful and effective IM communication:

- Check your organization's policy on IM software. Make sure it allows IMing on the job and that it authorizes you to download the software you want to use.
- Ask whether the other person is available to IM rather than assuming he or she is. Respect others' responses that they are busy.
- Save yourself from interruptions by using the "busy" or "away" feature to tell others you aren't available.
- Don't make IM your main form of communication. It can be the right channel for a quick answer or to open a door. For long conversations, delicate issues, or complex transactions, use the phone, e-mail, or have a face-to-face conversation.
- Keep messages brief and to the point.
- Use IMs for short, nonconfrontational messages, not for arguments or heated discussions.
- Don't write anything you wouldn't put on company letterhead because IMs can be permanent and they are easy to forward.
- Avoid acronyms that may not be widely understood by your correspondent. TTFN ("Ta ta for now") might be fine for casual personal exchanges; at work, this approach may not create the impression you want.
- Avoid poor grammar or general sloppiness that could create a bad impression of you and your company.
- Focus on what you're doing. Too much multitasking can lead to major slip-ups and embarrassments.

Source: After Frank Thorsberg, "Ten Tips for Proper IM Manners," AOL Computer Center, August 12, 2002, and from Kate Lorenz, *Six Rules for IM-ing at Work,* retrieved September 29, 2005, from **http://jobs.aol.com/article?id=20050808184709990048**.

Like voice mail, e-mail is asynchronous, so you can leave messages for others to pick up at their convenience. Because your ideas appear in writing, e-mail (like letters and faxes) makes it easier to comprehend lengthy, detailed messages. Along with speed and convenience, e-mail provides an astonishing degree of access to people you otherwise might not be able to reach.

The speed and easy-to-use nature of e-mail also make it a tool for improving personal relationships on the job.[80] Speeding up routine communication leaves more time for personal contacts, which the medium also makes more likely. Technology consultant Beau Carr explains: "It may sound backwards, but people who refuse to learn about technology are the ones losing the human touch. . . . Users can focus more energy and attention on relating to other people and at the same time deliver products and services faster, better, and probably less expensively."[81]

Along with its advantages, e-mail can easily become a drain on your productivity. The technology is so quick and easy that it is prone to overuse: Your in-box can fill up with unimportant messages, and you can go overboard in sending mail to others. At computer chip maker Intel Corp., employees spend an average of 2.5 hours per day sending and receiving e-mails.[82] See the appendix for more guidelines on composing and managing e-mail messages.

Computer conferencing allows individuals and groups who may be physically dispersed to speak and even collaborate on documents. Conferencing can take place in real time, with participants interacting via their computers at the same moment, or over different periods of time, with participants working independently but picking up on the comments and input of others in their group. Communication experts have developed computer software (called group decision support systems, or "groupware") that facilitates electronic conferencing.

Instant messaging (IM) is a tool that lets you exchange messages in real time via your computer. IM isn't just a tool for recreation: The technology has real utility on the job. Along with being quick and easy to use, the technology is free, which can help you reduce the number of expensive long-distance or international telephone calls. Instant messaging also allows users to send urgent information or queries to others currently logged on to the network or online. For example, customer support agents at many companies can instantly get help from their colleagues when stumped by a customer's problem. When speed is important, instant messaging can beat both e-mail and telephones in efficiency. Connecting is almost instantaneous, and there is less need to socialize when time is of the essence. "One thing about the telephone is the first thing you're supposed to say is 'how's the wife and kids?' With instant messaging you can just say, 'I want this.'"[83]

For all these reasons, instant messaging has grown from a chat room for teenagers and lonely adults to a valuable tool in business and the professions, used by groups as diverse as international scientists, computer manufacturers, retailers, and the Internal Revenue Service.[84] In one poll of 50 Fortune 1000 companies, 36 percent had employees who used instant messaging to keep in touch.[85] Another survey revealed that almost a quarter of American workers use instant messaging on the job, often informally.[86]

Along with its advantages, instant messaging does have drawbacks. Typing is certainly more cumbersome than talking on the phone, and text-only messages lack the richness of spoken conversations. Also, instant messages that pop up on the screen demand your attention and can be a distraction from other tasks. Instant messaging can make you available to others almost constantly. Failure to respond quickly to others' messages can be perceived by senders as lack of interest, especially if they know you are logged on at your computer. Like other technologies, instant messaging has its advantages, but it isn't the perfect medium for all occasions.

Which Channel to Use

New technologies have given businesspeople a wider range of choices for communication than ever before, and choosing the most efficient and effective way to communicate a message can mean the difference between success and failure. Recognizing this fact, a new start-up firm, Tello, helps businesses determine the best ways to contact customers and suppliers. Tello serves its clients by helping them figure out the best channels for reaching business prospects and partners.[87]

The question is not which communication channel to use, but when to use each one most effectively. As Table 1–3 shows, each communication channel has both advantages and drawbacks. Despite these pros and cons, there are guidelines that will help you decide how to deliver your message most effectively. Following these guidelines can produce dramatic results. In one survey, managers who were

Table 1–3 Considerations in Choosing a Communication Channel

	Time Required for Feedback	Richness of Information Conveyed	Sender's Control over How Message Is Composed	Control over Receiver's Attention	Effectiveness for Detailed Messages
Face-to-Face	Immediate (after contact is established)	High (verbal and nonverbal cues)	Moderate	Highest	Weak (listeners are likely to forget details of complicated messages)
Telephone	Immediate (after contact is established)	Vocal, but not visual cues	Moderate	Less than in face-to-face setting	Weakest
Voice Mail	Delayed	Vocal, but not visual cues	Higher (since the receiver can't interrupt)	Low	Weak
E-mail	Delayed	Lowest (when text only, no formatting)	High	Low	Better
Instant Messaging	Potentially quick (after contact is established)	Lowest (when text only, no formatting)	High	Modest	Weak
Hard Copy (e.g., handwritten or typed message)	Delayed	Words, numbers and images, but no nonverbal cues	Highest	Low	Good

identified as "media sensitive"—those who matched the channel to the message—were almost twice as likely to receive top ratings in their performance reviews when compared with less media-sensitive peers.[88]

Consider the Desired Tone In general, oral communication is best for messages that require a personal dimension. For example, relationships improve and problems decline when physicians and the administrators of hospitals and health care systems meet in person instead of exchanging messages through less personal channels.[89] Oral channels are also best for ideas that have a strong need for visual support—demonstration, photos or slides, and so on. Spoken communication is also especially useful when there is a need for immediate feedback, such as question-and-answer sessions or a quick reply to your ideas.

Written communication (with the exception of e-mail) works best when you want to create a relatively formal tone. Writing is almost always the best medium when you must choose your words carefully. Writing is also better than speaking when you want to convey complicated ideas that are likely to require much study and thought by the receiver. It is also smart to put your message in writing when you want it to be the final word, with no feedback or discussion. Finally, writing is best for *any* message if you want a record to exist. In business and the professions, sending confirming letters and memoranda is common practice, as is keeping minutes of meetings. These steps guarantee that what is said will be a matter of record, useful in case of later misunderstandings or disputes and in case anyone wants to review the history of an issue. Handwritten notes of thanks or sympathy express thoughtfulness and add a personal touch that typed messages lose.

Consider the Organization's Culture Besides message-related considerations, the culture of the organization in which you work may favor some communication channels over others.[90] For example, Microsoft Corporation is so e-mail intensive that some voice mail greetings include the directive "If you're from Microsoft, please try to send electronic mail." In other organizations, voice mail is the preferred channel. Kirk Froggatt, a vice president at Silicon Graphics, offers one explanation: "There's something fundamentally more personal about voice mail. You can get the tone of voice, the passion. People like that."[91] Along with an organization's overall preference for some channels, it's important to consider the preferences of departments, or even individuals. For example, the computer support staff in some organizations respond to e-mails, while in other companies a phone call to the help desk is the best way to get a quick response. And, if you know a co-worker or your boss only responds to face-to-face reminders, your best bet is to use that approach.

Consider using Multiple Channels In many cases, it is wise to send a message using both oral and written channels. This kind of redundancy captures the best of both media, and it works in a variety of settings:

- Distribute a written text or outline that parallels your presentation.
- Follow a letter, fax, or e-mail message with a phone call, or call first and then write.
- Send a report or proposal and then make appointments with your readers to discuss it.

You won't always have the luxury of choosing the communication channel. But when you do, the right decision can make your message clearer and more effective. The Career Tips on pages 26, 27, and 29 can help you use electronic channels with civility and effectiveness.

summary

No matter what the job, communication is both a frequent and a critically important process. It occupies more time than any other activity and often makes the difference between success and failure for the organization as a whole and for its individual members.

Communication, as the term is used in this book, is a process in which people who occupy differing environments exchange messages in a specific context via one or more channels and often respond to each other's messages through verbal and nonverbal feedback. The effectiveness of communication can be diminished by physical, physiological, or psychological noise, which can exist in the sender, receiver, message, or channel. Communication is an unavoidable, irreversible process. Although it is vitally important, it is not a panacea that can solve every personal and organizational problem.

Attending to the fundamental elements of the communication process can improve the chances of success: choosing the most credible sender, picking the optimal receivers and attending to their needs, developing messages strategically and structuring them clearly, minimizing communication noise, and taking advantage of feedback to clarify confusing messages.

Communication in business and professional life often presents ethical challenges. While no rule book exists to cover every situation, a set of ethical principles can provide a framework for making principled decisions about what to say and do.

Formal communication networks—which can be pictured in flowcharts and organizational charts—are management's way of establishing what it believes are necessary relationships among people within an organization. Formal communication flows in several directions: downward from superiors to subordinates, upward from subordinates to superiors, and horizontally among people of equal rank. Unlike formal relationships, informal communication networks consist of interaction patterns that are not designed by management. Informal networks can be based on physical proximity, shared career interests, or personal friendships. Informal networks serve many purposes: They can confirm, expand upon, expedite, contradict, circumvent, or supplement formal messages. Because these functions are so useful, it is important to cultivate and use informal contacts within an organization.

In business, communicators can exchange messages via a number of channels, some oral and others written. The channel used to deliver a message can have a strong influence on its effectiveness. Each channel has both advantages and drawbacks. The best choice in a given situation depends primarily on the nature of the message, the organizational culture, and the desired tone.

key terms

Test your understanding of these key terms by visiting the Online Learning Center Web site at www.mhhe.com/adler9.

channel 8
communication networks 13
computer conferencing 30
content messages 10
context 9
decoding 8
downward communication 13
electronic mail (e-mail) 28
encoding 8
feedback 8
formal communication networks 13
horizontal communication 17
informal communication networks 18
instant messaging 30
intranet 28
lateral communication 17
message 8
networking 21
noise 8
organizational charts 13
receiver 8
relational messages 10
sender 8
teleconferencing 25
upward communication 15
voice mail 26

activities

Go to the self-quizzes at the Online Learning Center at www.mhhe.com/adler9 to test your knowledge of chapter concepts.

1. Invitation to Insight

Keep a log of your work- (or school-) related communication over a 3-day period. Include who you have communicated with (superior, subordinate, peer, external) and your level of satisfaction. Based on your findings, analyze

a. How much time you spend communicating.
b. With whom you communicate.
c. Your level of satisfaction.
d. Areas where improving your communication skills would be desirable.

2. Invitation to Insight

Think about a situation you have experienced in which communication went wrong. Diagnose the problem by finding the parts of the communication process that contributed to the trouble. Suggest a remedy for each problem you identify:

a. Sender: Did the wrong person send the message?
b. Encoding: Did the sender use words or nonverbal cues that were confusing, inappropriate, or irrelevant?
c. Message: Was the message too short or too long? Were there too many messages? Was the timing wrong?
d. Channel: Was the most appropriate channel chosen?
e. Receiver: Was there no receiver at all? Was the message poorly formulated for the person(s) at whom it was aimed? Was it received by the wrong person?
f. Decoding: Did the receiver read in meanings that were not intended?
g. Feedback: Was feedback adequate to ensure understanding? What impact did the feedback have on the sender?
h. Noise: Did external, physiological, or psychological noise distort the message? Provide specific examples.
i. Context: In what ways did physical, social, chronological, and cultural contexts impede the interaction?

3. Skill Builder

Identify at least two possible relational meanings for the following statements. For each relational meaning, envision the context in which it might have been stated. Based on your chosen context, decide which relational dimensions the message involves: affinity, control, and/or respect.

a. What's the matter with you?
b. It's about time!
c. I spent two days on this job.
d. I'd rather do it this way . . .
e. Let me pick up the lunch check.
f. You were a half-hour late. Is something wrong?
g. Give me a call sometime.

4. Invitation to Insight

Learn about upward communication in the workplace by asking several employees what types of information they share with their supervisors. What types of information do they avoid sharing with their supervisors? How does the organization encourage or discourage accurate upward communication?

5. Skill Builder

Develop your skill at cultivating informal communication networks by following these instructions:

a. Choose one of the following information goals, or identify a school- or work-related goal of your own.
   i. Decide which instructors and/or courses in an academic department of your institution are worth seeking out and which you might want to avoid.
   ii. Identify the qualities that would help you get the job of your dreams.
   iii. Determine which software program best suits your needs for a given application (e.g., word processing, database) and context (e.g., customer tracking, report writing).

b. Identify the people who can help you acquire the information you are seeking. Locate people from a variety of positions within the organization so you will gain a complete perspective. For each person, decide which channel you could use to begin to develop your network.

6. Skill Builder

With your group members, formulate a hypothetical context for each message to the right. Then use the information on pages 30–32 to decide which communication channel would be best for each message. Use the criteria from Table 1–3 to explain your choice:

a. Informing your supervisor about difficulties with a co-worker.
b. Asking for a few days of leave from work to attend a special reunion.
c. Training a new employee to operate a complicated computer program.
d. Notifying the manager of a local business that you still haven't received the refund you were promised.
e. Reminding your busy boss about a long overdue reimbursement for out-of-pocket expenses.
f. Apologizing to a customer for a mistake your company made.
g. Getting your boss's reaction to the idea of giving you more responsibility.

resources

In Print

Badaracco, Joseph L., Jr. *Leading Quietly: An Unorthodox Guide to Doing the Right Thing*. Boston: Harvard Business School Press, 2002.

Badaracco focuses on the ethical challenges faced by middle managers. He presents eight "practical and counterintuitive guidelines for confronting situations in which right and wrong seem like moving targets." Each guideline includes a case study and the lessons derived from it. Learn about the ethical considerations of nonheroes and quiet leaders.

Collins, Sandra D. *Communication in a Virtual Organization*. Mason, OH: South-Western, 2003.

This book examines how to communicate in groups that are geographically dispersed. It offers tips on how to use new technologies to develop relationships and work effectively with fellow workers who are not co-located and who see each other infrequently.

Cross, Rob, and Andrew Parker. *The Hidden Power of Social Networks: Understanding How Work Really Gets Done in Organizations*. Cambridge, MA: Harvard Business School Press, 2004.

The authors argue that most organizational leaders have little understanding of how their employees actually interact to get work done and that formal organizational charts fail to reveal the often hidden social networks that truly drive—or hinder—an organization's performance. Based on their in-depth study of more than 60 informal networks within organizations around the world, the authors suggest how organizations can enhance the way their informal networks operate.

Dainton, Marianne, and Elaine Zelley. *Applying Communication Theory for Professional Life*. London: Sage, 2004.

The authors focus on communication theories that have clear value in the world of businesses, professions, and other organizations. Topics include persuasion, culture, leadership, groups, organizations, and mediated communication.

Eisenberg, E. M., and H. L. Goodall, Jr. "The Changing World of Work" and "Relational Contexts for Organizational Communication." In *Organizational Communication: Balancing Creativity and Constraint*, 4th ed. New York: Bedford/St. Martin's, 2004.

This excellent text on organizational communication illustrates how changing values and priorities, as well as issues like globalization and loyalty, lead to shifts in employees' views of work and work relationships. Chapter 9 develops ideas for communicating with superiors, subordinates, and peers, and avoiding some pitfalls of intimacy in office relationships, and Chapter 12 addresses integrity at work.

Klaus, Peggy. *Brag: The Art of Tooting Your Own Horn Without Blowing It.* New York: Warner Books, 2003.
Klaus suggests guidelines to promote yourself appropriately in a variety of situations, including suggestions to replace face time for telecommuters who rarely see their bosses. She gives tips on creating a coherent summary of your career: who you are, what you've done, and what you want to do. The book includes excellent sections on better e-mail and voice mails, and special tips for focusing on the skills you've learned if you have been out of the paid workforce for a while.

On the Web

Business Topics

BRINT, A Business Researcher's Interests (**www.brint.com**), contains information about business, management, and information technology in the form of articles, magazines, journals, and case studies. Other Web sites of interest to business communicators include Fast Company (**www.fastcompany.com**), *BusinessWeek* (**www.businessweek.com**), *Forbes* (**www.forbes.com**), Business.com (**www.business.com**), and Pertinent Information (**www.pertinent.com**). Current issues of business journals in over 40 U.S. cities are a click away at American City Business Journals (**www. bizjournals.com**).

Professional Communication Organizations

The Association for Business Communication Web site (**www.businesscommunication.org**) offers a way for you to learn more about business communication and your career interests.

Other professional organizations offer a wealth of information and informative links: the National Communication Association (**www.natcom.org**), the International Communication Association (**www.icahdq.org**), and the American Communication Association (**www.americancomm.org**).

Business and Professional Ethics

Ethics Updates (**http://ethics.sandiego.edu/index.html**) offers multiple links to ethical theory and applied ethics information. Click on "Case Studies" to choose from over 90 case studies and the opportunity to join online discussions for each.

The Institute for Business and Professional Ethics (**www.depaul.edu/ethics**) promotes ethical behavior through teaching, training, and research. Its Web site includes links to *Business Ethics Magazine*, *The Online Journal of Ethics*, a newsletter, and ethics articles.

The U.S. Office of Government Ethics' Web site (**www.usoge.gov**) includes specific ethics topics (gifts, honoraria, supplementing income), "What's New in Ethics?," workshops, and training materials.

The Center for the Study of Ethics in the Professions, CSEP (**www.iit.edu/departments/csep**), presents a newsletter, Ethics Across the Curriculum, Intercollegiate Ethics Bowl, and Online Ethics Codes (over 800 codes indexed by over 24 fields of study).

The University of British Columbia's Center for Applied Ethics (**www.ethics.ubc.ca/links/index.htm**) offers another variety of ethics resources.

Networking

The following sites are among the best for developing and managing personal networks:

- Company of Friends (**http://www.fastcompany.com**) gives lists of possible contacts in many geographical areas.
- WorldWIT (Women, Insights, Technology) is a global network on- and offline for women in business and technology (**www.worldwit.org**)
- Career Planning (**http://careerplanning.about.com**) offers articles on how to network and resources for finding people who can help you become more successful.
- BoardnetUSA (**www.boardnetusa.org**) lists boards of organizations that could use your talent and energy. You can develop leadership and teamwork skills while serving a cause you believe in.

For more about networking software, see reviews at **http://www.fastcompany.com/magazine/81/blog_sns.html** or read Katharine

Hansen's *Networking Timetable for College Students* (**www.quintcareers.com/networking_timetable.html**).

Finally, test your networking skills by taking the "Networking IQ" quiz at **http://www.careerbuilder.com/JobSeeker/CareerBytes/0403NetworkingIQ.htm**.

Mentoring Resources

MentorNet (**http://mentornet.net**) offers online resources, especially for women in engineering and science. Advancing Women (**www.advancingwomen.com/mentor/index.html**) and Leader Values (**www.leader-values.com**) answer questions and present links to articles about benefits of mentoring and how to get a mentor. Women entrepreneurs can find a mentor or support group through WNET (Women's Network for Entrepreneurial Training at **www.wnet.bz**). For more advice on finding a mentor, see *Fast Company* magazine's Web site **http://www.fastcompany.com/magazine/42/instill.html**. For issues related specifically to women, see **http://www.fastcompany.com/magazine/17/womentoring.html**.

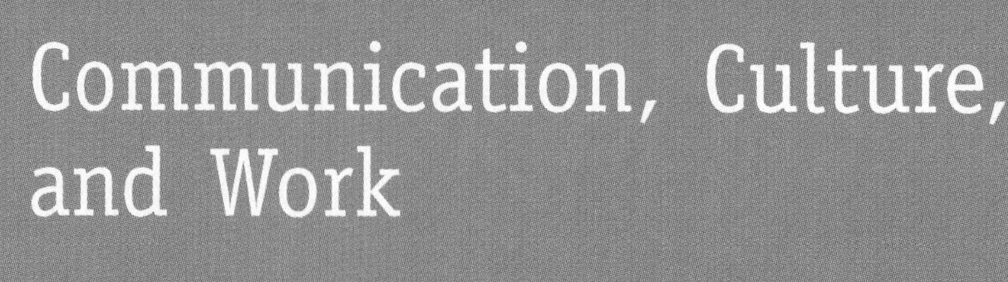

2 Communication, Culture, and Work

Chapter Outline

Chapter Objectives

After reading this chapter you should be able to

1 Identify the cultures and co-cultures in a specific organization, field, or community and describe how their norms and values shape communication in the workplace.

2 Use the guidelines on pages 58–61 to describe the ways you and others can communicate most effectively in a diverse work environment.

3 Describe the culture in a specific organization or field and explain how you can communicate most effectively within this culture.

Cultural Diversity and Communication

Diversity is a fact of life in today's working world. Consider the statistics. In the 1970s, roughly one American in eight was black, Hispanic, or Asian American. By the end of the 20th century one in four residents belonged to one of those groups. The population of Miami is two-thirds Hispanic; an equal percentage of Washington, DC, residents are black; and one-third of San Franciscans are Asian Americans.[1] As Figure 2–1 shows, the trend toward diversity will continue for the foreseeable future. According to U.S. Census Bureau, the nation's Hispanic and Asian populations will triple over the next half-century, and non-Hispanic whites will represent about one-half of the total population by 2050.[2] The growth is especially strong in some areas such as California, Texas, Florida, and New York. But diversity is also a fact of life in the U.S. heartland. Metropolitan areas including Salt Lake City, Minneapolis, Oklahoma City, and Colorado Springs are experiencing greater diversity as well.[3] Besides working with native-born people from different backgrounds, you can expect to communicate with people from other countries as well.

In fact, with the dramatic increase in international trade and immigration, the likelihood of working with people from different parts of the world is greater than ever. Over 10,000 foreign companies and their subsidiaries operate in the United States.[4] Eight of the 10 leading chemical companies, 9 of the 10 leading banks, and all of the leading construction companies are based outside the United States.[5] Some 300 Japanese companies operate in Michigan alone; German, British, and Dutch

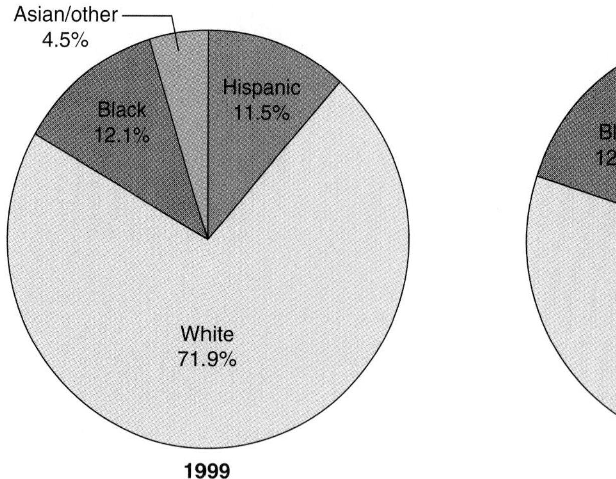

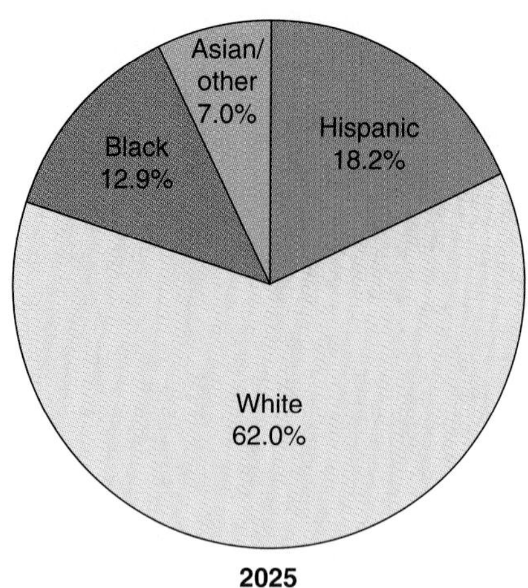

FIGURE 2–1 Racial and Ethnic Composition of the United States, 1999 and 2025

Note: White, black and Asian/other categories exclude Hispanics, who may be of any race. The Asian/other category includes American Indians, Eskimos, Aleuts, and Pacific Islanders. Totals may not add to 100 due to rounding.

Source: "The Changing American Pie, 1999 and 2025," Population Research Bureau, Washington, DC, 2000.

companies also have many U.S. sites. Immigrants accounted for over half of the growth in the U.S. labor force at the turn of the 21st century.[6] By 2016, experts predict that 2 million foreign-born workers will be moving to the United States every year.[7]

While overseas companies are part of the North American economy, Americans are moving abroad in growing numbers. Over 8 million were working overseas in 2003,[8] many for the 3,000 U.S. firms with global operations and others for over 36,000 foreign companies in more than 180 countries.[9] Among Fortune 500 corporations, the average U.S. multinational corporation has operations in about 17 countries, not to mention major interests in a number of affiliates worldwide.[10]

Given figures like these, it's no surprise that over 80 percent of the human resources executives surveyed say that global talent will be a priority in the coming years.[11] For companies and individuals who can take advantage of the trend toward increasing cultural diversity, the opportunities are great. DuPont has a policy of hiring men and women of a variety of ages and cultures because "diversity of experience and perspective gives DuPont a competitive edge."[12] Stona Fitch, vice president of manufacturing for Procter & Gamble, says, "Diversity provides a much richer environment, a variety of viewpoints, greater productivity. And, not unimportantly, it makes work more fun and interesting."[13] A spokesperson for the American Society of Civil Engineers states, "Without embracing diversity, the engineering profession will be unable to compete effectively in the global marketplace."[14]

The ability to work effectively with people from other countries is especially important if you plan a career in management, where international experience is rapidly moving from the "desirable" to the "essential." "We'd be blind not to see how critically important international experience is," says Colby H. Chandler, CEO of Eastman Kodak.[15] Whether you are working abroad, for or with foreign nationals at home, or with native-born people from different backgrounds, understanding cultural differences is an essential part of being an effective communicator.

The Nature of Culture

When most people use the word *culture*, they think of people from different national backgrounds. National cultures certainly do exist, and they play an important role

Table 2–1	**Some Cultural and Co-cultural Factors That Can Shape Communication**
	Race/ethnicity
	Nationality/geographic region
	Age
	Physical ability/disability
	Socioeconomic status
	Gender identity
	Language

in shaping the way people communicate. But as Table 2–1 shows, there are many other factors that define a culture and can shape the way people communicate. We therefore define **culture** as a learned set of shared interpretations about beliefs, values, and norms, which affect the behaviors of a relatively large group of people.[16]

It's important to realize that culture is learned, not innate. A Korean-born infant adopted soon after birth by American parents and raised in the United States will think and act differently from his or her cousins who grew up in Seoul. An African American may view the world differently depending on whether he or she was raised in a small town, an inner city, or middle-class suburbs—or in a country like France or Zaire, where African heritage has a different significance from that in the United States. A Jordanian who has lived in the United States since early childhood may subscribe to values and norms different from those of his brother-in-law visiting from Amman.

The book you are reading now is an example of the powerful, almost invisible force of culture. The fact that you are studying business and professional communication from a text rather than learning about it orally from an elder is just one example of a cultural standard. The assumption behind this book—that career success is important—is another. All the advice you will read here on how to operate in groups, how to negotiate differences with others, and how to organize and present your ideas embodies cultural assumptions. The overwhelming influence of culture on communication led famous anthropologist Edward Hall to assert that "culture is communication and communication is culture."[17]

Cultures are invisible to the people who are used to inhabiting them. But to people from different

From David W. Johnson and Frank P. Johnson, *Joining Together: Group Theory and Group Skills*, 8th ed. Published by Allyn and Bacon, Boston, MA. Copyright © 2003 by Pearson Education. Reprinted by permission of the publisher.

career tip

Getting a Job Overseas

Working abroad, even for a short period, can provide career advancement and personal growth. Along with paying jobs, short-term internships and volunteer positions offer chances to work overseas. Being bilingual or multilingual can be an advantage in landing a job abroad, although fluency in other languages is not always a requirement.

Web sites usually contain the most up-to-date information on overseas positions. Use the Internet Career Connection (**www.iccweb.com**), International Resources (**http://jobsearch.about.com/od/internationaljobs**), Jobs Abroad (**www.jobsabroad.com**), or Transitions Abroad (**www.transitionsabroad.com**). International Employment Gazette (**www.intemployment.com**) offers a print subscription for full information on overseas jobs. The University of Michigan provides information on work, volunteer, and internship positions overseas (**www.umich.edu/~icenter/overseas/work/waoverweb.html**) and International Opportunities (**www.cie.uci.edu/iop**) points the way to internships, research, study, teaching, volunteering, work, and summer programs.

The International Job Web site (**http://intljobs.about.com**) provides convenient links to at least 10 other major job banks with overseas positions. You can search for jobs by type (e.g., tourism, engineering, teaching), by region, or by specific country. To develop greater awareness of cultural networking differences as you search for a job, read "Networking Means Different Things in Different Countries" (**http://discussion.monster.com/articles/differentcountries**).

Print resources such as *Work Abroad* (Transitions Abroad Publishing, 2000) and the *Directory of American Firms Operating in Foreign Countries* (World Trade Academy Press, 2001) are also helpful. Besides offering job leads, these sources provide tips for constructing résumés for overseas employers. If you use a recruitment agency, be sure to check how it operates: Some are paid by employers to find employees in specific fields and locations, while others charge a fee from the new hire.

Before accepting an offer, check with reputable sources on finances, tax laws, insurance, moving, and cross-cultural and country-specific training.

Brint's International Business and Technology page (**www.brint.com/International.htm**) contains links to international corporations, travel, newspapers, law, business research, governments, banks, and currencies plus worldwide business and phone directories.

For a reality check on working abroad, read advice from those who've returned from overseas assignments. See, for example, P. Mandel, "Overseas Assignments: No Paradise," *BusinessWeek*, accessed June 20, 2006, from **www.businessweek.com/careers/content/oct2000/ca20001025_485.htm**.

backgrounds, the power of dominant norms is obvious. One account of a corporate training session illustrates this point:

> *[The trainer] would run a little experiment when she was talking to corporate audiences that were mixed—including white men, women, and minorities. She would ask the audience to do a simple task: "Please list," she would request, "the rules needed to be successful in a white male society." Immediately the women and the minorities would begin to write down all the things they had to do to "fit in." Meanwhile, the white males in the audience just sat there, doing nothing, looking around at the women and the minorities writing for all they were worth.*[18]

The author describing this experiment explains the important truth it reveals:

> *[Cultural] paradigms are like water to fish. They are invisible in many situations because it is "just the way we do things." Often they operate at an unconscious level. Yet they determine, to a large extent, our behavior. As a white male, I cannot write down all those rules. My wife can. My minority friends can.*[19]

Cultural Differences in Doing Business

Some cultural differences in customs and behavior are obvious. For example, your work life will be simpler once you understand that punctuality is important in Switzerland and Germany but less important in most parts of Africa. Other differences, though, are much more subtle. We'll begin this section by looking at the more obvious differences in customs and behavior that distinguish cultures. Next we'll explore some fundamental dimensions of diversity that are less obvious but at least as important.

Differences in Customs and Behavior Browse the travel and business sections of any decent bookstore and you're likely to find many volumes detailing the cultures and business practices around the world. The following categories are not an exhaustive list of differences between countries, but they suggest the importance of learning rules of the cultures in which you will operate.

Before going on, though, it is important to keep a sense of perspective about cultural influences on communication. Along with important differences, people from varied backgrounds also share many similarities. For example, computer engineers from Singapore, Lima, Tel Aviv, and Vancouver would find plenty of mutual interests and perspectives. Even when we acknowledge cultural variation, the fact remains that not everyone in a culture behaves identically. Figure 2–2 shows both the overlap in communication practices and the range of behavior within each one. Ignoring cross-cultural similarities and intracultural variation can lead to stereotyping people from different backgrounds, exaggerating and caricaturing the other culture, and judging its communication practices as radically different and implicitly wrong.

Formality U.S. Americans take pleasure in their informality and their quickness in getting on a first-name basis with others. With the exception of a few countries, including Thailand and Australia, business exchanges with persons from other countries tend to be much more formal, especially toward the beginning of a relationship. In the United States and Canada, first names are seen as friendly and indicative of

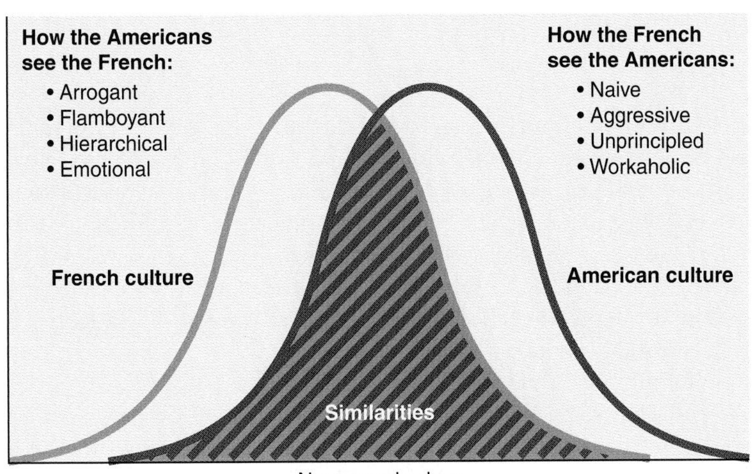

FIGURE 2–2
Culture and Stereotyping

Source: F. Trompenaars, *Riding the Waves of Culture* (New York: McGraw-Hill/Irwin, 1994), p. 28.

fondness and attachment. In many other countries—Mexico, Germany, and Egypt, for example—titles are an important way of showing respect, and it's best to use them until you are invited to move to a first-name basis.[20]

Names and titles aren't the only way to express degrees of formality. The way people do—or don't—converse with strangers varies from one culture to another. In North America, it's not uncommon to strike up a conversation with a stranger; but this custom isn't universal. The U.S. retailing giant Wal-Mart made the strategic decision not to hire greeters at its German stores for reasons expressed by a public relations expert from that country: "As a German, I find the idea of being greeted at the door uncomfortable. I would feel astonished if someone I didn't know started talking to me."[21]

Social customs Cultural differences begin as soon as communicators encounter one another. Greetings range from the bow (lower is more respectful) in Japan, to the *wai* (pressed palms with a head bow) in Thailand, to the handshake in Europe and South America.

In many countries, exchanging business cards is an important ritual. In Japan, especially, cards are given and received with care: The recipient should use two hands and study the card carefully, treating it with the same respect he or she would give its owner.[22] One U.S. businessperson lost a deal in Japan because his inattention to the Japanese businessmen's cards was taken as a measure of the lack of attention he would give to their business.[23]

In many cultures, gift giving is a part of business protocol. Knowing the details of a specific culture can be important. For example, in India, where cows are sacred, gifts of leather are to be avoided. In China, it is important to avoid giving gifts in sets of four since the sound of that number is the same as the word for "death." Consider gifts that are unique to your home region—Amish handicrafts from Pennsylvania, maple syrup from Vermont, Native American pottery from the Southwest—if they conform to the social customs of the recipient.

Styles of dress As travel and communication make the world feel like a smaller place, regional differences in clothing are becoming less pronounced. For men, the standard Western business suit is common in many urban settings. For both men and women abroad, conservative dress will take you much further than the latest fad or fashion. In Muslim countries, women can show respect with modest dress, including longer sleeves and lower hemlines than may be fashionable elsewhere.

Time In international business, the first shock for travelers from the United States may be the way members of other cultures understand and use time. North Americans, like most northern Europeans, have what anthropologists term a **monochronic** view of time, seeing it as an almost tangible substance. American speech reflects this attitude when people talk about saving time, making time, having time, wasting time, using time, and taking time. In U.S. culture, time is money, so it is rationed carefully. Appointments are scheduled and rigidly adhered to. Tasks are performed in a scheduled order, one at a time.

This monochronic orientation is not universal. Cultures with a **polychronic** orientation see time as taking a backseat to personal relationships. Meetings go on for as long as they take; they don't abruptly end because "it's time." Most Latin American cultures, as well as southern European and Middle Eastern cultures, have

a polychronic orientation. In Mexico, for example, "you make friends first and do business later," according to R. C. Schrader, who heads California's trade office in Mexico City.[24]

International management consultant Fons Trompenaars describes how the difference between monochronic time and polychronic time can make a strong impression when people from different cultures interact:

> *People who do only one thing at a time can, without meaning to, insult those who are used to doing several things. A South Korean manager explained his shock and disappointment upon returning to the Netherlands to see his boss:*
>
> *"He was on the phone when I entered his office, and as I came in he raised his hand slightly at me. Then he rudely continued his conversation as if I were not even in the room with him. Only after he had finished his conversation five minutes later did he get up and greet me with an enthusiastic, but insincere, 'Kim, happy to see you.' I just could not believe it."*
>
> *To a synchronic [monochronic] person, not being greeted spontaneously and immediately, even while still talking on the telephone, is a slight. The whole notion of sequencing your emotions and postponing them until other matters are out of the way suggests insincerity. You show how you value people by giving them time, even if they show up unexpectedly.*[25]

Members of polychronic cultures are less concerned with punctuality than those raised with monochronic standards. It is not that being punctual is unimportant; it is just that other relational factors may take priority. This fact helps explain why the notion of being "on time" varies. Extremely monochronic cultures view even small delays as an offense. In polychronic cultures, varying degrees of lateness are acceptable—from roughly 15 minutes in southern Europe to part, or sometimes even all, of the day in the Middle East and Africa.[26]

Conflict styles In some cultures, each person is responsible for helping to maintain harmony of a group and of society. The Korean term *kibun* embodies ideas of internal harmony or aura of harmony surrounding each person.[27] The maintenance and pursuit of harmony is expressed in the Japanese term *wa*. In other places—the Middle East and southern Europe, for example—harmony takes a backseat to emotional expression. Figure 2–3 illustrates how the rules for expressing emotions vary around the world.

The cultural avoidance of conflict means a Korean businessperson will probably not say "no" directly to you, fearing that you will lose face and suffer embarrassment. To help you maintain your *kibun*, he might spare you unpleasant news or information; it will be softened so that you don't suffer disgrace or shame, especially in front of others. You may be told that he will consider the matter or that it would be very difficult. Mexican business culture also values harmony and discourages confrontation. This attitude creates problems when it clashes with more aggressive standards that U.S. businesspeople usually bring to transactions. As

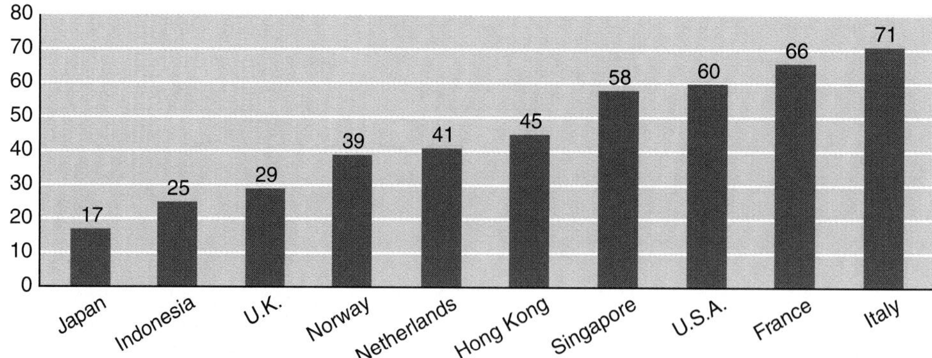

FIGURE 2–3 Percentage of Employees Who Would Openly Express Feeling Upset at Work

Source: F. Trompenaars, *Riding the Waves of Culture* (New York: McGraw-Hill/Irwin, 1994), p. 70.

president of Black & Decker Latin America, José Maria Gonzales is used to working with colleagues and suppliers from north of the border. Despite that fact, he says that coping with the difference between U.S. and Mexican approaches to conflict doesn't come easily:

> *In a meeting Americans can argue, hit the table and leave as if nothing happened, while a Mexican might not forgive you for three months. I have to make sure not to personalize things sometimes.*[28]

This sort of accommodation works both ways. People from cultures that seek harmony can learn to adapt to and accept conflict, and communicators from more aggressive societies like the United States can learn to appreciate the importance of harmony when communicating cross-culturally. Once communicators learn to appreciate different sets of rules about how to express and handle disagreements, conducting business becomes much easier.

Gender roles Women from North America, western Europe, and Australia/New Zealand who travel internationally are likely to be astonished and chagrined by the way they are regarded in some overseas cultures, where ideas of appropriate feminine behavior can be quite different. In some countries, a woman who outranks a man may not be treated that way by hosts; they may still speak to and prefer to negotiate with the male, assuming he is her superior. In Asian countries and Muslim countries women may find they are omitted from substantive conversation or overlooked in negotiations because of designated gender roles. Sometimes, a woman can establish greater credibility by clarifying her title, role, and responsibilities in writing before a personal visit, but even this step won't guarantee the desired effect.

The kinds of differences described here can present challenges when workers from different cultures work together. Table 2–2 is based on observations made at two Japanese-owned factories operating in the San Diego–Tijuana area, employing both U.S. and Mexican workers. It illustrates some of the challenges communicators face in today's international marketplace, where working with people from dramatically different backgrounds is a fact of life.

Fundamental Dimensions of Cultural Diversity

So far we have discussed obvious differences between cultures. As important as customs and norms are, they are only the tip of the cultural iceberg. Underlying what might appear to be idiosyncrasies in behavior are a number of fundamental values

Table 2–2 Cultural Traits Influencing Communication on the Job

	U.S.	Japan	Mexico
Social unit	Individual	Group	Family
Authority structure	Egalitarian	Hierarchical	Hierarchical
Basis for authority	Competence	Seniority	Trust
Style of negotiation	Direct	Indirect	Indirect
Decision making	Individualistic	Consensus	Authoritarian
Attitude toward conflict/competition	Seeks	Avoids	Avoids
Importance of personal relationships	Beneficial	Essential	Essential
Basis for status	Money/competence	Title/position	Title/position
Role of formality	Medium/low	High	High
Sense of history	Low	High	High
Importance of time	High	High (in business) Low (in personal matters)	Low

Source: Adapted from E. R. McDaniel and L. A. Samovar, "Cultural Influences on Communication in Multinational Organizations: Maquiladora Case Study," in *Intercultural Communication: A Reader,* 8th ed., eds. L. A. Samovar and R. E. Porter (Belmont, CA: Wadsworth, 1997).

that shape the way members of a culture think, feel, and act. In the following pages, we will look at some of these fundamental differences. Once you appreciate them, you will understand how and why people from different backgrounds behave as they do, and you will have ideas of how you can adapt to improve the quality of your communication with others.

High- versus Low-Context Anthropologist Edward Hall identified two distinct ways in which members of various cultures deliver messages.[29] A **low-context culture** uses language primarily to express thoughts, feelings, and ideas as clearly and logically as possible. To low-context communicators, the meaning of a statement is in the words spoken. By contrast, a **high-context culture** relies heavily on subtle, often nonverbal cues to convey meaning, save face, and maintain social harmony. Communicators in these societies learn to discover meaning from the context in which a message is delivered: the nonverbal behaviors of the speaker, the history of the relationship, and the general social rules that govern interaction between people. When delivering difficult or awkward messages, high-context speakers often convey meaning through context rather than plainly stated words to avoid upsetting their listeners. Mainstream culture in the United States and Canada falls toward the low-context end of the scale. Longtime residents generally value straight talk and grow impatient with "beating around the bush." By contrast, most Middle Eastern and Asian cultures fit the high-context pattern. In many Asian societies, for example, maintaining harmony is important, so communicators avoid speaking directly if that would threaten another person's dignity. One U.S. project manager describes how her insensitivity to high-context communication almost derailed an international team in developing a Japanese-language version of an Internet search service:

> *As an American project manager, I was expecting that if I was proposing something stupid, I would hear it from the people on the team. In reality, I had a plan with a fatal flaw, and the Japanese team members knew it, but it was not their style of communication to embarrass me by telling me.*[30]

Even within a single country, co-cultures can have different notions about the value of direct speech. For example, Puerto Rican language style resembles high-context Japanese or Korean more than low-context English. As a group, Puerto Ricans value social harmony and avoid confrontation, which leads them to systematically speak in indirect ways to avoid giving offense.[31] The same holds true for Mexican Americans, as communication researcher Don Locke explains:

> *Whereas members of the dominant culture of the United States are taught to value openness, frankness, and directness, the traditional Mexican-American approach requires the use of much diplomacy and tact when communicating with another individual. Concern and respect for the feelings of others dictate that a screen be provided behind which an individual may preserve dignity. . . . The manner of expression is likely to be elaborate and indirect, since the aim is to make the personal relationship at least appear harmonious, to show respect for the other's individuality. To the Mexican-American, direct argument or contradiction appears rude and disrespectful.*[32]

Even the relatively straightforward African American style of communicating isn't totally direct. In many cases it is "characterized by a speaker's use of innuendoes, insinuations, inferences, implications and suggestions to make the point" so that "the indirect message might not be a result of what is actually said, but of the meaning assigned to it by the hearer."[33] For example, rather than asking for a change of office outright, a person might describe the advantages of a different office, give a history of how long he or she has been in the present office, and add details or stories, taking a circular route to the main point.

A preference for high- or low-context communication isn't the only factor that distinguishes one culture from another. One survey of 160,000 employees in 60 countries revealed several other ways in which the world views of one national culture can differ from those of another.[34] Table 2–3 lists those dimensions and the styles that are most common in some countries. We will look at those differences now.

Individualism and Collectivism Members of **individualistic cultures** are inclined to put their own interests and those of their immediate family ahead of social concerns. Individualistic cultures offer their members a great deal of freedom, the belief being that this freedom makes it possible for each person to achieve personal success. **Collectivist cultures**, however, have tight social frameworks in which members of a group (such as an organization) feel primary loyalty toward one another and the group to which they belong. Japan, like most East Asian cultures, is highly collective.

In collectivist societies, members are expected to believe that the welfare of the organization is as important as their own.[35] Workers are less likely to strive to become organizational "stars," since that approach would dishonor other members

Table 2–3 Cultural Values in Selected Countries

Long-Term Orientation	Short-Term Orientation
China	Pakistan
Hong Kong	Philippines
Taiwan	Norway
Japan	Canada
South Korea	East Africa*
Individualistic	**Collectivistic**
U.S.	Guatamala
Australia	Ecuador
United Kingdom (England)	Panama
Canada	Venezuela
New Zealand	Pakistan, Indonesia
Avoid Uncertainty	**Tolerate Uncertainty**
Greece	Singapore
Portugal	Jamaica
Uraguay	Denmark
Guatemala	Sweden
Belgium and El Salvador	Hong Kong
High Power Distance	**Low Power Distance**
Malaysia	Austria
Philippines	Israel
Mexico	Denmark
Arab world**	New Zealand
China	Ireland
Task Oriented	**Socially Oriented**
Japan	Sweden
Hungary	Norway
Austria	Netherlands
Italy	Denmark
Switzerland	Costa Rica

**Ethiopia, Kenya, Tanzania, Zambia.*

***Egypt, Iraq, Kuwait, Lebanon, Libya, Saudi Arabia, United Arab Emirates.*

Source: Adapted from *Cultures and Organizations: Software of the Mind* by G. Hofstede. (New York: McGraw-Hill, 1997). Accessed from **http://www.geert-hofstede.com/hofstede-dimensions.php?culture1=95&culture2=14.**

of the team. "You seldom see an individual Japanese executive who stands above the rest until he is the most senior individual in the company," says international corporate recruiter Richard M. Ferry.[36] The power of collectivist beliefs was illustrated when PepsiCo rewarded one of its managers in China with a sizable cash bonus which he divided equally among his subordinates.[37]

Power Distance The term **power distance** refers to attitudes toward differences in authority. Cultures with high power distance, such as Mexico and the Philippines, accept the fact that power is distributed unequally—that some members have greater resources and influence than others. In these cultures, differences in organizational status and rank are expected, routine, and clear-cut. Employees respect those in high positions. Other cultures, such as the U.S., downplay differences in power. Employees are more comfortable approaching—and even challenging—their superiors and may expect to gain greater power.

Colleagues with different notions of power distance might find it difficult to work together. Imagine, for example, how a young business school graduate from a U.S. firm might grow frustrated after being transferred to the Guadalajara branch office, where the same relentless questioning that marked her as a free thinker in school is regarded as overly aggressive troublemaking.

Uncertainty Avoidance The world is an uncertain place. International politics, economic trends, and the forces of nature make it impossible to predict the future with accuracy. **Uncertainty avoidance** is a measure of how accepting a culture is of a lack of predictability. Some cultures (e.g., Singapore and Hong Kong) are comfortable with this fact. Their acceptance of uncertainty allows them to take risks, and they are relatively tolerant of behavior that differs from the norm. Other cultures (e.g., Japan, Greece, and Portugal) are less comfortable with change. They value tradition and formal rules, and show less tolerance for different ideas.

Task versus Social Orientation* Groups in societies with a strong **task orientation** (e.g., Japan, Austria, Switzerland, and Mexico) focus heavily on getting the job done. By contrast, groups in cultures with a high degree of **social orientation** (Scandinavian countries, Chile, Portugal, and Thailand) are more likely to be concerned about the feelings of members and their smooth functioning as a team. When compared to other countries, the United States falls slightly toward the task-oriented end of the spectrum and Canada is almost exactly in the middle, balanced between task and social concerns.[38]

Task-oriented societies focus on making the team more competent through training and use of up-to-date methods and are highly concerned with individual success: advancing to more responsible jobs, better training, and so on. By contrast, groups in socially oriented societies focus more on collective concerns: cooperative problem solving, maintaining a friendly atmosphere, and good physical working conditions.

Short- versus Long-Term Orientation Cultures with a **short-term orientation** look for quick payoffs, while people with **long-term orientations** defer gratification in pursuit of long-range goals. The willingness to work hard today for a future payoff is especially common in East Asian cultures, while Western industrialized cultures are much more focused on short-term results.

As long as employees and employers share the same orientation toward payoffs, the chances for harmony are good. When some people push for a quick fix while others urge patience, conflicts are likely to arise.

It's easy to see how a society's task or social orientation, attitudes toward uncertainty, individuality, power distance, and short- or long-term results can make a tremendous difference in how work situations evolve. Cultural values shape what persons communicate about and how they interact. Cultural differences don't account for every aspect of workplace functioning, of course, but they do provide a set of assumptions that exert a subtle yet powerful effect on each person's workplace communication.

Co-cultural Dimensions of a Diverse Society

It isn't necessary to travel abroad to find cultural differences. Diversity at home exerts a powerful effect on communication at work. Society is made up of a variety of **co-cultures**—groups that have a clear identity within the majority culture.

Regional Differences It is a mistake to think that members of one country all communicate identically. In the United States, for example, the unwritten rules about smiling differ from one part of the country to another. Communication researcher Ray Birdwhistell found that Midwesterners from Ohio, Indiana, and Illinois smiled more than New Englanders from Massachusetts, New Hampshire, and Maine. None of those people smiled as much as people from southern and border states like Georgia, Kentucky, and Tennessee.[39] Given these differences, it is easy to imagine how a manufacturer from Memphis might regard a banker from Boston as unfriendly, and how the New Englander might view the southerner as overly demonstrative.

**These categories were originally labeled "masculine" and "feminine," based on traditional views that men are assertive and results-oriented, while women are nurturing. In an era of increasingly flexible sex roles these terms are considered sexist and misleading, so we have substituted different labels.*

Ethnicity It is an oversimplification to describe a single "Hispanic," "Asian," "white," or "black" style of communication, just as it is dangerous to claim that all Arabs, baby boomers, Israelis, or women are alike. Each person's communication style is a combination of both individual and cultural traits. Keeping in mind the risks of overgeneralizing, scholars have found some patterns of communication that are common for many members of various groups. Understanding how communication is affected by cultural conditioning can help prevent jumping to mistaken conclusions about what a certain kind of behavior means. Table 2–4 highlights a few key cultural behaviors that are often misinterpreted.

The amount of talk and silence that is appropriate can differ from one co-culture to another. For example, most Native American and many Asian American cultures value silence more than mainstream U.S. culture does. By contrast, African American

Table 2–4 Co-cultural Differences Can Lead to Misunderstandings

Behaviors that have one meaning for members of the same culture or co-culture can be interpreted differently by members of other groups.

Behavior (in Traditional Co-culture)	Probable In-Group Perception	Possible Out-Group Perception
Avoidance of direct eye contact (Latino/a)	Used to communicate attentiveness or respect.	A sign of inattentiveness; direct eye contact is preferred.
Aggressively challenging a point with which one disagrees (African American)	Acceptable means of dialogue; not regarded as verbal abuse, or a precursor to violence.	Arguments are viewed as inappropriate and a sign of potential imminent violence.
Use of finger gestures to beckon others (Asian American)	Appropriate if used by adults for children, but highly offensive if directed at adults.	Appropriate gesture to use with both children and adults.
Silence (Native American)	A sign of respect, thoughtfulness, and/or uncertainty/ambiguity.	Interpreted as boredom, disagreement, or refusal to participate/respond.
Touch (Latino/a)	Normal and appropriate for interpersonal interactions.	Deemed appropriate for some intimate or friendly interactions; otherwise perceived as a violation of personal space.
Public display of intense emotions (African American)	Accepted and valued as measure of expressiveness. Appropriate in most settings.	Violates expectations for self-controlled public behaviors; inappropriate in most public settings.
Touching or holding hands of same-sex friends (Asian American)	Acceptable behavior that signifies closeness in platonic relationships.	Perceived as inappropriate, especially for male friends.

Source: Adapted from M. P. Orbe and T. M. Harris, *Interracial Communication: Theory into Practice* (Belmont, CA: Wadsworth, 2001), p. 65.

career tip

Communicating across Generations

Along with factors like ethnicity and regional differences, the era in which people have been raised can shape the way they communicate. Demographers, marketers, and social scientists often categorize people born in the Western world in the 20th century into four groups: "Matures," "Boomers," "Generation X," and "Generation Y."

Matures (born 1900–1945)
Matures have been called "The Greatest Generation." Their formative experiences included the Depression, World Wars I and II, and the dawn of the atomic era. These events led to a strong sense of self-control and self-sacrifice. Matures commonly have a strong respect for authority. In the workplace, they have traditionally been loyal to the organizations for which they work. They follow the rules, which they assume exist for good reason. Their work ethic includes timeliness and productivity.

Boomers (born 1946–1964)
Boomers benefited from growing up in the post–World War II era of prosperity. They witnessed and participated in an era of social reform and upheaval that included the Civil Rights revolution. Social upheaval surrounding the Vietnam War and the degradation of the environment led many Boomers to question the claims of authority figures—an ironic position now that they have become the authorities. Boomers have an optimistic, can-do belief in themselves and in the potential for society and organizations to change for the better. As a group, Boomers have grown used to getting their way.

Generation X (born 1965–1982)
For Gen-Xers, the 1969 moon landing was history and technological advances have been a fact of life. During their youth, gender roles for women became more flexible, contributing to the notion that anything is possible. Because of their many options, Generation X-ers characteristically explore what is desirable for themselves as individuals. They are adept with technology, skeptical, and independent, seeking a good balance between work and the rest of life. They don't accept orders uncritically, and they expect work and life to be meaningful. They respect performance over tenure and are loyal to people, not organizations.

Generation Y (born 1982–1991)
This group goes by a number of descriptive labels: the Why Generation, Net Generation, and Digital Natives. When compared to the preceding generation, they are hopeful and determined. They are technologically adept, and they like to learn by doing. They have high—sometimes unrealistic—expectations for salary, job, and duties. They are remarkably able to shift attention rapidly from one task to another. As a result, they are excellent at multitasking. On the other hand, they may ignore what doesn't interest them—at their own expense and that of their work.

Generalizations can, of course, by risky. Still, knowledge of these characteristics can help people from different generations understand and communicate better with one another.

Sources: Eisner, S. P. Managing "Generation Y." *Advanced Management Journal* 70(2005), pp. 13–17. Lyons, S., Duxbury, L., and Higgins, C. "Are Gender Differences in Basic Human Values a Generational Phenomenon?" *Sex Roles: A Journal of Research* 53 (2005), pp. 763–779. Oblinger, D. G., and Oblinger, J. L. *Educating the Net Generation*, Boulder, CO: Educause 2005. Online at **http://www.educause.edu/Books/635**. Rodriguez, R. O., Green, M. T., and Ree, M. J. "Leading Generation X: Do the Old Rules Apply?" *Journal of Leadership & Organizational Studies* 9 (2003), pp. 67–76.

and Euro-American cultures place a high value on verbal skills, and their members tend to speak more. It is easy to imagine how the silence of, say, a Japanese American or Native American employee could be viewed by an African American or Euro-American colleague as a sign of dislike.

Attitudes toward conflict also differ from one ethnic co-culture to another. Because Asian cultures place a high value on saving face, some Asian Americans can display a preference for not disagreeing assertively and directly. Native Americans may prefer to deal with conflict through silence rather than direct confrontation. By contrast, many (though certainly not all) people with a Greek, Israeli, Italian, French, or South American background may prefer a direct, open conflict style.[40]

Even when communicators from different backgrounds speak roughly the same amount, the degree of personal information they reveal can differ dramatically. For example, Euro-Americans disclose more than African Americans or Puerto Ricans, who in turn reveal more than Mexican Americans.[41] (Of course, varying social and cultural contexts may create different disclosure patterns.)

Nonverbal standards also vary by co-culture. Most communicators unconsciously assume that their rules for behaviors such as eye contact are universal. Researchers, however, have found that eye behavior can vary significantly. One study found that widely opened eyes are often interpreted in mainstream U.S. culture as a sign of surprise or wonder and in Hispanic culture as a call for help, signifying "I don't understand." To some African Americans, the same kind of gaze is often regarded as a measure of innocence.[42]

Since Euro-Americans often associate eye contact with honesty and respect, it is easy to misjudge others for whom steady eye contact would be a sign of disrespect. There are many cases where attempts by Puerto Ricans and Native Americans to show respect to persons in authority by not looking at them have been interpreted as dishonesty or disrespect by those accustomed to greater eye contact. Traditionally, Hopi and Navajo people generally avoid steady eye contact, as it is considered offensive, disrespectful, and rude. Blacks tend to make more eye contact when speaking but will not have such a steady gaze at someone they are listening to. Whites tend to make more continuous eye contact while listening to someone.[43]

Disabilities Belonging to a co-culture based on ethnicity or nationality requires years of immersion. By contrast, says columnist Karen Stone, "Disability is a club anyone can join, anytime. It's very easy. Have a stroke and be paralyzed. . . . Be in a car wreck and never walk again."[44] The Americans with Disabilities Act of 1990 (ADA) seeks to guarantee that people with disabilities receive reasonable accommodations and equal access to employment, buildings, transportation, and services. These legal guarantees are important, but they don't change the fact that, in many ways, having a disability may change how one is regarded. Typical language habits reflect this fact. The tendency is to use labels like "blind," "wheelchair-bound," or "deaf" to describe a person, putting him or her in a category that emphasizes physical condition over all other attributes.

Advocates urge terms that treat a disability as one feature, not as a defining characteristic. Describing Mike as "a person who is blind" is both more accurate and less constricting than calling him a "blind person." The difference between "deaf person" and "person who is deaf" might seem subtle—until you imagine which label you would prefer if you lost your hearing.

There are no hard-and-fast rules about communicating with people who have disabilities. After 11 years of research, communication researcher Dawn Braithwaite found that strategies preferred by some were rejected by others.[45] This variability showed up in situations in which an able-bodied person might appropriately offer help. About half of the survey respondents were open to offers of assistance, while others preferred that able-bodied persons wait until they receive a request for help. In either case, though, one message came through clearly: It is important for the self-esteem and safety of a person with a disability to maintain control over if, when, and how help is given. If your offer of help is turned down, accept that fact. If it is accepted, either ask "How can I help?" or ask whether your intentions are acceptable: "Would you like me to open the door?"

Despite the lack of specific overall rules, there are some guidelines for interacting with people who have disabilities:

1. Speak directly to people with disabilities, rather than looking at and talking to their companion or sign language interpreter.
2. When introduced to a person with a disability, offer to shake hands. People with limited hand use or who wear an artificial limb can usually shake hands. (Shaking hands with the left hand is an acceptable greeting.)
3. When meeting a person who is visually impaired, identify yourself and others who may be with you. When conversing in a group, remember to identify the person to whom you are speaking. If you are leaving a group, tell the other person.
4. If you offer assistance, wait until your offer is accepted. Then listen to or ask for instructions.
5. Treat adults as adults. Address people who have disabilities by their first names only when extending the same familiarity to all others. Never patronize people who use wheelchairs by patting them on the head or shoulder.
6. Leaning on or hanging on to a person's wheelchair is similar to leaning or hanging on to a person and is generally considered annoying. The chair is part of the personal body space of the person who uses it.
7. Listen attentively when you're talking with a person who has difficulty speaking. Be patient and wait for the person to finish, rather than correcting or speaking for the person. If necessary, ask short questions that require short answers, a nod, or shake of the head. Never pretend to understand if you are having difficulty doing so. Instead, repeat what you have understood and allow the person to respond. The response will clue you in and guide your understanding.
8. When speaking with a person who uses a wheelchair or a person who uses crutches, place yourself at eye level in front of the person to facilitate the conversation.
9. To get the attention of a person who is deaf, tap the person on the shoulder or wave your hand. Look directly at the person and speak clearly, slowly, and expressively to determine whether the person can read your lips. Not all people who are deaf can read lips. For those who do lip read, be sensitive to their

needs by placing yourself so that you face the light source and keep hands, cigarettes, and food away from your mouth when speaking.

10. Relax. Don't be embarrassed if you happen to use accepted, common expressions such as "See you later" or "Did you hear about that?" that seem to relate to a person's disability. Don't be afraid to ask questions when you're unsure of what to do.[46]

So far we have focused on guidelines for able-bodied communicators. People with disabilities also can take steps to improve communication. Braithwaite identified several strategies that can minimize the impact of the disability and help put able-bodied people at ease. They include:

- *Initiating a transaction:* "Excuse me. Would you mind looking up a phone number?"
- *Modeling behavior:* "If you move your lips more like this, I can understand you better."
- *Establishing normalcy:* "Don't you hate waiting in lines like this?"
- *Confronting the issue:* "I may have trouble speaking, but I can understand just fine!"
- *Using humor:* "Tony, they tell me your singing is so awful that even a guy like me who can't hear would hate it!"

Diversity and Ethical Issues

Some cultural differences may challenge your sense of what is normal or proper behavior without raising ethical questions. For example, you probably could readjust your sense of promptness or what to wear to a business meeting without facing

Self-Assessment Diagnosing Your Cultural Intelligence

These statements reflect different facets of cultural intelligence. For each set, add up your scores and divide by four to produce an average. Our work with large groups of managers shows that for purposes of your own development, it is most useful to think about your three scores in comparison to one another. Generally, an average of less than 3 would indicate an area calling for improvement, while an average of greater than 4–5 reflects a true CQ strength.

Rate the extent to which you agree with each statement, using the scale:
1 = strongly disagree, 2 = disagree, 3 = neutral, 4 = agree, 5 = strongly agree.

_______ Before I interact with people from a new culture, I ask myself what I hope to achieve.

_______ If I encounter something unexpected while working in a new culture, I use this experience to figure out new ways to approach *other* cultures in the future.

_______ I plan how I'm going to relate to people from a different culture before I meet them.

+ _______ When I come into a new cultural situation, I can immediately sense whether something is going well or something is wrong.

Total _______ ÷ 4 = [ ] **Cognitive CQ**

any sort of moral dilemma. In other cases, though, doing business in an unfamiliar culture might challenge your fundamental sense of right and wrong. You might be offended by differing notions of gender equality. You could be shocked to learn that bribes or payoffs are considered a normal part of doing business. You could encounter favoritism toward friends and family members that offends your sense of fair play. You might see a profound disregard for the environment.

There is growing recognition that businesses that operate in a worldwide economy need a universal code of business ethics. Toward that end, a collaboration of business leaders in Japan, Europe, and the United States have developed a code of ethics based on ideals from both East Asia and the West. Called the Caux Round Table Principles for Business, this code includes many communication-related principles, such as treating all employees with honesty and dignity, listening to employee suggestions, avoiding discriminatory practices, dealing with all customers fairly, and avoiding industrial espionage and other dishonest means of acquiring commercial information.[47]

Despite this admirable effort, you may encounter ethical challenges arising out of cultural differences. In cases like these, you can respond in a variety of ways:

Avoiding: You might refuse to do business in cultures which operate according to ethical principles that are different from yours.

Accommodating: You could accept the different ethical system and conform to practices that are fundamentally different from yours.

	_____	It's easy for me to change my body language (for example, eye contact or posture) to suit people from a different culture.
	_____	I can alter my expression when a cultural encounter requires it.
	_____	I modify my speech style (for example, accent or tone) to suit people from a different culture.
+	_____	I easily change the way I act when a cross-cultural encounter seems to require it.
Total	_____ ÷ 4 = ☐	**Physical CQ**

	_____	I have confidence that I can deal well with people from a different culture.
	_____	I am certain that I can befriend people whose cultural backgrounds are different from mine.
	_____	I can adapt to the lifestyle of a different culture with relative ease.
+	_____	I am confident that I can deal with a cultural situation that's unfamiliar.
Total	_____ ÷ 4 = ☐	**Emotional/ motivational CQ**

Source: P. C. Earley and E. Mosakowski, "Cultural Intelligence," *Harvard Business Review*, October 2004, pp. 139–146.

Forcing: You could insist on doing business in a way that you believe is ethically proper.

Educating–Persuading: You could try to convince the people with whom you want to do business why your set of ethical principles is more appropriate.

Negotiating–Compromising: Both parties could give up something to negotiate a settlement.

Collaboration–Problem Solving: The parties could confront the conflict directly and work together to develop a mutually satisfying solution.[48]

All of these approaches have obvious drawbacks. It's easy to imagine a situation in which you may have to choose between compromising your principles to please your bosses and customers or being true to yourself and risking your career.

Facing ethical dilemmas you never anticipated can be especially hard. You can begin to prepare yourself by grounding yourself in ethical principles and learning about the ethical practices of a new culture. When you do encounter new situations, ask yourself the following questions to help you make the best possible decision:

- *How morally significant is this situation?* Not all ethical conflicts have the same moral significance. For example, while giving contracts to friends or family members may offend the sensibilities of a businessperson used to awarding jobs on the basis of merit, the practice may not be as morally offensive as one exploiting child labor or irreparably damaging the environment.[49]
- *Is there home culture consensus regarding the issue?* If there is not widespread agreement in your home culture about the ethical principle, you justifiably may have more latitude about how to act. For example, since corporations in the United States have a wide range of policies about supporting the families of employees, there might be less obligation for a company to provide family benefits in a host country.[50]

Communicating across Diversity

By now it should be clear that communicating with others from different backgrounds isn't always easy. Matters including culture, race, and gender may have made others' experiences quite different from yours.[51] Some of the responsibility for building bridges rests with management, and a growing number of businesses are taking this job seriously. But you don't need to join a corporate training program to benefit from cultural diversity. Figure 2-4 shows the range of attitudes about

Denial	Defense	Minimization	Acceptance	Adaptation	Integration
No perception of differences	Hostility toward other cultures	Belief that cultural differences are superficial	Recognition and exploration of differences	Ability to empathize, shift frame of reference	Recognizing and embracing differences

Self-centered ◄——————————————► Other-centered

FIGURE 2–4
Stages of Intercultural Sensitivity

Source: Conceptualized by Chris Maxwell and Ann M. Greenhalgh, Undergraduate Leadership Program, The Wharton School, University of Pennsylvania. Adapted from *Module 6: Intercultural Communication for Business*, by O'Rourke/Yarbrough. © 2005. Reprinted with permission of South-Western, a division of Thomson Learning: **www.thomsonrights.com.** Fax 800-730-2215.

Table 2–5 Attitudes and Behaviors That Block or Promote Intercultural Relations

Assumptions That Block Authentic Relations	
Assumptions Majority Makes	**Assumptions Minorities Make**
• Differences should not affect performance.	• All members of the majority have the same attitudes about minorities.
• Minorities will always welcome inclusion in the majority culture.	• There are no majority members who understand minorities.
• Open recognition of differences may embarrass minorities.	• Majority members are not really trying to understand minorities.
• Minorities are using their situation to take advantage of the majority.	• The only way to change the situation is by confrontation and force.
• "Liberal" members of the majority are free of discriminatory attitudes.	• All majority members will let you down in a "crunch."
• Minorities are oversensitive	
Behaviors That Block Authentic Relations	
Behaviors of Majority Cultures	**Behaviors of Minority Cultures**
• Interruptions.	• Confrontation too early and too harshly.
• Condescending behavior.	• Rejection of offers to help and friendship.
• Expressions of too-easy acceptance and friendship.	• Giving answers majority members want to hear.
• Talking about, rather than to, minorities who are present.	• Isolationism.
Assumptions and Behaviors That Promote Authentic Relations	
• Treating people as individuals as well as members of a culture.	• Staying with and working through difficult confrontations.
• Demonstrating interest in learning about other cultures.	• Acknowledging sincere attempts (even clumsy ones).
• Listening without interrupting.	• Dealing with others as they are, instead of expecting them to be perfect.
• Taking risks (e.g., being first to confront needed differences).	• Recognizing that interdependence is needed between members of majority and minority cultures.
• Expressing concerns directly and constructively.	

Source: From Philip R. Harris and Robert T. Moran, *Managing Cultural Differences*, 2nd ed. (Houston: Grid, 1987), pp. 245–247.

cultural differences, and Table 2–5 lists attitudes and behaviors that can promote more satisfying, productive relationships among members of different cultures. These principles can be summarized in the five categories on pages 60–61. Adopting a more perceptive attitude can go a long way toward opening the door to more rewarding and productive communication.

Become Culturally Literate Many cultural problems are not caused by malice but by a lack of knowledge. Trainers in cultural sensitivity cite examples of how mistaken assumptions can lead to trouble.[52] In one West Coast bank, officials were dismayed when Filipino female employees didn't cooperate with the new "friendly teller" program. Management failed to realize that in Filipino culture, overtly friendly women can be taken for prostitutes. A Taiwanese executive who was transferred to the Midwestern offices of a large company was viewed as aloof and autocratic by his peers, who did not understand that Asian culture encourages a more distant managerial style.

Misunderstandings like these are less likely to cause problems when mainstream workers understand each other's cultural backgrounds. As Paulette Williams, former senior manager at Weyerhauser's nurseries in southern California, put it, "If you don't learn how other people feel, you can hurt them unintentionally."[53]

Timothy Weiss, a U.S. professor who spent a year teaching at the Chinese University of Hong Kong, illustrates the kind of open-minded, inquiring attitude that can make communicators more effective when they encounter different cultural practices.

> *Why, in a culture that so dearly values every second and minute saved, will meetings and conversations last for what Americans would consider such inordinately long periods? . . . In these departmental meetings—which I find excruciating—I suspect that something else is going on that a Westerner such as myself will understand sooner or later. Although I certainly am not ready to abandon my American sense of how departmental meetings should be conducted, in allowing myself to remain open-minded about other ways of conducting these meetings, I begin to learn something about other ways of approaching departmental issues and of communicating messages within a group.*[54]

View Diversity as an Opportunity It is easy to think of cultural differences as an annoyance that makes it harder to take care of business. Dealing with others who have different attitudes or customs takes patience and time—both scarce commodities in a busy work schedule. But with the right attitude, cultural diversity can stop being just a necessary cost of doing business and can become an opportunity.[55]

People with differing backgrounds can bring new strengths to a business. Women, for instance, are generally more skilled than men at reading nonverbal cues.[56] This makes them ideal members of a negotiating team, where they may be especially skilled at interpreting how the other people are feeling. Workers from diverse ethnic groups can offer new insights into how customers or other workers with similar backgrounds can be reached. A Hispanic supervisor, for example, may be especially effective at motivating and training other Hispanics, and a Korean team member can give new insights into how a Korean-managed competitor operates.

Avoid Ethnocentrism **Ethnocentrism** is the inclination to see all events from the perspective of your own culture and to evaluate your own culture as superior. Ethnocentrism is evident when you judge someone to be less intelligent or less important because he or she doesn't keep up with your national teams, critique others as less sophisticated because their dress doesn't match your culture's notion of fashion, or assume others have less business acumen because they use different software programs.

Don't Condescend It's easy to view people who are different as unequal. Your first reaction to a physically challenged colleague might be sympathy or pity. Immigrants who are learning English as a second language might sound less intelligent than native speakers. Even white males, members of the traditional majority, might seem like members of the "good old boy" club, undeserving of respect since their success seemingly owes more to personal connections than to merit.

Even excessive efforts to demonstrate an attitude of equality can come across as condescending. One African American woman listed three statements that white women who want to treat black women with respect and friendship should never utter: (1) "I never even notice that you're black"; (2) "You're different from most black people"; (3) "I understand what you're going through as a black woman, because I'm (Jewish, Italian, etc.)."[57]

Create Dialogue Intercultural communication experts Judith Martin and Thomas Nakayama advise that an important first step toward intercultural competence is to enter into dialogue.[58] Dialogue occurs when persons acknowledge each other's common humanity and engage with each other authentically and spontaneously. Dialogue requires an attitude of mutual respect in which each person is listening to the other without preplanned agendas or past prejudices and distortions.

When people from differing backgrounds don't listen to and talk with one another constructively, misperceptions can take root. In a study of American corporations, Charles Kelly found that blacks perceived whites as being reserved and ambitious and having an attitude of superiority. He found that whites perceived blacks as being easygoing and ambitious and feeling as if they are owed something.[59] Without understanding each other's concerns, attitudes like these are less likely to disappear.

Not all talk about differences is constructive: The way people talk about differences can make a tremendous difference in whether relationships improve or suffer. Journalist Ellis Cose describes two nonproductive styles:

> *Discussions tend to be conducted at one of two levels—either in shouts or whispers. The shouters are generally so twisted by pain or ignorance that spectators tune them out. The whisperers are so afraid of the sting of truth that they avoid saying much of anything at all.*[60]

Experts agree with Cose that ignoring differences can be just as dangerous as emphasizing them. The challenge, then, is to discuss differences openly without using the kinds of inflammatory language described in Chapter 4. If you approach others with a constructive attitude, the odds of positive outcomes increase.

Organizational Culture and Communication

So far we have explored culture as a matter of geography, ethnicity, and physical condition. But even people with identical personal backgrounds can find themselves in very different cultures, depending on the organizations to which they belong. Just like individuals, organizations have personalities. Some are casual, energetic, even zany; others are formal, slow-moving, and serious. Social scientists call this personality an **organizational culture**—a relatively stable, shared set of rules about how to behave and set of values about what is important. In everyday language, culture is the insiders' view of "the way things are around here."

Like human personalities, organizational cultures that appeal to one kind of person repel others. Many people abhor bureaucracies, with their clearly defined job

"After the merger, you may notice a few changes in our corporate culture."

hierarchies and voluminous rules; others feel most comfortable in that sort of setting. Some people welcome the chaotic disorganization and constant change that often characterize new companies in emerging fields; others feel more at home in organizations with clearly defined jobs and products. Some people like a working environment in which employees are one big family; others prefer to keep their working and personal lives separate.

Belonging to an organizational culture means choosing a way of life. Consider one example of how cultures—and their effects—can differ.

Tattoos, piercings, long hair and good books. It's an odd combination that helps bookselling superstore Borders distinguish itself from the competition. Borders goes for funky, edgy employees who use their personality and passion to sell the products. Barnes & Noble, its closest competitor, prefers clean-cut employees in pressed shirts who smile brightly while helping customers find whatever they're looking for.[61]

Another example shows how the culture that suits one person might not be right for another.

Take an up-and-coming executive at General Electric who is being wooed by Xerox—more money, a bigger office, greater responsibility. If his first reaction is to grab it, he's probably going to be disappointed. Xerox has a totally different culture than GE. Success (and even survival) at Xerox is closely tied to an ability to maintain a near frenetic pace, the ability to work and play hard, Xerox-style.

By contrast, GE has a more thoughtful and slow-moving culture. The GE culture treats each business activity seriously—almost as though each activity will have an enormous impact on the company. Success at GE is a function of being able to take work seriously, a strong sense of peer group respect, considerable deference for authority, and a sense of deliberateness. . . . But these same values might not be held in high esteem elsewhere.

Bright young comers at GE could, for example, quickly fizzle out at Xerox—and not even understand why. They'll be doing exactly what they did to succeed at GE—maybe even working harder at it—but their deliberate approach to issues large and small will be seen by insiders at Xerox as a sign they "lack smarts."[62]

Cultures aren't limited to large corporations. Every organization has its own way of doing business and treating people. Anyone who has worked for more than one restaurant or retail store, attended more than one college or university, belonged to more than one team, or volunteered for more than one worthy cause knows that even when the same job is being performed, the way of doing business can be radically different. Furthermore, the culture of an organization can make all the difference between a satisfying and a disappointing job. Research shows that employees are more satisfied and committed to their jobs when their values match those of their supervisors and the organization.[63] They are also more successful. Harvard Business School professors John Kotter and James Heskett flatly claim that people who conform to the norms of their organization's culture will be rewarded, while those who do not will be penalized.[64]

ethical challenge

Corporate Culture Supports Ethical Behavior

Electronics manufacturer Texas Instruments wants employees to ask themselves the following questions whenever they have a concern about whether a business action is ethical. Note how these questions reflect an organizational culture of integrity.

1. *Is it legal?* If not, then don't do it.
2. *Is it consistent with the company's stated values?* Texas Instruments has a clearly stated set of corporate values. Actions that don't fit with them shouldn't be undertaken.
3. *If you do it, will you feel bad?* If so, there's probably something wrong.
4. *How would it look in the newspapers?* If having people find out will be embarrassing, there's a problem.
5. *Do you think it's wrong?* If so, don't do it.
6. *If you're not sure—ask.* Never feel you have to make a decision on ethics by yourself. Get help from others.
7. *If you don't get a clear answer, keep asking until you do.* Don't fudge an ethical problem by saying you tried to get help but couldn't. Keep asking—the boss, the company's lawyers, human resources personnel—until you get a clear answer.

Source: *Bottom Line/Business* 1 (September 1995). Courtesy of Texas Instruments.

Some of the rules for communicating in organizational settings are spelled out: "Customers come first" is one example. But in other cases, rules aren't made explicit. For instance, "don't complain" or "document *everything*" can be powerful rules, even though they aren't ever discussed.[65] One study revealed that the costs of employees not understanding the unspoken rules of an organization can be high—running into millions of dollars in lost time, reduced productivity, quality problems, and ill will.[66] Another study suggests that it is mid-level managers who best know, understand, and transmit company culture, perhaps making them the best source of information for new hires.[67]

The Importance of Organizational Culture

It's hard to overstate the importance of organizational culture. The cost of having a workforce that doesn't understand and play by the rules can be staggering. In one survey, respondents reported that the annual cost of workers not "knowing the ropes" ranged from less than $100 to as much as $10 million.[68] When employees didn't understand or accept their organization's culture, the results included lost time, lowered productivity, bad publicity for the firm, lowered morale and trust, lost customers, and lost opportunity. Poor fit between cultures may even cause organizational mergers to fail.[69]

Organizational culture can affect you in a variety of ways, both large and small. Among other things, the culture of your organization can determine where and how long you work, including options such as flextime and telecommuting. It can shape the emotional environment, including the degree of cooperation or competition, and notions of how much and what kinds of fun are appropriate. Culture will surely

Table 2–6 Theory X and Theory Y Organizational Cultures

Theory X Organizations	Theory Y Organizations
• Work is inherently distasteful to most people, and they will attempt to avoid work whenever possible. • Most people are not ambitious, have little desire for responsibility, and prefer to be directed. • Most people have little aptitude for creativity in solving organizational problems. • Most people are self-centered. As a result, they must be closely controlled and often coerced to achieve organizational objectives. • Most people resist change. • Most people are gullible and unintelligent.	• Work can be as natural as play, if the conditions are favorable. • People will be self-directed and creative to meet their work and organizational objectives if they are committed to them. • The capacity for creativity spreads throughout organizations. • Most people can handle responsibility because creativity and ingenuity are common in the population. • Under these conditions, people will seek responsibility.

influence the way you and others dress and the space in which you work: its size, degree of privacy (or lack thereof), and decoration. Organizational culture will govern the amount and type of interaction you have (both on and off the job) with other employees, both co-workers and management.[70]

Dimensions of Organizational Culture

What elements distinguish one culture from another? In his well-known management book, *The Human Side of Enterprise*, Douglas McGregor proposed two theories which shape organizational cultures. He referred to these opposing motivational theories as **Theory X** and **Theory Y**.[71] As Table 2–6 shows, the assumptions behind each theory are different. It's easy to imagine how the top-down, authoritarian structure in a Theory X organization would differ from the more optimistic, supportive culture in a Theory Y operation.

Several dimensions distinguish organizations, even those doing the same kind of work.

1. *Sociability*. Are employees involved with one another on a personal level, or do they limit interaction to job-related tasks? A "one big family" culture isn't necessarily superior to a less personal one, but shared notions about how much sociability is appropriate is an important ingredient of job satisfaction.
2. *Power distribution and job autonomy*. What is the degree of power distance between people at different levels within the organization? What are the demands to report and justify actions to higher management? How much freedom do employees have to make decisions themselves? Some workers are most comfortable when they have both limited authority and responsibility; others prefer more freedom.
3. *Degree of structure*. Are job roles highly defined, with people operating within their own area of responsibility, or is it considered acceptable to get involved

on your feet

Describing Organizational Cultures

The culture of an organization can be a powerful influence on the experience members have in it and the public has with it.

In 2 minutes or fewer, brief your class on the culture of an organization (e.g., a place where you have worked or an organization you have belonged to) or a field (e.g., construction, software design) that you are familiar with.

Begin with a brief description of the organization or field and your experience with it. Then use the qualities listed on pages 64–65 that best describe the kinds of communication that shape this culture and how the culture shapes the way communication operates in the organization or field. Include at least one example of an incident or practice that illustrates the culture you are describing.

in other areas of the organization's work? Does the organization have a large number of policies and procedures or are issues handled less formally?

4. *Achievement rewards.* How (if at all) are the accomplishments of employees acknowledged and rewarded? Are praise and other types of reinforcement commonplace or infrequent? Is recognition based on true ability or other, less fair reasons? Is the level of reinforcement suitable to meet your personal needs?
5. *Opportunities for growth.* Does the company encourage workers to develop their skills and take on new responsibilities, or does it focus exclusively on employees' handling their present jobs competently? Does it encourage education and training? Are you satisfied with the opportunities for growth provided by the organization?
6. *Tolerance for risk and change.* Does management encourage employees to take well-reasoned chances or is avoiding risk a high priority? Is change expected and welcomed, or are tradition, predictability, and stability highly valued?
7. *Conflict tolerance.* Does the company believe that disagreement is not necessarily a sign of disloyalty or is harmony stressed? Are the organizational norms for managing conflict compatible with your personal style?
8. *Emotional support.* Does management show a genuine interest in the well-being of employees by seeking out and responding to their concerns? Do you feel as if you are receiving the emotional support you want and deserve?[72]

Creating and Maintaining Organizational Cultures

Whether the culture is created deliberately or evolves without a grand design, the earliest phase of an organization's life is the best time to set the tone for its lifelong culture. Early events are enshrined in stories that can take on the quality of legends.[73] One of the most famous of these tales is told at IBM about former chairman of the board Thomas Watson, Jr. Watson was barred from entering a high-security area of one of the company's plants because he was not wearing the proper identification badge. Rather than firing the assertive guard who blocked his entry, Watson acknowledged the policy and waited at the gate until the proper identification was found. The story confirms a policy central to IBM's culture: Everybody at the company obeys the rules.

An organization's culture takes on a life of its own. Customs and rituals develop that perpetuate a company's values.[74]

- The "work hard, play hard" culture of the Los Angeles Dodgers baseball club is apparent by a long history of practical jokes which included locking former manager Tommy Lasorda in his office, stealing the clothes of rookies while they are showering, and smearing shoe polish inside an unwitting player's cap in order to give him a black "halo." Players who have misconstrued these pranks as personal insults have overreacted until they understood the team's culture.[75]
- At Southwest Airlines, management cheerleads its employees with colorful streamers hanging from the ceiling at company meetings.
- At Tupperware, the president and senior managers spend fully 1 month per year at celebrations honoring top salespersons and managers.[76]
- Some cultural practices involve changing labels. Employees are called crew members at McDonald's, hosts at Disney Productions, and associates at JCPenney, reflecting those companies' shared belief that every worker plays an important role in the corporation's success.

Practices like these both reflect a company's culture and continue to shape it, but they are nothing more than gimmicks unless they are backed up by day-to-day activities.

Not all cultural traditions are so positive. Supervisors often try to prod unproductive workers by issuing more and more rules, feeding the flames of unhappiness that they are trying to extinguish. In some organizations, negative customs perpetuate an unhappy state of affairs. Complaining can become a part of a company's culture: Bitter employees may spend time over coffee ridiculing management and criticizing the company. Unavailability is sometimes an organizational trait as well: Managers who dislike and fear subordinates often barricade themselves in offices, cutting off communication with the rank-and-file employees, who, in turn, feel increasingly alienated. One observer pointed out how corporate downsizing can be the ultimate measure of management's attitude toward employees.

> *Perhaps the most dramatic and egregious gestures companies make are layoffs. On one level, it looks as though the corporation has just gone feral and is chewing off its right leg because its left leg is in a trap. But when layoffs are particularly callous, an additional message is sent, one that speaks of arrogance, omnipotence and impunity. It's as if a gang of executives, clad in navy suits, were walking down a city sidewalk four abreast, bumping hapless strangers into gutters or shop windows. Downsizing's subtext is this: "We have the power and the money. We can do what we like, and there's not much you can do about it except whine."*[77]

Organizational Culture and Career Planning

As a prospective employee, you might be tempted to select a company on the basis of its most obvious characteristics. What is the starting salary? How are the working conditions? What are the chances for promotion? If you consider only these factors, you could wind up with an impressive title and income—but miserable.

When you are thinking about going to work for an organization, make an effort to pin down its personality, just as you would if you were choosing a mate. After all, you are likely to spend more hours per year at work than you will with a spouse. You can get a sense of a company's culture in five ways.[78]

Study the Physical Setting An organization's physical plant says something about its personality. Even though most organizations don't make statements by building their environment, they do say something about themselves by choosing the space in which they operate. For example, choosing to locate in a high-rent or low-rent district might say something about the prosperity of the organization, its concern with controlling costs, the public it wants to serve, or even its competence. Likewise, the physical condition of the facilities makes a statement. Is the workplace clean or dirty? Are workers' areas personalized or standardized?

Read What the Company Says about Itself Press releases, annual reports, and advertisements can all be revealing. Companies with strong values are proud to publicize them. An emphasis on only profit and loss raises doubts about the company's concern for its personnel. Pride about innovation, service to customers, and commitment to the community—all are clues about an organization's culture. Of course, noble statements may only be lip service to praiseworthy values. Use the other suggestions in this section to see whether a company practices what it preaches.

Test How the Company Greets Strangers How are you treated when you visit a company or deal with its employees? Do they seem happy or grumpy? Are they willing to deal with you promptly, or are you left cooling your heels? Do they seem helpful, or do they seem unconcerned with your needs? A walking tour of the working areas can help give a feel for the organization's personality. "Vibrations" may not be a scientific term, but companies do have them.

Interview Company People An employment interview probably isn't the best place to explore how a company treats its employees. Talking with employees off the record can provide valuable insights about the way the company operates. See what they say about the company. Even rehearsed answers can be revealing: The apparent enthusiasm and sincerity with which they are delivered offer a clue about whether employees believe in the company line. Even if you don't learn much about the organization as a whole, you'll get a good picture of the kind of people you will be working with. Ask yourself how happy you would be working with these people day in and out.

Learn How People Spend Their Time During your interview and observations, find out how employees spend their time at work: A surprising amount of effort might go into activities that are only remotely related to getting the job done: dealing with paperwork, playing office politics, struggling with balky equipment, or attending one unproductive meeting after another.

Check out the parking lot or garage on evenings and weekends: Lots of vehicles can be a tip-off that you will be expected to work long hours. Decide whether you are willing to accept this lifestyle. The way a company goes about its business reveals more about its culture than the kind of work it does.

summary

As American society becomes increasingly diverse, the ability to communicate across cultures becomes a business necessity. Diversity has many dimensions: nationality, physical ability, language, and ethnicity are a few. Astute business communicators demonstrate awareness of cultural differences with regard to formality, social customs, dress, time, conflict styles, and gender roles. Diversity manifests itself in a great variety of norms and cultural values, such as high or low context, individualism versus collectivism, power distance, task or social orientation, long- or short-term focus, and degree of uncertainty avoidance. Effective communicators also allow for co-cultural variations that stem from regional differences, ethnicity, and physical abilities.

Communicators who succeed in a diverse workplace must educate themselves about different cultures and co-cultures. Viewing diversity as an opportunity instead of a problem is an important attitude, along with avoiding ethnocentrism. Treating people from different cultural backgrounds with respect is essential. Finally, being willing to acknowledge and develop dialogues around cultural differences can help communicators understand and appreciate one another.

Every organization has a distinct culture—a relatively stable picture of the organization's personality shared by its members. Cultures are usually shaped in the organization's early days, often by its earliest leaders. Theory X and Theory Y organizations develop very different organizational cultures, and everyday customs and rituals both reflect the culture and continue to shape it. When evaluating an organization, a prospective employee can consider whether that culture is a comfortable fit. Good salary and working conditions are not enough to guarantee job satisfaction if the company's personality doesn't suit the employee. Firsthand observation and informal contact with current employees are good ways to analyze an organization's culture.

key terms

Test your understanding of these key terms by visiting the Online Learning Center Web site at www.mhhe.com/ adler9.

co-cultures 51
collectivist cultures 48
culture 41
ethnocentrism 60
high-context culture 47
individualistic cultures 48
long-term orientation 51
low-context culture 47
monochronic time orientation 44
organizational culture 61
polychronic time orientation 44
power distance 50
short-term orientation 51
social orientation 51
task orientation 51
Theory X 64
Theory Y 64
uncertainty avoidance 50

activities

Go to the self-quizzes at the Online Learning Center at www.mhhe.com/adler9 to test your knowledge of chapter concepts.

1. Invitation to Insight

a. Either through personal interviews or research, identify several differences in communication practices between your own culture and another culture that interests you.
b. If you were interacting with a person from that culture, how would you bridge the differences?

2. Invitation to Insight

Choose one set of cultural values described on pages 46–51 and identify the characteristic that is not representative of your own culture. For example, if you are used to a low-context culture, you might focus on high-context communication. Now consider both the advantages and the disadvantages of working in an environment in which this unfamiliar norm is the dominant one. For instance, how might interaction be more effective or otherwise desirable if most people communicated in a high-context manner?

3. Skill Builder

Select one form of disability. Collaborate with several of your classmates to create two role plays, illustrating effective and ineffective communication with a person who is challenged by the disability. Act out your role plays in front of the class.

4. Skill Builder

Develop your ability to identify and communicate effectively within an organization's culture. Choose an organization in a field that interests you or focus on an organization to which you already belong. By analyzing the organization's physical setting and literature, interviewing others, and making your own observations, construct a description of the organizational culture that addresses the dimensions listed on pages 46–51. On the basis of your findings, describe an optimal way to communicate in the following areas:

a. Introducing new ideas.
b. Interacting with superiors.
c. Dealing with conflict.
d. Managing time.
e. Socializing with fellow workers.
f. Using preferred methods of exchanging information (e.g., telephone, e-mail, face-to-face interaction).

5. Skill Builder

Choose three cultures around the world with which you are likely to interact in the course of your career. Use the Internet sites listed in On the Web, World Cultures, on page 71 to discover the keys to effective intercultural communication in your three chosen cultures. For each of the three cultures describe

a. The culture in general.
b. Business protocol for that culture.
c. The language(s).
d. Sources you could go to for additional training and/or e-mail contacts.

6. Skill Builder

Representatives from Japan, the United States, and European nations collaborated in an attempt to create an international code of business ethics. Read about the Caux Round Table by using a search engine to find articles on this process begun in 1994. Read the document at **http://www.cauxroundtable.org** and then

a. List the seven principles found in the document.
b. Describe how these seven principles relate to the ethical standards on page 12 of Chapter 1.
c. Write a short essay describing how your own personal sense of ethics corresponds to each of the seven principles.

7. Invitation to Insight

Choose one of the following options to better understand the importance of organizational culture. In each case, use the most relevant dimensions of communication described on pages 64–65 to structure your analysis and description.

a. Interview someone familiar with an organization or field that interests you to learn about its culture. Identify the kinds of communication that shape this culture and how the culture shapes the way communication operates in the organization or field.

b. Assume the administration of your college or university has asked you to brief newly hired faculty members about the academic culture of your school from an undergraduate student's perspective. Describe how communication practices at your school both shape and reflect its culture. You can make your remarks more clear and interesting by including one or more brief examples to illustrate how the culture operates.

resources

In Print

Blank, R., and S. Slipp. *From the Outside In: Seven Strategies for Success When You're Not a Member of the Dominant Group of Your Workplace*. New York: AMACOM, 2000.

As the title indicates, the authors provide excellent examples of employees in contexts where they are aware of their difference and lack of dominance, whether that difference is ethnicity, gender, or culture. The focus is on defining one's workplace objectives and devising strategies to meet them.

Brown, D. W. *Organization Smarts: Portable Skills for Professionals Who Want to Get Ahead*. New York: AMACOM, 2002.

This book imparts practical advice for the workplace. Chapter 2, "Understanding the 'Real' Organization," describes how to look for the visible and invisible culture in an organization, the power relationships, and how to learn the customs of an organization you are entering.

Conrad, C., and M. S. Poole. Chapter 10, "Communication and Diverse Workplaces" and Chapter 11, "Communication, Globalization and Organizations," in *Strategic Organizational Communication in a Global Economy*, 6th ed. Belmont, CA: Wadsworth, 2005.

These chapters explain how workplaces have responded in different ways to diversification and globalization. The authors offer valuable insights on culture's impact on organizations and efforts by workplaces to be responsive rather than reactive to the changing dynamics of the workforce.

Hofstede, G. *Cultures and Organizations: Software of the Mind*. New York: McGraw-Hill, 1997.

Hofstede's original research in organizations around the world identified the fundamental dimensions of culture outlined in this chapter: individualism-collectivism, power distance, task and social orientation, and so on. This book describes those dimensions in detail and offers valuable tips for dealing with them in today's multinational, multicultural economy.

Keyton, Joann, *Communication and Organizational Culture*. Thousand Oaks, CA: Sage, 2005.

This scholarly book summarizes research findings and offers practical advice about managing, developing, and changing organizational cultures.

Ryan, D. J. *Job Search Handbook for People with Disabilities*. Indianapolis: Jist, 2000.

The author has spent 10 years helping persons with disabilities in their job searches. He examines job preparation strategies, career goals, and self-assessment, when and how to disclose a disability, and how to make accommodations.

Tuleja, Elizabeth A. *Intercultural Communication for Business*. Mason, OH: South-Western, 2005.

The author is a faculty member at the University of Pennsylvania's Wharton School, where she is responsible for managing courses for MBA executives. This book provides a brief overview of the issues and skills that business communicators need in an increasingly diverse world.

Zwell, M. *Creating a Culture of Competence*. New York: John Wiley & Sons, 2000.

Chapter 2, "The Building Blocks of Culture," describes six categories of competence that lead to outstanding organizational cultures: teamwork, service orientation, interpersonal awareness, organizational savvy, relationship building, and attention to communication

On the Web

World Cultures

Brigham Young University's Kennedy Center has produced a series of "Culturegrams"—brief profiles of key information for travelers visiting over 100 countries and regions, from Afghanistan to Zimbabwe. Each pamphlet begins with a simple map and background on geography, history, climate, and other basic information. Communication-related information profiles personal appearance, gestures, greetings, visiting, eating, and other useful topics. For example, in Somalia, men greet each other by firmly shaking hands three times before putting that hand to their hearts. More information about Culturegrams is available on the World Wide Web at **www.culturegrams.com**.

Finding information about a variety of cultures within the United States and internationally can be a challenge. For culture-specific information about traveling and doing business in other countries you can use Web sites of the U.S. State Department (**http://travel.state.gov**), United Nations (**www.un.org**), and National Geographic Society (**www.nationalgeographic.com**). Also see International Business Consortium (**http://cobe.boisestate.edu/ib**), Virtual Tourist (**www.vtourist.com**), Global Business Basics (**www.getcustoms.com**), and Executive Planet (**www.executiveplanet.com**).

For an interesting account of 10 faux pas in intercultural communication, go to **www.marybosrock.com/fauxpas.htm**. For excellent books on intercultural business and living in general and in specific countries, visit Intercultural Press (**www.interculturalpress.com**). Click on "Hot Links" for even more informative intercultural sites.

Global Ethics

The discussion of global ethics can be tangled and complex. At the Center for Global Ethics (**www.globalethics.org**) thinkers, scholars, and activists from a variety of business and religious backgrounds promote a global ethic. From this home page you can link to several business codes of ethics. This site also contains a library of ethical dilemma case studies, which are searchable by category (environment, biomedical) or by key word.

Additionally, use these Web sites for international ethics information: Caux Round Table (**www.cauxroundtable.org**), Center for Ethical Business Cultures (**www.cebcglobal.org**), and the International Society of Business, Economics, and Ethics (**www.isbee.org**).

part two: strategic case

Computer Solutions

From the outside, Marissa and Tran's partnership looks like a classic entrepreneurial success story. Their business, Computer Solutions, has doubled its volume annually in every 1 of the 4 years since it began in an extra room of Tran's apartment. Tran has always been the technical expert, and Marissa has dealt with landing customers and making sure they are satisfied. Besides Tran and Marissa, Computer Solutions now has 16 talented employees and needs at least 4 more to cope with the backlog of business.

Despite their success, both Tran and Marissa feel like they are facing a crisis in their partnership—although each one views the problem differently. Tran sees Marissa as failing to carry her share of the load: "I work 12-hour days to give our customers the solutions they need," he complains. "While I'm trapped here in the office, Marissa is off having 2-hour lunches or traveling to all sorts of great places." When we started this business, we agreed we would split the responsibilities 50-50, and now I'm doing much more than my share of work. And Marissa keeps saying we need to talk about this. But I'm too busy to talk. If I don't keep working, we're going to lose some of our customers."

Marissa sees the problem quite differently. "Tran doesn't seem to appreciate that I'm the one who brings in the business," she complains. "We have plenty of good, strong competitors out there, and I have the job of making sure customers choose and stay with us. Believe me—all the business meals, travel, and trade shows aren't fun. I'd much rather stay near home and live a normal life." Marissa also has another concern: "Tran doesn't recognize how our chief engineer, Carlo, is making our female employees very uncomfortable. Three of the women who work for us have complained privately to me about how Carlo's stares and jokes with sexual content are affecting their ability to work. Tran is Carlo's manager, and he needs to deal with this problem soon. I'm afraid we're at risk of losing some of these women. I can even imagine a sexual harassment lawsuit in our future. I've tried to explain to Tran how important it is to have a positive climate in the office, but he doesn't seem to think feelings are worth considering. A typical engineer!"

Until recently, Tran and Marissa hadn't spoken openly about their feelings toward one another. Despite this fact, they know each other well enough to realize that the tension was growing thicker by the week. Finally, at the end of an especially grueling month, the storm burst and they had the first shouting match of their partnership. Tran called Marissa a "glory hog," and she accused him of being a "sexist nerd." Since then, they have both suffered through a period of frigid politeness.

The strains of the unresolved conflict are beginning to affect the operation of Computer Solutions. Both partners realize that the success of the business depends on working through their differences. Marissa doubts they will be able to accomplish this without some outside help, and she is thinking about proposing to Tran that they hire a consultant to help them develop more productive ways of behaving. She also wants to propose that the company start a formal performance review process so problems like Carlo's can be managed and good employee performance is recognized. Tran is skeptical about "touchy-feely human relations types" becoming involved. He thinks they can use logic to solve their problems without bringing in outsiders.

As you read the chapters in this unit, consider the following questions:

Chapter 3

1. Which barriers to listening described in Chapter 3 might have contributed to Marissa and Tran's problems?
2. Describe how Marissa and Tran might have used the guidelines in Chapter 3 to deal more effectively with their disagreements.

Chapter 4

1. Describe a series of messages, ranging from highly ambiguous to highly specific, that Tran and Marissa could use to express their concerns to one another. Which approach(es) might have the best chance of success?

2. Give an example of how Marissa or Tran could use each type of inflammatory language described in this chapter to confront one another. For each statement, provide a noninflammatory alternative.
3. What kinds of behavior—verbal and nonverbal—might Carlo's subordinates have perceived as harassing? What options did they have for reducing these problem behaviors?

Chapter 5

1. What types of disconfirming messages do you suspect Marissa and Tran have been exchanging as their dispute escalated? How would you describe the communication climate of their relationship at this point?
2. Which types of confirming messages outlined on pages 139–143 could the partners use to improve the climate of their relationship?
3. How could Marissa, Tran, and Carlo use praise to improve the situation they are facing?
4. How might Marissa, Tran, and Carlo use the skills introduced on pages 146–149 to respond to criticism from one another and the other employees at Computer Solutions?
5. Describe likely scenarios if Tran and Marissa used each of the following approaches to dealing with their conflict: win–lose, compromise, win–win.

3 Listening

Chapter Outline

Chapter Objectives

After reading this chapter you should be able to

1 Identify how effective listening can contribute to your career success.

2 Describe barriers to your listening effectively and outline strategies for overcoming each barrier.

3 Identify your listening style(s), and describe how you might modify them as necessary.

4 Describe the best listening approaches you can use in a given situation to promote understanding, accomplish your goals, and enhance your relationship with others.

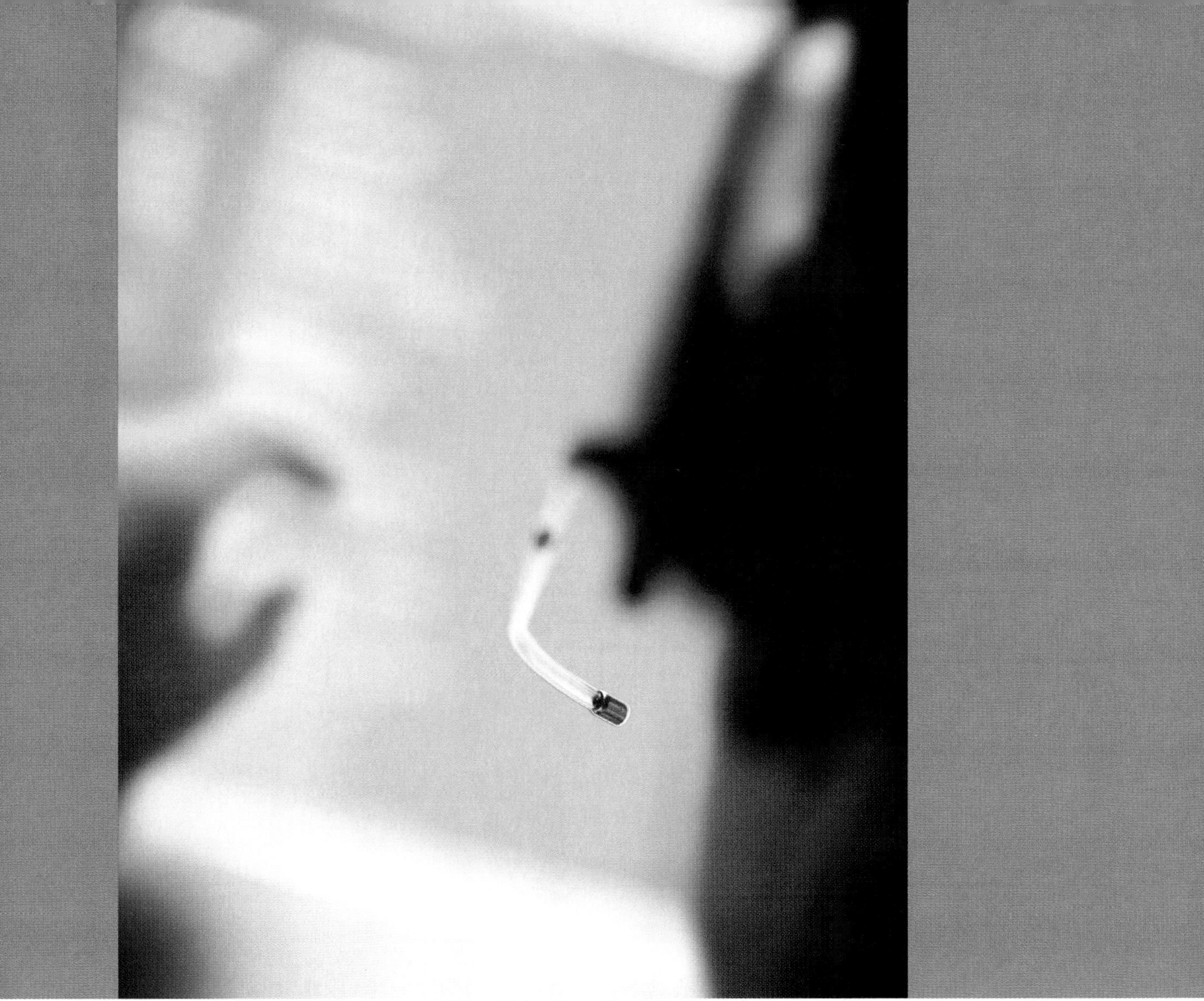

> "I told her we were meeting *this* Tuesday, not next Tuesday. Now we have to reschedule the meeting, and we may not make the deadline."
>
> "He said he was listening, but he didn't give me a minute to talk before he started interrupting. That's the last time I'll try to present a better way to do anything around here!"
>
> "Something went wrong down the line. I warned those people to watch the temperature carefully, but they don't listen. Now a whole batch is spoiled. What does it take to get them to understand?"

Situations like these are disturbingly common in business. They show how frequent listening failures are and how costly they can be. You may not be able to make others listen better, but you can boost your own ability to listen carefully to the scores of important messages you are likely to hear every business day.

As you will learn in the following pages, listening effectively is hard work. It involves far more than sitting passively and absorbing others' words. It occurs far more frequently than speaking, reading, or writing and is just as demanding and important.

The Importance of Listening

Business experts agree that listening is a vitally important skill. In today's highly competitive global marketplace, most theorists agree that management has to listen to everyone—customers, employees, scholars, government, and the public at large—in order to survive and prosper. Theorist Peter Senge coined the term "learning organization" to describe the importance of being open to input.[1] One characteristic of learning organizations is *dialogue* among everyone involved. This is why companies like Boeing and Ford have invested thousands of dollars to create cultures that welcome an exchange of ideas.[2]

Stephen Covey, in his best-selling book, identifies listening—understanding others' messages before making one's own understood—as one of the "seven habits of highly effective people."[3] Tom Peters, business consultant and co-author of *In Search of Excellence* and *A Passion for Excellence*, is sometimes called the guru of excellence. He emphasizes that one key to effective leadership is listening:

> *Leaders listen to what the market is saying, to what the customer is saying, and to what the team is saying. No, you don't have to do everything that your constituents demand that you do. But just by showing that you're listening, really listening, you demonstrate the respect that you accord to them.*[4]

Dennis Hastert, the Speaker of the U.S. House of Representatives echoed Peters's sentiment about the value of paying attention when describing how he spends most of his time: "They call me the Speaker, but they ought to call me the Listener."[5]

Business writer Kevin Murphy sums up the opinion of most business professionals when he says, "The better you listen, the luckier you will get."[6]

Research backs up the claims of business leaders. When 1,000 executives were asked to list the ideal manager's skills, listening ranked number one.[7] Another study asked business executives what skills were most important on the job. Listening was mentioned more than any other talent, including technical competence, computer knowledge, administrative talent, and creativity.[8]

Why is listening so important? One major reason is time: Listening is the most frequent—and, arguably, the most important—type of on-the-job communication. Studies conducted over 60 years ago indicated that adults spent an average of

29.5 percent of their waking hours listening. This is almost a third more time than they spent talking and virtually twice as much time as they spent reading.[9] A more recent study focused on listening in business settings. Personnel at all levels—including top-, middle-, and lower-level managers as well as workers with no managerial responsibilities—were asked to note the time they spent engaged in various types of communication during a typical week.[10] The results were impressive:

Listening 32.7%	Writing 22.6%
Speaking 25.8%	Reading 18.8%

Top executives spend even more time listening than other employees. Researchers have found that executives spend between 65 and 90 percent of the working day listening to someone.[11] Another piece of research revealed that effective managers almost constantly ask questions of their subordinates; in a half-hour conversation, some ask literally hundreds.[12]

Listening on the job is not only frequent but also important. When 282 members of the Academy of Certified Administrative Managers were asked to list the skills most crucial for managerial ability, "active listening" was rated number one and was placed in the "supercritical" category.[13] In another survey, 170 businesspeople were asked to describe the communication skills that they considered most important and that they wished had been taught in college; in each category, listening was the number-one response.[14] After the 2001 terrorist attacks in New York, thousands attended a town hall meeting called "Listening to the City" in which decision makers invited participation in redeveloping the World Trade Center site.[15] Effective listening is vital to organizations. It can improve quality, boost productivity, and save money. Poor listening can have the opposite effect. As one consultant says:

> *With more than 100 million workers in this country, a simple $10 listening mistake by each of them, as a result of poor listening, would add up to a cost of a billion dollars. And most people make numerous listening mistakes every week.*
>
> *Because of listening mistakes, letters have to be retyped, appointments rescheduled, shipments rerouted. Productivity is affected and profits suffer.*[16]

Moreover, as shown in Table 3–1 good listening skills require that not only the speaker's message content but also his feelings, intent, and the context are carefully considered. Consider the following example of the costs of poor listening on each of these levels. A devout Hindu ordered a snack at his local Taco Bell. Because eating beef is forbidden in his religion, he emphasized twice to the counter person that he wanted a burrito containing only beans, and not meat. After taking a bite of his order, he realized to his horror that the burrito contained beef. The customer later sued the food company, claiming emotional distress, as well as medical expenses and loss of wages.[17]

Beyond avoiding costly and embarrassing errors, good listening skills can play a major role in career success. Job hunters can respond best in employment interviews by keeping their ears open.[18] Listening is just as important once you have found a new job. Career consultant Andrea Sutcliffe argues that listening should be the predominant communication style for new employees: "If you had to choose one interpersonal skill to work on in your first year on the job, pick listening. It will be the single most important tool you will have for getting along and getting ahead."[19]

A study of employees in the insurance industry revealed that better listeners occupied higher levels in their company and were more upwardly mobile.[20] In problem-solving groups, people who listen well are rated as having the best leadership skills.[21] In a study of managerial effectiveness, listening skill was the best factor in distinguishing good bank managers from poor ones.[22] Along with advancing

Table 3–1 Listening at Different Levels

Listen for Content

Are you understanding the speaker's words? Do you need to ask questions or paraphrase for clarification?

Are your own filters (e.g., your opinions, biases) interfering?

Listen for Feelings

What feelings are verbally expressed?

What feelings are expressed nonverbally?

What isn't being said that offers clues about the speaker's feelings?

Should you ask the speaker to express or clarify his/her feelings?

Listen for Intent

What does the speaker want to do?

What does the speaker want you to do?

Listen for Context

How does the setting help you understand the message?

How do the speaker's remarks fit into the chronology of his/her life?

How does the speaker's sociocultural background help you understand the message?

in their careers, good listeners report being happier on the job, and others are more satisfied working with them.[23]

Listening skills are important in a variety of careers, and selling is a prime example: Writer and management professor David J. Schwartz makes the point more succinctly:

> *In an office recently I noticed a sign which said, "To sell John Brown what John Brown buys, you've got to see things through John Brown's eyes." And the way to get John Brown's vision is to listen to what John Brown has to say.*[24]

Listening to what people want and focusing on their needs helps you to avoid sounding "canned" and helps you focus on what you have to sell. "The great salespeople ask questions and have great listening skills. Poor salespeople get locked into script mode," according to Kevin Hogan, sales trainer and author. "Our job as salespeople is to listen and acquire an understanding of the needs of the prospect."[25]

Listening well is just as important for health care providers. It enables them to build rapport, show empathy, gather information, and identify patients' concerns.[26] A Harris poll found that 97 percent of adult patients said a physician's ability to listen to concerns and discuss them in an understandable way was an "extremely important" or "very important" ingredient in satisfying care.[27] Listening to the patient is considered so important that medical students in the United States now must demonstrate their ability to listen to patients in clinical exams before receiving their licenses to practice medicine.[28]

From hotels to high-tech computer services, from auto repair to financial institutions, service industries are the fastest-growing segment of the U.S. economy.

"Good service, in many respects, is good listening," according to Judi Brownell of Cornell University. "In order to thrive in highly competitive, rapidly changing environments, service employees must learn to listen well."[29] Feargal Quinn, entrepreneur and founder of the successful Superquinn grocery chain, believes that listening to the customers creates success. He expects all managers to "jump the counter" once a month. They shop, ask questions, wait in line, and "become" the customer so they learn to listen from a customer's point of view. According to Quinn, "Listening is not an activity you can delegate—no matter who you are."[30]

Barriers to Effective Listening

Despite the importance of understanding others, research suggests that misunderstandings are the rule, rather than the exception. Conversational partners typically achieve no more than 25 to 50 percent accuracy in interpreting each other's remarks.[31] Listening expert Ralph Nichols echoes this grim assessment. He estimates that the average white-collar worker listens at about a 25 percent efficiency level.[32] This dismal figure is supported by research showing that immediately after a 10-minute presentation, a normal listener can recall only 50 percent of the information presented. After 48 hours, the recall level drops to 25 percent.[33]

Despite the widespread problem of poor listening, most business communicators don't see themselves as lacking in this skill. In one study, subordinates were asked to rate the listening ability of their bosses. More than half put their managers in the "poor" category. When the same managers were asked to rate themselves, 94 percent described themselves as "good" or "very good" listeners! A number of studies have revealed reasons why people listen poorly, despite the advantages of doing just the opposite.[34]

Physiological Barriers

Chapter 1 described the various types of noise that can interfere with the decoding of a message. Of all these types, physiological noise is the easiest to recognize. Sometimes physical problems make it difficult to listen effectively. Fortunately, virtually all of these physiological limitations can be dealt with and overcome.

Hearing Problems Hearing isn't the same thing as listening. You can hear all sorts of background sounds—and even some speech—without listening. But for some people, poor listening results from actual hearing deficiencies. Once recognized, they can usually be treated. An undetected hearing loss may cause employees to get annoyed about the boss ignoring them or cause a supervisor to get angry when her instructions are bungled. Other people may have auditory processing difficulties, such as auditory discrimination, sequencing, or memory, which create the appearance of not listening or paying attention to what is said but are actually the result of physiological involvement, not intentional disregard.

"He'll see you, but he won't listen."

Rapid Thought Listeners can process information at a rate of about 500 words per minute, while most speakers talk at around 125 words per minute. This

ethical challenge

Golden and Platinum Rules

The Golden Rule tells us to treat others the way we would like to be treated, and the "Platinum Rule" is to treat others the way *they* would like to be treated. The best way to honor the Platinum Rule is to listen to others, discovering what they want. On the other hand, realists acknowledge that it is impossible to give equal attention to every message and still accomplish the multitude of tasks that occupy every workday.

How can you, as a busy worker, respond to nonessential messages without alienating the people who deliver them?

difference leaves us with a great deal of mental spare time. While it is possible to use this time to explore the speaker's ideas, we most often let our minds wander to other matters—from the unfinished business just mentioned to romantic fantasies. Management expert Peter Senge puts it this way: "Ears operate at the speed of sound, which is far slower than the speed of light the eyes take in. Generative listening is the art of developing deeper silences in yourself, so you can slow your mind's hearing to your ears' natural speed, and hear beneath the words to their meaning."[35]

Environmental Barriers

Some listening challenges reside outside the listener, in the environment. While none of these challenges can be eliminated, you can learn to deal with them.

Physical Distractions A stuffy room, noisy machinery, the cold you feel developing, or a conversation going on nearby are only a few of the distractions that can make listening difficult.

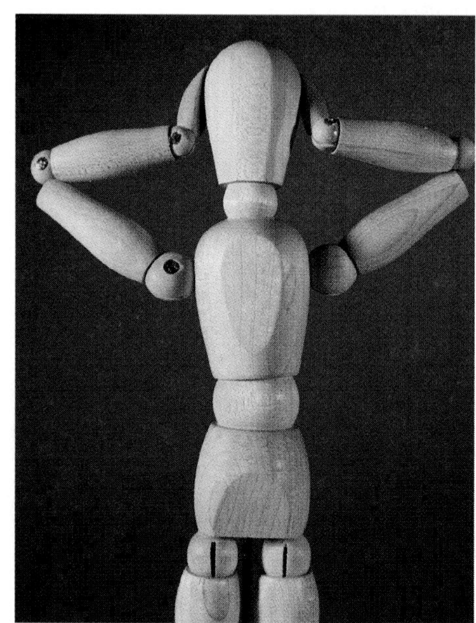

Problems in the Communication Channel Listening can be difficult when the communicators lack face-to-face contact. It's harder to receive ideas accurately over

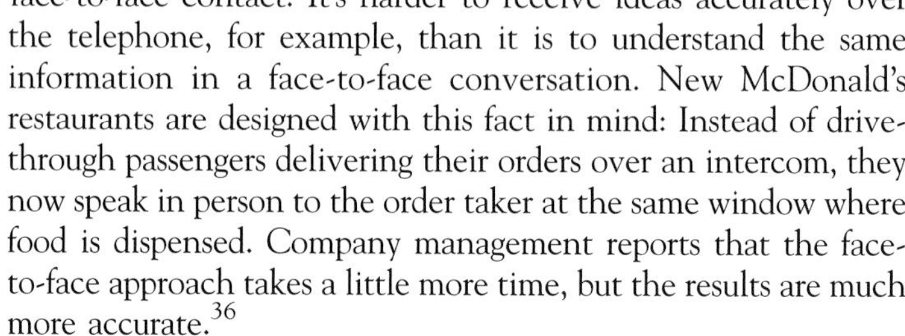

the telephone, for example, than it is to understand the same information in a face-to-face conversation. New McDonald's restaurants are designed with this fact in mind: Instead of drive-through passengers delivering their orders over an intercom, they now speak in person to the order taker at the same window where food is dispensed. Company management reports that the face-to-face approach takes a little more time, but the results are much more accurate.[36]

Message Overload It is hard to listen carefully when the phone rings every few minutes, people keep dropping in to give you quick messages, a co-worker has just handed you cost estimates on a new product line, and your computer continuously beeps to let you know you have incoming mail or scheduled appointments. Coping with a deluge of information is like juggling—you can keep only a few things going at one time.

Attitudinal Barriers and False Assumptions

Some of the most daunting barriers to understanding come from attitudes and assumptions that discourage careful listening.

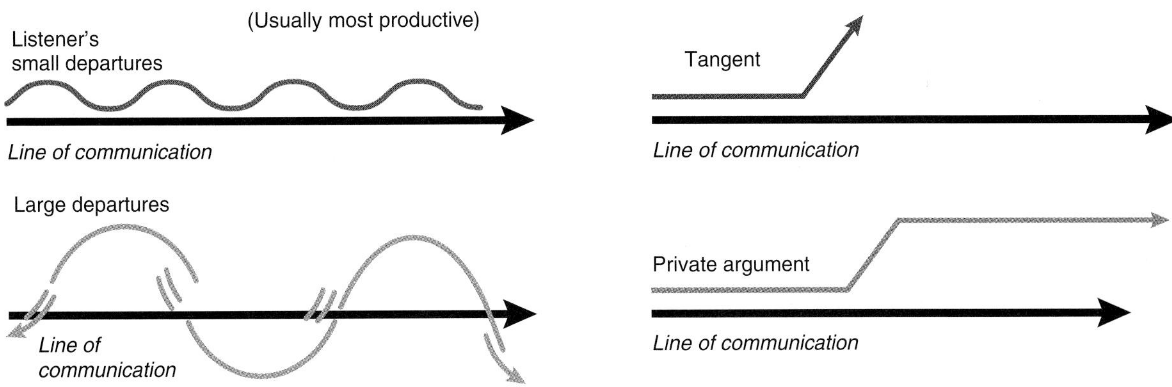

FIGURE 3–1
Thought Patterns
These four thought patterns represent different ways in which preoccupied listeners can ignore a speaker's message.
Source: A. D. Wolvin and C. G. Coakley, *Perspectives on Listening* (Norwood, NJ: Ablex, 1993), p. 115.

Preoccupation Business and personal concerns can make it difficult to keep your mind on the subject at hand. Even when your current conversation is important, other unfinished business can divert your attention: the call to an angry customer, the questions your boss asked about your schedule delays, the new supplier you heard about and want to interview, and the problems you have with the baby-sitter or the auto mechanic. Figure 3–1 illustrates several ways in which preoccupation can cause listeners to lose focus on understanding a speaker. Some preoccupation is inescapable, but keeping your focus on the speaker as much as possible will have benefits for you, the other person, and your relationship.

Egocentrism One common reason for listening poorly is the belief—usually mistaken—that your own ideas are more important or valuable than those of others. Besides preventing you from learning useful new information, this egocentric attitude is likely to alienate the very people with whom you need to work. Self-centered listeners are rated lower on social attractiveness than communicators who are open to others' ideas.[37] While a certain amount of self-promotion can be helpful in career advancement, advancing your own ideas at the expense of others' can cause you to slip down a rung or two as you climb the career ladder. As an old saying puts it, Nobody ever listened themselves out of a job.

Fear of Appearing Ignorant Some businesspeople think asking for clarification is a sign of ignorance. Rather than seek clarification, they pretend to understand others—often with unfortunate consequences. In truth, a sincere desire to seek clarification can pay dividends, as management guru Tom Peters explains:

> *My first boss . . . is one of the smartest people I know. He was smart enough and comfortable enough with himself to ask really elementary (some would say dumb) questions. The rest of us were scared stiff; we assumed that since we were being paid an exorbitant fee, we shouldn't ask dumb questions. But the result was we'd lose 90 percent of the strategic value of the interview because we were afraid to display our ignorance.*
>
> *Mostly, it's the "dumb," elementary questions, followed up by a dozen more elementary questions, that yield the pay dirt.*[38]

Assuming That Effective Communication Is the Sender's Responsibility Management expert Peter Drucker recognized that communication depends on the receiver as well as the sender when he wrote: "It is the recipient who communicates. The so-called communicator, the person who emits the communication, does not communicate. He utters. Unless there is someone who hears . . . there is only noise."[39]

As Drucker suggests, even the most thoughtful, well-expressed idea is wasted if the intended receiver fails to listen. The clearest instructions won't prevent mistakes if the employee receiving them is thinking about something else, and the best of products will never be made if the client or the manager isn't paying attention to the presentation. Both the speaker *and* the listener share the burden of reaching an understanding.

Assuming That Listening Is Passive Some communicators mistakenly assume that listening is basically a passive activity in which the receiver is a sponge, quietly absorbing the speaker's thoughts. In fact, good listening can be hard work. Sometimes you have to speak while listening—to ask questions or paraphrase the sender's ideas, making sure you have understood them. Even when you remain silent, silence should not be mistaken for passivity. Famous attorney Louis Nizer described how he would often emerge dripping with sweat from a day in court spent mostly listening. Sperry executive Del Kennedy, commenting on his company's well-known listening training program, says, "Most people don't know how exhausting listening can be."[40]

Assuming That Talking Has More Advantages Than Listening At first glance, it seems that speakers control things while listeners are the followers. Western society seems to correlate listening with weakness, passivity, and lack of authority or power.[41] The people who do the talking are the ones who capture everyone's attention, so it is easy to understand how talking can be viewed as the pathway to success.

Despite the value of talking, savvy businesspeople understand that listening is equally important. Consider the advice of communication consultant Bill Acheson: "For every minute a salesperson spends listening, he or she will save four minutes overcoming objections."[42]

Communication expert Susan Peterson reinforces the value of superior listening skills:

> *Too many times, whether it's with e-mail, voice mail or Internet, we are concentrating on the art of telling, not listening. Yet good listening, in my opinion, is 80 to 90 percent of being a good manager and an effective leader. . . . Listening is one of the best ways to keep high touch in your organization. In your day-to-day meetings with customers, clients, or employees, if you listen—really listen with full eye contact and attention—you can own the keys to the communication kingdom.*[43]

Writer and management professor David J. Schwartz makes the point more succinctly:

> *In hundreds of interviews with people at all levels I've made this discovery: The bigger the person, the more apt he is to encourage you to talk; the smaller the person, the more apt he is to preach to you.*
>
> *Big people monopolize the listening.*
>
> *Small people monopolize the talking.*[44]

career tip

Listening to Complaints

Listening is especially difficult when you are under attack. When criticism comes, the following tips can help you keep your cool and understand the other person.

1. *Take notes*. In a business setting, recording the facts of the case can prove important later. Writing can also give you something to do instead of becoming defensive.
2. *Allow the critic to "vent" for a while before responding*. Giving the complainer a chance to unload can help relieve his or her frustration. Remind yourself that listening to this sort of catharsis doesn't mean you agree with the complaints.
3. *Try to understand the critic*. Use questioning and paraphrasing to clarify the critic's problem. Again, remember that understanding doesn't necessarily mean accepting blame.
4. *Empathize with the complainer*. When possible, show that you understand how he or she feels: "I can see why you're frustrated."
5. *Tell them what you are going to do*. Once the complainer has calmed down, let him or her know how you will try to help. Then, do what you promised!
6. *Follow up with the complainer*. Let him or her know what has been done.

Sociocultural Differences

Some listening problems come from the differing styles of each communicator. Some arise from cultural communication styles, while others come from differences between typically masculine and feminine communication styles.

Cultural Differences Accent is often the most obvious difference when people from different cultures communicate. A different accent can be a source of psychological noise when it interferes with your ability to understand and appreciate the words of someone whose pronunciation differs from yours. Some communicators mistakenly assume that accented speakers are less intelligent and less able to understand spoken words.[45] Differing accents aren't just a problem in international communication. They can also interfere with communication between speakers from different co-cultures. For example, researchers have found that African American and Euro-American women hear very different things when speaking to each other.[46] White women tend to hear their own speech as being "normal or universal," and focus on African American women's pronunciation and grammar (instead of focusing on the message itself), whereas African American women (who are more used to hearing different styles of speech) find it easier to accept each accent as legitimate.

Some cultural differences are much more subtle than accent. The amount of time that should be spent listening is an example of one such difference. Monochronic Euro-Americans tend to put great value on time. Communicators raised with this orientation may view listening as wasting time, because it is not immediately clear what has been produced by taking the time to hear out another person. When interacting with Asians, U.S. businesspeople may find it very difficult to listen, as much time is spent engaging in small talk or having tea, rather than getting down to business.[47] The same issues may arise in U.S. business relationships with Latin Americans and Middle Easterners, who also value time spent on speaking and listening to information about families before business; however, time spent on listening in this way is of great importance to the overall relationship.

Culture also influences a communicator's attitude about silence—a big part of listening. African Americans and Euro-Americans tend to value speaking over listening and talk over silence.[48] Westerners often feel uncomfortable with long silences and want to fill them in with speech. By contrast, Native Americans and Japanese and other Asians regard silence as an important part of communication.[49] It is easy to imagine how a Westerner, uncomfortable with an Asian's silence, would fill in conversational gaps that seemed perfectly normal to a Korean or Navajo. In the same way, an Asian who wants to communicate successfully with a Euro-American would need to spend more time vocalizing.

Gender Differences Popular magazines are fond of asking, Who listens better, men or women? This question is not as helpful as asking, Do men and women listen differently? Research shows that, to at least some degree, the answer is yes.[50] By understanding the differences, men and women can do a better job of listening to and understanding one another.

Women often pay more attention to the kinds of relational messages described in Chapter 1, while men often pay more attention to information on the content level. Both men and women may not recognize important messages because they listen for different purposes. Consider a simple example: A computer programmer, when asked by two users if a particular software package will work, may reply, "Sure." The male user may focus on the content of the answer and take the statement at face value. The female user may tune in to the speaker's vocal tone and hear some hesitation or annoyance. Later on, the two users might disagree about what the programmer meant because they listened to different aspects of the response.

Another gender-related difference involves "listening noises"—vocalizers such as "uh-huh" and "ummm" that signal attention. Researchers have discovered that men and women often use and interpret listening noises differently.[51] Women may use them to signal attention; men, to signal agreement. Thus, a woman who says "uh-huh" may mean "I'm listening," while a man hearing this utterance would think that his female partner agrees. Once communicators are aware of differences like these, they can clarify the meaning of ambiguous vocal cues: "You seem interested in the idea I'm presenting. Do you agree that we should get started on it?"[52]

Men and women may hear different parts of a message because they listen for different purposes. Women are more likely to catch the feelings behind a speaker's words, while men tend to listen for the facts.[53] For example, at a committee meeting, a colleague is asked to redo a report. He says, "Sure." After the meeting, a female colleague may comment on how upset the person was and his reluctance to redo the report. She "heard" the feelings. A male colleague may respond, "What's the problem? He said he'd do it." Communicators who recognize this difference may choose to make any important feelings explicit when they are speaking to one or more men.

Gender differences don't just affect *how* we listen to one another; they also influence *whether* we listen at all. Well-known sociolinguist Deborah Tannen states: "All else being equal, women are not as likely to be listened to as men, regardless of how they speak or what they say."[54] In business meetings, it is not uncommon for an idea presented by a woman to be ignored or downplayed, while the same idea presented by a man receives more attention. Listeners who are aware of this tendency can train themselves to give equal attention to the messages of every communicator regardless of sex. One way to be more attentive to the ideas of everyone in a meeting is to systematically give equal time and attention to each person or to post the ideas in writing.

Lack of Training

Listening may seem like a natural ability—like breathing. "After all," you might say, "I've been listening since I was a child." We could all say the same thing about talking; but even though almost everyone does it, this doesn't mean most people do it well. Former Chrysler chairman Lee Iacocca recognized the need for organized programs to train personnel to become better listeners:

> *I only wish I could find an institute that teaches people how to listen. After all, a good manager needs to listen at least as much as he needs to talk. Too many people fail to realize that real communication goes in both directions. . . .*
>
> *You have to be able to listen well if you're going to motivate the people who work for you. Right there, that's the difference between a mediocre company and a great company. The most fulfilling thing for me as a manager is to watch someone the system has labeled as just average or mediocre really come into his own, all because someone has listened to his problems and helped him solve them.*[55]

Some businesses spend thousands of dollars on training, yet they fail to include training on listening in their workshops.[56] Most organizations, including major corporations such as 3M, American Telephone and Telegraph, General Electric, and Dun and Bradstreet, know better. They have included listening skills in their training programs.[57] Xerox Corporation's program for improving listening has been used by over 1.5 million employees in 71,000 companies, and Sperry Corporation invested more than $4 million to advertise its message: "We know how important it is to listen." In addition, Sperry set up listening seminars for its 87,000 employees in an effort to make its advertising campaign more than a string of empty slogans.

Listening Styles

Not everyone listens the same way. Two decades of research have identified four common ways people listen to others' messages.[58] You can identify your own preferences by completing the Self-Assessment: Listener Preference Profile on page 86.

People-Oriented

People-oriented listeners are most concerned with creating and maintaining positive relationships. They are sensitive to others' moods, and they respond to speakers' feelings as well as their ideas. People-oriented listeners usually are nonjudgmental about what others have to say: They are more interested in understanding and supporting people than in evaluating them.

Along with the obvious strengths of a people-oriented style, a strong concern for relationships has some drawbacks. It is easy to become overinvolved with others' feelings, and even to internalize and adopt them. People-oriented listeners may lose their ability to assess the quality of information others are giving in an effort

Self-Assessment Listener Preference Profile

Instructions: Think of a specific listening role or situation that you are often in. For example, you may focus on your listening at work, as a friend, as a spouse, or as a parent. (Note: You can complete the instrument more than one time, with different roles and situations in mind.) As you read the series of statements below, keep the particular listening role or situation you have chosen in mind. Circle the appropriate number for each item, using the key below:

Always 5 Frequently 4 Sometimes 3 Infrequently 2 Never 1

1.	I focus my attention on other people's feelings when listening to them.	5 4 3 2 1
2.	When listening to others, I quickly notice if they are pleased or disappointed.	5 4 3 2 1
3.	I become involved when listening to the problems of others.	5 4 3 2 1
4.	I try to find common areas of interest when listening to new acquaintances.	5 4 3 2 1
5.	I nod my head and/or use eye contact to show interest in what others are saying.	5 4 3 2 1
6.	I am frustrated when others don't present their ideas in an orderly, efficient way.	5 4 3 2 1
7.	When listening to others, I focus on any inconsistencies and/or errors in what's being said.	5 4 3 2 1
8.	I jump ahead and/or finish thoughts of speakers.	5 4 3 2 1
9.	I am impatient with people who ramble on during conversations.	5 4 3 2 1
10.	I ask questions to help speakers get to the point more quickly.	5 4 3 2 1
11.	I wait until all the facts are presented before forming judgments and opinions.	5 4 3 2 1
12.	I prefer to listen to technical information.	5 4 3 2 1
13.	I prefer to hear facts and evidence so I can personally evaluate them.	5 4 3 2 1
14.	I like the challenge of listening to complex information.	5 4 3 2 1
15.	I ask questions to probe for additional information.	5 4 3 2 1
16.	When hurried, I let others know that I have a limited amount of time to listen.	5 4 3 2 1
17.	I begin a discussion by telling others how long I have to meet.	5 4 3 2 1
18.	I interrupt others when I feel time pressure.	5 4 3 2 1
19.	I look at my watch or clocks in the room when I have limited time to listen to others.	5 4 3 2 1
20.	When I feel time pressure, my ability to concentrate on what others are saying suffers.	5 4 3 2 1

Scoring:

Tally the number of times you circled 4 or 5 for statements 1–5:

People-oriented = ________

Tally the number of times you circled 4 or 5 for statements 6–10:

Action-oriented = ________

Tally the number of times you circled 4 or 5 for statements 11–15:

Content-oriented = ________

Tally the number of times you circled 4 or 5 for statements 16–20:

Time-oriented = ________

Source: Adapted from L. Barker and K. Watson, *Listen Up* (New York: St. Martin's Press, 2000). Reprinted with permission.

to be congenial and supportive. They also risk being perceived as overly expressive and even intrusive by speakers who don't want to connect on a personal level.

Action-Oriented

Unlike people-oriented listeners who focus on relationships, **action-oriented** listeners are most concerned with the task at hand. Their main goal is to understand the facts and ideas that are being communicated. They want to get to the heart of the matter quickly, and so they appreciate clear, concise messages and often translate others' remarks into well-organized mental outlines.

Action-oriented listeners are most welcome when taking care of business is the primary concern: They help others focus on the task at hand and encourage them to be organized and concise. Their no-nonsense approach may not be welcomed by speakers who don't have the skill or inclination to be clear and direct. They appear to minimize emotional issues and concerns, which may be an important part of business and personal transactions.

Content-Oriented

Content-oriented listeners are evaluators. They want to hear details and analyze an issue from a variety of perspectives. They prefer to listen to experts and other credible sources of information. Content-oriented listeners often enjoy ideas for their own sake and are willing to spend time exploring them in thorough exchanges of ideas.

Content-oriented listeners can be a big help when the goal is to assess the quality of ideas, and when there is value in looking at issues from a wide range of perspectives. They are especially valuable when the issues at hand are complicated. On the other hand, their detail-oriented approach may annoy others who don't share their analytical orientation. Their thorough approach can take more time than others may be willing to give and their frequent challenging can be perceived as overly critical, or even hostile.

Time-Oriented

As the label suggests, **time-oriented** listeners are most concerned with efficiency. They view time as a scarce and valuable commodity and get impatient with people whom they view as wasting it. In a fast-paced business environment, time-oriented listeners can help keep things functioning efficiently. On the other hand, their displays of impatience can sometimes put a strain on relationships. Also, an excessive focus on time can hamper the kind of thoughtful deliberation that some jobs require.

If you completed the Self-Assessment on page 86, you may have found that you have more than one of the four listening preferences. If so, you aren't alone: 40 percent of the people who have used this instrument indicate at least two strong listening preferences.[59] The key to success as a listener is to recognize that you can control the way you listen and to use the approaches that best suit the situation at hand. When your relationship with the speaker needs attention, adopt a people-oriented approach. When clarity is the issue, be an action-oriented listener. If analysis is called for, put on your content-oriented persona. And when the clock is what matters most, become a model of time-orientation.

Just as important, try to assess the listening preferences of your conversational partners and adapt your approach accordingly.

Listening More Effectively

Regardless of your listening style, the following guidelines will enhance your effectiveness.

Minimize Distractions and Take Time to Listen

In Chapter 1 you read how noise—both physical and psychological—can interfere with communication. Even when you genuinely want to listen, it's hard to ignore the tug of incoming e-mails, the distractions of passersby, and the ring of your phone. Resist the urge to multitask; it gives a clear message that you are not listening.

Some kinds of noise are inescapable, but you can minimize other intrusions. When you really need to listen, do whatever it takes to get rid of distractions: Clear your desk, turn away from the computer, turn off the phone ringer, and close the door.

Taking time to listen may seem impossible in the face of other demands, but it can be an investment worth making. As author Stephen Covey puts it, dedicated listening "takes time, but it doesn't take anywhere near as much time as it takes to back up and correct misunderstandings when you're already miles down the road, to redo, to live with unexpressed and unsolved problems."[60]

If you simply can't take time to listen be honest rather than faking attention: It is better to say, "I'm really preoccupied with this budget. It's due by 4:00 this afternoon, but I do want to hear what's on your mind. Could we meet for coffee at 4:30?" Then be sure you follow up.

Talk and Interrupt Less

Sometimes the best approach to listening is to stay out of the way and encourage the other person to talk. One marketing expert explained how, even in selling, silence can be more effective than talking:

> *The 20/80 rule is a standard in small-business principles. Twenty percent of your customers account for 80 percent of your business. Here's a variation of the theme. . . . When meeting with prospective customers for the first time, listen 80 percent of the time and talk the other 20 percent. Your job is to listen attentively and determine what your prospects require. Before they are prepared to listen to your pitch, they want to tell you what they're looking for.*[61]

If you are a normally talkative person, consider rationing your comments when trying to listen. Imagine that you have only a finite number of words available, so that you speak only when it is absolutely necessary. You may be surprised at how the quality of your conversations and your level of understanding improve.

career tip

Minimizing Interruptions

Interrupting someone who expects to be listened to will usually annoy that person—whether a co-worker, customer, or supervisor. Although some interruptions are signs of involvement and interest ("Really?" "That's great!") and others are genuine requests for information ("Hold on: Did you say Jane or Joan?"), interruptions are rarely appreciated. When you cut others off, speakers may think that you don't care about their ideas or that you believe your ideas are better than theirs. You can be perceived as rude, egocentric, and controlling—someone who believes that what you have to say is more important than others' ideas.

You can cut back on interrupting by using several strategies:

- Count to three after the speaker seems to be finished. You may be surprised by how much more the other person has to say.
- Concentrate on what the speaker is saying and then paraphrase it back when s/he is finished.
- When you catch yourself interrupting, apologize and ask the speaker to continue.
- Ask a co-worker to count the number of times you interrupt in a day. You and your colleague might even agree on a subtle signal (e.g., a cough) to alert you about interruptions.

Source: Adapted from L. Barker and K. Watson, *Listen Up* (New York: St. Martin's Press, 2000), p. 88.

Seek and Observe Feedback

In the fast-paced world of business, you aren't likely to get all the information you need without seeking feedback. This can come as a rude shock after the much more structured messages that college students are accustomed to hearing. One intern described the difference between school and the workplace:

> *I was so used to professors basically telling you what they want from you that I expected to be, if not taught, then told, exactly what it was that they wanted. . . . [Instead] they just put things on my desk with only a short note telling me when they needed it done. No directions or comments were included.*[62]

In circumstances like these, you need to seek out feedback from the sender. There are three ways to do this: by asking questions, paraphrasing, and paying attention to nonverbal cues.

Ask Questions **Sincere questions** are genuine requests for information. They can be a terrific way to gather facts and details, clarify meanings, and encourage a speaker to elaborate. Former University of Kentucky basketball coach Rick Pitino learned the importance of asking questions after he lost a key recruit by trying to sell the virtues of his program instead of listening to what concerned his prospect. Later, when he courted another potential star (named Tony Delk), he used a more effective approach:

> *This time, instead of trumpeting Kentucky's virtues, he asked questions: what Delk wanted from a coach, what the family wanted for their son in college. For an hour, he just asked questions and nodded a lot, listening to their answers. . . .*
>
> *Not only did Pitino get Delk, but four years later, Delk helped lead Kentucky to its sixth national championship and Pitino's first. "That's one of my favorites," Pitino says. "That's one I like to tell business groups because it illustrates how important it is to listen to people."*[63]

"You haven't been listening. I keep telling you that I don't want a product fit for a king."

While sincere, focused questions can be a powerful tool, poor ones can do more harm than good. Avoid irrelevant questions ("Couldn't we have installed an automatic verifying system and avoided this problem?") that can leave the person angry and confused Also avoid **counterfeit questions** that are really disguised forms of advice or subtle traps: "Have you ever considered offering more money to get experienced people?" or "Why haven't you told me about this?"

No question is inherently counterfeit. Each of the examples above could be a sincere request for information. Furthermore, indirect questions can be a face-saving way to avoid embarrassing confrontations. But when the speaker's motive doesn't seem genuine, or if it doesn't seem to be in the receiver's best interests, counterfeit questions can pollute a communication climate just as quickly as any direct attack.[64]

Paraphrase **Paraphrasing** involves restating a speaker's ideas in your own words to make sure that you have understood them correctly and to show the other person that fact. Paraphrasing is often preceded by phrases such as "Let me make sure I understand what you're saying . . ." or "In other words, you're saying . . ." When you are paraphrasing, it is important *not* to become a parrot, repeating the speaker's statements word for word. Understanding comes from translating the speaker's thoughts into your own language and then playing them back to ensure their accuracy. After paraphrasing, it is important that you invite the speaker to *verify* your paraphrase so you know if you accurately understood him or her or to *clarify* your paraphrase and clear up what you have misunderstood.

The following conversations illustrate the difference between effective and ineffective paraphrasing:

Ineffective

Print Supervisor: I'm having trouble getting the paper to run that job. That's why I'm behind schedule.

Plant Manager: I see. You can't get the paper to run the job, so you're running behind schedule.

Print Supervisor: Yeah. That's what I said.

After this exchange, the plant manager still doesn't have a clear idea of the problem—why the print supervisor can't get the paper, or what he means when he says he can't get it. Effective paraphrasing, however, could help to get to the root of the problem:

Effective

Print Supervisor: I'm having trouble getting the paper to run that job. That's why I'm running behind schedule.

Plant Manager: In other words, your paper supplier hasn't shipped the paper you need for this job.

Print Supervisor: No, they shipped it, but it's full of flaws.

Plant Manager: So the whole shipment is bad?

Print Supervisor: No, only about a third of it. But I've got to get the whole batch replaced, or the dye lots won't match—the paper won't be exactly the same color.

Plant Manager: No problem—the colors can be a little off. But I have to have at least half of that order by Tuesday; the rest can wait a couple of weeks. Can you print on the good paper you have now, then do the rest when the new paper comes in?

Print Supervisor: Sure.

At first glance, questioning and paraphrasing may seem identical, but a closer look reveals that they are different tools. Questions seek new, additional information ("How far behind are we?" "When did it begin?"), while paraphrasing clarifies what a speaker has said. This is an important difference.

There are three types of paraphrasing. Although each of them reflects the speaker's message, each focuses on a different part of that statement.

Paraphrasing content The example above illustrates this most basic kind of paraphrasing, which plays back the receiver's understanding of the explicit message. It is easy to think you understand another person only to find later that you were wrong. At its most basic level, paraphrasing is a kind of safety check that can highlight and clarify misunderstandings. People who practice paraphrasing are astonished to find out how many times a speaker will correct or add information to a message that had seemed perfectly clear.

Paraphrasing intent Besides helping you understand *what* others are saying, paraphrasing can help you learn *why* they have spoken up. Imagine that, at a staff meeting, the boss announces, "Next week, we'll start using this display board to show when we're out of the office and where we've gone." It's easy to imagine two quite different reasons for setting up this procedure: (1) to help keep customers and colleagues informed about where each person is and when he or she will return, or (2) to keep track of employees because the boss suspects that some are slacking off on company time. Paraphrasing intent can help you understand what people mean when they make statements that can be interpreted in more than one way.

Paraphrasing feeling Often, the speaker's feelings are the most important part of a message. Despite this fact, most people don't express—or even recognize—their emotions. Ask yourself which emotions might be contained in these statements:

"That's the third time he canceled an appointment on me—who does he think he is?"

"Whenever a deadline comes, I get excuses instead of results—this can't go on much longer."

"One minute she says we have to spend money to make money, and the next minute she talks about cutting costs—I can't figure out what she really wants."

In each example there are at least two or three possible emotions:

Anger, hurt, and self-doubt.

Anger, frustration, and worry.

Anger and confusion.

Paraphrasing the apparent emotion can give the speaker a chance to agree with or contradict your interpretation: "Yeah, I guess it did hurt my feelings," or "I'm more worried than mad." In either case, this sort of response can help the other person to clarify how he or she is feeling and to deal with the emotions.

Attend to Nonverbal Cues Focusing on a speaker's nonverbal cues may tell you more than his or her words. Watch for the "iceberg tips" that let you know if the speaker might say more, especially if encouraged to do so.[65] Chapter 4 explains in detail the wealth of nonverbal cues that are always available to you: gestures, postures, vocal tones, facial expression, and more.

Nonverbal cues can be especially useful in figuring out another person's feelings and attitudes. You can get a sense of how emotions are communicated nonverbally by imagining all the different messages that might be conveyed by the following statements. How many different ways can you imagine each could be expressed? What different meaning might each set of nonverbal cues convey?

"No, nothing's the matter."

"We should get together one of these days."

"I'd like to talk with you in my office."

"Nobody's ever had that idea before."

Withhold Judgment

In his study of highly effective people, Stephen Covey said it best: "Seek first to understand, then to be understood."[66] It is often difficult to try to understand another person's ideas before judging them, especially when you hold strong opinions on the matter under discussion. For example, you might ask for a customer's reaction to your company's product or service and then spend your mental energy judging the answer instead of trying to understand it. ("Doesn't this guy have anything better to do than make petty complaints?" "Yeah, sure, he'd like us to deliver on a tighter schedule, but he'd scream his head off if we billed him for the overtime.") Or you might find yourself judging the ideas of a boss, co-worker, or subordinate before he or she has finished explaining them. ("Uh-oh. I hope this doesn't mean I have to spend a week in the field, trying to get market information." "These college kids come in and want to take over right away.") Listen first. Make sure you understand. Then evaluate.

Listen for Key Points

We are often tempted to ask a long-winded speaker "What are you getting at?" Sometimes it is appropriate to ask—politely—for the speaker's thesis: "I'm trying to pull together what you've been saying about the problems you've been having meeting your quotas. Could you summarize for me?"

Sometimes, however, it isn't appropriate to ask for the speaker's thesis outright. When you're 1 of 500 employees sitting in a darkened banquet room while senior executives try to promote corporate unity by giving short descriptions of what each of their divisions has done that year, you probably shouldn't ask, "Overall, then, would you say your division is losing its market share?" You can still do your own mental job of organizing and looking for patterns in this kind of situation.

career tip

Use a Telephone Log

E-mail provides a virtually automatic record of your correspondence, but telephone conversations are ephemeral. Recording phone calls is inconvenient and sometimes illegal, but a simple written log can help you maintain your records, prevent false claims, and re-establish contacts. For example, a log can remind you the name of the customer service agent to whom you spoke in a service call, the date and time of an appointment you've set up, or the model number of a product you're researching. Weeks later it may be important to tell a client, co-worker, or supervisor of all the attempts (successful and unsuccessful) you made to contact them or someone else.

You can also rely on your notes to remind others about information and commitments they have made, such as a reservation, promised delivery date, or a price quote: "The job won't be ready until November 15? But last Friday, Rose in your office promised me it would be done by the first of the month." A log can even remind people about what they *didn't* say or do. For example, you might respond to a complaint that you haven't kept a customer informed by explaining, "Actually I've phoned three times before today: On April 4, 11, and 18. Each time your voice mail picked up and I left a message telling you the job was ready."

For most purposes, a phone log doesn't have to be elaborate. Just make sure it contains all the information that you may need later:

- Date and time the call was placed.
- Subject of the call.
- Phone number called.
- Whether this call is a part of a series (i.e., a follow-up or response to an earlier call).
- Unsuccessful attempts to contact (busy signal, no answer, malfunctioning voice mail).
- Messages left on voice mail or with another person.
- Name of person you spoke with.
- Key points you and the other person made.

Keep your notes organized so you can use them later. If your notes are brief, you can jot them on a Post-it note attached to the other paperwork related to the subject in question. For more detailed and important matters, you may even choose to type up a record of the call, either on paper or in a computer file. It's probably best to file notes along with the other records for a given project. Whatever format you use, make your notes legible: the notes you hurriedly scribbled during a conversation won't be helpful if you can't read them later.

Take Notes and Repeat Information

Students know they need notes to recall important information for a test. Note taking can be just as valuable in business settings, both face to face and in phone conversations and teleconferences.[67] (See the Career Tip on this page.) You are unlikely to remember every deadline, every comment, or even every topic in a meeting or conversation unless you jot it down. This doesn't mean that you have to scribble every word in every setting: Some information doesn't need to be recorded, and writing down important information shouldn't distract you from listening. But when the topic is important, put it in writing.

It isn't always possible to take notes, and repetition works well in such cases. Remember that untrained listeners remember only about half of what they hear immediately after hearing it and then only half of that after 48 hours. One way to minimize this loss is to go over the important parts of a message aloud as soon as possible after you've heard it. For best results, talk about these ideas aloud—to a co-worker, your assistant, or a friend.

Analyze the Speaker's Evidence

As a good critical listener, you need to ask yourself several questions about the evidence a speaker gives to support her or his statements. What evidence does the order fulfillment manager give that the current computer system is causing problems or that a new one will be better? Does a sales representative back up the claim that a product will pay for itself in less than a year?

Once you have identified the evidence, you need to make sure it is valid. The success of the flexible-hours program instituted in the New York office doesn't mean that the same program will work as well in the factory in West Virginia, where a certain number of people have to be operating the machinery at any given time. The two or three employees unhappy with the new office furniture might be the exceptions rather than representative of the majority, while the one or two satisfied customers you hear about could be the only happy ones. Carefully researched statistics that look at more than a few isolated cases are a much stronger form of proof than are a few random examples.

The following questions can help you to examine the overall validity of supporting material:

Is the evidence given true?

Are enough cases cited?

Are the cited cases representative of the whole being considered?

Are there any exceptions to the points the speaker is making?

Do these exceptions need to be considered?

Examine Emotional Appeals

Sometimes emotional reactions are a valid basis for action. The sympathy we feel for underprivileged children is a good reason for donating money to their welfare. The desire to cut down on your own fatigue may be a good reason to hire an assistant.

In some cases, though, emotional appeals can obscure important logical considerations that might dissuade you from accepting a proposal. We can see this by thinking about fund-raisers who seek money for underprivileged children. Your sympathy might not justify allowing a fund-raiser to wander around your building soliciting funds from employees: Your employees could resent being asked to give money to *your* favorite cause rather than one of theirs, especially if they have just been asked to donate to another cause. The particular agency asking for your donation might not be the best vehicle for helping underprivileged children: It may have excessive overhead so that much of your contribution never reaches any children, or other organizations might serve needier people.

summary

For most workers, listening is the most frequent type of communication on the job, occupying more time than speaking, writing, or reading. Effective listening is important for several reasons. First, it aids the organization in carrying out its mission. In addition, effective listening helps individuals to advance in their careers. It provides information that helps them to learn about important happenings in the organization, as well as assisting them in doing their own jobs well. Listening also helps build strong personal relationships. Despite these advantages, most workers are poor listeners for a variety of reasons: physiological, environmental, attitudinal, sociocultural, and educational.

Most people have one or two preferred ways of listening that focus on people, content, action, or time. Understanding your own and others' listening styles gives you tools to analyze and improve your own listening and tailor messages to suit others' styles.

Listening effectively requires that the listener minimize distractions, talk less, and seek and observe feedback. A listener can seek feedback by asking genuine questions and by paraphrasing content, feelings, and intentions. Besides listening to others' words, insights can come from paying attention to their vocal and nonverbal cues. Listeners improve their effectiveness by listening for the key points, taking notes, and analyzing the speaker's evidence and emotional appeals.

key terms

Test your understanding of these key terms by visiting the Online Learning Center Web site at www.mhhe.com/adler9.

action-oriented listening style 87
content-oriented listening style 87
counterfeit questions 90
paraphrasing 90
people-oriented listening style 85
sincere questions 89
time-oriented listening style 87

activities

Go to the self-quizzes at the Online Learning Center at www.mhhe.com/adler9 to test your knowledge of chapter concepts.

1. Invitation to Insight

a. Recall three on-the-job incidents in which you had difficulty listening effectively. For each incident, describe which of the following factors interfered with your listening effectiveness:
   - i. Physiological barriers
     - Hearing problems
     - Rapid thought
   - ii. Environmental barriers
     - Physical distractions
     - Problems in the communication channel
     - Message overload
   - iii. Attitudinal barriers and faulty assumptions
     - Preoccupation
     - Egocentrism
     - Fear of appearing ignorant
     - Assuming that effective communication is the sender's responsibility
     - Assuming that listening is passive
     - Assuming that talking has more advantages than listening
   - iv. Sociocultural differences
     - Culture
     - Gender
   - v. Lack of training

b. Develop a list of ways you could overcome the greatest barriers that prevent you from listening more effectively.

2. Invitation to Insight

For each of the listening styles listed below (see text pp. 85–87), describe a specific work situation in which this style would be effective and one situation in which the style would probably not be appropriate. Defend your answers:

People-oriented
Action-oriented
Content-oriented
Time-oriented

3. Skill Builder

a. How can we differentiate between sincere questions and counterfeit questions?
b. What impact do counterfeit questions have on the receiver? On the interaction?
c. Write three examples of counterfeit questions. Supply a context that explains why the questions are counterfeit.
d. Convert the counterfeit questions to sincere questions.

4. Skill Builder

Practice your skill at questioning and paraphrasing in groups of four. Each group member should assume one of the following roles: speaker, listener1, listener2, and observer.

a. The **speaker** will talk about a problem he or she has recently experienced. If you can't think of a problem, talk about *one* of the following topics: how to perform a task you are familiar with, how to improve your chances for landing the job you want, or how to politely talk to a coworker about a behavior you disapprove of.
b. The **listeners** should use vocalizers, sincere questions, and paraphrasing to *understand* the speaker's content, intent, and feeling.
c. After the conversation ends, the speaker will describe the degree to which s/he feels satisfied that the paraphrasing reflected his or her meaning accurately. This is the measure of success of the interaction.
d. The **observer** should point out specific examples of effective and ineffective techniques used by the listeners.
e. Listeners should answer the following questions:
   i. Was paraphrasing difficult or awkward? Why?
   ii. How does this type of listening compare to your typical manner of responding?
   iii. What types of useful information did you gain from the conversations? Would you be likely to gain the same quality of information by responding in your more usual manner?
   iv. How could you use paraphrasing and sincere questioning to help in your everyday work?

5. Skill Builder

Practice your evaluative listening skills by following these steps:

a. Listen to a short persuasive presentation. Identify what the speaker is asking the listeners to believe or do.
b. Evaluate the speaker's evidence by answering the following questions.
   i. Does the speaker support the claim with evidence?
   ii. Does the speaker cite references for the evidence?
   iii. How accurate is the evidence? Explain.
   iv. Does the speaker represent opposing evidence fairly?
c. Identify at least two emotional appeals used by the speaker.
   i. Do any of the emotional appeals obscure important logical considerations?
   ii. Do the emotional appeals stretch the truth? Why or why not?
d. Based on this analysis, do you believe the speaker's argument is trustworthy?

resources

In Print

Barker, Larry, and Kitty Watson. *Listen Up: How to Improve Relationships, Reduce Stress, and Be More Productive by Using the Power of Listening.* New York: St. Martin's Press, 2000.

Many topics in this comprehensive book are especially useful for business communicators: How good listeners can control a situation, how to acquire important information by "listening around," and how to use various listening styles to build better relationships with others.

Borisoff, Deborah, and M. Purdy, eds. *Listening in Everyday Life: A Personal and Professional Approach*, 2nd ed. Lanham, MD: University Press of America, 1997.

This book includes specific sections on gender and cultural issues in listening and presents separate sections on listening in various occupations: education, business, service industries, legal, medical, and the helping professions. For business and professional readers who want career-specific help, these chapters are lively and practical.

Brownell, Judi. *Listening: Attitudes, Principles, and Skills*, 3rd ed. Boston: Allyn & Bacon, 2006.

This text explores many aspects of the process and challenges of listening, understanding, and responding in organizational and other relationships. Additionally, it addresses topics of listening between genders and cultures, and listening to media and in high-technology environments.

Covey, Stephen R. *The Seven Habits of Highly Effective People*. New York: Fireside Books, 1989.

Stephen Covey is noted for his principled approach to personal and professional communication. His classic and often-quoted "Habit 5: Seek First to Understand, Then to Be Understood" demonstrates how listening empathically to others can enable us to more effectively communicate our point of view.

Rogers, Carl R., and F. J. Roethlisberger. "Barriers and Gateways to Communication." *Harvard Business Review* 69 (November–December 1991), pp. 105–112.

This classic article argues that the primary barrier to communication is the tendency to evaluate another person's statements instead of first attempting to understand them. The authors urge readers to develop a habit of listening openly to ideas.

Shafir, Rebecca Z. *The Zen of Listening: Mindful Communication in the Age of Distraction*. Wheaton, IL: Quest Books, 2000.

The author describes techniques to create a mind-set for listening to ourselves and to others and shows us ways to increase our attention and memory while listening to the whole message. We can enhance our listening if we filter out distractions and practice Zen mindfulness to overcome the distractions of this high-tech, multitasking world.

Steil, Lyman K., and Richard K. Bommelje. *Listening Leaders: The Ten Golden Rules to Listen, Lead & Succeed*. Minneapolis, MN: Beavers Pond Press, 2004.

"Outstanding leaders are outstanding listeners." Starting with this thesis, the authors describe 10 rules for listening leaders and illustrate each of the 10 rules (chapters) with plenty of real-life examples and advice drawn from the lives of leaders who listen well.

On the Web

Businesslistening.com (**www.businesslistening.com**) is a collaborative effort of business consultants. This online reference center has ample resources for improving listening in all aspects of business. "The 'Talking Stick' Circle: An Ancient Tool for Better Decision Making and Strengthening Community" (**www.vision-nest.com/btbc/kgarden/tscircle.shtml**) offers insight into the Native American Talking Stick method for listening. High Gain (**www.highgain.com**) conducts listening training for businesses and provides immediate feedback for their listening self-assessment and other listening instructional tools.

Effective Listening offers tips and quotations on listening (**www.1000ventures.com/business_guide/crosscuttings/listening_main.html**). For listening quizzes at various levels of difficulty, go to Randall's Cyber ESL Listening Lab (**www.esl-lab.com**).

The International Listening Association (ILA) is dedicated to researching and understanding listening. Their Web site (**www.listen.org**) offers a variety of resources from members who work toward effective listening in business, government, the arts, human resources, health care, and more.

4

Verbal and Nonverbal Messages

Chapter Outline

Chapter Objectives

After reading this chapter you should be able to

1 Describe business situations in which ambiguous or specific language is preferable and create each type of statement.

2 Define, identify, and remedy examples of inflamatory language described in these pages.

3 Compare and contrast characteristically male and female speech and describe the potential benefits and problems arising from differences.

4 Describe how you can apply the information on nonverbal behavior in these pages in your own career.

5 Define and give examples of eight types of nonverbal behavior and summarize the importance of each in a specific organization or career field.

6 Predict the outcomes of various verbal and nonverbal behaviors with regard to sexual harassment and explain communication options for targets of harassment.

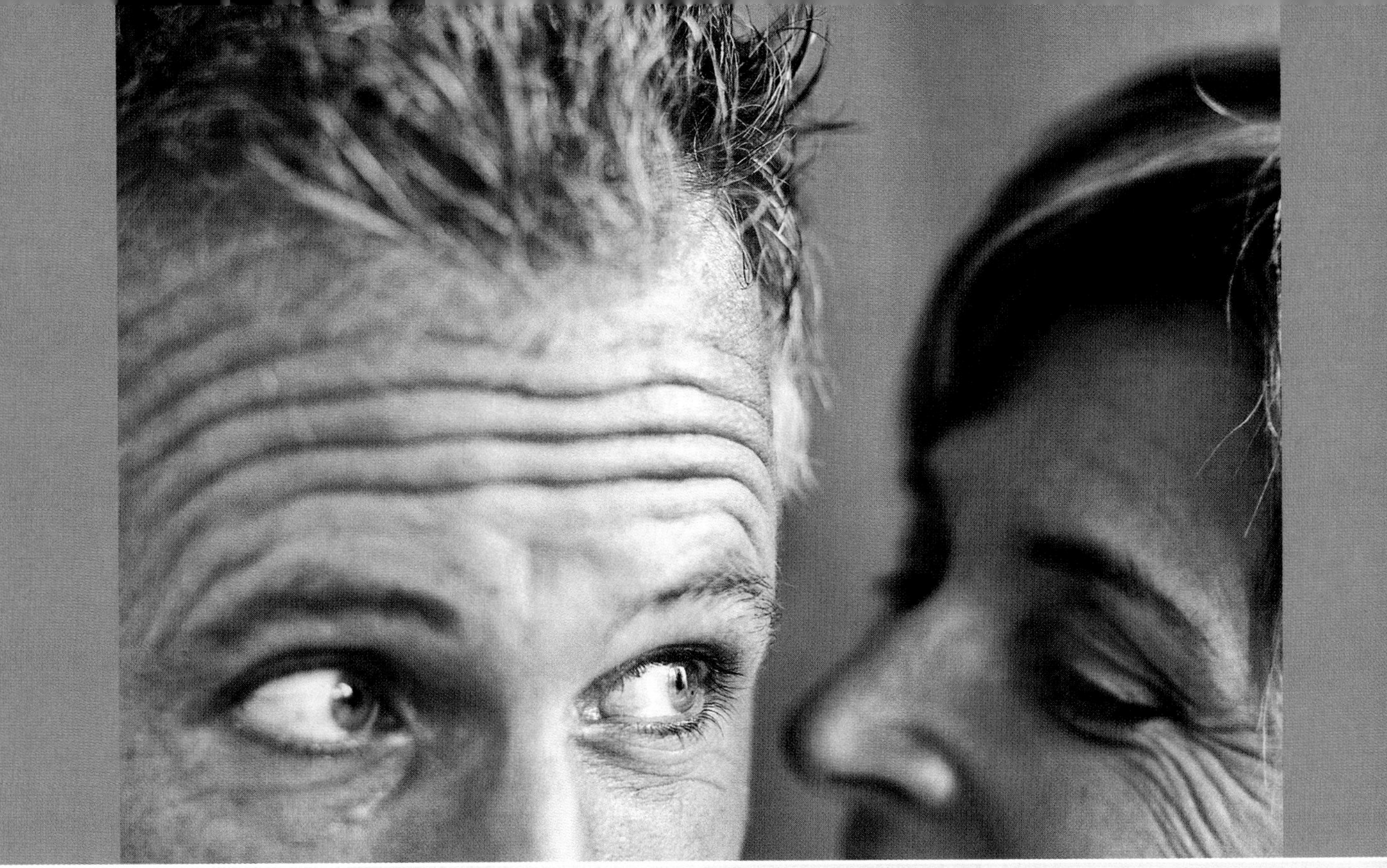

Although they are neighbors and see each other almost every day, Bob and Carolyn rarely speak to each other. Ever since their partnership broke up, the hard feelings have made even casual conversation painful.

"We both should have known better," Bob lamented. "It was such a simple misunderstanding. We went into the partnership agreeing that we would be 'equal partners,' but now I can see that we had different ideas about what being 'equals' meant. I saw each of us taking charge of the areas that we did best: I'm good at marketing and sales, and Carolyn knows product design and production backward and forward. So it made sense to me that, while we were each equally responsible for the business and deserving an equal share of the profits, we would each make the final decisions in the areas where we were experts."

"That's not what I meant by 'equal partners,'" stated Carolyn flatly. "Bob wasn't willing to take responsibility for the hard work of production. He kept saying, 'That's where you're the expert.' And he didn't have any faith in my ideas about sales and marketing. He wanted to make those decisions himself, whether or not I agreed. To me, being equal means you have just as much say as the other person in every part of the business."

In hindsight, both Bob and Carolyn realize that there had been signs of trouble from the beginning of their partnership. "Even before we opened for business, I could tell that Carolyn was unhappy," sighs Bob. "I always saw the venture as a chance to make a fortune. But whenever I'd get excited and talk about how much money we could make, Carolyn would clam up and get this grim look on her face."

Carolyn also remembers early, unspoken signs of trouble. "I've always wanted to have a business that my kids could be proud of," she said. "But when I'd talk about that, Bob wouldn't have much to say. Even though he never said so, at times I got the feeling that he was laughing at my high ideals."

This story illustrates the importance of paying close attention to verbal and nonverbal messages. The ill-fated partnership between Bob and Carolyn could have been avoided if they had paid more attention to the unspoken but powerful nonverbal clues that warned of trouble. Examining more carefully just what an equal partnership meant also could have helped them avoid the clash that finally led to their breakup.

How well you communicate your ideas will make the difference between success and failure. Expressing yourself effectively will boost your chances for a positive reaction, while a bungling delivery will torpedo even the best ideas. This chapter will look at the two channels by which you communicate: your words and your nonverbal behavior. In the following pages, you will gain a healthy respect for the advantages of using these channels effectively and the pitfalls of using them poorly. By the time you have finished this chapter, you will recognize that significant problems can lurk in even the simplest statements, and you will discover some ways to avoid or overcome such problems. You will also become more aware of the wordless messages that each of us constantly sends and receives.

Verbal Messages

As the case study on page 72 and the story that opened this chapter suggest, misunderstandings are a fact of life. In fact, most people vastly overestimate how well their explanations get through, and how well they understand others.[1] Linguistic theorists C. K. Ogden and I. A. Richards constructed a simple but profound model that explains the nature of many misunderstandings.[2] The broken line in their famous **triangle of meaning** model (Figure 4–1) shows that there is no direct relationship between an object, idea, process, or other referent and the word (or other symbol) used to represent it. Rather, the pathway to understanding—or misunderstanding—passes through the mind of the sender or receiver. As Table 4–1 on page 101 shows, the listener can understand the meaning of every word perfectly and still interpret a message in a way that is completely different from its intended meaning.

Clarity and Ambiguity

Since the most basic language problems involve misunderstandings, we will begin our study of language by examining how to prevent this sort of miscommunication. We will also look at times when a lack of clarity can actually be desirable.

FIGURE 4–1 Ogden and Richards's Triangle of Meaning

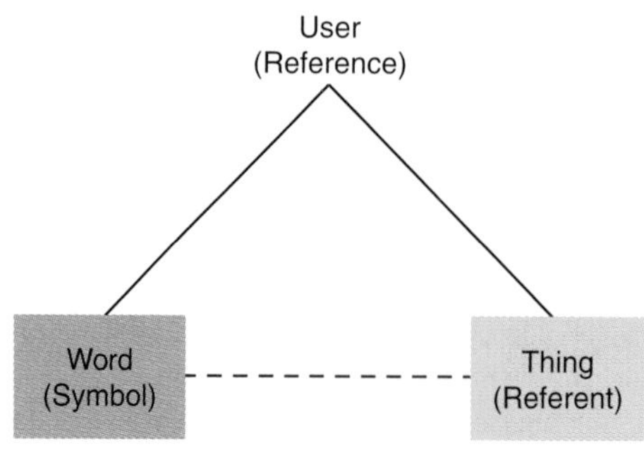

Table 4–1 Even Simple Messages Can Be Misunderstood

What the Manager Said	What the Manager Meant	What the Subordinate Heard
I'll look into hiring another person for your department as soon as I complete my budget review.	We'll start interviewing for that job in about 3 weeks.	I'm tied up with more important things. Let's forget about hiring for the indefinite future.
Your performance was below par last quarter. I really expected more out of you.	You're going to have to try harder, but I know you can do it.	If you screw up one more time, you're out.
I'd like that report as soon as you can get to it.	I need that report within the week.	Drop that rush order you're working on and fill out that report today.
I talked to the boss, but at the present time, due to budget problems, we'll be unable to fully match your competitive salary offer.	We can give you 95 percent of that offer, and I know we'll be able to do even more for you next year.	If I were you, I'd take that competitive offer. We're certainly not going to pay that kind of salary to a person with your credentials.
We have a job opening in Los Angeles that we think would be just your cup of tea. We'd like you to go out there and look it over.	If you'd like the job, it's yours. If not, of course you can stay here in Denver. You be the judge.	You don't have to go out to L.A. if you don't want to. However, if you don't, you can kiss good-bye to your career with this firm.
Your people seem to be having some problems getting their work out on time. I want you to look into this situation and straighten it out.	Talk to your people and find out what the problem is. Then get together with them and jointly solve it.	I don't care how many heads you bust, just get me that output. I've got enough problems around here without you screwing things up too.

Source: From Steven Altman, Enzo Valenzi, and Richard M. Hodgetts, *Organizational Behavior: Theory and Practice* (Academic Press, Inc., 1985).

Use Unequivocal Terms to Avoid Misunderstandings **Equivocal terms** are those with two different, but equally acceptable or common, meanings:

> A shipment ordered for Portland goes to Oregon instead of Maine.
>
> A client asks a contractor: "Can you move that door from here to there?" The contractor replies, "No problem." Later, the client is astonished to find that she has been charged for the change order. She thought "No problem" meant "No additional cost," but the contractor meant "I can do it . . . for a price."
>
> You agree to call on a client at home at "dinner time" in a part of the country where "dinner" is midday and "supper" is in the evening. When you appear at 6:00 P.M., the client asks why you didn't arrive at the promised time.

Most equivocal misunderstandings arise in casual conversation, where statements seem perfectly clear . . . until you discover that others can interpret them differently.[3] Sometimes equivocal problems arise because communicators from different fields use the same term in specialized ways. Hollywood agent Jerry Katzman describes just such a situation. In a meeting with representatives of a Silicon Valley software publisher, he used the phrase "in development" to mean a project that was at the rough-idea stage. By contrast, the software people were used to using that phrase to describe a project that had been funded and was being created. Katzman reported "It was like when the Japanese first came to Hollywood. They had to use interpreters, and we did too."[4]

Equivocation sometimes comes from different cultural values. Compared with U.S. businesspeople, Mexicans are less inclined to express conflict and are more polychronic and relaxed about managing time. The Spanish word *ahorita* means "right now" or "immediately" in English. Despite its dictionary meaning, North Americans have found that their Mexican counterparts use the term quite differently:

> When are those photocopies going to be ready?
>
> "*Ahorita,*" answers the secretary who knows the copy machine is broken.
>
> When will that delivery be made?
>
> "*Ahorita,*" answers the salesman who has no truck.
>
> One U.S. financial officer sheepishly admits he finally prohibited his Mexican staff from giving him *ahorita* as an answer.[5]

At least some equivocation problems can be avoided if you double-check your understanding of terms that might be interpreted in more than one way. When you agree to meet "Wednesday" with someone, mention the date to be sure that you're both thinking of the same week. When your supervisor says that your ideas are "OK," make sure that the term means "well done" and not just "adequate."

Use Lower-Level Abstractions When Clarity Is Essential Any object or idea can be described at various levels, some very general and others quite specific. Consider the following list of complaints about a fellow worker. Note that the same complaint is expressed but in various levels of abstraction, from highly abstract to low abstraction. Which is most helpful to the manager who must deal with this situation and to the employee being counseled?

problem

attitude problem

overly critical

finds fault with others

criticizes co-workers behind their backs, doesn't acknowledge any positive traits.

Low-level abstractions are highly specific statements that refer directly to objects or events that can be observed. By contrast, **high-level abstractions** cover a broader range of possible objects or events without describing them in much detail.

High-level abstractions can create problems because they are often subject to a wide variety of interpretations. For example:

Statement	Clarification
The job will take a little longer.	How much longer: Hours? Days? Weeks?
Straighten up the area.	A quick cleanup or a spit-and-polish job?

We need some market research.	A short questionnaire for a few of our biggest customers or lengthy personal interviews of thousands of potential customers?
Keep up the good work!	Which parts of the work are good?
Bring me a list of your costs on this job.	General categories of costs or an itemization of every expenditure, including postage and my secretary's overtime? A handwritten list for discussion purposes or a formal report?
Give me your honest opinion.	Speak my mind completely or only answer the questions you have specifically asked? Be diplomatic or blunt?

Since both abstract language and specific language have their advantages, it is often best to use both. One way to achieve maximum clarity is to begin explaining your proposal, problem, request, or appreciation with an abstract statement, which you then qualify with specifics:

> "I'm worried about the amount of time we seem to be spending on relatively unimportant matters [abstract]. In our last meeting, for instance, we talked for 20 minutes about when to schedule the company picnic and then had only 15 minutes to discuss our hiring needs [specific]."
>
> "I'd like to take on more responsibility [abstract]. Until now, the only decisions I've been involved in are about small matters [still abstract], such as daily schedules and customer refunds [more specific]. I'd like a chance to help decide issues such as buying and advertising [specific requests]."

One common type of overly abstract language is the use of excessively broad terms. Consider a few examples:

all	each	any	never	nothing
every	always	none	no one	nobody

When faced with a statement containing one of these words, an astute communicator can politely question its use by echoing the phrase with stress on the overly broad term or ask specifically about the term:

A: Our needs *never* get considered around here.

B: *Never?*

A: I can't understand *anything* he's saying.

B: What exactly didn't you understand?

Another type of ambiguous language that causes problems is the use of **relative words** such as *soon, often, large, short* that only have meaning in relationship to other (unspecified) terms. Telling your supervisor that you'll have the memo done *soon* or agreeing to do a *short* report can cause problems. If soon means "in a few weeks" to you, but it means "in a few days" to your boss, a conflict is brewing. If your boss expects a four-paged report and you thought you'd agreed to write two paragraphs or a page, you might both be upset with what transpires. Replacing relative words with numeric words can eliminate most of these problems. Use "in two days" rather than "soon" and "two paragraphs" rather than "short," for example.

Use Slang with Caution Casual, slang-laden speech may be fine off the job, but it can create the wrong impression with bosses, clients, and even colleagues. Some slang simply won't be understandable to others. For example, the British term "gobsmacked" is likely to draw a blank stare when used in conversation with someone outside the U.K. ("I was gobsmacked when they gave me that assignment"). Other language is likely to cast you in an unprofessional light. You may call your friends "dude" and label anything that's positive as "totally awesome," but it's smart to talk more professionally in business and other professional settings.

Use Jargon Judiciously Every profession has its own specialized vocabulary, often termed **jargon.** People who order office supplies talk about "NCR paper" and "three-up labels." Computer users talk about "64-bit architecture" and "image-compression boards."

In many cases, jargon serves a useful purpose. For one thing, it can save time. It's quicker for an accountant to use the term *liquidity* than to say "the degree to which an asset can be converted into cash." In the same way, *CPM* is a handy term that advertisers use to stand for "the advertising cost to make a thousand impressions." A specialized vocabulary is particularly vital when the subject matter is technical and complex. The phrase *sleeping pill* simply won't do for physicians, nurses, and other health professionals because it says nothing about the dosage, the particular drug, or the circumstances under which it should be used. Similarly, geologists can't discuss their findings by talking about "rocks."

A certain amount of jargon has its value for outsiders as well. Speakers who sprinkle their comments with jargon will appear more credible to some listeners.[6] While incomprehensible language may *impress* listeners, it doesn't help them to *understand* an idea. Thus, if your goal is to explain yourself (and not merely to build your image), the ideal mixture may be a combination of clear language sprinkled with a bit of professional jargon.

Problems arise when insiders use their specialized vocabulary without explaining it to the uninitiated. According to one survey, people in computer support industries are the worst offenders when it comes to jargon.[7] A customer shopping for a computer might be mystified by a dealer's talk about bus speed, onboard circuitry, and data transfer rates. When the same information is translated into language the buyer can understand—the length of time it takes to download a file, for example—a sale is more likely.[8]

"O.K. What part of 'malignant regression and pathogenic reintrojection as a defense against psychic decompensation' don't you understand?"

Certain words are used so often that they become clichés.[9] As one communication expert says, they "are brief and snappy, roll off the tongue easily, and can fool us into thinking that we know what we're talking about."[10] If you overuse buzzwords like "mission focused," "push the envelope," "paradigm shift," and "cutting edge," you run the risk of not clarifying your ideas in your own mind and not being clear to others.

Use Ambiguous Language When It Is Strategically Desirable In low-context cultures like the U.S. and Canada, speaking directly is valued. "Don't beat around the bush," we are tempted to say. Vague language can be a sign of deliberate deception, as an old joke shows. A reporter warned a state senator, "Sir, your constituents were confused by today's speech." "Good," the senator replied. "It took me two days to write it that way."

Despite its bad reputation, ambiguous language does have its place. High-context cultures have made an art of strategic ambiguity, finding ways to express difficult messages indirectly. One U.S. author describes how indirectness works:

> *Instead of criticizing a report, the manager asks for more information. . . . When they say "I'd like to reflect on your proposal a while," when the decision must be [made] soon, it means "You are dead wrong, and you'd better come up with a better idea very soon. But I don't tell you so, because you should know that yourself!"*
>
> *It seems to me that such indirectness in interpersonal communication is a virtue; it is just as efficient, and it is certainly more mature and polite than the affront, "You are dead wrong." We need not talk to one another as if we were children (or characters out of the pages of pulp fiction)—yes, children need clarity—but adults can deal with indirectness and multiple meanings.*[11]

Even in the normally low-context cultures like the United States, Canada, Israel, and Germany, there are many times when indirect speech helps communicators achieve two useful goals.[12] The first is *to promote harmony*. A group of workers who have been feuding over everything from next year's budget to funding the office coffee supply can at least reach consensus on abstractions like "the need to work well together" or "finding solutions we all can live with." While vague statements such as these might seem meaningless in light of everyday conflicts, they do provide a point upon which everyone can agree—a small but important start toward more cooperation.

A second function of ambiguous speech is *to soften the blow of difficult messages*. Business communicators face the constant challenge of delivering difficult messages: "This work isn't good enough." "You let me down." "We don't want to do business with you anymore." While statements like these may be honest, they can also be brutal. Ambiguous language provides a way to deliver difficult messages that softens their blow and makes it possible to work smoothly with the recipients in the future. For example:

Brute Honesty	Strategic Ambiguity
This work isn't good enough.	I think the boss will want us to back up these predictions with some figures.
You're not making any sense.	I'm having a hard time understanding that idea.
I don't want to work with you.	Right now I don't see any projects on the horizon.

A final function of strategic ambiguity is to make a *point indirectly that can't be expressed overtly*. In the current litigation-prone environment, business communicators often use strategic ambiguity to communicate critical messages without exposing themselves to lawsuits.[13] For example, consider this humorous letter of reference "endorsing" a former employee who was fired for being a slow, lazy, unmotivated worker with an inflated ego and who lacked qualifications, causing the company to lose money:

> *I am pleased to say John Doe is a former colleague of mine. John left this job the same way he came, fired with enthusiasm. We are deeply indebted for the services he has given our firm over the years.*
>
> *John will do nothing which will lower your high regard for him. His job requires few skills which he lacks. I honestly don't think he could have done a better job for us if he had tried. I most enthusiastically recommend John Doe with no qualifications whatsoever. It will not take John long to get up to speed. No salary would be too much for him. You won't find many people like John.*
>
> *In my opinion, you will be very fortunate to get this person to work for you. I would urge you to waste no time in making Mr. Doe an offer of employment.*[14]

One problem with strategic ambiguity, of course, is that it can easily be misunderstood. This problem can be especially acute in medical settings, when health care providers try to deliver bad news to patients in a way that softens its impact. For example,

> *[A surgeon] took one look at a patient's badly infected foot and recognized that it would have to be amputated. "I don't think we're going to be able to deal with this with local treatments," he told the patient.*
>
> *When the surgeon left the examining room, the woman turned to the doctor and asked: "Does that mean I'm going to have to go to Los Angeles for treatment?"*[15]

Even when misunderstandings aren't a problem, strategic ambiguity only works when both the sender and receiver are willing to tolerate a deliberate lack of clarity. Without that understanding, the result can be confusion, and often feelings of being betrayed or manipulated.[16]

Choose the Optimal Degree of Powerful Language Some types of language make a speaker sound less powerful, while other types create an air of power and confidence.

Less Powerful Speech	More Powerful Speech
Tag questions	
"This report is good, *isn't it?*"	"This report is good."
Hesitations	
"I, *uh*, think we should, *um*, use the newer format."	"I think we should use the newer format."
Qualifiers	
"*I don't know if you'll like this idea*, but we could hire an outside consultant."	"We could hire an outside consultant."
Intensifiers	
"That was *such* a good job!"	"That was a good job!"
Questions	
"*Do you think we should* shorten the report?"	"I think we should shorten the report."

ethical challenge

Strategic Ambiguity

a. Develop strategically ambiguous ways to rephrase each of the following statements:
   i. You've done a sloppy job here.
   ii. I can't understand what you're trying to say in this letter.
   iii. Nobody likes your idea.
   iv. Would you please hurry up and get to the point?

b. On the basis of your responses here, decide how honest strategically ambiguous statements are. If they are not completely honest, can they be considered ethical?

Speakers who use more powerful speech are rated as more competent, dynamic, and attractive than speakers who sound powerless.[17] One study revealed that even a single type of powerless speech mannerism can make a person appear less authoritative.[18] So, when your goal is to create an impression of power and conviction, it's best to avoid powerless speech.

On the other hand, there are times when powerful individuals might intentionally use less powerful language to avoid throwing their weight around. In some situations less powerful forms of speech can even enhance a speaker's effectiveness.[19] For example, a boss might say to her assistant, "Would you mind making copies of these files before you go home?" Both the boss and assistant know this is an order and not a request, but the questioning form is more considerate, and leaves the assistant feeling better about the boss.[20] The importance of achieving both content and relational goals helps explain why a mixture of powerful and polite speech is usually most effective.[21]

Inflammatory Language

Language has the power to stir intense emotions. It can motivate, inspire, and amuse audiences. Unfortunately, it can also generate negative feelings: antagonism, defensiveness, and prejudice. You can prevent these negative outcomes by following two guidelines.

Avoid Biased Language Emotional problems arise when speakers intentionally or unintentionally use **biased language**—terms that seem to be objective but actually conceal an emotional bias. Consider, for example, the range of words you could use to refer to a 25-year-old man who disagrees with your proposal: *gentleman*, *fellow*, *guy*, *young man*, or *person*. All of these are accurate, yet each one paints a different picture in the listener's mind. None of them is neutral.

"Sorry, Chief, but of course I didn't mean 'bimbo' in the pejorative sense."

When faced with biased language, it's wise to recognize that the speaker is editorializing. Tactfully restate the term in language that doesn't contain an evaluation, paraphrase with neutral language, or use terms that quantify:

Speaker's Biased Language	Listener's Restatement
It's a *gamble*.	So you don't think the idea is a reasonable risk. Is that it? (paraphrase)
He's *long-winded*.	Bill *has* been talking for a half hour. (quantify)
She's so *wishy-washy*.	You think Susan isn't willing to make a decision? (rephrase in nonbiased language)

Beware of Trigger Words Some terms have such strong emotional associations that they act almost like a trigger, setting off an intense emotional reaction in certain listeners. These **trigger words** can refer to specific people (your boss, the president), groups or categories of individuals (union stewards, the personnel department, customers with complaints), issues (right-to-work laws, affirmative action, flexible scheduling), or other topics (sexual harassment, Japanese imports, downsizing).

What is the best way to deal with trigger words? The first thing to realize is that, like others, you almost certainly have your own trigger words. You, therefore, ought to begin by recognizing them, so that when one comes up you'll at least be aware of your sensitivity and, thus, avoid overreacting. If, for example, your parents are farmers and you are sensitive about people speaking condescendingly about farmers, you might catch yourself before you overreact when a co-worker refers to someone on Casual Friday as "dressed like a farmer." It could be an innocent or uninformed remark.

Sometimes, however, you will discover too late that a term which seems innocuous to you is a trigger word for others. The best reaction when faced with such an emotional response is to let the other person get the strong feelings out of his or her system. At that point, you can choose a more agreeable term and proceed with the discussion.

Masculine and Feminine Language Use

Chapter 2 described how culture affects communication. Some social scientists have suggested that conversation between men and women is a kind of cross-cultural communication in which members of each sex are not speaking different dialects but **"genderlects."**[22] They have argued that these different approaches affect the way men and women interact with one another in ways that are powerful but usually unnoticed.

As you read about differences in male and female speech, understand that the descriptions don't characterize all men and women. The relationship between gender and language is like the one between gender and height: Men are generally taller than women, but some women are taller than some men. In fact, the difference between the tallest man and the shortest man (or the tallest woman and the shortest woman) is greater than the difference between the average man and the average woman. For this reason, the words "masculine" and "feminine" are actually better adjectives to describe language differences, since they refer to traits characteristically linked to each gender and not to biological sex. Remember also that gender isn't the only factor that influences conversational style. Cultural, geographical, and occupational influences also play a role. Finally, understand that the differences outlined in this section reflect past communication patterns. As the roles of men and women in society evolve, speech styles may change as well.

Feminine Speech From childhood, females learn to use speech for what Tannen and others refer to as **rapport talk:** to create connections, establish goodwill, show support, and build community.

For many women an important part of building rapport is using language as an *expressive tool:* to articulate emotions ("I'm worried about finishing those reports today"; "I'm glad everybody had a chance to speak") and clarify relationships ("We don't seem to be working well together").

Characteristically feminine speech often goes beyond just expressing emotions; it also is *supportive*. Women are most likely to listen and respond to spoken and unspoken conversational clues about the other person's feelings. One form of support is "troubles talk": sharing one's own problems as a way of showing solidarity. A characteristically feminine reply to a description of difficulties at work would be "I know what that's like. Last year I had so much trouble with a client on the Bustos case. . . ." This response lets the speaker know that she is not alone, that she is understood.

Another characteristic of feminine conversational style is its *tentative* nature. This is reflected in questioning forms ("Could we go now?" "Would you type that for me?"), hedges and disclaimers ("I'm not sure about these figures . . ."; "This might not be a good time to bring this up, but . . ."), and tag questions ("The report is due today, isn't it?"). While these forms exhibit the powerless characteristics described earlier in this chapter on pages 106–107, Tannen describes them more as a bid for solidarity than a sign of weakness:

> *Many women are frequently told, "Don't apologize" or "You're always apologizing." The reason "apologizing" is seen as something they should stop doing is that it seems synonymous with putting oneself down. But for many women, and a fair number of men, saying "I'm sorry" isn't literally an apology; it is a ritual way of restoring balance to a conversation. "I'm sorry," spoken in this spirit, if it has any literal meaning at all, does not mean "I apologize," which would be tantamount to accepting blame, but rather "I'm sorry that happened." To understand the ritual nature of apologies, think of a funeral at which you might say, "I'm so sorry about Reginald's death." When you say that, you are not pleading guilty to a murder charge. You're expressing regret that something happened without taking or assigning blame. In other words, "I'm sorry" can be an expression of understanding—and caring about—the other person's feelings rather than an apology.*[23]

Speech forms like apologizing, especially when used by women, can create the impression of less authority, status, certainty, accuracy, or credibility. However, tentative speech doesn't have to be regarded as weak: Another interpretation is that it builds rapport by avoiding dogmatism and suggesting equality.

These two interpretations of tentative speech show that language doesn't have any absolute meaning; rather, it is a product of the relationships and expectations of the people who use it. This explains why men who use tag questions may be perceived as more affiliative and cordial (because these forms are not expected), while women who use them may be viewed (especially by men in a business environment) as less self-assured.

Conversational initiation and maintenance are also characteristic of feminine speech. Women have long been taught to ask questions to get a conversation going, to find out what others are interested in, and to show interest in a conversational partner. So, many women ask questions to start and maintain conversations: "Did you hear about . . . ?" "Are you going to . . . ?" "Did you know that . . . ?" In addition, women use "listening noises" ("Uh, huh." "Oh really?" "Is that right?") to show interest. If women do interrupt, it is often to support or affirm the speaker, not to challenge or threaten.

Masculine Speech Whereas women use talk to build rapport, men are more comfortable with what linguists have labeled **report talk:** speech that focuses less on feelings and relationships and more on information, facts, knowledge, and competence. Men are more inclined to use language to claim attention, assert a position, establish status, and show independence.

Characteristically masculine speech uses language *instrumentally* (as opposed to expressively) to get things done: report information, solve visible problems, achieve, accomplish, attain, execute, perform. The results are often tangible and the reward is visible: "Fax these reports to accounting"; "I'll make reservations at Sara's"; "Finish that proposal by Monday." Language is often used by men to define status.

When dealing with personal problems, a characteristically masculine approach is to offer *advice* that will lead to a solution. Empathizing to show sympathy and establish solidarity just doesn't seem helpful or appropriate to many men.

Characteristically masculine speech is more *assertive, certain, direct,* and *authoritative.* Men often use statements of fact rather than opinion: "That deduction belongs on Schedule C" rather than "I think that's a Schedule C deduction." Declarative sentences and dropped pitch at the end create a sense of sureness and authority. Men are more likely to speak directly, giving clear and unambiguous commands or directions rather than couching requests in the form of questions.

Men's speech style typically includes several characteristics of conversational *dominance* or *control:* verbosity, topic control, and interruptions. Most research supports the statement that in conversations between men and women, men talk at greater length. Often in response to questions from women, men decide which topic of conversation to pursue and talk longer than the women in the same conversation. Research on interruptions is mixed as to who interrupts more, but it appears that the purpose of men's interruptions is often to gain control of the conversational topic or the conversation itself.

Table 4–2 summarizes the characteristics of feminine and masculine speech styles.

Meeting Gender-Related Language Challenges

Problems can arise when stereotypically masculine and feminine language styles clash on the job—often without anyone knowing exactly why. For instance, a woman who says, "I'm having difficulty with the Garcia account," may want to hear her concerns acknowledged and know that others have experienced similar problems. Her goal may be to gain support, establish connection, and seek rapport. Or she may just want to talk about the situation. A man, conditioned to use speech to solve problems,

Table 4–2 Characteristics of Feminine and Masculine Speech Styles

Characteristically Feminine Speech	Characteristically Masculine Speech
Builds rapport	Reports facts
Is expressive	Is instrumental
Offers support	Offers advice
Sounds tentative	Sounds certain
Initiates and maintains conversation	Controls conversation

might respond with advice: "Here's one way you could handle it. . . ." If the woman wanted support and connection, being given advice might produce an effect that is just the opposite of the rapport she was looking for: The woman might feel that her male colleague was trying to appear "one-up," coming across as a superior. From his frame of reference, the man *was* being helpful: He offered useful information at the request of someone in need.

Another gender-related problem can arise when a man pays attention to the content of a message while a woman focuses on the relational dimension of the words. If a male supervisor says, "I can't do anything about your hours; the boss says they're set and can't be changed," a woman may hear a relational message of "I don't care" or "I don't want to be bothered." The man, used to dealing with communication at the content level, isn't being unsympathetic; he is just responding to a request.

Both masculine and feminine language styles work well—as long as speakers operate by the same rules. Frustrations result when people expect others to use the same style as theirs. The following suggestions can help communicators understand and adapt to one another's differing uses of language:

- *Be aware of different styles.* Once you are aware that men and women have been taught to use language differently, there's less likelihood of being dismayed at a style that doesn't match yours. The cultural analogy is apt here: If you were traveling in another country, you wouldn't be offended by the customs of its inhabitants, even if they were different from yours. In the same way, accepting gender differences can lead to smoother relationships—even if members of the other sex behave differently from you.
- *Switch styles, when appropriate.* Being bilingual is an obvious advantage in a multicultural world. In the same way, using a communication style that isn't characteristic of you can be useful. If you routinely focus on the content of others' remarks, consider paying more attention to the unstated relational messages behind their words. If you generally focus on the unexpressed-feelings part of a message, consider being more task-oriented. If your first instinct is to be supportive, consider the value of offering advice; and if advice is your reflexive way of responding, think about whether offering support and understanding might sometimes be more helpful.

- *Combine styles.* Effective communication may not be an either-or matter of choosing one style. In many situations, you may get the best results by combining typically masculine and feminine approaches. Research confirms what common sense suggests: A "mixed-gender strategy" that balances the traditionally masculine, task-oriented approach with the characteristically feminine, relationship-oriented approach is rated most highly by both male and female respondents.[24] Choosing the approach that is right for the other communicator and the situation can create satisfaction far greater than that which comes from using a single stereotypical style.

Nonverbal Communication

Words are not the only way we communicate. You can appreciate this fact by imagining the following scenes:

> Your boss has told the staff that she welcomes any suggestions about how to improve the organization. You take her at her word and schedule an appointment to discuss some ideas you have had. As you begin to outline your proposed changes, she focuses her gaze directly on you, folds her arms across her chest, clenches her jaw muscles, and begins to frown. At the end of your remarks, she rises abruptly from her chair, says "Thank you for your ideas" in a monotone, and gives you a curt handshake.
>
> You are on a committee interviewing applicants for the job of customer relations representative. You notice one résumé that seems far superior to the others: The candidate received almost perfect grades at a top-flight university, had a similar position with a leading company in a distant city, and came with enthusiastic letters of recommendation. During the interview, you notice that he rarely looks you in the eye.
>
> Despite the expense, you have decided to have a highly regarded CPA handle your tax matters. While waiting for the accountant to appear, you scan the impressive display of diplomas from prestigious universities and professional associations. The accountant enters, and as the conversation proceeds, he yawns repeatedly.

Most people would find these situations odd and disturbing. This reaction would have nothing to do with the verbal behavior of the people involved. In each case, nonverbal behavior sends messages above and beyond the words being spoken: The boss doesn't really seem to want to hear your suggestions and you wonder whether the job applicant would in fact be good at dealing with customers, despite his credentials, or possibly even whether those credentials are genuine.

In the following pages we'll examine the role of nonverbal communication in the working world. For our purposes, **nonverbal communication** involves messages expressed by other than linguistic means.

Characteristics of Nonverbal Communication

Now that we have defined nonverbal communication and discussed its importance, we need to take a look at some of its characteristics. Nonverbal communication resembles verbal communication in some ways and is quite different in others.

Nonverbal Behavior Always Has Communicative Value You may not always *intend* to send nonverbal messages, but everything about your appearance, every movement, every facial expression, every nuance of your voice has the potential to convey meaning.[25] You can demonstrate this fact by imagining that your boss has "called you on the carpet," claiming that you haven't been working hard enough. How could you not send a nonverbal message? Nodding gravely would be a response; so would blushing, avoiding or making direct eye contact, or shaking your head affirmatively or negatively. While you can shut off your linguistic channels of communication by refusing to speak or write, it is impossible to avoid behaving nonverbally.

One writer learned this fact from movie producer Sam Goldwyn while presenting his proposal for a new film. "Mr. Goldwyn," the writer implored, "I'm telling you a sensational story. I'm only asking for your opinion, and you fall asleep." Goldwyn's reply: "Isn't sleeping an opinion?"

Nonverbal Communication Is Powerful Despite folk sayings like "you can't judge a book from its cover," we form impressions of others mostly from nonverbal observations—about physical appearance and behavior. Once we form these impressions, they influence our subsequent impressions and judgments. Canadian communication consultant Lee McCoy gives an example:

> *If I meet Susan and initially perceive her to be professional, attractive and intelligent, I'm also likely to begin to attribute other positive characteristics to her. I might see her as organized, successful and warm. This is not to suggest that I'll ignore negative characteristics, but it will take me longer to become aware of something negative if my initial perceptions of her are very positive. If, on the other hand, Susan presents herself to me as sloppily dressed, with bitten fingernails and a lack of eye contact, I may begin to attribute equally negative characteristics to her—insecurity, lack of knowledge, coldness.*[26]

Even after first impressions have been made, the impact of nonverbal behavior is powerful. In fact, when nonverbal behavior seems to contradict a verbal message, the spoken words carry less weight than the nonverbal cues.[27]

Nonverbal Behavior Is Ambiguous While nonverbal communication can create powerful impressions, the messages it conveys are ambiguous.[28] You don't have to be as clueless as the boss in the cartoon below to misinterpret nonverbal cues. Does a customer's yawn signal boredom or fatigue? Are your co-workers

Dilbert: © Scott Adams/ Dist. by United Feature Syndicate, Inc. Reprinted by permission.

laughing with or at you? Does your boss's frown reflect disapproval or preoccupation? Most nonverbal behaviors have a multitude of possible meanings, and it is a serious mistake to assume that you can decide which is true in any given case.

Nonverbal Communication Primarily Expresses Attitudes While it is relatively easy to infer general interest, liking, disagreement, amusement, and so on, from another's actions, messages about ideas or concepts don't lend themselves to nonverbal channels. How, for instance, would you express the following messages nonverbally?

Sales are running 16 percent above last year's.

I need more change at checkstand 2.

Management decided to cancel the sales meeting after all.

Let's meet at two to plan the agenda for tomorrow's meeting.

It's apparent that such thoughts are best expressed in speech and writing. It's also apparent, though, that nonverbal behavior will imply how the speaker *feels* about these statements: whether the speaker is pleased that sales are up or worried that they're not as high as expected, how urgently the cashier at checkstand 2 needs change, and so on.

Much Nonverbal Behavior Is Culture-Bound Certain types of nonverbal behavior seem to be universal. For example, there is strong agreement among members of most literate cultures about which facial expressions represent happiness, fear, surprise, sadness, anger, and disgust or contempt.[29] Many nonverbal expressions do vary from culture to culture, however. For instance, the hand sign that means "OK" in the United States and Canada has a different and obscene meaning in some other cultures. The nod that means "yes" in some cultures means "no" in others, while in still other cultures it means only that the other person understood the question.

In this age of international communication in business, it is especially important to understand that there are cultural differences in the meaning assigned to nonverbal behaviors. Consider the different rules about what distance is appropriate between speakers. One study revealed that the "proper" space between two speakers varied considerably from one culture to another: To Japanese, a comfortable space was 40.2 inches; for a U.S. resident, 35.4 inches; and to Venezuelans, 32.2 inches.[30] It's easy to see how this could lead to problems for a native of the United States doing business overseas. To a Latin American, the North American would seem too withdrawn, whereas a Japanese might see the same businessperson as too aggressive.

Types of Nonverbal Communication

We have already mentioned several types of nonverbal messages. We will now discuss each in more detail.

Voice Your own experience shows that the voice communicates in ways that have nothing to do with the words a speaker utters. You may recall, for instance, overhearing two people arguing in an adjoining room or apartment; even though you couldn't make out their words, their emotions and the fact that they were arguing were apparent from the sound of their voices. Similarly, you have

Models of Nonverbal Effectiveness

Think of an especially effective communicator you have encountered in business or professional settings. This may be someone you know (e.g., a boss, colleague, instructor) or a person you don't know personally but have dealt with (e.g., a medical professional, salesperson, public safety official). The person you choose may even be a character in a film.

Describe to your audience

1. Who this person is and the context in which you encountered him or her.
2. The nonverbal behaviors and attitudes that contribute to his or her effectiveness. Be as specific as possible: Give examples of how the person you are describing has used the types of behaviors described in this chapter: facial expression, voice, attire, etc.
3. What lessons you have learned from the person you've chosen, and how you can apply them in your life.

If time and the facilities permit, you may even share a photo of the person you are describing with your audience.

probably overheard people talking in a language you didn't understand; yet the speakers' feelings—excitement, delight, exhaustion, boredom, grief—were conveyed by their voices.

Social scientists use the term **paralanguage** to describe a wide range of vocal characteristics, each of which helps express an attitude:

pitch (high–low)
range (spread–narrow)
articulation (precise–imprecise)
rhythm (smooth–jerky)
volume (loud–soft)
resonance (resonant–thin)
tempo (rapid–slow)
dysfluencies (*um*, *er*, etc.)
pauses (frequency and duration)

Harvard University leadership expert Ronald Heifetz points out that the "music" of the voice can say more than the "lyrics" that are spoken:

> *It's difficult for someone who lost the last six arguments to say in a policy paper, "I've lost the last six arguments. If I don't win the next one, what am I going to tell people?" But in a conversation, the tone of voice and intensity of the argument give clues to that subtext. Listening musically enables leaders to get underneath and behind the surface to ask, "What's the real argument that we're having?"*[31]

While paralanguage reflects feelings, the *emphasis* a speaker puts on certain words can also change the meaning of a statement radically. Notice the differences in this one statement:

I need this job done right now. (Others might not.)

I *need* this job done right now. (It's important!)

I need *this* job done right now. (Forget the other jobs.)

I need this job done *right now*. (Immediately!)

Appearance Appearance plays a tremendous role in determining how a communicator's messages will be received in business and elsewhere.[32] As a rule, people who *look* attractive are considered to be likable and persuasive, and they generally have successful careers.[33] For example, research suggests that beginning salaries increase about $2,000 for every 1-point increase on a 5-point attractiveness scale and that more attractive men (but not more attractive women) are given higher starting salaries than their less handsome counterparts.

A number of factors contribute to how attractive a person seems. For instance, potential employers, customers, and co-workers are usually impressed by people who are trim, muscular, and in good shape. One study, in fact, shows that people who are overweight have more trouble getting job offers.[34] Some aspects of physical appearance cannot be changed very easily. One very significant factor in appearance, though—and one over which you may have the most control—is clothing.

The kind of clothing one wears can influence how people react. Boeing Aircraft CEO Philip Condit is aware of this fact. Having discovered that discussions were hard to get going when he appeared in a business suit and tie, Condit routinely dressed down when making trips to the shop floor to talk with the men and women who build Boeing aircraft.[35]

Attitudes about what clothing is acceptable keep changing. By the mid-1990s, even conservative IBM abandoned its decades-long policy of requiring employees to wear a dark business suit, even allowing male workers in some jobs to show up for work without a suit and tie. A spokesperson for IBM explained, "You try to dress like your customers do."[36] But the casual dress trends brought on by the 1990 dot-coms seem to be in decline.[37]

Whether to dress up or dress down depends on several factors, including the industry or field of work. California's outdoor gear clothing manufacturer, Patagonia, Inc., may have one of the most liberal dress codes: Even shoes aren't required.[38] By contrast, financial services and public administration businesses have some of the most conservative dress standards, while high-tech, utilities, and natural resources tend to be the most informal.[39]

Geography also makes a difference in determining an appropriate working wardrobe. In one survey, Washington, DC, proved to be the most conservative attire, with New York and Philadelphia close behind. California and New England—the location of many high-tech companies—had more liberal standards.[40] Knowing an office has a "business casual" dress code isn't enough. As business etiquette expert Dana Casperson notes, business casual "means one thing on the West Coast, another thing on the East Coast, and no one knows in the middle."[41] The culture of an individual organization also makes a difference in how to dress. Two companies in the same field might have quite different appearance codes.

When choosing your wardrobe, consider the following tips:

- *Look around.* The best guide to an appropriate wardrobe is right in front of you. Look at key people in the industry and country where you work. Wearing a conservative, dark business suit in a freewheeling start-up company where everyone else comes to work in jeans would look just as odd as wearing wrinkled Levis in a Wall Street stock brokerage.
- *Be flexible.* Within your company's dress code, choose an outfit that fits your daily activities. If you are seeing an important client, a business suit may be the best look. If you will be working all day at your desk, more casual dress may be fine.
- *Don't confuse "casual" with "sloppy."* A T-shirt and grubby denims send a different message than well-fitting khakis and a sharp shirt or sweater. Looking good in casual dress can be at least as challenging (and expensive) as a more formal look.
- *Dress for the job you want.* If you are seeking advancement, consider dressing in a way that makes it easy for the people who have the power to promote you to visualize you in a position of more responsibility.

The Face and Eyes On an obvious level, a person's face communicates emotions clearly: a subordinate's confused expression indicates the need to continue with an explanation; a customer's smile and nodding signal the time to close a sale; and a colleague's frown indicates that your request for help has come at a bad time. Facial expressions, like other nonverbal signals, are ambiguous (a co-worker's frown could come from a headache rather than the timing of your request). Nonetheless, researchers have found that accurate judgments of facial expressions can be made.[42]

The eyes themselves communicate a great deal. A skilled nonverbal communicator, for example, can control an interaction by knowing when and where to look to produce the desired results. Since visual contact is an invitation to

"You have until he rolls his eyes and looks at his watch."

speak, a speaker who does not want to be interrupted can avoid looking directly at people until it is time to field questions or get reactions.

Eye contact can be a good indicator of how involved a person is in a situation, although the advice to always look people straight in the eye has been partially contradicted by research. In most two-person conversations, people seem to look at their partners somewhere between 50 and 60 percent of the time, often alternating short gazes with glances away. Still, a person who makes little or no eye contact may seem to have little involvement in the situation.

The rules for eye contact and facial expressions vary from one culture to another. In some cultures—Diné (Navajo), for example—lack of eye contact may indicate respect for elders, not a lack of interest. In Japan, smiling is less common than in North America, which can confuse visitors who mistakenly perceive formality for unfriendliness. Clerks greet customers with a simple "Irasshaimase"—"Welcome"—but typically don't accompany the greeting with a smile.[43] Some foreign companies, including McDonald's Corp., have created "smile schools" to teach employees how to greet customers in a manner that seems more friendly.

Even among communicators who follow the rules of Euro-American culture, eye contact can be deceptive; some people *can* lie while looking you right in the eye. And even barely perceptible changes in eye contact can send messages that may or may not be accurate. The following story illustrates how eye contact can be misleading—with serious repercussions:

> *Discussing his corporation's financial future in front of television cameras, the chief executive officer of a Fortune 500 company lowered his eyes just as he began to mention projected earnings. His downcast eyes gave the impression—on television—that the executive wasn't on the level. Wall Street observers discounted the CEO's optimistic forecast, and the company's stock price dropped four points over the next few trading days. It took two years to build it up again—even though the projection had proved to be accurate.*[44]

Posture and Movement A person's body communicates messages in several ways. The first is through posture. The way you sit at your desk when you're working can reflect your attitude toward your job or how hard you're working to anyone who cares to look. A less obvious set of bodily clues comes from the small gestures and mannerisms that every communicator exhibits at one time or another. While most people pay reasonably close attention to their facial expression, they are less aware of hand, leg, and foot motions. Thus, fidgeting hands might betray nervousness; a tapping foot, impatience; and clenched fists or white knuckles, restrained anger. Table 4–3 describes the way others may be likely to interpret some of your gestures.

A study on privacy in the workplace by GF Business Equipment Company describes ways in which such gestures can be used to discourage visits from co-workers. In addition to avoiding eye contact with your visitor, the company suggests that you shuffle papers or make notes to indicate a desire to return to work . . . keep pen or pencil poised—that communicates an aversion to engage in conversation . . . and if interrupted when dialing a call, don't hang up the receiver.[45]

Good communicators are sensitive to small cues like this and tailor their behavior accordingly. They will notice a forward-leaning position as an indication that their remarks are being well received and will capitalize upon the point that led to this reaction. When a remark results in a pulling back, a smart communicator will uncover the damage and try to remedy it. Awareness of such subtle messages can

Table 4–3 Common Gestures and Their Possible Perceived Meanings

Gesture	In Moderate Form	When Exaggerated
Forward lean	Friendly feelings	Hostile feelings
Direct eye contact	Friendly feelings	Hostile feelings
Unique dress and hairstyle	Creativity	Rebelliousness
Upright posture	Expertise; self-confidence	Uprightness; hostility
Variability in voice pitch, rate, and loudness	Lively mind	Nervousness; anxiety; insecurity
Smiling	Friendliness; relaxed and secure composure	Masking hostility; submissiveness
Averting gaze	Shyness; modesty	Guilt; unreliability
Knitted brow	Involvement	Hostility
Nodding and reaching out the hands while talking	Self-confidence	Uncertainty

Source: Adapted from University of Northern Iowa College of Business Administration. Accessed from **http://www.cba.uni.edu/buscomm/nonverbal/body%20Language.htm**.

make the difference between success and failure in a variety of business settings: interviews, presentations, group meetings, and one-to-one interactions.

Body relaxation or tension is a strong indicator of who has the power in one-to-one relationships. As a rule, the more relaxed person in a given situation has the greater status.[46] This is most obvious in job interviews and high-stake situations in which subordinates meet with their superiors—requesting a raise or describing a problem, for example. The person in control can afford to relax, while the supplicant must be watchful and on guard. While excessive tension does little good for either the sender or receiver, total relaxation can be inappropriate for a subordinate. A job candidate who matched the interviewer's casual sprawl would probably create a poor impression. In superior-subordinate interactions, the best posture for the one-down person is probably one that is slightly more rigid than the powerholder's.

Height also affects perceptions of power: Tallness usually equates with dominance. Standing up tall can help you appear more authoritative, whereas a slumped posture or slouched shoulders creates an appearance of submissive or passive demeanor. Getting your body at the same level as others is a way of nonverbally diminishing status whether speaking with a colleague in a wheelchair or with others shorter than you. To literally have to look up to someone may make the shorter person feel like a subordinate. Sitting down with someone could signal your desire for collegiality rather than status, while standing over or behind someone signals power or status. Since women and persons from some minority co-cultures may not be as tall as the average American male, and since persons in wheelchairs interact at a shorter height, your relative height is a factor worth considering in professional interactions. If you are taller than others or are standing when others are sitting, they may be seeing you as an authority figure or higher-status individual, even if you don't wish to appear as one.[47]

Personal Space and Distance The distance we put between ourselves and others also reflects feelings and attitudes, and thus it affects communication. Anthropologist Edward Hall has identified four distance zones used by middle-class Americans: intimate (ranging from physical contact to about 18 inches), casual-personal (18 inches to 4 feet), social-consultative (4 to 12 feet), and public (12 feet and beyond).[48]

In some cases the distance zones don't apply at all—or at least the distances aren't flexible enough to reflect the attitudes of the parties. Dentists and barbers, for instance, work within intimate distance—actual physical contact; yet the relationship between dentist and patient or barber and client may be rather impersonal.

In other cases, though, the distance that people put between themselves and others is significant. For example, distance can reflect the attitude of the person who does the positioning. Research shows that a person who expects an unpleasant message or views the speaker as unfriendly takes a more distant position than does someone expecting good news or viewing the speaker as friendly.[49] An observant communicator can thus use the distance others choose with respect to him or her as a basis for hunches about their feelings. ("I get the feeling you're worried about something, Harry. Is there anything wrong?")

Besides reflecting attitudes, distance also creates feelings. In one study, subjects rated people who communicated at a greater distance as less friendly and understanding than those who positioned themselves closer.[50] (Closeness has its limits, of course. Intimate distance is rarely appropriate for business dealings.) Thus, an effective communicator will usually choose to operate at a casual-personal distance when a friendly atmosphere is the goal.

Interpersonal distance is another nonverbal indicator of power. One unspoken cultural rule is that the person with higher status generally controls the degree of approach. As Mehrabian puts it, "It is easy enough to picture an older person in this culture encouraging a younger business partner by patting him or her on the back; but it is very difficult to visualize this situation reversed; that is, with the younger person patting the older and more senior partner."[51] This principle of distance explains why subordinates rarely question the boss's right to drop in to their work area without invitation but are reluctant to approach their superior's office even when told the door is always open.

When a subordinate does wind up in the office of a superior, both tension and distance show who is in charge. The less powerful person usually stands until invited to take a seat and, when given the choice, will be reluctant to sit close to the boss. Wise managers often try to minimize the inhibiting factor of this status gap by including a table or comfortable easy chairs in their offices so that they can meet with subordinates on a more equal level.

Some managers try to promote informal communication by visiting employees in the employees' own offices. David Ogilvy, head of one of the largest advertising agencies in the country, says, "Do not summon people to your office—it frightens them. Instead, go to see them in *their* offices."[52]

Physical Environment So far we have discussed how personal behavior sends nonverbal messages. The physical environment in which we operate also suggests how we feel and shapes how we communicate.

Consider the way space is allocated in an organization. Power locations become apparent when we look at the amount and location of existing space given to various employees and groups. In many organizations, for instance, an employee's status may be measured by whether his or her office is next to the boss's or is in a dark alcove. An office with a window or an office on the corner often indicates higher status than an inside office with no window, and any office usually signals higher status than a cubicle.

In addition to reflecting status and power, the physical layout of an organization also shapes the ways its members interact with one another. For example, the temperature and humidity of a room can have profound effects on the success of communication. One study revealed that as temperatures and humidity increase, impressions of a speaker's attractiveness decline.[53] Understanding this fact can help you avoid scheduling presentations or meetings in hot, stuffy rooms, where the results may be doomed before a word is spoken.

Another way in which environments shape communication is proximity. The distance that separates people is perhaps the most important factor in shaping who talks with whom. Other things being equal, officemates will talk with one another more than with the people next door, and workers in the same area deal with one another more than with similarly employed people in another area. Researcher Thomas J. Allen studied workers in research facilities, medical laboratories, and business schools. He found that the frequency with which a person spoke to colleagues was a direct function of the distance between their desks.[54] In addition to the simple distance separating people, the difficulty of navigating that distance can also reduce interaction.[55] Corners that must be turned, doors that have to be wrestled open, and counters that block access keep people apart. One manager described the obstacle course that separated him from his boss's office:

> *I go from my office past the receptionist and down the hall to the other end of the building. I take the elevator to twelve, get off, and take another one to twenty-one. I get off and walk to the other end of the building, and pass through three doors, and I'm at his office—about a hundred feet straight above where I started!*[56]

Furniture arrangement also plays a big role in the way people communicate. For example, in one study of a medical office, only 10 percent of the patients were "at ease" when conversing with a doctor seated behind a desk, while the figure rose to 55 percent when the desk was removed.[57] Even when the location of furniture is fixed, choices about seating can influence interaction. Dominant, high-status persons often select the position at a table where they can see and be seen. This allows more interaction and more influence over the interactions at the table. Not surprisingly, the person who is seated at the head of a table is more often perceived as a leader. Persons who want to diminish their potential for interaction and leadership often seat themselves in less visible spots along the sides of a table.[58]

This sort of information can be useful on the job. You may be able to relocate your work to an area that will give you the interaction you want. Beyond this, realize that several places in your working environment will probably allow you to interact informally with desirable communication partners. Employee lounges, elevators, and dining areas are a few examples. Even restrooms can be handy places to establish contact, though you will probably want to continue your business in a more congenial spot. If you are interested in making your bosses more aware of your work, it's important to be visible to them. On the other hand, if you would just as soon be left alone, the old axiom "Out of sight, out of mind" applies here.

career tip

Cubicle Etiquette

As the comic character Dilbert has shown the world, daily life in a cubicle (or cube) has its challenges. These tips can help you manage the communication dynamics of cubicle life.

Privacy

Treat others' cubicles as if they were private offices. Knock gently to avoid startling occupants. Don't enter without verbal invitation or eye-contact permission—act as if there were a door. Never read the occupant's computer screens or borrow items from their desks just because you have access. Let others know when you aren't available by a "Do Not Disturb" sign or by your lack of eye contact. Resist the urge to shout out an answer to another cube dweller's question just because you overheard it. Avoid popping up over the top of cubicles to talk to others; instead, walk over or send an e-mail or instant message. Remember that whatever you say can be heard by others, so conduct meetings and personal conversations elsewhere. Keep conversations with your banker, family, doctor, and/or sweetheart out of the cubicle. Be polite enough to not listen to others' conversations, and certainly don't repeat anything overheard. Don't use a speaker phone in a cubicle; it is rude to the person on the other end and to your colleagues.

Noise

Don't add to the noise of a cube farm. Keep your voice on the low side. Set your phone ringer on low and turn it off when you are away from your desk. Don't let your cell phone ring when you are on another call. Use head phones for radios or CDs, and use a screen saver without sounds.

Odors

Your favorite scent (whether perfume, lotion, after-shave, or hair product) may be someone else's allergen, so think about its effect on others. Don't bring strong-smelling foods or gym bags with dirty sweats into the cubicle. Keep your shoes on. Try to eat in lunch areas, not at your desk as your hungry or sick colleagues may not appreciate the odor of your food.

Children

In most organizations, children (especially if they are too young for school) are best kept away from work except on special occasions. No matter how well-behaved, children may not be welcome or allowed by company policy to a shared cubicle.

Illness

Your determination to work when sick may be commendable, but you aren't doing any favors if you infect everybody in the office. This is a situation where the Golden Rule applies: If you wouldn't want someone in your state of health coming to work, try to stay away yourself. Consider alternatives like the telephone, e-mail, and instant messaging. No one will appreciate your sharing germs or illness and creating health risks for others.

Note: For more information see G. M. Smith, "Cubicle Etiquette" *Intercom*, November 2000, pp. 12–13, retrieved June 23, 2006, from **http://www.stc.org/intercom/PDFs/2000/200011_12-13.pdf**; J. Bremmer, "Cubicle Etiquette," at **www.bremercommunications.com/Cubicle_Etiquette.htm**; and "Cube and Cubicle Etiquette," at **http://papa.essortment.com/cubicleetiquett_ppb.htm.**

If you are a manager, think about arranging your subordinates' working areas to increase communication between people who should interact and to separate those who don't need to talk to one another. You can encourage communication between groups of workers by arranging gathering spots where congregation is easy. A good setting for informal contact needs to meet three criteria.[59] First, it ought to be centrally located so that people have to pass through it on their way to other places. Second, it should contain places to sit or rest, to be comfortable. Finally, it must be large enough so that the people gathered there won't interfere with others passing through or working nearby. Of course, if you want to discourage contact at a central spot (the copying machine, for example), simply change one or more of these conditions.

When it comes to managing interaction between members of an organization and its public, you can create the most desirable degree of accessibility by use of space and barriers. Proximity and visibility encourage contact, while distance and closure discourage it.

Time The way we use time provides a number of silent messages.[60] Leonard Berlin, senior financial analyst at ExxonMobil, attributes his reputation as a hard worker to the fact that he routinely arrives at work half an hour early. "That's a big thing to my boss," he says. "It doesn't matter that I leave at the regular time; getting here early shows an interest. I think that if I stayed to seven every night it would make less impression."[61]

Many business advisors recommend that you be particularly scrupulous about your use of time during the first few months you are on the job:

> *If . . . in that first ninety days, you're late or absent frequently, or seen as a clock watcher, you may earn yourself . . . negative scrutiny for a long time thereafter by your superiors. Rather than excusing any "infractions" of the rules, they'll be looking for slip-ups and a reason potentially to discharge you.*[62]

The amount of time we spend on a task or with a problem is also a good indication of how much importance we give it. The manager who never has time to talk over a problem with an employee or who postpones performance reviews because he or she "doesn't have time" is saying something about his or her regard for subordinates—as is the manager who takes time to converse casually with employees. The person who cuts one meeting short to attend another is making a statement about the relative importance of the two meetings.

Rules and customs about time vary widely from one culture to another. Whereas most North Americans and northern Europeans value punctuality, other cultures value taking time for important relationships more highly than routine appointments and deadlines. In monochronic cultures, speaking within the allotted time generally shows good planning and concern for the audience. Speaking longer inconveniences the listeners and communicates lack of regard for their schedules. But in some polychronic cultures, speaking only for the allotted time would indicate lack of excitement or actual indifference toward the audience or the issue. Getting down to business quickly can be seen as a rude and insulting move on the part of a potential business associate. In many polychronic cultures, the relationship not only is much more important than the business at hand but is also the foundation of the business venture and therefore determines whether there will be any business conducted. If the personal relationship is not established by taking time for dialogue and discussion, there will be no business relationship.

Chris Pagliaro, an American football coach, learned this lesson the hard way when he spent a season leading Milan's team in the Italian league. His realization that time is treated differently began to dawn on him when he arrived for the first practice sessions, scheduled for 8:30 P.M.:

> *We got out there at 8:30 P.M. I'm dressed, I've got my whistle, my (American) assistant coach is there, the two American players are there.*
>
> *And there's no Italians. It's ten 'til nine and I don't see anybody: [not] the owner, nobody. Around 9 o'clock, a couple of them start trickling in.*

Self-Assessment Your Nonverbal Immediacy

Indicate in the space at the left of each item the degree to which you believe the statement applies to you, using the following five-point scale:

1 = Never
2 = Rarely
3 = Occasionally
4 = Often
5 = Very often

____ 1. I use my hands and arms to gesture while talking to people.
____ 2. I touch others on the shoulder or arm while talking to them.
____ 3. I use a monotone or dull voice while talking to people.
____ 4. I look over or away from others while talking to them.
____ 5. I move away from others when they touch me while we are talking.
____ 6. I have a relaxed body position when I talk to people.
____ 7. I frown while talking to people.
____ 8. I avoid eye contact while talking to people.
____ 9. I have a tense body position while talking to people.
____ 10. I sit close or stand close to people while talking with them.
____ 11. My voice is monotonous or dull when I talk to people.
____ 12. I use a variety of vocal expressions when I talk to people.
____ 13. I gesture when I talk to people.
____ 14. I am animated when I talk to people.
____ 15. I have a bland facial expression when I talk to people.
____ 16. I move closer to people when I talk to them.

I had made a practice schedule—typical American coach: at 8:30 we do this, at 8:35 this, at 8:50 this. You might as well throw that one out the window. We got started around 9:20 or 9:30.[63]

The coach was smart and flexible enough to realize that he couldn't fight against a lifetime of cultural conditioning. He developed a compromise between the American need for punctuality and the casual Italian attitude about time:

By Friday, I knew it was useless. So what I did, I made a schedule and waited around. While the team ran laps, we set our watches back to 8:30. That's the only way I could do it. So we were always starting at 8:30, regardless of what time it was.

Improving Nonverbal Effectiveness

Now that you understand the elements of nonverbal communication, you can use the following guidelines to help achieve your professional goals.

____ 17. I look directly at people while talking to them.
____ 18. I am stiff when I talk to people.
____ 19. I have a lot of vocal variety when I talk to people.
____ 20. I avoid gesturing while I am talking to people.
____ 21. I lean toward people when I talk to them.
____ 22. I maintain eye contact with people when I talk to them.
____ 23. I try not to sit or stand close to people when I talk with them.
____ 24. I lean away from people when I talk to them.
____ 25. I smile when I talk to people.
____ 26. I avoid touching people when I talk to them.

Scoring Procedure:

1. Start with a score of 78. Add to that the scores from the following items: 1, 2, 6, 10, 12, 13, 14, 16, 17, 19, 21, 22, and 25.
2. Add only the scores from the following items: 3, 4, 5, 7, 8, 9, 11, 15, 18, 20, 23, 24, and 26.
3. Subtract your total score in step 2 from your total score in step 1. This is your final score.

When using this instrument it is important to recognize that the difference in these self-reports between females and males is statistically significant and socially significant (that is, substantial variance in the scores on this instrument can be attributed to biological sex). Whether these differences are "real" (that is, females may actually be more nonverbally immediate than males) or a function of social desirability (that is, females think they should be more immediate than males think they should be) or a function of actual behavior has not yet been determined.

Source: Adapted from V. P. Richmond, J. C. McCroskey, and A. D. Johnson, "Development of the Nonverbal Immediacy Scale (NIS): Measures of Self- and Other-Reported Nonverbal Immediacy," *Communication Quarterly* 51 (2003), pp. 505–517.

Monitor Your Nonverbal Behavior If you have ever asked yourself "how am I doing?" you know something about **self-monitoring**—the process of paying close attention to your behavior and using these observations to shape the way you behave.

High self-monitors are good at knowing when to adapt their nonverbal behavior to suit the situation.[64] By contrast, low self-monitors don't even recognize the negative impact of some of their behaviors. One study found low self-monitors were blissfully ignorant of their shortcomings and more likely to overestimate their skill than were better communicators.[65] For example, experimental subjects who scored in the lowest quartile on joke-telling skills were more likely than their funnier counterparts to grossly overestimate their sense of humor.

It's easy to see how self-monitoring can help you manage your nonverbal behavior. In a meeting or delivering a presentation, you might catch yourself droning on and losing your audience. When dealing with a difficult situation, your mental alarm will go off if you are losing your patience and showing irritation. Dealing with an unhappy client or customer, you can monitor and control your defensiveness.

ethical challenge

Consideration vs. Candor

Part of being professional is acting politely and showing interest even when you may not feel like doing so. What obligation do you have to present yourself as being interested and respectful when you're bored or dislike another person? How do you balance honesty and professionalism?

While too much self-monitoring can make you overly self-conscious; keeping an eye on how you may look and sound to others is likely to enhance your image as a professional.

Demonstrate Interest in Others Social scientists use the term **immediacy** to describe verbal and nonverbal behaviors that indicate closeness and liking. Among the nonverbal cues are closer proximity (within social conventions, of course), more direct eye gaze, more forward lean, more relaxed posture, positive facial expression, and warmer vocal qualities.[66]

There's a strong link between high immediacy and career success.[67] For example, supervisors perceived as having high immediacy are regarded by their subordinates as more competent, credible, and attractive than less immediate bosses, and the subordinates are more cooperative. By contrast, low immediacy cues can be a put-off. Recall from your own experience how you reacted when you encountered someone with an unfriendly expression, flat or hostile voice, and lack of animation.

Immediacy cues are especially important in the beginning states of a relationship. First impressions are powerful, particularly when strangers don't have much other information available to form opinions of you. Even after you know someone well, there are times when immediacy is especially important.[68]

With practice and self-monitoring, you can manage your nonverbal immediacy most effectively. You can begin by evaluating your current level of immediacy using the Self-Assessment inventory on pages 124–125.

Be Positive Emotions can be contagious. As one writer put it, "We catch feelings from one another as though they were some kind of social virus."[69] Psychologists use the term *emotional contagion* to describe this phenomenon. They have discovered that we can "infect" one another with our moods in as little as two minutes.[70]

As you read earlier in this chapter, we are most likely to show our feelings nonverbally. This means that if you are in a sour mood, it's likely that others will become unhappy just by being around you. Likewise, if your nonverbal cues are upbeat, you are more likely to get the same sort of reaction from others. Insincere cheerfulness probably won't get you very far, but a professional identity that reflects calmness, confidence, and goodwill will serve you well.

Just as others might "catch" an emotional state from you, you can be infected by the tone of others' nonverbal behavior. That's not a problem when you are around positive communicators, but sometimes you will need to struggle not to be overcome by the attitude of negative people.

Observe Conventions In your personal life, you may win friends by being a unique personality who stands out in a crowd. In your career, this approach can be risky.

Your best chances of success are to follow the nonverbal conventions of the group in which you find yourself.

As you read in Chapter 2, some conventions are cultural. For example, in Northern Europe you can expect to greet associates with a handshake, while in Mediterranean countries and Latin America, a hug and even a ritual kiss might be more appropriate. Likewise, an American woman traveling in an Islamic country probably would dress more conservatively and be more likely to wear a head covering than she would at home.

Some nonverbal conventions are just as strong within certain fields or organizations. The style of dress worn by software programmers in Silicon Valley would probably look out of place at a meeting of investment bankers on Wall Street, and the way you would dress at a company picnic or weekend retreat would probably differ from the clothes you would wear or the way you would act back in the office on Monday morning.

Actually, violating others' expectations can be effective, as long as your unexpected behavior is judged positively.[71] Dressing better, acting more friendly, appearing more interested, and being more enthusiastic can all generate positive reactions—as long as you don't overdo it so that your violation is regarded as negative or phony.

Sexual Harassment

Verbal and nonverbal sexual harassment on the job has always existed, but in recent decades it has been identified as a problem requiring governmental response. The Civil Rights Act of 1964 and subsequent legislation and court decisions have identified two types of sexual harassment:

- ***Quid pro quo*** (a Latin term meaning "this for that"). Examples of this form of harassment include directly or indirectly threatening not to promote someone who won't date you or implying that employment depends on the exchange of sexual favors.
- ***Hostile work environment.*** This category includes any verbal or nonverbal behavior that has the intention or effect of interfering with someone's work or creating an environment that is intimidating, offensive, or hostile. Unwelcome remarks ("babe," "hunk"), humor, stares ("elevator eyes"), signs, and invasions of physical space all can create a hostile work environment.

Of the two types of harassment, there is less confusion about blatant quid pro quo propositions, and most people agree on what constitutes blatant harassment.[72] There is less agreement, though, on what kinds of behavior create a hostile working environment. One person's harmless joke can be deeply offensive to someone else, and what seems like a sincere compliment to the person who offers it can sound like a come-on to the receiver.

Sexual harassment can occur in a variety of circumstances. It may arise between members of the same sex or between men and women. The harasser can be the target's supervisor, an agent of the employer, a supervisor in another area, a co-worker. Even behavior by non-employees (e.g., customers or people from other organizations) can be grounds for a harassment claim. The target does not have to be the person harassed but could be anyone affected by the offensive conduct. (Situations like this are termed "third-party harassment.") Unlawful sexual harassment may occur without economic injury to or discharge of the target.[73]

Reports of harassment are widespread. In fiscal year 2000, a total of 15,836 complaints were filed in the United States.[74] For example, in addition to a $7.75 million cash settlement in a suit against Ford Motor Company by 900 female employees, sensitivity training must now be given at Ford plants across the nation, at an estimated cost of $10 million.[75] Furthermore, sensitivity training is now provided at every organizational level of every federal government agency.[76] In Los Angeles, harassment was so widespread that the mayor ordered training programs for every city worker.

Avoiding Sexual Harassment Problems

Beyond the normal precautions and courtesy, it is smart to be especially sensitive in situations where others might take offense at your words or behaviors. Look at the situation from the other person's point of view. Could your language be considered offensive? Could your actions lead to discomfort? Read your company's sexual harassment policies carefully, know what the EEOC guidelines are, and be very familiar with any training and other information provided by your human resources professionals. If you wonder whether a behavior might be construed as harassment, not engaging in it is probably the safest course of action.

Responding to Sexual Harassment

Most organizations have developed policies prohibiting sexual harassment and procedures for people who feel they are being harassed. In addition to company policy, targets of sexual harassment are entitled to legal protection. The EEOC, state and local agencies, and the court system all enforce civil rights acts relating to harassment.

Despite the determination of government to protect employees, fighting sexual harassment through legal channels can take stamina. The process can be time-consuming, and targets sometimes experience depression, ridicule, isolation, and reprisal.[77] For these reasons, taking care of harassment at the lowest, most informal level possible may solve the problem in a way that doesn't punish the target. Listed below are several options, in escalating order. They aren't meant as a step-by-step guide as to how to respond, but they will help you decide which options may best suit a given situation.

1. *Consider dismissing the incident.* This approach is appropriate only if you truly believe that the remark or behavior isn't worth worrying about. Pretending to dismiss incidents that you believe are important can lead to repetition of the offensive behavior, self-blame, and diminished self-esteem.
2. *Compare your experiences with others.* Co-workers may have had experiences that will help you decide how to respond. As with any sensitive matter, make your

ethical challenge

Responding to Sexual Harassment

Imagine that the following incident happened to you, or to a female colleague who seeks your advice. Decide which of the eight alternatives listed on pages 128–130 is the most effective and appropriate response.

Susan Carter is one of the few female partners in a New York consulting firm. During an out-of-town planning meeting in her hotel room, the client makes a clumsy pass, knocking her over. He later apologizes, but Susan is unable to simply forget the incident.

The next day, Susan's boss, Justin Peale, calls to ask how her meeting went. She knows from the office grapevine that Justin only put her on this key account with reluctance, feeling that the clients would feel more comfortable working with a male account representative. Susan knows that telling her boss about the incident could prejudice him against giving her future assignments. On the other hand, she knows that keeping quiet compromises her dignity and that not reporting the incident may result in the client's firm being exposed to future lawsuits. What should she do?

Note: For a more detailed account of this incident and commentary by several executives, see J. Margetta, "Will She Fit In?" *Harvard Business Review*, March/April 1997, pp. 18–32.

inquiries discreet: You have little to gain by having your complaint become public unless and until you are sure it is worth pursuing.

3. *Tell the harasser to stop*. Inform the harasser early that the behavior is unwelcome, and ask him or her to cease immediately. Your statement should be firm, but unless the offense is clearly deliberate, it doesn't have to be angry. Remember that many words or deeds that make you uncomfortable may not be deliberately hostile remarks. (See Chapter 5 for details on how to be assertive without being aggressive.)
4. *Keep a diary*. If the harassment persists, keep a record of every incident. Detail the date, time, place, and exactly what happened. Describe how you responded and how you felt.
5. *Write a personal letter to the harasser*. A written statement may help the harasser to understand what behavior you find offensive. Just as important, it can show that you take the problem seriously. Put the letter in a sealed envelope (keeping a copy for yourself). Use information from your diary to detail specifics about what happened, what behavior you want stopped, and how you felt. Keep a record of when you delivered the letter. If you want to be certain that the delivery of the letter will be acknowledged, take a friend along when you present it.
6. *Ask a friend to intervene*. Perhaps a mutual acquaintance can persuade the harasser to stop. The person you choose should be someone who you are convinced understands your discomfort and supports your opinion. Be sure this intermediary is also someone the harasser respects and trusts.
7. *Complain through channels*. Report the situation to your supervisor, personnel office, or a committee that has been set up to consider harassment complaints. Think about what results you are seeking. Usually, having the harasser stop is

enough, but decide if you want more action: a transfer, reimbursement for medical bills, and so on.

8. *File a legal complaint*. You may file a complaint with the federal EEOC or with your state agency. You have the right to obtain the services of an attorney regarding your legal options. For example, some targets request a letter from the EEOC authorizing them to pursue a lawsuit on their own. (See **www.eeoc.gov** for detailed explanations of this procedure.)

summary

Whatever the goal and whatever the context, business and professional communication involves both verbal and nonverbal messages. Verbal messages are clearest when they contain unequivocal and nonabstract language and a minimum of unfamiliar jargon. While clarity is usually the goal, strategically ambiguous messages are sometimes useful ways of promoting harmony, facilitating change, and softening the blow of difficult messages.

Language can sometimes communicate and generate undesirable emotions. Biased terms seem to be objective but actually convey the speaker's attitudes. Trigger words arouse strong emotional reactions in a listener. Effective communicators avoid biased language and trigger words and monitor their own responses to others' use of this language.

Social scientists have discovered that men and women typically use speech for different purposes and in different ways. Feminine language emphasizes rapport, the creation and maintenance of relationships, to a greater degree than masculine speech, which is focused more on the report function of communication: accomplishing the task at hand and asserting control over the situation.

Nonverbal communication also carries a great deal of meaning, but where words normally express ideas, nonverbal behavior conveys attitudes and emotions. Nonverbal messages are always available, since it is impossible to avoid communicating nonverbally. These messages should be interpreted with caution, however, since they are usually ambiguous and are often culture-bound. Nonverbal messages can be expressed vocally, through appearance (physical stature and clothing), and through the face, eyes, posture, gesture, distance, physical environment, and time.

Some guidelines to help you achieve your workplace goals include monitoring your nonverbal behavior, demonstrating interest in others through immediacy, remaining positive and aware of emotional contagion, and observing nonverbal cultural and organizational conventions.

Sexual harassment is a combination of verbal and nonverbal behavior that has been recognized as illegal and inappropriate in the workplace. What counts as harassment depends in great part on the perceptions of the person who sees himself or herself as the target. This means that communicators must be sensitive to others' reactions, since their good intentions are not enough to avoid accusations of harassment. People who perceive themselves as targets of harassment in the workplace have a number of options available, ranging from informal to formal.

key terms

Test your understanding of these key terms by visiting the Online Learning Center Web site at www.mhhe.com/adler9.

biased language 107
equivocal terms 101
feminine style of speech 109
genderlects 108
high-level abstractions 102
hostile work environment 127
immediacy 126
jargon 104
low-level abstractions 102
masculine style of speech 110
nonverbal communication 112
paralanguage 115
quid pro quo sexual harassment 127
rapport talk 109
relative words 103
report talk 110
self-monitoring 125
triangle of meaning 100
trigger words 108

activities

Go to the self-quizzes at the Online Learning Center at www.mhhe.com/adler9 to test your knowledge of chapter concepts.

1. Skill Builder

Practice your skill at using unequivocal language by describing how each of the following sentences is likely to be misunderstood (or not understood at all). Then improve the clarity of each message by introducing your message with a high-level abstraction and qualifying it with low-level abstractions. To invent meaningful low-level abstractions, you will have to imagine a specific scenario.

a. You did a heck of a job on that proposal.
b. There are just a few small problems to clear up.
c. I just need a little more time to finish the job.
d. Your job performance hasn't been good this year.

2. Skill Builder

Practice clarifying your understanding of another person's ambiguous messages. For each sentence below, construct a polite question you could ask the speaker to help clarify the meaning.

a. I need this report right away.
b. This presentation needs to be perfect.
c. Whenever I leave to go to a meeting, nothing gets done in this office.
d. I'm on my own around here!

3. Invitation to Insight

Identify jargon in your own line of work, or interview a worker in a field that interests you and identify jargon that he or she uses. Then answer the following questions:

a. How does each term make communication more efficient?
b. What confusion might arise from the use of each term with certain listeners?
c. In cases where confusion or misunderstandings might arise, suggest alternative words or phrases that could convey the meaning more clearly.

4. Skill Builder

Describe a former co-worker three times. In your first account, use positively biased terms. In the second description, discuss the same person, using words with negative connotations. Finally, describe the co-worker in low-level abstractions without using biased language of any sort.

5. Invitation to Insight

Become more aware of your own emotional triggers by following these instructions:

a. In each category shown, identify two words that trigger positive reactions for you and two other words you react to negatively:
   i. A person's name.
   ii. The label for a category of people (e.g., "fanatic").
   iii. A rule, policy, or issue (e.g., gay marriage).

b. How do you react, both internally and observably, when you hear these terms? Ponder the source of your reactions (the way you were raised? past experiences?). How might your reactions impact your communication?

c. Use the same categories to identify words that trigger positive and negative reactions in a person you work with. What are the consequences of using these emotion-laden words with that person? Suggest neutral words you could use to replace the trigger words.

6. Invitation to Insight

Explore the characteristics of nonverbal communication as communicative yet ambiguous.

a. Observe the nonverbal behaviors of a person you work with. What interpretations do you attach to your observations? Describe an alternative interpretation for each nonverbal behavior you have noticed. Speculate on which of your interpretations might be more accurate. Verify your perceptions by asking your co-worker what the behavior means.

b. Ask a co-worker to observe you during a meeting. After the meeting, have your co-worker describe some of your nonverbal behaviors and speculate what meanings you intended. Did your co-worker's perceptions match your intentions?

7. Skill Builder

Demonstrate the impact of nonverbal communication by describing effective and ineffective examples of behaviors in each of the following categories.

a. Voice.
b. Dress.
c. Face and eyes.
d. Posture and movement.
e. Personal space and use of distance.

8. Skill Builder

Using the Web sites in Nonverbal Communication around the World on page 134, choose two countries that are likely to be a part of a specific career field or organization you may work for. Find two or more gestures that have different meanings in those countries. Categorize the gestures into those that appear similar to a gesture in your culture but have a different meaning, those that appear unlike any gesture that would be recognized in your culture, and those that are very different from the gestures with the same meaning in your culture.

9. Invitation to Insight

Visit the Indiana University Human Resource Web site at **http://www.indiana.edu/~uhrs/policies/uwide/sexual_harass.html**. Scroll down to Appendix A. Choose one of the examples of behavior that could lead to allegations of sexual harassment and answer the following questions.

a. Do you agree that this situation could lead to allegations of sexual harassment? If so, identify whether this behavior would be classified as quid pro quo or hostile work environment.

b. Use the guidelines in the text on pages 128–130 to decide how you would respond if you were the recipient of the harassment.

10. Invitation to Insight

Explore your present level of nonverbal effectiveness and how you might improve it.

a. Using the format below, identify an important business or professional context from your life (e.g., in meetings, with customers, on the phone). If you are not currently working, choose a context from school (e.g., in class discussions, meeting with professors).

b. Using the information in this chapter, describe in the format below both the aspects of your nonverbal behavior that are effective and also those you could improve.

c. Interview someone who has seen you operate in the context you are analyzing (e.g., a colleague, supervisor, professor, fellow student). Explain the types of nonverbal behavior described on pages 114–124. Then learn your interviewee's opinion of your effective nonverbal communication in this context, and how you could communicate more effectively.

d. Based on the information you have compiled, develop an action plan that describes how you can improve your nonverbal effectiveness in the context you are analyzing.

Context ______________________________

	Effective	Could Do Better (Describe How)
Self-appraisal		
Other's appraisal		
Action plan	1.	
	2.	
	etc.	

resources

In Print

Elgin, S. *The Gentle Art of Verbal Self-Defense at Work*. Englewood Cliffs, NJ: Prentice Hall, 2000.

If you work with people who have "malpractice of the mouth" (yelling, cursing, verbally attacking) this author gives plenty of pointers on discovering the meaning and intent behind the remarks and dealing with them in effective ways. Her real-life examples include information on handling sexual harassment, gender discrimination, e-mail, and voice mail.

Hickson, M. III; D. W. Stacks; and N. Moore. *Nonverbal Communication: Studies and Applications*, 4th ed. Los Angeles: Roxbury Publishing Company, 2004.

This is an excellent up-to-date review of nonverbal communication foundations, methods, and codes. Of particular interest for business and professional communication students is Chapter 14 ("Nonverbal Communication at Work"), which offers research on impression management, leadership, and performance appraisals.

Kegan, Robert, and Lisa Laskow Lahey. *How the Way We Talk Can Change the Way We Work: Seven Languages for Transformation*. San Francisco: Jossey-Bass, 2001.

Language is powerful and changing the language we use can change our work environments. The authors show how to move from the language of complaint to that of commitment, from blame to personal responsibility, from assumptions that hold us to assumptions we hold. The book includes plenty of interactive exercises and examples.

Martin, D. W. *Office-Speak: The Win-Win Guide to Touching Base, Getting the Ball Rolling, and Thinking Inside the Box*. Simon Spotlight, 2005.

The chapter "Why Business People Speak Like Idiots" captures the overblown use of jargon and clichés in the working world.

Riggio, R. E., and R. S. Feldman. *Applications of Nonverbal Communication*. Mahwah, NJ: Erlbaum, 2005.

A number of chapters in this edited collection are of interest to business and professional communicators. They deal with the role of nonverbal communication in medical, political, legal, and business settings as well as topics including the role of culture, detecting deception, and sexual harassment.

On the Web

Plain English

Get rid of jargon and other unnecessary words. See Plain English (**www.plainlanguage.gov**) sponsored by PLAIN, the Plain Language Action and Information Network and the Plain English Campaign (**www.plainenglish.co.uk**).

Gender and Language

For a list of guidelines on nonsexist language, visit **www.ncte.org/about/over/positions/category/lang/107647.htm**. The Institute for Teaching and Research on Women (**www.towson.edu/~vanfoss/wmcomm.htm**) provides a well-organized series of questions on gender communication. Read about the issues involved in the search for gender-free language (**www.eei-alex.com/eye/gender.html**) and discover more ways to use nondiscriminatory, positive business language (**www.pnl.gov/ag/usage/bias.html**).

Nonverbal Communication around the World

The Nonverbal Communication Research Page (**http://euphrates.wpunj.edu/faculty/wagnerk/webagogy/hecht.htm**) and Ohio State's nonverbal page (**http://library.osu.edu/sites/thegateway/display.php**) provide an exhaustive array of material on the study of nonverbal communication including journals, scholars, articles, organizations, and links to a variety of other germane sites.

Advice for business and professional persons on subjects from eating to gestures to gift-giving can be found at **http://nonverbal.ucsc.edu**. Click on "articles" at **www.getcustoms.com** for intercultural business advice on how to avoid choosing the wrong colors, the wrong tie, and the wrong gifts as well as guides to international customs regarding holidays, time, names, and money.

Business Casual

Articles on professional dress at Dressing Well (**www.dressingwell.com**) offer explanations and illustrations of business casual. Another consultant offers a "scale" illustration to help you sort out degrees of business casual (**http://conselle.com/whats_new/style_scale.html**). At Empowerment Enterprises (**www.casualpower.com**) explore case studies that describe relationships between dress and power, authority and trust, including sketches of clothing and links to articles on business casual from papers around the country. The article "Dress for Success" (**www.getcustoms.com/2004GTC/Articles/new003.html**) reviews the meaning of conservative, formal, and casual in five different countries. The Business Casual Dress Code (**http://wlb.monster.com/articles/women**) provides specific information for men and women as does this career center site: **http://www.career.vt.edu/JOBSEARC/BusCasual.htm**. For more illustrations, go to **http://businesscasualdress.com/illustrations.htm**.

Learning about Sexual Harassment

The consequences of a sexual harassment claim are serious, so it is important to be aware of what behavior might result in such an accusation. Test your knowledge of this area with *BusinessWeek*'s Web-based quiz at **www.businessweek.com/1997/41/b3548040.htm**.

For accurate and up-to-date information regarding recent court cases, rulings, and laws, visit the EEOC Web site (**www.eeoc.gov**) where you'll also find resources for employees, employers, and trainers. The Feminist Majority Foundation (**www.feminist.org/911/harass.html**) offers nationwide and state hotlines as well as resources geared explicitly to school, work, and the military. Included are a timeline and an annotated bibliography that cites sources on harassment in global (not just U.S.) workplaces. Explore excellent information on state laws with regard to harassment and find answers to questions such as What if I'm not sure? What if I have to arrange training? What if my child is being harassed? What if I'm accused? at **www.de.psu.edu/harassment**.

5 Interpersonal Skills

Chapter Objectives

After reading this chapter you should be able to

1 Describe the communication climate in a working environment, identify the messages that have helped create it, and suggest ways of communicating that can improve that climate.

2 Use the guidelines in this chapter to give constructive feedback.

3 Use the guidelines in this chapter to respond to criticism in a nondefensive manner.

4 Identify various approaches to conflict and steps to conflict management.

5 Describe four styles of negotiating solutions in work-related conflicts and predict likely consequences of using each style.

6 Demonstrate how to seek a win–win solution in a work-related negotiation.

What does it take to succeed in your career? Talent, good ideas, a good education, technical expertise, skills, hard work, motivation, initiative—all of these are important. In addition, because all jobs require you to get things done through other people—co-workers, customers, managers, people in other companies—career success also depends on your ability to communicate effectively. That ability, often called people skills, is the ability to work with other people, solve problems, negotiate differences, and handle conflicts so that you can do your job effectively.

Building Positive Relationships

Numerous studies have revealed just how important communication skills are in a career. In one survey, 1,000 personnel directors in the United States were asked to describe the "ideal management profile." The number-one characteristic was "ability to work well with others one-on-one."[1] Even CEOs who manage technical workers need people skills to succeed and often poor interpersonal skills are blamed for "derailed" CEOs.[2]

The ability to work well with others is just as important for newcomers as it is for managers. A survey of chief executive officers and human resource managers from leading organizations rated the ability to work cooperatively with others as a most desirable quality in college graduates.[3] Good interpersonal communication skills are important in careers as diverse as engineering, real estate, and franchise management.[4]

Table 5–1 Some Communication Traits of Unpleasant Co-workers

Busybody
- Butts in to conversations
- Butts in to others' business
- Expresses opinion on matters that don't concern him/her

Controlling/Bossy
- Tries to control, boss others around
- Gives orders without having the proper authority
- Is condescending/talks down to others
- Wants his/her own way

Self-promotion
- Competitive, wants to be number one
- Tries to promote him/herself
- Is self-centered
- Tries to make him/herself look good

Unprofessional Behavior
- Is rude
- Gossips and bad-mouths others to a third party
- Criticizes others
- Yells or screams

Unprofessional Focus of Attention
- Talks about personal problems at work
- Brings personal problems to work
- Talks about non-work-related issues

Distracting
- Distracts others from work
- Behaves in irritating ways

Defensive and Judgmental
- Sees others as a threat to his/her job
- Attacks others' behavior and judgments
- Critical, rather than constructive

Source: After J. M. H. Fritz, "How Do I Dislike Thee? Let Me Count the Ways: Constructing Impressions of Troublesome Others at Work," *Management Communication Quarterly* 15 (2003), pp. 410–438.

Everyone can tell stories about co-workers, bosses, and customers whose communication style made life unpleasant. Table 5–1 details some types of communication that surveys have found are especially unpleasant. You can probably recognize at least some of these behaviors in people you have worked with, and possibly even in yourself.

Former Chrysler chairman Lee Iacocca summed up the importance of maintaining good interpersonal working relationships when he said:

> *There's one phrase I hate to see on any executive's evaluation, no matter how talented he may be, and that's the line: "He has trouble getting along with other people." To me that's the kiss of death.*[5]

Some social scientists have coined the term **emotional intelligence** to describe the ability and skills of interacting well with others.[6] According to emerging research, cognitive IQ takes a backseat to emotional intelligence in determining outstanding job performance.[7] Across the job spectrum, from copier repair technicians to scientists, IQ accounts for no more than 25 percent of entrepreneurial failure and success. The more difficult the job and the higher it is in an organization's hierarchy, the more important emotional intelligence becomes. Consultant Robert Dilenschneider contrasts emotional intelligence with intellectual aptitude:

> *Your cognitive IQ could be 145, and you could get a doctorate in business, but you'll never break away from the pack unless your interpersonal skills are top-drawer.*[8]

This chapter focuses on how to develop and improve the personal communication skills that are so important for individuals and organizations. It describes the ingredients that foster a positive communication climate between people, and then it goes on to offer advice about how to communicate in a variety of important person-to-person situations: giving praise, delivering and receiving criticism without defensiveness, managing conflict constructively, and negotiating in a manner that delivers the best possible outcome.

© Tribune Media Services, Inc. All Rights Reserved. Reprinted with permission.

Communication Climate

Social scientists use the term **communication climate** to describe the quality of personal relationships in an organization. Do people feel respected? Do they trust one another? Do they believe that they are appreciated? The weather metaphor suggested by the term *climate* is apt. Your own experience shows that the mood of a workplace can be described as sunny and calm, cold and stormy, or in similar terms. Organizations create an overall climate, which can be healthy or polluted, but within that environment individual relationships have their own microclimates. For example, your interactions with one colleague might be described as icy, while you and another person enjoy a warm relationship. There's no question that communication climate is a key factor in job satisfaction and commitment to the organization.[9] For this reason, communicators need to understand how to create positive climates.

The climate of an organization comes not so much from the specific tasks that members perform as from the feelings they have about those tasks and each other. In fact, a positive climate can exist under the worst working conditions: in a cramped, poorly furnished, understaffed office; during the graveyard shift of an urban newspaper; or even in a road gang cleaning up trash by the highway. Conversely, the most comfortable, prestigious settings can be polluted by a hostile climate.

While communication climates are created by a variety of messages, they do share a common denominator. Positive climates result when people believe they are valued, and negative climates occur when people don't believe they are appreciated. Scholars have labeled messages that express feelings of value as **confirming** and those that fail to express value—or those that explicitly show a lack of value—as **disconfirming.**[10] Psychologist Jack Gibb described six kinds of messages that are likely to promote a supportive, confirming climate and six types of disconfirming messages that are likely to generate a defensive climate (see Table 5–2). Gibb's supportive categories provide a list of ways to promote positive, confirming relationships.

Use Descriptive "I" Language Many communicators unnecessarily attack the other person when delivering a message:

"Your report is too sloppy. You'll have to retype it."

"This is the third time this month that you've been late for work. You'll have to be more punctual."

"That was a dumb promise you made. We can never have the job done by the end of the month."

Table 5–2 Confirming and Disconfirming Message Identifiers

Supportive, Confirming Messages Are	Defense-Arousing, Disconfirming Messages Are
Descriptive (Use "I" language)	Evaluative
Focused on solving the problem	Controlling
Honest	Manipulative
Concerned with another's position	Indifferent
Equal	Superior
Open-minded, provisional	Dogmatic, certain

Statements like these are often called **"you" language** because they point a verbal finger of accusation at the receiver: "You're lazy." "You're wrong." By contrast, **descriptive statements** are often termed **"I" language** since they focus on the speaker instead of judging the other person. Notice how each of the evaluative statements above can be rephrased in descriptive "I" language:

> "I'm afraid the boss will get angry at both of us if we turn in a report with this many errors. We'll get a better reaction if it's retyped."
>
> "Since you've been coming in late, I've made a lot of excuses when people call asking for you. I'm uncomfortable with that, and that's why I hope you'll start showing up on time."
>
> "I'm worried about the promise you made. I don't see how we can get the job done by the end of the month."

Statements like these show that it's possible to be nonjudgmental and still say what you want without landing any verbal punches. In fact, descriptive statements like the ones you just read are *more* complete than are typical everyday complaints since they express both the speaker's feelings and the reason for bringing up the matter—things most evaluative remarks don't do.

Focus on Solving Problems, Not Controlling Others Some messages try to force others to do something they don't agree with or understand. If you're up against a tight deadline, for example, it's easy to say, "Look, I don't have time to explain—just do it my way." Because control shows a lack of regard for the other person's needs, interests, or opinions, it can cause problems in the relationship even if it gets you what you want now.

In contrast, **problem-oriented messages** aim at solving both persons' needs. The goal isn't to solve a problem my way or your way but rather to develop a solution that meets everyone's needs. You will learn more about how to achieve problem-oriented solutions when we discuss win–win negotiating strategies later in this chapter.

Be Honest: Don't Manipulate Once people discover that they have been manipulated, a defensive reaction is almost guaranteed. As Roger Fisher and Scott

ethical challenge

Is Total Honesty Always the Best Policy?

In principle, few people would dispute the ethical principle that honesty is the best policy. At the same time, it is hard to imagine a world in which everyone told the whole truth all the time.

Explore how you can reconcile the need to be honest with other goals by re-creating a list of all the opportunities you had to tell the truth during a typical day. Identify each occasion when you chose to either:

1. Tell even a partial lie (e.g., saying "Nothing's wrong" when you are bothered).
2. Hedge the truth by equivocating (e.g., saying "That's an unusual idea" instead of saying "I don't think that idea will work").
3. Keep quiet instead of volunteering the truth.

Based on your self-analysis, construct a principled yet pragmatic code of ethics involving honesty.

Brown explain, "If one statement of mine in a hundred is false, you may choose not to rely on me at all. Unless you can develop a theory of when I am honest and when I am not, your discovery of a small dishonesty will cast doubt over everything I say and do."[11]

By contrast, simple honesty is less likely to generate defensiveness, even when the news isn't welcome. Even though others might sometimes dislike what you have to say, your reputation for candor can earn you the respect of subordinates, co-workers, and management.

Show Concern for Others Indifference—lack of acknowledgment or concern for others—is a strong disconfirming message. By contrast, a genuine message of interest can make a tremendous difference. A simple apology for making you wait can do wonders. The secretary who takes the time to find the right person to answer your questions can leave you feeling grateful and worthwhile, encouraging you to do business with that company again. The manager who seems genuinely concerned with your opinions—even if she doesn't agree with them—is easier to work with than one who brushes your concerns aside.

Demonstrate an Attitude of Equality As the cartoon to the right suggests, a superior manner is both disconfirming and offensive. The kind of superiority that arouses defensiveness isn't based as much on intelligence, talent, or skill as on the dignity and respect that

"It's a vice-president thing, Berger. You wouldn't understand."

Best and Worst Communication Climates

Be prepared to describe to your group two organizations to which you have belonged:

- One with the most positive, confirming climate
- One with the most negative, disconfirming climate

The organizations you describe may be a work group, team, class, volunteer group, or any other group of people formed with the purpose of accomplishing a task.

Make sure your account of each group includes

- A description of how the communication qualities listed on pages 139–143 (or the absence of these qualities) helped create the climate you are describing.
- One or more specific examples that captures the kinds of communication that created the positive or negative climate.
- The lessons you've learned about communication from the experiences you have described.

everyone deserves. Talent doesn't justify arrogance. You have probably encountered bureaucrats who acted as though their jobs made them superior to the people they serve, or physicians who couldn't be bothered to explain test results to you. This sort of superior attitude causes defensiveness. Al Neuharth, founder of *USA Today,* earned a reputation as a tough, abrasive boss. His superior, evaluative comments like the following one suggest why: "When I criticize a female or when I criticize a grossly overweight person or anybody else, it's because, damn it, I think they ought to do better, just as I do."[12]

The essence of a more positive attitude is *respect*. Communication expert Kerry Patterson explains that respect is essential, just like the air we breathe: "if you take it away, it's all people can think about. At that point, the conversation is all about defending dignity."[13] Respect often comes from how we construct messages. Consider, for example, the difference between saying, "Could you get me the files?" and the demand, "Get me the files." As this example illustrates, *how* we speak and act can be more important than the words themselves. Pay close attention not only to what you say but also to your nonverbal behavior, including your vocal tone and facial expression, when expressing yourself.

Keep an Open Mind Listening with an open mind makes good sense. Whether the people you're dealing with are in your department or another, subordinates or customers, they probably have knowledge that you don't. Hearing them out may teach you something useful.

Besides providing useful information, listening open-mindedly can promote good relationships. Consider how you would feel if you had carefully researched a proposal to avoid raising the price on a product line, only to be told, "I see no evidence that we should keep the price down." Suppose, instead, that your supervisor had said, "I have strong reasons for raising the price, but maybe you'll change my mind," or had at least listened carefully to your idea and promised to give it some thought. Even if your supervisor eventually decides against your proposal, you will probably feel that your ideas are heard and respected—provided that the supervisor gives you good reasons for rejecting your plan.

A tentative approach also works well when you are bringing up ideas. Paradoxically, you may get a better hearing if you present them as ideas, and not facts. As one business newsletter put it, "There's a certain irony here—the more forceful we are, the less influential we're likely to be."[14]

Giving Praise

There's truth to the old saying, You can catch more flies with honey than with vinegar. Sincere praise, delivered skillfully, can produce dramatic results and leave you and the other person feeling better as well.

Communication consultants Peter and Susan Glaser offer several tips about how to take advantage of the power of praise.[15]

Make Praise Specific Almost any sincere praise will be appreciated, but describing exactly *what* you appreciate makes it easier for the other person to continue that behavior. Notice how the following specific compliments add clarity:

Broad	Specific
Good job on handling that complaint.	You really kept your cool when the customer complained.
I appreciate the support you've given me lately.	Thanks for being so flexible with my schedule while I was sick.
You've really been on top of your work lately.	You've finished every job this month within 2 days.

Being specific doesn't mean you have to avoid giving broad comments like the ones above. But along with giving general praise, consider the value of adding enough particulars to help the other person understand exactly what you appreciate.

Praise Progress, Not Just Perfection You might wonder whether some people do much of anything that deserves sincere praise. If you look for outstanding performance, the answer may be no; but you can still deliver genuine compliments by looking for progress. Consider a few examples:

> "This draft of the report is a lot clearer. Adding a detailed budget really helps explain where the money will go. I think the same kind of detail would help make the schedule clearer."
>
> "I know we still see things differently, but I'm glad we were able to work so well together on the Baretti job."

Praise Intermittently Too much praise can become as uncomfortable as too much rich food or too many jokes. Constant praise is also likely to sound insincere. In

ethical challenge

When You Can't Think of Praise

The value of praise is clear, and the guidelines in this section offer advice for when and how to compliment others. But what can you do when you cannot think of anything about another person's performance to praise?

"I don't want a raise, Mr. Harlingen. I just want bouquets and accolades and tokens of esteem and bravos and huzzahs and a piece of the action."

Reprinted by permission of *The Saturday Review.*

addition, social scientists have discovered that it isn't even as effective as occasional compliments. Praise others from time to time, when your remarks will have the best effect, but don't go overboard.

Relay Praise If you already believe that complimenting someone sincerely can improve the communication climate in your relationship, wait until you see the benefits of singing their praises to others who deserve to know. You will win the undying gratitude of the person you are complimenting; you will show your own sense of security and team spirit; and you will be informing others about information they will probably find valuable. Praising others takes little time, and it benefits everyone.

You can also become a "praise messenger" by letting people know that you've heard others saying complimentary things about them. They will be more likely to continue the behavior, and they will feel better both about the person who praised them and about you for delivering the good news.

Praise Sincerely Insincere praise is worse than no praise at all. It casts doubt on all your other compliments. It suggests that you can't think of anything the other person has done that deserves genuine acknowledgment, and it suggests that you think the recipient is naive enough to believe in your phony compliments.

As you consider when and how to praise, it is important to be aware of the cultural rules that may influence both the person receiving compliments and the audience to whom you are delivering them. In some collectivist cultures, it can be embarrassing to be singled out for praise, especially in front of others. In such cases, giving private reinforcement is probably wiser than lavishing compliments publicly.

Dealing with Criticism

Praise is a pleasure to give and receive, but it isn't always possible. In the real world of work, criticism is a fact of life. Sometimes you have to deliver a complaint, and other times you are on the receiving end of others' gripes. Either way, criticism can

Table 5–3 Some Differences between Constructive and Unhelpful Feedback

Constructive Feedback	Destructive Feedback
Specific Describes the other's problematic behavior in clear terms: "When you didn't return my calls and e-mails . . ."	**Vague** Criticism lacks specifics, making it more difficult for others to understand: "I just can't depend on you!"
Speaker-oriented Explains how the other's behavior is problematic for you: "I get embarrassed when you tease me in front of the boss."	**Blaming** Attacks the critic without explaining how/why his behavior is problematic for you: "You were out of line teasing me in front of the boss."
Problem-oriented Demonstrates a desire to improve the situation: "Let's figure out a way to work this out."	**Threatening** Attacks the other person: "If you can't do better, forget about our working together from now on."
Timely Delivers the message as soon as possible after the problem occurs.	**Gunnysacking** Holds on to resentments, becoming increasingly resentful.

Source: Adapted from H. Weisinger, *The Critical Edge: How to Criticize Up and Down Your Organization and Make It Pay Off* (Boston: Little, Brown, 1989).

start a cycle of defensiveness that pollutes the communication climate between people or working groups. Despite their risks, critical messages don't have to create problems. With enough skill, you can learn to both deliver and respond to them in ways that can maintain—or even improve—working relationships.

Offering Constructive Feedback

Despite its faultfinding nature, criticism doesn't have to trigger a defensive reaction. As Table 5–3 illustrates, the way you present your comments can make the difference between their being accepted and considered or being disputed and rejected.[16] You can maximize the chances of your comments being understood and accepted by carefully considering how they can be expressed.

Consider the Content The first concern is to edit your remarks so that they follow some important guidelines:

- *Limit the criticism to one topic.* You may have several complaints, but it is smart to focus on only one at a time. Your respondent may be able to handle a single problem, but he or she could grow understandably defensive if you pile on one gripe after another.
- *Make sure the criticism is accurate.* Be absolutely sure you get the facts straight before speaking out. If even a small detail is out of line, the other person can argue about that, sidetracking the discussion from the real problem at hand.
- *Define the problem clearly.* List the facts in enough detail so that the recipient knows exactly what you are talking about. Be prepared to give some examples to back up your point but don't overwhelm the other person with an avalanche of examples.
- *Show how your criticism can benefit the recipient.* Whenever possible, describe the payoffs for responding to your remarks. At the very least, the other person will get you off his or her back by heeding your complaints!

Consider the Sender Who delivers the criticism can be as important as the content of the remarks. Two guidelines will help you in this area:

- *Choose the most credible critic.* Sometimes the recipient will be more receptive to one person than to another. If a choice is available, make sure that the message comes from whoever can deliver it most effectively.
- *Make sure the criticism is appropriate to the critic's role.* Even accurate criticism is likely to be rejected if you have no business delivering it. For example, most comments about someone's personal life are out of place unless they affect a working relationship. Job-related comments should be appropriate for your relationship to the other person.

Consider the Relational Climate The framework in which your remarks are delivered can have an important impact on how they are received. Paying attention to three context-related factors can boost the odds of getting the desired reaction:

- *Deliver remarks as part of a positive relationship.* Let the other person know that your specific criticism doesn't diminish your respect or appreciation for the person in other areas. Sincerely acknowledging the positives can make the negatives easier to accept.
- *Accept partial responsibility for the problem.* If possible, show that you may have contributed in some degree to the issue. If nothing else, you might be able to say, "I probably should have brought this up sooner."
- *Accompany your criticism with an offer to help.* You can earn the goodwill of the other person by offering to play a role in solving the problem at hand.

Consider the Delivery How you express a criticism can make a big difference in the way it is received. Two delivery-related guidelines can help:

- *Deliver criticism in a face-saving manner.* Probably the most important consideration is to make sure your remarks are delivered privately. Criticizing someone in front of others is likely to trigger resentment and embarrassment.
- *Avoid sounding and looking judgmental.* Avoid using the kind of emotive language described in Chapter 4. Don't call names or use inflammatory labels, and don't attribute motives to the other person. Try to use the kind of descriptive "I" language described earlier in this chapter instead of defense-arousing "you" statements. Avoid condescending nonverbal behaviors such as shaking your finger, raising your voice, or rolling your eyes.

Responding to Criticism

When people are faced with criticism, the two most common responses are "fight" and "flight." Fighters react by counterattacking: "It's not my fault!" Another fighting response is to blame others: "I'm not the only one who's at fault here. I could have done better if I had gotten more support." Your own experience probably shows that fighting with your critics seldom persuades them to back down.

Flight is a second reaction to criticism. Most businesspeople are too mature to run away physically from a critic, but there are other ways of evading negative remarks. Sometimes you *can* physically avoid critics—steering clear of their offices or not returning their phone calls, for example. Even when you can't escape unpleasant remarks, you can mentally disengage by refusing to listen thoughtfully to the criticism.

career tip

The Art of the Apology

When you have made a mistake, nothing is as honest and potentially effective as a genuine apology. Besides being the right thing to do, apologizing can be a smart business strategy. Research suggests that sincerely acknowledging mistakes can drastically reduce both resentment and legal actions by offended parties.[17]

A complete apology contains several elements:

- ***Sincere regret.*** The fundamental part of an apology is a genuine expression of regret: "I feel bad about not showing up for yesterday's shift. I'm really sorry I let you down."
- ***Understanding that the person suffered harm.*** Show that you recognize how the other person was affected and that you're sorry. "I know it was busy, and it must have been a nightmare."
- ***An explanation of what happened.*** Without offering excuses, consider explaining how the offending behavior came to happen. "I got a panicky call from my grandmother, and felt like I had to get over there and see what the matter was. It turned out to be nothing, but by the time I got her calmed down it was too late to call you."
- ***Corrective action.*** Show that you intend to prevent future problems. "I've asked her to call my sister if anything like this happens again, so unless there's a real emergency there shouldn't be any more problems like this."
- ***Restoration.*** Do what you can to compensate the other person for the misdeed. "If it would help, I'm happy to cover tomorrow's shift, even though I'm not scheduled."

Source: After Patrick J. Kiger, "The Art of the Apology," *Workforce Management*, October 2004, pp. 57–62.

While keeping quiet can work in the short run, it seldom is a satisfying way to deal with an ongoing relationship in which you are constantly under attack.

Since neither fighting nor fleeing is likely to satisfy your critics or help you understand legitimate criticism, you need alternatives that allow you to listen nondefensively without losing face. Fortunately, two such alternatives exist.

Seek More Information Asking your critic to explain the problem gives you a constructive option to fighting or fleeing. By asking your critic for more information, you are showing that you take the criticism seriously but, at the same time, you aren't accepting blame for the problem. There are several ways to seek more information:

- *Ask for examples or clarification.* "You've said I'm not presenting a good attitude to customers. Can you describe exactly what I'm doing?"
- *Guess about details of the criticism.* Even if the critic isn't willing or able to offer specifics, you can guess: "Was it the way I handled Mr. Tyson when the bank sent back his check for insufficient funds?"
- *Paraphrase the critic.* "When you say I have a bad attitude toward customers, it sounds like you think I'm not giving them the service they deserve."
- *Ask what the critic wants.* "How could I behave in a better way around customers?"

Agree with the Criticism An obvious but often overlooked way of responding is to agree with the criticism. Although this approach might seem like a form of self-punishment, it can be extremely effective. There are three ways to agree with a critic:

- *Agree with the facts.* Sometimes you are confronted with facts that can't be disputed. In these cases, your best approach is probably to face up to the truth: "You're

right. I *have* been late three times this week." Notice that agreeing with the facts doesn't mean that you are accepting responsibility for every imaginable fault. In the case of being late to work, you might go on to point out that your lateness is a fluke in an otherwise spotless work record; but arguing with indisputable information isn't likely to satisfy your critic, and it will probably make you look bad.

- *Agree with the critic's right to his or her own perception.* Sometimes you can't honestly agree with the criticism. For example, a customer might unjustly accuse you of not caring about good service. After asking for more information to find out the basis of the criticism (a shipment didn't arrive on time, for example), you can acknowledge how the other person might view you as being at fault: "I can understand why it might seem that I don't care about your needs. After all, you did tell me that you absolutely had to have that shipment by last Friday, and I told you that it would be there. I'd be mad too if I were you." Notice that agreeing with the perception doesn't require you to *accept* your critic's evaluation as accurate, although you might indeed find that it does have some merit. What you are doing is acknowledging the other person's right to view the issue in a way that may differ from yours; you are agreeing that you can see how their perception makes sense to them, whether or not you see it the same way. To see the value of this approach, consider how offensive the alternative would be. To say or imply "Your view of the issue is completely wrong and mine is right" isn't likely to satisfy the other person, nor is it a reasonable position in most cases.
- *Emphasize areas of common ground.* As much as possible, point out areas where you and the other person share the same point of view. For example:

  Critic: The customers will never go for this idea!

  Response: I'm with you: We have to keep the customers satisfied. Maybe we can find a way to see how they'll respond to this idea. If they hate it, of course I'll drop the suggestion.

Even when the criticism is extreme, you can probably find something in the other person's position to agree with:

Hysterical Critic: You're going to ruin the whole job!

Response: I know how important it is to you. (Then let the critic talk about the job's importance, reinforcing your agreement.)

Work for a Cooperative Solution Once your critic believes that you've understood his or her position and acknowledged at least some parts of it, he or she will be as ready as possible to hear your point of view. A few strategies can maximize the chances for a constructive solution.[18]

- *Ask for the chance to state your point of view.* If you push ahead and state your position before the critic is ready to listen, your words probably won't get through. It's far more productive to give your critic a thorough hearing, agree with whatever points you can, and then ask, "May I tell you my perspective?" Doing so won't guarantee that you'll get a respectful hearing, but it gives you the best chance of one.
- *Focus on a solution, not on finding fault.* Your own experience will show that playing the blame game rarely works. A far more productive approach is to focus on finding a solution that will work for both you and the critic by asking, "What would make this situation better?" or "How can we handle this situation in a way that both of us can accept?"

Managing Conflict

Like it or not, conflict is part of every job. Even the most competent, intelligent, ethical people will disagree from time to time. Sometimes conflict involves work-related issues: scheduling, funds, work assignments, and so on. Other times, it focuses on personal issues: sexual harassment, the amount of socializing appropriate during working hours, or whether a shared assistant is doing his or her work efficiently. The dispute may be loud and argumentative, calm and rational, or so indirect that it is never mentioned outright.

Conflict may be equated with the common cold—unavoidable, unpleasant, and counterproductive. To most people, the fewer conflicts the better. But since conflict is unavoidable, an inability or refusal to face problems can lead to job-hopping. Brenda Richard, director of human resources for the Radisson Hotel New Orleans, describes people who fit this pattern: "They don't want to solve problems, they don't want conflict."[19] The problem isn't conflict itself, but rather *the way in which it is handled*. With the right approach, conflict can produce good results. Management consultant and Harvard Medical School psychologist Steven Berglos flatly argues that constructive conflict is an essential ingredient in organizational success:

> *If you're not looking for ways to promote healthful conflict between people of different backgrounds who cannot possibly see the world the same way, don't be surprised if anarchy ensues or if the best and the brightest abandon you.*[20]

The Chinese language represents the fact that conflict can lead to great benefits or great costs. In Chinese, the ideogram for the word *crisis* is made up of two characters: danger and opportunity. A poorly handled organizational conflict certainly can be dangerous; relationships suffer and productivity declines. On the other hand, a skillfully handled conflict can result in several benefits.[21] It can function as a safety valve, letting people ventilate frustrations that are blocking their effective functioning. It can lead to solving troublesome problems. James Baldwin said it best: "Nothing can be changed until it is faced." Problems seldom go away just because they are ignored; they usually grow worse. Facing them can promote group loyalty and cohesiveness. People who successfully overcome conflicts often feel that, together, they have made progress toward their mutual goals.

What Are Conflicts About?

Conflicts fall into several categories.[22] To understand them all, take another look at the dispute between business partners Marissa and Tran described in the "Computer Solutions" case study on page 72.

The Topic at Hand The most obvious source of conflicts is the subject at hand. Topic-related disagreements are a fact of life in the workplace. They involve issues including

pay and other compensation	job assignments
resources	the quality of products and services
scheduling	budgeting

In the Computer Solutions case, Marissa and Tran's dispute is over how to equalize the amount of work they do: Each partner complains that s/he works harder than the other.

The Process Some disputes are more about *how* to do something than what to do. For example,

Labor and management might acknowledge that differences are likely to occur over the life of a contract, but disagree on what to do when disputes arise.

A project team might all agree that the work at hand needs to be divided up, but they could disagree on how to decide who does what.

Members of a community nonprofit group might decide to hold a fundraiser, but disagree on how to choose the type of event.

In the Computer Solutions case study, Tran and Marissa know they need to resolve their feelings about each other's contributions to the partnership, but have trouble deciding how to proceed. Marissa wants to bring in an outside expert to mediate the problem, while Tran thinks they could work out the problems without any outsiders getting involved. So, the process has become a second area of conflict.

Relational Issues As you read in Chapter 1, along with substantive content issues are *relational* disputes that center on how parties want to be treated by one another.

Are we a big family, or a group of professionals who keep our personal lives separate from work?

Should bosses and their subordinates also be friends?

Does management really welcome ideas from rank-and-file employees, or is the suggestion box just a prop?

In the Computer Solutions case, Marissa and Tran aren't just disagreeing about who is working harder. As the conflict escalates, each is probably feeling unappreciated and resentful. Unless they can address and resolve these feelings, equalizing the workload won't resolve their conflict.

Ego/Identity Issues Social scientists use the term "face" to describe the identity each of us strives to present. In a work context, most people try to present a face of

competence	honesty
commitment	reasonableness
fairness	professionalism

Relationships do well when others acknowledge our presenting face, and conflicts intensify when others communicate in face-threatening ways.[23] Marissa's calling Tran a "sexist nerd" is an obvious face-threatening attack. Such accusations open a whole new front in the dispute, in addition to the original disagreement about equalizing the workload.

Even though the four types of conflicts are listed separately here, most disputes involve a combination of issues. As the preceding paragraphs show, Tran and Marissa have conflicts in each area. When you deal with a conflict, it's important to explore all of the dimensions on which it operates.

Approaches to Conflict

When faced with a conflict, you have several choices about how to respond. Each of these approaches has different results.[24]

Avoiding One way to deal with conflict is to avoid it whenever possible and withdraw when confronted. In some cases, avoidance is physical: refusing to take phone calls, staying barricaded in the office, and so on. In other cases, however, avoidance can be psychological: denying that a problem exists or that it is serious, repressing emotional reactions, and so on. In the workplace, a communicator who avoids conflicts might accept constant schedule delays or poor-quality work from a supplier to avoid a confrontation or might cover up for a co-worker's frequent absences even if it means doing the other person's work. As these examples suggest, avoidance may have the short-term benefit of preventing a confrontation, but there are usually long-term costs, especially in ongoing relationships. "I think it's better to face whatever the conflict is head on and deal with the situation as it comes up and not side-step it or go to someone else about the problem," advises Jean Stefani, a senior operations analyst at Comcast Communication.[25]

Despite its drawbacks, avoidance is sometimes a wise choice. Table 5–4 lists some circumstances in which keeping quiet may be the most appropriate course of action. For example, when standing up for your rights would be hopeless, silence might be the best policy. You might simply tolerate a superior's unreasonable demands while you look for a new job, or you might steer clear of an angry co-worker who is out to get you. In many cases, however, avoidance has unacceptable costs: You lose self-respect, you become frustrated, and the problem may only get worse.

Table 5–4 Factors Governing Choice of a Conflict Style

Consider Avoiding
1. When an issue is genuinely trivial, or when more important issues are pressing.
2. When you have no chance of winning.
3. When the potential for disruption outweighs the benefits of resolution.
4. To let others cool down and regain perspective.
5. When the long-term costs of winning may outweigh short-term gains.
6. When others can resolve the conflict more effectively.

Consider Accommodating
1. When you find you are wrong.
2. When the issue is important to the other party and not important to you.
3. To build social credits for later issues.
4. To minimize loss when you are outmatched and losing.
5. When harmony and stability are more important than the subject at hand.
6. To allow others to learn by making their own mistakes.

Consider Competing
1. When quick, decisive action is vital (e.g., emergencies).
2. On important issues where unpopular actions need implementing (e.g., cost cutting, enforcing unpopular rules).
3. When others will take advantage of your noncompetitive behavior.

Consider Collaborating
1. To find solutions when both parties' concerns are too important to be compromised.
2. When a long-term relationship between the parties is important.
3. To gain commitment of all parties by building consensus.
4. When the other party is willing to take a collaborative approach.

Consider Compromising
1. When goals are important but not worth the effort or potential disruption of more assertive modes.
2. When opponents with equal power are committed to mutually exclusive goals.
3. To achieve temporary settlements of complex issues.
4. To arrive at expedient solutions under time pressure.
5. As a backup, when collaboration is unsuccessful.

Source: Kenneth W. Thomas, "Toward Multi-Dimensional Values in Teaching: The Example of Conflict Behavior," *Academy of Management Review* 2, no. 3 (1987), p. 487.

Accommodating Whereas avoiders stay away from conflicts, accommodators give ground as a way of maintaining harmony. In many cases, accommodating is hard to defend. It can be equivalent to appeasement, sacrificing one's principles, and putting harmony above dealing with important issues. In her fascinating book *Talking from 9 to 5*, sociolinguist Deborah Tannen describes an extreme case in which accommodating led to disaster.[26] On January 13, 1982, Air Florida flight 90 crashed

career tip

How to Say No

There are times when even the most cooperative communicators feel compelled to decline the requests of a customer, colleague, or even a boss. Following these steps can help soften the blow when you choose to say no.

1. Acknowledge that the request is important to the person making it: "I can understand why you need help to meet the deadline. . . ."
2. Decline the request: "I won't be able to help you out on this one."
3. Give your reasons, if appropriate: "I'm using every minute of my time to finish the XYZ report."
4. Offer help in finding a solution: "I could show you the report format I used last year. It might help you figure out how to approach this job."

shortly after takeoff from Ronald Reagan National Airport in Washington, DC; 69 passengers were killed. The cause of the disaster was excessive ice on the airplane's wings. An analysis of cockpit recordings made on the heavily armored black box recovered after the accident revealed that the co-pilot had hinted about excessive ice several times to the pilot before takeoff but that his suggestions went unheeded. The command structure of aircraft operations dictates that the pilot has the final word on whether a plane is fit to fly. It is easy to imagine that a less accommodating approach might have caused the pilot to recheck the situation before making what turned out to be a catastrophic decision.

Though it has obvious drawbacks, accommodating, does have merit in some circumstances (see Table 5–4). If you are clearly wrong, then giving up your original position can be a sign of strength, not weakness. If harmony is more important than the issue at hand—especially if the issue is a minor one—then accommodating is probably justified. For example, if you don't care strongly whether the new stationery is printed on cream or gray paper and fighting for one color might be a big concern for others, then giving in is probably smart. Finally, you might accommodate if satisfying the other person is important enough to your welfare. You might, for example, put up with an overly demanding customer to make an important sale.

Competing A competitive approach to conflicts is based on the assumption that the only way for one party to reach its goals is to overcome the other. This zero-sum approach is common in many negotiations, as you will see later in this chapter. Sometimes a power-based approach to conflict is based on simply disregarding the other person's concerns. Unsympathetic management might turn a deaf ear to the request of employees to make provisions for on-site exercise facilities, implying—or even stating outright—that the physical condition of employees is not the concern of the employer and that providing easy access to exercise would require a cash outlay and reduce time spent on the job.

In many cases, a competitive attitude is unnecessary. As the section of this chapter on win–win negotiating shows, it often *is* possible for both sides in a conflict to reach their goals (see pages 157–162). For instance, an employer might find that the cost of providing on-site exercise equipment is more than offset by reduced absenteeism and greater appeal when recruiting new employees. Furthermore, a competitive orientation can generate ill will that is both costly and unpleasant. In our physical-fitness example, workers whose needs are ignored are likely to resent their employer and act in ways that ultimately wind up costing the company a great deal.

Despite its drawbacks, competition isn't always a bad approach. In some cases, an issue isn't important enough to spend time working it out. In other instances, there isn't time to collaborate on solutions. Finally, if others are determined to gain advantage at your expense, you might compete out of self-defense.

Collaborating Rather than taking a competitive approach, collaborative communicators are committed to working together to resolve conflicts. Collaboration is based on the assumption that it is possible to meet one's own needs and those of the other person. This approach is reflected in Rabbi Hillel's statement, "If I am not for myself, who will be? If I am only for myself, what am I? If not now, when?"

Whereas avoiding and accommodating are based on the assumption that conflict should be avoided, and competing is based on the belief that conflict is a struggle, collaboration assumes that conflict is a natural part of life and that working with the other person will produce the best possible solution. The benefits of collaboration are clear: Not only can the issue at hand be resolved, but the relationship between the parties can also be improved.

Despite its advantages, collaborative communication isn't a panacea. It takes time to work with others, and a mutually satisfactory outcome isn't always possible. Furthermore, collaboration requires the cooperation of everyone involved. If the other party isn't disposed to work with you, then you may be setting yourself up for exploitation by communicating openly and offering to work cooperatively.

Compromising In a **compromise,** each party sacrifices something he or she is seeking to gain an agreement. On one hand, this approach is cooperative, recognizing that both parties must agree to resolve a conflict. On the other, compromise is self-centered, since the parties act in their self-interest to get the best possible deal.

Compromise is a middle-range approach. It is more assertive than avoiding and accommodating yet less aggressive than competing. It is cooperative yet less so than collaboration. While it does not give any one of the parties in a dispute everything he or she seeks, it provides an outcome that, by definition, everyone involved can live with. As Table 5–4 shows, compromise may not be the perfect approach, but under many circumstances it produces the best possible outcome.

Handling Conflicts Constructively

When you avoid a conflict or accommodate another's demand, few communication skills are necessary. But if you decide to address an issue directly—either to collaborate, to compete, or to seek a compromise—you will need to negotiate.

Negotiation occurs when two or more parties—either individuals or groups—discuss specific proposals to find a mutually acceptable agreement. Although we don't always use the term, we negotiate every day. As one consultant explains, "Negotiations are seldom formal, sit-around-the-table affairs. In fact, almost any form of business problem or disagreement—from scheduling work shifts to 'Who's going to pay this $500 expense?'—is resolved by some form of negotiation."[27]

There's nothing magical about negotiation. When poorly handled, it can leave a problem still unsolved and perhaps worse than before. ("I tried to work things out, but he just tried to railroad me. I'm going to file a lawsuit this time.") When negotiation is handled skillfully, though, it can improve the position of one or even both parties. The remainder of this chapter will introduce communication strategies that can produce the best possible outcomes to your negotiations.

"It's not enough that we succeed, Cats must also fail."

Negotiation Strategies and Outcomes A common negotiating strategy is the competitive **win–lose** approach. It is based on the assumption that only one side can reach its goals and that any victory by that party will be matched by the other's loss. As Table 5–4 shows, you probably will need to take a competitive win–lose approach to protect your interests if others insist on gaining at your expense or when resources are truly scarce. For example, your company and another might compete for the same customers, and you might compete with another candidate for the same once-in-a-lifetime job.

Nobody seeks out **lose–lose** outcomes, but they can arise when competitors try to gain an advantage at one another's expense. Like armies that take mortal losses while trying to defeat their enemies, disputants who go for a competitive victory often find that they have hurt themselves as much as their opponents. For example, if you push for an unrealistically low price, you might antagonize the seller so much that you don't get the product you're seeking and the seller doesn't make the sale. On the job, feuding parties may ruin their own careers by gaining reputations as difficult employees or as poor team players.

Sometimes it seems better to *compromise* than to fight battles in a competitive manner and risk a lose–lose outcome. There certainly are cases in which compromise is the best obtainable outcome—usually when disputed resources are limited or scarce. If two managers each need a full-time assistant but budget restrictions make this impossible, they may have to compromise by sharing the services of one employee. While compromises may be necessary, they are less than ideal because both parties lose at least some of what they were seeking. Buyers, for instance, may pay more than they can afford, while sellers receive less than they need.

When negotiators collaborate, they can often—though not always—achieve a **win–win** outcome, in which everybody involved is satisfied. Win–win solutions are easiest when the needs of each party aren't incompatible, as in the following examples:

- *Shorter working hours*. Even though they were paid overtime, teachers at a preschool resented working weekends to keep school equipment clean and organized. A brainstorming session between the teachers and director produced a solution that satisfied everyone's needs: Substitutes covered for the teachers during some school hours while the teachers sorted and cleaned equipment. This approach had several benefits: Teachers' weekends were free, and teachers got a weekly change-of-pace from child care. Furthermore, the director was happy because the substitutes' pay was lower than the teachers' overtime.

career tip

Dealing with Difficult People

Sometimes you will be forced to work with people whose behavior can only be called difficult. While you can't change the way they act, you can respond in ways that prevent you from becoming one of their victims. If any of the following styles is familiar, consider trying the recommended ways of responding.

Sherman tanks try to get their way by attacking, intimidating, and trying to prove that they are right. They behave with aggression and impatience. To cope

- Stand up to them, but consider giving them some time to run down.
- Get them to sit or stand at the same level as you, and maintain eye contact.
- State your own opinions and perceptions clearly and forcefully, but don't argue or humiliate them.
- Be firm, but stay ready to be friendly.

Snipers use innuendoes, digs, "playful" teasing and other indirect approaches to express aggression. To cope

- Refuse to be attacked indirectly. Ask, "Are you trying to ridicule me?" or "That sounded like an attack. How did you mean it?"
- Get other points of view from group members. Do not allow the sniper's remarks to pass as truth. ("Does anyone else see it that way?")
- If you are the third party to sniping, don't take sides. Insist that it stop in your presence.

Complainers are less interested in resolving problems than with blaming others and shirking responsibility. Cope by

- Listening attentively to their complaints.
- Paraphrasing what they say so they can verify or clarify their perception.
- Not agreeing with or apologizing for their allegations.
- Moving to a problem-solving mode by asking specific, informational questions and asking for the complaints in writing.

Negativists tap the potential for despair in us because they are angry and resentful, convinced that they are powerless over much in their lives. To cope

- Be alert to the potential for being dragged into their despair.
- Make optimistic but realistic statements.
- Don't try to argue them out of their pessimism.
- Do not offer solutions or alternatives until there has been a thorough discussion of the problem.

A rich Internet resource for dealing with difficult people is Work911 (**http://www.work911.com**). It offers over 1,000 articles organized by topics such as communication, stress, and anger management. Additional help with difficult people and conflict at work is available from online discussion lists. You can join "Dealing with Difficult People" or "Conflict at Work" discussion lists by sending e-mails to **difficultpeople-subscribe@egroups.com** or **workcomm-subscribe@egroups.com**.

Sources: Robert Bacal, *The Complete Idiot's Guide to Dealing with Difficult Employees* (Indianapolis: Alpha Books, 2000); and Robert M. Bramson, *Coping with Difficult People* (New York: Anchor/Doubleday, 1981).

- *Increasing employee compensation.* A contractor's employees wanted a raise. The contractor recognized that the employees deserved more, but couldn't afford to increase his payroll. After considering alternatives together, the boss and employees came up with a plan that pleased everyone. Workers were allowed to use company vehicles during nonworking hours, saving them the expense of

Table 5–5 When to Use Competitive and Win-Win Negotiating Styles

Use a Competitive Approach	Use a Win-Win Approach
When your interests and the other party's clearly conflict.	When you and the other party have common interests.
When the other party insists on taking a win-lose approach.	When the other party is willing to consider a win-win approach.
When you do not need a long-term harmonious relationship.	When a continuing, harmonious relationship is important.
When you are powerful enough to prevail.	When you are weaker or power is approximately equal.
When short-term goals are more important.	When long-term goals are more important.

an extra car or truck. The owner rented his vacation home to employees at a bargain rate. Finally, the boss negotiated lower prices for his employees on home furnishings and appliances at local merchants. These changes increased the employees' buying power—at little cost to the boss.

- *Blending business goals and community beauty.* A cellular phone company wanted to install a tower in the middle of a town, but residents didn't want an eyesore. The company agreed to build a long-needed new steeple for a local church, with the transmitter concealed inside. Furthermore it paid the church $2,000 monthly rent. The result was a triple win: Expanded phone service, maintenance of the community's beauty, and both a new steeple and income for the church.[28]

As these few examples illustrate, the specific solutions that will work for a problem differ in each case. The important point is that parties working together *can* often find no-lose solutions to their problems. And, not surprisingly, research shows that a win–win approach is preferred to other problem-solving styles.[29] In one study, researchers compared the problem-solving styles used in six organizations. They found that the two highest-performing organizations used a win–win approach to a greater degree than did the less effective companies, while the lowest-performing organizations used that style less than the others.[30]

Win–win outcomes are ideal, but they aren't always realistic. Table 5–5 offers guidelines about when the chances are best for using this approach, as well as others.

Preparing to Negotiate Successful negotiations begin before you say a word to the other person. You can take several steps to think out your position and approach your negotiating partners in a way that boosts the odds of getting your message across and getting a constructive response.

Clarify your interests and needs Communicators can doom negotiations by prematurely focusing on means instead of ends. *Ends* are the goals you want, and *means* are ways of achieving those goals. In their best-selling book *Getting to Yes*, Roger Fisher and William Ury show that win–win results come from focusing on means instead of ends.[31] To illustrate the difference, we can adapt a story they tell.

Imagine a dispute between two office workers. John wants to open a window and Mary wants it closed. (This issue may seem trivial, but long-standing feuds have developed over smaller issues.) At this point the issue seems irreconcilable; but imagine that a colleague asks each worker what he wants. John replies, "To get some fresh air." To the same question, Mary replies, "To avoid a draft." "I have an idea," the mediating colleague suggests: "What if we open a window in the next room? That would give John the fresh air he needs and prevent the draft that Mary wants to avoid."

This simple example illustrates the difference between means and ends:

Issue	Ends	Means
John	Fresh air	Open window *or* Open window in adjoining room
Mary	No draft	Keep window closed *or* Open window in adjoining room

If Mary and John stayed focused on the first means that occurred to them, the issue would never be resolved to their satisfaction. But once they identified the ends each was seeking, the pathway to a mutually acceptable means was perfectly clear.

It's far better to identify the real end you are seeking and leave a discussion of means for later.

Consider the best time to raise the issue Raising a difficult issue when the other person is tired, grumpy, or distracted by other business is likely to threaten the odds of getting the results you are seeking. Review the variables about chronological communication contexts in Chapter 1 (page 9) when you consider when to raise an issue.

Prepare your statement Think over how you can best express yourself, following the advice for offering constructive feedback on pages 145–146 in this chapter. Practicing your message can help make your point quickly and clearly, and it will prevent you from blurting out an angry statement you'll regret later. When planning your remarks, be sure to think about how you can use "I" language instead of delivering defense-arousing "you" messages.

Rehearsing your statement doesn't mean you should memorize your remarks word for word; this approach would sound canned and insincere. Think about your general ideas and perhaps a few key phrases you'll use to make your ideas clear.

Conducting the Negotiation The win–win approach is most successful when it follows the steps described below.

Identify the ends both parties are seeking As you read earlier, seemingly irreconcilable conflicts can be resolved if negotiators focus on their needs, and not on positions. Consider the example of a parent who has found that the traditional work schedule isn't compatible with his child care responsibilities. Here are the ends that the employee and the boss identified:

Employee: Make sure the children are cared for after school.

Boss: Make sure employee's productivity doesn't drop.

Both: Keep the employee on the job. Keep a positive relationship.

Brainstorm a list of possible solutions Once both parties have identified the ends they are seeking, the next step is to develop a list of solutions that might satisfy each party's needs. Recall the problem-oriented approach introduced earlier in this chapter: Instead of working against one another (How can I defeat you?), the parties work together against the problem (How can we beat the problem?).

Consider again the case of the employee trying to have his child cared for after school. In this case, a number of potentially win–win solutions are worth exploring. For example:

- The employee could do some work at home during nonbusiness hours.
- The company could offer flexible work hours, so employees can get their jobs done when children are at school or being cared for by others.
- The employee could share his full-time position with another worker, giving the boss the coverage the boss needs and the employee the free time. If the employee needs additional income, he could take part-time work that could be done at home at his convenience.
- The boss could subsidize after-school child care, on the assumption that productivity would rise and absenteeism decline as children of employees are being cared for.

While not all of the above options are likely to be workable, the key to successful brainstorming is to avoid judging any possible solutions for the time being. Nothing deflates creativity and increases defensiveness as much as saying, "That won't work." You can judge the quality of each idea later; but for now, the key is quantity. Perhaps one person's unworkable idea will spark a productive suggestion.

Evaluate the alternative solutions After brainstorming as many ideas as possible, decide which ones are most promising. During this stage, it is still critical to work for an answer that meets the important needs of all the parties. Cooperation will come only if everyone feels satisfied with the solution.

Implement and follow up on the solution Once the best plan is chosen, make sure everyone understands it; then give it a try. Even the most appealing plans may need revision when put into action. After a reasonable amount of time, plan to meet with the other parties to discuss how the solution is working out. If necessary, identify the needs that are still unmet, and then repeat the problem-solving procedure.

A Case Study of Win–Win Problem Solving The case of Marta, a senior manager, and Kurt, her assistant, shows how win–win problem solving can work. Kurt has learned that his department is about to launch a particularly ambitious project. He feels ready to take on more responsibility and thinks this could be a good chance to show what he can do. Kurt is disappointed that Marta hasn't offered him the chance to lead the effort, but he wisely has thought about how to approach her instead of unassertively nursing his grudge or aggressively attacking her. Knowing from experience that

Marta is most receptive when not distracted by other matters, he makes an appointment to talk with her. They agree to meet at the end of the workday, after most employees have gone home and the office is quiet.

Identify the needs of both parties

Marta: What's up?

Kurt: I'm really excited about the KDM project, and I'd like a shot at taking the lead on managing it.

Marta: Kurt, that's a major project. I need someone with more experience, especially in public relations, to handle that job. I've asked Greta to handle it. *(Marta explains her need—to have the job managed by someone with more experience.)*

Kurt: Well, I guess I understand. But I'd really like to take on more responsibility. This is the second time a big job went to somebody else. I'd like to find some way of proving myself and showing what I can do for this company. *(Kurt wisely avoids arguing about the specific project and instead focuses on his real goal—to get a chance to show he can handle more responsibility.)*

Marta: Fair enough. Let's try to figure out a way that you can have the responsibility and recognition you want and I can feel confident that the job is the right size. *(Like Kurt, Marta focuses on ends—Kurt growing in his job—instead of means.)*

Brainstorm a list of possible solutions

Kurt: Great. What if you put me in charge of a major project—one not quite as big as this one, and I could just check everything with you along the way?

Marta: Or I might be able to team you up with someone who has experience in areas where you're weak, and you could run the project together. Or I could get you to assist Greta on this project, so you could get some experience under her supervision and see how the aspects all fit together.

Kurt: I'd really like to show I can take the lead. What if I took on a less important project—one that called for me to figure out problems in these areas? Or maybe I could manage just the public relations part of a bigger project, to show you that I can handle that. *(Notice that Kurt and Marta have brainstormed five options to consider, without judging any at this point.)*

Evaluate the alternative solutions

Marta: All of these are possibilities. Let's see which of them will best suit us both. I could put you in charge of a major project, I guess, but you would need a lot of support, and I'm afraid I don't have enough time to give it to you.

Kurt: Plus it would drive us both crazy if I had to check every detail with you. And I don't really want to team up with someone, either. The whole idea is for me to get some experience where I need it, and a

career tip

Ethical Communication Gets Positive Results

Stephen Covey, author of *The Seven Habits of Highly Effective People*, *Principle-Centered Leadership*, and *First Things First*, offers these guidelines for principled communication. Covey argues that, besides being ethical, this approach can increase your influence with others.

- *Refrain from saying the unkind or negative things.* When you are provoked or fatigued, the temptation to lash out at others is strong. Being kind under pressure will earn you the respect of others.
- *Distinguish between the person and the behavior or performance.* You may disapprove of bad behavior and poor performance, but separate your judgment of the work from the person who has done it.
- *Keep your promises.* Never make agreements unless you are prepared to keep them. Being known as a dependable person will generate trust that makes your word a powerful thing.
- *Reward open, honest expressions or questions.* Too often we punish honest, open expressions or questions. As a result others learn to hide their ideas, opinions, and feelings. You may not agree with someone, but you can always say, "Thank you for being honest with me."
- *Admit your mistakes.* Everyone makes mistakes. When you do, apologize. When personal problems occur, consider whether you are at least partly to blame. Resist the urge to offer excuses, explanations, or defenses: They rarely convince or impress anyone.
- *Accept the other person.* Nothing reinforces defensive behavior more than judgment, comparison, or rejection. Accepting others as they are frees them from the need to defend themselves. Acceptance doesn't necessarily require you to agree with the other person's opinion. Rather, it means accepting his or her right to hold a position, even when it is different from yours.

Source: Stephen Covey, "Seven Methods of Influence," *Incentive* 17 (October 1996), p. 22.

person who has that experience will just handle those concerns—which gets me nowhere.

Marta: On the other hand, I don't want to just put you on your own. How would you feel about handling the public relations on Greta's project? She could use some extra help, and having that help would give her time to train you. It would also help you get a sense of the whole project—not just part of it.

Implement the solution Kurt agreed to the idea of handling Greta's public relations:

Kurt: Just one thing. I want Greta to know that my job is to be responsible for that part of the project—not just be her assistant.

Marta: Sounds fair to me. I'll talk to Greta and make sure she's agreeable. I do think she has a lot of good advice to offer, though. You'd be foolish not to consider her opinions. And, of course, both she and I will have to support your decisions. But I'll be sure both of us give you the freedom to come up with your own plan—and the responsibility that goes with the freedom.

Follow up on the solution Marta, Kurt, and Greta met several weeks after developing their plan to check its progress:

Kurt: I'm feeling pretty good about the arrangement. I appreciate the chance to be responsible for one part of such a big project. Just one thing, Greta. When we agree on the way I'll do a job, I feel uncomfortable when you keep checking on how I'm doing. It makes me wonder whether you think I'll mess it up.

Greta: Not at all, Kurt. I thought you'd want to know that I'm available for support. Of course, I do want to keep posted, but I don't have any intention of being a snoop. What do you suggest?

Kurt: How about letting me come to you. I promise to keep you on top of things, and I do appreciate your advice. I'd just like to have a little more operating room.

Marta: Sounds like a good arrangement. Let's give it a try and get together next week at this time to see how it works.

Self-Assessment Personal Conflict Style Inventory

This survey will help you identify your preferred method of dealing with conflict, both when a difference first arises and when the issue intensifies.

Instructions: Consider your response in situations where your wishes differ from those of another person. Circle one number on the line below each statement. If you find it easier, you may choose one particular conflict setting and use it as background for all the questions.

When I First Discover that Differences Exist . . .

A I make sure that all views are out in the open and treated with equal consideration, even if there seems to be substantial disagreement.

Not at all characteristic ← 1 2 3 4 5 6 → *Very characteristic*

B I devote more attention to making sure others understand the logic and benefits of my position than I do to pleasing them.

Not at all characteristic ← 1 2 3 4 5 6 → *Very characteristic*

C I make my needs known, but I tone them down a bit and look for solutions somewhere in the middle.

Not at all characteristic ← 1 2 3 4 5 6 → *Very characteristic*

D I pull back from discussion for a time to avoid tension.

Not at all characteristic ← 1 2 3 4 5 6 → *Very characteristic*

E I devote more attention to feelings of others than to my personal goals.

Not at all characteristic ← 1 2 3 4 5 6 → *Very characteristic*

F I make sure my agenda doesn't get in the way of our relationship.

Not at all characteristic ⟵ 1 2 3 4 5 6 ⟶ *Very characteristic*

G I actively explain my ideas and just as actively take steps to understand others.

Not at all characteristic ⟵ 1 2 3 4 5 6 ⟶ *Very characteristic*

H I am more concerned with goals I believe to be important than with how others feel about things.

Not at all characteristic ⟵ 1 2 3 4 5 6 ⟶ *Very characteristic*

I I decide the differences aren't worth worrying about.

Not at all characteristic ⟵ 1 2 3 4 5 6 ⟶ *Very characteristic*

J I give up some points in exchange for others.

Not at all characteristic ⟵ 1 2 3 4 5 6 ⟶ *Very characteristic*

If Differences Persist and Feelings Escalate . . .

K I enter more actively into discussion and hold out for ways to meet the needs of others as well as my own.

Not at all characteristic ⟵ 1 2 3 4 5 6 ⟶ *Very characteristic*

L I put forth greater effort to make sure that the truth as I see it is recognized and less on pleasing others.

Not at all characteristic ⟵ 1 2 3 4 5 6 ⟶ *Very characteristic*

M I try to be reasonable by not asking for my full preferences, but I make sure I get some of what I want.

Not at all characteristic ⟵ 1 2 3 4 5 6 ⟶ *Very characteristic*

N I don't push for things to be done my way, and I pull back somewhat from the demands of others.

Not at all characteristic ⟵ 1 2 3 4 5 6 ⟶ *Very characteristic*

O I set aside my own preferences and become more concerned with keeping the relationship comfortable.

Not at all characteristic ⟵ 1 2 3 4 5 6 ⟶ *Very characteristic*

P I interact less with others and look for ways to find a safe distance.

Not at all characteristic ⟵ 1 2 3 4 5 6 ⟶ *Very characteristic*

Q I do what needs to be done and hope we can mend feelings later.

Not at all characteristic ⟵ 1 2 3 4 5 6 ⟶ *Very characteristic*

R I do what is necessary to soothe the other's feelings.

Not at all characteristic ⟵ 1 2 3 4 5 6 ⟶ *Very characteristic*

S I pay close attention to the desires of others but remain firm that they need to pay equal attention to my desires.

Not at all characteristic ⟵ 1 2 3 4 5 6 ⟶ *Very characteristic*

T I press for moderation and compromise so we can make a decision and move on with things.

Not at all characteristic ⟵ 1 2 3 4 5 6 ⟶ *Very characteristic*

(continued)

Style Inventory Tally Sheet

When you are finished taking the inventory, write the number you circled for each situation beside the corresponding letter on the tally sheet below. Add each of the 10 columns of the tally chart, writing the total of each in the empty box just below the double line.

A __ G __	K __ S __	B __ H __	L __ Q __	C __ J __	M __ T __	D __ I __	N __ P __	E __ F __	O __ R __
Calm	Storm	Calm	Storm	Calm	Storm	Calm	Storm	Calm	Storm
Collaborating		**Forcing (Competing)**		**Compromising**		**Avoiding**		**Accommodating**	

Now list your scores and the style names in order from highest score to lowest in both the calm and storm columns below.

Calm: Response when issues/conflicts first arise.

Storm: Response after the issues/conflicts have been unresolved and have grown in intensity.

Score	Style	Score	Style
____	____________________	____	____________________
____	____________________	____	____________________
____	____________________	____	____________________
____	____________________	____	____________________

Interpreting the Scores

This exercise gives you two sets of scores for each of the five approaches to conflict. *Calm* scores apply to your response when disagreement first arises. *Storm* scores apply to your responses if things are not easily resolved and emotions get stronger. The higher your score in a given style, the more likely you are to use this style in responding to conflict. The highest score in each of the columns indicates a "preferred" or primary style. If two or more styles have the same score they are equally "preferred." The second highest score indicates your "backup" style if the number is relatively close to the highest score. A fairly even score across all of the styles indicates a "flat profile." Persons with a flat profile tend to be able to choose easily among the various responses to conflict.

Read more about these five Styles of Conflict Management and take this inventory online at **http://peace.mennolink.org/resources/conflictstyle**.

Note: This is a partial version of *Style Matters: The Kraybill Conflict Style Inventory,* reprinted by permission of Ronald Kraybill. The full version has features that make it culturally sensitive. It also offers extensive practical strategies to bring out the best in each style and discussion questions for groups. More information and free trainers' notes at **www.RiverhouseEpress.com**.

summary

People skills are an essential ingredient for success in any career. These skills create a positive communication climate in which people feel valued. The key to building a positive climate is confirming communication, which conveys respect for the other person, even during a conflict. Confirming messages are phrased in descriptive "I" language. They focus on solving problems, not imposing solutions. They are honest, show concern for the other party, demonstrate an attitude of equality, and reflect the communicator's open-mindedness.

One way to create and maintain a positive communication climate is to offer praise. There are several guidelines for praising effectively: Make praise specific and sincere, praise progress, praise intermittently, and relay praise to others.

In the real world of business, however, praise is not always appropriate; sometimes criticism must be given. The climate of a relationship can be enhanced by offering criticism in the most constructive manner. The chances for acceptance of criticism are best when a critical message is framed in a way that considers the content by limiting remarks to one topic, making sure they are accurate, defining the problem clearly, and showing how attending to the criticism can benefit the recipient. Choosing the most credible critic and making sure the remarks are appropriate to the critic's role can also maximize the beneficial effects of the criticism. Attention to the context is another way to maximize the chances that criticism will be well received: delivering remarks as part of a positive relationship, accepting partial responsibility for the problem, and accompanying criticism with an offer to help. Finally, delivering the criticism in a face-saving manner and a nonjudgmental tone can lead to a nondefensive response.

When on the receiving end of another person's criticism, several responses can prevent defensiveness. One approach is to seek more information by asking for examples or clarification, guessing about details when necessary, paraphrasing the critic, and asking what the critic wants. Agreeing with the facts of the criticism or with the critic's perception are also potentially effective.

On-the-job conflicts are inevitable so it is important to handle them constructively. Understanding that conflicts are not all the same requires communicators to first explore whether the conflict is about a topic, a process, the relationship, or one's ego. Second, recognize that one can choose from five ways to handle conflict: avoiding, accommodating, competing, collaborating, or compromising. Each has both advantages and drawbacks, so situational factors will usually govern which one to use at a given time. Next, consider how you will negotiate a mutually acceptable agreement. Negotiations can take four forms: competitive, lose–lose, compromise, and win–win. The approach that parties take often determines the outcome. Successful negotiating includes these steps: clarify your interests and needs by distinguishing between ends and means, pay attention to timing, and prepare nondefensive ways to begin. Then follow steps of a win–win approach by identifying each parties' ends, brainstorming, evaluating possible solutions, implementing and following up on a solution.

key terms

Test your understanding of these key terms by visiting the Online Learning Center Web site at www.mhhe.com/adler9.

communication climate 139
compromise 154
confirming messages 139
descriptive statements 140
disconfirming messages 139
emotional intelligence 138

"I" language 140
lose–lose orientation 155
negotiation 154
problem-oriented messages 140
win–lose orientation 155
win–win orientation 155
"you" language 140

activities

Go to the self-quizzes at the Online Learning Center at www.mhhe.com/adler9 to test your knowledge of chapter concepts.

1. Invitation to Insight

Recall two or three instances in which you have enacted troublesome communicative behaviors (see Table 5–1).

a. Identify which types of behaviors you enacted. What circumstances led you to enact these behaviors?
b. What were the results of these behaviors for you and the other people involved?
c. Describe specifically how you could have behaved in a more confirming manner.

2. Skill Builder

Convert each of the following disconfirming messages into a confirming message. In your messages, use descriptive "I" language (pp. 139–140) and unequivocal terms (pp. 101–102). Invent details about the situation as necessary.

a. "I sure wish I had someone to help me with this project."
b. "Look . . . stop asking questions and just get it done."
c. "You may think you know how to handle the situation, but you really don't have enough experience. I'm the boss and I know when an assignment is over your head."
d. "What a tacky idea. A formal reception with paper plates! I can't believe you'd even suggest that."
e. "If you want to keep your job, you had better round up 10 new accounts by Monday."

3. Invitation to Insight

Familiarize yourself with effective praise by completing the following exercise:

a. Recall three situations in which someone has praised you. Using the guidelines on pp. 142–143, evaluate the praise you received. Was it specific? Sincere? How did the praise impact you?
b. Think of three co-workers or acquaintances you could praise sincerely. How could you deliver the praise effectively? For each, write a short statement or paragraph expressing your praise.

4. Skill Builder

Practice your ability to manage criticism constructively by creating a brief role play with a partner based on one of the scenarios below (or use any critical message you are likely to receive on the job).

A co-worker accuses you of trying to ingratiate yourself with (kiss up to) the boss.

A hard-to-please client snaps at you about not returning his phone calls in a timely manner.

You forgot to proofread the budget committee's minutes before you distributed them; you accidentally mistyped several of the budget figures and the boss is upset.

You walk through a co-worker's work area on the way to the drinking fountain. She barks, "Can't you give me some space to do my job?"

At a meeting, you present a proposal that angers one of your co-workers. He attacks you verbally, claiming that you don't have your facts right.

Your supervisor criticizes you for taking too long to finish a job.

Enact the role play three times as follows:

a. The sender of the message uses judgmental language and the receiver responds defensively.

b. The sender uses judgmental language. The receiver responds nondefensively, using the skills described on pages 148–149.
c. The sender delivers the criticism as constructive feedback, using the guidelines on pages 145–146. The receiver responds nondefensively.

Discuss the impact that each approach is likely to have (i) on the relational climate and (ii) on future interactions between these employees. Explain your answer by using the communication model in Chapter 1, pp. 8–10.

5. Invitation to Insight

Recall two conflicts you've been involved in recently.

a. For each, identify the primary source of conflict described on pages 150–151 (topic, process, relational, ego/identity). Do you think the other party(ies) would agree about the primary source of the conflict? Why or why not?
b. Next, identify any secondary sources of each conflict.
c. How did each dimension affect the way the participants approached the conflict?

6. Skill Builder

Describe an avoiding, accommodating, competing, collaborating, and compromising response to each of the following situations. Then decide which approach you would recommend. Because the meaning of a message varies with the context, you will need to decide on the specifics of the situation in order to make an informed choice. Explain your choice, using the information on pages 151–154.

a. At 4:30 P.M. a boss asks her assistant to work late to retype a 25-page report due the next morning. The assistant has already purchased nonrefundable tickets to attend a concert that evening.
b. The co-worker with whom you share a small cubicle habitually leaves papers, files, and books strewn all over her desk. The litter bugs you. Besides, you are concerned that it gives your clients a bad impression.
c. The assistant manager of a bookstore is faced with a customer demanding a refund for a book he claims was a gift. The book has several crumpled pages and a torn cover.
d. You are facilitator of a student group that is writing a research report worth half of your grade for the term. One group member misses two meetings without contacting you. When he returns, he explains that he had a family emergency and asks what he can do to make up the work.

7. Skill Builder

Sharpen your skill at knowing when and how to communicate assertively by following these steps:

a. Develop an assertive message for each of the following situations in your professional life:
   i. Making a request.
   ii. Describing a problem involving the recipient of your message.
   iii. Offering a suggestion.
b. Practice each message with a partner until you are confident that it is organized and delivered as effectively as possible. Recording your rehearsal can provide valuable feedback.
c. Now discuss with your partner the potential benefits and drawbacks of delivering each assertive message.

8. Skill Builder

In the following conflicts, identify the type(s) of conflict (topic, process, relational, ego/identity) and the ends desired by each party. For each situation, identify solutions (means to the end) that can satisfy the needs of everyone involved.

a. A landlord and tenant disagree about who should pay for an obviously necessary paint job for the office space.
b. Two co-workers contributed equally to developing a proposal for an important client. They both want to be the one who delivers the final proposal.
c. A sales manager and sales representatives disagree over the quota necessary to earn bonuses.
d. In a company with limited resources to spend on a new project, the marketing

manager wants more money to be spent on advertising, while the product development manager wants a greater budget for researching new product lines.

9. Skill Builder

With a partner, select one of the following situations. Plan how you would prepare for and conduct the negotiation, working through each step on pages 157–158. Provide details as necessary to explain the situation.

a. You want to ask for a raise.
b. You and your co-workers would like your boss to hire an additional worker so you can accomplish all the necessary work in a timely fashion, without burnout.
c. You want to rent office space for your small business at a rate that is 5 to 10 percent less than the advertised price.
d. You need an extra week to complete a long, complex assignment.

resources

In Print

Blanchard, Ken, and Margret McBride. *The One Minute Apology: A Powerful Way to Make Things Better*. New York: William Morrow, 2003.

The authors contend that it takes "common sense, wisdom, and strength" to ascertain and admit you've made a mistake. In a parable, the reader is presented with a sound method for dealing with mistakes.

Cloke, Kenneth, and J. Goldsmith. *Resolving Personal and Organizational Conflict: Stories of Transformation and Forgiveness*. San Francisco: Jossey-Bass, 2000.

Based on their mediation practice, the authors teach that listening closely to people's stories when they are in conflict is the first step to resolution. With rich examples from organizations and individuals, the authors demonstrate that listening to people tell their conflict stories and then creating a third story can move people from fear and hostility to understanding, forgiveness, and collaboration.

Covey, Stephen R. *The Seven Habits of Highly Successful People*. New York: Simon & Schuster, 1989.

In this classic book, Covey identifies the qualities of people who have led successful lives. "Habit 4: Think Win–Win" expands on the win–win approach to negotiating that we presented in this chapter and shows how it operates in a variety of contexts. Covey's description makes it clear that win–win problem solving and career success are compatible.

Crowe, Sandra A. *Since Strangling Isn't an Option: Dealing with Difficult People, Common Problems and Uncommon Solutions*. New York: Perigee, 1999.

The author divides her work into three parts: "Fundamentals of Understanding" addresses our perceptions of others' behaviors and our reactions to their behaviors. "Personality Types and Patterns of Behavior" discusses nine difficult personalities and stresses that you can only change how you perceive and respond, not how the other behaves. "Tools and Recipes" suggests ways to redirect difficult workplace conversations with difficult personalities.

Fisher, Roger, and Daniel Shapiro. *Beyond Reason: Using Emotions as You Negotiate*. New York: Viking, 2005.

The authors, from the Harvard Negotiation Project, contend that paying attention to the core issues that create the most emotion during negotiations—appreciation, affiliation, autonomy, status, and role—increases the chances of a win–win outcome. Taking these issues into consideration when preparing for negotiation is the key.

Fisher, Roger, and William Ury. *Getting to Yes: Negotiating Agreement without Giving In*. Boston: Houghton Mifflin, 1981.

In this readable, realistic introduction to what they call "principled negotiation," Fisher and Ury discuss communication skills that offer the prospect of accomplishing one's own goals in ways that preserve, or even improve, relationships with the other party.

Goleman, Daniel, and Cary Cherniss, eds. *The Emotionally Intelligent Workplace: How to Select for, Measure, and Improve Emotional Intelligence in Individuals, Groups, and Organizations.* San Francisco: Jossey-Bass, 2001.

Members of the Consortium for Research on Emotional Intelligence in Organizations contribute 15 models and 22 guidelines for assessing and promoting emotional intelligence in organizations. The book gives some basic definitions and information about emotional intelligence and has other parts that are quite scientific and analytical.

Lewicki, Roy J., David M. Saunders, and John M. Minton. *Essentials of Negotiation*, 2nd ed. New York: McGraw-Hill, 2000.

This book translates academic work on negotiation into practical terms. Separate chapters focus on cooperative and competitive approaches to negotiating. Also covered are strategies for finding and using leverage, ethics, and negotiating in a global economy.

Patterson, K., et al. *Crucial Confrontations: Tools for Resolving Broken Promises, Violated Expectations, and Bad Behavior.* New York: McGraw-Hill, 2005.

With experience and well-chosen examples, the authors demonstrate how to assess your own motives and needs, and to prepare for and conduct necessary confrontations while providing for the emotional safety for both parties.

Patterson, K., et al. *Crucial Conversations: Tools for Talking When the Stakes Are High.* New York: McGraw-Hill, 2002.

Based on years of experience with organizations, the authors lay out some steps to healthy dialogue and ways to make conversations safe even if you're angry or afraid of the conversation and even when others resort to "silence" or "violence."

Wilmot, W. W., and Joyce L. Hocker. *Interpersonal Conflict*, 7th ed. New York: McGraw-Hill, 2007.

This comprehensive and useful guide explains what researchers have learned about topics important to business communicators: styles and tactics, types of power, negotiation, and interventions by third parties.

On the Web

Principled Negotiation

The Center for the Study of Ethics in the Professions (**www.iit.edu/departments/csep/links.html**) lists extensive resources for ethics case studies in a variety of professions, ethics resource guides, and ethics organizations.

Interpersonal Competency

The Interpersonal Competency Scale provides a tool for assessing your motivation, knowledge, and skills in interpersonal communication. Subscales give you readings of your adaptability, involvement, conversation management, and empathy. Find this assessment instrument at **http://www.uamont.edu/facultyweb/roiger/write/competen.html**.

The Consortium for Research on Emotional Intelligence in Organizations (**www.eiconsortium.org**) presents a wealth of information on research, reports, best practices, and more.

For a guide to understanding defensive and supportive climates, go to **www.bsu.edu/classes/flint/climate.html**. Read the Appendix on Defensive and Supportive Communication Climates from Jack Gibb's writing, "Trust: A New Vision of Human Relationships for Business, Education, Family, and Personal Living."

Conflict and Conflict Management

The Gentle Art of Verbal Self-Defense (**http://adrr.com**) provides a method of using words to deal with conflict situations and these resources show you how. See an immense slate of mediation and conflict resolution organizations and resources at **www.uwec.edu/Sampsow/Links/Conflict.htm**.

Work 911 (**www.work911.com**) provides over 1,000 articles organized into categories of communication, anger management, work-related issues, and stress. Workplace Solutions (**www.wps.org**) is chock-full of resources and links to articles that deal with conflict resolution and reducing violence in the workplace.

The International Association for Conflict Management (**www.iacm-conflict.org**) brings scholars and practitioners together to study and develop conflict management skills in many settings. Find links to articles, research, and more organizations.

part three: strategic case

Platinum Sounds

Not bad for a 20-year-old, thinks Gina deSilva. I'm the youngest store manager in the history of Platinum Sounds. With this job it will take me a little longer to get my degree, but I won't have to take out student loans and I'll leave school with some real management experience. That should make me lots more employable after I graduate.

Gina knows this job won't be an easy one. As a start she begins a mental "to do" list of the people with whom she needs to interview.

- *Clarify Marty's expectations of me.* Now that I'm store manager, Marty (the regional manager) will be my boss. I don't know him very well, and I need to understand what he wants me to do. What are his priorities? What problems does he see with the store? What does he think of me? Better find out.
- *Hire assistant manager to replace me.* Interview Rashid and Samantha, the top candidates. Rashid is more experienced and sociable, but can I count on him to put the store first when it conflicts with his band? Samantha is very serious, but her in-your-face style rubs some clerks the wrong way. Can she learn to be a little less aggressive? Also, I need to be sure that whoever I hire is committed to staying with the job for at least a year.
- *Hire two new clerks.* We need to hire two new salesclerks really soon. What skills and attitudes are we looking for? How can I handle the interviews to be sure we get the best people?
- *Schedule performance reviews.* At Platinum Sounds, semiannual performance reviews are a requirement. They also help determine who gets salary increases. Most people view these reviews as a stressful chore. How can I take the stress out of these interviews and make them really work for the company and the clerks?
- *Figure how to cut employee turnover.* We've had to replace 7 of our 10 salespeople in the last year. I'm not sure why so many people have left. Training new staff takes a lot of time, and new people don't serve the customers too well until they have figured out our routine. I need to talk with the three old-time clerks who are still here and the new ones. Maybe I should also track down people who left the store and find out why they quit.
- *Do market research with customers.* I know sales have been off since Mega-Hits opened in the mall. I need to talk with our customers to find out how to keep them here. I also need to track down customers we've lost and find out how to get them back.
- *Become the best manager I can be.* I know I take things too seriously, and I'm weak on the financial side of the business. I need to find people who are good managers in retail stores like this one and see what they can tell me about how to do a good job here at Platinum Sounds.

As you read the chapters in this unit, consider the following questions:

1. Who are the people Gina needs to interview? For each person, identify the type of interview described in Chapter 7 that would be most appropriate.
2. What will be her goal for each type of interview?
3. What topics does she need to cover for each interview?
4. Within each topic area, what primary questions does she need to ask? What types of questions described in Chapter 6 will be most effective in meeting her goals?
5. How can she plan the opening and closing of each interview to help achieve her goals?

Principles of Interviewing

Chapter Objectives

After reading this chapter you should be able to

1 Prepare for each stage of an interview: opening, body, and closing.

2 Demonstrate knowledge of the uses and limitations of each type of interview question: open, closed, fact, opinion, primary, secondary, direct, indirect, hypothetical, and leading.

3 Describe and observe the ethical obligations of interviewers and interviewees.

Daniel and Cecilia are co-owners of a small bookstore. A large national chain has opened in a nearby mall and is drawing away business. The partners think adding a small café to their store could recapture customers. They decide to travel around the state, asking other independent booksellers with cafés how well their plans have worked.

Sharon, a marketing manager for a building-supplies manufacturer, is preparing for a trade convention. Although her firm produces more than a thousand products, she can show only a few at the convention. She calls the convention coordinator and asks questions that will help her plan the exhibit: Are the builders who attend the convention mostly concerned with large public buildings, mostly with private homes, or a combination of both? How large will her exhibit space be? Will electrical outlets be available, and can they handle large power demands?

Ravi has just been appointed as new manager of a restaurant that has dropped from the leading producer in the chain to the bottom of the list in just over a year. His job is to figure out where the problem lies and turn the situation around. He begins by talking with virtually every employee, from shift managers to dishwashers.

Susan had worked in the accounting department for 3 months when Lloyd, her supervisor, calls her into his office. "Is there a problem?" she asks nervously. "No, no," Lloyd replies. "I wanted to let you know we've been pleased with your performance and to find out how you feel about your work in the last 3 months. I'd also like to know more about how you see yourself in the company in the future."

Each of these conversations is an **interview,** a two-party conversation in which at least one person has a specific, serious purpose. This definition makes it clear that interviewing is a special kind of conversation, differing from other types in several ways. Most important, interviewing is always *purposeful*. Unlike more spontaneous conversations, an interview includes at least one participant who has a serious, predetermined reason for being there. Interviews are also more *structured* than most conversations. As you will soon learn, every good interview has several distinct phases and always involves some sort of question-and-answer format. Interviews also have an element of *control* not present in more casual interaction. The interviewer's job is to keep the conversation moving toward a predetermined goal. Interviews always involve *two parties*. While there may be several interviewers (as sometimes occurs in employment situations) or multiple respondents (as in a "meet the press" journalistic format), there are always two parties: interviewer and respondent. A final difference between interviewing and other conversation involves the *amount of speaking* by each party. While the speakers in most informal conversations speak equally, experts suggest that participation in most interviews (with the possible exception of sales and information-giving types) ought to be distributed in roughly a 70 to 30 percent ratio, with the interviewee doing most of the talking.[1]

Some people in business spend much of their time in interviews. For example, salespeople interview current and potential customers to assess their needs. Health care professionals, including nurses, doctors, dental hygienists, and emergency-room receptionists, interview patients to learn about their problems. Most managerial jobs also require some interviews. Many consultants recommend that managers practice "management by walking around" and regularly interview their subordinates about progress, problems, and concerns. In fact, communication authorities claim that interviews are the most common form of planned communication.[2]

There are many kinds of interviews. *Selection interviews* help organizations and prospective employees explore the fit between applicant and employer. *Performance appraisal interviews* review the performance of employees and help set targets for the future. *Disciplinary interviews* deal with misconduct or poor performance. *Survey interviews* gather information from a number of people. They are used to provide information from which to draw conclusions, make interpretations, and determine future action. Manufacturers and advertisers use them to assess market needs and learn consumer reactions to new products. Employers use them to gather employees' ideas about how space should be allotted in a new location or how much a new benefits program might be needed. *Diagnostic interviews* allow health care professionals, attorneys, counselors, and other business and professional workers to gather information that helps them to respond to the needs of their clientele. *Research interviews* provide information upon which to base future decisions. An entrepreneur who is thinking about opening a chain of restaurants might interview others with related experience when developing the concept and question people familiar with the target area to collect ideas about locations and clientele. On a more personal level, an employee thinking about a career change might interview several people who work in the field she is considering to seek advice about how to proceed. *Investigative interviews* gather information to determine the causes of an event, usually a problem. Finally, *exit interviews* help to determine why a person is leaving an organization.

Each type of interview calls for a special approach, and Chapter 7 will discuss several of them in detail. Despite the differences, all interviews share some common characteristics and communication strategies. This chapter will introduce the skills that you can use in virtually every interview you face in your career, either as interviewer or interviewee.

Planning the Interview

A successful interview begins before the parties face each other. Whether you are the interviewer or the respondent, background work can mean the difference between success and disappointment.

Define the Goal

Sometimes the purpose of an interview isn't as obvious as it seems at first. For instance, if you are a hotel manager and have received several complaints about the surly manner of a desk clerk, you would certainly speak to the employee. What would your purpose be?

An obvious answer would be to change the clerk's behavior, but this goal isn't precise enough. Will you reprimand the clerk, insisting on a change in behavior? Will you act as a counselor, trying to correct the problem by understanding the causes of the employee's rudeness? Or will you take the role of an explainer, teaching the clerk some new customer-relations skills? While the general goal of each approach is identical (changing the clerk's behavior), the precise goal influences your approach.

The same principle operates in other types of interviews. In a selling situation, is the goal to get a single order or to build a long-term relationship? Is your goal in a grievance interview to ask for specific changes or simply to have your past concerns acknowledged?

In any interview, you should make your goal as clear as possible, as in the following examples:

Vague: Improve clerk's behavior.

Better: Teach clerk how to handle registration problems.

Best: Teach clerk what to tell guests when rooms are not ready.

Vague: Turn prospect into a customer.

Better: Show customer features and benefits of my product.

Best: Identify prospect's needs and show how my product can satisfy them, resulting in trial order.

The interviewee should also have a clear purpose. Notice, for example, the interviewee's purposes in regard to grievance and employment interviews:

Vague: Complain about unfair supervisor.

Better: Protest unfair scheduling of assignments.

Best: Have supervisor develop fair method of scheduling future assignments.

Vague: Get job offer.

Better: Get job offer by demonstrating competence.

Best: Get job offer by describing work experience, referring to favorable references, and describing ideas for the position.

Identify and Analyze the Other Party

Whether you are the interviewer or the interviewee, your interviews will be more useful and successful if you select the right person to talk to whenever you have a choice. If you are looking for information, the person you select to interview may greatly influence the quality of the information you get. In sales, for example, identifying the appropriate interviewee—the person who makes purchasing decisions—is vital. Mark H. McCormack, owner of a sports promotion agency, describes the situation:

> *One of the biggest problems we have had as a sales organization is figuring out who within another company will be making a decision on what. Very often in our business we don't know if it's the advertising department, the marketing department, or someone in PR or corporate communications. It may very well turn out to be the chairman and CEO of a multibillion-dollar corporation if the subject is of personal interest to him.*[3]

Finding the right interviewee isn't only important in sales. For example, if you want to know more about the safety procedures in a manufacturing area, the plant manager or foreman can tell you more about them than, say, publicity staff—who probably get their information from the plant manager anyway. If you're preparing for a job interview, you'll want to know as much as possible about the person to whom you'll be talking.

As you decide who is ready, willing, and able to provide the information you need, consider several factors.

Knowledge Level As an interviewer, your questions should be tailored to the information the other person has. A sales representative who bombarded a prospective client with overly technical information would probably be making a mistake, as would a supervisor who sought managerial advice from an employee who has no experience in leading others. As an interviewee, the same principle applies: You need to figure out the knowledge level of the person asking you questions so your answers won't be too simplistic or complex.

The Other's Concept of Self The self-image of the other party can have a strong effect on what goes on in an interview. For example, if your boss is interviewing you about a project that isn't going well, consider whether she sees herself as a colleague who might be able to help you, an authority whose advice you should take, or an employee who will be in trouble if she has to defend a failure to her own superiors. Each attitude will call for a different approach on your part. If you're seeking career

Planning Your Dream Interview

Imagine that you could interview anyone you want regarding a business or professionally related topic. Describe to your group how you would approach this topic, addressing the following points:

1. Who would you interview? Why did you choose this person?
2. What would be your goal for the interview? (Be as specific as possible.)
3. What topics would you cover, and what questions would you ask in each topic area?
4. How would your self-analysis and analysis of the interviewee affect your approach?

advice from a potential mentor, that person's willingness (or unwillingness) to listen to your thoughts should dictate how much you take charge of the conversation, or how much you follow the veteran's lead.

Your Image Who you are isn't as important as who the other party *thinks* you are. In an employment interview, a knowledgeable applicant who *appears* uninformed is in trouble. In the same way, an employee may want to discuss constructively a problem with the boss, but if the boss thinks the subordinate only wants to complain, the employee's chances for success are limited.

Attitude You may find three sources of information useful for identifying the interviewee's attitudes. First, you can listen to *what other people say*. Co-workers, friends, and even the media can be sources for learning about the other person. "I'm going to ask for a raise," you might tell a friend with whom you work. "How do you think I should bring it up?" If you interview an executive about career opportunities, knowing your subject's career history or education might help you build rapport and ask useful questions.

If you have known the other person before the interview, *what that person has said* can be a good source of information. For instance, you may have once heard your boss comment favorably about an employee who really had facts and figures to back up what he said. If you are asking for a raise, this information could give you an important clue about how to present your arguments.

Finally, you can discover a great deal about the person you will interview by *observation*. If you have seen the other party dress casually, use informal language, or joke around, you might behave differently than if you had observed more straight-laced behavior. Does he or she seem to encourage drop-in visits or prefer prearranged appointments?

Even if you are meeting the person for the first time, you can still learn something from observation. One sales authority recommends:

> *Be observant. Many times there are clues all around the office that will give you ideas that may assist you in talking the prospect's language and, thus, making the sale. Look for trophies, pictures, books, decor, awards, and plaques. It's a safe bet that the prospect is very proud of anything that is on display in the office.*[4]

Prepare a List of Topics

Sometimes the topics an interview should cover will become clear as soon as you've listed your objectives. An insurance-claims investigator, for example, usually covers a standard agenda when collecting data on an accident: road conditions, positions of the vehicles, nature and extent of injuries, and so on. In other cases, however, some background research is necessary before you can be sure an agenda is complete. An office manager who is considering the purchase of new laptops might need to do some reading and talk with her staff before she can know which questions to ask the sales representatives who will be calling on her. She will probably want to learn about the topics listed below:

Objective: To purchase affordable wireless laptops that will be secure, reliable, and compatible with current equipment.

List of Topics:

Attitudes of the staff toward specific brands

Funds available.

The general price range of the products.

Whether vendors have fixed or negotiable prices and quantity discounts.

Interviewees, too, should have goals and agendas. A job seeker approaching an employment interview might have a program like this:

Objective: To have the interviewer see me as a bright, ambitious, articulate person who knows about and can serve the company's needs.

List of Topics:

Discuss my short-term and long-term career goals.

Answer all questions completely and in an organized way.

Share my knowledge of the company's products and financial condition.

Choose the Best Interview Structure

There are several types of interview structures. As Table 6–1 illustrates, each calls for different levels of planning and produces different results.

A **highly structured interview** consists of a standardized list of questions. In its most extreme form, it even specifies their precise wording and the order in which they are asked. Highly structured interviews are most common in market research, opinion polls, and attitude surveys. Most of the questions allow only a limited range

Table 6–1 Differences between Highly Structured and Nonstructured Interviews

Highly Structured Interview	Nonstructured Interview
Usually takes less time	Usually takes more time
Easier for interviewer to control	More difficult for interviewer to control
Provides quantifiable results	Results more difficult to quantify
Requires less skill by interviewer	Requires high degree of interviewer skill
Low flexibility in exploring responses	High flexibility in exploring responses

of answers: "How many televisions do you own?" "Which of the following words best describes your evaluation of the company?" The answers to closed questions such as these are easy to tabulate, which makes this approach convenient for surveying large numbers of respondents. Because of their detailed structure, highly structured interviews call for less skill by the questioner.

Highly structured interviews have drawbacks, however, that make them unsuitable for many situations. The range of topics is limited by a predetermined list of questions, and there is no chance for the interviewer to follow up intriguing or unclear answers that might arise during the conversation.

The **nonstructured interview** stands in contrast to its highly structured counterpart. It might consist of a topical agenda without specific questions or it might consist of just a few key questions and the interviewer builds on the answers given. Many managers make a point of regularly dropping in on their employees. The conversation may be generally directed at finding out how the employees are doing with their work, whether they are satisfied with their jobs, whether they have any problems—personal or work-related—that the manager should know about, but there are no specific, planned questions. Nonstructured interviews allow considerable flexibility about the amount of time and nature of the questioning in the various content areas. They permit the conversation to flow in whatever direction seems most productive.

Nonstructured interviewing looks easy when it's done with skill, but it's actually very difficult. It's easy to lose track of time or to focus too much on one topic and neglect others. When you're worried about what to ask next, you may forget to listen closely to the interviewee's answer and may miss clues to ask for more information.

The **moderately structured interview** combines features of the other types. The interviewer prepares a list of topics to be covered, anticipates their probable order, and lists several major questions and possible follow-up probes. These make up a flexible plan, which the interviewer can use or adapt as circumstances warrant. The planned questions ensure coverage of important areas, while allowing for examination of important but unforeseen topics.

"Next question: I believe that life is a constant striving for balance, requiring frequent tradeoffs between morality and necessity, within a cyclic pattern of joy and sadness, forging a trail of bittersweet memories until one slips, inevitably, into the jaws of death. Agree or disagree?"

Consider Possible Questions

After clarifying your purpose, setting an agenda, and deciding on a format, you are ready to think about specific questions. As you might expect, the type and quality of questions are the biggest factor in determining the success or failure of an interview.

The proper questions to ask might seem to be obvious once an agenda is finished, but this is not always the case. An interviewer should consider several types of questions when planning an interview.

Table 6–2 Advantages of Open and Closed Questions

When to Use Open Questions	When to Use Closed Questions
1. To relax the interviewee (if the question is easy to answer and nonthreatening)	1. To maintain control over the conversation
2. To discover the interviewee's opinions	2. When specific information is needed and you are not interested in the interviewee's feelings or opinions
3. To evaluate the interviewee's communication skills	3. When time is short
4. To explore the interviewee's possession of information	4. When the interviewer is not highly skilled
5. To discover the interviewee's feelings or values	5. When a high degree of standardization between interviews is important

Source: Gerald L. Wilson and H. Lloyd Goodall, Jr., *Interviewing in Context* (New York: McGraw-Hill, 1991), pp. 75–80.

Open and Closed Questions **Closed questions** restrict the interviewee's response. Closed questions form the backbone of most highly structured interviews, but they also have their place in moderately structured and nonstructured ones, too. Some ask the respondent to choose from a range of answers: "Which of the three shifts would you prefer to work on?" "Do you think Mary, Dave, or Leonard would be best for the job?" "Would you rather stay in this department or have a transfer?" Other closed questions ask for specific data: "How long have you worked here?" "When do you think the order will be ready?"

Open questions invite a broader, more detailed range of responses. Some questions are more open than others. Consider the difference between a wide-open one such as "What do you think is going on here?" and a more focused, but still open query like "What would you do if you were in my position?" or "What makes you interested in working for this company?" As Table 6–2 shows, both open and closed questions have their advantages.

As an interviewee, you may sometimes want to turn a closed question into an open one so that you can share more information:

Question: Do you have any experience as a manager?

Answer: Not on the job, but I've studied management in several college courses, and I'm looking forward to developing the skills I learned there. I'm especially excited about using the situational leadership approach I learned in my business communication course. I understand you've sent several of your people to workshops on the subject.

Factual and Opinion Questions **Factual questions** investigate matters of fact: "Have you taken any courses in accounting?" "Are you willing to relocate if we have an opening in another city?" "Can we apply lease payments to the purchase price, if we decide to buy?" **Opinion questions,** as their name implies, ask for the respondent's judgments: "Which vendor do you think gives the best service?" "Do you think Al is being sincere?" "Is the investment worth it?"

Whether you approach a topic seeking facts or opinions can greatly influence the results. A manager trying to resolve a dispute between two employees could approach each one subjectively, asking, "What's the source of this problem?" This is a broad opinion-seeking question that invites disagreement between the disputants. A more factual question would be "Tell me when you first noticed the problem, and describe what happened."

This doesn't mean that it is always better to ask factual questions. Opinions are often precisely what you are seeking. A client seeking financial advice from an investment counselor would be making a mistake by asking "How have energy stocks done in the past?" when the real question is "How do you expect they'll do in the future?" Your decision about whether to seek facts or opinions has to be based on your reason for asking the question.

Primary and Secondary Questions **Primary questions** introduce new topics or areas within topics: "How did you hear about our company?" "Do you have any questions for me?" "How often do you use the transit system?" **Secondary questions** aim at gathering additional information about a topic that has already been introduced: "Tell me more about it." "What do you mean by 'commitment'?" "Does that price include shipping costs?"

Secondary questions are useful in several circumstances:

- When a previous answer is *incomplete:* "What did Marilyn say then?"
- When a previous answer is *superficial* or *vague:* "What do you mean, you *think* the figures are right?"
- When a previous answer is *irrelevant:* "I understand that the job interests you. Can you tell me about your training in the field?"
- When a previous answer seems *inaccurate:* "You said everyone supports the idea. What about Herb?"

Direct and Indirect Questions The best way to get information is usually to ask **direct questions:** "What area of our business interests you most?" "I hear you've been unhappy with our service. What's the problem?"

Sometimes, however, a straightforward approach won't work. One such case occurs when the respondent isn't *able* to answer a direct question accurately. This inability may come from a lack of information, as when a supervisor's "Do you understand?" gets a "yes" from employees who mistakenly believe that they do. In another case, a respondent may not be *willing* to give a direct answer that would be risky or embarrassing. A boss who asks a subordinate "Are you satisfied with my leadership?" isn't likely to get a straight answer if the employee thinks the boss is incompetent or unfair. In these instances, an indirect approach would be better. **Indirect questions** elicit information without directly asking for it, as the following comparisons show:

Direct Question	Indirect Question
Do you understand?	Suppose you had to explain this policy to other people in the department. What would you say?
Are you satisfied with my leadership?	If you were manager of this department, what changes would you make?

Sometimes even the most skillful indirect questions won't generate a good response. But there is another indirect way of judging a response—the interviewee's nonverbal behavior. Facial expressions, posture, gestures, eye contact, and other nonverbal behaviors offer clues about another person's emotional state. Here is a description of how one attorney uses people's nonverbal behaviors as a guide when selecting members of a jury:

> *To gauge nonverbal clues, Fahringer may ask the potential juror, "Mr. Jones, I'm going to ask you to do me a favor. Will you look at my client, Billy Williams, right now, and tell me whether you can think of him as being innocent." At that instant, Fahringer concentrates on the juror's face. "If he has difficulty looking at my client, or, when he glances at him, drops his eyes, rejecting him, he has told me all that I need to know."*[5]

The same technique can work in the business world. For example, a manager who thinks an employee may be afraid to admit problems with a project can watch for clues by observing how the employee reacts nonverbally to a question such as "Is everything still on schedule for the September 15 opening?"

Hypothetical and Critical Incident Questions **Hypothetical questions** seek the respondent's answer to a what-if question. They can be a useful way of indirectly getting a respondent to describe beliefs or attitudes: "If we were to take a poll about the morale level around here, what do you think the results would be?"

Hypothetical questions are also a useful way of learning how people would respond in certain situations. A bank manager might test candidates for promotion by asking, "Suppose you became assistant operations manager and you had to talk to one of the tellers about her manner toward customers. What would you do if she accused you of acting bossy and forgetting your friends since your promotion?" Again, there is no guarantee that hypothetical answers will reflect a person's real behavior, but their specificity and realism can give strong clues.

Finally, hypothetical questions can be a useful way to get advice that will help you make a personal decision. For example, if your physician presents you with two options for treatment, you might ask, "Which one would you choose if you were me?" If you're talking to a trusted friend about whether to take a new job, you could ask, "What would you do?"

Critical incident questions ask the interviewee about a specific account of a real situation rather than a hypothetical one and are generally more reliable than hypothetical questions.[6] For example, a CEO may ask a "future" executive hopeful: "Think of a time when you felt you needed to break an implicit company policy in order to achieve the larger company vision. Describe the situation and how you handled it."

Leading Questions **Leading questions** force or tempt the respondent to answer in one way. They frequently suggest the answer the interviewer expects: "How committed are you to our company's philosophy of customer service?" "You aren't really serious about asking for a raise now, are you?"

Some questions are highly leading. Using emotionally charged words and name-calling, they indicate the only acceptable answer: "You haven't fallen for those worn-out arguments, have you?" Other highly loaded questions rely on a bandwagon effect for pressure: "Do you agree with everyone else that it's best to put this incident behind us and forget the whole thing?"

Conducting Telephone Interviews

Telephone interviews are often used in market research and other types of surveying to gather information when large numbers of people must be approached. They can also be essential when distance and time make a face-to-face conversation impossible. When you must conduct a telephone interview, consider these tips:

1. If possible, arrange the session in advance to be sure you have the undivided attention of the interviewee. If you must conduct an unplanned interview, ask the subject whether this is a good time for your conversation. It may be better to reschedule than to deal with a distracted interviewee.
2. Plan on a shorter interview than you might have if you were in a face-to-face setting. A 15- or 20-minute phone conversation feels much longer than the same encounter would in person.
3. Take advantage of the ability to use notes, which are less likely to distract you or the interviewee than in face-to-face settings. Be cautious about asking to tape-record an interview if there is any chance that doing so will inhibit the interviewee.
4. When interviewees must respond to visual information such as text or graphs, make sure they have received them in advance of the discussion. For example, consider mailing or faxing documents to the interviewee far enough in advance so he or she can examine them before your conversation.
5. Since you won't be able to observe the interviewee's nonverbal behavior, pay special attention to cues about his or her feelings and attitudes by listening to vocal cues such as tone, rate, and pitch.

Other leading questions signal the interviewer's position without being so intimidating: "Don't you think that idea is a little expensive?" In cases like this, you can consider the question as a chance to make the best argument to support your position: "Sure, it looks expensive at first, but in the long run this approach will save us money."[7]

A single question often falls into several categories. For instance, the question "Describe some experiences that demonstrate your leadership abilities" is open, direct, factual, and primary. A question could also be closed, hypothetical, and secondary: "You said you welcome challenges. If the chance arose, would you be interested in handling the next round of layoffs?"

Arrange the Setting

A manager at a major publishing company regularly interviews subordinates over lunch at a restaurant where company employees frequently eat together. The manager explains:

> *The advantage of meeting here is we're both relaxed. They can talk about their work without feeling as though they've been called on the carpet to defend themselves. They're also more inclined to ask for help with a problem than if we were in the office, and I can ask for improvements and make suggestions without making it seem like a formal reprimand. We also have time to talk without people dropping in or the phone ringing. Of course, if I'm not happy with the person, or if I'm about to fire them, I certainly wouldn't do it over lunch. If that happened, or if they had a serious, confidential problem to discuss, I'd take them in my office, close the door, and have my secretary hold all calls.*

The physical setting in which an interview occurs can have a great deal of influence on the results. With some planning of time and place, you can avoid the frustrations of trying to discuss a confidential matter with a co-worker within earshot of people who would love to overhear your conversation or of trying to stop your boss in the hall to ask for a raise when she's on her way to a meeting and the easiest way to get free of you is to say no.

Time When you plan an interview, give careful thought to how much time you will need to accomplish your purpose and let the other person know how much time you expect to take. If you ask a co-worker in another department to spend half an hour with you to answer some questions about a mutual project, he can schedule his time so that you won't have to cut the session short or try to cram an important discussion into 15 minutes.

Other things to consider are the time of day and what the people involved have to do before and after the interview. For example, if you know your boss has an important meeting this afternoon, you can reasonably assume she will be too preoccupied or too busy to talk to you right before it and perhaps immediately afterward. You may also want to avoid scheduling an important interview right before lunch so that neither person will be more anxious to eat than to accomplish the goal of the interview.

Place The right place is just as important as the right time. The first consideration here is to arrange a setting that is free of distractions. The request "Hold all my calls" is a good sign that you will have the attention of your interviewing partner. Sometimes it's best to choose a spot away from the normal habitat of either person. Not only does this lessen the chance of interruptions, but people often also speak more freely and think more creatively when they are in a neutral space, away from familiar settings that trigger habitual ways of responding.

The physical arrangement of the setting can also influence the interview. Generally, the person sitting behind a desk—whether interviewee or respondent—gains power and formality. On the other hand, a seating arrangement in which the parties face each other across a table or sit with no barrier between them promotes equality and informality. Distance, too, affects the relationship between interviewer and respondent. Other things being equal, two people seated 40 inches apart will have more immediacy in their conversation than will the same people discussing the same subject at a distance of 6 or 7 feet.

Isn't it usually desirable to create a casual atmosphere in an interview? As with other variables, the choice of closeness or distance depends on your goal. A supervisor who wants to assert his authority during a reprimand session might choose to increase distance and sit behind a desk. On the other hand, a sales representative who wants to gain the trust of a customer would probably avoid the barrier of a desk.

Conducting the Interview

After careful planning, the interview itself takes place. An interview consists of three stages: an opening (or introduction), a body, and a closing. We will now examine each one in detail.

Opening

A good introduction can shape the entire interview. Research suggests that people form lasting impressions of one another in the first few minutes of a conversation. Dave Deaver, a national management recruiter, describes the importance of first impressions in a job interview this way: "The first minute is all-important in an interview. Fifty percent of the decision is made within the first 30 to 60 seconds. About 25 percent of the evaluation is made during the first 15 minutes. It's very difficult to recover the last 25 percent if you've blown the first couple of minutes."[8] These initial impressions shape how a listener regards everything that follows.

A good introduction ought to contain two parts: a greeting and an orientation. The opening is also a time for motivating the interviewee to cooperate and giving a sense of what will follow.

Greeting and Building Rapport The interviewer should begin with a greeting and a self-introduction, if necessary. In formal situations—taking a legal deposition or conducting a highly structured survey, for example—it is appropriate to get right down to business. But in many situations, building rapport is both appropriate and useful. If the interviewer and interviewee are comfortable with one another, the results are likely to be better for both. This explains why a few minutes of informal conversation are often part of the opening of an interview. This small talk tends to set the emotional tone of the interview—whether it is formal or informal, nervous or relaxed, candid or guarded.

The most logical openers involve common ground: shared interests or experiences. "How are you coping with our record snowfall?" "Did you find your way around the airport construction?" Another type of common ground involves job-related topics, though usually unrelated to the subject of the interview itself. A manager interviewing employees to help design a new benefits package might start the conversation by asking, "How's the new parking plan we proposed last month working out?" Conversation in this rapport-building stage should be sincere. A phony-sounding compliment ("Are those pictures of your family? They certainly are attractive!") is likely to create the opposite reaction from what you want. On the other hand, you should be able to come up with genuine remarks: "What a great view!" "I'm really excited to be here!"

Orientation In this stage of the opening, the interviewer gives the respondent a brief overview of what is to follow. This orientation helps put the interviewee at ease by removing a natural apprehension of the unknown. At the same time, it helps establish and strengthen the interviewer's control, since it is the interviewer who is clearly setting the agenda. In the orientation, be sure to do the following things.

Explain the reason for the interview A description of the interview's purpose can both put the interviewee at ease and motivate him or her to respond. If your boss called you in for a "chat" about "how things are going," curiosity would probably be your mildest response. Are you headed for a promotion? Are you being softened up for a layoff? Did somebody complain about you? Sharing the reason for an interview can relieve these concerns: "As you know, we're thinking about opening a branch office soon, and we're trying to plan our staffing. I'd like to find out how you feel about your working situation now and what you want so we can consider your needs when we make the changes."

Explain what information is needed and how it will be used A respondent who knows what the interviewer wants will have a greater likelihood of supplying it. In our example, the boss might be seeking two kinds of information. In one case, a statement of needed information might be "I'm not interested in having you name names of people you like or dislike. I want to know what parts of the business interest you and what you'd consider to be an ideal job." A quite different request for information might be "I'd like to hear your feelings about the people you work with. Who would you like to work with in the future, and who do you have trouble with?"

A description of how the information will be used is also important. In our current example, the boss might explain, "I won't be able to tell you today exactly what changes we'll be making, but I promise you we'll do the best we can to give you what you want." In many situations, it's important to define the confidentiality of the information you are seeking: "I promise you that this talk will be off the record. Nobody else will hear what you tell me."

Clarify any ground rules Make sure that you and the other party understand any operating procedures. For example, you might say, "I'd like to tape our conversation instead of taking notes." An interviewer might say, "I'd like to spend the first part of our conversation going through the list of questions I've prepared. Then we can spend the rest of our time covering any questions or thoughts you might have."

Mention the approximate length of the interview An interviewee who knows how long the session will last will feel more comfortable and give better answers.

Motivation In some situations, such as a job interview, both people feel the interview is important to them personally. Sometimes, however, you need to give interviewees a reason that will make them feel the interview is worthwhile for them. In some cases, you can simply point out the payoffs: "If we can figure out a better way to handle these orders, it will save us both time." "We'd like to know what you'd like in the new office building so we can try to make everyone as comfortable as possible." If the interview won't directly benefit the other person, you might appeal to his or her ego or desire to help other people: "I'd like to try out a new promotional item, and you know more about them than anyone." "Although you're leaving the company, perhaps you can tell us something that will make it a better place for other people to work."

Body

It is here that the questions and answers are exchanged. While a smooth interview might look spontaneous to an outsider, you have already learned the importance of preparation.

It's unlikely that an interview will ever follow your exact expectations, and it would be a mistake to force it to do so. As an interviewer, you will think of important questions—both primary and secondary—during the session. As a respondent, you will probably be surprised by some of the things the interviewer asks. The best way to proceed is to prepare for the general areas you expect will be covered and do your best when unexpected issues come up.

Responsibilities of the Interviewer The interviewer performs several tasks during the question-and-answer phase of the discussion.

Control and focus the conversation If an interview is a conversation with a purpose, it is the interviewer's job to make sure that the discussion focuses on achieving the purpose and doesn't drift away from the agenda. A response can be so interesting that it pulls the discussion off track: "I see you traveled in Europe after college. Did you make it to Barcelona?" Such discussion about backgrounds might be appropriate for the rapport-building part of the opening, but it can get out of control and use up time that would better be spent achieving the interview's purpose.

A second loss of control occurs when the interviewer spends too much time in one legitimate area of discussion, thereby slighting another. Difficult as it may be, an interviewer needs to allot rough blocks of time to each agenda item and then to follow these guidelines during the interview.

Listen actively Some interviewers—especially novices—become so caught up in budgeting time and planning upcoming questions that they fail to hear what the respondent is saying. Multitasking can present problems. It can be hard to juggle the tasks of asking and answering questions, taking notes, keeping eye contact, and budgeting time. With all these challenges, you can forget the most important task: To listen carefully and thoughtfully to what the other person is saying.

Use secondary questions to probe for important information Sometimes an answer may be incomplete. At other times, it may be evasive or vague. Since it is impossible to know in advance when probes will be needed, the interviewer should be ready to use them as the occasion dictates.

An interviewer sometimes needs to *repeat* a question before getting a satisfactory answer:

Interviewer: Your résumé shows you attended Arizona State for 4 years. I'm not clear about whether you earned a degree.

Respondent: I completed all the required courses in my major field of study, as well as several electives.

Interviewer: I see. Did you earn a degree?

When a primary question doesn't deliver enough information, the interviewer needs to seek *elaboration:*

Interviewer: When we made this appointment, you said Bob has been insulting you. I'd like to hear about that.

Respondent: He treats me like a child. I've been here almost as long as he has and I know what I'm doing!

Interviewer: Exactly what does he do? Can you give me a few examples?

Sometimes an answer will be complete but unclear. This requires a request for *clarification:*

Respondent: The certificate pays 6.3 percent interest.

Interviewer: Is that rate simple or compounded?

A *paraphrasing* probe restates the answer in different words. It invites the respondent to clarify and elaborate upon a previous answer:

Interviewer: You've been with us for a year now and already have been promoted once. How do you feel about the direction your career is taking?

Respondent: I'm satisfied for now.

Interviewer: So far, so good. Is that how you feel?

Respondent: Not exactly. I was happy to get the promotion, of course. But I don't see many chances for advancement from here.

Often *silence* is the best probe. A pause of up to 10 seconds (which feels like an eternity) lets the respondent know more information is expected. Depending on the interviewer's accompanying nonverbal messages, silence can indicate interest or dissatisfaction with the previous answer. *Prods* ("Uh-huh," "Hmmmm," "Go on," "Tell me more," and so on) accomplish the same purpose. For example:

Respondent: I can't figure out where we can cut costs.

Interviewer: Uh-huh.

Respondent: We've already cut our travel and entertainment budget 5 percent.

Interviewer: I know.

Respondent: Some of our people probably still abuse it, but they'd be offended if we cut back more. They think of expense accounts as a fringe benefit.

Interviewer: (silence)

Respondent: Of course, if we could give them something in return for a cut, we might still be able to cut total costs. Maybe have the sales meeting at a resort—make it something of a vacation.

The Interviewee's Role The interviewee can do several things to help make the interview a success.

Listen actively Careful listening can assure that you understand the questions asked, so you do not go off on tangents or give answers unrelated to what is asked. Connecting your answers to what the interviewer has previously said shows both listening and critical thinking skills.

Give clear, detailed answers A piece of obvious advice interviewees often ignore is to answer the question the interviewer has asked. An off-the-track answer suggests that the respondent hasn't understood the question, is a poor listener, or might even be evading the question. Put yourself in the interviewer's position, and think about what kind of information you would like to have. Then supply it.

Correct any misunderstandings Being human, interviewers sometimes misinterpret comments. Most interviews are important enough for the respondent to want to be sure that the message given has been received accurately. Obviously, you can't ask the interviewer "Were you listening carefully?" but two strategies can help get your message across. First, you can orally restate your message. This can be done either in the body or conclusion phase of the interview. For instance, in the body phase, while reporting on a list of exhibit preparations, the interviewee might mention that the brochures will have to be hand-carried; the following exchange could come later in the body phase or at the conclusion:

Interviewer: So, everything will be at the exhibit booth when we get to the convention, and all we have to do is set up the exhibit.

Interviewee: Not quite. The brochures won't be ready in time to ship to the convention, so you'll have to carry them with you on the plane.

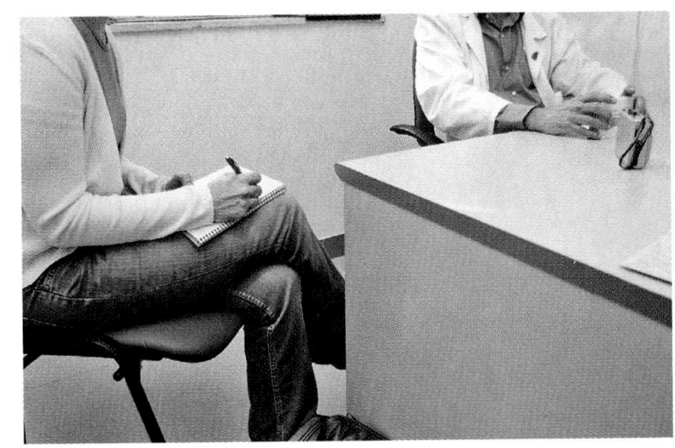

Second, you can *put your ideas in writing*. It is sometimes wise to summarize important ideas in a memo that can be delivered before, during, or after the session. This enables the recipient to have a permanent record of your message.

Cover your own agenda Interviewees often have their own goals. In a selection interview, the employer's goal is to pick the best candidate, while the applicant's aim is to prove that his or her qualifications make him or her the best. This may

Self-Assessment **Rating Your Interview Skills**

Rate your skills in interview basics using the following scale:

1 = Not at all competent
2 = Somewhat comfortable
3 = Moderately competent
4 = Usually comfortable and competent
5 = Very comfortable and capable

1 2 3 4 5 1. I am able to greet the other person and introduce myself with sincere enthusiasm.

1 2 3 4 5 2. I am able to build rapport by establishing common ground and other ice-breaking conversation.

1 2 3 4 5 3. I am able to clarify the reason for the interview, the information that will be covered, and the estimated length of the interview.

4. *As an interviewer I understand how to (or I can)*

1 2 3 4 5 a. Control and focus the conversation.

1 2 3 4 5 b. Listen actively.

1 2 3 4 5 c. Use secondary questions, paraphrases, prods, and silence to gain elaboration and/or clarification.

5. *As an interviewee I understand how to*

1 2 3 4 5 a. Listen attentively to questions.

1 2 3 4 5 b. Give clear, detailed answers to the questions asked without getting sidetracked.

1 2 3 4 5 c. Correct any misunderstandings about me or my answers that the interviewer appears to have.

1 2 3 4 5 d. Cover my own agenda in addition to the interviewer's agenda.

1 2 3 4 5 6. Review and clarify the results of the interview and establish future actions

1 2 3 4 5 7. Conclude with pleasantries.

The closer to 60 your score is, the more competent and comfortable you see yourself with interviewing basics.

involve redefining the concept of best. For instance, a relatively inexperienced candidate might have the goal of showing the employer that experience isn't as important as education, enthusiasm, or social skills.

Closing

An interview shouldn't end with the last answer to the last question. As with most other types of communication, certain functions need to be performed to bring the interview to a satisfactory conclusion.

Review and Clarify the Results of the Interview Either party can take responsibility for this step, though in different ways. The person with the greater power (usually the interviewer) is most likely to do so in the most forthright manner. For example, in an interview exploring a grievance between employees, a manager might say, "It sounds like you're saying that both of you could have handled it better." When the party with less power (usually the interviewee) does the reviewing and clarifying, the summary often takes the form of a question. A sales representative might close by saying, "So the product sounds good to you, but before you make your final decision you'd like to talk to a few of our clients to see how it has worked out for them. Is that right?"

Establish Future Actions When the relationship between interviewer and respondent is a continuing one, it is important to clarify how the matter under discussion will be handled. A sales representative might close by saying, "I'll put a list of our customers in the mail to you tomorrow. Then why don't I give you a call next week to see what you're thinking?" A manager might clarify the future by saying, "I'd like you to try out the arrangement we discussed today. Then let's all get together in a few weeks to see how things are going. How does the first of next month sound?"

Conclude with Pleasantries A sociable conclusion needn't be phony. You can express appreciation or concern, or you can mention future interaction:

"Your ideas were terrific. I know I can use them."

"I appreciate the time you've given me today."

"Good luck with the project."

The Ethics of Interviewing

The exchange of information that goes on between interviewer and interviewee should be guided by some basic ethical guidelines and responsibilities.[9] In addition to the moral reasons for following these guidelines, there is often a pragmatic basis for behaving ethically. Since the interview is likely to be part of an ongoing relationship, behaving responsibly and honorably will serve you well in future interactions. Conversely, the costs of developing a poor reputation are usually greater than the benefits of gaining a temporary advantage by behaving unethically or irresponsibly.

Obligations of the Interviewer

A conscientious business communicator will follow several guidelines when conducting an interview.

Make Only Promises You Are Willing and Able to Keep Don't make offers or claims that may later prove impossible to honor. For example, an employer should not encourage a job applicant about the chances of receiving an offer until he is sure an offer will be forthcoming. To make this sort of promise and then be overruled later by the boss or find out that the budget doesn't permit hiring at this time would be both dishonest and unfair. Likewise, a candidate should not indicate a willingness to start work immediately if she cannot begin work until she has sold her home and moved to the town where her new job is

ethical challenge

Handling Difficult Questions

1. You know that an employee has been leaving work early for the past several months. You hope he will volunteer this information, without your having to confront him. During a performance appraisal, how can you raise the issue with this employee?
2. You are conducting a series of half-hour interviews with consumers, exploring their attitudes toward a variety of social issues, as part of a market research project for your employer. In the first few minutes of one session, the interviewee makes several racist comments. How do you respond?
3. You are interviewing for a job you really want. The employer asks about your experience with a particular type of database software. You don't know much about this type of program, but you are confident that you can teach yourself before the job begins. How do you reply to the interviewer?

located. Despite the temptations, avoid making any commitments that sound good but are not firm.

Keep Confidences Interviewers should not reveal confidential information to interviewees, nor should they disclose any private information gained during a session to people who have no legitimate reason to have it. For example, a supervisor who learns about an employee's personal problems should reveal them only with the employee's permission. Likewise, employees who learn confidential information in the course of their jobs—income levels, company plans, and so on—are obliged to make sure that such information stays private.

Allow the Interviewee to Make Free Responses An interview that coerces the subject into giving unwilling answers is a charade of an honest conversation. For example, a supervisor conducting a performance appraisal who asks a subordinate "Who do you think is responsible for the problems in your area?" should be willing to accept whatever answer is given and not automatically expect the employee to accept the blame. Trying to *persuade* an interviewee is a normal part of doing business, but coercing one is not ethical.

Treat Every Interviewee with Respect With rare exceptions, the interviewer's job is to help the interviewee do well. This means making sure that the interviewee feels comfortable and understands the nature of the session. It also means the interviewer must design questions that are clear and must help the interviewee answer them as well as possible.

Obligations of the Interviewee

The interviewee is also obliged to behave in an ethical and responsible way during a session. Several guidelines apply here.

Don't Misrepresent the Facts or Your Position Whether the setting is an employment interview, a performance review session, or an information-gathering survey, it can be tempting to tell interviewers what they want to hear. The temptation is especially great if your welfare is at stake. But besides being unethical, misrepresenting the facts is likely to catch up with you sooner or later and harm you more than telling the truth in the first place would have.

Don't Waste the Interviewer's Time If the choice exists, be sure you are qualified for the interview. For example, it would be a mistake to apply for a job you have little chance of landing or to volunteer for a customer survey if you aren't a member of the population being studied. If preparation for the interview is necessary, be sure to do your homework. Once the interview has begun, be sure to stick to the subject to use the time most wisely.

Sample Interview Plan

The following plan shows the kind of work that should go on before an interviewer and interviewee sit down to or even schedule a meeting. Every important interview requires the kind of planning exhibited here to achieve its goals. As you read this account, notice that it follows the advice outlined in this chapter.

Analysis and research

I know that I'll never build the kind of financial security I am seeking by relying only on the income I earn from my job. Investing successfully will be the path to financial success. I also know that I'm very unsophisticated when it comes to investing, so I want to get a financial advisor who can teach me about the world of finance and who can help me set up and follow a plan.

Picking a financial advisor is like choosing a doctor. Skill is important, but it's not the only thing that matters. I need to find someone who has a personal style that I'm comfortable with and whose philosophy matches mine. I also need to find someone who is willing to devote time to me even though I don't have a great deal of money to invest . . . yet!

I've compiled a list of possible advisors from friends, newspaper articles, and listings in the phone directory. I will call several of the people on this list to set up appointments for interviews.

Goal

Based on my needs, the goal for my interviews will be to identify a financial planner with expertise in the field, whose investment philosophy matches mine, and who has a personal style that I am comfortable with.

Interview strategy

I definitely want to conduct these interviews in the offices of each financial planner. Seeing where and how they do business will probably give me a good idea of my comfort level before asking any questions. For instance, seeing a shabby or disorganized office would cause me to doubt the competence of an advisor. On the other hand, a very plush office might make me wonder if I was being charged too much just to support a lavish lifestyle.

I'll also be interested in seeing how much time each person gives me for the interview. If the person is rushed when trying to get a new client, this could mean I won't get the time or attention I need once my money is in the planner's hands.

It will be interesting to see how much each person lets me explain my concerns and how much each controls the conversation. I'm no financial expert, but I don't like the attitude "I'm the expert, so don't waste time asking too many questions." Since I would like someone who is willing to explain investing to me in a way that I can understand, I'll be looking for a good teacher.

Topics and questions *As my goal suggests, I want to explore three topics. The following list shows the questions I'm planning to ask in each topic area as well as follow-up questions I can anticipate asking. I'm sure there will be a need for other secondary questions, but I can't predict all of them. I'll have to think of them on the spot.*

TOPIC A: Expertise in Investments and Financial Planning

[This series of open questions explores the interviewee's qualifications and also provides an opportunity for her to talk about herself.]

1. What credentials do you have that qualify you as a financial planner? How important are credentials? If they aren't important, what is the best measure of a financial planner's qualifications?

[These questions move from a narrow to broader focus.]

2. Do you have any areas of specialization? How and why did you specialize in this area?

[These indirect questions are a way of finding out whether the advisor's performance has been satisfactory.]

3. How many clients have you served in the last 5 years? What is the length of the relationship with your clients? How many have you retained, and how many are no longer with you?

[The average portfolio size is one measure of the advisor's expertise.]

4. What's the average amount of money you have managed for your clients?

[A closed question, designed to give interviewer references.]

5. May I see a list of your past and current clients and call some of them for references?

[The first question is a broad, open one. The second, closed question will produce a specific answer that can be compared with those of other potential advisors.]

6. How would you describe your track record in terms of investment advice? Specifically, what has been the ratio of successful to unsuccessful advice?

TOPIC B: Investment Philosophy

[This broad, open question gives the advisor a chance to describe his or her approach.]

1. How would you describe your investment philosophy?

[This hypothetical question will provide specific information about how a client–advisor relationship might operate.]

2. If I became your client, what steps would you recommend to start and maintain a financial program?

[This sequence of questions moves from specific to broad topics in a logical order.]

3. What kind of products do you like to deal in? Which specific ones might you recommend for me? Why?

[This two-question sequence again moves from a narrow to broader focus. The most important information for the client is contained in the second question.]

4. I've read that some financial advisors make their income from commissions earned when their clients buy and sell investments. Other advisors charge a fee for their time. What approach do you take? Can you explain how this approach is in my interest as well as yours?

[Although this sounds like a closed question, it is likely to generate a long answer.]

5. How much should I expect to pay for your advice?

TOPIC C: Personal Style

[This indirect question really asks, "Would we work well together?"]

1. What kind of clients do you like to work with? What kinds don't you work well with?

[The first question here is really an indirect way of discovering how much attention the advisor has paid to the potential client.]

2. Have you looked over the papers I sent you about my financial condition? What did you think of them?

[This clever hypothetical question has a better chance of generating a useful answer than the more direct "What can you tell me about the kind of service I can expect?"]

3. If I were to call one of your clients at random, what would he or she tell me about the type of service and frequency of communication I can expect with you?

[This is a straightforward, open question.]

4. If we were to develop a relationship, what would you expect of me?

[This hypothetical question anticipates an important issue.]

5. Suppose I were to disagree with your advice. What would you say and do?

summary

Interviewing is a face-to-face conversation in which at least one party has a specific, serious purpose. As such, it is perhaps the most common form of planned communication. Interviewing differs from other types of conversation in its purposeful nature, its degree of structure, its imbalance of control and speaking by one party, and its bipolarity.

A good deal of planning should occur before an important interview begins. The first step involves defining the objective as clearly as possible. At the same time, each party should analyze the other, tailoring the interview to the other's self-concept, knowledge level, image of the interview partner, and attitude toward the topic. The best way to obtain this information is through what others say, what the person in question says, and what you observe.

Having defined the objectives, both interviewer and respondent should prepare agendas, listing the areas they want to cover during the meeting. The interviewer should decide whether a highly structured, moderately structured, or nonstructured format is most desirable. It is also critical to plan important primary and secondary questions in advance of the interview. When forming questions, the interviewer should consider desired depth, open versus closed nature, direct or indirect approach, whether fact or opinion is sought, and whether hypothetical or actual inquiries will be most productive. Leading and loaded questions ought to be avoided. Finally, the interviewer and interviewee ought to choose a setting that promotes the best possible outcome.

The interview itself consists of three parts. The opening establishes rapport, orients the respondent, and offers motivation for contributing. During the body, the interviewer should keep the conversation focused, listen actively, and probe for additional information when necessary. The respondent should give clear and detailed answers, correct any misunderstandings, and cover his or her own agenda. The closing ought to review and clarify what has occurred, establish what actions will occur in the future, and conclude with pleasantries.

Besides attending to practical considerations, participants in an interview are obliged to behave in an ethical manner. Interviewers should treat every interviewee with respect, keep confidences, make only promises they are prepared to honor, and avoid coercing the respondent. Interviewees should prepare for the session to avoid wasting the interviewer's time and should represent both facts and their positions honestly.

key terms

Test your understanding of these key terms by visiting the Online Learning Center Web site at www.mhhe.com/adler9.

closed questions 180
critical incident questions 182
direct questions 181
factual questions 180
highly structured interview 178
hypothetical questions 182
indirect questions 181
interview 174
leading questions 182
moderately structured interview 179
nonstructured interview 179
open questions 180
opinion questions 180
primary questions 181
secondary questions 181

Imagine an interview in which limited eye contact, much silence, and no exaggerated claims about one's abilities are valued. This article tries to help interviewers see how the cultural framework creates a paradigm for a successful interview which might be in direct conflict with other (than U.S. mainstream) cultural values.

Stewart, C. J., and W. B. Cash. *Interviewing: Principles and Practices*, 11th ed. New York: McGraw-Hill, 2006.

The latest edition of this venerable book provides a comprehensive, thorough introduction to the many types of interviews common in business and the professions.

On the Web

The University of Kansas's "Virtual Interviewing Assistant" **(www.ku.edu/~coms/virtual_assistant/ via)** contains a variety of information on interviewing strategies and techniques. The home page provides links to information on the nature of effective interviewing, influences on the interviewer and the interviewee, pre- and postinterview strategies, and conducting the interview. Other links offer guidelines on specific interviewing types such as employment, performance appraisal, counseling, discipline, and focus groups.

7 Types of Interviews

Chapter Outline

Chapter Objectives

After reading this chapter you should be able to

1 Plan and conduct an information-gathering interview that will help you clarify and/or achieve your career-related goals.

2 Identify and demonstrate the steps to prepare for, participate in, and follow up after an employment interview.

3 List various types of employment interviews and describe how you can prepare for each one.

4 Distinguish between legal and illegal employment interview questions and identify several methods of responding to illegal ones.

5 Describe how you can prepare for and effectively participate in a performance appraisal.

Of all the interview types described in Chapter 6, four are essential in almost every occupation: information-gathering, career research, employment, and performance appraisal. This chapter outlines the skills required for each of these important types of interview.

The Information-Gathering Interview

Information-gathering interviews come in many forms. For example, **investigative interviews** help answer the question, "What happened?" **Survey interviews** are used for various types of research to sample large groups of people. **Diagnostic interviews** are used by professionals in health care, law, counseling, and other areas to assess and treat clients. **Research interviews** turn up information that can help individuals and organizations perform more effectively. Finally, **exit interviews** help an organization learn why employees are leaving.

Many businesspeople owe their success in great part to the lessons they learned in information-gathering interviews. Sam Walton, founder of the Wal-Mart empire, explains how he used this approach early in his career to interview executives who had information that would help him:

> *I would just show up and say, "Hi, I'm Sam Walton from Bentonville, Arkansas. We've got a few stores out there, and I'd like to speak with* Mr. *So-and-So"—whoever*

the head of the company was—"about his business." And as often as not, they'd let me in, maybe out of curiosity, and I'd ask lots of questions about pricing and distribution, whatever. I learned a lot that way.[1]

Another start-up tale reinforces the value of informational interviews. Three years out of college and jobless, entrepreneur Michael Mellinger created a thriving computer programming business in Barbados, where a staff of talented workers from second- and third-world Asian countries develop software for clients from wealthy, industrialized economies. He developed this idea by interviewing executives of Fortune 500 companies, whom he asked what services they needed. Despite his inexperience, Mellinger's approach captured the interest of top-level people. Before long, his mentors included the chief information officers of Pepsi, Merrill Lynch, and Chase Bank.[2]

Whatever their form, all types of information-gathering interviews follow the same general approach described in the following pages.

Collect Background Information

In many cases, pre-interview research is well worth the effort. Suppose, for instance, that you are interested in proposing a job-sharing plan—a system in which two people would share the responsibilities and salary of one full-time job. You decide you need to interview several people in your company before presenting your idea formally. Before conducting these interviews, however, you need to research the answers to some basic questions: How common is job sharing? In what industries does it occur? What forms does it take? Has it been tried by any firms in your field? What have the results of such arrangements been? Until you know at least the rough answers to these questions, you won't be ready to bring up the idea in your company.

Besides conducting traditional library research, you can get answers to questions like these by interviewing knowledgeable people. In this sense, talking about a single information-gathering interview is really an oversimplification, for you will usually conduct several during various stages of a task. You might, indeed, collect some fundamental background information during your first round of interviews. Perhaps you know someone who worked for a company that already has a job-sharing policy. An acquaintance might have mentioned a recent newspaper article on the subject, and you can get the reference that will help you locate it. During this phase, your questions will be necessarily vague, similar to the request you might make of a reference librarian: "I'm looking for information about job sharing. How do you think I ought to go about it?"

Once you have collected the necessary background information, you can use this knowledge to plan an intelligent approach to your second round of interviews—perhaps with people suggested by your earlier research or with the key decision makers who are your ultimate target.

Define Interview Goals and Questions

Defining the specific goal of your interview is always a key step. Your goal ought to be as specific as possible and be worded in a way that will tell you whether you have

career tip

Informational Interviewing and Searching for Company Information

Preparing for an Informational Interview

Quintcareers offers a tutorial on informational interviewing (**www.quintcareers.com/informational_interviewing.html**) and guidelines for planning and conducting interviews. You will also find links to over 20 related Web sites that cover informational interviewing from beginning (reasons to conduct an interview) to end (sending a thank-you note). Other useful sites are **www.apsu.edu/careers/interview/interviewing.htm** and **http://danenet.wicip.org/jets/jet-9407-p.html**. Rivier College's informational interviewing site (**www.rivier.edu/departments/cardev**) includes sample scripts and question lists.

You can read the transcripts of hundreds of informational interviews in the fields of computers and information technology at **www.santarosa.edu/~lhemenw/interview**.

Using Search Engines and Directories

There are many occasions when you need to learn about a company before an interview. The World Wide Web contains a wealth of information about organizations. You can find it by using two basic strategies:

Directories like Yahoo (**www.yahoo.com**) are the electronic equivalent of the card catalog in a traditional library. Typing the name of a particular company into a directory will produce a list of Web pages that have been identified as focusing on the organization in question. For example, a Yahoo search for "McGraw-Hill" (the publisher of this book) produced 58 Web sites, most of which contained information on various divisions of the company. You can also use a *search engine* like AltaVista (**www.altavista.com**) to generate a far larger list of pages in which the name of a company is *mentioned*. An AltaVista search for "McGraw-Hill" produced over 473,000 sites in which the company was mentioned, including company sites, reviews of books published by the company, syllabi of academic courses for which McGraw-Hill books are used as texts, transcripts of speeches by McGraw-Hill employees, and biographies of McGraw-Hill authors. Such an enormous list of sites gives you too much information. Fortunately, every search engine provides a tool for refining the original number of "hits." If these tools aren't clear, advice is only a mouse click away when you take advantage of the search engine's "help" feature.

If you are looking for the address or phone number of companies, consider using a lookup tool like the global Yellow Pages (**www.yellowpages.com**) or White Pages (**www.whitepages.com**).

Using Company Locators

A number of Web-based tools are specifically designed to locate information about organizations. For example,

- CorpTech (**www.corptech.com**) provides free access to information capsules on 45,000 U.S. high-technology companies, including demographic information, employment statistics, and product analysis.
- Hoover's company profiles online (**www.hoovers.com**) provides in-depth information on more than 2,700 public and private companies in the United States and around the world.

For tips about the employment process, interviewing skills, as well as information on specific companies, visit sites including Quintessential Careers Guide (**www.quintcareers.com**), Career Builder (**www.careerbuilder.com**), and WetFeet.com (**www.wetfeet.com**). For a tutorial on using the Internet to research companies and nonprofit organizations, go to **www.learnwebskills.com/company**.

the answers you were seeking. Here are examples of how you might define a goal for an information-gathering interview:

Vague	Specific
I want to learn about tax-free municipal bonds.	Will tax-free municipal bonds give me liquidity, appreciation, safety, and tax shelter better than my present investments?
What happened at the accident yesterday?	What caused the accident, and could it have been prevented?
Should I buy a database management system?	Will a database management system improve my efficiency enough to justify the purchase?

Once you have identified your purpose, you must develop questions that will help you achieve it. For example:

> *Purpose:* To learn what steps I need to take to have a job-sharing arrangement approved by management.
>
> *Questions:*
>
> Whom should I approach first?
>
> Who will be the key decision maker on this issue?
>
> Should I present my formal proposal first, or should I start by mentioning the subject informally?
>
> What objections might management have to the proposal?
>
> Is anyone else in the company (nonmanagement personnel) likely to oppose or support the idea?
>
> What arguments (such as precedent, cost savings, employee morale) will most impress management?
>
> What influential people might support this idea?

As you develop your questions, use the guidelines in Chapter 6. Make sure you gather both facts and opinions—and recognize which is which. Be prepared to follow up your primary questions with secondary queries as necessary.

Choose the Right Interviewee

The ideal respondent within an organization will be part of an informal communication network and may have no official relationship with you on the organizational chart. It might be naive to talk with your boss about the job-sharing proposal until you have consulted other sources who could suggest how to broach the subject: Perhaps a politically astute co-worker, someone who has experience making proposals to management, or even the boss's administrative assistant, if you are friends, will be helpful.

After you have established the purpose and the appropriate person to interview, follow the guidelines in Chapter 6 to plan and conduct the interview.

The Career Research Interview

The **career research interview** is a special type of informational interview in which you meet with someone who can provide information that will help you define and achieve your career goals. It is based on the principle that speaking with the right people can give you valuable ideas and contacts that you simply can't find from books, magazines, the Internet, or any other source.

The Value of Personal Contacts

The old phrase "It isn't what you know, it's who you know" is certainly true when it comes to getting a job. Over 30 years of research confirm that the vast majority of people don't find jobs from advertisements, headhunters, or other "formal" means.[3] Like these traditional sources, Web-based services like Monster.com aren't as useful as they might seem: Job-finding expert Richard Bolles cites research suggesting that less than 10 percent at best of job seekers find employment by using the Internet.[4] Instead of using impersonal means, the majority get offers for employment through personal contacts. The reverse is also true: Most employers find good employees through their personal networks.[5] The results of one survey, displayed in Table 7–1, show the important role of personal contacts in looking for new jobs.

Table 7–1 Success Rates of Sources for Job Opportunities

Source	Success Rate (%)
Professional associates, former colleagues, friends	75%
Fellow students	60
People holding a similar job	50
Professional association placement services	40
Former teachers	30
Newspaper or magazine advertisements	25
Relatives	25
University placement offices	10
Social acquaintances	10
Letters to corporate officers	5
Leads from former employers	5
Mass mailings to employers	5
State placement offices	2
Professional placement agencies	1

Source: After C. J. Stewart and W. B. Cash, Jr., *Interviewing: Principles and Practices,* 4th ed. (Dubuque, IA: Wm. C. Brown, 1985), p. 213.

career tip

Networking Organizations

Much personal networking occurs informally among friends and business associates. Along with these casual connections, though, there are a number of organizations that provide a structured way to make and cultivate connections with people with whom you can offer mutual support.

Invitation-only Groups

Most urban areas contain a number of small, private groups dedicated to networking. These groups typically contain between 15 and 30 members, each of whom is usually from a different field. Events may include guest speakers, day-long seminars with consultants, brainstorming sessions in which members can get career advice from one another, and lunches or dinners in which seating is arranged to ensure that members will talk with people they don't already know well. Since invitation-only groups usually don't advertise their existence, you may need to ask friends and acquaintances to help you locate one.

Open Networking Groups

A growing number of groups don't require formal membership and allow visitors to drop in on meetings. Open groups may consist of several people (or none) from a given field: realtors, attorneys, computer programmers, and so on. Their activities are often listed in the community calendar or business sections of your local newspaper.

Trade Associations

Trade organizations provide industry-specific information to members who share an interest in a specific field. There are over 18,000 such associations in the U.S. alone. Besides their basic purpose, these organizations provide a terrific way to identify people with whom to build a network. Association meetings and directories provide an easily accessible way to find people whose interests and talents can be helpful. Find the groups that meet your needs in Carol A. Schwartz, *Encyclopedia of Associations*, 31st ed. (Detroit: Gale Research Inc., 1997). Volume 1 gives a brief abstract of each association, and Volume 2 lists these organizations by geographical area.

Web Resources

The Art of Networking Web site at **www.quintcareers.com/networking.html** offers excellent resources and links to others. Find newsgroups and mailing lists at **www.synapse.net/~radio/finding. htm**. Read various newsletters on networking at **www.emediawire.com/releases/2005/11/emw304743.htm**. Also see the "Resources: On the Web" section on page 249 of this chapter for more networking resources.

Another study of over 150,000 jobs found that more people were hired by referrals than by any other source.[6]

Finding a job is only one goal of career research interviews. These conversations can serve three purposes:

To conduct research that helps you learn more about the field and specific organizations that interest you.

To be remembered by making contacts who will recall you at an appropriate time and either offer you a position, inform you of employment opportunities, or suggest you to a potential employer.

To gain referrals to other people whom you might contact for help in your job search. These referrals can easily lead to meetings with more useful contacts, all of whom might mention you to *their* friends and associates.

Choosing Interviewees

The key to finding the wealth of unadvertised positions is to cultivate a network of contacts who can let you know about job opportunities and pass along your name to potential employers. Chapter 1 (pages 21–24) offered tips on how to build and nurture a personal network.

There's no doubt that the people in your immediate networks can be helpful; but surprisingly, you can benefit even more from more-distant connections. In his classic study titled "The Strength of Weak Ties," Mark Granovetter surveyed over 280 residents of a Boston suburb who had taken a new job within the past year. While only 17 percent of the people surveyed found their jobs through close friends or relatives, the majority learned about their new positions from people who were only distant associates—old college friends, former colleagues, parents of a child's playmate, and so on.[7] Weak ties are often more useful than close acquaintances in finding jobs because your close associates rarely know more than you do about career opportunities. Distant acquaintances, however, are connected to other, less familiar communication networks, networks that often contain valuable information about new jobs.[8]

You might wonder why the kind of important person you would like to interview would be willing to meet with you. There are actually several reasons. First, if you have made contact through a referral, your subject will probably see you in deference to your mutual acquaintance. If you can gain a referral, you are most likely to get a friendly reception. Second, interviewees might be willing to see you for ego gratification. It is flattering to have someone say "I respect your accomplishments and ideas" and difficult for even a busy person to say no to a request that accompanies such a comment. A third reason is simple altruism. Most successful people realize they received help somewhere along the line, and many will be willing to do for you what others did for them. Finally, you may get an interview because the person recognizes you as ambitious, someone who might have something to offer his or her organization.

Contacting Prospective Interviewees

When you approach a career research interviewee—especially one you don't know well—it can be smart to make your first contact in writing. A telephone call runs the risk of not getting through; and even if you do reach the interviewee, your call may come at a bad time. While e-mail can be quick and efficient, a traditional letter can make a strong, positive first impression. Your first letter, like the one in Figure 7–1, should introduce yourself, explain your reason for the interview (stressing that you are *not* seeking employment), state your availability for a meeting, and promise a follow-up telephone call.

Unless you'll be conducting the interview within a day or two of the time your interviewee agrees to meet with you, a second letter, e-mail, or phone call should precede the interview and confirm its date, place, and time. This sort of follow-up can save you the frustration of being stood up by a forgetful interviewee. Just as important, it shows that you know how to handle business engagements in a professional manner.

Giving your interviewee an advance list of topic areas and questions you hope to cover will distinguish you as a serious person, worth the interviewee's time and effort. Also, supplying this list will give your interviewee a chance to

FIGURE 7–1
Letter Requesting an Informational Interview

Emily Park
9971 Washoe St., NE
Albuquerque, NM 87112
(505) 793–3510 eprk112@sunnet.net

May 25, 2007

Vanessa J. Yoder
Daniels, Grenz, & Hickman
11000 Arvilla Road SE
Albuquerque, NM 87106

Dear Ms. Yoder:

I am currently a junior at the University of New Mexico and am majoring in political science and communication. After graduating from UNM, I plan to attend law school and focus my studies on immigration law.

I understand from news accounts and from several of my professors that you are an expert in immigration law and have a stellar reputation for representing women when the cases involve both domestic violence and immigration issues. I also heard of your work during my internship at the Women's Workforce Training Center.

I would appreciate the opportunity to meet with you to discuss how I might best prepare myself for an eventual career in immigration law. I would also like to know which law schools you would recommend and hear about the challenges and rewards of this type of practice.

I will call your office next week hoping to schedule an appointment. I know you are a busy person and I would be grateful for 30-45 minutes of your time.

I look forward to benefiting from your advice.

Sincerely,

Emily Park

Emily Park

think about the areas you want to discuss and ideally come to your meeting best prepared to help you. Figure 7–2 illustrates a confirming e-mail with list of questions.

Following Up

In a post-interview letter or e-mail, express thanks for the interviewee's time and mention how helpful the information was. Besides demonstrating common courtesy, these messages become a tangible reminder of you and provide a record of your name

FIGURE 7–2
Confirming E-mail with List of Questions

Subject: Interview confirmation and questions
Date: Wed, 11 June 2007, 8:26 a.m. (MDT)
From: Emily Park <eprk112@sunnet.net>
To: Vanessa Yoder <Vanessa.Yoder@dgh.com>

Dear Ms. Yoder:

Thank you again for agreeing to speak with me about how I can best prepare myself for a career in immigration law. I am looking forward to our meeting at your office this coming Thursday, June 14, at 2:00 p.m. I know how busy you must be, and I'm grateful for your giving me 45 minutes of your time.

In order to use our time together most efficiently, here is a list of some questions I hope we can discuss at our meeting:

TRENDS IN IMMIGRATION AND LAW
- What trends do you anticipate in immigration patterns?
- How do you view the field of immigration law changing to reflect these conditions?

EDUCATION
- What law schools do you recommend for someone interested in practicing immigration law?
- Do you recommend any courses I should take in my senior year at the university?

EXPERIENCE
- What types of work experience (paid or volunteer) could help prepare me for law school and eventual employment?
- Can you recommend ways I might pursue positions in these areas?

EMPLOYMENT
- What types of jobs are there for attorneys who specialize in immigration law?
- How easy/difficult do you anticipate it will be to secure employment in these sorts of jobs?
- What, if any, are the pros and cons I might expect as a woman practicing law in this area?

LIFESTYLE
- How would you describe the benefits and challenges of working in the field of immigration law?
- How compatible is a career in this area with being a parent?

OTHER CONTACTS
- Can you recommend other people who might be willing to talk with me about preparing for a career in immigration law?

and address that will be useful if the interviewee wants to contact you in the future. Of course, all correspondence should be typed neatly with impeccable format, spelling, and grammar: Your letters are a reflection of you.

The Employment Interview

An **employment interview** is designed to explore how well a candidate might fit a job. The exploration of fit works both ways: Employers certainly measure prospective candidates during this conversation, and prospective employees can decide whether the job in question is right for them. The Bureau of Labor Statistics reports that the typical American worker holds nearly nine different jobs before age 32, so the probability of facing at least one employment interview in the near future is high.[9]

CLOSE TO HOME BY JOHN McPHERSON

How personnel managers actually make their hiring decisions.

The short time spent in an employment interview can have major consequences. Consider the stakes: Most workers spend the greatest part of their adult lives on the job—roughly 2,000 hours per year or upward of 80,000 hours during a career. The financial difference between a well-paid position and an unrewarding one can also be staggering. Even without considering the effects of inflation, a gap of only $200 per month can amount to almost $100,000 over the course of a career. Finally, the emotional results of having the right job are considerable. A frustrating job not only makes for unhappiness at work but these dissatisfactions also have a way of leaking into nonworking hours as well.

How important is an interview in getting the right job? The Bureau of National Affairs, a private research firm that serves both government and industry, conducted a survey to answer this question. It polled 196 personnel executives, seeking the factors that were most important in hiring applicants. The results showed that the employment interview is the single most important factor in landing a job.[10] Further research revealed that the most important factor during these critically decisive interviews was communication skills. Employers identified the ability to communicate effectively as more important in shaping a hiring decision than grade-point average, work experience, extracurricular activities, appearance, and preference for job location.[11]

Even though interviews can play an important role in hiring, research shows that potential employers—at least those who aren't trained in employment interviewing—are not very good at using interviews to choose the best applicant for a job.[12] They fail to recognize the potential in some candidates who would make fine employees, and they are impressed by others who prove to be less than satisfactory as workers. In other words, the best candidate does not necessarily get the job offer.

In many situations, the person who knows the most about getting hired gets the desired position. "Chemistry is the paramount factor in hiring," states Wilhelmus B. Bryan, III, executive vice president of William H. Clark Associates, a New York recruiting firm.[13] While job-getting skills are no guarantee of qualifications once the actual work begins, they are necessary to get hired in the first place.

Pre-Interview Steps

Scanning the newspaper for openings and then filing an application with the company's personnel or human resources department is one way of looking for a job but often not the most effective. Many employers never advertise jobs and, depending on the salary sought, only 5 to 24 percent of job seekers find a job solely through local newspaper ads.[14] Employment expert Richard Bolles explains:

> *I know too many stories about people who have been turned down by a particular company's personnel department, who then went back to square one, found out who, in that very same company, had the power to hire for the position they wanted, went to that woman or man, and got hired—ten floors up from the personnel department that had just rejected them.*[15]

Even when a company does advertise, the odds don't favor an applicant who replies with an application and résumé. Since most job announcements attract many more applicants than an employer needs, the job of the personnel department becomes *elimination*, not selection. The goal is to reduce the pool of job seekers to a manageable number by rejecting as many applicants as possible. Given this process of elimination, any shortcoming becomes welcome grounds for rejecting the application and the applicant. Many consultants, therefore, suggest identifying and contacting the person who has the power to hire you *before* an opening exists. The process has several steps.

Conduct Background Research The first step is to explore the types of work and specific organizations that sound appealing to you. This involves doing Internet research, reading magazines and newspaper articles, taking classes, and simply fantasizing about jobs you might find interesting. The result of your research should be a list of organizations and names of people who can tell you more about your chosen field.

Besides helping you find organizations where you want to work, your knowledge of a company will distinguish you as a candidate worth considering for a job. Desiree Crips of Salus Media in Carpinteria, California, reflects the view of most potential employers: "If someone walks in here and doesn't know anything about our company, that's a real negative. There's just no excuse for not being up to speed on any company you're applying to these days."[16] Doing your homework is just as important in the workforce as in school.

Contact Potential Employers At some point, your research and networking will uncover one or more job leads. You might read a newspaper story about the need of a local employer for people with interests or training like yours. Perhaps a career research interview subject will say, "I know someone over at _______ who is looking for a person like you." You might learn through a friendly contact that a desirable firm is about to expand its operations. In such a case, it is time to approach the person who has the power to hire you and explore how you can help meet the company's needs.

Whether the job lead comes from a formal announcement or a contact from your personal network, your first step is to let the organization know about your interest in a job. In most cases, the best way to do this is with written correspondence, usually a cover letter and a copy of your résumé. The Appendix of this book has advice on constructing and formatting résumés. A cover letter like the one in Figure 7–3 that takes the following approach will serve you well.

In the first paragraph, introduce yourself to the reader. Clearly state your purpose for writing (e.g., in response to an advertisement, at the suggestion of a mutual acquaintance, as a result of your research) and describe your ability to meet the company's needs. When appropriate, mention any mutual acquaintances that the addressee will recognize. If you are writing to the human resources department of a medium- or large-sized organization, be sure to give the job number if there is one; a company that has many job openings won't know which one you're applying for unless you identify it.

In the next paragraph or two, highlight one or two of your most impressive accomplishments that are *relevant to the job at hand*. Don't just say you can help the organization: Offer some objective evidence that backs up your claim.

In the closing paragraph, describe the next step you hope to take—usually requesting an interview. Detail any information about limits on your availability (though you should keep these to an absolute minimum). Supply any other information that

FIGURE 7–3
Sample Letter Requesting an Employment Interview

387 Blythe St.
Aurora, CO 80017
(303) 654-7909
kad@zcom.net

April 17, 2007

Mr. John Waldmann, Executive Director
Boulder Arts Council
2987 Seventh St.
Boulder, CO 90302

Dear Mr. Waldmann:

[The writer identifies her reason for writing, and makes reference to a mutual acquaintance, who presumably can vouch for her.]

Our mutual friend Marcia Sherwood recently alerted me to the open position of Events Coordinator for the BAC, and I am writing to express my interest in that position.

[This paragraph links the writer's experience to the job being sought.]

I would welcome the chance to use skills acquired over the past 12 years planning events for a variety of community organizations in the Denver area to help the Council extend its reach in the community.

[This paragraph details professional accomplishments that are relevant to the job being advertised.]

As a person who has coordinated a wide range of community events for nonprofit organizations, I can bring the Arts Council demonstrated ability to motivate and coordinate the work of volunteers and to generate widespread publicity for events on a limited budget. Most recently, I was chairperson for Aurora's Earth Day festival, and I was the public information coordinator for last year's Halloween auction and dance to benefit Denver's Shelter Services for Women. The enclosed résumé details a variety of other activities that have helped prepare me for the position of Events Coordinator.

[The applicant closes by clearly expressing her desire to meet and discuss the job, indicating when she will be available.]

I would welcome the chance to discuss how I might help the Boulder Arts Council. I will be available any time in the next month, except for the weekend of April 28-29.

I look forward to hearing from you soon.

Sincerely,
Kristina Dudley
Kristina Dudley

the prospective employer may have requested. Finally, close with a cordial expression of gratitude.

Most career counselors recommend directing your request for an interview to the person who has the ability to hire you, rather than to the company's personnel department. We have already discussed why personnel departments aren't the best avenue for getting hired: Employees there usually are screening large numbers of applicants, so they are looking for reasons to reject as many as possible to arrive at a manageable number of finalists to interview. Also, personnel screeners usually are not familiar with the position, so they may reject candidates for superficial or mistaken reasons.

The mechanical nature of this screening process is best illustrated by the growing use of **scannable résumés.** These documents are "read" by document scanning devices, not humans. The software searches for key words and phrases that describe the skills and education required for the position. Applications that contain these words are passed on to a human who evaluates them further. The Appendix of this book offers tips on creating effective scannable résumés; but even the best document may not capture the unique traits you can offer an employer. For this reason, you will maximize your chances at being recognized by developing a relationship with people who know both your talents and the characteristics of the job.

Prepare for Possible Interview Formats The standard one-on-one, question-and-answer interview format isn't the only one you may encounter. A variety of interview formats is used by employers. If you are prepared for all of them, you aren't likely to be surprised.

In a **panel interview** (sometimes called a **team** or **group interview**), the candidate is questioned by several people. Panel interviews save the company time and provide the people with whom you may work an opportunity to compare their perceptions of you. When setting up an interview, it is appropriate to ask whether you will be facing a team of questioners. If you are, do your best to learn and use the names of each person. When you answer questions, make sure you look at everyone in the group. Some employers use a **stress interview** to evaluate your behavior under pressure; you can find tips to prepare for this in the Resource section at the end of this chapter.

In an **audition interview** you will be asked to demonstrate whatever skills the employer is looking for. You might be asked to create a project, solve a problem, or respond to a typical scenario in the job, such as dealing with a difficult client. The audition shows the potential employer how you are likely to do on the job. The prospect of an audition can be especially helpful if you will be competing against candidates with more experience or stronger credentials. For that reason, you might even volunteer for an audition if you are confident you can handle the job well.[17]

A **behavioral interview** is based on the assumption that past experience is the best predictor of future performance. In this approach interviewers explore specifics about the candidate's past accomplishments. John Madigan, a vice president at The Hartford Financial Services Group, explains the way behavioral interviews work: "We actually ask what you did in specific situations. Concrete examples will demonstrate a person's preferred way of dealing with those situations and give you a better idea of that person and how they're likely to act on the job."[18]

Here are some questions you might hear in a behavioral interview:

- Give me a specific example of when you sold your supervisor or professor on an idea or concept. What was the result?
- Tell me about a time when you came up with an innovative solution to a challenge you or your company was facing. What was the challenge? What role did others play?
- Describe a situation where you faced multiple projects. How did you handle it?[19]

If you have a proven record of accomplishments that will clearly work well in the job you are seeking, a behavioral interview should sound ideal. If you don't have work experience that is clearly relevant to the new position, find ways to demonstrate how

Preparing for Behavioral Interviews

Interviewers often ask questions about your past behavior in order to judge the way you are likely to handle a job if hired.

Each answer to a behavioral question should include (a) one or more specific examples of what you did and (b) what the example(s) you've chosen say about you as a prospective employee. Choose examples that showcase some of your best qualities. If it is a question about something you did wrong or a mistake you made, show how you learned something or how something positive resulted from the experience. For example, if asked to describe a time when you were faced with a stressful situation that demonstrated your coping skills, you might answer: "In the middle of my last semester as a senior, my father had emergency surgery. That put a big load on my family, and I moved back home for about 2 months to lend a hand. During that time I managed to finish all my classes with As and Bs, and I also covered every shift on my job after the first week. It wasn't fun, but that experience taught me that I can handle a lot of demands."

Practice your skill at behavioral interviews by answering the questions below in a group:

- Describe a time that you needed to work as part of a team.
- Tell about a time that you had to use creativity and problem-solving skills to solve an important problem.
- Explain how you handled a situation when you had to make an important ethical decision.
- Describe a time when you didn't succeed at something you were trying to accomplish.
- Give an example of a time when you took on a greater share of responsibility or decision making than was required by your job.

For more examples of behavioral interview questions, see **www.quintcareers.com/sample_behavioral.html**.

things you have done in other contexts apply to the job you are seeking. For example, you might be able to show how experience in retail sales taught you how to deal with difficult customers you'll encounter in a customer service job, or how being a volunteer for a nonprofit charity gave you an appreciation for working with limited resources—an attitude most employers will welcome.

Think Constructively The way you think about an upcoming interview can affect how you feel and act during the session. A research team at Washington State University interviewed both highly anxious and more confident students to discover what causes some people to become especially apprehensive during the process of meeting prospective employers.[20] The differences between the groups were startling. Anxious students avoided thinking about an interview in advance, so they did little in the way of research or preparation. When they did think about an upcoming interview, they dwelled on negative self-talk: "I won't do well" or "I don't know why I'm doing this." It's no surprise that thoughts like these created negative self-fulfilling prophecies that led to poor interview performances. Students who handled interviews better weren't anxiety-free, but they thought about the upcoming challenge in more productive ways. We can imagine them thinking, "The interviewer isn't trying to trick me or trip me up" and "I'll do a lot better if I prepare."

Dress Appropriately and Act Professionally Looking good when you meet a potential employer is vitally important. In one survey, recruiters ranked clothing as the leading factor in shaping their initial impressions of applicants (ahead of physical attractiveness and résumé). Furthermore, 79 percent of the recruiters stated that their initial impressions influenced the rest of the interview.[21] The best attire to wear will depend on the job you are seeking: The professional business suit that would be appropriate for a banking job would almost certainly look out of place if you were interviewing for a job in the construction industry, and it might look overly formal at many software companies. When in doubt, it is always safest to dress on the conservative side. Of course, cleanliness and personal hygiene are essential.

Be sure to arrive at the interview 5 to 10 minutes early. Be polite to everyone in the office. While you wait, choose reading material about the business or company, not about current TV personalities. When introduced, shake hands firmly, no more than three shakes, avoiding limpness or a hand-crushing grip. Smile, make eye contact, and take your lead from the interviewer about how to proceed.

During the Interview

If your fate in the selection process were determined by a skilled, objective interviewer, the need for strategic communication might not be essential. Research shows, however, that the rating you are likely to receive from an interviewer can be influenced by a variety of factors as varied as the time of day, the sex of the interviewer and interviewee, whether the candidates before you did well or poorly, and the employer's mood.[22] Since the interview is not a scientific measure of your skills, it is especially important to do everything possible to make the best impression. Interviewing expert Anthony Medley describes one memorable job candidate who illustrates the importance of first impressions:

> *She was attractive, presentable, and had good references. But after showing up ten minutes late, she called me "Mr. Melody" throughout the interview.*
>
> *The two things I remembered about her were that she had kept me waiting and constantly mispronounced my name. I finally offered the position to someone whose . . . skills were not nearly so good.*[23]

Your background research will pay dividends during the employment interview. One criterion most interviewers use in rating applicants is "knowledge of the position," and a lack of information in this area can be damaging. One example illustrates the advantages that come from knowing even a small amount about a position:

> *When I first took a job as a young attorney for Litton Industries, I was interviewing for the position as an assistant division counsel for their Guidance Control Systems Division. That name alone was enough to boggle my mind. A scientist I was not. After a little research, I found that they made something called an inertial navigation system. That was worse than the name of the division. What was an inertial navigation system?*

Table 7–2 Most Frequent Interviewer Complaints about Interviewees

1. Poor personality, manners; lack of poise, confidence; arrogant; egotistical; conceited
2. Poor appearance, lack of neatness, careless dress
3. Lack of enthusiasm, shows little interest, no evidence of initiative, lack of drive
4. Lack of goals and objectives, lack of ambition, poorly motivated, does not know interests, uncertain, indecisive, poor planning
5. Inability to express self well, poor oral expression, poor habits of speech
6. Unrealistic salary demands, overemphasis on money, more interested in salary than opportunity, unrealistic concerning promotion to top jobs
7. Lack of maturity, no leadership potential
8. Lack of extracurricular activities, inadequate reasons for not participating in activities
9. Failure to get information about our company, lack of preparation for the interview, inability to ask intelligent questions
10. Excessive interest in security and benefits, "what can you do for me" attitude
11. Objects to travel, unwilling to relocate

Source: Victor R. Lindquest, *The Northwestern Endicott Report 1988* (Evanston, IL: The Placement Center, Northwestern University, 1988).

Finally I went to a fraternity brother who had majored in engineering and asked him if he knew what it was all about. He explained to me that inertial navigation was a method of navigating whereby the system allows you, if you know your starting point, to measure speed and distance and therefore know where you are at all times. He also explained the components of the system.

When I went into my interview with the division counsel, I astounded him by my ability to talk the jargon of inertial navigation. . . .

He later told me that I was the first person he had interviewed for the job to whom he did not have to explain inertial navigation. Since he didn't understand it any better than I did, his being relieved of this obligation was a big plus in my favor. Also he said that he knew that it was not an easy task for me to find someone who could explain the subject and understand it well enough to have the confidence to discuss it. My initiative and interest in going to this extent to prepare for the interview had impressed him.[24]

Table 7–2 lists common interviewer complaints about interviewees.

Anticipate Key Questions Most employment interviewers ask questions in five areas:

Educational background. Does the candidate possess adequate training for a successful career? Do the candidate's grades and other activities predict success in this organization?

Work experience. Do any previous jobs prepare the candidate for this position? What does the candidate's employment history suggest about his or her work habits and ability to work well with others?

Career goals. Does the candidate have clear goals? Are they compatible with a career in this organization?

Personal traits. Do the actions and attitudes of the candidate predict good work habits and good interpersonal skills?

Knowledge of organization and job. Does the candidate know the job and organization well enough to be certain that he or she will feel happy in them?

While the specifics of each job are different, many questions will be the same for any position. Table 7–3 lists the most common questions asked by interviewers. In addition, knowledge of the company and job should suggest other specific questions to you.

You can't anticipate every question a prospective employer will ask. Still, if you go into the interview with a clear sense of yourself—both strengths and limitations—and the nature of the job you are seeking, you can probably handle almost any question. Consider a few examples of unusual questions, and what the interviewers who asked them were seeking.

Question	What the Interviewer Was Seeking
What's the biggest career mistake you've made so far?	Have you learned from your errors? What mistakes are you not likely to make if you work for us?
If I asked your previous co-workers what I'd better watch out for from you, what would they say?	How aware are you of your own strengths and weaknesses?
Who else are you interviewing with, and how close are you to accepting an offer?	How committed are you to our organization? How do others view your potential as an employee?[25]

Since most employers are untrained in interviewing, you can't expect them to ask every important question.[26] If your interviewer doesn't touch on an important area, look for ways of volunteering information that he or she probably would want to have. For instance, you could show your knowledge of the industry and the company when you respond to a question about your past work experience: "As my résumé shows, I've been working in this field for 5 years, first at Marston-Keenan and then with Evergreen. In both jobs we were constantly trying to keep up with the pace you set here. For example, the VT-17 was our biggest competitor at Evergreen. . . . "

"Will my office be near an ice machine?"

Respond to the Employer's Needs and Concerns While you may need a job to repay a college loan or finance your new Porsche, these concerns won't impress a potential employer. Companies hire employees to satisfy *their* needs, not

Table 7–3 Commonly Asked Questions in Employment Interviews

Educational Background

How has your education prepared you for a career?

Why did you choose your college or university?

Describe your greatest success (biggest problem) in college.

What subjects in school did you like best? Why?

What subjects did you like least? Why?

What was your most rewarding college experience?

Work Experience

Tell me about your past jobs. (What did you do in each?)

Which of your past jobs did you enjoy most? Why?

Why did you leave your past jobs?

Describe your greatest accomplishments in your past jobs.

What were your biggest failures? What did you learn from them?

How have your past jobs prepared you for this position?

What were the good and bad features of your last job?

This job requires initiative and hard work. What in your experience demonstrates these qualities?

Have you supervised people in the past? In what capacities? How did you do?

How do you think your present boss (subordinates, co-workers) would describe you?

How do you feel about the way your present company (past companies) is (were) managed?

Career Goals

Why are you interested in this position?

Where do you see yourself in 5 years? 10 years?

What is your eventual career goal?

Why did you choose the career you are now pursuing?

yours. Although employers will rarely say so outright, the fundamental question that is *always* being asked in an employment interview is "*Are you a person who can help this organization?*" That is, "*What can you do for us?*" One career guidance book makes the point clearly:

> *It is easy to get the impression during an interview that the subject of the interview, the star (so to speak) of the interview is, well, you. After all, you're the one in the hot seat. You're the one whose life is being dissected. Don't be too flattered. The real subject of the interview is the company. The company is what the interviewer ultimately thinks is important.*

What are your financial goals?

How would you describe the ideal job?

How would you define success?

What things are most important to you in a career?

Self-Assessment

In your own words, how would you describe yourself?

How have you grown in the last years?

What are your greatest strengths? Your greatest weaknesses?

What things give you the greatest satisfaction?

How do you feel about your career up to this point?

What is the biggest mistake you have made in your career?

Do you prefer working alone or with others?

How do you work under pressure?

What are the most important features of your personality?

Are you a leader? (a creative person? a problem solver?) Give examples.

Knowledge of the Job

Why are you interested in this particular job? Our company?

What can you contribute to this job? Our company?

Why should we hire you? What qualifies you for this position?

What do you think about __________ (job-related topic)?

What part of this job do you think would be most difficult?

Other Topics

Do you have any geographical preferences? Why?

Would you be willing to travel? To relocate?

Do you have any questions for me?

> *Of course, you will be very concerned about what opportunities and skills the company has to offer you, but if you're smart, you'll keep that to yourself. It's not that it isn't proper to be interested in advancement and money—in fact, that's a given. What is not a given is your ability to put the interests of your company ahead of your own from time to time; to make personal sacrifices for the good of an important project. The interviewer will be extremely interested in these things if you can find a way to communicate them.*[27]

Your approach in an interview, then, should be to show your potential employer how your skills match the company's concerns. Background research will pay off here, too: If you have spent time learning about what the employer needs, you will be in a good position to show how you can satisfy company needs and concerns. Consider an example:

Interviewer: What was your major in college?

Poor Answer: I was a communications major.

Better Answer: I was a communications major. I'm really glad I studied that subject, because the skills I learned in school could help me in this job in so many ways: Dealing with customers, working with you and the other people in the department, and also with all the external contractors who are part of the job. . . .

Interviewer: Tell me about your last job as a sales rep.

Poor Answer: I handled outside sales. I called on about 35 customers. My job was to keep them supplied and show them new products.

Better Answer: (elaborating on previous answer) I learned how important it is to provide outstanding customer service. Even though the products I sold in my last job are different from the ones I'd be selling here, I know that the competitive edge comes from making sure the customers get what they want, when they need it. I know that this company has a reputation for good service, so I'm really excited about working here.

Just because you respond to the employer's needs doesn't mean you should ignore your own goals; but as you are in an interview, keep in mind that you need to demonstrate how you can help the organization or you won't have a job offer to consider.

Because most employers have had bad experiences with some of the people they have hired, they are likely to be concerned about what might go wrong if they hire you. In Richard Bolles's words, employers worry that

> *you won't be able to do the job, you lack the skills, you won't work full days, regularly, you'll quit unexpectedly, it will take you a long time to master the job, you won't get along with others, you'll do the minimum, you'll need constant supervision, you'll be dishonest, irresponsible, negative, substance abuser, incompetent, you'll discredit the organization or cost them a lot of money.*[28]

You can allay these fears without ever addressing them directly by answering questions in a way that showcases your good work habits:

Interviewer: What were the biggest challenges in your last job?

Answer: The work always seemed to come in spurts. When it was busy, we had to work especially hard to stay caught up. I can remember some weeks when we never seemed to leave the office. It was hard, but we did whatever it took to get the job done.

Interviewer: How did you get along with your last boss?

Answer: My last manager had a very hands-off approach. That was a little scary at times, but it taught me that I can solve problems without a lot of supervision. I was always glad to get guidance, but when it didn't come, I learned that I can figure out things for myself.

Negotiating a Salary

It is usually best to save a discussion of salary until you have been offered a job. Compensation is almost always negotiable to some degree. It becomes increasingly so for positions that require more expertise and experience. The way you handle this issue can make a significant difference in the pay and benefits you receive. The following tips can help you negotiate the best possible compensation package.

Find Out the Prevailing Compensation for Your Type of Job

Discover what others are paid for the kind of work you do. Begin by exploring compensation levels in your field or industry. Several strategies will help you come up with realistic figures:

- *Online information:* The World Wide Web contains a variety of sites with salary information. Useful Web sites include JobSmart (**http://jobsmart.org**), Career Builder (**www.careerbuilder.com**), and Career City (**www.careercity.com**). You can also use a search engine like MetaCrawler (**www.metacrawler.com**) to seek out compensation. Combine terms like "wages" or "salary" with the name of your field (e.g., "sales" or "programming") to find the numbers you are seeking. The Salary Calculator (**www.homefair.com/calc/salcalc.html**) and Salary.com (**www.salary.com**) provide additional salary comparisons and information. At Jobstar (**http://jobstar.org/index.php**) you can check your salary IQ and link to over 300 salary surveys.
- *Personal contacts:* Your personal network can provide very useful information on prevailing salaries and benefits. Career counselors, recruiters, and outplacement counselors can be useful sources of information. An informational interview with people like this can be extremely useful. Contacts within a specific geographical area or company where you hope to work can be especially helpful. Rather than embarrassing people by asking for personal information ("How much do you earn?") or proprietary data ("What's the top salary the company would pay for a job like this?"), it's better to ask questions like, "What is the salary range in this company for a job like mine?" A good follow-up is, "What might lead an employer to offer a salary at the top end of this scale?"

Learn How Much the Company Wants You

Your leverage will be greatest under two conditions: first, if the company needs to hire someone quickly; and second, if it is specifically interested in you. Your personal network is, again, the ideal way to determine whether these conditions exist. You can also determine how motivated the company is to hire you from your knowledge of the job market—both nationally and locally—for positions like the one you are seeking.

Consider Negotiating for Nonsalary Compensation

Even if the salary offer isn't everything you hope for, you may be able to get other benefits that improve the overall compensation package. Items you might ask for include:

- Nonsalary financial gains: commissions, bonuses (for signing or future performance), money in lieu of unneeded benefits (e.g., health insurance when you already have coverage), profit sharing, stock options.
- Time: personal leave days, extra vacation, flexible scheduling of work hours, telecommuting, job sharing.
- Educational benefits: tuition reimbursement, training programs.
- Perquisites: better office, expense account, company car, reserved or paid parking.
- Relocation expenses: house-hunting trips, moving costs, realty fees for home purchase/sale.
- Support: free on-site child care, company time for volunteering in your child's school.
- Lifestyle: use of company apartment, upgraded business travel (hotel, air), company tickets to sporting events and theaters, health club membership.

ethical challenge

Promoting Yourself with Honesty

Think of a job that you are probably capable of handling well but for which you would most likely not be the candidate hired. Develop a list of questions you would probably be asked in an interview for this position. Then develop a list of answers that show you in the best possible light while being honest.

Be Honest Whatever else an employer may be seeking, honesty is a mandatory job requirement. If an interviewer finds out that you have misrepresented yourself by lying or exaggerating about even one answer, then everything else you say will be suspect.[29]

Being honest doesn't mean you have to confess to every self-doubt and shortcoming. As in almost every type of situation, both parties in an employment interview try to create desirable impressions. In fact, some ethicists have noted that the ability to "sell" yourself honestly but persuasively is a desirable attribute, since it shows that you can represent an employer well after being hired.[30] So, highlight your strengths and downplay your weaknesses, but always be honest.

Emphasize the Positive Although you should always be honest, it is also wise to phrase your answers in a way that casts you in the most positive light. Consider the difference between positive and negative responses to this question:

Interviewer: I notice you've held several jobs, but you haven't had any experience in the field you've applied for.

Negative Answer: Uh, that's right. I only decided that I wanted to go into this field last year. I wish I had known that earlier.

Positive Answer: That's right. I've worked in a number of fields, and I've been successful in learning each one quickly. I'd like to think that this kind of adaptability will help me learn this job and grow with it as technology changes the way the company does business.

Notice how the second answer converted a potential negative into a positive answer. If you anticipate questions that have the ability to harm you, you can compose honest answers that present you in a favorable manner.

Even if you are confronted with comments that cast you in a negative light, you can recast yourself more positively. Notice how each negative trait below could be reframed as a positive attribute:[31]

Negative Trait	Positive Attribute
Overly detailed	Thorough, reliable
Cautious	Careful, accurate

Intense	Focused
Slow	Methodical, careful
Naive	Open, honest
Aggressive	Assertive

Don't misunderstand: Arguing with the interviewer or claiming that you have no faults isn't likely to win you a job offer. Still, reframing shortcomings as strengths can shift the employer's view of you:

Employer: If I were to ask your colleagues to describe your biggest weaknesses, what do you think they'd say?

Candidate: Well, some might say that I could work faster, especially when things get frantic. On the other hand, I think they would agree that I'm very careful about my work and that I don't make careless errors. In the long run, I think that saves the company and our customers a lot of grief. I want to work faster, but never at the cost of making mistakes.

Another important rule is to avoid criticizing others in an employment interview. Consider the difference between the answers below:

Interviewer: From your transcript, I notice that you graduated with a 2.3 grade-point average. Isn't that a little low?

Negative Answer: Sure, but it wasn't my fault. I had some terrible teachers during my first 2 years of college. We had to memorize a lot of useless information that didn't have anything to do with the real world. Besides, professors give you high grades if they like you. If you don't play their game, they grade you down.

Positive Answer: My low grade-point average came mostly from very bad freshman and sophomore years. I wasn't serious about school then, but you can see that my later grades are much higher. I've grown a lot in the past few years, and I'd like to think that I can use what I've learned in this job.

Most job candidates have been raised to regard modesty as a virtue, which makes it hard to toot their own horns. Excessive boasting certainly is likely to put off an interviewer, but experts flatly state that showcasing your strengths is essential. Florida State University management professor Michele Kacmar found that job seekers who talked about their good qualities were rated higher than those who focused on the interviewer.[32] Pre-interview rehearsals will help you find ways of saying positive things about yourself in a confident, nonboastful manner.

Back Up Your Answers with Evidence As you read a few pages ago, behavioral interviewers figure that the best predictor of a potential employee's performance is what he or she has done in the past. Even if you aren't in a behavioral interview, it is usually effective to back up any claims you make with evidence of your performance.

career tip

Creating a Portfolio

Showing a prospective employer what you can do is much more effective than simply talking about your qualifications. This is especially true for jobs that involve tangible products like graphic design, commercial art, journalism, and technical writing. Portfolios can also work in less obvious fields. You might, for example, demonstrate your ability to do solid work by sharing a report you helped create or a collection of letters from happy customers praising your work. In occupations like these, a well-designed and thoughtfully constructed portfolio showcases your skills and actual accomplishments.

You can present your portfolio in person during an interview, present it on a CD or DVD, or make it available online. You can find extensive guides to constructing portfolios at the career centers of many colleges and universities, including

- Ball State University **http://www.bsu.edu/art/article/0,25305--,00.html** and **http://www.bsu.edu/commstudies/article/0,,16720--,00.html**
- University of Wisconsin—River Falls **http://www.uwrf.edu/ccs/portfolio-steps.htm**
- EFolio Minnesota **http://www.efoliomn.com**

One good framework for answering questions is the "PAR" approach. These initials stand for the three parts of a good answer: Identifying the *problem*, describing the *action* you took, and stating the *results* that your actions produced. You can see the value of this approach by comparing the two answers below:

Interviewer: What strengths would you bring to this job?

Weak Answer: I'm a self-starter who can work without close supervision [unsupported claim].

Stronger Answer: I'm a self-starter who can work without close supervision [claim]. For example, in my last job, my immediate supervisor was away from the office off and on for 3 months because of some health issues [problem]. We were switching over to a new accounting system during that time, and I worked with the software company to make the change [action]. We made the changeover without losing a single day's work, and without any loss of data [results].

Keep Your Answers Brief It is easy to rattle on in an interview out of enthusiasm, a desire to show off your knowledge, or nervousness, but in most cases highly detailed answers are not a good idea. The interviewer probably has a lot of ground to cover, and long-winded answers won't help. A general rule is to keep your responses under 2 minutes. An interviewer who wants additional information can always ask for it.

Be Enthusiastic If you are applying for jobs that genuinely excite you, the challenge isn't to manufacture enthusiasm, but to show it. This can be difficult when you are feeling nervous in what feels like a make-or-break session. Just remember that the interviewer wants to know how you really feel about the job and organization, so all you have to do is share the enthusiasm you feel. Sharing your interest

Table 7–4 Questions to Consider Asking the Interviewer during an Employment Interview

Why is this position open?

How often has it been filled during the past 5 years?

What have been the reasons for people leaving in the past?

Why did the person who most recently held this position leave?

What would you like the next person who holds this job to do differently?

What are the most pressing issues and problems in this position?

What support does this position have (people, budget, equipment, etc.)?

What are the criteria for success in this position?

What might be the next career steps for a person who does well in this position?

What do you see as the future of this position? This organization?

What are the most important qualities you will look for in the person who will occupy this position?

and excitement in the job and company can give you a competitive edge. Career Center Director Gregory D. Hayes says, "If I talk to five deadbeat people and have one who is upbeat, that's the one I'm going to hire."[33]

Have Your Own Questions Answered Any good employer will recognize that you have your own concerns about the job. After you have answered the interviewer's questions, you should be prepared to ask a few of your own. Realize that your questions make indirect statements about you just as your answers to the interviewer's inquiries did. Be sure your questions aren't all greedy ones that focus on salary, vacation time, benefits, and so on. Table 7–4 lists some questions to consider asking when you are invited to do so.

Rehearsing an Interview No athlete would expect to win without practicing, and no performer would face an audience without practicing long and hard. The same principle holds when you are facing an important employment interview: You should practice enough to be your very best when facing a prospective employer.

Effective practicing involves several steps:

1. Use your pre-interview research to identify the nature of the job you are seeking. What skills are required? What personal qualities are most desirable for this position? What kind of person will fit best with the culture of the organization?
2. Draft a series of questions that explore the job description you have created; use the lists in Table 7–3 as a guide. Be sure to include questions in each key area: educational background, work experience, career goals, personal traits, and knowledge of the organization and job.
3. Think about how you can answer each question. Each answer should contain a *claim* ("I have experience making presentations using Microsoft PowerPoint") and *evidence* to back it up ("I learned PowerPoint in a college business

Self-Assessment Your IQ (Interview Quotient)

Assess how ready you are to handle employment interviews skillfully by answering the questions below, using the following scale:

5 = strongly agree; 4 = agree; 3 = maybe, not certain; 2 = disagree; 1 = definitely not.

Pre-Interview Planning

1.	I have conducted background research and understand the organization and the field in which it operates.	5 4 3 2 1
2.	I know the nature of the job for which I am being interviewed (responsibilities, necessary skills, how it fits in the organization).	5 4 3 2 1
3.	When possible and appropriate, I have asked members of my personal network to give the prospective employer favorable information about me.	5 4 3 2 1
4.	I am prepared for any interview format.	5 4 3 2 1
5.	I think constructively about the upcoming interview, rather than dwell on negative thoughts.	5 4 3 2 1
6.	I will be groomed and dressed in a way that is appropriate for this organization and the position I am seeking.	5 4 3 2 1
7.	I know what is required to arrive at the interview site comfortably in advance of the scheduled interview time.	5 4 3 2 1

During the Interview

8.	I can handle the small talk that arises in the opening phase of the interview.	5 4 3 2 1
9.	I nonverbally communicate my interest and enthusiasm for the job.	5 4 3 2 1
10.	I am prepared to answer the kinds of questions likely to be asked (see Table 7-3) in a way that shows how I can meet the employer's needs.	5 4 3 2 1
11.	I back up all my answers with examples that help clarify and prove what I'm saying.	5 4 3 2 1
12.	I give concise answers to the interviewer's questions.	5 4 3 2 1
13.	I present myself confidently and with enthusiasm.	5 4 3 2 1
14.	I am prepared to respond to illegal questions the interviewer might ask.	5 4 3 2 1
15.	I know when and how to deal with salary questions.	5 4 3 2 1
16.	I can provide a list of references who will respond favorably if contacted by my prospective employer.	5 4 3 2 1
17.	I am prepared to ask questions of my own about the job and organization.	5 4 3 2 1
18.	I have practiced asking and answering questions so I can feel comfortable and be articulate in the interview.	5 4 3 2 1

After the Interview

19.	I know how to write an effective thank-you letter.	5 4 3 2 1
20.	I am prepared to follow up with the interviewer to determine my status, if necessary.	5 4 3 2 1

(continued)

Scoring

Total the numbers you have circled. If your score is between 80 and 100, you appear to be well-prepared for interviews. If your score is between 60 and 80, you are moderately prepared. If your score is below 60, you would do well to make additional preparations before any employment interviews.

Source: After Ron and Caryl Krannich, *Interview for Success: A Practical Guide to Increasing Job Interviews, Offers, and Salaries*, 8th ed. (Manassas Park, VA: Impact Publications, 2003), pp. 12–17.

communications course and used it to train customer service reps in my last job"). In every case, make sure your answer shows how you can satisfy the employer's needs.

4. Role-play the interview several times with the help of a friend. Be sure you include the orientation and conclusion phases of the interview, as well as practice the questions you plan to ask the interviewer. If possible, videotape and review your performance twice: once to evaluate the content of your answers and again to check your appearance and the image you are projecting.

Many colleges have student job placement centers that have tremendous print resources on interviewing as well as a way of scheduling and videotaping a mock interview with a professional job counselor who will go over your videotape with you and give you constructive advice. Alternatively, to practice your answers to interview questions (with multiple-choice responses) go to Monster's career center Web site (**www.interviewmastery.com/index.cfm?affiliate5monster-ic**). The virtual interview gives you an opportunity to get feedback about a variety of responses.

Post-Interview Follow-up

Without exception, every employment interview should be followed immediately by a thank-you letter to the person who interviewed you. As Figure 7–4 shows, this letter serves several purposes:

- It demonstrates common courtesy.
- It reminds the employer of you.
- It gives you a chance to remind the interviewer of important information about you that came up in the interview and to provide facts you may have omitted then.
- It can correct any misunderstandings that may have occurred during the interview.
- It can tactfully remind the interviewer of promises made, such as a second interview or a response by a certain date.

If you don't get the job, consider contacting the person who interviewed you and asking what shortcomings kept you from being chosen. Even if the interviewer isn't comfortable sharing this information with you (it might not have anything to do with your personal qualifications), your sincere desire to improve yourself can leave a positive impression that could help you in the future.

FIGURE 7–4
Sample Thank-You Letter

8975 Santa Clarita Lane
Glendale, CA 90099
(818) 214-0987

March 30, 2007

Ms. Leslie Thoresen
The Think Tank
23262 Wilshire Blvd.
Los Angeles, CA 90076

Dear Ms. Thoresen:

I left our meeting yesterday full of excitement. Your remarks about the value of my experience as a student journalist and volunteer writer of newsletters were very encouraging. I also appreciate your suggestion that I speak with Mr. Leo Benadides. Thank you for promising to tell him that I'll be calling within the next week.

Since you expressed interest in the series of articles I wrote on how Asian women are breaking cultural stereotypes, I am enclosing copies with this letter. I hope you find them interesting.

Your remarks about the dangers of being typecast exclusively as a writer on women's issues were very helpful. Just after we spoke I received an assignment to write a series on e-mail romances. I'll be sure you receive a copy when these articles are published.

Thank you again for taking time from your busy day. I will look forward to hearing from you when the job we discussed is officially created.

Sincerely,

Susan Mineta

Susan Mineta

Unlike most business correspondence, a thank-you letter doesn't have to be typewritten. Because it is a personal expression of gratitude, handwriting is considered acceptable. Depending on the formality of your relationship and the image you want to create, you may still choose to use a regular business-letter format. Whatever style you choose, the letter should be neat, error-free, and carefully composed.

Interviewing and the Law

Many laws govern which questions are and are not legal in employment interviews, but the general principle that underlies them all is simple: Questions may not be asked for the purpose of discriminating on the basis of race, color, religion, sex, disabilities, national origin, or age. Employers may still ask about these areas, but the

U.S. government's Equal Employment Opportunity Commission (EEOC) permits only questions that investigate a **bona fide occupational qualification** (**BFOQ** in bureaucratic jargon) for a particular job. This means any question asked should be job-related. The Supreme Court has said that "the touchstone is business necessity."[34] Table 7–5 lists questions that are generally not considered BFOQs as well as those that are legitimate.

The Americans with Disabilities Act of 1990 (ADA) requires equal access to employment and provision of "reasonable accommodations" for persons with disabilities. It defines *disability* as a "physical" or "mental impairment" that "substantially limits" one or more "major life activities." As with any other job-related issue, the key question is what is "reasonable." The law clearly states, however, that disabled candidates can be questioned only about their ability to perform "essential functions" of a job and that employers are obligated to provide accommodations for disabled candidates and employees. If a person indicates a need for reasonable accommodation during the application process, the company is required to provide it. For example, a person who is deaf can request an interpreter at company expense for the interview.[35]

There are several ways to answer an unlawful question:[36]

1. *Answer without objection*. Answer the question, even though you know it is probably unlawful: "I'm 47."
2. *Seek explanation*. Ask the interviewer firmly and respectfully to explain why this question is a BFOQ: "I'm having a hard time seeing how my age relates to my ability to do this job. Can you explain?"
3. *Redirection*. Shift the focus of the interview away from a question that isn't job-related and toward the requirements of the position itself: "What you've said so far suggests that age is not as important for this position as is willingness to travel. Can you tell me more about the travel requirement?"
4. *Refusal*. Explain politely but firmly that you will not provide the information requested: "I'd rather not talk about my religion. That's a personal matter for me."
5. *Withdrawal*. End the interview immediately and leave, stating your reasons firmly but professionally: "I'm very uncomfortable with these questions about my personal life, and I don't see a good fit between me and this organization. Thank you for your time."

Choosing the best response style depends on several factors.[37] First, it is important to consider the probable intent of the interviewer. The question may indeed be aimed at collecting information that will allow the employer to discriminate, but it may just as well be a naive inquiry with no harm intended. Some interviewers are unsophisticated at their job. A study reported in *The Wall Street Journal* revealed that over 70 percent of 200 interviewers in Fortune 500 corporations thought that at least 5 of 12 unlawful questions were safe to ask.[38] In another survey, employers at 100 small businesses were presented with five illegal interview questions. All of the respondents said they either would ask or had asked at least one of them.[39] Results like these suggest that an illegal question may be the result of ignorance rather than malice. The interviewer who discusses family, nationality, or religion may simply be trying to make conversation. Be careful not to introduce these topics yourself as it may open the door to conversations and questions you would rather not deal with.

Table 7–5 Questions Interviewers Can and Cannot Legally Ask

Federal law restricts employer interviewer questions and other practices to areas clearly related to job requirements. The following are some questions and practices that are generally considered legitimate and others that are not.

Subject	Unacceptable	Acceptable
Name	What is your maiden name? Have you ever changed your name?	Name "Is there another name I'd need to check on your work and education record?"
Residence	"Do you own or rent your home?"	Place of residence
Age	Age Birth date Dates of attendance or completion of elementary or high school Questions that tend to identify applicants over age 40	Statement that hire is subject to verification that applicant meets legal age requirements "If hired, can you show proof of age?" "Are you over 18 years of age?" "If under 18, can you, after employment, submit a work permit?"
Birthplace, citizenship	Birthplace of applicant, applicant's parents, spouse, or other relatives "Are you a U.S. citizen?" *or* citizenship of applicant, applicant's parents, spouse, or other relatives Requirement that applicant produce naturalization, first papers, or alien card *prior to employment*	"Can you, after employment, submit verification of your legal right to work in the United States?" *or* statement that such proof may be required after employment
National origin	Questions as to nationality, lineage, ancestry, national origin, descent, or parentage of applicant, applicant's parents, or spouse "What is your mother tongue?" *or* language commonly used by applicant How applicant acquired ability to read, write, or speak a foreign language	Languages applicant reads, speaks, or writes, if use of a language other than English is relevant to the job for which applicant is applying
Sex, marital status, family	Questions that indicate applicant's sex Questions that indicate applicant's marital status Number and/or ages of children or dependents Provisions for child care Questions regarding pregnancy, childbearing, or birth control Name or address of relative, spouse, or children of adult applicant "With whom do you reside?" or "Do you live with your parents?"	Name and address of parent or guardian if applicant is a minor, statement of company policy regarding work assignment of employees who are related
Race, color	Questions as to applicant's race or color Questions regarding applicant's complexion or color of skin, eyes, hair	

Subject	Unacceptable	Acceptable
Religion	Questions regarding applicant's religion Religious days observed *or* "Does your religion prevent you from working weekends or holidays?"	Statement by employer of regular days, hours, or shifts to be worked
Arrest, criminal record	Arrest record *or* "Have you ever been arrested?"	"Have you ever been convicted of a felony?" Such a question must be accompanied by a statement that a conviction will not necessarily disqualify an applicant from employment
Military service	General questions regarding military service such as dates and type of discharge Questions regarding service in a foreign military	Questions regarding relevant skills acquired during applicant's U.S. military service
Organizations	"List all organizations, clubs, societies, to which you belong."	"Please list job-related organizations or professional associations to which you belong that you believe enhance your job performance."
References	Questions of applicant's former employers or acquaintances that elicit information specifying the applicant's race, color, religious creed, national origin, ancestry, physical handicap, medical condition, marital status, age, or sex	"By whom were you referred for a position here?" Names of persons willing to provide professional and/or character references for applicant
Physical description, photograph	Questions as to applicant's height and weight Requirement that applicant affix a photograph to application Request that asks applicant, at his or her option, to submit a photograph Requirement that calls for a photograph after interview but before employment	Statement that photograph may be required after employment
Physical condition, handicap	Questions regarding applicant's general medical condition, state of health, or illnesses Questions regarding receipt of workers' compensation "Do you have any physical disabilities or handicaps?"	Statement by employer that offer may be made contingent on applicant's passing a job-related physical examination "Do you have any physical condition or handicap that may limit your ability to perform the job applied for? If yes, what can be done to accommodate your limitation?"

For further information about illegal questions consult these online sources:

http://jobsearchtech.about.com/od/interview/l/aa022403_2.htm
http://www.jobweb.com/Resources/Library/Interviews/Handling_Illegal_46_01.htm
http://www.collegegrad.com/ezine/23illega.shtml
http://www.usatoday.com/careers/resources/interviewillegal.htm
http://www.careerbuilder.com/JobSeeker/CareerBytes/Hints1199.htm?cbRecursionCnt=1&cbsid=cb781b8e848941068d065692fdf7abc0-191287698-r0-1

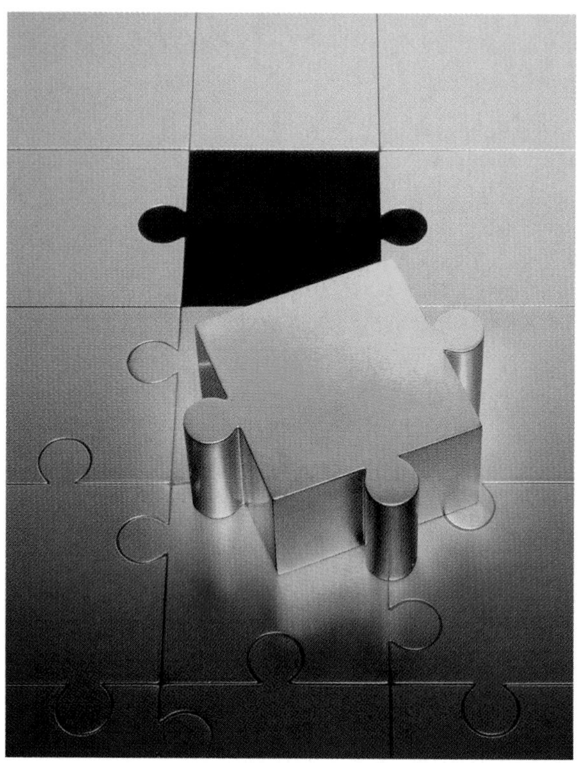

A second factor when considering how to respond to an illegal question is your desire for the job at hand. You may be more willing to challenge the interviewer when a position isn't critical to your future. On the other hand, if your career rides on succeeding in a particular interview, you may be willing to swallow your objections. A third factor to consider is your feeling of comfort with the interviewer. For example, a female candidate with school-age children might welcome the chance to discuss child care issues with an interviewer who has identified herself as a single mother who faces the same challenges. A fourth item to consider is your own personal style. If you are comfortable asserting yourself, you may be willing to address an illegal question head-on. If you are less comfortable speaking up, especially to authority figures, you may prefer to respond less directly.

Being interviewed does not mean you are at the mercy of the interviewer; laws do govern your rights as a candidate. If you choose to take more assertive approach to illegal questioning that you believe resulted in discrimination, you have the right to file a charge with the EEOC and your state Fair Employment Practices Commission within 180 days of the interview. In practice, the EEOC will withhold its investigation until the state commission has completed its inquiry. Federal and state agencies have a backlog of cases, however, so it may take years to complete an investigation. The commission may mediate the case, file a suit, or issue you a letter to sue.[40] Keep in mind that just because you can file a lawsuit doesn't mean this will always be the best course of action: A suit can take many months, or even years, to be settled and a ruling in your favor may not result in a large settlement. Furthermore, knowledge that you've filed a suit is not likely to make you an attractive candidate to other employers who hear of your action. Seeking professional counsel can help you make a decision that balances your personal values and practical considerations.

Sample Employment Interview

The following transcript is based on a real interview. As you read it, pay attention to both the interviewer's questions and the applicant's responses. In both cases, notice the strengths and the areas needing improvement. What parts of this interview would you like to incorporate in your style? What parts would you handle differently?

[The interview begins with an exchange of pleasantries]	**Interviewer:**	Monica Hansen? I'm Chris Van Dyke. Welcome.
	Applicant:	It's good to meet you.

career tip

Cleaning Up Your Digital Dirt

In spite of your best efforts to create a résumé and present yourself as a qualified job applicant, prospective employers have other ways of forming impressions of you, including all of the information available online. To discover what others can easily see about you, try these options:

1. Google yourself by typing your name into the search engine at **www.google.com**. Employers do it and so can you. The only hits may be advice you gave about training your Jack Russell Terrier or a review you wrote about a great restaurant. On the other hand, you may find comments you made at meetings you attended, information about you in newspaper articles, public hearings, or court actions. You may be able to get site owners to remove things you would rather not have on record. If not, at least be aware of what others can see.
2. Review your profile on Web sites like Facebook (**www.facebook.com**) or MySpace (**www.myspace.com**), and/or Web sites you have created. Imagine the impression your profiles would make on prospective employers and consider editing references and photos you no longer want to share with the world—or at least change your privacy settings. The photo of you from the Halloween party your sophomore year or the comments others wrote about you might not create the best impression.
3. Use technology to see what others are saying about you. Pubsub.com or Feedster.com can help you track and monitor what is said about you in blogs or newsgroups, providing you the opportunity to correct false information.

Source: After J. Flesher, "How to Clean Up Your Digital Dirt Before It Trashes Your Job Search," retrieved January 26, 2006, from **www.careerjournal.com**.

[... and small talk.]	**Interviewer:**	Did you have any trouble finding us?
	Applicant:	The directions were perfect. And thanks for the parking pass.
[The interviewer briefly previews the approach of the interview and the anticipated amount of time.]	**Interviewer:**	Oh, yes. That's a necessity. The garage costs $12 per day if you don't have one. We'll have about a half-hour this morning to talk about the personnel administrator's position you've applied for. I'd like to learn about you. And, of course, I want to answer any questions you have about us.
	Applicant:	Great. I'm looking forward to it.
[Body of interview begins with an open question about employment history.]	**Interviewer:**	Good. Let's begin by having you tell me about your most recent position. Your résumé says you were at ITC in Springfield. Is that right?
[Interviewee uses question to showcase	**Applicant:**	That's right. My official job title was personnel assistant, but that really

the skills acquired in past job that could help in the one being offered here.]

doesn't describe very well the work I did. I recruited nonexempt employees, processed the payroll, oriented new employees, and maintained the files.

[Follow-up questions explore areas of interest in the new job.]

Interviewer: Were you involved with insurance?

[The applicant uses this answer to point out another skill that she brings to the job.]

Applicant: Yes. I processed workers' compensation claims and maintained the insurance reports for our health care plans. I learned a lot about dealing with government regulations.

Interviewer: And you said you were involved in hiring?

Applicant: Yes. I was responsible for recruiting and interviewing all clerical and administrative support people.

[Another open question, this time exploring the applicant's ability to analyze her own performance.]

Interviewer: How did that go?

[The applicant fails to use this answer to showcase her abilities . . .]

Applicant: It was tough in Springfield. There's actually a shortage of talented support people there. It's an expensive town to live in, and there aren't a lot of people who can afford living there on an administrative assistant's salary. It's not like Atlanta, where there's plenty of good help.

[so the interviewer follows up with another question.]

Interviewer: What did you learn about hiring from your experiences at ITC?

[This answer is better, since it describes insights and skills the applicant brings to this job.]

Applicant: I learned to look further than the résumé. Some people seem great on paper, but you find there's something wrong when you hire them. Other people don't have much experience on paper, but they have a lot of potential.

Interviewer: How did you get beyond paper screening?

Applicant: Well, if someone looked at all promising, I would phone the former employers and talk to the people the applicant actually worked for. Of course a lot of former employers are pretty noncommittal, but they usually would give clues about what they really thought about the person I was investigating—giving an indirect opinion without saying it outright.

Interviewer: What would you do if this was the person's first job?

[The applicant demonstrates resourcefulness here, spelling out her skill in the last sentence of her answer.]

Applicant: I found that almost everyone had done some kind of work—part-time or vacation. And I could check up on that. Or I would even ask for the names of a few teachers and phone them up, if the person was just graduating. I learned that there's almost always a way to find what you're looking for, if you get creative.

Interviewer: Didn't that take a lot of time?

[This is a subtle way of saying, "I have good judgment."]

Applicant: Yes, it did. But it was worth it in the long run, since we got much better employees that way. We almost never had to dismiss someone whom we'd done a phone check on.

Interviewer: You were promoted after a year. Why?

[Again, the applicant's answer introduces a trait that would be valuable in the new job: The desire for self-improvement.]

Applicant: I was lucky to be in the right place. The company was growing, and we were very busy. I tried to take advantage of the situation by offering to do more and by taking classes at night.

Interviewer: What classes did you take?

[Presumably the skills acquired in these courses would be useful if the applicant is hired. In any case, she demonstrates the desire to learn skills useful in the business world.]

Applicant: I took an applied human relations class last spring. And before that, a couple of computer classes: one in database management and one in desktop publishing. Our department was thinking about starting an employee newsletter, and I wanted to see if we could produce it in-house.

Interviewer: It sounds like you've done very well at ITC. Why do you want to leave?

[The response begins with a provocative statement, and then

Applicant: In some ways I *don't* want to leave. The people are great—most of them—and I've enjoyed the work. But I'm looking

goes on to supply a solid reason for seeking a new job.]		for more challenges, and there isn't much chance for me to take on more responsibility there.
	Interviewer:	Why not?
	Applicant:	Well, my boss, the personnel director, is very happy in her job and has no plans to leave. She's young, and there's very little chance I'll be able to advance.
[The interviewer seeks specifics to elaborate on the broad statement "I'm looking for more challenges"]	**Interviewer:**	I see. Well, that is a problem. And what kind of responsibilities are you looking for?
[. . . and the candidate supplies answers.]	**Applicant:**	I'd say the biggest one is the chance to help make policy. In my past jobs, I've been carrying out policies that other people—management—have made. That's been fine, but I'd like to be involved in setting some policies myself.
[Again, the interviewer follows up by seeking more specifics]	**Interviewer:**	What kinds of policies?
[. . . and the candidate is prepared with detailed responses.]	**Applicant:**	Oh, there are several. Designing benefits packages. Coming up with a performance review system that people will take seriously. Teaching our supervisors how to interview and hire more systematically.
[The interviewer makes a smooth transition to a new topic.]	**Interviewer:**	I see. Well, the position you've applied for certainly does have those sorts of responsibilities. Let me ask you another question. What do you enjoy most about personnel work?
[The stock answer "I like to work with people" is so broad that it has little meaning]	**Applicant:**	Well, I really enjoy the chance to work so much with people. Of course, there's a lot of paperwork, too, but I especially like the chance to work with people.
[. . . so the interviewer seeks clarification.]	**Interviewer:**	When you say "people," what kinds of work are you thinking of?

Applicant: I guess the common denominator is making people happy. Lots of employees get involved with the personnel department—once they've been hired, that is—because they have problems. Maybe it's an insurance claim or a problem with their performance review. It makes me feel good to see them leave feeling satisfied, or at least feeling better after they've come in so upset.

Interviewer: Are you always able to help them?

Applicant: No, of course not. Sometimes a person will want the impossible, and sometimes there just won't be any answer.

[Again, the interviewer uses a situational approach, seeking specifics.]

Interviewer: Can you give examples of these times?

[The applicant does a good job of describing a situation that illustrates her previous answer.]

Applicant: Well, one example of an impossible request comes up a lot with health insurance. At ITC we could choose from two plans. With one plan you could use any doctor you wanted. You had to make a co-payment with that one. With the other plan, you had to choose a doctor from a list of preferred providers, but there was no co-payment. If an employee chose the preferred-provider plan and later decided he or she wanted to use a doctor that wasn't on the list, we just couldn't do anything about it.

Interviewer: We've had that problem here, too. How did you handle it?

Applicant: Being sympathetic helped a little. Even if I couldn't give them what they wanted, at least saying I was sorry might have made it seem less like a total rejection. I also pointed out that they *could* switch plans during the open-enrollment period, which comes every year. I've also suggested to my boss that we do a better job of informing people about the restrictions of the preferred-provider plan before they sign up and maybe even get them to sign a statement that says they understand them. I think that would reduce the surprises that come up later.

[With this new topic, the interviewer shifts from fact to opinion questions.]

Interviewer: That's a good idea. Monica, what qualities do you think are important for a personnel officer?

Applicant: Knowing the job is definitely important, but I'd say getting along with people might be even more important.

Interviewer: And how would you describe your ability to get along?

Applicant: Sometimes I think I deserve an Academy Award for acting the opposite of the way I feel.

Interviewer: Really? Tell me about it.

[The applicant offers a specific example to illustrate her provocative statement about acting the opposite of the way she feels.]

Applicant: Every so often people will come in with an attitude problem, and I try to calm them down by acting more pleasant than I feel. For example, we've had people who think they're entitled to take 6 months off for a workers' compensation claim, when the doctor has said they're ready to come back after a few weeks. They come in and yell at us, and it's tough to be pleasant at times like those. But I don't think there's any point in being blunt or rude. It just makes them more angry.

[This indirect question really asks, "What kind of manager might you be?"]

Interviewer: I see what you mean. Let's shift gears, Monica. If you were to pick a boss, what are the important traits that he or she should have?

Applicant: Let me see . . . certainly lots of follow-up—letting people know where they stand. The ability to give criticism constructively and to compliment good work. Giving people a task and then leaving them alone, without nagging.

Interviewer: But still being there to help if it's needed, right?

Applicant: Sure. But also giving me the space to finish a job without staying *too* close.

Interviewer: Anything else?

Applicant: Being available for help, as you said. Being consistent. And being willing to train employees in new jobs, letting them grow. And considering the personal goals of employees.

[The interviewer turns to a new topic area.]

Interviewer: In personnel work, there's a need for confidentiality. What does that mean to you?

Applicant: That's an important area. You see lots of personal information, and it's easy to make offhand remarks that could upset someone.

Interviewer: What kinds of things do you have to be careful about?

Applicant: Oh, even something as simple as a person's birthday. Most people wouldn't care, but some people might be offended if their birthdays got out. I've learned to be constantly on guard, to watch what I say. I'm a private person anyway, so that helps.

[This question explores the candidate's personal attitudes.]

Interviewer: Monica, I've been asking you a lot of questions. Let me ask just one more; then it can be your turn. What are the factors that motivate you?

Applicant: Well, I like to be busy. If things aren't busy, I still work, but I like to be stimulated. I seem to get more work done when I'm busy than when there's plenty of time. It's crazy, but true. I'm also motivated by the chance to grow and take on as much responsibility as I can handle.

[Almost every employment interview includes a chance for the interviewee to ask questions.]

Interviewer: Monica, what questions do you have for me? What can I tell you about the job or the company?

[The applicant wisely begins by asking about the company, not focusing on personal questions such as compensations.]

Applicant: What kind of growth do you see for the company?

Interviewer: Well, we have 155 employees now. As I think you know, we're 5 years old, and we started with five employees. Our sales were up 14 percent last year, and it looks like we'll be expanding more.

Applicant: How many employees do you think will be added?

Interviewer: Well, we hired 20 new people last year, and we expect to hire almost the same number this year.

Applicant: And what's the turnover like?

Interviewer: That's a good question for a personnel person to ask! We've been growing so much, and people have been able to move into more responsible jobs, so they've been satisfied for the most part. Our turnover has been pretty low—about 15 percent annually.

[This question focuses on responsibilities of the job.]

Applicant: Will the person you hire be involved in making policy?

Interviewer: Yes, definitely. We're still trying to catch up with ourselves after growing so fast. A big project for this year is to put together an employee handbook. Too many of our policies are verbal now, and that's not good. Developing that handbook would mean working directly with the president of the company, and that definitely involves developing policy.

[Finally, the applicant asks about compensation and benefits.]

Applicant: Of course, I'm interested in learning about the benefits and salary.

[The interviewer appropriately defers a complete answer until the company has a clearer idea of the candidate's desirability.]

Interviewer: Of course. Here's a copy of our benefits summary for you to study. We can talk about salary later. Right now I'd like you to meet a couple of our managers. After you've spoken with them, we can get back together to discuss salary and other matters.

[The interviewer wraps up the conversation by

We will definitely be making our decision within the next 10 days, so I *describing when the hiring decision will be made.]*

promise you you'll have an answer before the first of next month. It's been a real pleasure talking to you, Monica. You certainly express yourself well. I'll talk with you again soon.

Applicant: Thanks. I've enjoyed the talk, too. I'll look forward to hearing from you.

The Performance Appraisal Interview

A working group is like an athletic team: Even the best players need the guidance of a coach to help them do their individual best and work with other members. Managers are the coaches in most organizations, and the performance appraisal interview is one way they help their team members.

Definition and Importance

Performance appraisal interviews are scheduled regularly between superior and subordinate to discuss the quality of the subordinate's performance. More specifically, these interviews have several functions, including the following:

- *Letting the employee know where he or she stands.* This kind of feedback includes praising good work, communicating areas that need improvement, and conveying to the employee his or her prospects for advancement.
- *Developing employee skills.* The review can be a chance for the employee to learn new skills. Among their other roles, managers and supervisors should be teachers. The performance appraisal interview can be a chance to show an employee how to do a better job.

Dilbert: © Scott Adams/Dist. by United Feature Syndicate, Inc. Reprinted by permission.

- *Improving employment relationship.* Performance reviews should improve superior–subordinate relationships and give employees a sense of participation in the job. Ideally, employees will leave the interview feeling better about themselves and the organization.
- *Helping management learn the employee's point of view.* A performance appraisal should include upward as well as downward communication. It provides a chance for subordinates to explain their perspective to managers.
- *Counseling the employee.* An appraisal interview provides the chance for managers to learn about personal problems that may be affecting an employee's performance and to offer advice and support.
- *Setting goals for the future.* One result of every performance appraisal interview should be a clear idea of how both the superior and the subordinate will behave in the future.

Some bosses and employees complain that performance reviews are a nuisance. Management guru Robert Townsend agrees—to a point. "Printed forms for performance appraisal and MBOs are used by incompetent bosses in badly managed companies," he claims.[41] Performance appraisals appear to be increasingly unpopular and a recent survey of HR professionals found that 32 percent were unsatisfied with their company's process.[42] Despite criticisms of this sort, authorities on communication agree that most managers and supervisors need to give employees *more* feedback, not less. "Day-to-day coaching is the most overlooked step of the performance process," says *One Minute Manager* co-author Kenneth Blanchard.[43] Townsend agrees. "Real managers manage by frequent eyeball contact," he insists, quoting one good boss's description of the process: "Half our meetings are held in the hall, the other half in the washroom."

Perhaps these management experts have a point. If bosses spent more time giving employees informal feedback and setting goals on a day-to-day basis, there might be less need for quarterly or semiannual formal meetings. But one way or the other, performance review is one of the most important responsibilities a manager has.

Despite the potential threat of being evaluated, performance appraisals can be welcomed by employees. One of the greatest hungers that workers have is to know where they stand with management. Researchers have found that receiving personal feedback correlates highly with job satisfaction,[44] and appraisal interviews offer a periodic session dedicated to providing just that feedback. Despite this fact, 40 percent of all employees report that they don't receive a regular performance review.[45]

Just because employees want feedback doesn't mean that they are always satisfied with the performance appraisals they do receive. Sometimes performance reviews can be contaminated by organizational politics, generating resentment and undermining morale.[46] This sort of bias isn't new: Over 18 centuries ago in 3rd-century China, a member of the Wei dynasty's court complained about a manager: "The Imperial Rater of Nine Grades seldom rates men according to their merits but always according to his likes and dislikes."[47] Intentionally or not, many unskilled managers turn appraisal sessions into criticisms of past shortcomings that do little besides arouse resentment and defensiveness in employees. The interviewing skills outlined in this section can help make sure that a performance review meets the needs of both management and employees.

Performance review should be an ongoing process, not something that happens only at infrequent intervals during a scheduled interview.[48] The functions of performance appraisal listed on pages 241–242 can and should be performed constantly in the kind of process pictured in Figure 7–5. This doesn't mean that formal

FIGURE 7–5
The Performance Appraisal Process

interviews are useless, for they provide a chance to focus on how well the ongoing job of judging and improving performance is proceeding. The value of a formal review is captured by former Chrysler chairman Lee Iacocca, who describes how the procedure works in his company:

> *Every three months, each manager sits down with his immediate superior to review the manager's past accomplishments and to chart his goals for the next term. Once there is agreement on these goals, the manager puts them in writing and the supervisor signs off on it. . . . The discipline of writing something down is the first step toward making it happen. In conversation, you can get away with all kinds of vagueness and nonsense, often without even realizing it. But there's something about putting your thoughts on paper that forces you to get down to specifics. That way, it's harder to deceive yourself—or anybody else.*[49]

Steps in the Appraisal Process

After an initial exchange of pleasantries—usually brief—the manager should provide a rationale for the interview, an outline of what information will be covered and how it will be used, and a preview of the interview's probable length. After the preliminaries, the body of an appraisal interview should go on to cover three areas: a review of the criteria established in past meetings, a discussion of the employee's performance, and a setting of goals for the future.

Review Progress The first step in the body of any appraisal interview should be to identify the criteria by which the employee is being evaluated. Ideally, these criteria will already be clear to both the manager and employee, but it is wise to restate them. A manager might say:

> *Bill, as I'm sure you remember, we decided at our last meeting to focus on several targets. We agreed that if you could reach them, you'd be doing your present job very well and you'd be setting yourself up for an assistant sales manager's position. Here's the list of targets we developed last time [shows employee list]. So these are the areas we need to look at today.*

Discuss Successes, Problems, and Needs After the criteria have been defined, the discussion can focus on how well the employee has satisfied them. Discussion will be easiest when the goals are measurable: Are sales up 15 percent? Have jobs been completed on time? If the employee has explanations for why targets were not reached, it is the manager's job to consider these fairly. Some goals are subjective, so the evaluation of their performance will be a matter of judgment as well. Even seemingly vague goals like "being more patient with customers" can be at least partially clarified by turning them into simple behavioral descriptions such as "letting customers talk without interrupting them."

When evaluating past performance, it is important to maintain a balance among the points under consideration. Without meaning to let it happen, a manager and employee can become involved in discussing (or debating) a relatively unimportant point at length, throwing the overall look at the employee's performance out of perspective. A skillful interviewer will focus only on the most important criteria, usually dealing with no more than three areas that need work. Even the most demanding manager will realize upon reflection that changing old habits is difficult and that it is unrealistic to expect dramatic improvement in too many areas within a short time.

Even when an appraisal is conducted with the best of intentions, its evaluative nature raises the odds of a defensive response. Feedback will be best received when it meets several criteria. Observing these guidelines can boost the chances of keeping the interview's tone constructive:

- *Feedback should be accurate.* Perhaps the worst mistake an evaluator can make is to get the facts wrong. Before you judge an employee, be sure you have an accurate picture of his or her performance and all the factors that affected it. A tell-and-listen approach can help the manager understand an employee's performance more fully.
- *Feedback should be relevant to the job.* For example, it may be legitimate to comment on an employee's appearance in a job that involves contact with the public, but it is out of line to be critical about the way he or she handles personal matters after business hours.

The best chances of success occur when the review offers a balance of praise and constructive suggestions for improvement. Both everyday experience and research have demonstrated the power of positive reinforcement. One study revealed that the commitment level of employees dropped when their behavior was identified as only "satisfactory."[50] A manager who uses praise in appraisal interviews should remember the tips for praising outlined in Chapter 5 (pages 143–144).

Sooner or later, even the most outstanding employee will need to hear criticism about his or her work. Delivering negative information is one of the biggest challenges a manager or supervisor can face. The guidelines in Chapter 5 (pages 145–146) offer tips on how to offer negative feedback supportively. Handling critical situations well isn't just the boss's responsibility; the subordinate needs to behave responsibly too. The guidelines for coping nondefensively with criticism outlined on pages 146–149 should be helpful when it is your turn to receive critical messages. While following these guidelines won't guarantee a successful performance review, it can increase the chances that the meeting will be genuinely constructive and serve the interests of both the superior and the subordinate.

Set Goals Once the employee and manager have discussed past successes, problems, and needs, the task becomes defining goals for the future. The goals should meet several criteria:

- They should focus on the most important aspects of the job. The tried-and-true 80:20 rule applies here: Changing 20 percent of a worker's behavior will usually solve 80 percent of the problems.
- They should be described as specifically as possible so that both manager and employee will know what actions constitute the target.
- A time period should be stated for each target. People often work best when faced with a deadline, and setting dates lets both parties know when the results are due.
- The targets ought to provide some challenge to the worker, requiring effort yet being attainable. A manageable challenge will produce the greatest growth and leave workers and managers feeling pleased with the changes that occur.

Table 7–6 Checklist for Performance Appraisal Interviewing

a. Interview covers key areas
   i. Orients employee
   ii. Establishes positive climate
   iii. Reviews past achievement of goals
   iv. Identifies successes, problems, and needs in employee's area of responsibility
   v. Establishes new goals with employee

b. Feedback delivered constructively
   i. Information accurate
   ii. Feedback appropriate to critic's role
   iii. Balance of praise and constructive criticism

c. Praise delivered effectively
   i. Praise sincere
   ii. Specific behaviors identified
   iii. Emphasis on progress, not perfection
   iv. Praise communicated by deeds as well as by words

d. Criticism expressed constructively
   i. Criticism limited to key areas
   ii. Criticism delivered in face-saving manner
   iii. Criticism accompanied by offer to help
   iv. Benefits of cooperating emphasized

e. Interview accomplishes all necessary functions
   i. Lets employee know where he or she stands
   ii. Develops employee skills
   iii. Improves communication climate, boosts morale
   iv. Helps management understand employee's point of view
   v. Counsels employee as appropriate
   vi. Sets goals for future

Review and Respond to the Written Record The appraisal process commonly has a written dimension in addition to the interview itself. Before the meeting, the manager often completes an evaluation form listing characteristics or behaviors important to the job. Ideally, the information on this form is taken from the goals set at the previous interview. In some organizations, the subordinate also fills out a self-rating form covering similar areas. In most companies, a performance review is summarized and documented with a written evaluation. In most cases, the manager completes a final report that summarizes the results of the session. The employee usually has the option of adding his or her own response to the manager's report. This document then becomes part of the employee's records and is used as a basis for future evaluations and as a source of information for decisions about promotions. (See Table 7–6.)

summary

This chapter focuses on four important types of interviews: information-gathering, career research, employment, and performance appraisal. The most common type of information-gathering interview aims at conducting research. The research interviewer should begin by collecting background information on the subject and the interviewee. This information is used to define the general goals of the interview and identify the specific questions that should be asked. Equally important is identifying whom to interview to get the desired information.

A career research interview is conducted to research a career field, to be remembered by the interviewee, and to gain referrals to others who might be able to assist in beginning and shaping that career. Personal contacts are vital to choosing interviewees, and professionalism in written and oral communication are vital in contacting an interviewee, conducting the interview, and following up after the interview.

Employment interviews are critically important for even the most qualified job applicant, since the person who receives a job offer is often the one who knows the most about how to get hired. Since many positions are never advertised, a job seeker should begin the selection process long before an official job interview. The first step involves conducting background research, then contacting potential employers appropriately, usually with a cover letter and résumé. Candidates should rehearse for panel, behavioral, and audition interview formats. They should also think constructively, make initial contact professionally, and dress appropriately. Whatever the format, interviewees should be prepared to answer key questions and constantly focus on showing how they can help the organization reach its goals by responding to the employer's needs and concerns. Candidates should also answer honestly, emphasize the positive while briefly and enthusiastically backing up answers with evidence, and ask pertinent questions. Finally, they should follow up with a letter of thanks to the interviewer.

Federal and state laws restrict interviewers from asking questions that are not related to the bona fide occupational qualifications of a job. In this chapter, we listed both acceptable and unacceptable questions and practices and suggested strategies for responding to illegal questions.

Performance appraisal interviews give superiors and their subordinates a structured way to look at the quality of the subordinate's performance. When conducted skillfully, these sessions offer a chance for employees to learn how they are viewed by management and to jointly set goals.

Appraisal interviews should begin with a review of the employee's performance, clearly stating the criteria used to evaluate the employee. Next, the employee's performance should be compared to these criteria, citing successes and problems. Finally, the manager and employee should set goals for the next evaluation period.

key terms

Test your understanding of these key terms by visiting the Online Learning Center Web site at www.mhhe.com/adler9.

audition interview 213
behavioral interview 213
bona fide occupational qualification (BFOQ) 229
career research interview 205

diagnostic interview 201
employment interview 209
exit interview 201
investigative interview 201
panel interview 213
performance appraisal interview 241
research interview 201
scannable résumé 213
stress interview 213
survey interview 201

activities

Go to the self-quizzes at the Online Learning Center at www.mhhe.com/adler9 to test your knowledge of chapter concepts.

1. Invitation to Insight

Consider the four types of interviews common to most occupations. For each type:

a. Identify a specific interview you have taken part in or will encounter.
b. Describe the goal of the interviewee and the interviewer in each situation. Is it similar or conflicting? If conflicting, what extra preparations would be advisable?
c. For the past interviews, describe how satisfied you were with your behavior. For future interviews, predict how satisfied you expect to be with your behavior, given your present level of interviewing skill.
d. Use concepts you have learned in this chapter to suggest at least two improvements you can enact in your next interview.

2. Invitation to Insight

Select a person in your chosen career who plays a role in hiring new employees. Conduct an information-gathering interview to discover the following:

a. What methods are used to identify job candidates?
b. What format is used to interview applicants?
c. What formal and informal criteria are used to hire applicants?
d. What personal qualities of applicants make a positive or negative impression?

3. Invitation to Insight

Brainstorm 5 to 10 specific actions you have taken (in classes, on the job, or in volunteer activities) that demonstrate your ability to perform well. Include specific evidence for each. Recall the positive results of your actions.

For added practice, team up with a classmate. Use the PAR approach (see p. 224) to role-play asking and answering interview questions. As your classmate asks questions, answer with actions and results. Then switch roles.

4. Skill Builder

For each of the following topics identify at least two people you could interview to gather information and write one or more specific objectives for each interview:

a. Learning more about a potential employer. (Name a specific organization.)
b. Deciding whether to enroll in a specific class. (You choose which one.)
c. Deciding which type of personal computer or software application to purchase.
d. Exploring career opportunities in a city of your choice.
e. Determining the best savings or investment vehicle for you at this time.
f. Comparing health insurance plans available to students.

5. Skill Builder

You can develop your skill and gain appreciation for the value of the informational interview by doing one of the following activities:

a. Conducting an informational interview with a professional in a career field that interests you. Possible goals are to learn more about the field, to learn how to advance in your current job, or to learn what it would take to switch fields. Follow these steps:

i. Identify a promising interviewee.
ii. Write a letter requesting an interview.
iii. Follow up your letter with a phone call to arrange a date.
iv. Develop a list of questions that will achieve your stated purpose. Be sure that these questions follow the guidelines in Chapter 6.
v. Conduct the interview and report your results. Analyze how well you performed and suggest how you could improve in conducting future interviews.
vi. Write a thank-you letter to your subject.

b. Identifying a specific organization you would like to work for, and completing the following pre-interview steps:

i. Identify the person—by title and name, if possible—who has the power to hire you.
ii. Using research and the results of informational interviews, analyze the requirements for the position you would like to hold.
iii. Develop a list of questions a potential boss might ask in a selection interview.
iv. Prepare answers to those questions.

c. Role-playing an actual interview, with a companion filling the role of your potential employer.

6. Skill Builder

Imagine that a supervisor or instructor is preparing an evaluation of your performance. Four areas will be covered:

a. Quality of work.
b. Productivity.
c. Communication skill.
d. Attitude.

i. For each area, write one or two measurable objectives that could be used as assessments in your area of work.
ii. Based on your actual behavior on the job, prepare a verbal explanation describing how well you have met these assessments during the last month.
iii. Identify several areas in which you could improve. From this information compose several measurable behavioral objectives for the coming month.

resources

In Print

Allen, J. G. *The Complete Q&A Job Interview Book*, 4th ed. Hoboken, NJ: John Wiley & Sons, Inc. 2004.
This book leads you into a thorough preparation for thinking through the reasons behind and possible answers to typical interview questions. The author provides suggestions for improving your verbal and nonverbal responses.

Bolles, R. N. *Job-Hunting on the Internet*, 3rd ed. Berkeley, CA: Ten Speed Press, 2005.
The author of *What Color Is Your Parachute?* presents a comprehensive guide to Internet job-hunting. Annotated sites are categorized by job postings, résumés, career counseling, and specialized sites for women, minorities, persons with disabilities, and more. Excellent general job-searching advice, too.

Fry, R. *Your First Interview: For Students and Anyone Preparing to Enter Today's Tough Job Market*, 4th ed. Franklin Lakes, NJ: Career Press, 2002.
Ron Fry shows the reader step-by-step how to take charge of the interview process from presenting yourself positively at first contact through negotiating a salary. He presents concise and updated information on networking, as well as on informational and employment interviewing.

Hansen, Katherine. *A Foot in the Door: Networking Your Way into the Hidden Job Market*. Berkeley, CA: Ten Speed Press, 2000.
A useful guide to networking. Hansen begins by describing the "hidden job market" of unadvertised positions, and how networking operates to fill them. She then goes on to explain how to

identify potential network members, how to make contact with them, how to ask for help, and how to keep track of information gleaned from the network. Specific sections offer advice for women, minorities, older workers, former military personnel, and those who have been fired or laid off.

Schmidt, Wallace V., and Roger N. Conway. *Results Oriented Interviewing: Principles, Practices, and Procedures*. Boston: Allyn & Bacon, 1999.

This book contains useful chapters on a variety of interview types: employment, performance appraisal, counseling, sales, and focus group research.

Stewart, Charles J., and William B. Cash, Jr. *Interviewing: Principles and Practices*, 11th ed. New York: McGraw-Hill, 2006.

Chapter 8 offers useful advice about employment interviews, including information on legal and illegal questions. Chapter 9 explores performance reviews in depth.

On the Web

Job Leads

Even if you plan to base your job campaign on personal networking, using Web-based job announcements can give you a feeling for the marketplace in the field of your choice. Beyond just describing vacancies, many of the following sites offer a variety of career planning tools such as résumé building, career counseling, and interview tips. Some of the best job sites on the Web are listed below.

Job Hunters Bible (**www.jobhuntersbible.com**), the megasite developed by career and job-hunting expert Richard Nelson Bolles, offers extensive links to sites for job-hunting tasks such as searching for job listings; posting your résumé; getting career counseling; researching jobs, companies, and cities; and making contacts with people who can help you.

The following sites are worth considering for job postings and extensive job-search resources:

- *Career Magazine:* **www.careermag.com**
- *CareerLab:* **www.careerlab.com**
- *CareerShop:* **www.careershop.com**
- *Career Builder:* **www.careerbuilder.com**
- *HotJobs:* **www.hotjobs.com**
- *JobOptions:* **www.joboptions.com**
- *Monster:* **www.monster.com**

Interviewing Self-Quizzes

Prepare yourself for employment interviews by taking the interview quiz from the Connecticut Department of Labor at **http://www.chesgroup.com/dynamic/quiz.htm** or the interview quiz from Thomas More College at **http://www2.thomasmore.edu/career/job.cfm?group=Job%20Search**.

Preparing for Stress Interviews

Some employers subject applicants to stress interviews to see how well they can handle the pressures that typically occur on the job. Although many HR professionals and career experts don't find these interviews helpful, you may find an interviewer challenging you with prolonged silence or hostile questions like "What makes you think you can do this job?" or "What makes you think the theories you learned in college work in the real world?"

If you aren't ready for this sort of grilling, you can easily get rattled. Prepare yourself by reading about stress interviews and seeing sample questions at any of these sites:

- **www.workopolis.com/servlet/News/torontostar/20011208/ts10194**
- **http://candocareer.com/job-interview-questions/stress.htm**
- **http://www.asktheheadhunter.com/hastress.htm**
- **http://careercenter.tamu.edu/Students/S1/S1B1A5.shtml**

Problem-Solving and Behavioral Interviews

For a look at the use of "puzzle questions" in employment interviews, a trend begun by Microsoft, see William Poundstone's *How Would You Move Mount Fuji?: Microsoft's Cult of the Puzzle: How the World's Smartest Companies Select the Most Creative Thinkers* (Boston: Little, Brown and Company, 2003) at **www.techinterview.org**.

part four: strategic case

Museum of Springfield

Paul Georgakis is the new media coordinator at the Museum of Springfield. He is working on the biggest assignment of his career: developing the Web site for the museum's forthcoming new show "Images of Springfield." The exhibit is being underwritten by Midwestern Industries, and museum curator Mary Weston has told Paul that the board of trustees is counting on the exhibit's success to open the door to more corporate support. "If that happens we'll have a shot at becoming a top-quality regional museum," Mary tells Paul. "I don't have to tell you how important that is to the board of trustees." Mary might as well have said, "I don't have to tell you how important this is to your career."

Along with Paul, the project team for the Web site includes four other members:

Elaine Dorsch is the site's designer. Bringing San Francisco–based Elaine onboard was a coup for Paul. She has created sites for several world-class organizations, and she took the museum job for a deeply discounted fee because she grew up in Springfield and wants to give something back to the community.

Roger Chilton, a history professor at the local branch of the state university, is the content expert on the exhibit and the accompanying Web site. His specialty is the influence of business and government institutions on underprivileged groups in 19th-century U.S. society.

Julia Winger is the corporate liaison with Midwestern Industries. She has made it clear that her company is glad to support the museum and that it expects to be recognized for doing so. "Doing good can help Midwestern Industries do well," she told Paul.

Mary Weston, Paul's boss, represents the museum's administration and board of trustees.

The Web site project got off to a good start. But lately, several problems have developed. On a practical level, it has proved almost impossible to get all members to attend the last few meetings. Because Elaine is based in San Francisco and Julia's office is in Minneapolis, it has proved difficult for both of them to squeeze in visits to Springfield.

Even more disturbing has been the growing tension, as it has become clear that Roger's exhibit includes some disturbing images and stories. Julia recently sent the team an e-mail saying "Midwestern Industries isn't contributing several hundred thousand dollars to upset the community." Roger replied, "It isn't a historian's job to make people happy." Paul is growing worried that either Roger or Julia may pull out of the project, and either scenario would be a disaster.

Finally, it has become clear that Elaine views any suggestion for revising her design as an assault on her artistic talent. "I don't tell you how to run your museum or Midwestern Industries," she says. "You're the experts in your own fields, and I am in mine. I know what I'm doing, and you just have to trust me."

Paul's boss Mary has made it clear that she is counting on him to keep the team together and the project on track.

As you read the chapters in this unit, consider how answers to the following questions might help Paul manage this difficult job:

1. What types of power listed in Chapter 8 does each team member have? How can the members use their power to help the group achieve its goal?
2. What approach to leadership outlined in Chapter 8 can Paul use to keep the group functioning well?
3. What are the personal goals of each member? How do these goals contribute to and/or interfere with the group's job?
4. How can the group use the systematic problem-solving method outlined in Chapter 8 to overcome the challenges it faces?
5. What decision-making method(s) should the members use in deciding how to resolve their disagreements?
6. Are there ways the team can handle some of its tasks without meeting in person?
7. What might an agenda for the team's next meeting look like?
8. What techniques outlined in Chapter 9 can Paul use when he chairs face-to-face meetings?

8 Working in Teams

Chapter Outline

Chapter Objectives

After reading this chapter, you should be able to

1 Diagnose a group and identify the kind of communication that can transform it into a true team.

2 Analyze the advantages and drawbacks of whether a group should meet face-to-face or work as a virtual team.

3 Compare various approaches to centralized leadership, self-directed teams, and power distribution.

4 Identify the stages and characteristics of each stage of group problem solving and the roles that help groups function.

5 Explain various decision-making methods and the circumstances in which each is most appropriate.

6 Apply the guidelines for effective communication in groups and teams to a group to which you belong.

In his book *Tales of a New America,* Robert Reich describes the importance of teamwork in an increasingly technological age:

> *Rarely do even Big Ideas emerge any longer from the solitary labors of genius. Modern science and technology is too complicated for one brain. It requires groups of astronomers, physicists, and computer programmers to discover new dimensions of the universe: teams of microbiologists, oncologists, and chemists to unravel the mysteries of cancer. With ever more frequency, Nobel prizes are awarded to collections of people. Scientific papers are authored by small platoons of researchers.*[1]

The Nature of Teams

Working with others is a vital part of virtually every job.[2] In a national survey of architects and landscape architects, over 75 percent of these professionals reported that they "always" or "often" worked in teams.[3] In the burgeoning field of multimedia, the ability to work as a team member has been identified as the top nontechnical job skill.[4] Motorola, Ford, 3M, USAA Insurance, and Chase Manhattan Bank have used teams to become leaders in their fields.[5]

Teams Are Essential

No matter how brilliant you are, being a solo player is not an option in today's business world. Gary Kaplan, owner of a Pasadena, California, executive recruiting firm, offers one explanation of why team players are valued over rugged individualists: "The single-combat warrior, that bright, purposeful worker, tends to suck up a lot of oxygen in an organization. And now they're often seen as too innovative and too difficult."[6]

Just because groups *can* be effective doesn't guarantee that they always *will* succeed. Table 8–1 lists the conditions where groups are superior to individuals working alone, as well as those where they are not the best approach. You can see that, in the right circumstances, groups have several advantages over the same number of individuals working alone.[7] One of these advantages is *productivity*. Research shows that the old saying "Two heads are better than one" can be true: Well-conceived and efficiently operating groups produce more solutions than individuals working alone, and the solutions are likely to be better. Social scientists use the term *synergy* to describe how the capability of a group can be greater than the output all of its members could produce individually.[8]

Along with greater productivity, the *accuracy* of an effective group's work is higher than that of individuals. Consider the task of creating a new product. A group of people from sales, marketing, design, engineering, and manufacturing is likely to consider all the important angles, while one or two people without this breadth of perspective would probably miss some important ideas.

Table 8–1 Group vs. Individual Performance

Group Superior to Individuals	Individuals Superior to Group
Task requires broad range of talents and knowledge	Task requires limited knowledge, information (which individuals possess)
Complicated task (requires division, coordination of labor)	Simple task (can be done by one person or individuals working separately)
Time available for deliberation	Little time available
Members are motivated to succeed	Members don't care about job
High standards of performance	"Social loafing" is the norm

Source: Adapted from J. D. Rothwell, *In Mixed Company*, 5th ed. (Belmont, CA: Wadsworth, 2004), p. 76; and A. P. Hare, "Roles, Relationships, and Groups in Organizations: Some Conclusions and Recommendations," *Small Group Research* 34 (April 2003), pp. 123–154.

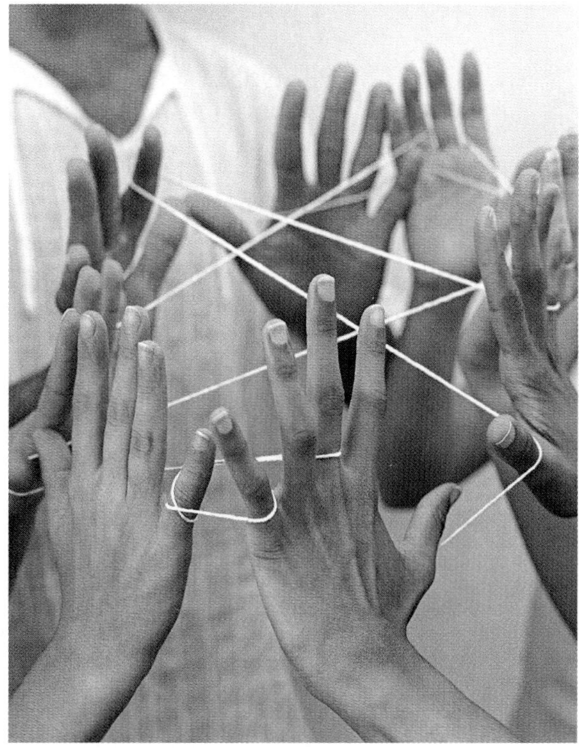

Teams not only produce better products but also generate more *commitment* and *enthusiasm* from the members who created them. People are usually more committed to a decision if they have had a part in making it. Recognizing this principle, many American companies create participatory management programs and quality circles that involve employees in important decisions. For example, William Deardon, chief executive officer of Hershey Foods Corporation, established a corporate planning committee to make the major plans and decisions for the company: "I figured that if we worked it out together," he explained, "the members of the group would feel that it was their plan and our plan—not my plan—and they'd work harder to implement it."[9]

Working effectively in groups calls for many of the skills described in earlier chapters of *Communicating at Work*. Chapter 1 discussed when to meet face-to-face and when to use other communication channels—telephone, electronic mail, and so on. Chapter 2 emphasized the importance of adapting to cultural norms when working with others. The listening skills outlined in Chapter 3 are essential when working in teams, as are the interpersonal skills described later in Chapter 5. Chapter 4 offered tips on using language effectively and being sensitive to nonverbal cues. The fundamental communication skills described so far in this book are important, but there are also special characteristics that distinguish communication in groups. In the following pages you will learn about those characteristics and how to apply them when you work in groups and teams.

Characteristics of Work Groups

The word *group* is often used to refer to any assembly of people—the commuters on the morning train, the sightseers gathering for a walking tour of the downtown area, the rock band at a local nightspot. When we talk about people interacting at work, we use the label differently. But not all collections of people—even people who come together in working settings—are groups.

For our purposes, a **work group** is a small, interdependent collection of people with a common identity who interact with one another, usually face-to-face over time, to reach a goal. Using this definition, we can single out several significant characteristics of work-centered groups that can help you develop ways to work more effectively with others on the job.

Size Most experts say that a twosome is not a group since the partners do not interact in the same way that three or more people do. For instance, two people working together can resolve disputes only by persuading one another, giving in, or compromising. In groups, however, members can form alliances and outvote or pressure the minority.

Although less agreement exists about when a collection of people becomes too large to be considered a group, virtually every small-group expert argues that any collection much larger than 20 people loses many of the properties that define groups—at least effective ones.[10] Research on a number of companies has found that 10-person teams often produce better results at a quicker rate and with higher profits than do groups of several hundred.[11] There are several reasons why size doesn't translate into effectiveness: People begin to act in formal ways. Members have fewer chances to participate, since a few talkative members are likely to dominate the group. Quieter members lose their identity and become less committed to the team. Coalitions also can form, leading members to become more concerned with having their side win than with tackling the challenge at hand.

Most communication experts suggest that the optimal size for small decision-making groups is either five or seven members.[12] The odd number of participants eliminates the risk of tie votes. Teams with fewer than five members lack the resources to come up with good ideas and to carry them out, while larger groups suffer from the problems of anonymity, domination, and lack of commitment.

Interaction A collection of people studying in a library or working out at the gym is merely co-acting. Likewise a roomful of trainees at a seminar isn't a group unless and until the individuals start interacting. It isn't the number of people but rather interaction and the exchange of information that makes a collection of individuals a group.

Shared Purpose Interaction alone doesn't create a working group. Guests at a reception or attendees at a convention might talk with one another, but unless they share a collective goal, they won't be able to collectively accomplish anything. One challenge facing anyone leading a newly created group is to give members a clear sense of shared purpose.

Interdependence Group members don't just interact; they depend on one another. A roomful of telemarketers who are working on commission have little effect on one another, and thus they can hardly be called a group, let alone a team. By contrast, consider the workers in a restaurant: If the kitchen crew fails to prepare orders promptly or correctly, the servers' tips will decline. If the employees who clear tables don't do their jobs quickly and thoroughly, the servers will hear complaints from their customers. If the waiters fail to take orders accurately, the cooks will have to fix some meals twice. In a restaurant, as in any real team, the employees are part of an interdependent system.

One manager let employees know how valuable they are with the following memo:

You Arx a Kxy Pxrson

My kxyboard works vxry wxll—xxcxpt for onx kxy. You would think that with all thx othxr kxys functioning propxrly, onx kxy not working would hardly bx noticxd; but just onx kxy out of whack sxxms to ruin thx wholx xffort.

You may say to yoursxlf—Wxll I'm only onx pxrson. No onx will noticx if I don't do my bxst. But it doxs makx a difxrxncx bxcausx to bx xffxctivx an organization nxxds activx participation by xvxry onx to thx bxst of his or hxr ability.

So thx nxxt timx you think you arx not important, rxmxmbxr my kxyboard. You arx a kxy pxrson.

Regular Interaction and Communication A group that interacts over a period of time develops particular characteristics. For example, a group will tend to develop shared standards of appropriate behavior that members are expected to meet. Typical expectations involve how promptly meetings begin, what contribution each member is expected to make to certain routine tasks, what kind of humor is appropriate, and so on.

career tip

What Makes a Group a Team?

The term **team** appears everywhere in the business world. The positive connotations of a team—spirit, cooperation, hard work—lead some managers to give every collection of workers the team label. You don't have to be an athlete to appreciate the value of teams, and you don't need to be a cynic to know that calling a group of people a team doesn't make them one.[13] True teams have all the attributes of a group, but they have other qualities that distinguish them and make them more satisfying to work in and more productive. Communication researchers Carl Larson and Frank LaFasto spent nearly 3 years interviewing members of over 75 teams that were clearly winners. The groups came from a wide range of enterprises including a Mount Everest expedition, a cardiac surgery team, the presidential commission that studied the space shuttle *Challenger* accident, the group that developed the IBM personal computer, and two championship football teams. Although the groups pursued widely different goals, they all shared eight important characteristics. You can understand both why your team functions as it does and how to improve its effectiveness by analyzing how well your group fits the profile of these winning teams.

- *Clear and inspiring shared goals*. Members of a winning team know why their group exists, and they believe that purpose is important and worthwhile. Ineffective groups have either lost sight of their purpose or do not believe that the goal is truly important.
- *A results-driven structure*. Members of winning teams focus on getting the job done in the most effective manner. They do whatever is necessary to accomplish the task. Less effective groups either are not organized at all or are structured in an inefficient manner, and their members don't care enough about the results to do what is necessary to get the job done.
- *Competent team members*. Members of winning teams have the skill necessary to accomplish their goals. Less effective groups lack people possessing one or more key skills.
- *Unified commitment*. People in successful teams put the group's goals above their personal interests. While this commitment might seem like a sacrifice to others, for members of winning teams the personal rewards are worth the effort.
- *Collaborative climate*. Another word for collaboration is *teamwork*. People in successful groups trust and support one another.
- *Standards of excellence*. In winning teams, doing outstanding work is an important norm. Each member is expected to do his or her personal best. In less successful groups, getting by with the minimum amount of effort is the standard.
- *External support and recognition*. Successful teams need an appreciative audience that recognizes their effort and provides the resources necessary to get the job done. The audience may be a boss, or it may be the public the group is created to serve.
- *Principled leadership*. Winning teams usually have leaders who can create a vision of the group's purpose and challenge members to get the job done. Finally, they have the ability to unleash the talent of group members.

You may not be able to single-handedly transform your entire organization into a team-friendly environment, but it still is possible to influence the group of people with whom you work. Examine the characteristics of teams listed above and ask yourself whether you are communicating in a manner that makes that small but important leap possible.

Identity Both members and outsiders view groups as distinct entities. Some groups have a formal title such as "benefits committee" or "accounting department." Others have an informal identity like "lunchtime power walkers" or "those guys who carpool together." In either case, the fact that the group is seen as distinct has important consequences. To a greater or lesser extent, members feel their own image is tied to the way the group is regarded. In addition, the group's identity means that the addition or loss of a member feels significant to the people involved, whether the change in membership is cause for celebration or disappointment.

Virtual Teams

Virtual teams interact and function as groups without being in the same place at the same time.[14] Technology permits virtual groups to transcend boundaries of location and time. Barry Caldwell, supervisor of computer-aided industrial design technologies at Ford Motor Company's Corporate Design division, concurs, explaining how Ford's virtual teams span the globe: "We can't change the fact that Europe is five or six hours ahead [of Michigan]," he says. "But virtual teams can be extremely effective if you can have people working in Italy or Germany—five hours ahead of you—and they can hand work off to Dearborn at the end of their day, and you can carry it further and then pass it back. Instead of an eight-hour day, you can get 14 hours."[15]

Virtual teamwork can be just as valuable for busy people who work near one another. Some human resources experts claim that, when people work more than 50 feet apart, their likelihood of collaborating more than once a week is less than 10 percent.[16] Given this fact, virtual meetings can boost the efficiency of people who work under the same roof.

Another advantage of virtual teams is the leveling of status differences. On networked teams, rank is much less prominent than in face-to-face groups.[17] In e-mail, the ideas of a new or mid-level worker look identical to those of a senior manager. Back-and-forth dialogue is much less intimidating in mediated format than it might be when you have to face the boss in person.

Sometimes a virtual group needs to communicate in real time. Teleconferencing and instant messaging (IMing) make it easy and inexpensive to conduct synchronous virtual meetings. In other cases, working asynchronously can be more effective. Michael Charnow, vice president at California software developer Ontek Corp., describes the value of asynchronous conferencing for his staff: "We wanted telecommunications capabilities because work such as programming and research is done at all hours of the day and night, and we don't feel that people have to be physically present to do their best work."[18] For asynchronous meetings, Web-based discussion tools provided by Google, Yahoo, and others are simple to set up and manage. (See page 296 in Chapter 9 for details.)

Despite the advantages of virtual teamwork, computer networking can't replace all of the functions of personal contacts. Frank Carrubba, executive vice president and chief technical officer of Philips Electronics NV in the Netherlands, explains the need for what some wags have called "face time": "You have to figure out how to deal with people other than in the terminal of a computer and keep them spirited over long distances, especially when failures arise. And you have to know how to use the brief times when people are brought together."[19]

Leadership and Influence in Groups and Teams

Throughout most of the history of organizations, the importance of centralized leadership in groups went unquestioned. The common thinking was that one ingredient in effective group functioning was the presence of a leader who could

career tip

Working in Virtual Teams

1. *Strive for some "face time," especially during the group's formation.* Virtual teams are most cohesive, trusting, and successful when members have had a chance to spend time together in person, especially during the group's development.
2. *Be mindful of time zone differences.* When members of a virtual team are dispersed across time zones, it's especially important to schedule meetings so no members are inconvenienced. Time differences can be especially challenging when groups span several continents. For example, if some members are in California and others in India are time shifted by a half day, the only times that may work for people with normal schedules are early morning and early evening. Remember Asia is a day *ahead* of the United States; Europe is a half to a full day *behind.*
3. *Use time zones to your advantage.* Consider handing off tasks that members in other time zones can tackle while you are off work. For example, a member in Seattle can request information at the end of the workday, and teammates in Florida can respond at the start of their next workday, so an answer will be in the sender's in-box when s/he logs on 3 hours later.
4. *Keep a personal touch.* Express some of the same emotions and personal thoughts that you would in face-to-face communication. Doing so can build camaraderie and the human feeling that virtual teams may lack without face-to-face communication.
5. *Consider using "back channels."* Use telephone, personal e-mail, and instant messaging to confer directly with one or more team members when you need to deal with issues and relationships personally in a way that will save the group time and effort.
6. *Do a trial run of technology.* Make sure in advance of meetings that all the technology upon which your team relies is working. It can be frustrating and discouraging to waste meeting time dealing with glitches.
7. *Seek input from all team members.* Sometimes members who are more comfortable with the technology of the virtual team will "speak" more than those who have more expertise in the team area, but not with the technology being used.
8. *Be aware of cultural differences in communication style.* These exist in cyberspace as well as in face-to-face communication. Remind yourself of style differences in high- and low-context cultures, expectations of leaders and team members, preferences for direct and indirect means of expression. Learn to read between the lines of those who may not directly criticize your ideas or offer advice.

Sources: Kathleen Melymuka, "Tips for Teams," *Computerworld* 31 (April 28, 1997), p. 72; and J. Dan Rothwell, *In Mixed Company: Communicating in Small Groups and Teams,* 6th ed. (Belmont, CA: Wadsworth, 2006), pp. 386–387.

motivate members and make final decisions. Recently, however, experts in business and professional communication have come to recognize another approach to group functioning that puts most or all of the power into the hands of members. Since both of these approaches—centralized and decentralized—are common in today's workplace, the following pages will look at how communication operates in each one.

Centralized Leadership

The difference between effective and ineffective leaders can be dramatic: A losing team gets a new coach and, with the same players, begins winning against the same opponents; a demoralized division gets a new sales manager and orders increase;

a production crew gets a new supervisor and workers who once spent their time complaining find new enjoyment and productivity. Whatever the nature of the organization, we count on the person in charge to make the enterprise work.

What qualities make leaders effective? Sometimes that question is difficult to answer. Many effective leaders seem to perform their role effortlessly, and people seem to follow them naturally; others seem to rule by sheer force. Scholars and researchers have studied leadership from many perspectives. Following are some leadership approaches.

Trait Approach The **trait approach** is based on the belief that all leaders possess common traits that lead to their effectiveness. The earliest research sought to identify these traits, and by the mid-1930s scores of studies pursued this goal. Their conclusions were contradictory. Certain traits did seem common in most leaders, including physical attractiveness, sociability, desire for leadership, originality, and intelligence.[20] Despite these similarities, the research also showed that these traits were not *predictive* of leadership. In other words, a person possessing these characteristics would not necessarily become a leader. Another research approach was necessary.

Style Approach Beginning in the 1940s, researchers began to consider the **style approach.** They asked whether the designated leader could *choose* a way of communicating that would increase effectiveness. This research identified three managerial styles. Some leaders are **authoritarian,** using legitimate, coercive, and reward power at their disposal to control members. Others are more **democratic,** inviting members to help make decisions. A third leadership style is **laissez-faire:** The designated leader gives up the power of that position and transforms the group into a leaderless collection of equals.

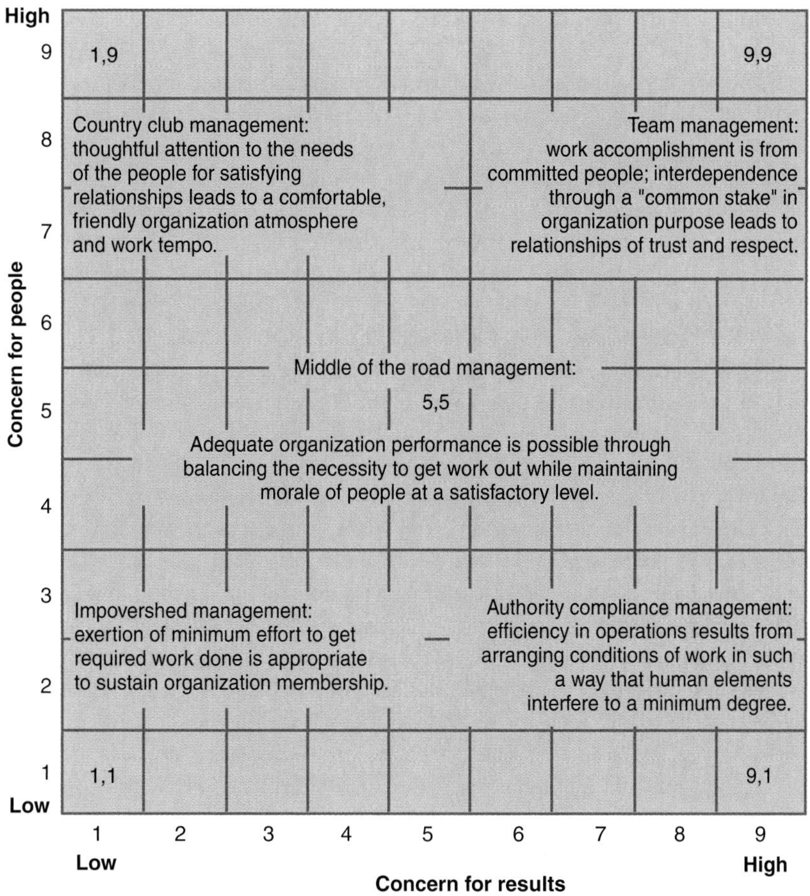

FIGURE 8–1
The Leadership Grid®

Source: From *Leadership Dilemmas—Grid Solutions* by Robert R. Blake and Anne Adams McCanse (formerly the *Managerial Grid* by Robert R. Blake and Jane S. Mouton). Houston: Gulf Publishing Company, p. 29. Copyright 1991 by Scientific Methods, Inc. Reproduced by permission of Grid International Inc.

Early research seemed to suggest that the democratic style produced the best results,[21] and contemporary studies suggest that members of groups with democratic leadership are slightly more satisfied than those run by autocratic leaders.[22] Still, it is an oversimplification to say that a democratic approach always works best. For instance, groups with autocratic leaders were more productive in stressful situations, while democratically led groups did better when the conditions were nonstressful.[23]

One of the best-known stylistic approaches is the *Leadership Grid®* by Robert Blake and Jane Mouton (see Figure 8–1),[24] which shows that good leadership depends on skillful management of the task and the relationships among group members. The horizontal axis of the grid measures a manager's concern for task or production—getting the job done. The vertical axis measures the leader's concern for people and relationships. Blake and Mouton's grid counteracts the tendency in some naive managers to assume that if they focus solely on the task, good results will follow. They argue that the most effective leader is one who adopts a 9,9 style, showing high concern for both product *and* people.

Contingency Approaches Unlike the style approach, **contingency approaches** are based on the idea that the "best" leadership style is flexible—it changes from one situation to the next. For instance, a manager who successfully guides a project team developing an advertising campaign might flop as a trainer or personnel officer.

Psychologist Fred Fiedler conducted extensive research in an attempt to discover when a task-oriented approach works best and when a relationship-oriented style is most effective.[25] He found that a decision about whether to emphasize task or relationship issues in a situation depends on three factors: (1) *leader–member relations*, including the attractiveness of the manager and the loyalty of the followers; (2) *task structure*, involving the degree of simplicity or complexity of the job; and (3) *the leader's power*, including job title and the ability to coerce and reward.

Generally, Fiedler's research suggests that a task-oriented approach works best when circumstances are extremely favorable (good leader–member relations, highly structured tasks) or extremely unfavorable (poor leader–member relations, unstructured task, weak leader power). In moderately favorable or unfavorable circumstances, a relationship-oriented approach works best. While these findings are useful, it is important not to overstate them. In most cases, good leadership requires a mixture of relationship and task concerns. The question is not which dimension to choose, but which one to *emphasize*.

Another model of situational leadership is the life-cycle approach developed by Paul Hersey and Kenneth Blanchard.[26] The **life-cycle theory** suggests that a leader's concern for tasks and relationships ought to vary, depending on the readiness of the subordinate or subordinates to work independently. According to the life-cycle theory, a worker with a low level of readiness needs a style of leadership that is highly directive and task-related. As the group member becomes more competent and motivated, the manager ought to offer rewards in terms of social reinforcement. As the subordinate becomes able to perform the task without the guidance of the boss, the manager ought to withdraw the task-related supervision even more, while encouraging the employee's new ability. Finally, when the worker's ability to handle a task is superior, the boss can cut back the amount of socioemotional support, knowing that the worker is functioning at the highest level and that any reinforcements are now primarily internal.

Becoming a Leader

Sometimes leaders are appointed by higher-ups, but in many cases they emerge from a group. **Emergent leaders** may be chosen by the members of a group either officially or informally. An athletic team may elect a captain. The owners' association of a condominium chooses a head. Union members pick a team to represent them in contract negotiations with management. Volunteers organizing a fund-raising drive for the local school or church nominate a chairperson.

Emergent leaders don't always have official titles. A group of disgruntled employees might urge one person to approach the boss and ask for a change, for example. A team of students assigned to develop a class project might agree that one person is best suited to take the lead in organizing and presenting their work. Sometimes emergent leaders are officially recognized, but other times their role is never acknowledged overtly. In fact, there are often cases where the designated leader may be the titular head, while an emergent leader really runs the show. Fans of late-night movies recall how the young, inexperienced lieutenant learns to defer to the grizzled, wise sergeant. This pattern often repeats itself in everyday working situations, when new managers or supervisors recognize the greater knowledge of

career tip

How to Emerge as a Group Leader

If you are interested in seeking a leadership position—and you almost certainly will be at one time or another—research has demonstrated that the following types of behavior will help you assert your influence.

- *Participate early and often*. Talking won't guarantee that you will be recognized as a leader, but failing to speak up will almost certainly knock you out of the running.
- *Demonstrate your competence*. Make sure your comments identify you as someone who can help the group succeed. Demonstrate the kinds of expert, connection, and information power described later in this chapter.
- *Don't push too hard*. It's fine to be assertive, but don't try to overpower other members. Even if you are right, your dogmatism is likely to alienate others.
- *Provide a solution in a time of crisis*. How can the group meet a deadline? Gain the sale? Get the necessary equipment? Members who find answers to problems like these are likely to rise to a position of authority.

Source: Reprinted by permission of Waveland Press, Inc. from M. Z. Hackman and C. E. Johnson, *Leadership: A Communication Perspective*, Long Grove, IL: Waveland Press, Inc., 2004.

old-timers who are subordinates on the organizational chart. In cases like these, the new manager is smart to defer to the unofficial, emergent leader—at least until he or she gains some experience and wisdom.

Communication researcher Ernest Bormann has studied how emergent leaders gain influence, especially in newly formed groups.[27] According to Bormann, a group selects a leader by the *method of residues*—a process of elimination in which potential candidates are gradually rejected for one reason or another until only one remains. This process of elimination occurs in two phases. In the first, members who are clearly unsuitable are rejected. The surest path to rejection is being quiet: Untalkative members were never chosen as leaders in the groups Bormann studied. Failing to participate verbally in a group's work leaves the impression of indifference and lack of commitment. Another ticket to early rejection is dogmatism: Members who express their opinions in strong, unqualified terms are usually perceived as being too extreme and inflexible to take a leading role. A third cause of elimination as leader is a lack of skill or intelligence: Competence is obviously a necessary condition for successful leadership, and members who lack this quality are rejected early.

Quietness, dogmatism, and incompetence are almost always grounds for disqualification. Beyond these factors, a communication style that members find irritating or disturbing is likely to knock a member out of consideration as a leader. A variety of behaviors fall into this category, depending on the composition of the group. In one case being too serious might be grounds for rejection, while in a different situation a joker would earn disapproval. Using inappropriate language could be a disqualifier. In a group with biased members, gender or ethnicity might be grounds for rejection.

After clearly unsuitable members have been eliminated, roughly half of the group's members may still be candidates for leadership. This can be a tense time, since the jockeying for a role of influence may pit the remaining candidates against one another. In some groups, the contenders for leader acquire what Bormann calls "lieutenants," who support their advancement. If only one candidate has a lieutenant, his or her chances of becoming leader are strong. If two or more contenders have supporters, the process of leader emergence can drag out or even reach a stalemate. The Career Tip box on page 263 offers advice for the times when you want to take on leadership of a group.

In their book, *Getting It Done: How to Lead When You're Not in Charge,* Roger Fisher and Alan Sharp describe "lateral leadership" as a way to avoid the extremes of doing nothing or taking charge and bossing others. They suggest that a group member can lead others by doing three things: *asking* thoughtful, sincere questions to get others to think creatively and contribute their ideas; *offering* ideas to help the group while inviting others to challenge your thoughts; and *doing* something constructive needed by the group and modeling the behavior needed.[28]

Power and Influence of Members

Most working groups have what social scientists call a **designated leader**—the boss, chairperson, coach, or manager who has formal authority and responsibility to supervise the task at hand. Other groups, called **self-directed work teams** are responsible for managing their own behavior to get a task done.[29] For example, at one General Mills cereal plant, teams schedule, operate, and maintain machinery so effectively that the plant runs with no managers present during night shifts. The company reports that productivity at plants that rely on self-managed teams is as much as 40 percent higher than at traditional factories. At Federal Express, a group of clerks spotted and solved a billing problem, saving the company $2.1 million in just 1 year. Harley-Davidson successfully organizes operations at its Kansas City, Missouri, motorcycle assembly plant using self-directed teams.[30]

Whether or not a group has a designated leader, every member has the power to shape events. Over a half century ago, John French and Bertram Raven identified several forms of power that are usually possessed by one or more members of a group—not necessarily just the designated leader.[31] Depending on how they are used, these forms of power can make or break the success of a working group.

Position Power

Position power is the ability to influence that comes from the position one holds. We often do things for the boss precisely because he or she holds that title. While legitimate power usually belongs to designated leaders, people in lesser positions sometimes have jobs that involve telling higher-ups what to do. For example, a media expert might tell the CEO or board chairman what will and won't work in a presentation to stockholders.

Coercive Power

The power to punish is known as **coercive power,** since we often follow another's bidding when failure to do so would lead to unpleasant consequences. Designated leaders have coercive power: They can assign unpleasant tasks, deny pay raises, and even fire us. Other members have coercive power, too, though it is usually subtle. A committee member or officemate who acts as a blocker when things don't go his way is coercing others to take his views into account, implying, "If you don't follow at least some of my suggestions, I'll punish the group by continuing to object to your ideas and refusing to cooperate with you."

Reward Power

The flip side of coercive power is **reward power**—the ability to reward. Designated leaders control the most obvious rewards: pay raises, improved working conditions, and the ability to promote. But, again, other members can give their own rewards. These come in the form of social payoffs, such as increased goodwill, and task-related benefits, like voluntary assistance on a job.

Expert Power **Expert power** comes from the group's recognition of a member's expertise in a certain area. There are times when one expert is better suited to make a decision than is an entire team. Designated leaders aren't always the experts in a group. In a manufacturing firm, for example, a relatively low-ranking engineer could influence management to alter a project by using her knowledge to declare that a new product won't work. Problems can arise either when management doesn't recognize a knowledgeable member as an expert or when unqualified people are granted expert status.

Referent Power The term **referent power** alludes to the influence members hold due to the way others in the group feel about them: their respect, attraction, or liking. It is here that the greatest difference between designated leaders and members with true influence occurs. An unpopular boss might have to resort to his or her job title and the power to coerce and reward that comes with it to gain compliance, while a popular person, with or without a leadership title, can get others to cooperate without threatening or promising.[32] Mike Zugsmith, co-owner of a commercial real-estate brokerage, captures the importance of referent power, even for a boss: "When I started this company in 1979, I was 28. I was supervising salespeople who were 20 to 30 years my senior. It readily became apparent that simply because your name is on the door doesn't mean you'll get respect. You have to earn it."[33]

Information Power **Information power** is the ability of some members to influence a group because of the information they possess. This information is different from the kind of knowledge that gives rise to expert power. Whereas an expert possesses some form of talent based on training or education, an information-rich group member has access to otherwise obscure knowledge that is valuable to others in the group. A new employee who was hired away from a competitor, for example, is likely to play a key role in the decisions of how his new company will compete against the old one. Likewise, a member who is well connected to the organizational grapevine can exert a major influence on how the group operates: "Don't bring that up now. Smith is going through a divorce and he's saying no to everything." "I just heard there's plenty of money in the travel and entertainment budget. Maybe this is the time to propose that reception for the out-of-town distributors we've been thinking about."

Connection Power In the business world, a member's influence can often come from the connections he or she has with influential or important people inside or outside the organization—hence the term **connection power.** The classic example of connection power is the son or daughter of the boss. While the official word from the top may be "Treat my kid just like any other employee," this is easier said than done. Not all connection power is harmful. If one member sees a potential customer socially, he is in a good position to help the business. If another one knows a government official, she can get off-the-record advice about how to handle a government regulation.

If we recognize the influence that comes with connection power, the old saying "It isn't what you know that counts, it's who you know" seems true. If we look at all the types of power described in this section, we can see that a more accurate statement is "What counts is whom you know [connection power], what you know [information and expert power], who respects you [referent power], and who you are [legitimate power]." This range of power bases makes it clear that the power to influence a group is truly shared among members, all of whom have the ability to affect how well a group works as a unit and the quality of the product it turns out.

Problem-Solving Communication

In the past decades, researchers have developed several methods for helping groups solve problems and make decisions effectively. By taking advantage of these methods, groups can come up with the highest-quality work possible.

Systematic Problem Solving

The range of problems that groups face on the job is almost endless. How can we cut expenses? Increase market share? Reduce customer complaints? Offer a better employee-benefits program? Not all groups approach problems like these systematically,[34] but most researchers agree that groups have the best chance of developing high-quality solutions to problems like these when they follow a systematic method for solving problems.[35]

The best-known problem-solving approach is the **reflective-thinking sequence,** developed over 80 years ago by John Dewey and used in many forms since then.[36] In its most useful form, the reflective-thinking sequence is a seven-step process.

1. *Define the problem.* A group that doesn't understand the problem will have trouble finding a solution. Sometimes the problem facing a group is clear. It doesn't take much deliberation to understand what's necessary when the boss tells you

Dilbert: © Scott Adams/Dist. by United Feature Syndicate, Inc. Reprinted by permission.

to work out a vacation schedule for the next 6 months. On the other hand, some problems need rewording because they are too broad as originally presented. The best problem statements are phrased as probative questions, ones that encourage exploratory thinking:

Too Broad	Better
How can we reduce employee turnover?	How can we reduce turnover among new employees? (This suggests where to look for the nature of the problem and solutions.)
How can we boost the morale of the office staff?	How can we reduce the complaints about too much work?

2. *Analyze the problem.* At this stage, the group tries to discover the causes and extent of the problem, probably by doing some research between meetings. Questions that are usually appropriate in this stage include: (a) How bad is that problem? (b) Why does it need to be resolved? and (c) What are its causes? It can be just as useful to focus on the positive aspects of the situation during this phase to consider how they can be strengthened. Questions in this area include: (a) What forces are on our side? (b) How do they help us? and (c) How can we strengthen them?

   A group analyzing the question "How can we reduce complaints about too much work?" might find that the problem is especially bad for certain staffers. It might discover that the problem is worst when staffers have to type long reports at the last minute. It might learn that the major complaint doesn't involve hard work as much as it does resentment at seeing other people apparently having a lighter load. Positive research findings might be that the staffers understand the importance of their role, that they view being chosen to do important jobs as a sign of respect for the quality of their work, and that they don't mind occasional periods of scrambling to meet a deadline.
3. *Establish criteria for a solution.* Rather than rushing to solve the problem, it's best to spend some time identifying the characteristics of a good solution. Who would it have to satisfy? What are the cost constraints? What schedule needs to be met? Sometimes criteria like these are imposed from outside the group. Other requirements come from the members themselves. Regardless of the source of these requirements, the group needs to make them clear before considering possible solutions. Without defining the criteria of a satisfactory solution, the group may waste time arguing over proposals that have no chance of being accepted.
4. *Consider possible solutions to the problem.* This is the time for using the creative thinking techniques described later in this chapter. A major hazard of group problem solving is that it may get bogged down in arguing over the merits of one or two proposals without considering other solutions that might exist. Besides limiting the quality of the solution, such squabbling also leads to personal battles among members.[37]

The most valuable feature of brainstorming is the emphasis on generating many ideas before judging any of them. This sort of criticism-free atmosphere encourages people to volunteer solutions that, in turn, lead to other ideas. A brainstorming list for the overworked staffers might include the following:

- Cut down on the number of jobs that have to be done over; create a company style book that shows how letters are to be set up, how contract clauses should be phrased, and so on.
- Have staffers help each other out—someone with too much work to do can ask someone else to take over a project.
- Establish a typing pool: Instead of assigning a staffer to a specific person or group, turn over all typing tasks to a group leader who will distribute them. Since the typists will be working as a group, they can train new typists themselves.

5. *Decide on a solution.* Once the group has considered all possible solutions to a problem, it can go back and find the best answer to the problem. This is done by comparing each idea to the list of criteria developed earlier by the group. In addition to measuring the solution against its own criteria, the group should judge any potential solutions by asking three questions: First, will the proposal bring about all the desired changes? If it solves only part of the problem, it isn't adequate without some changes. Second, can the solution be implemented by the group? If the idea is good but is beyond the power of this group to achieve, it needs to be modified or discarded. Finally, does the idea have any serious disadvantages? A plan that solves one set of problems while generating another probably isn't worth adopting.
6. *Implement the solution.* Inventing a solution isn't enough. The group also has to put the plan into action. This probably involves several steps. First, it's necessary to identify the specific tasks that must be accomplished. Second, the group must identify the resources necessary to make the plan work. Third, individual responsibilities must be defined: Who will do what, and when? Finally, the group should plan for emergencies. What will happen if someone is sick? If the project runs over budget? If a job takes longer than expected? Anticipating problems early is far better than being caught by surprise.
7. *Follow up on the solution.* Even the best ideas don't always work out perfectly in practice. For this reason, the group should check up on the implementation of the solution to see whether any adjustments are needed.

Stages in Group Problem Solving

The systematic problem-solving approach described above is certainly sensible, but it doesn't consider how the relationships among individual members can make it difficult for them to follow this kind of rational approach faithfully.[38] As groups conduct business, their discussions are likely to move more or less regularly through several phases characterized by different types of communication. Aubrey Fisher identified four of these stages: orientation, conflict, emergence, and reinforcement.[39]

The first stage in a group's development is the **orientation phase,** sometimes called **forming.**[40] This is a time of testing the waters. Members may not know one another very well and so are cautious about making statements that might offend. For this reason, during the orientation stage team members aren't likely to take strong positions even on issues they regard as important. It is easy to mistake the lack of conflict during this phase as harmony and assume that the task will proceed smoothly. Peace and quiet are often a sign of caution, not agreement. Despite the tentative nature of communication, the orientation stage is important since the norms that can govern the group's communication throughout its life are often formed at this time.

After the team members understand the problem and have a feel for one another, the group typically moves to the **conflict phase,** which has been called **storming.** This is the time when members take a strong stand on the issue and defend their positions against others. Disagreement is likely to be greatest during this phase, and the potential for bruised egos is strongest. The norms of politeness that were formed during orientation may weaken as members debate with one another, and there is a real risk that personal feelings will interfere with the kind of rational decision making described in the preceding section. Conflict does not have to be negative, however. If members adopt the kinds of constructive approaches outlined in Chapter 5, they can come up with high-quality solutions that have the potential to get the job done and leave everyone satisfied.[41]

Some groups never escape from the conflict stage. Their interaction—at least about the problem at hand—may end when time pressures force a solution that almost no one finds satisfactory. The boss may impose a decision from above, or a majority might overrule the minority. Time may even run out without any decision being made. Not all groups suffer from such unhappy outcomes, however. Productive teams manage to work through the conflict phase and move on to the next stage of development.

The **emergence phase** of problem solving, sometimes called **norming,** occurs when the members end their disagreement and solve the problem. The final decision may be enthusiastically supported by every member. In some cases, though, members may compromise or settle for a proposal they didn't originally prefer. In any case, the key to emergence is acceptance of a decision that members can support (even if reluctantly). Communication during the emergence phase is less polarized. Members back off from their previously held firm positions. Comments like "I can live with that" and "Let's give it a try" are common at this point. Even if some people have doubts about the decision, there is a greater likelihood that they will keep their concerns to themselves. Harmony is the theme.[42]

The fourth stage of discussion is the **reinforcement phase.** This stage has also been called **performing** because members not only accept the decision but also actively endorse it. Members who found arguments against the decision during the conflict stage now present evidence to support it. In school, the reinforcement stage is apparent when students presenting a group project defend it against any complaints the instructor might have. On the job, the same principle applies: If the boss finds fault with a team's proposals, the tendency is to band together to support them.

In real life, groups don't necessarily follow this four-step process (summarized in Table 8–2) neatly. In an ongoing team, the patterns of communication in the past can influence present and future communication.[43] Teams with a high degree of conflict might have trouble reaching emergence, for example, whereas a group that is highly cohesive might experience little disagreement.

Table 8–2 Characteristics and Guidelines for Problem-Solving Stages

	Member Behaviors	Member Concerns	For Higher Performance
Forming	Most comments directed to designated leader. Direction and clarification frequently sought. Status accorded to members based on their roles outside the group. Issues discussed superficially.	Why am I in this group? Why are the others here? Will I be accepted? What is my role? What jobs will I have? Will I be able to handle them? Who is the leader? Is s/he competent?	Provide structure. Clarify tasks, roles, and responsibilities through discussion. Encourage participation and questions by all and discourage domination by any. Facilitate learning about one another's expertise, needs, values, and preferences.
Storming	Some members try to gain disproportionate share of influence. Subgroups and coalitions form with conflicting interests, goals, values. Expertise and power of designated leader may be tested and challenged. Members overzealously judge one another's ideas and personalities, resulting in ideas and people being shot down.	How much autonomy will I have? Will I be able to influence others? What is my place in the pecking order? Who are my friends and allies? Who are my enemies? Do my ideas get any support here? Why don't some of the others see things my way? Is this aggravation worth the effort?	Use joint problem solving. Discuss group's problem-solving ideas. Have members explain how other ideas are useful and how to improve them. Establish norm supporting expression of different viewpoints.
Norming	The group establishes and follows rules and procedures. Members sometimes openly disagree.	How can we get organized well enough to stay on top of our tasks?	Challenge the team, fight complacency.

Sometimes a group can become stuck in one phase, never progressing to the phases that follow. Members might never get beyond the superficial, polite interaction of orientation. If they do, they might become mired down in conflict. Ongoing groups might move through some or all of the stages each time they tackle a new problem, as pictured in Figure 8–2. In fact, a group that deals with several issues at one time might be in different stages for each problem.

Knowing that a group to which you belong is likely to pass through these stages can be reassuring. Your urge to get down to business and quit wasting time during the orientation phase might be tempered if you realize that the cautious

	Member Behaviors	Member Concerns	For Higher Performance
	The group laughs together, has fun, tells occasional jokes at one another's and leader's expense. Members have a sense of "we-ness." The group feels superior to other groups. Groupthink may be a risk.	How close should I get to other members? How can we work in harmony? How do we compare to other groups? What is my relationship to the leader? How do we keep conflicts and differences under control? How can we structure things to run smoothly?	Conduct consensus-seeking discussions of challenging problems. Establish norms of high performance. Request and provide both positive and constructive feedback on individual and team actions. Encourage open discussions about individual ideas and concerns.
High Performing	Members trust one another and are honest with one another. Roles are clearly assigned, yet members step into one another's roles as needed. Members openly discuss and accept differences. Members challenge one another's ideas, leading to effective problem solving. Members challenge one another to do better and support one another. Members seek feedback from one another.	How can we continue at this pace? How might we share our learnings with one another? What will I do when this process is over? How will I find another team as good as this one?	Jointly set challenging goals. Look for opportunities to increase group's scope. Question assumptions, norms, and traditional approaches. Develop mechanism for ongoing self- and group assessment.

Source: After Ed Kur, "The Faces Model of High Performing Team Development," *Management Development Review* 9, no. 6 (1996), pp. 32–41.

communication is probably temporary. Likewise, you might be less distressed about conflict if you know that the possibility of emergence may be just around the corner.

Functional Role Analysis

Another way every member can shape the way a group operates is by acting in whatever way is necessary to help get the job done. This approach has been labeled the "functional perspective" because it defines influence in terms of fulfilling essential functions, not formal titles. These essential contributions have earned the name

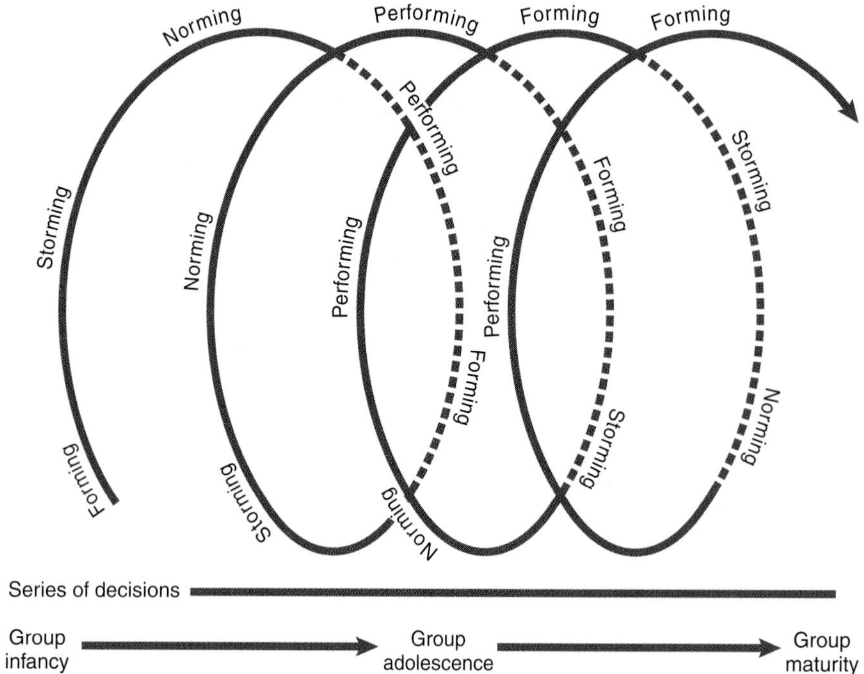

FIGURE 8–2 Cyclical Stages in an Ongoing Group

Source: From G. J. Galanes, K. Adams, and J. K. Brilhart, *Effective Group Discussion*, 11th ed. (New York: McGraw-Hill, 2004).

functional roles because they involve functions that are necessary for the group to do its job. Table 8–3 lists these functional roles, as well as noting some dysfunctional behaviors that reduce the effectiveness of a group. As the table shows, there are two types of functional roles. **Task roles** play an important part in accomplishing the job at hand. **Relational roles** help keep the interaction between members running smoothly.[44]

Table 8–3 is a valuable diagnostic tool. When a group isn't operating effectively, you must determine which functions are lacking. For instance, you might note that the group has several good ideas but that no one is summarizing and coordinating them. Or perhaps the group lacks a crucial piece of information, but no one realizes this fact.

In some cases, your diagnosis of a troubled group might show that all the necessary task functions are being filled but that the social needs of members aren't being met. Perhaps members need to have their good ideas supported ("That's a terrific idea, Neil!"). Maybe personal conflicts need to be acknowledged and resolved ("I know I sound defensive about this. I've worked on this idea for a month, and I hate to see it dismissed in 5 minutes"). When social needs like these go unfilled, even the best knowledge and talent often aren't enough to guarantee a group's smooth functioning.

Sometimes a group will transform important functional roles into formal ones. For example, at financial services giant Charles Schwab, one person in every meeting serves as an observer-diagnoser.[45] This person doesn't take part in the discussion; instead he or she creates a list of what went right (e.g., "Good creativity," "Excellent use of time") and what went wrong (e.g., "Lots of digressions," "Personal criticism created defensiveness") in the meeting. This list gets included in the minutes, which are reviewed by management. It's easy to imagine how the observer's comments can help a group work effectively.

Having too many people fill a functional role can be just as troublesome as having nobody fill it. For example, you might discover that several people are acting as

Table 8–3 Functional Roles of Group Members

Task Functions

1. *Information or opinion giver.* Offers facts or opinions relevant to group task.
2. *Information or opinion seeker.* Asks others for task-related information or opinions.
3. *Starter or energizer.* Initiates or encourages task-related behavior (e.g., "We'd better get going on this").
4. *Direction giver.* Provides instructions regarding how to perform task at hand.
5. *Summarizer.* Reviews what has been said, identifying common themes or progress.
6. *Diagnoser.* Offers observations about task-related behavior of group (e.g., "We seem to be spending all of our time discussing the problem without proposing any solutions").
7. *Gatekeeper.* Regulates participation of members.
8. *Reality tester.* Checks feasibility of group ideas against real-world contingencies.

Relational Functions

1. *Participation encourager.* Encourages reticent members to speak, letting them know that their contribution will be valued.
2. *Harmonizer.* Resolves interpersonal conflicts between members.
3. *Tension reliever.* Uses humor or other devices to release anxiety and frustration of members.
4. *Evaluator of emotional climate.* Offers observations about socioemotional relationships between members (e.g., "I think we're all feeling a little defensive now," or "It sounds like you think nobody trusts you, Bill").
5. *Praise giver.* Reinforces accomplishments and contributions of group members.
6. *Empathic listener.* Listens without evaluation to personal concerns of members.

Dysfunctional Roles

1. *Blocker.* Prevents progress by constantly raising objections.
2. *Attacker.* Aggressively questions the competence or motives of others.
3. *Recognition seeker.* Repeatedly and unnecessarily calls attention to self by relating irrelevant experiences, boasting, and seeking sympathy.
4. *Joker.* Engages in joking behavior in excess of tension-relieving needs, distracting members.
5. *Withdrawer.* Refuses to take stand on social or task issues; covers up feelings; does not respond to others' comments.

Source: After Kenneth D. Benne and Paul Sheats, "Functional Roles of Group Members," *Journal of Social Issues 4* (1948), pp. 41–49.

opinion givers but that no one is serving as an opinion seeker—like a series of radio stations broadcasting but no one receiving. If two or more people compete for the role of direction giver, the results can be confusing. Even social roles can be overdone. Too much tension relieving or praise giving can become annoying.

Once you have identified the missing functions, you can fill them. Supplying these missing roles often transforms a stalled, frustrated group into a productive team.[46] Other members probably won't recognize what you're doing, but they will realize that you somehow know how to say the right thing at the right time.

Functional Roles in Action

Either individually or in a group,

1. Identify a task that would likely be addressed in a group discussion (e.g., planning a fund-raising event, developing a policy on personal use of computers). Or, choose a task that you are already working on in a group.
2. Present examples of how each of the functional roles (task and relational) listed in Table 8–3 could be performed in the group's discussion. Explain how each role can lead to higher-quality solutions.
3. Present examples of how each of the dysfunctional roles in Table 8–3 might be enacted in the group's discussion. Describe the consequences of each of these roles.

Decision-Making Methods

Disagreement may be a healthy, normal part of solving problems on the job, but sooner or later it becomes necessary to make a decision as a group. Whether the issue is who will work over the weekend, how to split the year-end bonus money among members, or which approach to advertising is best, there usually has to be one answer to a problem. As business instructor Joel Baum puts it, "*How* you decide is just as important as *what* you decide. The process you use has a direct impact on how members feel about the decision. It can influence commitment, excitement, and buy-in; or it can create feelings of resentment and exclusion."[47] There are a number of ways to make business decisions like these.

Consensus **Consensus** is a collective group decision that every member is willing to support. The purest form of consensus is unanimous, unequivocal support: the belief of every member that the decision reached is the best possible one. An entire employee search committee might, for instance, agree that a particular candidate is perfect for a job. This state of unanimity isn't always possible, however, and it isn't necessary for consensus. Members may support a decision that isn't their first choice, accepting the fact that it is the best one possible for the group at that time. In the case of the new employee, the committee members might agree on a candidate who is the second choice of some members since the people who will actually be working with her are her most enthusiastic supporters.

Consensus is valued more highly in some cultures than others. For example, British and Dutch businesspeople value the "team must be aboard" approach. On the other hand, Germans, French, and Spanish communicators depend more on the decision of a strong leader and view a desire for consensus as somewhat wishy-washy.[48]

Cultural norms aside, consensus has both advantages and drawbacks. While it has the broadest base of support from members, reaching consensus takes time. It requires a spirit of cooperation among group members, a willingness to experience temporary disagreements, a commitment to listening carefully to other ideas, and a win–win attitude. While consensual decisions are often superior to other types, the cost in time and frustration isn't always worth the effort, especially for relatively minor issues. Furthermore, there are times when it simply isn't possible to reach consensus.

THE FAR SIDE® By GARY LARSON

"Okay, Williams, we'll just vote. ... How many here say the heart has four chambers?"

Majority Vote Whereas consensus requires the agreement of the entire group, deciding by a **majority vote** needs only the support of a plurality of the members. Thus, majority voting decisions are much quicker and easier to reach. A 10-person staff choosing a decorating scheme for the new office might talk almost endlessly before reaching consensus, but with a majority vote, the decision would require the agreement of only 6 members. While majority vote works well on relatively minor issues, it is usually not the best approach for more important decisions (at least not in small groups), since it can leave a substantial minority unsatisfied and resentful about being railroaded into accepting a plan they don't support.

Minority Decision In a **minority decision,** a few members make a decision affecting the entire group. This is frequently the case in business situations. For instance, the executive committee of a corporation often acts on behalf of the board of directors, which, in turn, represents the shareholders. Minority decisions are also made in less exalted circumstances. A steering group responsible for planning the company picnic might delegate tasks like publicity, entertainment, and food to smaller collections of members. As long as the minority has the confidence of the larger group, this method works well for many decisions. While it doesn't take advantage of the entire group's creative thinking, the talents of the subgroup are often perfectly adequate for a task.

Expert Opinion When a single person has the knowledge or skill to make an informed decision, the group may be best served by relying on his or her **expert opinion.** As one observer puts it, "If you want a track team to win the high jump, you find one person who can jump seven feet, not seven people who can jump one foot." Some group members are experts because of specialized training: a structural engineer working with a design team on a new building, a senior airline mechanic who decides whether a flight can depart safely, or a systems analyst involved in the development of a new data control system. Other people gain their expertise by experience: the purchasing agent who knows how to get the best deals or a labor negotiator seasoned by years of contract deliberations.

Despite the obvious advantages, following an expert's suggestions isn't always as wise an approach as it might seem. First, it isn't always easy to tell who the expert is. Length of experience isn't necessarily a guarantee, since the business world abounds with old fools. Even when a member clearly is the expert, the other members must *recognize* this fact before they will willingly give their support. Unfortunately, some people who are regarded as experts don't deserve the title, while some geniuses may be ignored.

Self-Assessment Evaluating Your Group's Communication Effectiveness

Use the inventory below to identify how well your group is performing these important communication practices.

As a Group, How Well Did You	Not Well				Very Well
Define or clarify the task	1	2	3	4	5
Exchange and share information	1	2	3	4	5
Encourage expression of various points of view	1	2	3	4	5
Evaluate and analyze data	1	2	3	4	5
Use the best decision-making approach (consensus, majority rule, etc.)	1	2	3	4	5
Focus on tasks, not individuals	1	2	3	4	5
Demonstrate respect for all	1	2	3	4	5
Encourage feedback	1	2	3	4	5
Encourage expression of opinion	1	2	3	4	5
Build on others' ideas	1	2	3	4	5
Ask for clarification of ideas	1	2	3	4	5
Demonstrate equality	1	2	3	4	5
Address disagreements or misunderstandings	1	2	3	4	5
Stay on task	1	2	3	4	5

Authority Rule In many business groups, decision making is often a matter of **authority rule:** The designated leader makes the final decision. This doesn't mean that such leaders must be autocratic: They often listen to the ideas and suggestions of members before making the decisions themselves. The owner of a family business might invite employees to help choose a new company logo, while selecting the final design after hearing their opinions. A store manager might consult with employees about scheduling work hours, while reserving the final decisions for herself. The input from group members can help an authority to make higher-quality decisions than would otherwise be possible. One major risk of inviting suggestions from subordinates, however, is the disappointment that might follow if these suggestions aren't accepted.

Choice of a Decision-Making Method Each decision-making method has its advantages and disadvantages. The choice of which one to use depends on several factors.

What type of decision is being made? If the decision can best be made by one or more experts or if it needs to be made by the authorities in charge, then involving other group members isn't appropriate. If, however, the task at hand calls for creativity or requires a large amount of information from many sources, then input from the entire group can make a big difference.

How important is the decision? Trivial decisions don't require the involvement of the entire group. It's a waste of time and money to bring everyone together to make decisions that can easily be made by one or two people.

How much time is available? If time is short, it simply may not be possible to consult everyone in the group. This is especially true if the members are not all available—if some are away from the office or out of town, for example. Even if everyone is available, the time-consuming deliberations that come with a group discussion may be a luxury you can't afford.

What are the personal relationships among members? Even important decisions might best be made without convening the whole group if members are on bad terms. If talking things out will improve matters, then a meeting may be worth the emotional wear and tear that it will generate. But if a face-to-face discussion will just make matters worse, then the decision might best be made in some other way.

Effective Communication in Groups and Teams

Whether you are in a group with centralized leadership or one with shared decision-making power, you can communicate in ways that help the group work effectively and make the experience satisfying. For the group to function well, each member must take into account the issues and problems that may arise whenever people try to communicate.

Recognize Both Group and Personal Goals

Every business and professional group operates to achieve some specific goal: selling a product, providing a service, getting a job done, and so on. In addition to pursuing a group's goals, members usually also have their own *individual* goals. Sometimes an individual's goal in a group is identical (or nearly identical) to the shared goal of the group. For example, a retailer might join the community Christmas fund-raising campaign out of a sincere desire to help the needy. In most cases, however, people also have more personal motives for joining a group. The retailer, for instance, might realize that working on the fund-raising campaign will improve both his visibility and his image in the community—and ultimately lead to more business. Notice the relationships between some common group and individual goals:

Group Goal	Individual Goal
Athletic team wants to win league championship.	Athlete wants to be star for social rewards.
Sales department wants to meet annual sales target.	Sales representative wants to earn bonus.
Retailer wants to expand hours to attract new business.	Employees want to avoid working nights and weekends.
Company wants employee to attend seminar in Minneapolis.	Employee wants to visit family in Minneapolis.

As some of these examples show, personal goals aren't necessarily harmful to a group or an organization if they are compatible with the group's objectives. In fact, under these circumstances they can actually help the group to achieve its goals. For instance, sales representatives who want to increase their commissions will try to sell more of the company's products. Similarly, an otherwise reluctant employee might volunteer to attend a January seminar in Minneapolis to see her family during the visit.

Only when an individual's goals conflict with the organization's or group's goals do problems occur. If Lou and Marian hate each other, their arguments could keep the group from getting much done in meetings. If Bill is afraid of losing his job because of a mistake that has been made, he may concentrate on trying to avoid being blamed rather than on solving the problem.

The range of personal goals that can interfere with group effectiveness is surprisingly broad. One or more team members might be concerned with finishing the job quickly and getting away to take care of personal business. Others might be more concerned with being liked or appearing smart than with doing the job as quickly or effectively as possible. Someone else might want to impress the boss. All these goals, as well as dozens of others, can sidetrack or derail a group from doing its job.

As Table 8–4 shows, groups will be happiest and most efficient when the members are also reaching their personal goals. You can boost the effectiveness of your

Table 8–4 Group Process Variables Associated with Productivity

1. Members are clear about and agree with group goals.
2. Tasks are appropriate for group versus individual solutions.
3. Members are clear about and accept their formal roles.
4. Role assignments match member abilities.
5. Level of leader's direction matches the group's skill level.
6. All group members are free to participate.
7. Group gets, gives, and uses feedback about its effectiveness and productivity.
8. Group spends time defining and discussing problems it must solve or decisions it must make. Members also spend time planning how they will solve problems and make decisions.
9. Group uses effective decision-making strategies that were outlined in advance.
10. Group evaluates its solutions and decisions.
11. Norms encourage high performance and quality, success, and innovation.
12. Subgroups are integrated into the group as a whole.
13. The group contains the smallest number of members necessary to accomplish its goals.
14. Group has enough time to develop cohesiveness and accomplish its goals.
15. Group has cooperative orientation.
16. Periods of conflict are frequent but brief and the group has effective ways of dealing with conflict.

Source: Research summarized in S. A. Wheelan et al., "Member Perceptions of Internal Group Dynamics and Productivity," *Small Group Research 29* (1998), pp. 371–393.

ethical challenge

Dealing with Offensive Humor

You are a new employee in a close-knit accounting department. You soon find that not-so-subtle racist and ethnic jokes are the order of the day. Your fellow workers use derogatory terms when they refer to clients and others. For you, this is an ideal job in terms of responsibility and salary; however, you are offended by the bigoted comments. What will you do?

group by doing everything possible to help members satisfy those goals. If the people in your group are looking for fun and companionship, consider ways to tackle the job at hand that also give them what they want. On the other hand, if they are in a hurry because of busy schedules, concentrate on keeping meetings to a minimum. If some members like recognition, stroke their egos by offering compliments whenever you can sincerely do so. The extra effort that you spend catering to the individual needs of members will pay dividends in terms of the energy and loyalty that the group gains from happy members.

In some cases, group members announce their personal goals. In other cases, though, stating a personal goal outright could be embarrassing or counterproductive. A committee member wouldn't confess, "I volunteered to serve on this committee so I could find new people to date." An employee would never say openly, "I'm planning to learn everything I can here and then quit the firm and open my own business." Personal goals that are not made public are called **hidden agendas.**

Hidden agendas are not necessarily harmful. The dating goals of a member needn't interfere with group functions. Similarly, many other personal motives are not threatening or even relevant to a group's business. Some hidden agendas are even beneficial. For instance, an up-and-coming young worker's desire to communicate competence to the boss by volunteering for difficult jobs might well help the group. International team consultant Frank Heckman sees that the "bottom line is that we all have personal agendas and to some degree, some are hidden even to us."[49] Other hidden agendas, however, are harmful and Heckman adds that "the problem will come in if the individual is duplicitous and undermines what the team is trying to achieve."[50] Two feuding members who use meetings to disparage each other can only harm the group, and the person collecting ideas to go into business himself will most likely hurt the organization when he takes its ideas elsewhere.

There is no single best way to deal with harmful hidden agendas. Sometimes the best course is to bring the goal out into the open. For example, a manager might speak to feuding subordinates one at a time, let them know she recognizes their problem, and work with them to solve it directly and constructively (probably using the conflict management skills described in Chapter 5). When you do decide to bring a hidden personal goal into the open, it's almost always better to confront the member privately. The embarrassment of being unveiled publicly is usually so great that the person becomes defensive and denies that the hidden goal exists.

At other times, it is best to treat a hidden personal goal indirectly. For example, if a member's excessive talking in meetings seems to be a bid for recognition, the best approach might be to make a point of praising his valid contributions more frequently. If two feuding subordinates continue to have trouble working together, the manager can assign them to different projects or transfer one or both of them to different groups.

Promote Desirable Norms

Norms are informal, often unstated rules about what behavior is appropriate in a group.[51] Some norms govern the way tasks are handled, while others shape the social interaction of the group. A group's norms often are shaped by the culture of the organization to which it belongs. For example, 3M's success has been attributed to its "bias for yes": When in doubt, employees are encouraged to take a chance instead of avoiding action for fear of failure.[52] Likewise, Motorola's turnaround has been attributed to its changing norms for conflict. The company's culture now makes it acceptable to disagree strongly (and loudly) in meetings, instead of keeping quiet or being overly diplomatic.[53] As Table 8–5 shows, the norms in some groups are constructive, while other groups have equally powerful rules that damage their effectiveness.[54]

The challenge of establishing norms is especially great when members come from different cultural backgrounds.[55] For example, group members from a low-context culture (such as the United States or Canada) would be more likely to address conflicts directly, while those from high-context backgrounds (East Asia or the Middle East, for example) would be inclined to use indirect approaches. Likewise, members from a background where high power distance is the norm would be less likely to challenge a group's leader than those from a background where low power distance is the norm.

Once norms are established, members who violate them create a crisis for the rest of the team, who respond in a series of escalating steps.[56] Consider, for example,

Table 8–5 Typical Constructive (and Destructive) Norms for a Working Group

- Handle (Ignore) business for co-workers who are away from their desks.
- Be willing (Refuse) to admit your mistakes.
- Occasional time off from work for personal reasons is (isn't) okay, as long as the absence won't harm the company.
- Do (Don't) be willing to work overtime without complaining when big, important deadlines approach.
- Say so (Keep quiet) if you disagree. Don't (Do) hint or go behind others' backs.
- Avoid (Hold) side conversations during meetings.
- Don't (Do) interrupt or ignore others' ideas.
- Arrive on time (Be late) for meetings.
- Celebrate (Don't celebrate) successes.
- Honor (Shirk) your commitments.

Source: After Joel A. C. Baum, "Avoiding Common Team Problems," HomePage for Game Theory and Competitive Strategy MGT 2056–Fall 2003, retrieved August 26, 2003, from **http://www.rotman.utoronto.ca/~baum/mgt2003/avoid.html**.

ethical challenge

The Unproductive Teammate

You are a member of what was once a dream team of productive workers. Until recently, everyone worked well together to meet the team's goals. When one member took time off to care for a child in the hospital a few months ago, everyone was happy to cover for him. Over the next months the same member began missing more work because of other problems—a spouse needing care, a sports injury, and moving to a new home. The rest of the group has begun to doubt that their unproductive colleague will ever contribute his fair share to the group again, and they agree that it's time to raise this issue.

Describe how the team can deal with this issue in a way that acknowledges both the unproductive member's legitimate problems and the group's need for the member to do his share.

a worker who violates the norm of not following up on her obligations between group meetings. Her teammates might react with increasing pressure:

- *Delaying action.* Members talk among themselves but do not approach the deviant, hoping that she will change without pressure.
- *Hinting about the violation.* Members tease the violator about being a "flake" or about being lazy, hoping that the message behind the humor will cause her to do her share of work.
- *Discussing the problem openly.* Members confront the nonconformist, explaining their concerns about her behavior.
- *Ridiculing and deriding the violator.* Persuasion shifts to demands for a change in behavior; the group's pressure tactics may well trigger a defensive response in the nonconforming member.
- *Rejecting or isolating the deviant.* If all other measures fail, the team member who doesn't conform to group norms is asked to leave the group. If she cannot be expelled, other members can effectively excommunicate her by not inviting her to meetings and by disregarding any attempts at communicating she might make.

There are two ways in which an understanding of norms can help you to function more effectively in a group.

Create Desirable Norms Early Norms are established early in a group; and once they exist, they are difficult to change. This means that when you participate in a group that is just being established, you should do whatever you can to create norms that you think will be desirable. For example, if you expect members of a committee to be punctual at meetings, it's important to begin each session at the appointed time. If you want others to be candid about their feelings, it's important to be frank yourself and encourage honesty in others at the outset.

Comply with Established Norms Whenever Possible In an established group, you have the best chance of reaching your goals if you handle the task and social relationships in the group's customary manner. If your co-workers are in the habit of exchanging good-natured insults, you shouldn't be offended when you are the target—and you will be accepted as one of them if you dish out a few yourself. In a group in which the norm is never to criticize another member's ideas directly, a blunt approach probably won't get you very far. When you are entering an established group, it's wise to learn the norms by personal observation and by asking knowledgeable members before plunging in.

A national or regional culture can also shape the way group members communicate with one another. Differences in managing conflict are a good example. The straight-talking low-context style that is accepted in many parts of the English-speaking world is not the norm in other places.[57] It may not always be possible to follow established norms. If a group is in the habit of cracking racist jokes, doing shabby work, or stealing company property, for example, you probably would be unwilling to go along just to be accepted. This sort of conflict between personal values and group norms can lead to a major crisis in values. If the potential for conflict is great enough and the issue is sufficiently important, you may decide to do whatever you can to join a different, more compatible group.

Promote an Optimal Level of Cohesiveness

Cohesiveness can be defined as the degree to which members feel themselves part of a group and want to remain with that group. You can think of cohesiveness as a magnetic force that attracts members to one another, giving them a collective identity. As you might suspect, highly cohesive groups have happier members than less closely knit groups. Workers who belong to cohesive groups are likely to have higher rates of job satisfaction and lower rates of tension, absenteeism, and turnover than those who belong to less cohesive groups.[58] They also make better decisions.[59]

Not all cohesive work groups are productive—at least not in terms of the organization's goals. In strikes and slowdowns, for example, highly cohesive workers can actually shut down operations. (Of course, the workers' cohesiveness in such cases may help them to accomplish other group goals, such as higher pay or safer working conditions.) In less dramatic cases, cohesiveness in observing anti-organization norms ("Don't work too hard," "Go ahead and report our lunch as a business expense—we always do that," "If you need some art supplies for your kids, just take them from the supply closet") can leave group members feeling good about each other but harm the interests of the organization.

Cohesiveness develops when certain conditions exist in a group. Once you understand these conditions, you can apply them to groups on or off the job. You can also use them to analyze why a group's cohesiveness is high or low and choose ways to reach and maintain a desirable level of cohesiveness. Here are seven factors that promote an optimal level of cohesiveness.[60]

Shared or Compatible Goals Group members draw closer together when they have a similar aim or when their goals can be mutually satisfied. For instance, the members of a construction crew might have little cohesiveness when their pay is based on individual efforts, but if the entire crew receives a bonus for completing stages of the building ahead of schedule, the members are likely to work together better.

Progress toward Goals When a group makes progress toward its target, members are drawn together; when progress stops, cohesiveness decreases. Members of

the construction crew just mentioned will feel good about each other when they reach their target dates or can reasonably expect to do so. But if they consistently fall short, they are likely to get discouraged and feel less attraction to the group; when talking to their families or friends, there will be less talk about "us" and more about "me."

Shared Norms or Values Although successful groups tolerate or even thrive on some differences in members' expressed attitudes and behaviors, wide variation in what members consider appropriate behavior reduces cohesiveness. For example, a person who insists on wearing conservative clothes in a business where everyone else dresses casually probably won't fit in with the rest of the group.

Minimal Feelings of Threat among Members In a cohesive group, members usually feel secure about their status, dignity, and material and social well-being. When conflict arises over these issues, however, the results can be destructive. If all of the junior executives in a division are competing for the same senior position—especially if senior positions rarely open—the cohesiveness of the group is likely to suffer, at least until the job is filled.

Interdependence among Members Groups become more cohesive when members need one another to satisfy group goals. When a job can be done by one person alone, the need for unity decreases. An office team in which each member performs a different aspect or stage of a process will be less cohesive than one in which members rely on one another.

Competition from outside the Group When members perceive an external threat to their existence or dignity, they draw closer together. Almost everyone knows of a family whose members seem to fight constantly among themselves until an outsider criticizes one of them. The internal bickering stops for the moment, and the group unites against the common enemy. An uncohesive work group could draw together in a similar way when another group competes with it for such things as use of limited company resources or desirable space in a new office building. Many wise managers deliberately set up situations of competition between groups to get tasks accomplished more quickly or to generate more sales dollars.

Shared Group Experiences When members have been through an experience together, especially an unusual or trying one, they draw closer together. This is why soldiers who have gone through combat together often feel close for the rest of their lives. Work groups that have accomplished difficult tasks are also likely to be more cohesive. Some organizations also provide social events such as annual "retreats" for their executives; retreats might include workshops to discuss particular aspects or problems of members' jobs, sports events, and parties. Annual sales meetings are often partially intended to increase group cohesiveness, since these meetings are not the most cost-efficient way to distribute sales information.

Avoid Excessive Conformity

Bad group decisions can also come about through too much agreement among members. Irving Janis calls this phenomenon **groupthink,** an unwillingness, for the sake of harmony, to examine ideas critically.[61] Janis describes several characteristics of groups that succumb to groupthink:

- *Illusion that the group is invulnerable:* "We can afford to raise the price on our deluxe-model kitchen appliances because they're so much better than anything else on the market. Even if our competitors could develop comparable models, we'd still outdo them on style."
- *Tendency to rationalize or discount negative information:* "I know the market research says people will buy other brands if our prices go up any more, but you know how unreliable market research is about things like that."
- *Willingness to ignore ethical or moral consequences of the group's decision:* "The waste we're dumping in the river may kill a few fish, but look, this company provides jobs and a living for all the people who live in this town."
- *Stereotyped views of other groups:* "The only thing those people at the head office care about is the bottom line. They don't give a damn about what we think or what we need."
- *Group pressure to conform:* "Come on, none of the rest of us is interested in direct-mail marketing. Why don't you forget that stuff?"
- *Self-censorship:* "Every time I push for an innovative ad campaign, everybody fights it. I might as well drop it."
- *Illusion of unanimity:* "Then we all agree: cutting prices is the only way to stay competitive."
- *"Mindguards" against threatening information:* "They're talking about running the machines around the clock to meet the schedule. I'd better not bring up what the supervisor said about how her staff feels about working more overtime."

career tip

Devil's Advocate and Other Anti-conformity Tools

Since medieval times, the Catholic Church has appointed a "Devil's Advocate" to present all possible arguments—even seemingly slight ones—against promoting a candidate toward sainthood. The Church recognizes the danger of one-sided enthusiasm and relies on the advocate to make sure that decision makers consider all sides of the issue. This approach can serve nonreligious groups just as well, especially when there is an undisputed consensus toward making an important decision. If your group doesn't have the foresight to appoint a devil's advocate, you can take on this role by challenging the majority's thinking.

Other approaches can serve as antidotes to groupthink. If the group has enough members, it can be helpful to set up two (or more) subgroups to consider approaches independently. Another approach is to request the opinions of respected outsiders who haven't been influenced by the collective enthusiasm of members.

A second type of harmful conformity has been labeled **risky shift:** the likelihood of a group to take positions that are more extreme than the members would choose on their own.[62] A risky shift can work in two directions. When members are conservative, their collective decisions are likely to be more cautious than their individual positions. More commonly, groups are prone to taking positions that are riskier than the choices members would have taken had they been acting separately. Thus, risky shift results either in taking risks that aren't justified and suffering the costs or avoiding necessary steps that the team needs to take to survive and prosper.

Paradoxically, cohesive teams are most prone to groupthink and risky shift. When members like and respect one another, the tendency to agree is great. The best way to guard against this sort of collective blindness—especially in very cohesive groups—is to seek the opinions of outsiders who may see things differently. In addition, leaders who are highly influential should avoid stating their opinions early in the discussion.[63]

Encourage Creativity

One advantage of broadly based participation in groups is the greater chance for creativity. As more members bring their different perspectives to a task, the chances of coming up with a winning solution increase.

Of course, the quantity of people involved doesn't guarantee the quality of their contributions. One way to boost the creativity of the group is through **brainstorming**—an approach that encourages free thinking and minimizes conformity. The term was coined by advertising executive Alex Osborn, who noticed that groups were most creative when they let their imaginations run free.[64] He also realized that creativity was stifled when members began criticizing either their own ideas or those of others. As one observer put it, "Throwing away ideas too soon is like opening a package of flower seeds and then throwing them away because they're not pretty."[65]

Out of these observations came a series of steps that, with variations, are now used widely.

Conduct a Warm-up Session During this phase the group is reminded of brainstorming's cardinal rules:

1. All evaluation and criticism of ideas is forbidden during the early phases of the process.
2. Wild and crazy ideas are encouraged.
3. Quantity—not quality—of ideas is the goal.
4. New combinations of ideas are sought.

Once members understand these rules, they practice them with some nonsense issue, such as uses for a paper clip (high-tech tie clip, lightning rod for an anthill) or a brick (heat and use as a foot warmer in bed, freeze and use as a beer cooler on picnics). This sort of wild thinking loosens the group up to approach the real problem creatively.

Generate Possible Solutions Now the group applies the brainstorming rules, as described above, to the task at hand. During this stage, a recorder lists all the ideas generated by the group on a chalkboard or flip chart that everyone can see. The leader encourages "hitchhiking" on previous ideas, so that one suggestion leads to variations. The leader should also keep the level of enthusiasm high to spur more contributions.

Eliminate Duplicate Ideas After the brainstorming session is completed, duplicate suggestions are eliminated. No evaluation of ideas is made at this stage; the group simply clarifies and simplifies the list of ideas it has developed.

Evaluate Ideas Once the group has generated all the ideas it can think of, it can begin to decide which are worth considering seriously. Unless only one or two ideas stand out as winners, it's usually best to prune the unworkable ones in several passes. Begin by scratching the clearly unworkable ideas, leaving any that have even some merit. After discussing the remainder, the group can pick the top two or three ideas for serious consideration and then decide which one is best.

Brainstorming can be even more effective in virtual groups than in face-to-face meetings.[66] Furthermore, more ideas are generated when brainstorming is anonymous than when members know who is contributing suggestions.

summary

When used effectively, small groups are more productive, their results more accurate, and their decisions more enthusiastically supported by members. Small groups share characteristics of size, interaction, shared purpose, interdependence, regular interaction and communication, and identity. Virtual teams transcend time and space boundaries and present both advantages and challenges.

The best approach to leading a group varies, depending on circumstances. In groups with a designated leader, the optimal style depends on leader–member relations, the structure of the task, and the amount of power the leader possesses. In groups without a designated leader, a predictable process occurs in which a single leader often emerges. In many groups, leadership is often shared among members, who may each possess one or more types of power , stemming from position, ability to coerce and reward, expertise, information possessed, connections, and esteem of other members.

Groups often solve problems together in a systematic way that involves moving through stages that can be called forming, storming, norming, and performing. For better or worse, members can influence the effectiveness of the group by enacting various functional roles, both task and relational. Dysfunctional roles contribute to group ineffectiveness. Carefully choosing a decision-making method ensures that the group uses time effectively and generates an outcome that members are most likely to support.

Groups can be more successful when members recognize and try to fulfill both personal and group goals, promote desirable norms, promote an optimal level of cohesiveness, avoid excessive conformity, and boost creativity.

key terms

Test your understanding of these key terms by visiting the Online Learning Center Web site at www.mhhe.com/adler9.

authoritarian leadership style 260
authority rule 276
brainstorming 285
coercive power 264
cohesiveness 282
conflict phase 269
connection power 265
consensus 274
contingency approaches to leadership 261
democratic leadership style 260
designated leader 264
emergence phase 269
emergent leader 262
expert opinion 275
expert power 265
forming stage 268
functional roles 272
groupthink 284
hidden agenda 279
information power 265
laissez-faire leadership style 260
life-cycle theory of leadership 262
majority vote 275
minority decision 275
norming stage 269
norms 280
orientation phase 268
performing stage 269
position power 264
referent power 265
reflective-thinking sequence 266
reinforcement phase 269
relational roles 272
reward power 264

risky shift 285
self-directed work teams 264
storming stage 269
style approach to leadership 260
task roles 272
team 257
trait approach to leadership 260
virtual team 258
work group 255

activities

Go to the self-quizzes at the Online Learning Center at www.mhhe.com/adler9 to test your knowledge of chapter concepts.

1. Invitation to Insight

Consider an effective team you have observed or participated in. Identify the characteristics that contributed to this team's productivity. Provide an example of each. Then use concepts from this chapter to suggest at least one way the team could have improved.

2. Invitation to Insight

Analyze the types of power that exist in your class or some other working group. Which members use each type of power? Who exerts the most influence? What kinds of power do you possess?

3. Skill Builder

Using Table 8–3, identify the role each of these statements represents.

a. "Debby, could you hold on and let Martin speak first?"
b. "So far we have discussed six funding sources . . ."
c. "Although you seem to disagree, both of you are concerned with . . ."
d. "I think you're really on to something. That seems like the information we need."
e. "What else do you think we should consider?"

4. Skill Builder

With three to six of your classmates, decide which method of decision making would be most effective for your group in each of the following situations:

a. Choosing the safest course of action if you were lost in a dangerous area near your city or town.
b. Deciding whether and how to approach your instructor to propose a change in the grading system of your course.
c. Designing the most effective campaign for your school to recruit minority students.
d. Duplicating for distribution to your instructor and classmates the solutions to this exercise that your group developed.
e. Hiring an instructor for your department.
f. Choosing the name for a new brand of breakfast cereal.
g. Selecting a new computer system.
h. Deciding which of three employees gets the desirable vacant office.
i. Planning the weekend work schedule for the upcoming month.
j. Deciding whether the employees should affiliate with a labor union.

5. Invitation to Insight

Although it may be larger than most of the groups discussed in this chapter, your class is a good model of the principles described here. Answer the following questions about your class or about a group that you participate in:

a. What are the stated goals of the class or group? Does the group have any unstated, shared goals?
b. What are your individual goals? Which of these goals are compatible with the group's goals, and which are not compatible? Are any of your individual goals hidden agendas?
c. What are your instructor's or the group leader's individual goals? Were these goals stated? If not, how did you deduce them?

How compatible are these goals with the official goals of the class or group?

d. How do the individual goals of other members affect the functioning of the group as a whole?

6. Skill Builder

Suggest several norms that would be desirable for each of the following groups. In your list, include norms that address tasks, relationships, and procedures. How could you promote development of these norms as the group's leader? As a member?

a. A student fund-raising committee to develop scholarships for your major department.
b. The employees at a new fast-food restaurant.
c. A group of new bank tellers.
d. A company softball team.

7. Invitation to Insight

Which of the functional roles in Table 8–3 do you generally fill in groups? Do you fill the same role in most groups at most times, or do you switch roles as circumstances require? Do you tend to fill task roles or relational roles? How could you improve the functioning of one group you belong to by changing your role-related behavior?

8. Skill Builder

Use the skills you learned in Chapters 6 and 7 to interview one member of a work-related group. Identify the following:

a. What is the level of the group's cohesiveness? Is this level desirable, too high, or too low?
b. Which of the factors on pages 282–284 contribute to the level of cohesiveness in this group?
c. On the basis of your findings, develop a report outlining specific steps that might be taken to improve the degree of cohesiveness in this group.

9. Skill Builder

Recall a group you've participated in that demonstrated an excessive level of conformity. Identify negative outcomes that resulted from the excessive conformity. Which characteristics of groupthink did the group exhibit? What allowed these characteristics to exist? Write at least three suggestions that might have helped the group prevent overconformity.

resources

In Print

Donnellon, Anne. *Team Talk: The Power of Language in Team Dynamics*. Boston: Harvard Business School Press, 1996.

This book uses everyday team conversations to explain how and why teams, especially cross-functional teams, work. The author explores the language of teams to understand the challenges and successful ways of meeting the challenges of teams whether you are a team member or manager. A team talk audit can be used to analyze team talk and demonstrate the power of language and listening.

Frey, Lawrence F.; Dennis Gouran; and Marshall Scott Poole. *Handbook of Group Communication Theory and Research*. Newbury Park, CA: Sage, 1999.

This book offers a wealth of knowledge about how small groups function. Separate chapters explore topics including the role of individuals and cultural background in groups, how members are socialized into teams, how the decision-making process operates, the role of relational communication in teams, how members influence one another, and how groups can communicate using technology.

Godar, Susan H., and Sharmila P. Ferris. *Virtual and Collaborative Teams: Process, Technologies and Practices*. Hershey, PA: Idea Group, 2004.

Each of the four sections of this book provides several well-researched chapters on these aspects of virtual teams: their makeup, leadership, communication processes, and effective uses.

Hirokawa, Randy Y., et al. *Small Group Communication: Theory & Practice: An Anthology*, 8th ed. Los Angeles, CA: Roxbury, 2003.

This anthology consists of 24 chapters prepared by leading small-group communication scholars. Sections include the nature of groups, theories of small groups, organization of groups, group processes, groups and teams, leadership, and diversity in groups. Additionally there are three chapters on observing, analyzing, and evaluating group communication.

Katzenbach, Jon R. *Teams at the Top*. Boston: Harvard Business School Press, 1998.

Katzenbach's classic book on teams, *The Wisdom of Teams*, is a primer for teams around the world. Now, *Teams at the Top* offers more information and insight to enhance your teamwork. The glossary of team terms and the short diagnostic guide for teams are particularly useful.

Kostner, Jaclyn. *Bionic Teamwork: How to Build Collaborative Virtual Teams at Hyperspeed*. Chicago: Dearnborn, 2001.

The author is an international expert on collaborative virtual teamwork. She draws on her experiences with diverse multinational corporations to describe some of the best practices in virtual teams. Kostner insists that it is not technology that makes a team, but rather trust and communication.

Maxwell, John C. *The 17 Indisputable Laws of Teamwork: Embrace Them & Empower Your Team*. Nashville: Thomas Nelson, Inc., 2001.

Using examples from famous and not-so-famous men and women, leadership expert Maxell illustrates 17 laws of teamwork such as "The Law of Communication: Interaction Fuels Action" and "The Law of Identity: Shared Values Define the Team." Other laws are about roles, morale, leadership, trust, attitudes, and teamwork.

Northouse, Peter G. *Leadership: Theory and Practice*, 3rd ed. Thousand Oaks, CA: Sage, 2005.

This is a comprehensive guide to many approaches to leadership explored by social scientists. Separate chapters explore various perspectives on leadership covered in this chapter (trait, style, situational, and contingency) and teams. A final chapter explores the ethical dimension of leadership.

Rothwell, J. Dan. *In Mixed Company—Communicating in Small Groups and Teams*, 6th ed. Belmont, CA: Wadsworth, 2007.

This popular text presents essential concepts of communicating in groups. Chapter 11 focuses on virtual teams and new technologies that influence small group communication.

Surowiecki, James. *The Wisdom of Crowds*. New York: Doubleday, 2004.

The author draws examples from fields including psychology, ant biology, economics, artificial intelligence, and history to show that groups of people often devise solutions that are superior to even the smartest individuals. While the focus is on large groups, the principles here reinforce the concept that collective wisdom is a valuable tool for decision makers in business and the professions.

Wheelan, Susan A. *Creating Effective Teams*. Newbury Park, CA: Sage, 1999.

This book outlines how groups can progress, through the stages described in the chapter you have just finished, from their original formation toward solving the problems they are designed to address. The book is full of strategies for creating and maintaining effective teams. Examples and checklists back up the well-researched information in this useful book.

On the Web

For over 10 years the nonprofit Center for the Study of Work Teams, housed at the University of North Texas, has been researching and educating all areas of collaborative work teams. Its home page (**www.workteams.unt.edu**) is an outstanding place to begin your study. Check out their superb links (well categorized and organized), free articles, careers, participation, newsletter, and more.

Team Builders Plus (**www.teambuildersplus.com**) links to articles and organizations on over 25 relevant team topics: assertiveness, 360-degree feedback, facilitating, online surveys, quotes, and newsgroups.

Explore Team Management Systems' international research bibliography of team processes and linking skills (active listening, problem solving) at **www.tms.com.au/reference.html**.

Go to **www.uwec.edu/Sampsow/Links/Group.htm** for an excellent annotated list of group and team process links. For information about group dynamics and skills, including vast resources about virtual teams, check out **www.mapnp.org/library/grp_skll/meetings/meetings.htm#anchor1492512**. A helpful Team Effectiveness Checklist is available at **www.workforce.com/archive/article/23/17/54.php** and tools for collaboration and leadership development are at **www.abetterworkplace.com**.

If you are looking for *tools* for your group to use, try **http://www.Intranets.com**. This site allows you to create your own team intranet. The free standard edition includes the capability to circulate announcements, build and modify a team calendar, create a library of documents, and post a member list. It also allows your team to set up an online discussion board where members can post comments and respond to one another's ideas and a polling capability that can be useful for larger groups. For a monthly fee, the professional edition provides e-mail addresses, instant messaging, document sharing, a task manager, and wireless access.

A more modest site for groups is **http://groups.yahoo.com**. Finally, if your team has a complicated project, you can create a flowchart to clarify the critical jobs and deadlines at the TeamFlow Web site—**http://www.teamflow.com**.

Effective Meetings

Chapter Outline

Chapter Objectives

After reading this chapter you should be able to

1 Describe various types and purposes of meetings.

2 Identify reasons to hold a meeting and determine when a meeting is not necessary.

3 Construct a complete meeting agenda.

4 Analyze participant behavior at meetings and identify several methods to encourage full participation of all members, keep discussion on track, create a positive atmosphere, and promote understanding.

5 Effectively bring a meeting to a close and follow up appropriately.

As they do every week, the agents of a real estate firm meet to discuss the latest trends in the market and to share information that will help them increase their sales.

The tenants in an apartment building gather to discuss the need for better maintenance and security.

A group of employees meets with top management to discuss a list of important issues, including the need for child care, a potential series of layoffs, and health benefits.

The owner of a small business meets over lunch with the director of a local advertising agency, who outlines how her firm can increase the client's market share.

Examples like these show that meetings are a fact of life on the job. They also help explain why we so often hear that someone we want to contact is "in a meeting." A moment's thought will reveal why *group* and *meeting* are not identical terms. A team of assembly-line workers or of firefighters fits the characteristics of a group outlined in Chapter 8, but these people spend very little time in meetings. The members of some groups work in separate offices, separate buildings, or separate cities; they communicate with one another about their group efforts, but only occasionally do they confer at once to discuss shared concerns. In this chapter, we will focus specifically on how groups operate in meetings, that is, on those occasions when their members communicate simultaneously to deal with common concerns.

Table 9–1 Hourly Costs of Meetings*

Average Annual Salary of Attendees	Number of People Attending Meeting 2	4	6	8	10
$100,000	$112	$224	$236	$448	$560
75,000	84	168	252	336	420
62,500	70	140	210	280	350
50,000	56	112	168	224	280
37,500	42	84	126	168	210
25,000	28	56	84	112	140

**Figures do not include cost of employee benefits, lost productivity, facility, and equipment.*

Meetings really are ubiquitous. In one study of 15 corporations, researchers gave pocket recorders to a wide range of key workers—from sales representatives to vice presidents—and asked these workers to list what they were doing every 20 minutes on the job. An analysis of almost 90,000 working days showed that an impressive 46 percent of the time was spent in meetings of one sort or another.[1] Other estimates confirm this figure. The number of times people meet as they do business is staggering: Between 11 and 20 million business meetings take place each day in the United States, and businesspeople spend an average of half their time attending them.[2] In one corporation alone, managers spend an astonishing 4.4 million hours per year in meetings.[3] As Table 9–1 shows, the cost of meetings—even for small organizations—is considerable. If you include the time spent planning and following up on face-to-face interaction, the costs are even higher. For example, the Dow Jones Travel Index indicates that the average cost of an overnight business trip is $1,250 to $1,400.[4]

Just because meetings are common doesn't mean that they are always productive. A survey by one marketing research company showed that executives consider one-third of the gatherings they attend to be unnecessary.[5] Another study found that unproductive meetings cost U.S. businesses as much as $37 billion annually.[6] While unambitious workers may find that meetings break up a busy workday, more-focused employees view unnecessary and inefficient meetings as a frustrating waste of time.[7]

Organizations in which this cynicism is justified are in trouble. Beyond wasting precious time, pervasively inefficient meetings contribute to an overall atmosphere that isn't in anybody's best interests. "Meetings matter because that's where an organization's culture perpetuates itself," says William R. Daniels, senior consultant at American Consulting & Training.[8] Meetings—whether they are good or bad—are a sign of an organization's health.

Since meetings are so common and so important, this chapter will take a closer look at them. By the time you have finished reading these pages, you should understand some methods for planning and participating in meetings that will produce efficient, satisfying results.

Types of Meetings

People meet for many reasons. In most business and professional settings, meetings fall into three categories: information-sharing, problem-solving, and ritual activities. Of course, some meetings may serve more than one purpose.

Information-Sharing Meetings

In many organizations, people meet regularly to exchange information. Police officers and nurses, for example, begin every shift with a meeting in which the people going off duty brief their replacements on what has been happening recently. Members of a medical research team experimenting with a new drug may meet regularly to compare notes on their results. In many office groups, the Monday morning meeting is an important tool for informing group members about new developments, emerging trends, and the coming week's tasks. Perkin Elmer Corporation, a producer of scientific measuring instruments and precision optical equipment, is a typical example. The firm schedules a weekly meeting of all corporate and top executives to keep them up-to-date on the activities of the more than 20 divisions the company has around the world.

Problem-Solving or Decision-Making Meetings

In other meetings, a group may decide to take some action or make a change in existing policies or procedures. Which supplier should we contract? Should we introduce a new product line? Should we delay production so we can work out a design flaw in our new keyboard? Where can we cut costs if sales don't improve this year? How can we best schedule vacations?

Problem solving of one sort or another is the most common reason for a business meeting. Because problem-solving and decision-making meetings are the most challenging types of group activity, the bulk of this chapter discusses how to conduct them effectively.

Ritual Activities

In still other meetings, the social function is far more important than any specific task. In one firm, Friday afternoon "progress review sessions" are a regular fixture.

career tip

Technology for Virtual Meetings

For simple teleconferences, most phone companies provide a service where three or more people can hold a conference call. Users can set up these conversations on a pay-per-use basis or in some cases have unlimited teleconferencing for a single monthly fee. Check with your telephone provider for details. With Web-based services like Skype (**www.skype.com**) you can host conference calls for no cost using an Internet connection.

Many services now provide free tools that allow groups to meet and share information on the Web. For example, Yahoo Groups (**http://groups.yahoo.com**) and Google Groups (**http://groups.google.com**) make it easy to create, read, and reply to messages in a discussion. With them, you can create an archive of messages, share photos with group members in your own photo album, coordinate events for your group with a shared calendar, and post links to Web sites related to your group. With an inexpensive Webcam and microphone, members can see and talk with one another via their Web-based group. Wikis take the concept of Web-based meetings a step further by allowing users to freely create and edit Web page content using any Web browser. For a primer on wikis, see **http://c2.com/cgi/wiki?WikiWikiWeb**.

Several commercial sites offer more robust features for virtual meetings. An excellent one is WebEx Meeting Center (**www.webex.com**). It allows users to create teleconferences, add video to meetings, give software demonstrations, deliver presentations via the Web, and share computer applications. Anyone in the meeting can view and edit shared documents or take meeting participants on a Web tour. Microsoft's Live Meeting (**www.microsoft.com/office/rtc/livemeeting/default.mspx**) provides similar features and allows users to share any application on their desktop.

Their apparently serious title is really an insider's tongue-in-cheek joke: The meetings take place in a local bar and to an outsider look like little more than a T.G.I.F. party. Despite the setting and apparently unbusinesslike activity, however, these meetings serve several important purposes.[9] First, they reaffirm the members' commitment to one another and to the company. Choosing to socialize with one another instead of rushing home is a sign of belonging and caring. Second, the sessions provide a chance to swap useful ideas and stories that might not be appropriate in the office. Who's in trouble? What does the boss really want? As you read in Chapter 1, this sort of informal communication can be invaluable, and the meetings provide a good setting for it. Finally, ritual meetings can be a kind of perk that confers status on the members. "Progress review committee" members charge expenses to the company and leave work early to attend. Thus, being invited to join the sessions is a sign of having arrived in the company.

Virtual Meetings

The term *meeting* conjures up images of people seated around a table, transacting business. But technology has made meetings possible even when the participants are half a world apart. *Virtual meetings* can take several forms.

Teleconferences (also called *conference calls*) are essentially multiparty telephone conferences. Intraorganization phone systems usually have a teleconferencing capability, and most telephone companies provide a similar feature for a modest monthly fee. With this approach, the person who calls the meeting dials the first

participant, then briefly taps the hang-up button and calls other numbers. When all parties have come on the line, the caller sends another signal and everyone is able to talk freely with one another.

Videoconferences allow users in distant locations to see one another. The number of locations with videoconferencing is surprisingly large: over half a million sites worldwide, by one estimate.[10] Videoconferencing is especially valuable in organizations with widespread operations. For example, CKE Restaurants of Santa Barbara, California, operates over 3,400 restaurants including Hardee's, Carl's Jr., Sa Salsa, and Timber Lodge Steakhouse. The company uses Web-based conferencing to link members spread across the United States, saving thousands of dollars over the cost of face-to-face meetings.[11]

You don't need an elaborate organizational network to hold a videoconference. With low-cost Webcams and microphones, free software, and a high-speed Internet connection, you can hold virtual meetings with people anywhere on Earth. See the Career Tip box on page 296 for details. Commercial centers like Kinko's offer for-rent videoconferencing, and computer users with a modestly priced camera and the right software can hold videoconferences from their desks.

Whether you are having a teleconference or videoconference, following some basic guidelines will help the meeting run smoothly:

- Before the meeting, send your agenda and copies of any documents that will be discussed to all participants. Number pages of longer documents to avoid unnecessary paper shuffling.
- At the beginning of the meeting, have participants introduce themselves and state their location.
- In phone conversations, parties should identify themselves whenever necessary to avoid confusion. ("Ted talking here: I agree with Melissa. . . .")
- Avoid interrupting others or leaving out persons simply because you can't see them.

ethical challenge

Dealing with Opposing Viewpoints

Your manager has asked you to provide suggestions from your department with regard to the company's policy on flex time. These suggestions will be taken seriously and have a strong chance of being adopted. You are in a position to call a meeting of key people in your department to discuss the issue.

Two of the most vocal members of the department have diametrically opposed positions on flex time. One of them (whose position on the issue is different from yours) will be out of the office for a week, and you could call the meeting while he is gone. What do you do?

- Keep distractions (ringing phones, slamming doors, etc.) to a minimum.
- Use the best equipment possible. Cheap speakerphones and computer cameras may make it difficult to understand one another.[12]

Online meetings allow computer users to use the Internet to create their own private conversation, in which they exchange typed messages in real time. As with teleconferences, in-house computer networks can make chat sessions easy. Free instant messaging is the quickest and easiest way to hold an online meeting. Just create a "buddy list" of the people with whom you want to talk, and you can meet online whenever you want. Sophisticated programs for meetings include a document-sharing capability, which allows users to view and add to the same computer file.

Virtual meetings have many advantages when compared to the face-to-face variety.[13] Most obviously, they allow people to interact far more quickly, easily, and affordably than would otherwise be possible. Virtual meetings are easier to schedule, and they take less time than in-person sessions since participants don't have to worry about getting to and from the meeting site. The relative ease of holding virtual meetings makes it possible to include people who otherwise wouldn't be able to attend. Finally, the less-personal nature of meetings encourages lower-status members to participate in discussions more freely and stand their ground on controversial issues.

Along with these advantages, virtual meetings have some important drawbacks when compared to the in-person variety. Participants have less access to one another's nonverbal feedback, increasing the chances of misunderstandings. Just as important, they may exclude participants who don't have access to the necessary technology. Even when they do have all the technology, some participants who don't use teleconferencing or videoconferencing regularly may be uncomfortable or clumsy when using it.

Planning a Problem-Solving Meeting

Successful meetings are just like interviews, presentations, letters, and memos: They must be planned.

When to Hold a Meeting

Given the costs of bringing people together, the most fundamental question is whether to hold a meeting at all. In one survey, middle and upper managers reported that over 25 percent of the meetings they attended could have been replaced by a memo, e-mail, or phone call.[14] Other experts report that roughly half of all business meetings are unproductive.[15] There are many times when a meeting probably isn't justified:[16]

- The matter could be handled just as well over the phone.
- You could send a memo, e-mail, or fax to achieve the same goal.
- Key people are not available to attend.
- The subject would be considered trivial by many of the participants.
- There isn't enough time to handle the business at hand.
- Members aren't prepared.
- The meeting is routine, and there is no compelling reason to meet.
- The job can be handled just as well by one or more people without the need to consult others.
- Your mind is made up or you've already made the decision.

Keeping these points in mind, a planner should call a meeting (or appoint a committee) only when the following questions can be answered "yes."[17]

Is the Job beyond the Capacity of One Person? A job might be too much for one person to handle for two reasons: First, it might call for more *information* than any single person possesses. For example, the job of improving health conditions in a food-processing plant would probably require the medical background of a physician or other health professional, the firsthand experience of employees familiar with the work, and a manager who knows the resources available for developing and implementing the program.

Second, a job might take more *time* than one person has available. For instance, even if one employee were capable of writing and publishing an employee handbook, it's unlikely that the person would be able to handle the task and have much time for other duties.

Are Individuals' Tasks Interdependent? Each member at a committee meeting should have a different role. If each member's share of the task can be completed without input from other members, it's better to have the members co-acting under the supervision of a manager.

Consider the job of preparing the employee handbook that we just mentioned. If each person on the handbook team is responsible for a separate section, there is little need for the group to meet frequently to discuss the task: Meetings would be little more than show-and-tell sessions. A more efficient plan might be for the group to meet at the outset to devise an outline and a set of guidelines about style, length, and so on, and then for a manager or group leader to see that each person completes his or her own section according to those guidelines.

There are times when people who do the same job can profit by sharing ideas in a group. Members of the handbook team, for example, might get new ideas about how the book could be made better from talking to one another. Similarly, sales representatives, industrial designers, physicians, or attorneys who work independently might profit by exchanging experiences and ideas. This is part of the purpose of professional conventions. Also, many companies schedule quarterly or

career tip

Opting Out of Meetings

What should you do when you are expected to attend a meeting that you know will be a waste of time? There are some occasions when you can't escape worthless meetings: when you are formally obligated to attend, when your absence would damage your reputation, or when your boss insists that you show up.

On other occasions, though, you may consider using one of the following strategies to make your nonattendance acceptable:

- *Provide written input.* If your sole reason for showing up is to provide information, a memo or written report may be a good substitute for your physical presence.
- *Suggest a productive alternative.* There may be other ways for you—and maybe even other attendees—to achieve objectives without actually having a face-to-face meeting: an exchange of e-mails, teleconferencing, or delegating the job to a smaller group. Suggesting these alternatives may earn you the gratitude of others who don't want to attend the meeting any more than you do.
- *Tell the truth.* In some cases you may choose to explain your reasons for not wanting to attend. Of course, you should do so diplomatically. Instead of saying, "These meetings are always a waste of time," you might say, "I'm not sure my attendance would serve any useful purpose."

Source: Adapted from S. M. Lippincott, *Meetings: Do's, Don'ts, and Donuts*, 2nd ed. (Pittsburgh, PA: Lighthouse Point Press, 1999).

annual meetings of people who do similar but independent work. While this may seem to contradict the requirement for interdependence of members' tasks, there is no real conflict. A group of people who do the same kind of work can often improve their individual performance through meetings by performing some of the complementary *functional roles*. For example, one colleague might serve as reality tester. ("Writing individual notes to each potential customer in your territory sounds like a good idea, but do you really have time to do that?") Another might take the job of being information giver. ("You know, there's a printer just outside Boston who can do large jobs like that just as well as your regular printer, but he's cheaper. Call me, and I'll give you the name and address.") Others serve as diagnosers. ("Have you checked the feed mechanism? Sometimes a problem there can throw the whole machine out of whack.") Some can just serve as empathic listeners. ("Yeah, I know. It's tough to get people who can do that kind of work right.")

Is There More than One Decision or Solution? Questions that have only one right answer aren't well suited to discussion in meetings. Whether the sales force made its quota last year and whether the budget will accommodate paying overtime to meet a schedule, for instance, are questions answered by checking the figures, not by getting the regional sales managers or the department members to reach an agreement.

Tasks that don't have fixed outcomes, however, are appropriate for committee discussion. Consider the job facing the members of an advertising agency who are planning a campaign for a client. There is no obvious best way to sell products or ideas such as yearly physical examinations, office equipment, or clothing.

Agenda for Your "Dream Team" Meeting

Imagine you could assemble a meeting with several of the people who would be best equipped to help you advance in your career. This group could include people from organizations that interest you, experts you have seen in the media, academics, and people in your community. Use the guidelines in these pages to create an agenda for this hypothetical meeting. To your class group, present

- A description of your career goals.
- A list of the people you want to include in your hypothetical meeting, and why you chose them.
- An agenda for the meeting that follows the format in Figure 9–1.

Tasks such as these call for the kind of creativity that a talented, well-chosen group can generate.

Are Misunderstandings or Reservations Likely? It's easy to see how meetings can be useful when the goal is to generate ideas or solve problems. But meetings are often necessary when confusing or controversial information is being communicated. Suppose, for instance, that changing federal rules and company policy require employees to document their use of company cars in far more detail than was ever required before. It's easy to imagine how this sort of change would be met with grumbling and resistance. In this sort of situation, simply issuing a memo outlining the new rules might not gain the kind of compliance that is necessary. Only by talking out their complaints and hearing why the new policy is being instituted will employees see a need to go along with the new procedure. "I can write down the vision of the company a thousand times and send it out to people," says Dennis Stamp, chairman of Vancouver's Priority Management Systems, Inc. "But when I sit with them face-to-face and give them the vision, for some reason it is much more accepted."[18]

Setting an Agenda

An **agenda** is a list of topics to be covered in a meeting. A meeting without an agenda is like a ship at sea without a destination or compass: No one aboard knows where it is or where it's headed. Smart organizations appreciate the importance of establishing agendas. At computer chip giant Intel, company policy requires meeting planners to circulate. You can start building an agenda by asking three questions:

1. What do we need to do in the meeting to achieve our objective?
2. What conversations will be important to the people who attend?
3. What information will we need to begin?[19]

Agenda items can come from many sources: the group leader, minutes from previous meetings, group members, or standing items (e.g., committee reports).[20]

FIGURE 9–1
Format for a Comprehensive Agenda

AGENDA

Date: December 19, 2007

To: Pat Rivera, Fred Brady, Kevin Jessup, Monica Flores, Dave Cohn

CC: Ellen Tibbits, Louisville Design Group (invited presenter)

From: Ted Gross

Subject: Planning meeting for new Louisville office

Meeting time: Tuesday, April 2, 9:30-11:30 a.m.

Location: Third-floor conference room.

Background: We are still on target for an August 10 opening date for the Louisville office. Completing the tasks below will keep us on schedule—vital if we're to be ready for the fall season.

We will discuss the following items:

1. **Office Equipment** 15 minutes
   Please come with a list of equipment you think will be needed for the office. At the meeting we'll refine this list to standardize our purchases as much as possible. Let's try to start out with compatible equipment!
2. **Office Decoration** 20 minutes
   Ellen Tibbits of the Louisville Design Group will present a preliminary design for our reaction. She will come up with a final plan based on our suggestions.
3. **Promotion** 15 minutes
   Kevin wants to prepare a series of press releases for distribution to Louisville media a month or so before the office opens. *Please come with suggestions of items that should be mentioned in these releases.*

As Figure 9–1 illustrates, a complete agenda contains this information: a list of the attendees (and whoever else needs to see the agenda), the meeting's time and location, necessary background information, and a brief explanation of each item. If you post an agenda on the Web, it is possible to attach annotations, or even entire documents, to supplement items. (For an example, see **http://grammar.ccc.commnet.edu/grammar/corresp/agenda.pdf**.)

Time, Length, and Location To avoid problems, all three of these details need to be present on an agenda. Without the *starting time,* you can expect to hear such comments as "I thought you said 10, not 9," or "We always started at 3 before."

Dilbert © Scott Adams/Dist. by United Feature Syndicate, Inc. Reprinted by permission.

Unless you announce the *length,* expect some members to leave early. Failure to note the *location* results in members' stumbling in late after waiting in the "usual place," wondering why no one showed up.

If your group needs to meet regularly, the best way to schedule meetings may be to build the time and place into everyone's schedule. At the Ritz-Carlton chain of luxury hotels, everyone in the organization starts the workday with a briefing. At company headquarters, top managers meet with the president of the company. Around the world, local employees start their daily shifts by covering the same points addressed in the headquarters meeting.[21]

Participants The overall size of the group is important: When attendance grows beyond seven members, the likelihood of some members' falling silent increases. If the agenda includes one or more problem-solving items, it's best to keep the size small so that everyone can participate in discussions. If the meeting is primarily informational, a larger group may be acceptable.

Be sure to identify on the agenda the people who will be attending. By listing who will attend, you alert all members about whom to expect in the meeting. If you have overlooked someone who ought to attend, a member who received the agenda can tell you. It is frustrating and a waste of time to call a meeting and then discover that the person with key information isn't there.

Background Information Sometimes participants will need background information to give them new details or to remind them of things they may have forgotten. Background information can also provide a description of the meeting's significance.

Items and Goals A good agenda goes beyond just listing topics and describes the goal for the discussion. "Meetings should be outcome- rather than process-driven," says Anita Underwood, Dun and Bradstreet's vice president of organizational management.[22] Most people have at least a vague idea of why they are meeting. Vague ideas, however, often lead to vague meetings. A clear list of topics and goals like the ones in Figure 9–1 will result in better-informed members and more productive, satisfying meetings.

The best goals are *result-oriented, specific,* and *realistic.* Notice the difference between goals that do and don't meet these criteria:

Poorly Worded	Better
Let's talk about how we can solve the sales problems in the northwestern region.	We will brainstorm and create a list of specific ways our product can be shown to be useful in the special climate conditions of the Northwest.
We're going to talk about the new income-savings plan.	We will explain the advantages and disadvantages of our two income-savings plans so employees can decide which best suits their needs.
Joe Fishman will tell you about his trip to the new supplier's plant.	Joe will explain the facilities of our new supplier and how we can use them to cut costs.

Goals like these are useful in at least two ways: First, they help to identify those who ought to attend the meeting. Second, specific goals also help the people who do attend to prepare for the meeting, and they help to keep the discussion on track once it begins.

The person who calls the meeting isn't the only one who can or should set goals. There are many times when other members have important business. The planner is often wise to use an "expectations check" to identify members' concerns.[23] Members can be polled before the meeting, so that their issues can be included in the agenda or at the start of the meeting. The fact that a member wants to discuss something does not mean that the topic should automatically be considered though. If the issue is inappropriate, the planner may choose to postpone it or handle it outside the meeting.

Pre-meeting Work The best meetings occur when people have done all the necessary advance work. The agenda is a good place to tell members how to prepare for the meeting by reading information, developing reports, preparing or duplicating documents, or locating facts or figures. If all members need to prepare in the same way (for example, by reading an article), adding that fact to the agenda is advised. If certain members have specific jobs to do, the meeting organizer can jot these tasks on their individual copies: "Sarah, be sure to bring last year's sales figures"; "Wes, please duplicate copies of the annual report for everyone."

The order of agenda items is important. Some experts suggest that the difficulty of items should form a bell-shaped curve, with items arranged in order of ascending and descending difficulty (see Figure 9–2). The meeting ought to begin with relatively simple business: minutes, announcements, and the easiest decisions. Once members have hit their stride and a good climate has developed, the group can move on to the most difficult items. These should ideally occupy the middle third of the session. Then the final third of the meeting can focus on easier items to allow a period of decompression and goodwill.

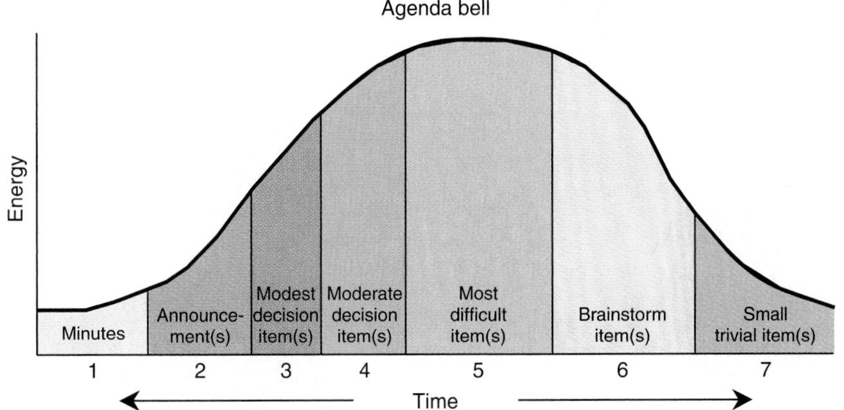

FIGURE 9–2
A Bell-Shaped Agenda Structure

Source: From John E. Tropman, "The Agenda Bell." Copyright © John E. Tropman. Used with permission.

Conducting the Meeting

To the uninitiated observer, a well-run meeting seems almost effortless. Time is used efficiently, the tone is constructive, and the quality of ideas is good. Despite their apparent simplicity, results like this usually don't just happen: They grow from some important communication skills.

Beginning the Meeting

Effective openings get the meeting off to a good start. First, they give everyone a clear picture of what is to be accomplished. Second, they define how the group will try to reach its goal. Finally, they set the stage for good teamwork and, thus, good results. The first few remarks by the person who called the meeting can set the stage for a constructive session. They should cover the following points.[24]

Identify the Goals of the Meeting This means repeating the information listed in the agenda, but mentioning it here will remind everyone of the meeting's goals and help to focus the discussion. For example:

> "We're faced with a serious problem. Inventory losses have almost doubled in the last year, from 5 to 9 percent. We need to decide what's causing these losses and come up with some ideas about how to reduce them."

Provide Necessary Background Information Background information explains the context of the meeting and gives everyone the same picture of the subject being discussed. It prevents misunderstandings and helps members to understand the nature of the information the group will consider. Clarifying key terms is often helpful:

> "By 'inventory losses,' we mean materials that are missing or damaged after we receive them. These losses might occur in the main warehouse, en route to the stores, or within the stores themselves."

Show How the Group Can Help Outline the contributions that members can make during the meeting. Some of these contributions will come from specific people:

> "Tom's going to compare our losses with industry figures, so we can get an idea of how much of the problem is an unavoidable cost of doing business. Chris

will talk about his experiences with the problem at Sterling, where he worked until last year. That firm had some good ideas we may be able to use."

Other contributions can be made by everyone present. This is the time to define specifically how each member can help make the meeting a success:

"We're counting on everybody here to suggest areas where we can cut losses. Once we've come up with ideas, I'll ask each of you to work out a schedule for putting the ideas to work in your department."

Preview the Meeting If you have not already done so, outline how the meeting will run. For instance:

"We'll begin by hearing the reports from Tom and Chris. Then we'll all work together to brainstorm a list of ways to cut losses. The goal here will be to get as many ideas as possible. Once we've come up with a list, we can decide which ideas to use and how to make them work."

Identify Time Constraints Clarify how much time is available to prevent wasting time. In some cases, it's only necessary to remind the group of how much time can be spent in the meeting as a whole ("We can develop this list between now and 11 o'clock if we keep on track"). In other cases, it can be useful to preview the time available for each agenda item:

"Tom and Chris have promised to keep their remarks brief, so by 10 o'clock we should be ready to start brainstorming. If we get our list put together by 10:30, we'll still have a half hour to talk about which ideas to try and how to put them into action."

career tip

Members Can Be Leaders, Too

Good leadership promotes successful meetings, but members can also play an important role in making a meeting successful. The following tips can be used by every person involved in a meeting:

- Ask that an agenda be sent out before the meeting or agree on an agenda at the beginning of the meeting.
- Ask for help at the beginning of the meeting. Seek clarification on the meeting's goal. Is it to present information? To make a decision?
- Be tactfully bold and suggest canceling an unnecessary or badly planned meeting. Convene it when there is a need and an agenda.
- Volunteer to be a record keeper. A written set of minutes reduces the chance for misunderstandings, and keeping notes yourself leads to a record that reflects your perception of events.
- Suggest that a timekeeper be appointed, or volunteer yourself. This person advises the group when time for addressing each issue—and the meeting itself—is nearly over and alerts the group when time runs out.
- Ask for help before the meeting closes: "Exactly what have we decided today?" "What do we need to do before our next meeting?"

Source: Adapted from Ana M. Keep, *Moving Meetings* (New York: Irwin, 1994).

Following these guidelines will get your meeting off to a good start. Even if you are not in charge of the meeting, you can still make sure that the opening is a good one by asking questions that will get the leader to share the kind of information just listed:

"How much time do you expect we'll need?"

"How far do you expect we'll get today?"

"What can we do to help solve the problem?"

And so on.

Conducting Business

No meeting will be successful without committed, talented participants. But even the best attendees do not guarantee success. Someone—either the leader or a responsible member—has to be sure that all important business is covered in a way that takes advantage of the talents of everyone present.

Parliamentary Procedure

Parliamentary procedure is a set of rules that governs the way groups conduct business and make decisions in meetings. The term may bring up images of legislators using obscure rules to achieve political goals. ("Madam Chairperson, I move we set aside the order of business and refer this motion to the committee of the whole. . . .")

While parliamentary procedure can be a form of gamesmanship, when used sensibly it can be a useful tool for managing group meetings. This approach can keep discussions clear and efficient while safeguarding the rights of everyone involved in deliberations.

When to use parliamentary procedure There are several situations when parliamentary procedure is an appropriate way to operate a meeting:

- *When a group's decisions will be of interest to an external audience.* This approach provides a record of the group's operations (the "minutes" of meetings), so interested observers can learn about the input of each member and the decisions made by the group as a whole.
- *When haste may obscure critical thinking.* Because it slows down the pace of discussions, parliamentary procedure can help groups deliberate before making decisions. Of course, there is no guarantee that this approach will help a group avoid making bad decisions, but it can help.
- *When emotions are likely to be strong.* Parliamentary procedure gives members with minority viewpoints a chance to speak, and its rules (when properly enforced) discourage uncivil behavior.

Order of business It's always a good idea to have an agenda. Under the rules of parliamentary procedure, the agenda provides a plan to handle business in a logical manner. The standard meeting agenda has the following parts:

1. *Reading of the minutes.* A good set of minutes is more than a formality: It gives everyone involved a chance to make sure the record describes what *really* happened and helps future groups learn from the decisions of this group.
2. *Reports.* Smart groups use committees to handle tasks. This is the time when these groups, as well as individual members, share information with the rest of the group.
3. *Unfinished business.* The group now addresses matters that haven't yet been settled.
4. *New business.* This is the time when members can bring up new issues for the group to discuss and decide on.

Motions When a member wants the group to deliberate, he or she introduces a **motion:** a specific proposal for action.

> "I move we redirect 10 percent of contributions to the Annual Fund to the endowment."
>
> "I move that we send two delegates to the annual convention in Chicago, with the goal of interviewing candidates for the position of associate director."
>
> "I move we go on record opposing the city's proposal to convert open parkland into parking."

Good motions address a single issue in a brief, clear way. Once introduced, a motion must be seconded by someone other than its sponsor. This procedure ensures that only those motions deemed worthy by at least two members are discussed by the group. Motions can be discussed and amended by other members. Once discussion is complete, a motion is decided by a public vote.

Using parliamentary procedure isn't an all-or-nothing proposition. Many groups use some of its elements without binding themselves to learning and using the full

career tip

Getting Credit for Your Ideas

It can be frustrating to see others get credit for your good ideas. Here are some nonaggressive strategies for making sure you get the recognition you deserve:

- In advance of the meeting, share your ideas with others who will be present. Securing their buy-in before the formal session can help ensure that your point of view is recognized.
- Put your proposal in writing and circulate it before the meeting. At the very least, this approach will ensure that people who may miss the meeting will see your ideas. Also, a well-written document can often lay out ideas more clearly than you might do in the meeting. Finally, your written message creates a record that the ideas were yours.
- If another person seems to be taking credit for an idea you raised, ask in a sincere manner, "Is this the same idea I raised earlier, or are you suggesting a modification?" Whatever the answer, you have reminded others where the original idea came from.

set of rules. Resources at the end of this chapter provide more detailed advice on using this approach.

Encouraging Participation Loosely structured, informal meetings may appear to give everyone an equal chance to speak out, but because of gender, culture, and style differences, every member may not, in fact, have the same access.[25] Group members' relative status or rank, ages, gender, and cultural backgrounds all influence interaction patterns in groups. Unbalanced participation can cause two sorts of problems: First, it discourages people who don't get a chance to talk. Second, it prevents the group from considering potentially useful ideas. There are several ways to improve participation at meetings.

Use the nominal group technique One method for giving every member's ideas an equal chance to be considered is the **nominal group technique (NGT)**.[26] (The method's name comes from the fact that, for much of this process, the participants are a group in name only, since they are working independently.) The NGT method consists of five phases:

1. Each member writes down his or her ideas, which are then collected by a discussion leader. This method ensures that good ideas from quiet members will have a chance for consideration.
2. All ideas are posted for every member to see. By keeping the authorship of ideas private at this point, consideration is less likely to be based on personal factors such as authority or popularity.
3. Members discuss the ideas to understand them better, but criticism is prohibited. The goal here is to clarify the possibilities, not to evaluate them.
4. Each member privately rank-orders the ideas from most to least promising. Individual ranking again prevents domination by a few talkative or influential members.

5. Items that receive the greatest number of votes are discussed critically and thoroughly by the group. At this point, a decision can be made, using whichever decision-making method described in Chapter 8 (e.g., consensus, majority rule) is most appropriate.

This approach lends itself nicely to computer-mediated meetings. With most groupware packages, members can anonymously input ideas via computer and have their contributions displayed for consideration by everyone. This anonymity can empower normally quiet group members, who might be too intimidated to speak up.

The NGT method is too elaborate for relatively unimportant matters but works well for important issues. Besides reducing the tendency for more talkative members to dominate the discussion, the anonymity of the process lessens the potential for harmful conflicts.

Have members take turns Another approach is to give every member a turn to speak. While it probably isn't wise to conduct an entire meeting this way, the technique can be useful at the beginning of a meeting to start members off on an equal footing, or in the middle if a few people are dominating the discussion, or at the end if some people have not been heard.

Use questions Questions that draw out listeners are another way to encourage participation. Four types of questions can balance the contributions of members.

Overhead questions are directed toward the group as a whole, and anyone is free to answer:

> "Sales have flattened out in the western region. Can anybody suggest what's going on?"
>
> "We need to find some way of rewarding our top producers. I'd like to hear your ideas."

As long as overhead questions draw a response from all members, it's wise to continue using them. When a few people begin to dominate, however, it's time to switch to one of the following types.

Direct questions are aimed at a particular individual, who is addressed by name:

> "How would that suggestion work for you, Kim?"
>
> "Greg, how's the new plan working in your department?"

Direct questions are a useful way to draw out quiet members, but they must be used skillfully. Never start a discussion with a direct question. This creates a schoolroom atmosphere and suggests the rule "Don't speak until you're called on"—hardly a desirable norm in most meetings. It's also important to give respondents a way out of potentially embarrassing questions. For example, a chairperson might ask, "Tony, can you give us the figures for your department now, or will you need to check them and get back to us?"

Reverse questions occur when a member asks the leader a question and the leader refers the question back to the person who originally phrased it:

> "Suppose the decision were up to you, Gary. What would you do?"
>
> "That's a good question, Laurie. Do you think it's a practical idea?"

Reverse questions work well when the leader senses that a member really wants to make a statement but is unwilling to do so directly. It's important to use reverse questions with care: The member could be asking for information, in which case a direct answer is appropriate.

Relay questions occur when the leader refers a question asked by one member to the entire group:

"Cynthia has just raised a good question. Who can respond to it?"

"Can anyone offer a suggestion for Les?"

Relay questions are especially useful when the leader wants to avoid disclosing his or her opinion for fear of inhibiting or influencing the group. Relays should usually be rephrased as overhead questions directed at the entire group. This avoids the suggestion that one member is smarter than the others. Of course, if a particular person does have special expertise, it is appropriate to direct the inquiry to him or her:

"Didn't you have a problem like that once with a distributor, Britt? How did you work things out?"

Keeping Discussions on Track Sometimes the problem isn't too little discussion but too much. Like the wolves in the cartoon on this page, groups often talk on and on without moving any closer to accomplishing a goal. When this happens, the leader or some other member needs to get the discussion back on track by using one of the following techniques.

"My question is: Are we making an impact?"

Remind the group of time pressures When the group is handling an urgent topic in a leisurely manner, you can remind everyone about the importance of moving quickly. But when doing so, it is important to acknowledge the value of the comments being made:

"Radio ads sound good, but for now we'd better stick to the newspaper program. John wanted copy from us by noon, and we'll never make it if we don't get going."

Summarize and redirect the discussion When members ramble on about a topic after the job is done, you can get the discussion moving again by tactfully summarizing what has been accomplished and mentioning the next task:

"It seems as if we've come up with a good list of the factors that might be contributing to absenteeism. Can anybody think of more causes? If not, maybe we should move on and try to think of as many solutions as we can."

Use relevancy challenges When a discussion wanders away from the business at hand, summarizing won't help. Sometimes the unrelated ideas are good ones that just don't apply to the group's immediate job. In other cases, they are not only irrelevant but also worthless. In either situation, you can get the group back on track by questioning the idea's relevancy. In a **relevancy challenge,** the questioner tactfully asks a member to explain how an apparently off-the-track idea relates to the group's task. Typical relevancy challenges sound like this:

> "I'm confused, Tom. How will leasing new equipment instead of buying it help us to boost productivity?"
>
> "Fran asked us to decide which word-processing package to buy. Does the graphics package you mentioned have something to do with the word-processing decision?"

At this point the member who made the original remark can either explain its relevance or acknowledge that it wasn't germane. In either case, the advantage of this sort of challenge is that it isn't personal. It focuses on the *remark* and not on the *person* and thus reduces the chance of a defensive response.

Promise to deal with good ideas later Another way to keep the goodwill of a member who has brought up an irrelevant idea is to suggest a way of dealing with it at the appropriate time:

> "That equipment-leasing idea sounds promising. Let's bring it up to Jeff after the meeting and see what he thinks of it."
>
> "A graphics package seems important to you, Lee. Why don't you look into what's available, and we can decide whether the change would be worth the cost."

As with relevancy challenges, your suggestion about dealing with an idea later has to be sincere if the other person is going to accept it. One way to show your sincerity is to mention exactly when you would like to discuss the matter. This might be a specific time ("after lunch"), or it might be when certain conditions are met ("after you've worked up the cost"). Another way to show your sincerity is to inquire about the idea after the meeting: "How's the research going on the graphics package?"

Keeping a Positive Tone Almost everyone would agree that getting along with people is a vital ingredient in a successful career. In meetings, getting along can be especially tough when others don't cooperate with your efforts to keep the meeting on track—or, even worse, attack your ideas. The following suggestions can help you handle these irritating situations in a way that gets the job done and keeps potential enemies as allies.

Ask questions and paraphrase to clarify understanding Criticizing an idea—even an apparently stupid one—can result in a defensive reaction that will waste time and generate ill will. It's also important to remember that even a seemingly idiotic remark can have some merit. Given these facts, it's often wise to handle apparently bad ideas by asking for some clarification. And the most obvious way to clarify an idea is to ask questions:

"Why do you think we ought to let Marcia go?"

"Who would cover the store if you went skiing next week?"

"What makes you think we shouldn't have a Christmas party this year?"

You can also paraphrase to get more information about an apparently hostile or foolish remark:

"It sounds as if you're saying Marcia's doing a bad job."

"So you think we could cover the store if you went skiing?"

"Sounds as if you think a Christmas party would be a waste of money."

This sort of paraphrasing accomplishes two things: First, it provides a way to double-check your understanding. If your replay of the speaker's ideas isn't accurate, he or she can correct you: "I don't think Marcia's doing a bad job. I just don't think we need so many people up front." Second, even if your understanding is accurate, paraphrasing is an invitation for the other person to explain the idea in more detail: "If we could find somebody to work a double shift while I was skiing, I'd be willing to do the same thing for him or her later."

Enhance the value of members' comments It's obvious that you should acknowledge the value of good ideas by praising or thanking the people who contribute them. Surprisingly, you can use the same method with apparently bad ideas. Most comments have *some* merit. You can take advantage of such merits by using a three-part response:[27]

1. Acknowledge the merits of the idea.
2. Explain any concerns you have.
3. Improve the usefulness of the idea by building on it or asking others for suggestions.

Notice how this sort of response can enhance the value of apparently worthless comments:

"I'm glad you're so concerned about the parking problem, Craig [acknowledges merit of comment]. But wouldn't requiring people to carpool generate a lot of resentment [balancing concern]? How could we encourage people to carpool voluntarily [builds on original idea]?"

"You're right, Pat. Your department could use another person [acknowledges merit of comment]. But Mr. Peters is really serious about this hiring freeze [balancing concern]. Let's try to come up with some ways we can get you more help without having to hire a new person [builds on original idea]."

Pay attention to cultural factors Like every other type of communication, the "rules" for conducting productive, harmonious meetings vary from one culture to another. For example, in Japan problem-solving meetings are usually preceded by a series of one-to-one sessions between participants to iron out issues, a process called *nemawashi*.[28] The practice arises from the Japanese cultural practice that two people may speak candidly to one another, but when a third person enters the discussion, they become a group, requiring communicators to speak indirectly to maintain harmony. By contrast, in countries where emotional expressiveness is the norm, volatile exchanges in meetings are as much the rule as the exception. "I've just come back from a meeting in Milan," stated Canadian management consultant Dennis Stamp. "If people acted the same way in North American meetings you'd think they were coming to blows."[29]

Concluding the Meeting

The way a meeting ends can have a strong influence on how members feel about the group and how well they follow up on any decisions that have been made or instructions that have been given.[30]

When to Close the Meeting There are three times when a meeting should be closed.

When the scheduled closing time has arrived Even if the discussion has been a good one, it's often best to close on schedule to prevent members from drifting off to other commitments one by one or losing attention and becoming resentful. It's wise to press on only if the subject is important and the members indicate willingness to keep working.

When the group lacks resources to continue If the group lacks the necessary person or facts to continue, adjourn until the resources are available. If you need to get cost figures for a new purchase or someone's approval for a new idea, for example, it is probably a waste of time to proceed until the data or go-ahead has been secured. In these cases, be sure to identify who is responsible for getting the needed information, and set a new meeting date.

When the agenda has been covered It seems obvious that a meeting should adjourn when its business is finished. Nonetheless, any veteran of meetings will testify that some discussions drag on because no one is willing to call a halt. Unless everyone is willing to socialize, it's best to use the techniques that follow to wrap up a meeting when the job is completed.

How to Conclude a Meeting A good conclusion has three parts. In many discussions, the leader will be responsible for taking these steps. In leaderless groups or in groups with a weak leader, one or more members can take the initiative.

Signal when time is almost up A warning allows the group to wrap up business and gives everyone a chance to have a final say:

> "We have about 15 minutes before we adjourn. We still need to hear Bob's report on the Kansas City conference, so let's devote the rest of our time to that."
>
> "It's almost time for some of you to leave for the airport. I'd like to wrap up our meeting by putting the list of suggestions Mr. Moss has asked us to send him into its final form."

Summarize the meeting's accomplishments and future actions For the sake of understanding, review what information has been conveyed and what decisions have been made. Just as important is reminding members of their responsibilities:

> "It looks like we won't have to meet again until the sales conference next Tuesday in San Juan. We'll follow the revised schedule that we worked up today. Chris will have copies to everyone first thing tomorrow morning. Nick will call the hotel to book the larger meeting room, and Pat will take care of having the awards made up. Let's all plan to meet over dinner at the hotel next Tuesday night."

Thank the group Acknowledging the group's good work is more than just good manners. This sort of reinforcement shows that you appreciate the group's efforts and encourages good performance in the future. Besides acknowledging the group as a whole, be sure to give credit to any members who deserve special mention:

> "We really got a lot done today. Thanks to all of you, we're back on schedule. Bruce, I appreciate the work you did on the specifications. We never would have made it without you."
>
> "You were all great about coming in early this morning. The extra rehearsal will make a big difference in the presentation. Those charts are terrific, Julie. And your suggestion about using the slide projector will make a big difference, Lou. Let's all celebrate after we get the contract."

Following Up the Meeting

It's a mistake to assume that even a satisfying meeting is a success until you follow up to make sure that the desired results have really been obtained. A thorough follow-up involves three steps.

Build an Agenda for the Next Meeting Most groups meet frequently, and they rarely conclude their business in one sitting. A smart leader plans the next meeting by noting which items need to be carried over from the preceding one. What unfinished business must be addressed? What progress reports must be shared? What new information should members hear?

Follow Up on Other Members You can be sure that the promised outcomes of a meeting actually occur if you check up on other members. If the meeting provided instructions—such as how to use the new long-distance phone service—see whether the people who attended are actually following the steps that were outlined. If tasks were assigned, check on whether they're being performed. You don't have to be demanding or snoopy to do this sort of checking. A friendly phone call or personal remark can do the trick: "Is the new phone system working for you?" "How's it going on those sales figures?" "Did you manage to get ahold of Williams yet?"

Take Care of Your Own Assignments Most homework that arises out of meetings needs continued attention. If you wait until the last minute before tackling it, the results are likely to be sloppy and embarrassing.

Self-Assessment Team Meeting Effectiveness Checklist

Evaluate the effectiveness of your meetings by using this format: 0 = never; 1 = rarely; 2 = sometimes; 3 = usually; 4 = often; 5 = always.

Planning

1. Are meetings held when (and only when) necessary? 0 1 2 3 4 5
2. Is membership well chosen?
   a. Is the size of the group appropriate? 0 1 2 3 4 5
   b. Are the necessary knowledge and skills represented? 0 1 2 3 4 5
3. Have unproductive members been excluded (if practical)? 0 1 2 3 4 5
4. Is enough time allotted for tasks at hand? 0 1 2 3 4 5
5. Is the meeting time convenient for most members? 0 1 2 3 4 5
6. Is the location adequate?
   a. Is the size appropriate? 0 1 2 3 4 5
   b. Are the facilities appropriate? 0 1 2 3 4 5
   c. Is there freedom from distractions? 0 1 2 3 4 5
7. Is a complete agenda created and circulated?
   a. Is it distributed far enough in advance of the meeting? 0 1 2 3 4 5
   b. Does it include particulars (meeting data, time, length, location, attendees)? 0 1 2 3 4 5
   c. Does it contain background information as necessary? 0 1 2 3 4 5
   d. Does it list goals for each item supplied? 0 1 2 3 4 5

During the Meeting

8. Opening the meeting
   a. Have goals for the meeting been identified? 0 1 2 3 4 5
   b. Has necessary background information been reviewed? 0 1 2 3 4 5
   c. Are expectations for members' contributions clear? 0 1 2 3 4 5
   d. Has the sequence of events for the meeting been previewed? 0 1 2 3 4 5
   e. Have time constraints been identified? 0 1 2 3 4 5
9. Encouraging balanced participation
   a. Have leader and members used questions to draw out quiet members? 0 1 2 3 4 5
   b. Are off-track comments redirected with references to the agenda and relevancy challenges? 0 1 2 3 4 5
   c. Do leader and members suggest moving on when an agenda item has been dealt with adequately? 0 1 2 3 4 5
10. Maintaining positive tone
    a. Are questioning and paraphrasing used as nondefensive responses to hostile remarks? 0 1 2 3 4 5
    b. Are dubious comments enhanced as much as possible? 0 1 2 3 4 5
    c. Does the meeting reflect the cultural norms of attendees? 0 1 2 3 4 5
11. Solving problems creatively
    a. Is the problem defined clearly (versus too narrowly or broadly)? 0 1 2 3 4 5
    b. Are the causes and effects of the problem analyzed? 0 1 2 3 4 5

c. Are clear criteria for resolving the problem established?	0 1 2 3 4 5
d. Are possible solutions brainstormed without being evaluated?	0 1 2 3 4 5
e. Is a decision made based on the previously established criteria?	0 1 2 3 4 5
f. Are methods of implementing the solution developed?	0 1 2 3 4 5

Concluding and Following Up

12. Concluding the meeting	
a. Does the meeting run the proper length of time (versus ending prematurely or continuing after excessive length or wasted time)?	0 1 2 3 4 5
b. Is a warning given shortly before conclusion to allow wrap-up of business?	0 1 2 3 4 5
c. Are a summary of the meeting's results and a preview of future actions given?	0 1 2 3 4 5
d. Does the leader acknowledge contributions of group members?	0 1 2 3 4 5
e. Are assignments for future meetings clarified?	0 1 2 3 4 5
13. Follow-up activities	
a. Does the leader build an agenda for the next meeting upon results of the previous one?	0 1 2 3 4 5
b. Does the leader follow up on assignments of other members?	0 1 2 3 4 5
c. Do members follow through on their own?	0 1 2 3 4 5

summary

Meetings are a common event in most organizations. They occupy large amounts of time and cost the business a great deal of money. Some meetings are aimed at sharing information; others are of a problem-solving nature; still others serve a ritual function that confers status on members, builds cohesiveness, and provides an informal channel of communication. Virtual meetings provide advantages and challenges for leaders and participants.

Meetings should be held only when the job at hand is beyond the capacity of one person to handle, requires a division of labor, and has more than one right answer. If misunderstanding or resistance to a decision is likely, it is also wise to hold a meeting to overcome those hazards. Well in advance of each meeting, members should receive an agenda that announces the time, length, and location of the session; those who will attend; background information on the topic; goals for the meeting; and any advance work members need to do.

Once the meeting is called to order, the chairperson should announce the goals of the session, review necessary background information, show how members can help, preview how the session will proceed, and identify any time constraints. The participation of quiet members can be encouraged by using the nominal group technique, giving everyone a chance to speak, and using questions. When discussions wander off track, the chairperson and other members can regain focus by referring to time pressures, summarizing and redirecting the remarks of the members who have digressed, using relevancy challenges, and promising to deal with tangential issues after the meeting. The tone of meetings can be kept positive if members make an attempt to understand one another by asking questions and paraphrasing and if they enhance the value of one another's comments. Effective meetings are conducted in a manner that reflects the rules of the cultural norms of the participants.

The meeting should be closed when its scheduled time is completed, when the group lacks resources to continue, or when the agenda has been completed—whichever comes first. The chairperson should give the group warning that time is almost up and then summarize the meeting's accomplishments and future actions. Group members should also be thanked for their contributions. The chairperson's activities after the meeting has concluded include building an agenda for the next session, following up on other members, and honoring his or her own commitments.

key terms

Test your understanding of these key terms by visiting the Online Learning Center Web site at www.mhhe.com/adler9.

agenda 301
direct question 310
motion 308
nominal group technique (NGT) 309
online meeting 298
overhead questions 310
parliamentary procedure 307
relay questions 311
relevancy challenge 312
reverse questions 310
teleconference 296
videoconference 297

activities

Go to the self-quizzes at the Online Learning Center at www.mhhe.com/adler9 to test your knowledge of chapter concepts.

1. Invitation to Insight

You can gain an appreciation for the importance of meetings by interviewing one or more people in a career field that is of interest to you.

a. Ask questions such as:
   i. How frequent are meetings in your work?
   ii. How long do these meetings typically take?
   iii. What kinds of topics are covered in your meetings?
   iv. What formats are used (parliamentary procedure, following agenda, open-ended discussions with no clear agenda, virtual versus face-to-face)?
   v. How effective are meetings? What factors contribute to their effectiveness or ineffectiveness?

b. Compare your findings with your classmates' findings.
   i. Which types of meetings occur most frequently (informational, problem-solving, ritual)?
   ii. Which types of formats occur most frequently?
   iii. Are the advantages mentioned by interviewees similar to those identified in the text?

iv. Based on concepts from the text, suggest remedies for the challenges identified by the interviewees.

2. Skill Builder

Use the information in this chapter to decide which of the following tasks would best be handled by a problem-solving group and which should be handled by one or more individuals working separately. Be prepared to explain the reasons for each choice.

a. Developing procedures for interviewing prospective employees.
b. Tabulating responses to a customer survey.
c. Investigating several brands of office machines for possible purchase.
d. Choosing the most desirable employee health insurance program.
e. Organizing the company picnic.
f. Researching the existence and cost of training programs for improving communication among staff members.

3. Skill Builder

With a group of your classmates, simulate a group decision-making process using the nominal group technique. Use one of the following scenarios or create one of your own:

a. Choosing a topic from this class about which you could deliver a group oral presentation.
b. Deciding where you and your classmates might go for a field trip.
c. Selecting the next novel your book club will read and discuss.

After you complete the role play, discuss advantages and disadvantages of the nominal group technique as a decision-making procedure.

4. Invitation to Insight

Ask someone you know to provide you with a copy of an agenda from a workplace meeting, or provide one of your own from a meeting you have attended. With a group of classmates, analyze the agenda.

a. Which elements of an effective agenda are present? Which are absent?
b. To what degree does the agenda illustrate *result-oriented*, *specific*, and *realistic* goals?
c. Suggest improvements for future agendas. If result-oriented goals are missing, write some examples.

5. Ethical Challenge

You are chairing a meeting in which one member whom everyone dislikes is aggressively promoting an idea. Time is short, and everyone in the group is ready to make a decision that will go against the disliked member's position. You realize that the unpopular idea does have real merit, but lending your support and urging further discussion will put the group further behind and leave the other members annoyed with you.

Suggest three different ways you could handle the situation. For each, write out the specific comments you would make. Using vocabulary from this chapter, discuss advantages and disadvantages of each scenario.

6. Skill Builder

Use the skills introduced on pages 312–314 to describe how you would respond to the following comments in a meeting. Identify which skill you are using:

a. "There's no way people will work Sundays without being paid double overtime."
b. "No consultant is going to tell me how to be a better manager!"
c. "I don't think this brainstorming is worth the time. Most of the ideas we come up with are crazy."
d. "Talking about interest rates reminds me of a time in the 1980s when this story about President Carter was going around. . . ."
e. "Sorry, but I don't have any ideas about how to cut costs."

resources

In Print

Cochran, Alice C. *Roberta's Rules of Order.* San Francisco: Jossey-Bass, 2004.

Cochran provides a less formal, more flexible approach to using parliamentary procedure in running meetings. Most important, the approach here replaces debate with dialogue and puts the motion after discussion of a problem and various solutions.

Leigh, Judith. *Organizing and Participating in Meetings.* New York: Oxford University Press, 2003.

This book guides readers through each stage of planning and conducting both formal and informal meetings. Topics include telephone meetings, online meetings, videoconferencing, creating agendas, writing papers or reports, chairing meetings, and presenting a paper. Information here will be useful in both business and non-work meetings such as voluntary organizations, charities, and local groups.

Pape, William R. "A Meeting of Minds." *Inc.* 19 (September 16, 1997), pp. 29–30.

This article provides a clear description of electronic meetings. It is a good introduction, both for planners who are considering using this format and for first-time participants.

Snair, Scott. *Stop the Meeting! I Want to Get Off: How to Eliminate Endless Meetings While Improving Your Team's Communication, Productivity, and Effectiveness.* New York: McGraw-Hill, 2003.

The author provides guidelines to improve productivity and communication and to reduce meeting time, including ways to delegate and curtail meetings.

Tropman, John E. *Making Meetings Work: Achieving High-Quality Group Decisions.* Newbury Park, CA: Sage, 1996.

This practical guide offers both leaders and participants guidelines for making meetings more efficient and productive.

Wycoff, Joyce. *Mindmapping: Your Personal Guide to Exploring Creativity and Problem-Solving.* New York: Berkley Books, 1991.

Mindmapping is a visual and creative way to take notes, generate ideas, and encourage thinking. Chapter 7, "Managing Meetings," provides helpful ways to use mindmapping to set meeting goals and manage discussions.

On the Web

Making Meetings Work

Virtual Meeting Assistant (**www.ku.edu/~coms/virtual_assistant/vma/vms.htm**) is part of the University of Kansas's array of the "Virtual Communication Assistant" series. This Web site includes advice on a variety of useful topics to help you plan and conduct meetings. Separate sections address specific types of meetings (informational, problem-solving, training, and brainstorming). General advice is also available on constructing an agenda and leading meetings.

Interaction Associates (**www.interactionassociates. com**) offers meeting process technology and a comprehensive list of tips and techniques for meetings, including how to make meetings work.

See the Management Library (**www.managementhelp.org**) for a complete library of links to articles, self-assessments, and advice for managing meetings and more. The Meeting

Network (**www.3m.com/meetingnetwork**) presents articles and advice on such things as running effective meetings, maximizing participation, and keeping meetings on track. International Association of Facilitators (**www.iaf-world.org**) encourages professional facilitation and provides information and links on the subject.

Parliamentary Procedure

The National Association of Parliamentarians' Web site (**www.parliamentarians.org/parlipro.htm**) discusses principles of parliamentary law, describes groups that use it, offers a sample meeting agenda, and provides text and tables outlining the use of motions. Robert's Rules of Order Revised, the body of rules for groups using parliamentary procedure, can be found there or at **www.constitution.org/rror/rror--00.htm**. For questions and answers about parliamentary decision making, go to **http://jimslaughter.com/parliamentaryprocedure.htm**. Also see the description of the book *Roberta's Rules of Order* in the "In Print" section above.

part five: strategic case

Fresh Air Sports

Fresh Air Sports Rentals began 8 years ago in a southern California beachfront hut where Woody and Sandy Belmont rented out fat-tired cruiser bikes to tourists. Business was good, and within a year Fresh Air customers could also rent a variety of other outdoor gear including surfboards, mountain bikes, and paddleboats.

Over the years Fresh Air has grown into a network of 18 locations throughout the western United States and Canada. The company is big enough now that name recognition is feeding the business: Customers who have rented from Fresh Air in one location look for it in other vacation spots. Woody and Sandy are thinking seriously of expanding the business to resorts on the East Coast, in Mexico, and in Central America.

Next month, Fresh Air is having its first-ever associates' meeting in San Diego. Woody and Sandy need to develop several presentations for that conference:

- A keynote speech, welcoming the employees and building enthusiasm for the company and for the upcoming meeting. During this speech, Sandy and Woody will also introduce Fresh Air's new management team.
- An informative program on how to avoid sexual harassment claims. Fresh Air's new human relations director will deliver this talk, but Sandy wants to play a close role in its development.
- A session introducing the company's new incentive plan, in which employees will receive bonuses for increasing sales. While the potential for greater compensation is good, base salaries will decline under this arrangement. Woody knows that it's important to sell the plan to employees if it has a chance of succeeding.
- A series of awards presentations at the closing dinner. At this session, employees will be honored for their exceptional service. Woody and Sandy want to include enough employees to boost morale, without creating so many awards that they appear meaningless.

As you read the chapters in this unit, consider the following questions for each presentation:

1. What is the general goal for each presentation? Create a specific goal for each one.
2. What factors outlined in Chapter 10 (audience, occasion, speaker) should Sandy and Woody consider for each presentation?
3. Construct an outline for at least one of the presentations, based on your analysis in question 2 above. Include material for the introduction and conclusion and the main points in the body.
4. For each main point in the body of the presentation you developed in question 3 above, identify one type of supporting material that you could use to make the point cleaner, more interesting, and/or more persuasive.
5. Describe the style of delivery that would be most effective for each of the presentations to be delivered at the San Diego meeting. Besides the speaker's style, discuss ways in which the speaking environment could be arranged to help achieve the presentation's goal.

10 Developing and Organizing the Presentation

Chapter Outline

Chapter Objectives

After reading this chapter, you should be able to

1 Develop an effective strategy for a specific presentation based on a complete analysis of the situation.

2 Identify general and specific goals for a given speaking situation.

3 Construct a clear thesis based on an analysis of a specific speaking situation.

4 Choose and develop an organizational plan for the body of a presentation that best suits its goal and the audience.

5 Create an effective introduction and conclusion for a presentation, following the guidelines in this chapter.

6 Design a presentation that contains effective transitions between the introduction and body, between points in the body, and between the body and conclusion.

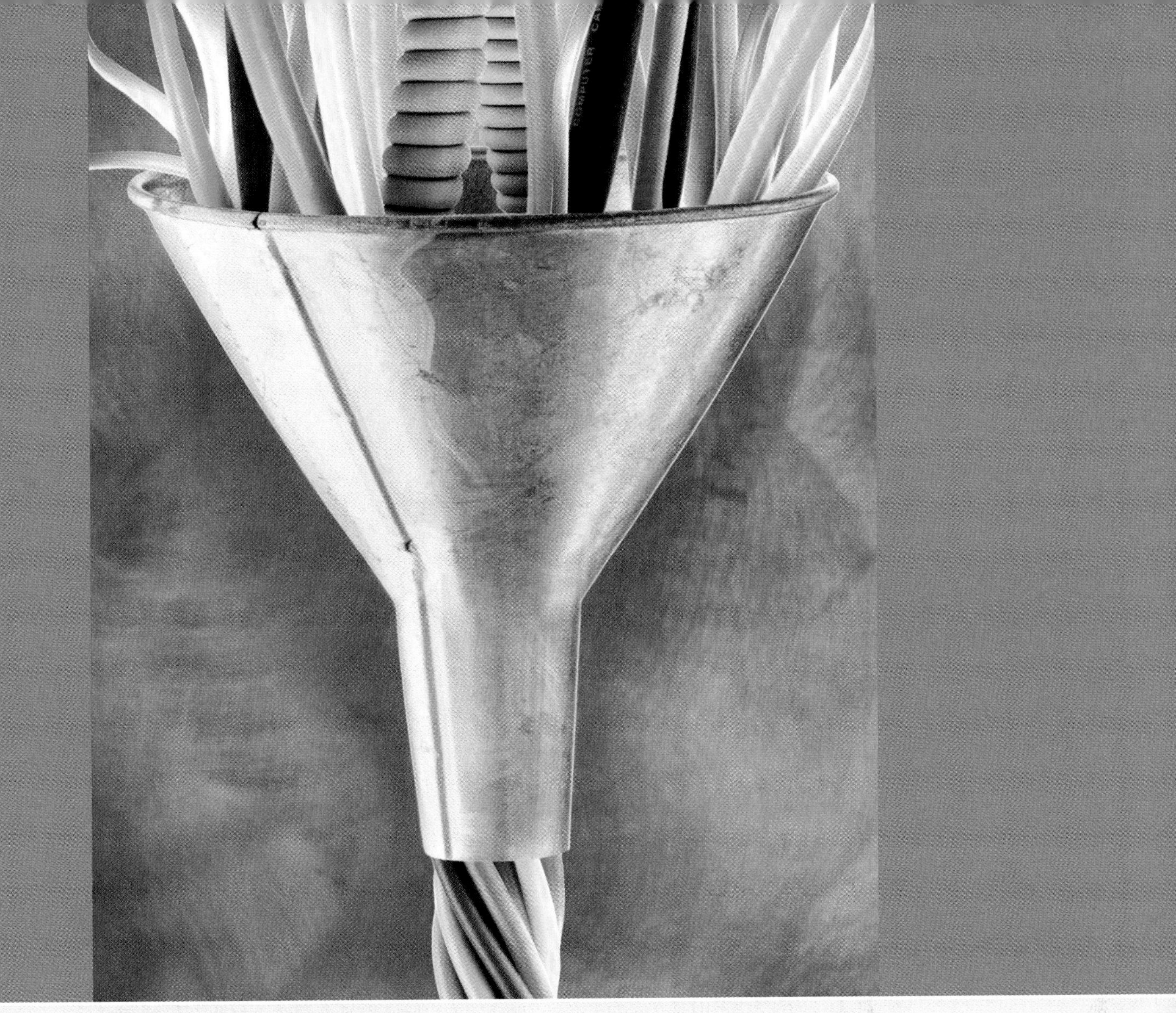

Whatever your field, whatever your job, speaking to an audience is a fact of life. Sales representatives and account executives deliver presentations to potential customers. Brand managers propose ideas to management and explain new product lines to the sales force. Department heads and supervisors brief superiors on recent developments and subordinates on new company policies. Computer specialists explain new systems and software to the people who will use them. Presentations are so pervasive that some experts have estimated that speakers address audiences an astonishing 33 million times each day.[1] According to one survey, businesspeople give an average of 26 presentations a year.[2] Table 10–1 offers a sample of the kinds of presentations that most people deliver sooner or later in their careers. Chapters 13 and 14 offer specific advice on planning and delivering specific types of presentations.

Table 10–1 Common Types of Presentational Speaking

Type of Presentation	Example
Briefing and informational announcements	Announcing new health insurance procedure
Orientation sessions	Conducting new-employee orientation
Training programs	Explaining how to operate new computer software
Research and technical reports	Describing a market research survey
Progress reports	Giving a status report on monthly sales
Civic and social presentations	Making a speech at a local service club
Convention and conference presentations	Reporting on company's technological breakthroughs
Television and radio interviews	Describing company's position on industrial accident or injury
Introductions	Introducing new employee to other workers
Sales presentations	Presenting product to potential customer
Project and policy proposals	Proposing new travel policy to management
Seeking resources	Making loan request to commercial lender
Ceremonial occasions	Speaking at retirement celebration for longtime employee

While some business and professional presentations are formal, full-dress performances before large audiences, most are comparatively informal talks to a few people or even a single person. If you drop into your boss's office and say, "Do you have a few minutes? I have some information that may help us cut down our travel expenses," you're arranging a presentation. You're also delivering a presentation when you teach the office staff how to use the new phone system, explain the structure of your department to a new employee, or explain to management why you need a larger budget.

Even when you create a written report, you will often introduce its contents in an oral presentation, and the quality of your spoken remarks may be the measure of your success. In fact, the quality of your presentation may determine whether anyone ever reads your documents. Furthermore, the highly public nature of presentations means that your reputation can rest or fall on how you handle yourself in front of an audience.

As your career progresses, presentational speaking skills become even more important.[3] As one automobile executive explained:

> *As an executive rose in management, he had to rely less on his technical training and more on his ability to sell his ideas and programs to the next level of management. When I was just an engineer somewhere down the line working on a technical problem, everything affecting me was in my grasp. All I had to do was solve this particular problem, and I was doing my job. But now, as head of advanced engineering, I have to anticipate and predict product trends and then sell my programs for capitalizing on those trends.*[4]

career tip

How Much Time Does It Take to Plan a Presentation?

Mark Twain once said, "It usually takes more than 3 weeks to prepare a good impromptu speech." This humorous observation highlights a truth about virtually every presentation: Success comes from careful planning, and planning takes time.

Almost every inexperienced speaker underestimates the amount of time necessary to create an effective presentation. Most experts use the hour-per-minute rule of thumb: Expect to spend about 1 hour of preparation time for every minute you will be speaking. Some professionals suggest a more modest 10-to-1 ratio between preparation and speaking time. "If I'm building a new presentation from scratch, you're probably talking about at least 10 hours of research and development for 1 hour of delivery time," says corporate trainer Bob Pike.

Experts agree that the way you spend preparation time is more important than the actual number of hours you spend. Most suggest that analyzing your audience is essential. Even for 1-hour speeches he has delivered many times before, Pike spends at least 2 to 3 hours researching the specific audience he will be addressing. He often asks key clients to fill out questionnaires that identify their specific interests, level of knowledge, any topics, or even specific words he should avoid.

Speakers are like athletes: Time spent planning and practicing is an investment that produces winning results.

Note: For more information on presentation planning, see Dave Zielinski, "Clock Work: How to Make the Most of Your Preparation Time," *Presentations*, February 2002, pp. 32–40.

Most people who work in organizations eventually find that their effectiveness and success depend on their ability to organize their ideas and present them effectively. Sometimes a written memo or report will do the job, but there are often important reasons for presenting your ideas in person. For example, if people don't understand a point in a proposal, they may put it aside for weeks or simply veto it. Delivering your message in person provides immediate feedback that helps you clarify points and answer questions. Oral presentations are often more persuasive as well. A speaker's knowledge, enthusiasm, and apparent confidence can influence people to accept or reject an idea in a way that a written document cannot.

In practice, you'll rarely get approval for an important idea without explaining it in person. As one executive put it:

> *The people who have the power and responsibility to say yes or no want a chance to consider and question the proposal in the flesh. Documents merely set up a meeting and record what the meeting decided. Anyone serious about an idea welcomes the chance to present it himself—in person. We wisely discount proposals whose authors are unwilling to be present at the launching.*[5]

Presentations aren't delivered only to internal audiences. Many people also give work-related addresses to listeners outside their organizations. Realizing that effective speakers carry their message to the public in ways that print and electronic media can't match, companies send representatives into the community to deliver speeches in a wide variety of settings.[6] Some of the world's biggest corporations sponsor training. Toastmasters International, a group dedicated to helping businesspeople present their ideas effectively, now has 190,000 members around the world.[7]

Research confirms that speakers can become more effective with training.[8] Even people who seem to work in fairly solitary jobs give speeches to clubs, professional organizations, and community groups.

Different kinds of presentations make different demands on the speaker. For example, a sales presentation to one customer may often seem more like a conversation because the customer may interrupt with questions, while a speaker addressing an audience of several hundred people may delay questions until the end. In spite of the differences, all presentations make many of the same demands on the speaker. The planning, structure, support, and strategy of each of them are very important, and a good speaker follows approximately the same steps in planning and developing almost any presentation. The material in the next four chapters applies to almost any presentation you will give in your career or profession.

Analyzing the Situation

Before you plan even one sentence of the actual presentation, you have to think about the situation in which you'll speak. A presentation that might fascinate you could bore or irritate the audience. You can make sure that your approach is on target by considering three factors: the audience, yourself as the speaker, and the occasion.

Analyzing the Audience

The saying "Different strokes for different folks" is never more true than when you are delivering a presentation. Having good ideas isn't enough. You have to present those ideas in a way that your listeners will understand and appreciate.[9] Former Chrysler president Lee Iacocca pinpointed the value of audience analysis:

> *It's important to be able to talk to people in their own language. If you do it well, they'll say "God, he said exactly what I was thinking." And when they begin to respect you, they'll follow you to the death. The reason they're following you is not because you're providing some mysterious leadership. It's because you're following them.*[10]

Asking yourself a number of questions about your listeners will shape the way you adapt your material to fit their interests, needs, and backgrounds.

Always tailor your presentation to your audience

Who Are the Key Audience Members? Not all audience members are equally important. Sometimes one or two listeners has the power to approve or reject your appeal. Abraham Lincoln made this point clearly when his cabinet unanimously opposed one of his ideas. "The vote is eight to one against the plan," the president stated. "The motion carries." In cases such as this, you need to identify the interests, needs, attitudes, and prejudices of the key decision makers and then focus your appeal toward them.

Sometimes it's easy to identify the key members. You don't have to be a communications expert to figure out that your boss has more power than the interns who are listening in on your

presentation. There are times, though, when you will need to do some prespeaking investigation to identify the opinion leaders and decision makers in your audience.

How Much Do They Know? A group of experts doesn't need the background information that less informed audiences would require. In fact, these people would probably be bored and offended by your basic explanation. Likewise, people who are familiar with a project don't need to be brought up-to-date—unless they have missed some late-breaking developments.

It's also important to ask yourself what your listeners do *not* know: Uninformed people or non-experts will be mystified (as well as bored and resentful) unless you give them background information.

What Do They *Want* to Know? People will listen to you if you address *their* interests, not yours. Asking for a promotion because you need the money isn't nearly as effective as demonstrating that you can help the company better in the new position. Asking for an assistant because you feel overworked isn't as likely to impress your boss as showing how the help will increase productivity or allow you to take on more business. Perhaps the most important key to effective selling is identifying the prospect's needs and showing how the product can satisfy them.

The job titles of your listeners can give you clues about what they want to know. If audience members are specialists—in engineering, finance, or marketing, for example—they'll probably be interested in the more technical aspects of your talk that pertain to their specialties. On the other hand, an audience of non-experts would probably be bored by a detailed talk on a subject they don't understand. Surprisingly, most managers fall into this category. Even an executive who came up through the ranks as an engineer takes a different perspective upon becoming responsible for an entire job. The details that might once have been fascinating are now less important—perhaps still interesting, but not suitable for an overall view of a project. "Just give me a quick description, a schedule, and the dollar figures" is a common attitude.

What Are Their Personal Preferences? The personal idiosyncrasies of your listeners can make all the difference in how your message is received. Some people insist on a formal presentation, while others prefer a more casual one. Some audiences appreciate humor, while others are straitlaced. Some people hate to waste time on casual conversation and digressions, while others are willing to work at a more leisurely pace. Knowing these preferences can make the difference between success and failure in a presentation. One business consultant described how attitudes can vary from one set of listeners to another:

> *We found . . . that in the same corporation engineers giving reports to different department heads were required to go about it in a totally different manner. One department head wanted every detail covered in the report. He wanted analyses of why the report was being done, complete background on the subject under discussion, and a review of the literature, and he expected the report to run twenty or thirty written pages. In addition, he wanted an oral presentation that covered almost every detail of the report. The man who ran the department right down the hall wanted just the opposite. He wanted short, comprehensive reports discussing only the elements that were new. He said he already knew what was going on in his department. He didn't want an analysis of the situation, and he didn't want any young engineer wasting his time. The reports that got an A in one department got an F in another and vice versa. Therefore, the first rule for anyone giving a report is to ask those who requested the report what form they would like it to take.*[11]

Audience attitudes can be hard to anticipate. One architect describes how he had to disguise the use of cost-saving technology to suit the mistaken assumptions of some clients.

> *When I [used to] prepare a preliminary design for a client, I often sketch[ed] a floor plan "free-hand": meaning that I quickly [drew] the design idea without a lot of detailed measurements. . . . With the advent of computer aided design (CAD), we can produce the same design on the computer . . . faster, more accurately, and at the same cost as before.*

Although this approach seems like a win–win scenario for the architect and the client, experience proves that this isn't the case.

> *Some of our clients have complained that we are spending too much time and money on these preliminaries . . . they want something fast and cheap. They assume that because of how the product looks, we are spending more time (and more of their money) too early in the process. No amount of explanation will appease them.*
>
> *So, what to do? We just purchased a new software product. It is called Squiggle. It takes the very accurate, crisp, straight lines of a computer design and actually makes it look hand-drawn. Now, the clients will look at a computer drawing, but see hand-drawn.*[12]

Which Demographic Characteristics Are Significant? A number of measurable characteristics of your listeners might suggest ways to develop your remarks. One such characteristic is *sex*. What is the distribution of men and women? Even in this age of relative enlightenment, some topics must be approached differently, depending on your audience's sex.

A second demographic characteristic is *age*. A life insurance salesperson might emphasize retirement benefits to older customers and support for dependent children to younger ones with families. A speaker promoting a company health plan would discuss different activities with listeners in their 20s and 30s than she would with employees who were nearing retirement.

Cultural background is often an important audience factor. You would use a different approach with blue-collar workers than you would with a group of white-collar professionals. Likewise, the ethnic mix of a group might affect your remarks. The points you make, the examples you use, and even the language you speak will probably be shaped by the cultural makeup of your audience.

Another demographic factor is the *economic status* of your audience. This factor is especially important in sales, where financial resources "qualify" potential customers as prospects for a product or service as well as suggest which features are likely to interest them. In real estate, for example, well-to-do customers would certainly be interested in properties different from those that would interest less affluent ones. They might also be more concerned about the tax consequences of a sale and less concerned with monthly payments than with the interest rate at which the mortgage is written.

Not every variable is important in planning every speech. For instance, an engineer speaking about recent advances in the field should consider her audience's level of knowledge (about engineering and those advances) and occupations (that is, what those advances have to do with her listeners' work), but matters such as sex, age, and economic status probably wouldn't be as important. On the other hand, a representative from Planned Parenthood speaking to a community organization would have to consider sex, age, and economic status as well as listeners' religious backgrounds and their attitudes toward the medical profession. The first step to good audience analysis is to recognize which dimensions of your listeners' background are important and to profile those dimensions accurately.

What Size Is the Group? The number of listeners will govern some very basic speaking plans. How many copies of a handout should you prepare? How large must your visuals be to be seen by everyone? How much time should you plan for a question-and-answer session? With a large audience, you usually need to take a wider range of audience concerns into account; your delivery and choice of language will tend to be more formal; and your listeners are less likely to interrupt with questions or comments. A progress report on your current assignment would look ridiculous if you delivered it from behind a podium to four or five people. You would look just as foolish speaking to a hundred listeners while reclining in a chair.

What Are the Listeners' Attitudes? You need to consider two sets of attitudes when planning your presentation. The first is your audience's attitude toward *you as the speaker*. If listeners feel hostile or indifferent ("Charlie is such a bore"), your approach won't be the same as the one taken if they are excited to hear from you

career tip

Speaking to International Audiences

Developing a presentation for any audience takes careful planning. When your listeners come from a background different from yours, extra thought is required. The following tips will boost the odds of achieving your goal with a diverse audience.

1. *If in doubt, address listeners more formally than usual.* As a rule, business is conducted more informally in the United States and Canada than in many other parts of the world. What seems friendly in much of North America may be perceived as disrespectful elsewhere.
2. *Make your presentation highly structured.* Be sure to follow the guidelines in this chapter for organizing a presentation. Have a clear introduction in which you identify your thesis and preview your remarks. Highlight key points during the body of your presentation, using a clear organizational pattern. Conclude with a summary of your main ideas.
3. *Use standard English.* Most non-native speakers learned English in school, so avoid idioms and jargon that may be unfamiliar. Whenever possible, use simple words and sentences. Also, use nouns instead of pronouns whenever possible to minimize confusion.
4. *Speak slightly more slowly than usual.* Don't, however, raise the volume of your voice: Shouting won't make you easier to understand.
5. *Use handouts.* Most non-native audience members will have higher reading than listening comprehension, so printed supporting materials will help them understand and remember your points. Providing listeners with printed information in advance of your presentation will make it easier for them to follow your remarks.
6. *Consult with a local coach.* Share your remarks with someone familiar with your audience before the presentation to make sure your ideas are clear and free of blunders that will undermine your credibility. When U.S. president John F. Kennedy announced his solidarity with the citizens of Germany's historic capital by proclaiming "Ich bin ein Berliner," any resident of the city could have told him the words translated as "I am a jelly doughnut."

The Getting Through Customs Web site (**www.getcustoms.com**) offers practical advice about cultural variations and cautions in public speaking. Go to "articles" and then to "first impressions in business" to read an interesting article. From the Advanced Public Speaking Institute (**http://www.public-speaking.org**) go to "international issues."

Source: Adapted from LaTresa Pearson, "Think Globally, Present Locally," *Presentations*, April 1996, pp. 20–27, 68; and Kathy Schmidt, "How to Speak So You're Open to Interpretation," *Presentations*, December 1999, p. 126.

("I'm glad he says he's going to simplify the paperwork; last year, he did a great job of speeding up the process for getting repairs done").

In addition to listeners' feelings about you, the audience's attitude about *your subject* should influence your approach. Do your employees think the benefits of the new pension plan are too far in the future to be important? Does the sales force think the new product line is exciting or just the same old line in a new package? Do the workers think the new vice president is a genius or just another figurehead? Attitudes such as these should govern your approach.

One way to discover the attitudes of your audience—and to gain the audience's approval of your idea—is to meet with listeners before your presentation. With this sort of preparation, you can make whatever adjustments are necessary to win over the key decision makers before you begin your formal presentation. A communications expert describes the value of this kind of advance work:

> *At one of the largest, publicly owned utilities in the United States senior officers of both Human Resources and Management Information Systems had prepared new program proposals for car pooling and a pilot electronic mail program. The research and development stages for each of these proposals had taken between four and six months. After extensive presentations, covering timeliness, costs both direct and indirect, and benefits to department heads and customers, the meeting participants were called upon for comment.*
>
> *Nearly everyone present at the meeting—between eight and ten other department heads—had suggestions for improvements and modifications. Why? Because they had not been given an opportunity to study the proposals in advance. Consequently, the discussion on these proposals alone took two or three times the allotted time for the entire meeting. So many changes were suggested by the other participants that the makers of the original proposals had to spend months revising them.*
>
> *. . . Obviously, if the chairman of the meeting (the chief executive officer) had been consulted before this meeting to help "bless" the projects, and other department heads had been briefed prior to the presentation to help buy them in, better results in a shorter period of time would have been achieved. My friend can attest to the effectiveness of this method because it's what he did before his own later presentation. The result was so fast that he had to hold himself back from suggesting that his proposal be further discussed before final acceptance.*[13]

Analyzing Yourself as the Speaker

No two presentations are alike. While you can learn to speak better by listening to other speakers, a good presentation is rather like a good hairstyle or sense of humor: What suits someone else might not work for you. One of the biggest mistakes you can make is to try to be a carbon copy of some other effective speaker. When developing your presentation, be sure to consider several factors.

Your Goal The very first question to ask yourself is why you are speaking. Are you especially interested in reaching one person or one subgroup in the audience? What do you want your key listeners to think or do after hearing you? How will you know when you've succeeded?

Your Knowledge It's best to speak on a subject about which you have considerable knowledge. This is usually the case, since you generally speak on a subject precisely because you *are* an authority. Regardless of how well you know your subject, you may need to do some research—on the last 3 years' sales figures, the number of companies that have used the flexible-hours program you're proposing, the actual maintenance costs of the new equipment your company is buying, and so on.

If you do need to gain more information, don't fool yourself into a false sense of security by thinking you know enough. It's better to overprepare now than to look like a fool later. Kenneth Clarke, Britain's finance minister, embarrassed himself due to faulty knowledge. While visiting the town of Consett in northern England, he praised its success as an industrial center, saying it had "one of the best steelworks in Europe." But the steel mill had closed down 15 years earlier, putting 3,000 employees out of work. To redeem himself for that gaffe, Clarke cited another Consett factory as a major competitor in the world of disposable diapers. The town's diaper plant had closed down 2 years before.[14]

Your Feelings about the Topic An old sales axiom says, You can't sell a product you don't believe in. Research shows that sincerity is one of the greatest assets a speaker can have.[15] When you are excited about a topic, your delivery improves: Your voice becomes more expressive, your movements are more natural, and your face reflects your enthusiasm. On the other hand, if you don't care much about your topic—whether it's a report on your department's sales, a proposal for a new program, a product you're selling, or a new method you're explaining—the audience will know it and think, If the speaker doesn't believe in it, why should I? A good test for your enthusiasm and sincerity is to ask yourself if you really care whether your audience understands or believes what you have to say. If you feel indifferent or only mildly enthusiastic, it's best to search for a new idea for your proposal or a new approach to your subject.

Analyzing the Occasion

Even a complete understanding of your audience won't give you everything you need to plan an effective presentation. You also need to adapt your remarks to fit the circumstances of your presentation. Several factors contribute to the occasion.

Facilities Figure 10–1 shows how you can adapt the layout of a room to suit the speaking situation. Whatever arrangement you choose, you need to consider some important issues. Will there be enough seating for all the listeners? What

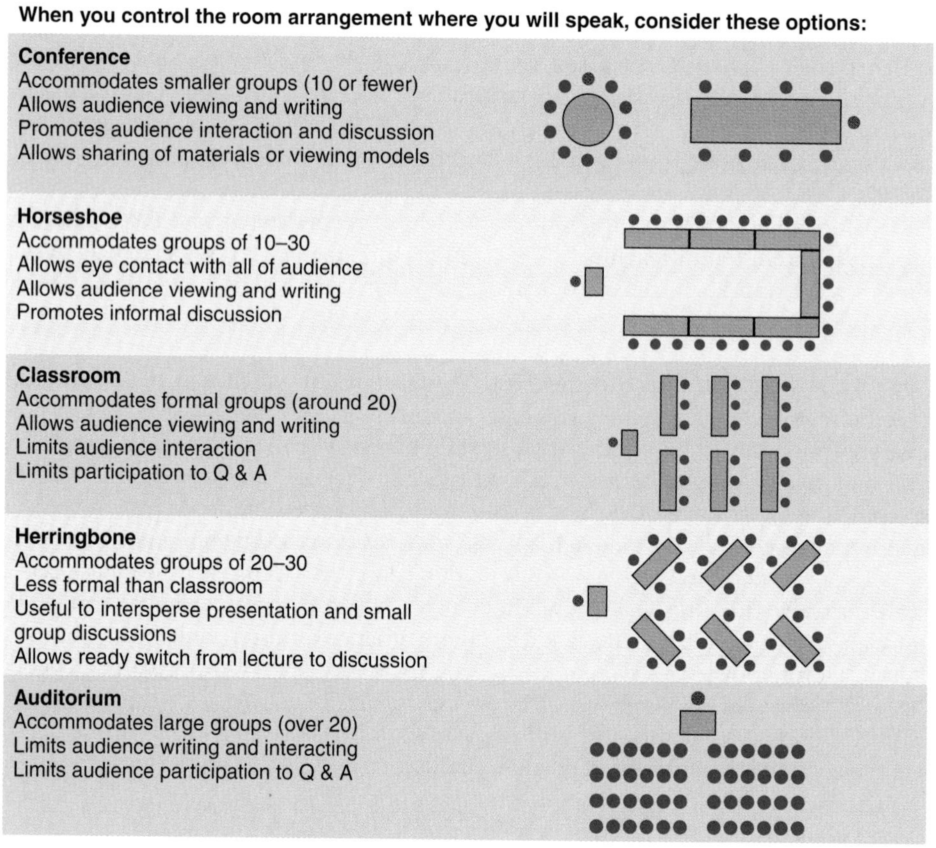

FIGURE 10–1
Room Arrangement Options

Source: After G. L. Morrisey, T. L. Sechrest, and W. B. Warman, *Loud and Clear: How to Prepare and Deliver Effective Business and Technical Presentations*, 4th ed. (Cambridge, MA: Perseus Books, 1997), pp. 146–147.

When you control the room arrangement where you will speak, consider these options:

Conference
Accommodates smaller groups (10 or fewer)
Allows audience viewing and writing
Promotes audience interaction and discussion
Allows sharing of materials or viewing models

Horseshoe
Accommodates groups of 10–30
Allows eye contact with all of audience
Allows audience viewing and writing
Promotes informal discussion

Classroom
Accommodates formal groups (around 20)
Allows audience viewing and writing
Limits audience interaction
Limits participation to Q & A

Herringbone
Accommodates groups of 20–30
Less formal than classroom
Useful to intersperse presentation and small group discussions
Allows ready switch from lecture to discussion

Auditorium
Accommodates large groups (over 20)
Limits audience writing and interacting
Limits audience participation to Q & A

type of equipment is available for you to use? Will there be distracting background noises?

Questions like these are critical, and failure to anticipate facility problems can trip you up. For example, the absence of an easel to hold your charts can turn your well-rehearsed presentation into a fiasco. Lack of a convenient electrical outlet can replace your PowerPoint show with an embarrassing blackout. Even the placement of doorways can make a difference. Most experienced speakers won't settle for others' assurances about facilities; they check out the room in advance and come prepared for every possible disaster.

Time There are two considerations here. The first is the time of day you'll be speaking. A straightforward, factual speech that would work well with an alert, rested audience at 10 A.M. might need to be more entertaining or emphatic to hold everyone's attention just before quitting time.

Besides taking the hour of day into account, you also need to consider the length of time you have to speak. Most business presentations are brief. One director of a Los Angeles shopping mall typically gives prospective vendors 20 minutes to make their pitch: "I automatically x-out anyone who is late or exceeds their time allotment. My experience has shown that people who have trouble adhering to parameters and deadlines are unreliable."[16] Alan Brawn, national sales manager for Hughes-JCC, reinforces the importance of keeping your remarks within the preset time limit: "Typically, if major points aren't made in about six minutes, a person's time in the sun is done."[17]

Despite an absolute claim like this, the amount of time you have to speak will vary. In any case, it's your job to find out what your time constraints are and stick within them. If you have only a little time to give a progress report to management, for example, you can only outline the major aspects of your most recent product; whereas if you have half an hour, you might be expected to go into more detail and discuss some of the alternatives you have considered along the way. Sometimes the length of your talk won't be explicitly dictated, but that doesn't mean you should talk as long as you like. Usually, factors in the situation suggest how long it's wise for you to speak. Notice, for example, how well speaker Hugh Marsh adapted his remarks to the after-dinner setting of his summary business report to a group of association members:

> *Good evening, ladies and gentlemen. Whenever I get on a podium this late, after a long day at the office, I remind myself of several immutable laws.*
>
> *First, There is Marsh's First Law of Oratory—on any platform, any speech will grow in length to fill the time available for its delivery. Well, take heart. I only have fifteen minutes.*
>
> *Then there is Marsh's Second Law of Oratory—the farthest distance between two points is a speech. Or, as we used to say in Texas, speeches too often are like a Longhorn steer—a point here and a point there and a lot of bull in between. Well, again, take heart. I will try to keep my two points close together.*
>
> *Another law I remind myself of is Marsh's Third Law of Oratory—no speech ever sounds as good at 7:00 P.M. as it did at noon.*
>
> *And, finally, there is Marsh's First Law of Meeting Attendance—everybody's gotta be someplace. As long as we're here, let's be friends. I'll be brief. You be attentive. I'll make my few points and get off so we can get back to the fun part of the meeting—socializing.*[18]

on your feet

Adapting to the Situation

Share with your group examples from your experience of excellent and/or terrible business and professional communication. Share the lessons you learned from each experience. Be prepared to explain how the examples and lessons you chose will be appropriate and useful for the members of your group.

Here are a few examples to get you started:

- "I once had a professor who was blind. After one day of class, he had memorized the names of all 30 students, and he could recognize them by voice and their position in the classroom. This experience reminded me how it's possible to do almost anything with enough focus and that I have no business complaining when things get a little hard for me. It also reminded me how much people like being remembered by name. Now I try to apply that lesson to people I meet."
- "I work at a local golf course. After being there for almost a year and getting lots of good feedback from our customers, I asked my boss for a small raise. He replied, Are you kidding? I could train a monkey to do your job. Even though I knew the comment wasn't fair, it hurt. I hope I remember never to toss off thoughtless comments without thinking about their potential to hurt others. The experience also taught me a lesson about how *not* to manage employees!"

Context As Chapter 1 explained, the context of your presentation also influences what you say or how you say it. For example, if others are speaking as part of your program, you need to take them into account. ("I had originally planned to discuss the technical aspects of our new express delivery system, but I think Carol has covered them pretty thoroughly. Let me just bring your attention to two things.") Preceding speakers may have left your audience feeling bored or stimulated, receptive or angry, thoughtful or jovial. Since that state of affairs will affect how the audience receives your presentation, you should try to adjust to it.

Current events could also affect what you say or how you say it. For example, if you're presenting your new budget proposal just after the company has suffered a major financial loss, you should be prepared to show how your budget will cut costs. As you'll read later in this chapter, one effective way to begin a speech is to talk about a recent occurrence: Beginning your talk to the sales force by mentioning Steve's major new account, for instance, is a good way to get attention and motivate your audience.

Setting Your Goal and Developing the Thesis

An absolutely essential step in planning any presentation is to define your goal—what you want to accomplish. Speaking without a clear goal is a recipe for failure. As speaking coach Sandy Linver put it:

> *Giving a presentation without recognizing, focusing on, and remembering your objective is the equivalent of dumping the contents of your briefcase all over your boss's desk. You don't speak to fill time by reeling off fact after unorganized fact, nor to show beautiful pictures that take the breath away, nor to impress the audience with*

your wit and skill as a dramatic speaker. You don't give speeches to win speech-making awards. You are there to make the best of an opportunity, just as you do in every other aspect of your business activities.[19]

There are two kinds of goals to consider: general and specific.

General and Specific Goals

As the name implies, a **general goal** (sometimes called a *general purpose*) is a broad indication of what you're trying to accomplish. There are three general speaking goals: to inform, persuade, and entertain. While one type of goal may be primary, a speaker often attempts to accomplish more than one. For example, a human resources officer might be smart to make an informative session on filing insurance claims as entertaining as possible to keep the audience's attention.

The goal of an *informative* presentation is either to expand your listeners' knowledge or to help them acquire a specific skill. Teaching a group of product managers about new developments in technology, training a new sales representative, or giving a progress report on regional sales to a senior sales manager are all typical examples of informative talks.

Persuasive presentations focus on trying to change what an audience thinks or does. Selling is the most obvious example, but there are others as well. A union organizer will try to persuade a group of employees to vote for a union. An accountant might try to convince management to adopt a different procedure for reporting expenditures. A marketing manager might try to convince sales representatives to be more enthusiastic about a product that has not sold well.

Sometimes a speaker's goal is to *entertain* the audience. The welcoming speaker at a convention might concentrate on getting the participants to relax and look forward to the coming events. After-dinner speakers at company gatherings or awards dinners usually consider themselves successful if their remarks leave the group in a jovial mood.

The **specific goal** (sometimes called the *specific purpose*) of your presentation describes the outcome you are seeking. If you think of a speech as a journey, your specific goal is your destination. Stating the specific goal tells you what you will have accomplished when you have "arrived." A good specific-goal statement usually describes *whom* you want to influence; what you want them to *think* or *do;* and *how, when,* and *where* you want them to do it. Your goal statement should combine the answers to these questions into a single statement: "I want (whom) to (do what) (how, when, where)." Here are some good examples of goal statements:

"I want the people who haven't been participating in the United Way campaign to sign up."

"I want at least five people in the audience to ask me for my business card after my talk and at least one person to schedule an appointment with me to discuss my company's services."

"I want at least five people in the department to consider transferring to the new Fort Worth office."

"I want the boss to tell the committee that he's in favor of my proposal when they discuss it after my presentation."

Like these examples, your goal statements should do three things: describe the reaction you are seeking, be as specific as possible, and make your goal realistic.

career tip

Invitational Rhetoric: Presentations as Dialogue

Informing, entertaining, and persuading are all goals that suggest speaking is a one-way affair—something that a presenter does *to* an audience. In recent years, some scholars have suggested a fundamentally different "invitational" approach. As its name suggests, invitational speaking involves a dialogue in which speaker and audience clarify positions and explore issues without trying to persuade one another.

Invitational speaking works best in a climate of equality and mutual respect. Both speaker and audience members recognize each other's perspectives as valuable and worthy of exploration. An invitational speaker also recognizes that listeners ultimately have the right and power to decide for themselves whether and how to accept the speaker's ideas.

At first an invitational approach might seem too weak for a hard-headed business world. In fact, its open-minded approach can be very effective in a variety of business and professional settings. As Chapter 3 explained, most sales professionals emphasize the importance of listening and responding to the customer's concerns. Chapter 7 described how employment and performance appraisal interviews can be more successful if you present yourself as willing to speak to and learn from an interviewer instead of just selling your position. In Chapter 13 you will learn the importance of responding thoughtfully and respectfully in question-and-answer sessions.

Note: For more information on invitational speaking, see Sonja J. Foss and Cindy L. Griffin, "Beyond Persuasion: A Proposal for an Invitational Rhetoric," *Communication Monographs* 62 (1995), pp. 1–18; Sonja K. Foss and Karen A. Foss, *Inviting Transformation: Presentational Speaking for a Changing World,* 2nd ed. (Prospect Heights, IL: Waveland Press, Inc., 2003); and Deborah Tannen, *The Argument Culture: Stopping America's War of Words* (New York: Ballantine, 1999).

Describe the Reaction You Are Seeking Your goal should be worded in terms of the *desired outcome:* the reaction you want from your audience. You can appreciate the importance of specifying the outcome when you consider a statement that doesn't meet this criterion: "I want to show each person in this office how to operate the new voice mail system correctly."

What's wrong with this statement? Most important, it says nothing about the desired audience response. With a goal such as this, you could give a detailed explanation of the whole system without knowing whether anyone learned a thing! Notice the improvement in this statement: "I want everyone in this group to show me that he or she can operate the voice mail system correctly after my talk." With this goal, you can get an idea of how well you've done after delivering your presentation.

Be as Specific as Possible A good goal statement identifies the who, what, how, when, and where of your goal as precisely as possible. For instance, your target audience—the who—may not include every listener in the audience. Take one of the statements we mentioned earlier: "I want the boss to tell the committee that he's in favor of my proposal when they discuss it after my presentation." This statement correctly recognizes the boss as the key decision maker. If you've convinced him, your proposal is as good as approved; if not, the support of less influential committee members may not help you. Once you identify your target audience, you can focus your energy on the people who truly count.

ethical challenge

Keeping Your Goals Private

Sometimes it can be ethical to withhold your goal from an audience, while doing so at other times is unethical. Check your ability to distinguish the difference by identifying three situations for each of the following:

1. When it is legitimate to withhold your goal.
2. When withholding your goal would be unethical.

The best goal statements describe your goals in *measurable terms*. Consider these examples:

Vague	Specific
I want to collect some donations in this meeting.	I want to collect at least $15 from each person in this meeting.
I want to get my manager's support for my idea.	I want my manager to give me 1 day per week and the help of a secretary to develop my idea.

Knowing exactly what you want to accomplish dramatically increases the chances that you will reach your goal. Suppose you need to convince a group of subordinates to stay within budget. You already know that the following statement is no good: "I want to talk about the importance of our new budget limitations." (If you're not sure why, take another look at the preceding section on describing reactions.) A more result-oriented goal would be "I want this group to stay within budget." But even this goal statement has problems. Whom are you going to encourage: people who are already holding the line on expenses or those who look like they might overspend? How many people do you hope to persuade? How will you appeal to them? When do you want them to do it: beginning immediately or when they get around to it? The latter may not be until after the fiscal year is over—too late to save this year's profits in your department. A comprehensive specific-goal statement can take care of questions such as these: "I want to convince the four people who had spent more than half their year's budgets by May 1 that the department's solvency depends on their cutting expenses and have them show me a revised plan by the end of the week that demonstrates how they intend to trim costs for the rest of the year." This statement gives you several ideas about how to plan your presentation. Imagine how much more difficult your task would be if you had settled for the first vague goal statement.

Developing the Thesis

The **thesis statement**—sometimes called the *central idea* or *key idea*—is a single sentence that summarizes your message. Table 10–2 offers some tips for formulating this sort of statement. Once you have a thesis, every other part of your talk

Table 10–2 Methods for Defining a Thesis Statement

1. Imagine that you met a member of your audience at the elevator and had only a few seconds to explain your idea before the doors closed.
2. Imagine that you had to send a one- or two-sentence e-mail that communicated your main ideas.
3. Ask yourself, if my listeners heard only a small portion of my remarks, what is the minimum they should have learned?
4. Suppose that a friend asked one of your listeners what you were driving at in your presentation. What would you want the audience member to say?

should support it. The thesis gives your listeners a clear idea of what you are trying to tell them:

"We're behind schedule, but we can catch up and finish the job on time."

"The credit rating you earn now can help—or hurt—you for decades."

"Investing now in a new system will save us money in the long run."

Presentations without a clear thesis leave the audience asking, What's this person getting at? And while listeners are trying to figure out the answer, they'll be missing much of what you're saying.

The thesis is so important that you will repeat it several times during your presentation: at least once in the introduction, probably several times during the body, and again in the conclusion.

Beginning speakers often confuse the thesis of a presentation with its goal. Whereas a goal statement is a note to *yourself* outlining what you hope to accomplish, a thesis statement tells your *audience* your main idea. Sometimes the two can be virtually identical. There are other cases, however, where goal and thesis differ. Consider a few examples:

Goal	Thesis
I want Krakos Grocery to order Sun Valley Bread.	Switching to Sun Valley Bread will increase your sales.
Parents will be confident that their children are being prepared for later schooling.	Our preschool curriculum is based on sound educational theory and research.
Audience members will be able to respond to sexual harassment instead of accepting it.	You don't have to accept sexual harassment.
I want to acquire new customers seeking state-of-the-art technology.	Recent advances have dramatically changed this industry in the past few years.

It may seem unethical to avoid mentioning your goal to an audience, but sometimes the omission is a matter of common sense and not deception. Mr. Krakos already knows the Sun Valley representative wants to sell him bread, but he's most interested in hearing *why* he should change suppliers. Similarly, an after-dinner speaker at a local service club might have the goal of getting the audience to relax, but sharing that goal would probably seem out of place.

There are other times, however, when hiding your goal would clearly be unethical. A speaker who began his presentation by saying, "I don't want to sell you anything; I just want to show you some aspects of home safety that every homeowner should know," and then went on to make a hard-sell pitch for his company's home fire alarms would clearly be stepping out of bounds. It usually isn't necessary to state your goal as long as you are willing to share it with your audience, if asked. It's very rare, however, not to state the thesis at the beginning of a presentation.

Organizing the Body

Inexperienced speakers make the mistake of starting to plan a talk by beginning at the beginning, by first writing an introduction. This is like trying to landscape a piece of property before you've put up a building. Even though it doesn't come first in a presentation, the body is the place to start your organizing. Organizing the body of a talk consists of two steps: identifying the key points that support your thesis, and then deciding what organizational plan best develops those points.

Brainstorming Ideas

Once you have figured out your thesis, you are ready to start gathering research to support your presentation. The first step is to pull together a list of all the information you might want to include. You'll probably have some ideas already in mind, while finding other possibilities will usually require further research. If, for example, you want to sell potential customers on your product, you'll want to find out which competing products they are using now and how they feel about them. You'll also want to discover whether they are familiar with your product and what attitudes they have about it. In other cases, the material you'll need to discuss may appear to be obvious. If you're giving a report on last month's sales, the figures might form the bulk of your remarks. If you are explaining how to use a new piece of equipment, the operating steps appear to be the obvious body of your talk.

Your brainstorming and research will produce a list of material from which you'll build your presentation. For example, suppose that you have been asked to address a group of employees about why you want them to use Mercury Overnight for letters and packages that need to be delivered quickly. Using your research on Mercury Overnight, you might make up a list that looks something like the one in Figure 10–2.

Notice that this list is a random assortment of points. In fact, your own collection of ideas probably won't even be neatly listed on a single piece of paper. More likely it will be scribbled on an assortment of index cards, check stubs, message pads, or whatever you had at hand when you came across a piece of promising information. Once you've assembled what seems like enough raw material, you're ready to organize it.

Basic Organizational Plan

Once you have a list of possible ideas, you are ready to organize them in a clear form that helps achieve your speaking goal. Most people will agree that clarity

- Mercury Overnight will pick up the package at your office instead of you having to go through the mailroom.
- It will also deliver right to your office if the label is marked properly, so you don't have to wait for the mailroom to process and deliver it to you.
- When we experimented with different delivery services, Mercury delivered every single package we gave it within 24 hours.
- Some of the companies we tried took 2 days or more about 25 percent of the time.
- One company we tried got the package in on time about 90 percent of the time.
- Other companies we've tried have held up packages for as much as a week for no good reason.
- Mercury will deliver into the rural areas where many of our customers are, while some of the other companies only deliver in the urban areas.
- Mercury will bill the departmental accounts, saving bookkeeping time.
- Some companies charge a lot of extra money for the odd-sized packages we send sometimes, but Mercury just charges by weight.
- Because we can't always count on overnight delivery with the delivery service we're using now, we often have to take time off to run a package across town.
- Mercury charges less than its competitors for heavy packages.
- If we send several things at once to the same place, Mercury will give us a lower "group rate."
- Mercury will come out at any time to pick up a package.
- Other companies will only make a regular daily stop, which doesn't do you much good if your package isn't ready when they come.
- Mercury will make pickups from 7 in the morning until midnight, which is nice if you're working early or late.
- If you send the package through the post office and don't put enough postage on it, the post office sends it back and the package won't get there in time.
- The packages that we've sent through some other shippers sometimes get so badly damaged that the contents have to be replaced. The shipper will pay for the contents if you insure the package, but that doesn't get it there on time.
- Sometimes you have to ship a one-of-a-kind item, like a prototype for an advertisement, and if it gets lost or damaged it can take weeks to make a new one.
- Mercury's best shipping fee includes insurance.
- It isn't easy to figure out which delivery service is best.
- When the company was smaller, we used to just send things by mail.
- We researched the idea of setting up our own delivery service, but management vetoed it because it cost too much.

FIGURE 10–2
Selling Points Produced by a Brainstorming Session

is important, but few realize just how critical it is. A substantial body of research indicates that organizing your remarks clearly can make your messages more understandable, keep your audience happy, and boost your image as a speaker.[20] Despite the benefits of good organization, most presentations suffer from a variety of problems in this area:

- Taking too long to get to the point.
- Including irrelevant material.
- Leaving out necessary information.
- Getting ideas mixed up.[21]

Problems like those above can lead to organizational chaos. Even experienced speakers can get into trouble when they speak without preparing their ideas. U.S. President George W. Bush was a more effective speaker when working from prepared notes than when speaking off the cuff. His answer to a question about his proposed Social Security plan illustrates the problem:

> *Because the—all which is on the table begins to address the big cost drivers. For example, how benefits are calculated, for example, is on the table; whether or not benefits rise based upon wage increases or price increases. There's a series of parts of the formula that are being considered. And when you couple that, those different cost drivers, affecting those—changing those with personal accounts, the idea is to get what has been promised more likely to be—or closer delivered to what has been promised.*[22]

Most speakers would find that some of their own remarks would look almost as disjointed. The key to avoiding a meaningless stream of ideas is to organize your ideas before speaking.

No matter what the subject or the goal, most effective presentations follow a well-known pattern: First, tell them what you're going to tell them; then, tell them; then, tell them what you told them. The format looks like this:

Introduction
- Attention getter
- Thesis
- Preview

Body (two to five main points)

I.
II.
III.
IV.
V.

Conclusion
- Review
- Closing statement

This linear, logical approach to organization isn't the only way to structure a presentation. Researchers have found that it works best with Euro-American audiences or listeners receptive to the Euro-American cultural standard. Listeners from other backgrounds may use less linear patterns, which have been given labels including "star," "wave," and "spiral."[23] Despite the value of these patterns in certain situations, the standard format is probably the safest approach with most business audiences who are part of Euro-American culture.

You have probably encountered this format many times. Despite its familiarity, many speakers act as if they have never heard of it. They launch into their subjects without any prefatory remarks about what they're about to say. Some finish their main ideas and then stop speaking without any summation or closing. Still others deliver what seems to be a model three-part talk but don't stop there; they continue tacking on new information after you have closed your mental files: "Did I mention that . . . ," "We had the same problem, by the way, last year when . . . ," or "Oh, another thing I should have mentioned . . ." Even worse, many speakers don't seem to have *any* organizational plan in mind. Their remarks sound as if the speakers had dropped their note cards and shuffled them together in random order before addressing the group.

Identify Main Points and Subpoints

The list of ideas you've compiled by brainstorming and research probably contains more material than you'll want to use in your talk. So the next step is to figure out which key points best support your thesis and help you achieve your purpose. Your analysis of the speaking situation will also help you to pinpoint your key ideas.

On the basis of this analysis, you might decide that the major reasons that would convince listeners to sign up to use Mercury are

I. Mercury is more reliable.

II. Mercury is more convenient.

III. Mercury is more economical.

None of these points was on the brainstorming list in Figure 10–2, but they emerge as themes from that list. Each of the points that did appear on that list will fit into one of these categories, so the speech can be organized around these three points.

How do you identify your main points? One way is by applying the "1-week-later" test: Ask yourself what main points you want people to remember 1 week after the presentation. Since most listeners won't recall much more than a few ideas, your 1-week-later points logically should be emphasized during your talk.

The basic ideas that grow out of your audience analysis or brainstorming list might work well as the main points of your talk, but this doesn't always happen. As with the Mercury delivery service example, there may be better ways to organize your material. Before you can decide, you need to think about the different ways the body of a presentation can be organized.

Once you have identified main points, you can fill in your plan with the subpoints that expand on each of them. These subpoints can be added to a standard outline like the one in Figure 10–4 on page 363. A more visual way to represent the relationship between a thesis, main points, and subpoints is by drawing a logic tree like the one in Figure 10–3.[24]

Choose the Best Organizational Pattern

There are many ways to organize the body of a presentation. Some work best for fundamentally informative subjects, and others are more effective when you want to persuade your listeners. You should choose the one that best develops your thesis and thus helps you to achieve your goal.

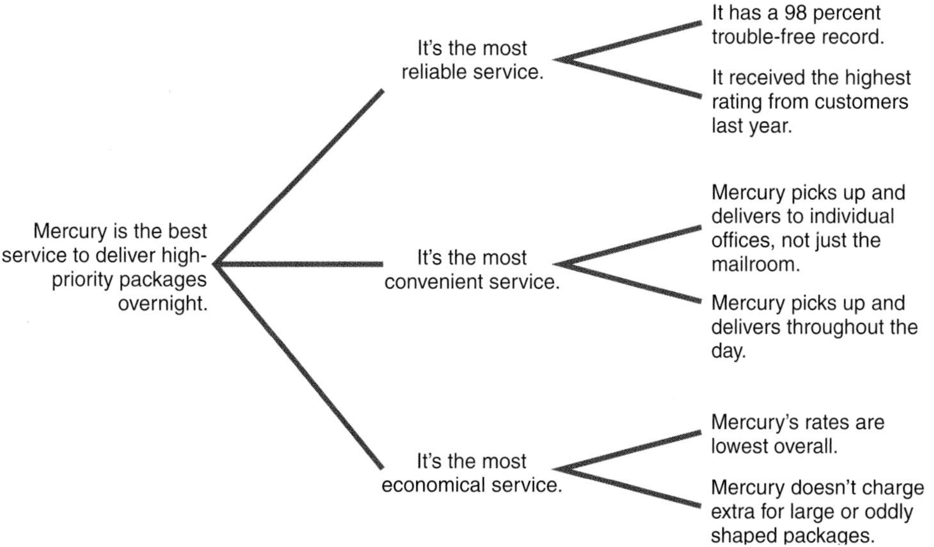

FIGURE 10–3
A logic tree illustrates the relationship between the thesis, main points, and subpoints in a presentation.

Chronological A **chronological pattern** arranges your points according to their sequence in time. You can use it to explain a process, such as the steps in putting an order through the order-fulfillment and shipping departments or the schedule for developing a new product. One of its most common uses is to give instructions:

Thesis: Downloading the software program is easy.

I. Click *Manual Download*.

II. When the *File Download* box appears, choose a folder location.

III. Close all applications including your Web browser.

IV. Double-click on the saved file icon to start the installation process.

Chronological patterns are also useful for discussing events that develop over time:

Thesis: We need to stay on schedule if we're to get the catalog out in time for the holidays.

I. A product list must be ready by March 1.

II. Photography and catalog copy have to be completed by May 6.

III. Page proofs have to be read and corrected by July 30.

IV. Final proofs have to be reviewed by department heads by August 30.

V. Catalogs have to be shipped no later than October 5.

Chronological patterns may be used for discussing history:

Thesis: A review of the past 5 years shows that we've been moving toward empowering our entire workforce to make decisions.

I. Five years ago, management introduced the Employee Advisory Council.

II. Four years ago, we started using project teams that include people from every level of the company.

III. Two years ago, the company started allowing department supervisors to make purchases within their areas without getting the approval of their managers.

IV. Over the past year, the company has followed the suggestions of several workers at the field level in making changes in our billing process.

Spatial A **spatial pattern** organizes material according to how it is put together or where it is located physically. You might use a spatial pattern to show the parts in a model for a new product, the location of various departments in your building, or the safety requirements of a piece of equipment—where safety shields should be placed, the support required in the floor, and so on. You might sell a piece of real estate with a spatially organized presentation like this:

Thesis: This home provides all the space you need.

I. The upstairs has enough bedrooms for every member of the family, plus a private study.

II. The main floor is spacious, with a large living room, a formal dining room, and an eat-in kitchen.

III. The basement has a finished playroom for the children and a utility room.

IV. The yard has large trees and lots of space for a garden.

You can also show the geographical nature of a subject by citing examples from many places:

Thesis: Business is better in some areas than in others.

I. Northeast regional sales are 50 percent ahead of last year's.

II. Mid-Atlantic regional sales are 10 percent ahead of last year's.

III. Southern regional sales are about the same as last year's.

IV. Midwest regional sales are down about 25 percent from last year's.

Topical A **topical pattern** groups your ideas around some logical themes or divisions in your subject. For example, you might organize a proposal for simplifying the expense-accounting procedures around the reasons for the change or a sales presentation for photocopiers around the three major types of copiers you think a customer might be interested in. An accountant might organize a proposal for a new inventory system this way:

Thesis: A just-in-time inventory system has three major benefits.

I. It eliminates excess inventory that may result from long-term ordering.

II. It cuts down on waste resulting from supplies becoming outdated or shopworn.

III. It saves on storage and computer-records costs.

The topical approach is sometimes termed a *catchall approach* because people occasionally describe a list of points as *topical* if they can't think of another pattern that will work. However, a jumbled list of ideas isn't organized just because you call it topical. A genuine topical approach has elements logically related according to some scheme an audience can easily recognize.

Cause–Effect A **cause–effect pattern** shows that certain events have happened or will happen as a result of certain circumstances. For example, you might show prospective life insurance customers how certain clauses will provide extra coverage if they are hospitalized or demonstrate how a new advertising program will help a product reach a wider market. You might also use it to demonstrate how certain circumstances are creating a problem:

Thesis: Redecorating the offices before raising salaries [*cause*] will damage morale and affect productivity [*effect*].

I. When employees see the offices being redecorated without having received a cost-of-living raise over the past year, they'll be discouraged.

II. Discouraged employees aren't as likely to give the company their best efforts during the upcoming season.

An alternative form of the cause–effect structure is an *effect–cause* structure. When you use this structure, you focus more on results: You begin with the result and how it came to pass or how you think it can be made to happen. For example, you might use an effect–cause pattern to explain why a company has a strict policy about absenteeism or to explain how you expect to accomplish a sales goal you have set. It may also be used to explain how a problem has been created:

Thesis: The decline in our car-rental profits [*effect*] is the result of several problems [*cause*].

I. Our profits have decreased 35 percent.

Table 10–3 Presentation Styles and Their Corresponding Organizational Patterns

Informative	Persuasive
Chronological	Problem-Solution
Spatial	Criteria Satisfaction
Topical	Comparative Advantages
Cause-Effect	Motivated Sequence

II. Several factors are responsible.
   A. Our competitors are offering better service at lower prices.
   B. Our maintenance costs have nearly doubled on newer cars.
   C. Our advertising is not effective.

As Table 10–3 shows, chronological, spatial, topical, and cause–effect plans are best suited to informative presentations. While they can be used when your goal is to persuade an audience, you will have better results if you use whichever of the following organizational plans best matches your topic and the speaking situation.

Problem-Solution A **problem–solution pattern** is the simplest persuasive scheme. As its name suggests, you begin by showing the audience that something is wrong with the present situation and then suggest how to remedy the situation.

This plan works especially well when your audience doesn't feel a strong need to change from the status quo. Since listeners have to recognize that a problem exists before they will be interested in a solution, showing them that the present situation is not satisfactory is essential before you present your idea. For example:

Thesis: Establishing a system of employee incentives can boost productivity.

I. Our level of productivity has been flat for over 2 years while the industry-wide rate has climbed steadily in that period. [*Problem*]

II. Establishing an incentive system will give employees a reason to work harder. [*Solution*]

A problem–solution pattern might also be used to show how updating a computer system will solve problems with inventory monitoring, why a potential customer needs a personal financial advisor, or why a department needs additional staff.

The problem–solution approach can be effective, but it isn't the best strategy for every persuasive situation. If your listeners already recognize that a problem exists, you may not need to spend much time proving the obvious. In such circumstances, you might do better to use one of the following three strategies.

Criteria Satisfaction A **criteria satisfaction** organizational strategy sets up criteria that the audience will accept and then shows how your idea or product meets them.

A venture capitalist used a criteria satisfaction plan when seeking investors for a business project. Notice that he introduced each criterion and then showed how his project would satisfy it:

Introduction: Being in the right place at the right time can be the key to financial success. I'm here to offer you a chance to reap substantial benefits from an extremely promising project. Like any investment, this project needs to be based on the sound foundation of a solid business plan, a talented management team, and adequate financing. Let me show you how the project meets all of these important requirements.

Body:

I. The first criterion is that the business plan must be solid. Extensive market research shows the need for this product. . . .

II. The second criterion is a talented management team. Let me introduce the key members of this management team and describe their qualifications. . . .

III. The third criterion is a solid, realistic financial plan. The following plan is very conservative yet shows strong potential for a substantial profit. . . .

Conclusion: Because it meets the conditions of a solid business plan, this project is worth your serious consideration.

In this example, the speaker introduced each criterion and then immediately showed how his plan satisfied it. A different approach is to present all the criteria first and then present your proposal. The strategy here is to gain the audience's acceptance first and boost your credibility. Having done this, you go on to show how your plan meets the criteria presented. With this approach, the thesis is deferred—which is especially smart when the audience may not be inclined to accept it without some powerful arguments.

A manager used a criteria satisfaction plan with a deferred thesis to announce a wage freeze to employees—hardly a popular idea. If she had announced her thesis first ("A wage freeze is in your best interest"), the employees probably would have been too upset to listen thoughtfully to her arguments. By leading her audience through the reasons leading up to the freeze, she increased the chances that the employees would understand management's reasoning. Notice how the thesis is first presented in the middle of the body and is restated in the conclusion:

Introduction: You know that we've faced declining revenues for the past year. During these hard times, we need a policy that is best both for the company and for you, the employees. That's the only way we will be able to survive.

Body:

I. There are three important criteria for selecting a policy. [*Introduces criteria first*]
   A. It should be fair.
   B. It should cause the least harm to employees.
   C. It should allow the company to survive this difficult period without suffering permanent damage.

II. A wage freeze is the best plan to satisfy these criteria. [*Satisfaction of criteria*]
   A. It's fair.
      1.
      2.
   B. It causes minimal harm to employees.
      1.
      2.
   C. It will enable the company to survive.
      1.
      2.

Conclusion: A wage freeze is the best plan at this difficult time.

Comparative Advantages A **comparative advantages** organizational plan puts several alternatives side-by-side to show why yours is the best. This strategy is especially useful when the audience is considering an idea that competes with the one you're advocating. In many such cases a head-on comparison that supports your case is far more effective than ignoring alternative plans. A purchasing agent made the case to her boss for leasing office equipment instead of borrowing to buy it outright:

Thesis: When we remodel the offices, we can use our budget far more efficiently by leasing equipment and furnishings instead of buying them.

Body:

I. Our up-front costs will be dramatically lower because there's no down payment.

II. The application process will be easier. To qualify for a loan, we have to give the bank 2–3 years of financial records. A lease only requires us to furnish 6 months of records.

III. We can keep pace with technology. Short-term leases will cost us less than buying new equipment every few years. We couldn't afford to do that if we buy equipment outright.

IV. We can buy more. Because lease costs are lower, we can get better quality equipment that will improve our productivity.

Conclusion: When it comes to value for our dollar, leasing is definitely the way to go.

Motivated Sequence The **motivated sequence** organizational plan is a five-step scheme designed to boost the involvement and interest of the audience.[25] Regardless of the topic, the sequence of steps is the same:

1. *Attention.* Capture the attention of the audience by introducing the problem in an interesting manner. (This functions as an introduction.)
2. *Need.* Explain the problem clearly and completely. Use a variety of supporting material to back up your claim, proving that the problem is serious. Ideally,

make your listeners feel that the problem affects them in some way. Make them eager to hear a solution.

3. *Satisfaction*. Present your solution to the problem. Provide enough support to prove that the solution is workable and that it will, indeed, solve the problem.
4. *Visualization*. Describe clearly what will happen if your proposal is adopted so that the audience has a clear mental picture of how your proposal will solve the problem. You may also paint a verbal picture of what will happen if your proposal is *not* adopted. In either case, the key to success in this step is to paint a vivid picture of the outcomes, showing how your proposal will make a real difference.
5. *Action*. Call for a response by your audience. Explain what listeners can do to solve the problem. (This functions as the conclusion.)

The motivated sequence plan provides a step-by-step approach for organizing a speech. It builds on the basic problem–solution plan: Step 1 arouses the interest of listeners so that they will be more receptive to the topic. Step 4 goes beyond simply providing a solution and helps the audience picture what a difference it will make. Step 5 guides the audience on how to bring the solution about, making it easier for listeners to take the necessary steps and arousing them to act. Unlike most presentations, this approach usually won't require a preview in the opening of your remarks.

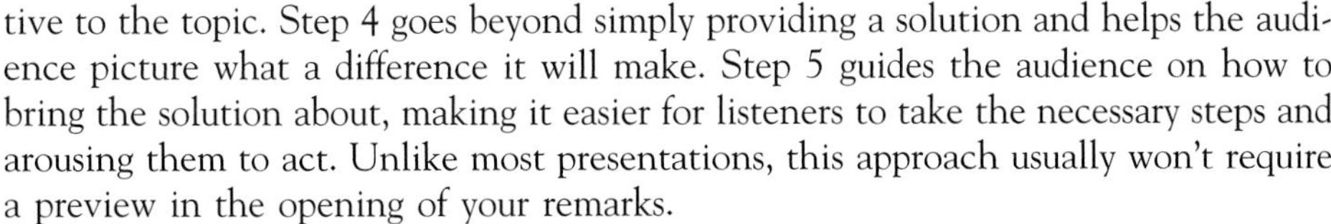

The motivated sequence approach works best when the problem that you present and the solution that you propose are easy to visualize. If your listeners can imagine the problem and see themselves solving it by following your plan, they'll be motivated to accept your reasoning. Recognizing this fact, a travel agent used the motivated sequence to capture the interest of audience members and show them the joys of cruising:

> *Imagine yourself cruising in tropical waters . . . visiting foreign ports . . . dancing all night . . . dining on gourmet cuisine without worrying about the size of the check. These are just a few of the joys of cruising.*
>
> *I'm sure all of you here would take a cruise if you could. But you're probably saying to yourself, "I can't afford it." You may be resigned to taking a vacation that costs plenty but doesn't give you the kind of special experience that's only possible on a vacation cruise.*
>
> *I'm happy to say that you can afford it. Let me show you that cruising can be no more expensive than other, much-less-exciting vacations. . . .*
>
> *What would a cruising vacation be like? Imagine yourself sailing on our ten-day "Sun and Sea Odyssey." Your trip would begin with a champagne bon voyage reception. . . .*
>
> *A few reservations are still available for this winter's cruises. If you let me know that you are interested today, I'll send you a brochure describing the cruises in detail. Then we can discuss how to plan the vacation of your dreams at a price you can afford.*

Because the motivated sequence approach closes with an appeal to action, it is especially well suited to getting an immediate response to your proposal. Recognizing this fact, a fund-raiser used it to generate pledges for an urgent appeal:

[Attention]	Here's a picture of the Myer family. Ted, the father, is a trained stonemason and proud of it. Anne, the mom, is a registered nurse. Little Chris is a normal kid who loves baseball and pizza. His teachers say he has a gift for math and languages.
[Need]	Since this photo was taken, the Myers have had a run of terrible luck. Last year, Ted fell at work and wrenched his back. He's been unable to work ever since, and his disability insurance has almost run out. Three months after Ted's accident, Anne was diagnosed as having leukemia. She's undergoing treatment, and the doctors are optimistic; but she can't work now, and there's no telling when she will be able to return to her job. The Myers lived on their savings for 6 months, but now all the money is gone. Last week they had to move out of their apartment, and they have nowhere else to go. Nowhere, that is, except Transition House.
[Satisfaction]	You can help provide temporary housing for the Myers and other neighbors who are in trouble by contributing to Transition House. Your donations will give these people a safe place to stay while they get back on their feet and save them from life on the street.
[Visualization]	We're hoping to raise enough money tonight to give the Myer family a month at Transition House. During that time, Ted can finish training for a new career as a bookkeeper and get back to work. He hopes to become a CPA. Once he's on the job, the Myers will be able to find a new apartment so that Anne can fight for her health and Chris can stay in his same school, where he's doing so well.
[Action]	What we need from you tonight is a donation. We're asking for anything you can afford: the price of an evening on the town or maybe a postponement of that new outfit you were thinking of buying. In just a moment, I'll be passing out pledge cards. . . .

At first glance, the motivated sequence approach seems to depart from the basic introduction-body-conclusion pattern of organizing a presentation. A closer look shows that the plan does follow the same pattern:

Introduction

- Attention

Body

I. Need

II. Satisfaction

III. Visualization

Conclusion

- Action

Each has an introduction that captures the attention of your audience and gives members reasons to listen. Each has a body that is arranged in a pattern that is easy to follow and helps achieve the purpose of the presentation. Each has a conclusion that reinforces the thesis of the talk and leaves the audience motivated to accept it.

Rules for Main Points

Whichever pattern of organization you use, your main points should meet the following criteria.

Main Points Should Be Stated as Claims A **claim** is a statement asserting a fact or belief. By stating your claims in full, grammatical sentences, they will probably satisfy the 1-week-later test and be remembered by your listeners. Notice how describing main points as claims in complete sentences is clearer and far more effective than using simple three- or four-word statements.

Fragment	Claim
Choosing a physician	It's essential to choose a health care provider from the list of approved doctors.
Sexual and ethnic discrimination	Allowing sexual or ethnic considerations to intrude into our hiring decisions isn't just bad judgment, it's illegal.
Demographic changes in the market	Due to demographic changes, we can expect our market to shrink in the next 10 years.

All Points Should Develop the Thesis Consider the following outline:

Thesis: Allowing employees more latitude in choosing their work hours is good for the company and for the workers.

I. Flexible scheduling can work in several ways.

II. Flexible scheduling improves morale.

III. Flexible scheduling reduces absenteeism.

The first point may be true but doesn't say anything about flexible scheduling's value and, therefore, ought to be dropped.

A Presentation Should Contain No More than Five Main Points Your main points are, after all, what you want your listeners to remember, and people have difficulty recalling more than five pieces of information when they are presented orally.[26] For that reason, it is imperative that your presentation contain no more than five main points. This requires some discipline. Consider the advice of David Dempsey, a trial attorney and a public speaking professor at Oglethorpe University in Atlanta, about the need to ruthlessly edit your ideas:

> *Make three points that stick, rather than 10 quick points that leave no lasting impression. Constantly ask yourself, "Is this the most important issue, the best example, the most compelling way to illustrate my point?"*[27]

Even when you have a large amount of material, it's usually possible to organize it into five categories or fewer. For example, if you were preparing an analysis of ways to lower operating expenses in your organization, your brainstorming list might include these ideas:

- Reduce wattage in lighting fixtures.
- Hire outside data processing firm to handle seasonal billing rather than expand permanent in-house staff.
- Sell surplus equipment.
- Reduce nonbusiness use of copying machines.
- Reduce temperature in less-used parts of the building.
- Pay overtime rather than add new employees.
- Retrofit old equipment instead of buying new machinery.

Your outline could consolidate this list into three areas:

Thesis: We can reduce operating costs in three areas: energy, personnel, and equipment.

I. We can reduce our energy costs.
  A. Reduce wattage in lighting fixtures
  B. Reduce temperature in less-used parts of the building

II. We can reduce money spent on new personnel.
  A. Hire outside data processing firm for seasonal billing
  B. Encourage overtime instead of adding employees

III. We can reduce our purchase and maintenance costs on equipment.
  A. Retrofit old equipment
  B. Sell surplus equipment
  C. Reduce personal use of copying machines

This outline contains all the items in your list, but organizing them into three broad categories makes your presentation much easier to comprehend than a seven-point presentation would be.

Each Main Point Should Contain Only One Idea Combining ideas or overlapping them will confuse audiences. Consider this outline:

Thesis: Many local businesses continue to discriminate against some job applicants.

I. Businesses discriminate on the basis of ethnic background.

II. Businesses discriminate on the basis of disability.

III. Businesses discriminate on the basis of age and sex.

Since discrimination can be related to either age or sex, there's no logical reason to put age and sex in the same category.

Main Points Should Be Parallel in Structure Whenever Possible Parallel wording can reflect your organization and dramatize your points. Consider how the repetition of "businesses discriminate" in the last outline helps drive the point home far more forcefully than does the following, less effective wording of your main points:

I. Most businesses discriminate against minorities.

II. Disability is another reason for discriminating against some job applicants.

III. Some businesses even refuse to hire employees who are over 65.

IV. Women often have extra trouble finding a job.

You won't always be able to state your main points using parallel construction, but a look at many of the examples in this chapter shows you that it can be used often.

Planning the Introduction and Conclusion

The body of a presentation is important, but the introduction that precedes it needs just as much attention. Your introduction should take between 10 and 15 percent of the speaking time. During this short time—less than 1 minute of a 5-minute talk—your listeners form their initial impression of you and your topic. That impression, favorable or not, will affect how they react to the rest of your remarks. To be most effective, an introduction should accomplish several purposes.

Functions of the Introduction

As you have already learned, an introduction should have two parts: an attention getter and a thesis statement and preview. These two parts should accomplish five things.

Capture the Listeners' Attention As you learned in Chapter 4, audiences don't always approach a presentation ready to listen. The topic may not seem important or interesting to them. Your listeners may have been ordered to attend your presentation.

Even when the presentation is obviously important, your listeners will usually have other matters on their minds. It's vital, therefore, to begin by focusing attention on you and your topic if there is any chance that the listeners' minds are elsewhere.

Give Your Audience a Reason to Listen The best way to grab and hold your listeners' attention is to convince them that your message will be important or interesting to them. For example, if company employees are generally satisfied with the insurance program the company has been using, they won't be interested in hearing about a new health plan that will be cheaper for the company unless you can begin by enumerating its advantages to them—for instance, that it will provide them with better emergency services. Similarly, management will be more interested in hearing your new ideas if you first say that the plans you're proposing will yield higher profits.

Set the Proper Tone for the Topic and Setting If you want potential customers to buy more fire insurance, your opening remarks should prepare them to think seriously about the problems they would encounter if they had a fire in the house. If you want to congratulate your subordinates about their recent performance and encourage them to perform even better on the next assignment, your opening remarks should put them in a good mood—not focus on the problems you must face. In any case, your introduction should establish rapport with your listeners. Robert Moran accomplished this goal when he began his remarks to a Japanese audience:

> *If I were an American and you were an American audience, I would probably begin my speech with a joke. If I were Japanese speaking to a Japanese audience, I would probably begin with an apology. Since I am neither American nor Japanese, I will begin with an apology for not telling a joke.*[28]

Establish Your Qualifications If the audience already knows that you are an expert on the subject, if a previous speaker has given you an impressive introduction, or if your authority makes it clear that you're qualified to talk, establishing credibility isn't necessary. In other cases, however, you need to demonstrate your competence quickly so that the listeners will take your remarks seriously. Nonverbal behaviors will also help boost (or diminish) your credibility. Recall the information on nonverbal communication in Chapter 4, and see additional advice on building credibility through nonverbal behavior in Chapters 12 and 14.

Introduce Your Thesis and Preview Your Presentation In most cases, you need to state your main idea clearly at the beginning of your remarks so that your listeners know exactly what you're trying to say. In addition to your thesis statement, a preview of your main points tells your listeners where you're headed.

Accomplishing these five goals in less than 1 minute isn't as difficult as it might seem because you can accomplish several functions at the same time. For example, notice how an insurance agent introduced a 30-minute talk on an admittedly difficult topic:

> *Being an insurance agent gives me a lot of sympathy for tax collectors and dog catchers. None of us has an especially popular job. After all, it seems that with life insurance you lose either way: If the policy pays off, you won't be around to enjoy the money. On the other hand, if you don't need the policy, you've spent your hard-earned savings for nothing. Besides, insurance isn't cheap. I'm sure you have plenty*

of other things you could use your money for: catching up on bills, fixing up your house, buying a new car, or even taking a vacation.

With all those negatives, why should you care about insurance? For that matter, why am I devoting my career to it? For me, the answer is easy: Over the years, I've seen literally hundreds of people—people just like you and me—learn what a difference the right kind of insurance coverage can make. And I've seen hundreds more suffer from learning too late that insurance is necessary.

Well, tonight I want to give you some good news. I'll show you that you can win by buying insurance. You can win by gaining peace of mind, and you can even win by buying insurance that works like an investment, paying dividends that you can use here and now.

Types of Opening Statements

Of all parts of a presentation, the opening words are the hardest for many speakers. You have to be interesting. You have to establish the right tone. Your remarks have to relate to the topic that's being discussed. And, finally, the opening statement has to feel right for you.

The kind of opening you choose will depend on your analysis of the speaking situation. With familiar topics and audiences, you may even decide to skip the preliminaries and give just a brief background before launching into the thesis and preview:

> "We've made good progress on Mr. Boynton's request to look into cost cutting steps. We've found that it is possible to reduce operating expenses by almost 10 percent without cutting efficiency. We'll be introducing six steps this morning."

In most cases, you will want to preface your remarks with some sort of opening statement. Following are seven of the most common and effective ways to begin a presentation.

Ask a Question Asking the right question is a good way to involve your listeners in your topic and establish its importance to them.

Many speakers try to capture attention by asking the audience a **rhetorical question:** one to which the answer is obvious, and which does not really call for a response. For example, a manager who wants to whip up employee enthusiasm for a proposal that will reduce paperwork might ask, "Is it just me, or does anybody else feel like we've spent too much time filling in forms?" Rhetorical questions work well when you can be sure the audience's reaction is the one you want.

Dilbert © Scott Adams/Dist. by United Feature Syndicate, Inc. Reprinted by permission.

When used poorly, rhetorical questions can be risky. Beware of asking questions that listeners won't care about ("Have you ever wondered what the Sherman Antitrust Act means to you?"). Other rhetorical questions can be so thought-provoking that your audience will stop listening to you: "If you had to fire three of the people who report to you, how would you decide which ones to let go?" When you decide to begin with a rhetorical question, be sure to avoid mistakes like these.

Other questions call for an overt response: "How many people here are from out of state?" "Who has had trouble meeting deadlines for sales reports?" "What do you see as the biggest threat facing the company?" If you *are* seeking an overt reaction from your listeners, be sure to let them know: "Let me see a show of hands by the people who . . ." "Hold up your program if you're among those who . . ." If you want them to respond mentally, let them know: "Answer this question for yourself. Are you sure that all of your expense reports would pass an Internal Revenue audit?"

Tell a Story Since most people enjoy a good story, beginning with one can be an effective way to get the audience's attention, set the tone, and lead into the topic. This example, from the introduction to a speech on time management, accomplishes all these functions in a few sentences:

> *In a biology class, I once read about a naturalist who was studying processionary caterpillars. These little guys line up in strings and move along through trees, eating leaves and insects.*
>
> *One day, the naturalist nudged the line of caterpillars onto the rim of an old flower pot. They wound up following one another round and round, never stopping. After a few days they starved to death, even though they were within inches of food. Why? Because they confused activity with accomplishment. They were as active as they could be, moving along staying busy. They just weren't getting anywhere.*
>
> *Unfortunately, sometimes we are no smarter than those bugs.*[29]

Present a Quotation Quotations have two advantages: First, someone else has probably already said what you want to say in a very clever way. Second, quotations let you use a source with high credibility to back up your message.

Not every quotation has to come from a distinguished person. As long as the character you quote is appropriate for the audience and the topic, he or she can be almost anyone—even a fictional character:

> "The comic strip character Pogo once said, 'We have met the enemy, and it's us.' If you think about all the paperwork that keeps us from being more productive, that comment could describe us."

Make a Startling Statement An excellent way to get listeners' attention is to surprise them. Sales presentations often include startling facts in their openings: "Do you know that half of all business calls never reach the intended party?" This approach will work only if your startling statement bears a clear relationship to your topic. Stephen Gardner, the assistant attorney general of Texas, used this approach in an exposé of the abuses of credit bureaus:

> *The whole credit system is frighteningly out of control. Not only are your financial matters virtually an open book, but it is an open book with a couple of pages missing, some lines crossed out, and some pieces in backwards!*[30]

Refer to the Audience Mentioning your listeners' needs, concerns, or interests clarifies the relevance of your topic immediately and shows that you understand your listeners. For example: "I know you're all worried by rumors of cutbacks in staff. I called you here today to explain just what the budget cuts will mean to this department."

Former California governor George Deukmejian used the technique of referring to the audience in a talk to the Los Angeles Rotary Club. Deukmejian acknowledged the fact that people who listen to after-lunch speakers—even famous ones—appreciate brevity:

> *I promise not to speak for too long this afternoon. It's worth noting that the Lord's Prayer is only 56 words long. The Gettysburg Address is 226. The Ten Commandments are 297. But the U.S. Department of Agriculture's order on the price of cabbage is 15,269 words. I'll try to finish somewhere in between.*[31]

Refer to the Occasion Sometimes the event itself provides a good starting point: "We're here today to recognize some very important people."

Sometimes you can begin by referring to some other aspect of the situation, for example, by relating your remarks to those of a previous speaker: "I was very interested in what Larry had to say about the way our expenses will rise in the next couple of years. Let's look at one way we can keep that increase as small as possible."

David M. Roderick of United States Steel used the technique of referring to a previous speaker in the introduction of his remarks to the National Press Club:

> *Thank you, Don, for your introduction. I feel privileged to have this renowned forum as a platform for stating the case for our nation's steel industry—its plight and the importance of its survival.*
>
> *I just hope this issue is not too drab when compared to your two most recent luncheon presentations by gourmet James Beard and economist Arthur Laffer—pie on the plate and pie in the sky. And now steelmaking.*
>
> *Certainly what happens to the nation's fourth largest industry has to be important. Its demise would certainly be news—bad news for almost everyone. I think, then, its struggle to survive and regroup and prosper should be equally newsworthy.*[32]

Use Humor The right joke can be an effective way to get attention, make a point, and increase your audience's liking for you. The vice president of an advertising agency, for example, might begin an orientation session for new management trainees with the following tale:

> *Maybe you've heard the story about the guy who smells awful all the time. When asked the reason for this he explains that it's because of his job—working in a circus giving enemas to elephants. The listener asks, "Why don't you get another job?" and the guy replies hotly, "What! And get out of show business?"*
>
> *Well, that story has some truth in our business too. Lots of people view advertising as glamorous: three-hour expense-account lunches and big commissions. Advertising is certainly a kind of show business, but along with all the glamour comes a lot of hard, messy work. I want to begin this orientation program by telling you about both the clean, easy parts and the tough, grubby ones. Then you'll have a better idea what to expect in the next months and years.*

Jokes aren't the only kind of humorous opener. Sometimes you can make an amusing remark that will set the tone perfectly for your message. For instance:

> *Some people say that problems are not problems, but rather, they are opportunities. If that's the case, then given the present situation, we are faced with a hell of a lot of opportunities.*[33]

Any humor you use should be appropriate to your topic and to the occasion. Telling a few knock-knock jokes before you launch into your financial report will draw attention—but not to your topic. The tone of your presentation could be ruined by a joke. For instance, you probably shouldn't tell a few jokes about smog and then say, "But seriously, folks, I want to talk about what we're doing to curb air pollution from our own factories."

Your jokes should also be appropriate for your audience. The inside jokes that work well with your office staff, for example, are likely to alienate clients at a contract negotiation because outsiders won't understand them. Jokes that are off-color or in any way make light of sexism, racism, or disabilities are likely to offend or embarrass someone in your audience. The risks of telling them aren't worth the laughs they might generate.

Functions of the Conclusion

With the end of your presentation in sight, it can be tempting to wrap things up with a lame comment like "That's about it." Resist the temptation to close quickly and weakly: Experts agree that your final words may create a lasting impression.[34] The conclusion of your presentation should be even shorter than the introduction: not much more than 5 percent of your total speaking time. Within those few moments, though, you must accomplish two important things: review and close. Let's look at each of these parts in detail.

The Review Your review should contain a restatement of your thesis and a summary of your main points. Sometimes these two elements will be presented almost exactly as they appear on your outline:

> "This afternoon, I've suggested that our merchandising approach needs changing to become more profitable. I've suggested three such changes: first, to increase our newspaper advertising; second, to feature higher-quality merchandise; and third, to expand our product line in all areas."

Your review can also be a subtler rewording of the same information:

> "By now I hope you agree with me that some basic merchandising changes can improve our balance sheet. When people find out that we have a broad range of high-quality products, I'm convinced that we'll have more customers who will spend more money."

The Closing Statement A strong closing will help your listeners to remember you favorably; a weak ending can nullify many of your previous

"Will your presentation have a bloopers part at the end?"

gains. Besides creating a favorable impression, the closing statement will give your remarks a sense of completion. You shouldn't leave your audience wondering whether you've finished. Finally, a closing statement ought to incite your listeners, encouraging them to act or think in a way that accomplishes your purpose. Let's look at several varieties of closing statements.

Types of Closing Statements

Several of the techniques used for getting attention in your introduction will also work well as closing statements. To refresh your memory, they are:

Ask a question.

Tell a story.

Give a quotation.

Make a startling statement.

Refer to the audience.

Refer to the occasion.

Use humor.

In addition, there are several other types of closing statements you might use.

Return to the Theme of Your Opening Statement Coming back to where you started gives a sense of completeness to your presentation. With this approach, you should refer to your opening statement but add a new insight, further details, or a different ending:

> "At the beginning of my talk, I asked whether you might not be paying more tax than you need to. I suspect you discovered that you've been overly generous with Uncle Sam. I hope I have helped you to understand your real liability and to take advantage of some of the tax shelters available to you."

One way to capture your audience's attention is to split your story. Start, but don't finish it in your introduction. Cut off your narrative at a key point, perhaps just before the climactic finish, promising your audience that you will wrap it up in the course of your remarks.

Appeal for Action When your goal involves getting the audience to act in a certain way, you can sometimes close your presentation by asking for your desired result:

> "So now that you know what these workshops can do, the only question is when you ought to enroll. We have openings on August 19 and on September 23. I'll be available in a moment to sign you up for either date. I'm looking forward to seeing you soon."

End with a Challenge Whereas an appeal asks for some action, a challenge almost demands it:

> "You can go on as before, not failing completely but not doing the best possible job. Or you can use the ideas you've heard this morning to become more creative, more productive, and more successful. Why be average when you can be superior? Why settle for a few hopes when you can reach your dreams? It's up to you."

Adding Transitions

Transitions are words or sentences that connect the segments of a presentation. As Figure 10–4 shows, they work like bridges between the major parts of your remarks and tell your listeners how these parts are related. Transitions should occur between the introduction and the body, between the main points within the body, and between the body and the conclusion. The examples below illustrate each of these instances:

> "Those are big promises. Let me talk about how we can deliver on them."
>
> "Not all the news is bad, however. Let me tell you about some good things that happened at the conference."
>
> "After hearing about so many features, you may have trouble remembering them all. Let's review them briefly."

Functions of Transitions

Transitions like the preceding examples serve three important purposes.

They Promote Clarity Clarity in speech—especially one-way speech like presentations—is more difficult to achieve than clarity in writing. The format of a letter, memo, book, or report makes its organization of ideas clear. Paragraphs, lists, different typefaces, and underlining can all emphasize how ideas are related to one another. In a presentation, however, listeners don't have the benefit of any of these aids to figure out how your ideas are put together. They have only what the verbal cues—transitional words and phrases—provide.

They Emphasize Important Ideas Transitions within presentations highlight important information the way italics and bold type emphasize it in print:

> "Now let's turn to a third reason—perhaps the most important of all—for equipping your field representatives with electronic pagers."
>
> "That's what company policy says about the use of expense accounts. Now let's take a look at how things *really* work."

They Keep Listeners Interested Transitions give momentum to a presentation. They make listeners want to find out what comes next:

> "So we gave them the best dog-and-pony show you've ever seen. And it was perfect—just like we planned. What do you think they said when we were finished?"
>
> "By now you're probably asking yourself what a product like this will cost. And that's the best news of all. . . ."

Characteristics of Effective Transitions

Transitions that promote clarity, emphasize important ideas, and keep listeners interested possess two characteristics. First, they refer to both preceding and upcoming ideas. A transition is like a bridge: To get listeners from one point to another, it must be anchored at both ends. By referring to what you just said and to what you'll

Purpose: After hearing this talk, the prospective customer will sign up to use Mercury as its exclusive overnight delivery service.

Thesis: Mercury is the best service to deliver your high-priority packages on time.

INTRODUCTION

A. Overnight delivery services aren't cheap, but they are worth the expense *if* they do the job of getting important materials into the right hands quickly. [*Attention getter*]

B. After comparing Mercury with the other delivery services, you'll see that it is the best one to do the job. [*Thesis*]

C. As I'll explain in the next few minutes, Mercury is more reliable, convenient, and economical than the competition. [*Preview*]

Transition: Let me start by explaining why Mercury is best with the most important feature of any delivery service: reliability.

BODY

I. Mercury is more reliable than other services.
   - A. Mercury's 98 percent trouble-free record beats every other service.
   - B. Other services have held up deliveries for as much as 1 week.
   - C. Other services have damaged packages.
   - D. In some cases, other services have even lost packages.

Transition: Besides being reliable, Mercury is the best service in another important way ...

II. Mercury is more convenient than other services.
   - A. Mercury picks up and delivers items to individual offices, not just to the mailroom like ABC Overnight.
   - B. Mercury picks up or delivers packages any time between 7:00 A.M. and midnight, instead of only coming by once a day like International Air Freight.
   - C. Mercury is the only service that will bill departmental accounts separately, saving you bookkeeping time.

Transition: Because it's so convenient and reliable, you might think that Mercury is more expensive than other services, but it's not.

III. Mercury is more economical than other services.
   - A. It doesn't charge extra for oddly shaped packages.
   - B. It charges less than every other service for heavy packages.
   - C. The shipping fee includes insurance.

Transition: By now you can see why it's worth considering Mercury as the provider of your overnight mail service ...

CONCLUSION

A. Mercury is reliable, convenient, and economical. [*Thesis/Review*].

B. With Mercury you won't just pay for the best service ... you'll get it.

FIGURE 10–4
A Complete Presentation Outline

Self-Assessment Checklist for Organizing a Presentation

Use this list to check how well your presentation is organized.

Does the **introduction**

____ 1. Capture the attention of your audience?
____ 2. Give your audience reasons to listen?
____ 3. Set an appropriate tone?
____ 4. Establish your qualifications, if necessary?
____ 5. Introduce your thesis and preview the content?

Does the **body**

____ 1. Use the most effective organizational pattern?
  a. Chronological
  b. Spatial
  c. Topical
  d. Cause–effect
  e. Problem–solution
  f. Criteria satisfaction
  g. Comparative advantages
  h. Motivated sequence
____ 2. State your main points in complete sentences?
____ 3. Use your main points to develop your thesis?
____ 4. Contain no more than five main points?
____ 5. Express only one idea in each main point?
____ 6. State your main points in parallel structure if possible?

Do you have **transitions** that

____ 1. Refer to both recent and upcoming material, showing relationships between the two?
____ 2. Emphasize your important ideas?
____ 3. Clarify the structure of your ideas?
____ 4. Exist in all necessary parts of presentation?
  a. Between introduction and body
  b. Between main points within body
  c. Between body and conclusion

Does the **conclusion**

____ 1. Review your thesis and your main points?
____ 2. Conclude with an effective closing statement?

say next, you are showing the logical relationship among those ideas. Notice the smooth connections between the ideas in these transitions:

> "Those are the problems. Now let's see what can be done about solving them."
>
> "Now you see that the change makes sense financially. But how will it be received by the people who have to live with it?"

If you have trouble planning a transition that links preceding and upcoming material smoothly, the reason may be that the ideas aren't logically related or the organizational plan you've chosen is flawed. Review the organizing patterns on pages 345–353 and the rules for main points on pages 353–355 to be sure that the structure of your presentation's body is logically suited to the topic.

Transitions should also call attention to themselves. You should let listeners know that you're moving from one point to another so that they will be able to follow the structure of your ideas easily. Notice how the examples you have read so far all make it clear that the presentation is shifting gears. This sort of highlighting is often due to the use of key words:

> "The *next* important idea is . . ."
>
> "*Another* reason we want to make the change . . ."
>
> "*Finally,* we need to consider . . ."
>
> "To *wrap things up* . . ."

Phrases like these are not in themselves good transitions, since they do not refer to both previous and upcoming material strongly enough. But when used as part of a transition like the ones illustrated in these pages, they do signal listeners that you are moving to a new part of your presentation. A presentation checklist, covering transitions and the other organizational concepts discussed in this chapter, is presented in the Self-Assessment on page 364.

summary

At one time or another, almost everyone makes on-the-job presentations: some formal and others informal, some for external and others for internal audiences. A speaker's reputation can affect the direction and success of his or her career.

Presentations should be based on a three-part analysis of the speaking situation. First, speakers should analyze the audience: Who are the key listeners; what do they already know; what do they want to know; and what are their preferences, significant demographics, size, reason for being there, and attitudes? Second, speakers should analyze themselves as speakers. To do so, they should consider their goal for speaking, their knowledge of the subject, and the sincerity they bring to the topic. Finally, speakers should analyze the speaking occasion by considering the facility, the time of day and length of time they will speak, and the context in which their remarks will occur.

After analyzing the situation, the speakers' next steps are to define both general and specific goals and to create the thesis. Is the general goal to inform or persuade? The specific goal identifies who the speakers want to reach, what they want them to do, and how, when, and where they want them to act. Clear goal statements define the desired audience reaction in a specific and attainable manner. After defining the goal, speakers must clearly structure the thesis as a single sentence. It is the central idea and will be repeated throughout the presentation, so it is essential to design it carefully.

Clearly organized presentations increase audience comprehension and speaker credibility by following a basic structure of introduction, body, and conclusion. Speakers may begin by brainstorming for ideas that might possibly fit into the talk. The goal statement and audience analysis then serve as devices for choosing the items that are appropriate for this specific presentation. These items can then be arranged into a series of main and subpoints and then put into the organizational pattern that works best for the goal and content. Common organizational patterns are chronological, spatial, topical, cause–effect, problem–solution, criteria satisfaction, comparative advantages, and motivated sequence.

After the body of the presentation has been developed, an introduction is created to capture the attention of the audience, give a reason to listen, and state the thesis. The conclusion reviews the thesis and main points and closes with a strong statement.

Finally, transitions connect the introduction to the body, the main points of the body, and the body to the conclusion. They call attention to themselves to keep listeners oriented and highlight material that precedes and will follow.

key terms

Test your understanding of these key terms by visiting the Online Learning Center Web site at www.mhhe.com/adler9.

cause–effect pattern 347
chronological pattern 345
claim 353
comparative advantages pattern 350
criteria satisfaction pattern 348
general goal 337
motivated sequence pattern 350
problem–solution pattern 348
rhetorical question 357
spatial pattern 346
specific goal 337
thesis statement 339
topical pattern 347
transition 362

activities

Go to the self-quizzes at the Online Learning Center at www.mhhe.com/adler9 to test your knowledge of chapter concepts.

1. Invitation to Insight

Gain insights about occasion and audience analysis by interviewing a professional who frequently delivers presentations to a variety of audiences in the workplace. Ask your interviewee questions such as

a. How do you gather information about your potential audience? About the expectations of the occasion?
b. Compare the expectations of some of the various audiences you address.
c. In what ways do you adjust your presentations for these audiences?
d. What do you do if you discover that your audience members' knowledge level about your topic will vary widely?
e. How do you appeal to an audience who will probably be bored by or opposed to your topic?
f. What are some strategies for tweaking your presentation so it's appropriate to the occasion?

In class, share answers gleaned from various interviews.

2. Skill Builder

Identify the most important factors about your audience, the occasion, and yourself as a speaker that you should consider when planning a presentation to

a. Ask your boss for a raise.
b. Give instructions to a trainee.
c. Interview for a job.
d. Announce a cost increase in employee health care benefits.
e. Brief a new supervisor on the key operating procedures within your group.

3. Skill Builder

Imagine that you have been asked to give a 15-minute description of your department's functions. How would your goal and approach differ for each of the following audiences?

a. A group of new employees from all over the company.
b. New employees within the department.
c. A group of managers from other departments.
d. Several of your superiors.
e. A supplier who is helping you update equipment.
f. A group of customers touring the company.

4. Skill Builder

Write a specific-goal statement for each of the following situations. Then translate your goal into an effective thesis:

a. A farewell speech honoring a not-too-popular manager at his retirement dinner.
b. A training session introducing a new emergency evacuation plan.
c. A kickoff speech for the United Way payroll deduction campaign.
d. An appeal to the boss to hire an additional employee in your department.
e. A proposal to your department head for changing course requirements for the major.
f. A banker's speech to an economics class on the topic "The Changing Banking Industry."
g. A request to your landlord for new office carpeting.

5. Skill Builder

Write a specific goal and thesis statement for a presentation about the value of learning communication skills introduced in this book. Imagine you will be addressing your presentation to an organization you work for or a college class you're taking. What demographic information would be important to know about your audience? Which demographic information would not be relevant to your presentation? Next, identify three to five key points you would cover in your presentation.

6. Invitation to Insight

How would you enhance your credibility if you were delivering a presentation to various businesses in your community, asking them to establish internships for communications students?

7. Skill Builder

What kinds of material would you gather for a presentation on each of the following topics? Where would you find your information?

a. How changes in the cellular telephone industry will affect consumers.
b. How to begin an investment program.
c. Changing trends in the popularity of various academic courses over the last 10 years.
d. Why students should (should not) buy a personal computer.
e. Career opportunities for women in the field of your choice.

8. Skill Builder

Which organizational plan (chronological, spatial, and so on) would you use for each of the following presentations?

a. Instructions on how to file a health insurance claim form.
b. A request for time and money to attend an important convention in your field.

c. A comparison of products or services between your organization and a competitor.
d. A report on an industrial accident.
e. Suggestions on reducing employee turnover.

9. Skill Builder

Develop outlines for three of the following topics or for a topic that you are knowledgeable about, applying the rules for main points given in this chapter:

a. When to use small claims court.
b. The importance of creativity in advertising.
c. Renting versus leasing a car.
d. The proper format for a business letter.
e. Types of sexual harassment.
f. The fastest-growing jobs in the 21st century.

10. Skill Builder

Prepare an introduction and a conclusion for each of the following presentations:

a. A talk to employees announcing personnel layoffs.
b. The last in a day-long series of talks to a tired audience on maintaining and operating equipment.
c. An appeal to co-workers for donations to the Community Holiday Relief Fund.
d. A talk, the topic of which is "What Employers Look for in a College Graduate," to your class by the president of the local chamber of commerce. (Plan your concluding remarks to follow a question-and-answer period.)

resources

In Print

Brody, M. *Speaking Your Way to the Top: Making Powerful Business Presentations*. Boston: Allyn & Bacon, 1997.

This book provides excellent information on business presentations. Chapter 2 presents information on analyzing and understanding your goal, audience, and logistics for any presentation. The author includes a list of questions to consider in the demographic and psychographic analysis of the audience.

Foss, S. K., and K. A. Foss, *Inviting Transformation: Presentational Speaking for a Changing World*, 2nd ed. Prospect Heights, IL: Waveland Press, Inc., 2003.

Chapter 5, "Framing," expands the reader's repertoire of organizational patterns with descriptions and examples of 18 methods of framing or organizing presentations. Chapter 7, "Beginning and Ending," presents as many possibilities for introductions and conclusions.

Inch, E. S., and B. Warnick. *Critical Thinking and Communication: The Use of Reason in Argument*, 4th ed. Boston: Allyn & Bacon, 2002.

This text provides an in-depth look at argument and its relationship to ethics, culture, and occasions. It explores reasoning and inferences, types of claims and evidence, and propositions of fact, value, and policy. Various models for analyzing arguments are included.

Jaffe, C. *Public Speaking: Concepts and Skills for a Diverse Society*, 5th ed. Belmont, CA: Wadsworth, 2007.

This is an asset for analyzing increasingly pluralistic audiences. Chapter 5 ("Audience Analysis") focuses on cultural variables that influence how speakers and audiences see themselves and each other.

Jeary, T. *Life Is a Series of Presentations*. New York: Simon & Schuster, 2004.

As the title suggests, this book argues that presentations are a fact of everyday business and personal life. When we write or speak to our boss, colleagues, friends, and family, we are usually making a case. Jeary's thesis is provocative and demonstrates the value of the skills covered in this section of *Communicating at Work*.

Kurtz, P. L. *The Global Speaker: An English Speaker's Guide to Making Presentations around the World*. New York: American Management Association, 1995.

This book offers tips on speaking to audiences around the world. It helps you to evaluate the language proficiency of your audience, as well as to avoid cultural taboos.

Wilder, C. "Concluding with Conviction." In *The Presentations Kit: 10 Steps for Selling Your Ideas*. New York: Wiley, 1994.

Conclusions are vital to the overall impact of a presentation. Wilder offers some forceful ideas that will help you pack all the punch you can into your conclusion. The book includes tips for organizing and delivering your conclusion.

On the Web

Introductions and Conclusions

From the Advanced Public Speaking institute (**www.public-speaking.org**), go to "openings and closings," "body," or "organization" for help on these topics. Power Pointers (**www.powerpointers.com**) hosts an abundance of articles on introductions and conclusions (as well as tips for organizing presentations). So You Wanna? (**www.soyouwanna.com**) presents general help in beginning a presentation. Look for well-categorized quotations that are useful for introductions and conclusions at **http://dir.yahoo.com/Reference/quotations**. Here you can also link to nearly 100 other sites of quotations. Another compendium of quotes is the famous Familiar Quotations by Bartlett (**www.columbia.edu/acis/bartleby/bartlett**). Motivating Moments (**www.motivateus.com**) presents useful ideas for closings: motivational and inspirational stories.

Brainstorming and Outlining

Sometimes the best way to organize ideas is visually. Until recently, the best approach was to write ideas on index cards, spread them out on the table or floor, and rearrange them until a clear plan emerged. Now, computer software makes the task quicker and easier.

"Inspiration" (**www.inspiration.com/general_biz.html**) is a visual tool for developing ideas. The program's diagram view provides an easy-to-use equivalent of the index card approach. Each idea you type into the computer appears onscreen inside its own box or circle. You can click on these ideas with your mouse and rearrange them until they fall into patterns that seem clear and effective. Then, with a simple command, the visual map is turned into a traditional outline, suitable for conversion into speaker's notes, handouts, or visual aids. Besides serving as an outlining tool, Inspiration makes it easy to create concept maps, process flows, knowledge maps, flowcharts, and other visual diagrams.

Other concept-mapping software programs include Decision Explorer (**www.banxia.com/demain.html**), MindManager (**www.mindjet.com**), IHMC's Concept Map (**http://cmap.coginst.uwf.edu**), and VisiMap (**www.visimap.com**).

Demographic Analysis

Resources for demographic analysis are plentiful. The Pew Research Center (**www.people-press.org**) conducts independent research on attitudes toward public policies and news. You'll find the interactive typology (**http://people-press.org/fit/**) useful to view characteristics of various types of voters/audiences and you can participate in an interactive exercise to "type" yourself.

The NES (National Election Studies) Guide to Public Opinion and Electoral Behavior hosts outstanding graphs and charts on characteristics of the electorate at **www.umich.edu/~nes/nesguide/nesguide.htm**. Additionally use Gallup Polls (**www.gallup.com**), U.S. Census Bureau (**www.census.gov**), and National Center for Health Statistics (**www.cdc.gov/nchs/nsfg.htm**).

Organizations and Aids for Speakers

The following organizations offer opportunities for members to develop their speaking skills and provide resources for members and nonmembers:

- Toastmasters International (**www.toastmasters.org**)
- National Speaker's Association (**www.nsaspeaker.org**)

Checklists can be a great time-saver and a help in analyzing an audience and speaking situation. Help organize your next presentation by using the Pre-Program Questionnaire, a great checklist to analyze audience and context, at **www.public-speaking.org/public-speaking-questionnaire-article.htm**. A valuable checklist for room setup is at **www.public-speaking.org/public-speaking-setupchecklist-article.htm**. If you are required to travel and speak, access a worthwhile travel checklist from the same site.

11

Verbal and Visual Support in Presentations

Chapter Outline

Chapter Objectives

After reading this chapter, you should be able to

1 Use each type of verbal aid to add interest, clarity, and/or proof to a main point.

2 Design a visual aid appropriate for a given situation.

3 Choose the most appropriate and effective medium for presenting visual aids in a given situation.

4 Design and/or critique a presentation using PowerPoint or similar software.

Tom Sutcliffe was frustrated. "I know I deserve that raise," he said firmly to his friend and co-worker Tina Agapito. "I laid out all the reasons to the boss as clear as day. I've been doing the work of two people ever since Van left. My productivity is higher than anybody else's in the place. My salary is way behind the industry average. And all my clients are happy. What else does he want?"

Tina tried to be supportive. "I know you deserve the raise, Tom. And I just can't believe the boss doesn't see that too. Did you back up your claims?"

"What do you mean?" Tom replied.

"Did you give him evidence about your productivity or about how your salary compares with the industry? And did you give him some proof about all your happy clients?"

"I guess not," said Tom. "But I shouldn't have to sell myself around here. The boss ought to appreciate a good employee when he has one!"

"Maybe so," Tina answered. "But the boss hears a lot of requests for money and resources. And he's really busy. Maybe if you can make your case clearer and more interesting, you've still got a chance."

Tina's advice to Tom was good. Solid ideas won't always impress an audience. Most listeners are busy and preoccupied, and they usually don't care nearly as much about your message as you do. The kind of clear organization described in Chapter 10 will help make your presentations a success, but you often need to back up your well-organized points in a way that makes your audience take notice, understand you, and accept your message. In other words, you need to use plenty of supporting material.

Functions of Supporting Material

Supporting material is anything that backs up the claims in a presentation. You can see the relationship between these claims and supporting material in the following examples:

Claim	Support
We could increase sales by staying open until 10 P.M. on weekday evenings.	An article in *Modern Retailing* cites statistics showing that stores with extended evening hours boost profits by more than 20 percent of the direct overhead involved with the longer business day.
Replacing the ink cartridge on the printer isn't as complicated as it seems.	Here's a diagram that shows how to do it.
Taking the time to help customers will boost their loyalty and increase your commissions.	Let me read you a letter written just last week by one satisfied customer.

As these examples show, a presentation without supporting material would still be logical if it followed the organizational guidelines in Chapter 10. But it probably wouldn't achieve its goal because it would lack the information necessary to develop the ideas in a way that the audience would understand or appreciate. Carefully selected supporting material can make a presentation more effective by adding three things: clarity, interest, and proof.

Clarity

Supporting material can make abstract or complicated ideas more understandable. Notice how the following analogy clarifies how computers with point-and-click user interfaces were such a revolutionary improvement over earlier generations that relied on arcane keyboard commands:

"And that's our plan. Any questions?"

> *Imagine driving a car that has no steering wheel, accelerator, brake pedal, turn signal lever, or gear selector. In place of all the familiar manual controls, you have only a typewriter keyboard.*
>
> *Any time you want to turn a corner, change lanes, slow down, speed up, honk your horn, or back up, you have to type a command sequence on the keyboard. Unfortunately, the car can't understand English sentences. Instead, you must hold down a special key with one finger and type in some letters and numbers, such as "S20:TL:A35," which means, "Slow to 20, turn left, and accelerate to 35."*
>
> *If you make typing mistakes, one of three things will happen. If you type an unknown command, the*

car radio will bleat and you will have to type the command again. If what you type happens to be wrong but is nevertheless a valid command, the car will blindly obey. (Imagine typing A95 instead of A35.) If you type something the manufacturer didn't anticipate, the car will screech to a halt and shut itself off.[1]

Interest

Supporting material can enliven a presentation by making your main points more vivid or meaningful to the audience. Notice how one attorney added interest to a summary aimed at discrediting his opponent's restatement of evidence:

It seems that when Abe Lincoln was a young trial lawyer in Sangamon County, Illinois, he was arguing a case with a lawyer whose version of the facts came more from his imagination than the testimony. Lincoln, in his argument, turned on him and said:

"Tell me, sir, how many legs has a sheep got?" "Why, four, of course," the fellow answered. "And if I called his tail a leg, then how many legs would that sheep have?" Lincoln asked. The answer came, "Then he'd have five." "No!" Lincoln roared, pounding the jury rail; "he'd still have just four legs. Calling his tail a leg won't make it a leg. Now let's look at the actual testimony and see how many tails you've been calling legs."[2]

Proof

Besides adding clarity and interest, supporting material can provide evidence for your claims and make your presentation more convincing. A speaker might use supporting materials this way to back up the claim "Employer-sponsored day care can boost productivity as well as help parents":

A survey of Union Bank employees in California showed the value of on-site, employer-sponsored day care. Turnover of employees using the bank's on-site center was only 2.2 percent, less than one quarter of the 9.9 percent turnover for workers who used other forms of day care. And that's not all: Employees using the day care center were absent from work an average of 1.7 days a year less than other parents of young children. This sort of center can even get parents back to work more quickly after a new baby is born: Mothers who used the bank's center took maternity leaves that were 1.2 weeks shorter than other parents'.[3]

Whenever you use work of others to back up your claims, be sure to cite the source. Some sources, of course, are more credible than others. In the preceding paragraph, for example, the claim that employer-sponsored day care is good for employers is strengthened by citing a survey done by a respected bank. The same claim wouldn't be as persuasive coming from a survey of employees who were seeking day care, since their motives would be more self-serving.

Verbal Support

As Table 11–1 shows, many kinds of verbal supporting material can be used to add interest, clarity, or proof to a presentation. The most common supports for business and professional presentations are definitions examples, stories, statistics, comparisons, and quotations. Consider the preferences of your audience when choosing the types of support you'll present.

Table 11–1 Types of Verbal Support

Type	Definition	Use	Comments
Definition	Explains meaning of a term	Clarify	Important when terms are unfamiliar to an audience or used in an uncommon way
Example	Brief reference that illustrates a point	Clarify Add interest (if sufficient number given)	Usually best in groups of two or more, if brief
Story	Detailed account of an incident	Clarify Add interest Prove (factual only)	Adapt to audience Must clearly support thesis Tell at appropriate length
Statistics	Numerical representations of point	Clarify Prove Add interest (when combined with other form of support)	Link to audience's frame of reference Use sparingly Round off Supplement with visuals, handouts
Comparisons	Examinations or processes that show how one idea resembles another	Clarify Add interest (figurative) Prove (literal)	Tailor familiar item to audience Make sure comparison is valid
Quotations	Opinion of expert or articulate source	Clarify Add interest (sometimes) Prove	May be paraphrased or read verbatim Cite source Use sources credible to audience Follow up with restatement or explanation

Definitions

You can appreciate the need for a speaker to define unclear terms by recalling times when someone began using unfamiliar language, leaving you confused and unable to understand:

> "BITNET hosts are a collection of IBM and Vax computers that use 80-character EBCDIC card images. Thus, they tend to mangle the headers and text of third-party traffic from the rest of the ASCII/RFC-822 world."

Definitions remove this sort of confusion by explaining the meaning of terms that are unfamiliar to an audience or are used in a specialized or uncommon way:

> "A *smart electrical meter* doesn't just measure how much energy a customer uses. It identifies when you used it, and sends that information back to the local utility for monitoring and billing purposes."
>
> "In finance, *a capital gain* is the profit that results when you sell assets like real estate or shares of stock for more than you paid for them. A *capital gains tax* is the amount government charges on that profit."
>
> "*Bollywood* is the informal name of the Hindi language film industry based in Mumbai, India. The term is a combination of the words 'Bombay' (the old name for Mumbai) and 'Hollywood.'"

Examples

Examples are brief illustrations that back up or explain a point. A speaker arguing for an enhanced package of employee benefits could cite examples of companies that already provide a variety of perks:

- Gasket maker Fel-Pro of Skokie, Illinois, contributes $3,500 annually for up to 4 years of college tuition for employees' children.
- Anheuser-Busch employees take home two free cases of beer a month. Employees of Ben & Jerry's take home three free pints of ice cream a day.
- Apple Computer gives its employees 6-week paid sabbaticals every 5 years.[4]

Likewise, a marketing consultant explaining how the name of a business can attract customers could back up the claim by citing examples of clever names:

- Totally Twisted, a Maryland pretzel company.
- Now Showing, a movie theater turned lingerie shop in Oklahoma.
- Access/Abilities, a California firm that helps people with disabilities.[5]

The same consultant could show how poor names can discourage business:

- Coffin Air Service.
- Big Bill's Plumbing.
- Bland Farms, a mail-order food company.[6]

In many cases you don't need to look outside your own experience for examples to back up a point. Union members claiming that "management cares more about buildings and grounds than employees" might back up their claim by offering examples:

> *We keep hearing that "employees are our most important asset," yet we don't see dollars reflecting that philosophy. In the 2.5 years since our last pay raise, we have seen the following physical improvements at this site alone: a new irrigation system for the landscaping, renovation of the corporate offices, expansion of the data processing wing, resurfacing of all the parking lots, and a new entrance to the building. Now all those improvements are helpful, but they show that buildings and grounds are more important than people.*

When they are used to prove a point, examples are most effective when several are given together. If you are supporting the claim that you are capable of taking on a more challenging job, it is best to remind your boss of several tasks you have handled well. After all, a single example could be an isolated instance or a lucky fluke.

Stories

Stories illustrate a point by describing an incident in some detail. Almost everyone loves to hear a good story. It adds interest and, when well chosen, it can drive home a point better than logic and reasoning alone. As one expert put it, "People don't want more information. They are up to their eyeballs in information. They want faith—faith in you, your goals, your success, in the story you tell . . . faith needs a story to sustain it."[7]

Stories come in three categories: Fictional, hypothetical, and factual. *Fictional stories* allow you to create material that perfectly illustrates the point you want to

Storytelling to Make a Point

Well-chosen and well-told stories can help you make a point in an interesting and compelling way. In a brief presentation of 2 minutes or less, use a story to illustrate an important lesson regarding professional communication. The story you tell may be based on your personal experience, something you observed, or something you read or heard about from others.

Organize your presentation in one of two ways: Either state your thesis first and then show how the story supports it or tell the story first, and then show how it illustrates your thesis. In either case, conclude by showing audience members how your thesis and the story that illustrates it relate to their professional lives.

make. This fictional story uses humor to help listeners understand the importance of being proactive in business:

> *In Greece there is an old monastery perched on top of a high mountain, with steep cliffs on every side. The only way to visit it is to get in a wicker basket and have a monk pull you up by ropes.*
>
> *One visitor noticed that this rope—the one his life depended on—was old and quite frayed. He asked the monk, "When do you change the rope?" The monk replied, "Whenever it breaks."*

After the laughter died down, the speaker used this story to make his point:

> *In this company we don't wait until the rope breaks. We don't even let it fray. We fix things before they become hazards.*[8]

Other stories are *hypothetical:* "Imagine yourself . . ."; "Suppose that you were . . ."; "What would you do if . . ." Besides being involving, hypothetical stories allow you to create a situation that illustrates exactly the point you are trying to make. You can adjust details, create dialogue, and use figures that support your case. But your account will be effective only if it is believable.

A representative explaining the concept of "Guaranteed Account Value" in a variable annuity investment might use a hypothetical example like this:

> *Suppose you have two kids who will be ready for college in 5 years. You have $50,000 saved, but you know that won't be enough to cover their expenses. So you want to invest your savings, hoping that it will grow. On the other hand, you don't want to risk losing some of your savings.*
>
> *If you purchase an annuity with a Guaranteed Account Value clause, your $50,000 will be safe no matter what happens to the stocks you've invested in. Suppose the stocks drop in value by half: Even then, you'd get back your full $50,000. On the other hand, if your stock portfolio grows in value—say it doubles to $100,000—you'd get the full amount.*

Factual stories can also add interest and clarity. The story below, from a frustrated consumer, illustrates the thesis that many businesses are more interested in making a sale than in supporting their products after the deal is closed. Notice how the last sentence restates the main idea so that the point of the story is clear:

> *Last Tuesday I decided to call the automobile dealership. There were two numbers listed in the phone book, one for "Sales," the other for "Service." I asked the service manager if I could bring my car in the following Saturday. Service managers always have a way of making you feel unwanted, and he seemed pleased to be able to tell me that they were closed Saturday and wouldn't be able to take me until a week from Thursday.*
>
> *I didn't make a date. Instead I called the other number, under "Sales." "Are you open Saturday?" I asked. "Yes, sir," the cheery voice said at the other end of the phone. "We're here Saturdays from eight in the morning till nine in the evening, and Sundays from noon until six."*
>
> *Now, if I can buy a car on Saturday, why can't I get one fixed on Saturday? What's going on here anyway? I think I know what's going on, of course. We're selling things better than we're making them, that's what's going on.*[9]

While both factual and hypothetical stories can make a presentation clearer and more interesting, only the factual type can prove a point:

> "Cutting the payroll by using temporary employees sounds like a good idea, but it has problems. Listen to what happened when we tried it at the place I used to work. . . ."
>
> "I'm sure Wes can handle the job. Let me tell you what happened last year when we assigned him to manage the Westco account. . . ."
>
> "You might think life insurance isn't necessary for a young, healthy person like you, but remember Dale Crandall, the linebacker from State? Well, he was about as healthy as they come, but . . ."

Whether they are fictional, hypothetical, or factual, effective stories possess several characteristics.[10] First, they should be relatively brief: Don't spin out a 5-minute yarn to make a minor point. They should also be interesting and appropriate for your audience: A story that offends your listeners will be memorable, but not in the desired way. Most importantly, a story must support the point you are trying to make. An amusing story that doesn't support your thesis will just distract your listeners.[11]

Statistics

Statistics are numbers used to represent an idea. Most statistics are collections of examples reduced to numerical form for clarity. If you were arguing that there was a serious manufacturing problem with a new product line, describing one or two dissatisfied customers would not prove that the problem went beyond the usual "acceptable" rate of error in manufacturing. The following statement, though, would constitute proof: "Our return rate on the new line is just over 40 percent—as opposed to the usual rate of 5 percent—and of all those returns, four-fifths are related to a flaw in the gear assembly." Statistics are probably the most common form of support in business presentations. They are used to measure the size of market segments, sales trends, decreasing or increasing profits, changes in costs, and many other aspects of business.

When handled well, statistics are especially strong proof because they are firmly grounded in fact and because they show that the speaker is well informed.[12] Consider this example:

> *The U.S. Census Bureau reports that people with a bachelor's degree earn an average of 62 percent more than those with only a high school diploma. Over a lifetime,*

> *the gap in earning potential between a high school grad and someone with a B.A. is more than a million dollars. These figures show that whatever sacrifices you make for a college education in the short term are worth it in the long term.*

Despite their potential effectiveness, poorly used statistics can spoil a presentation. One common mistake is to bury an audience under an avalanche of numbers like this speaker did at an annual stockholders' meeting:

> *Last year was an exciting one for our company. We earned $6.02 per share on a net income of $450 million, up from $4.63 per share on income of $412 million in the preceding year. This increase came in part from a one-time gain of $13 million from the sale of common stock to New Ventures group, our research and development subsidiary. Excluding this one-time gain, we increased our earnings per share 5.8 percent in the recent year, and we increased our net income 6.5 percent.*

These numbers would be very appropriate in a printed annual report, but when a speaker rattles them off one after another, there is little chance that audience members will follow them. Rather than smothering your listeners with detail, you can provide a few key numbers. (If backup information is important, you can supply it in written materials accompanying your presentation.) Notice how the following appeal uses figures to highlight the most persuasive reasons for extending a business trip, while making details available for anyone who might be interested:

> *Believe it or not, it's actually $600 cheaper for us to spend the weekend in San Francisco than to fly home on Friday after the conference. We'd save more on airfare by staying over Saturday night than the cost of meals and hotels. The difference comes from the plane tickets: $598 per person if we return on Friday versus $249 if we stay over until Sunday. Coupled with cheaper weekend rates at the hotel, we come out ahead. I've worked out the details on this fact sheet, which I'll circulate now.*

In addition to restricting the amount of statistical information you convey, it is usually best to simplify that information by rounding off numbers. It's easier to understand "almost two-thirds" than it is to absorb "64.3 percent," and "almost twice the cost" is easier to grasp than is "Item A costs $65.18, while item B runs $127.15."

Besides having too many numbers, statistic-laden presentations are too dry for all but the most dedicated and involved audiences to handle. When you are speaking to a group of nonspecialists, it's important to link your figures to a frame of reference the group will understand. Notice how the following statistics (presented in the form of examples) give new impact to the old principle that time is money:

> *For a manager who is earning $30,000 a year, wasting one hour a day costs the company $3,750 a year. For a secretary at $20,000, fifteen minutes at each of two coffee breaks costs $1,427.50. And for a $100,000-a-year executive, a two-hour lunch costs the company an extra $12,500 annually.*[13]

When a presentation contains more than a few statistics, you will probably need to use visual aids to explain them: Numbers alone are simply too confusing to understand. The material on pages 385–389 offers guidelines about how to present statistical data graphically.

Comparisons

Comparisons can make a point by showing how one idea resembles another. Some comparisons—called analogies—are *figurative*. They compare items from an unfamiliar area with items from a familiar one. By considering a few examples, you can appreciate the value of figurative comparisons to add clarity and interest to a presentation:

> "We think that sending people to one company for loans, another for insurance, and a third for brokerage services makes about as much sense as sending them to one store for eggs, a second for meat, and a third for bread."[14]
>
> "The cheap special fares advertised by some airlines are misleading, since the "mouse print" at the bottom of the page lists so many restrictions. No food chain could get away with advertising prime rib at $3 a pound, limited to six roasts per store, available only when bought in pairs Tuesday through Thursday afternoons."[15]
>
> "Corporate intelligence . . . can make you think your competitors are on to something when they may be just as rudderless as you are. It's like cheating on a test: Unless you're sitting next to the class ace, you're wasting your time."[16]

By linking the familiar with the unfamiliar, figurative analogies can also help listeners understand concepts that would otherwise be mystifying. One speaker used a figurative comparison to explain a limitation of cable modem Internet connections in terms easily understandable by non-experts:

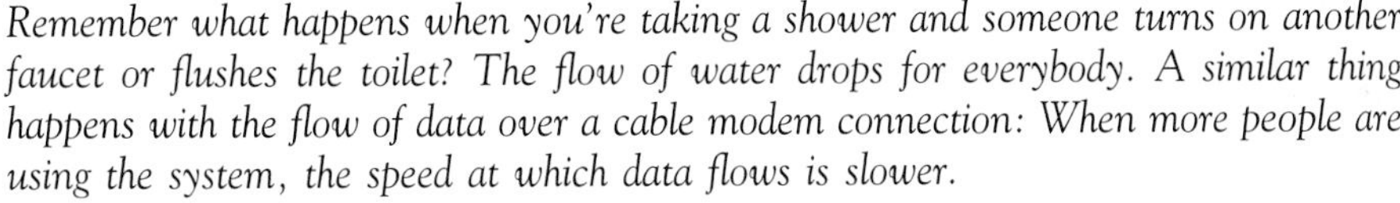

> *Remember what happens when you're taking a shower and someone turns on another faucet or flushes the toilet? The flow of water drops for everybody. A similar thing happens with the flow of data over a cable modem connection: When more people are using the system, the speed at which data flows is slower.*

Management consultants and authors have used a wide variety of comparisons to suggest how organizations can be more effective. For example, a book called *Judo Strategy* suggests that small organizations can out-compete giant competitors just like a lightweight judo master can defeat a larger opponent.[17] Other writers have shown how businesses can be more effective by resembling winning sports teams, military strategists, and even ant colonies.[18] It's easy to imagine how each of these comparisons helps clarify the concept being explained.

Other comparisons are *literal*, linking similar items from two categories. An account executive might use this sort of comparison to argue, "We need to spend more of our advertising budget on direct mail. That approach worked wonders on the NBT campaign, and I think it can do the same for us here." One critic of the banking industry used literal comparisons to show the abysmal compensation for most bank tellers:

> *If the tellers at your local bank seem a little surly these days, they've got a good reason. A comparison of their wages with those of other workers shows that they are among the worst paid workers around, according to a recent survey by the local consulting firm of Towers Perrin Foster and Crosby. Tellers earn about $16,200 annually: about*

> *$900 less than the take-home pay for mail clerks, $1,700 less than what the average custodian earns, and it's more than $6,000 less than what a computer operator brings home. When compared to secretaries, bank tellers' pay is pathetic: almost half of the $31,800 the average executive secretary earned in the 90 companies surveyed.*

After an explosion killed 12 in a West Virginia coal mine, some observers used a comparison to argue that weak federal laws make it financially worthwhile for mine owners to break safety rules:

> *Driving solo in a California carpool lane carries a bigger fine than allowing combustible materials to accumulate in a coal mine.*[19]

Whenever you propose adopting a policy or using an idea because it worked well somewhere else, you are also using comparisons as proof. The strength of this proof will depend on how clearly you can establish the similarity between the items you are comparing.

Whether their purpose is to add clarity, interest, or proof, comparisons should possess two characteristics: First, the familiar part of comparisons should be well known to the audience. For instance, it would be a mistake to say "Jumbo certificates of deposit are similar to Treasury bills in several ways" if your listeners don't know anything about Treasury bills. Second, you should be sure your comparisons are valid. You would be stretching a point if you tried to discourage employee abuse of the copying machine by claiming, "Using the machine for personal papers is a crime, just as much as robbery or assault." A closer match is both more valid and effective: "You wouldn't help yourself to spare change from a cash register; everybody with a conscience knows that would be a case of petty theft. But using the copying machine for personal papers costs the company, just as surely as if the money came out of the cash register."

Quotations

Quotations use the words of others who are authoritative or articulate to help you make a point more effectively than you could on your own. Some quotations add clarity and impact. You might, for example, add punch to a talk on the importance of listening to customer complaints by citing a successful businessperson like Bill Gates, founder of Microsoft: "Your most unhappy customers are your greatest source of learning." Likewise, you could emphasize the importance of getting agreements in writing by quoting movie producer Sam Goldwyn: "A verbal contract isn't worth the paper it's written on."

If you were trying to offer advice on how to become successful, your best bet would be to quote people who your audience recognizes as achievers. You might cite the words of Donald Trump on the importance of learning from others:

> *You can't know it all. No matter how smart you are, no matter how comprehensive your education, no matter how wide ranging your experience, there is simply no way to acquire all the wisdom you need to make your business thrive.*

Or you might repeat the words of Oprah Winfrey about taking responsibility for your own success:

> *I don't think of myself as a poor deprived ghetto girl who made good. I think of myself as somebody who from an early age knew I was responsible for myself, and I had to make good.*[20]

Some quotations are too long, boring, or confusing to read word-for-word. In these cases, you can still take advantage of the material by paraphrasing it, as in this example:

> *Before we go overboard on the idea of flexible scheduling, it's important to consider the research conducted recently by Professors Graham Staines of Rutgers University and Joseph Pleck of Wellesley College. In a survey of over 1,000 employees, they found that people who worked modified schedules were not as happy with their family lives as were people who worked a traditional Monday through Friday, 9-to-5 shift.*

Citing Your Sources

Whether you are quoting someone or using a statistic, it's both proper and effective to cite the source. Showing that your ideas are based on authoritative sources boosts your credibility.

Here is a simple four-step method for citing sources without interrupting the flow of your presentation:

1. *State your point:* "The trend of working from home is growing."
2. *Identify the source of your citation:* "In the March 12 edition of *USA Today* columnist Stephanie Armour states that . . ."
3. *State the content of your citation:* ". . . Just about anyone with a high-speed Internet connection and a telephone can become a virtual free agent, handling customer service calls for major corporations."
4. *Explain how and why the material is important for members of your audience:* "That means almost everybody in this room has the potential to work from home, whether while you are going to school, raising a child, or have limited mobility."

Use the following guidelines to cite sources.

Cite the Source in a Way That Adds to the Credibility of Your Presentation Notice how the citations in this section introduce their source, and consider how much less effective they would be without this sort of introduction.

Cite Sources That Have Credibility with Your Audience Citing Karl Marx about the abuse of workers won't impress an audience of Republican manufacturers, while a similar message from an article in *The Wall Street Journal* might be effective.

Restate the Point of Long Citations If your citation has taken a minute or two to deliver, summarize the point it makes before moving on:

> "After hearing Roberta's figures, you can see that our advertising dollars are well spent."
>
> "You can see from this research that there are hidden costs in this proposal."
>
> "Customer letters like those make it clear that we need to improve our service."

Visual Aids

The old cliché is true: A picture often *is* worth a thousand words. That is why charts, diagrams, and other graphic aids are part of most business presentations.

Researchers have verified what good speakers have always known intuitively: Using visual aids makes a presentation more effective. In one study, two groups of business students watched videotaped presentations describing upcoming time-management

Appeal to Varied Learning Styles

Not everyone learns the same way. Scholars have discovered three distinct learning styles.

Auditory learners absorb information best by listening and speaking. They benefit from hearing detailed descriptions and having the chance to recite or repeat information. You can help auditory learners by making sure your descriptions are clear and reinforced with plenty of verbal support, and by providing plenty of opportunities for audience feedback.

Visual learners thrive on visual aids of various types: video clips, charts, maps, pictures, slides, posters, charts, and graphs. For example, a visual learner would do better with maps and diagrams than with a set of written or spoken directions.

Tactile learners succeed by *doing*, rather than listening or observing. They like outlines to write on and time to take notes. These learners will volunteer to role play or demonstrate something you are teaching. They appreciate being able to move around while learning—passing out materials, handling models, and so on.

Most audiences will contain people with all three learning styles, so your best bet is to design presentations that include verbal, visual, and interactive types of supporting material.

Note: For more information on learning styles, instruments to assess your learning style, and suggestions for presenting to all learning styles, go to any of these sites:
www.vark-learn.com/english/index.asp
www.ldrc.ca/projects/miinventory/miinventory.php?eightstyles51
www2.ncsu.edu/ltc/guides/learning_styles/quiz.html
www.berghuis.co.nz/abiator/lsi/lsitestresults.html

seminars. One group saw a version of the talk with no visual support, while the other saw the same talk with a number of high-quality visuals. After the presentation, audience members were asked about their willingness to enroll in the time-management course and about their opinion of the speaker they had just viewed.

Audience members who saw the presentation with visuals were clearly more impressed than those who saw the same talk with no visual support. They planned to spend 16.4 percent more time and 26.4 percent more money on the time-management seminar being promoted. They also viewed the speaker as more clear, concise, professional, persuasive, and interesting.[21]

Well-designed graphics are also easier to understand than words alone. A chart listing a point-by-point comparison of two products is easier to follow than a detailed narrative. A plummeting sales curve tells the story more eloquently than any words. You can appreciate the value of visuals to make a point quickly and clearly by reading the following text alone and then seeing how the chart in Figure 11–1 makes the information so much clearer:

> *The power of tax-free accumulation is tremendous. Suppose you invested $10,000 at 10 percent. If you were taxed at a rate of 33 percent, your investment would grow to $35,236 over 20 years. If you were in the 28 percent tax bracket, your original nest egg would grow to $40,169. But with a tax-free investment, the original $10,000 would appreciate to a value of $67,275.*

Visuals can help make complicated statistics easier for you to explain and easier for your listeners to understand. Besides increasing the clarity of your material, visuals will make your presentations more interesting. For example, investment brokers often use an array of well-prepared charts, tables, models, and so on, to add variety to information that would be deadly dull without it.

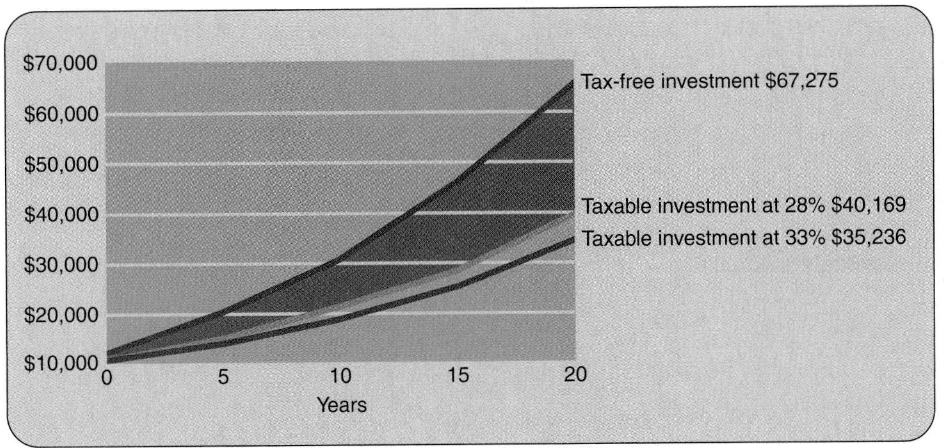

FIGURE 11–1

A visual aid is often clearer and more dramatic than words alone.

Visuals can also boost your image in ways that extend beyond the presentation itself. A professional display of visuals labels you as a professional person—a candidate for recognition in the future by superiors and the public. Finally, visuals can make your information more memorable. Researchers have discovered that audiences recall far more information when it is presented both verbally and visually than when it is presented in only one way:[22]

Visual aids perform many useful functions:

- They can *show how things look*. An architect might use a model or an artist's sketch to describe a project to potential clients, and an advertising director could use photographs of a new product as part of a campaign.
- They can *show how things work*. An engineer could include diagrams as part of the instructions for a piece of equipment, and a sales representative could use a model to show how a boat is designed for speed and safety.
- They can *show how things relate to one another*. An organizational chart provides a clear picture of the reporting relationships in a company; a flowchart pictures the steps necessary to get a job done.
- They can *emphasize important points*. You might use a chart to show customers the features of a new product or develop a graph to show the performance of a stock.

Types of Visual Aids

As a speaker, you can choose from a wide array of visual aids to make your presentations more effective. You won't use them all every time you speak, but sooner or later you will, in your presentations, use almost every type described in the following pages.

Objects and Models Sometimes the object you are discussing or a realistic model is the best kind of support. This is especially true in training sessions and in some types of selling, where hands-on experience is essential. It's difficult to imagine learning how to operate a piece of equipment without actually giving it a try, and few customers would buy an expensive, unfamiliar piece of merchandise without seeing it demonstrated.

When you do use an object or model, be sure the item is large enough for everyone to see. Small items like a microchip or a ring can work in a one-on-one presentation, but this approach will only frustrate a larger group of listeners. It is almost

FIGURE 11–2
Floor Plan

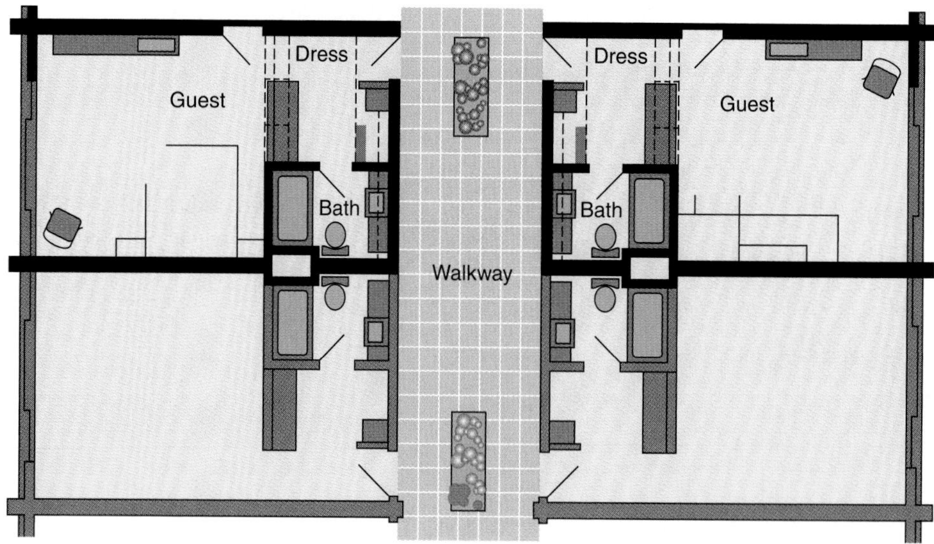

always a bad idea to pass an object around for the audience to examine. Doing so will probably distract both the person who has the object at a given moment and the other people who are craning their necks to get a preview.

Photographs Photographs can be the most effective means of illustrating a variety of images that need literal representation: an architectural firm's best work, a corporation's management team, or a stylish new product. Photographs also provide an excellent form of proof. For instance, an insurance investigator's picture of a wrecked auto may be all that exists of a car months later, when a claim is argued in court.

Diagrams Diagrams are abstract, two-dimensional drawings that show the important properties of objects without being completely representational. Types of diagrams you might use in presentations include floor plans (see Figure 11–2), drawings (see Figure 11–3), and maps (see Figure 11–4). Diagrams are excellent for conveying information about size, shape, and structure.

FIGURE 11–3
Drawing

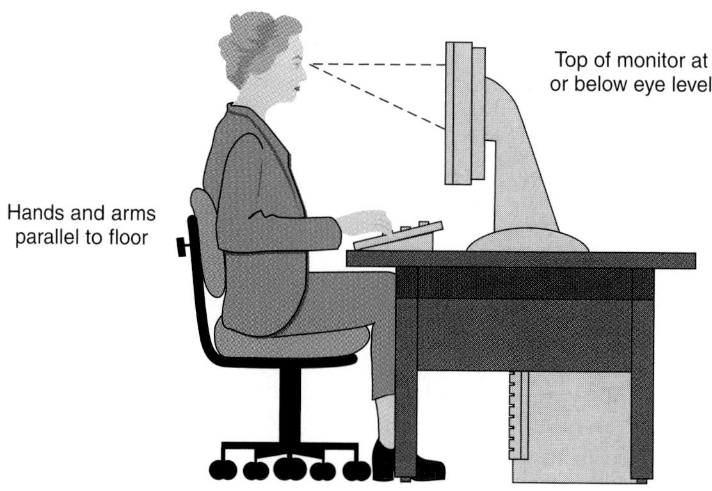

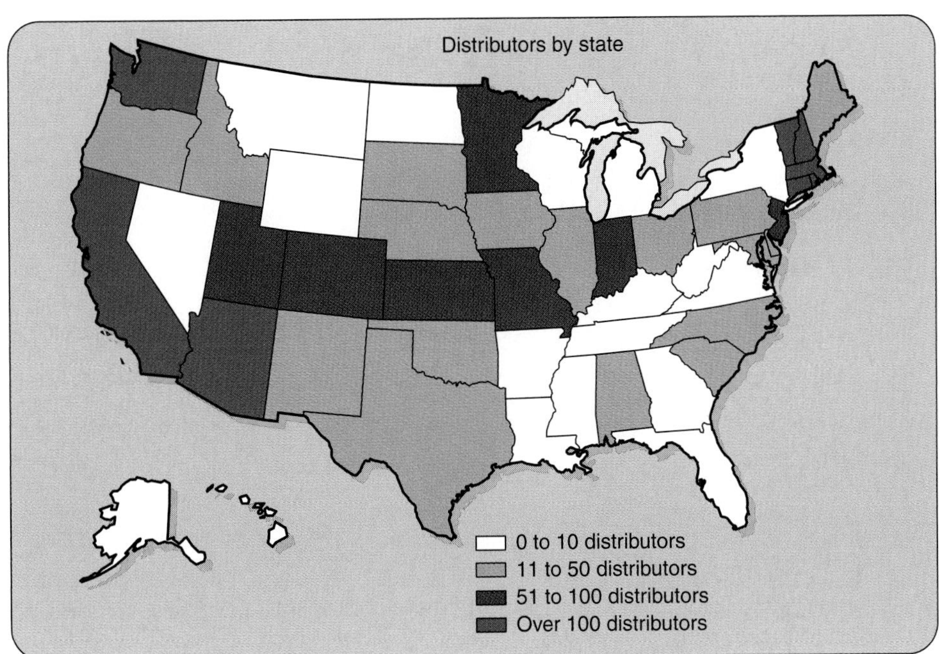

FIGURE 11–4
Map

Lists and Tables Lists and tables are effective means of highlighting key facts and figures. They are especially effective when you list steps, highlight features, or compare related facts: advantages and disadvantages, current and past performance, your product versus a competitor's, and so on. The table in Figure 11–5 clearly lists the added benefits available to employees of larger companies. A sales manager might use a similar chart to compare this year's sales performance and last year's in several regions. A human resources officer explaining the advantages and disadvantages of two different health insurance plans available to employees might use a list or table to help individual employees decide which plan might work best for them.

Amateur speakers often assume they need only enlarge tables from a written report for an oral presentation. In practice, this approach rarely works. Most written tables

College Costs, 1996–2006

	Private 4-Year	Public 4-Year	Community College
1996–97	$12,994	$2,975	$1,465
1997–98	$13,785	$3,111	$1,567
1998–99	$14,709	$3,247	$1,554
1999–2000	$15,518	$3,362	$1,649
2000–1	$16,072	$3,508	$1,642
2001–2	$17,377	$3,766	$1,608
2002–3	$18,060	$4,098	$1,674
2003–4	$18,950	$4,645	$1,909
2004–5	$20,045	$5,126	$2,078
2005–6	$21,235	$5,491	$2,191

FIGURE 11–5
Table

FIGURE 11–6
Pie Chart

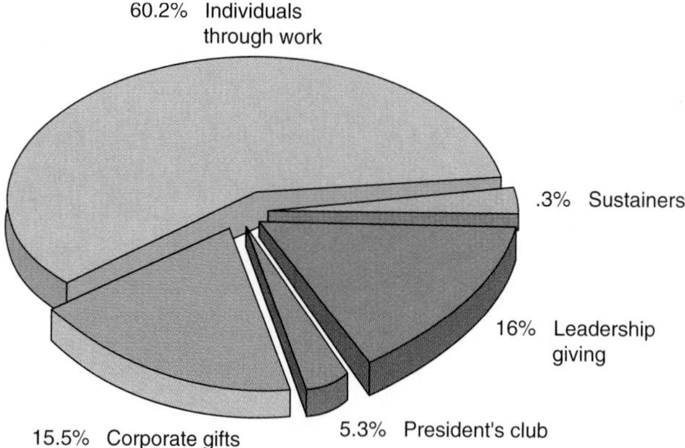

are far too detailed and difficult to understand to be useful to a group of listeners. As you design lists and tables for presentation, remember the following points:

- *Keep the visual aid simple.* List only highlights. Use only key words or phrases, never full sentences.
- *Use numbered and/or bulleted lists to emphasize key points.* Numbered lists suggest ranking or steps in a process, while bulleted lists work best for items that are equally important.
- *Use text sparingly.* If you need more than eight lines of text, create two or more tables. Lines of text should never exceed 25 characters across, including spaces.
- *Use large type.* Make sure that the words and numbers are large enough to be read by everyone in the audience.
- *Enhance the list's or table's readability.* Careful layout and generous use of white space will make it easy to read.

Pie Charts **Pie charts** like the one in Figure 11–6 illustrate component percentages of a single item. Frequently, they are used to show how money is spent. They also can illustrate the allocation of resources. For example, a personnel director might use a pie chart to show the percentage of employees who work in each division of the company.

Many computer graphics programs make it easy to produce attractive and dramatic pie charts by tilting the figure or removing one segment. While this highlighting can attract interest, it also risks distorting the data. Follow these guidelines when constructing pie charts:

- *Place the segment you want to emphasize at the top-center* (12 o'clock) *position* on the circle. When you are not emphasizing any segments, organize the wedges from largest to smallest, beginning at 12 o'clock with the largest one.
- *Label each segment,* either inside or outside the figure.
- *List the percentage for each segment* as well as its label.

Bar and Column Charts **Bar charts** like the one shown in Figure 11–7 compare the value of several items: the productivity of several employees, the relative amount of advertising money spent on different media, and so on. Simple **column charts** like the one in Figure 11–8 reflect changes in a single item over time. Multiple-column charts like the one in Figure 11–9 compare several items over time.

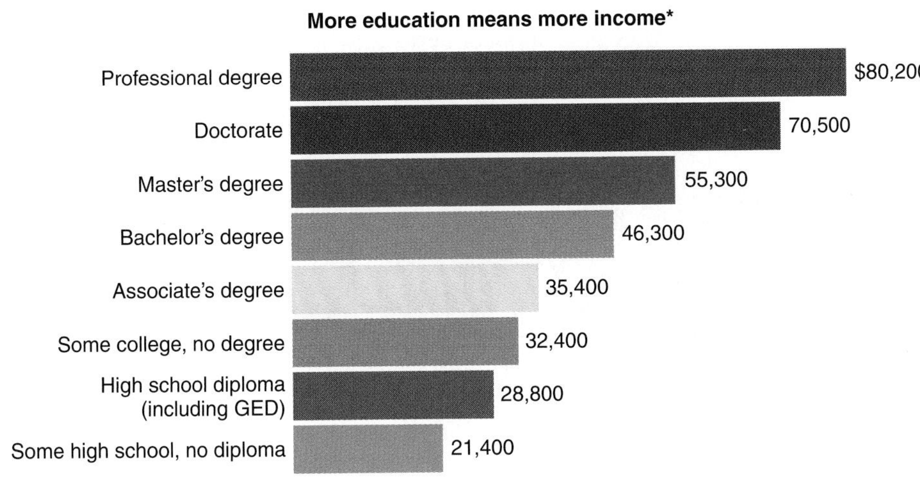

FIGURE 11–7
Bar Chart

**All figures are median income.*
Source: U.S. Bureau of Labor Statistics.

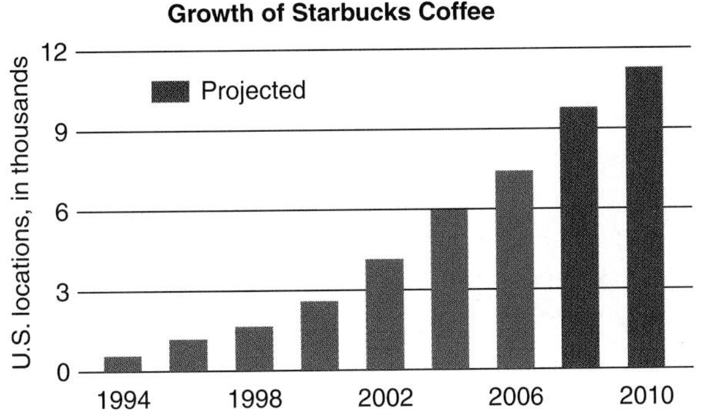

FIGURE 11–8
Simple Column Chart

Source for projections: CIBC World Markets.

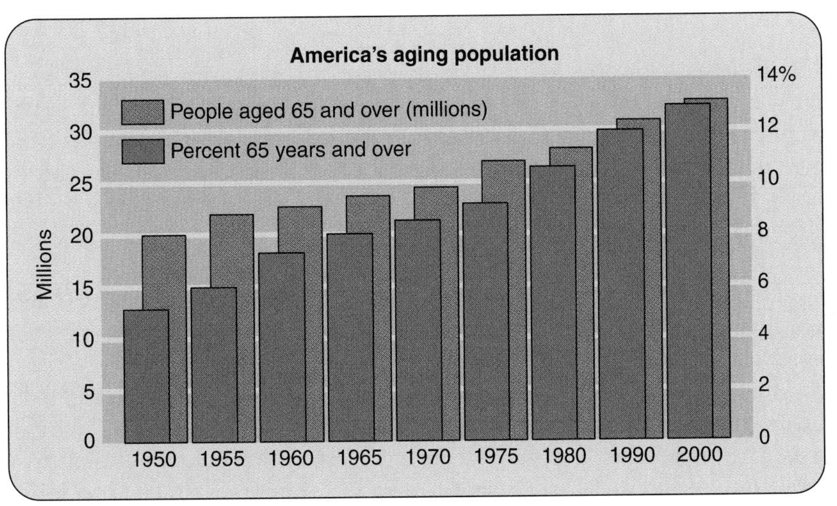

FIGURE 11–9
Multiple-Column Chart

FIGURE 11–10
Pictogram

Several tips will help you design effective bar and column charts:

- *Always represent time on the horizontal axis* of your chart, running from left to right.
- *Arrange the bars in a sequence* that best suits your purpose. You might choose to order them from high to low, from low to high, in alphabetical order, or in order of importance.
- *Make sure the numerical values represented are clear.* This may mean putting the numbers next to bars or columns. In other cases, the figures will fit inside the bars. In a few instances, the scale on the axes will make numbering each bar unnecessary.

Pictograms **Pictograms** are artistic variations of bar, column, or pie charts. As Figure 11–10 shows, pictograms are more interesting than ordinary bars. This makes them useful in presentations aimed at lay audiences such as the general public. Pictograms are often not mathematically exact, however, which makes them less suited for reports that require precise data.

Graphs **Graphs** show the correlation between two quantities. They are ideally suited to showing trends, such as growth or decline in sales over time. They can also represent a large amount of data without becoming cluttered. Graphs can chart a single trend, or show relationships among two or more trends like the one in Figure 11–11. Notice in Figure 11–12 how identical data can be manipulated by adjusting the horizontal and vertical axes.

Video There are times when video support is a plus. If you are illustrating action—the performance of an athletic team or the gestures of a speaker, for example—video may do the job better than any other medium.

Despite the benefits of video, including footage that you have created yourself can be risky. Even with easy-to-use digital editing software, there is likely to be a gap between what you can create yourself and professional-quality work. Common problems with amateur work include segments that last too long, that

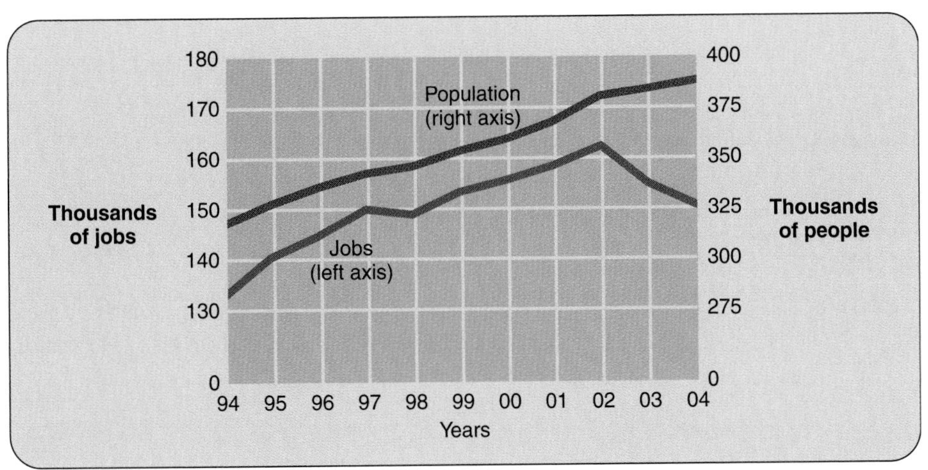

FIGURE 11–11
Multiple-Line Graph

lack the kind of narration and musical accompaniment that add continuity, and that are full of jerky images and awkward cuts between shots. The risk of using amateur videos containing flaws like these is that they will cast the rest of your message in an unprofessional light. This is why most business communication experts use only video programs that have been professionally prepared—usually at considerable expense.

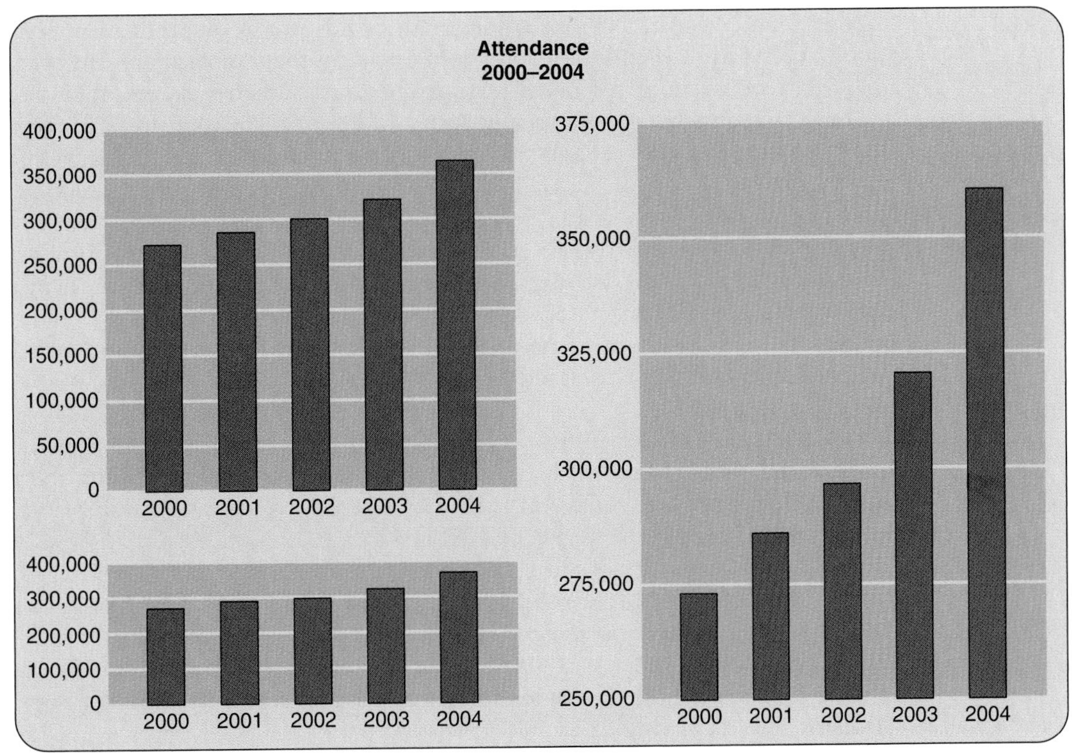

FIGURE 11–12
The same data can be distorted by varying the horizontal and vertical size and axes of a graph. These graphs were created using Microsoft PowerPoint.

ethical challenge

Fooling with Averages

Imagine that you are making a proposal about an investment opportunity to a potential client. The profit figures you are displaying in a column graph show fluctuating returns over the past few years:

- 2002: 5 percent
- 2003: 4 percent
- 2004: 7 percent
- 2005: 6 percent
- 2006: 9 percent

If you use only the even-numbered or only the odd-numbered years in your chart, you can suggest that there is an unbroken upward trend. The results look less impressive if you display every year's returns. What should you do?

Media for Presenting Visual Aids

Choosing the most advantageous way to present your visual aids is just as important as picking the right type. The best photograph, chart, or diagram will flop if it isn't displayed effectively.

Chalk- and Dry-Erase Marker Boards Every student is familiar with chalkboards and dry-erase marker boards. When these boards are available in a presentation room, they can be useful for recording information that comes up on the spot, such as a tally of audience responses to your questions. When you are presenting preplanned visuals, though, it's usually best to use a medium that doesn't require you to turn your back on the audience and write or draw freehand.

Sometimes you will be recording and organizing audience input, such as ideas in a brainstorming session. In cases like this, consider writing ideas on large-size Post-it notes instead of directly on a board. This makes it easy for you (or other participants) to recategorize the ideas without having to erase and rewrite them. Also, you can take the sticky notes with you at the end of your talk as a record of the points. By contrast, the words written on a chalk- or whiteboard dissolve into a mass of particles when you erase them.

Flip Charts and Poster Board **Flip charts** consist of a large pad of paper attached to an easel. You reveal visuals on a flip chart one at a time by turning the pages. You can also produce visuals on rigid poster board, which you can display on the same sort of easel.

A major advantage of flip charts and poster displays is that they are relatively simple to prepare and easy to use. Their low-tech nature eliminates the risk of equipment problems. Also, you can create them with familiar materials: pens, rulers, and so on. Most copy shops can also turn computer-generated files into high-quality posters. In addition, flip charts and poster boards are relatively portable (most easels collapse into a carrying case) and easy to set up.

Despite these advantages, flip charts and poster boards have several potential drawbacks: First, they may be too small for some members of a large audience to see easily. Second, they are relatively fragile and can become shabby after being handled in presentations. Finally, posters and large charts are clumsy. They don't fit in a briefcase or under an airplane seat, and they make it awkward to perform simple maneuvers like shaking hands or catching a taxi.

Transparencies and Photographic Slides **Transparencies** are clear sheets, usually the size of standard business paper, that are used with an overhead projector to cast an image on a screen. Transparencies have several advantages: They can be produced quickly—in seconds with the right printer or copying machine. They are often easier to create than other types of visuals, since you can copy professional-looking visuals from other sources instead of creating images from scratch. (Be sure to give credit to the original creator.) They can be projected to a large size for all members of a large audience to see. They are visible in a lighted room. Using special pens, you can draw on them as you speak, underlining key words, circling important numbers, completing graphs, and so on. After the presentation, you can erase your additions and reuse the same sheets in future presentations. Finally, but equally important, transparency projectors are usually available in meeting rooms.

Transparencies also suffer from several drawbacks: They may seem old-fashioned to audiences used to computer-based presentations and they require a bulky projector with a vertical arm that may have to be positioned in a special way so it doesn't block anyone's view.

Photographic **slides** have different uses and properties, although they are projected on a screen like overhead transparencies. They work best when you want to show an actual photographic image. They are easy to edit: You can add, delete, and rearrange them to suit the needs of a particular presentation.

The biggest drawback of slides is the need for a darkened room. While the projector is on, the speaker is only a shadowy figure to the audience.

Presentations using slides or an overhead projector will be most effective when you remember several points:

- *Show images only when you are discussing them.* Between transparencies or slides, shut off the projector or insert a blank screen.
- *Stand near the screen and face the audience as you speak.* Use a pointer to refer to the slide or transparency as it appears. (Use a remote control with a slide projector or have an assistant cycle through images on your command.) Don't turn your back on the audience and point to the screen.
- *Never remove or replace transparencies while the projector is on.* Position a sheet, and then turn on the machine. Turn it off, and then remove the sheet.
- *Cover the parts of a transparency you haven't discussed yet.* As you come to each point, move the cover (usually a piece of paper or cardboard) to reveal the new information. This technique prevents your audience from getting ahead of you. Be aware that particularly in a less formal setting, some audiences may see this technique as controlling or condescending.
- *Keep the slide show brief.* The distraction factor will be smallest if you don't keep the room dark for a long time. Don't dwell on each frame. Everyone has suffered through a seemingly endless narrative of boring frames, and the same abuses can occur in business presentations.

Computer Displays You can burn a CD-ROM or DVD that contains a wealth of material for your presentations: photos, charts, graphs, and video. With the right display, you can even use a computer to create visuals during your presentation: a Web site demonstration, for example, or a brainstorming list.

You have several options for displaying images produced by a computer. The cheapest and easiest output device is the screen of your own computer, but its small size limits you to an audience of only a few people. Data projectors allow the user to project images from the computer onto a large screen, where these images can be seen easily by an audience.

With all computer-assisted displays, keep Murphy's Law in mind: Whatever can go wrong with the system probably will. Beware of compatibility problems. Test all parts of the system together, just as you plan to use it, ideally in the place where you will speak. A sophisticated display is useless if it doesn't work when you are standing in front of an expectant audience.

Video Players If you don't have a computer with DVD capability handy, you can still include video in your presentations by using a DVD or videotape player (VCR) and a TV monitor or data projector. Video works especially well to illustrate real-world activity. The equipment is usually available in most meeting venues, and it can be used without having to darken the room.

Handouts **Handouts** provide a permanent record of your ideas. Intricate features of a product, names and phone numbers, or "do's and don'ts" are easier to recall when your listeners have a printed record of them. Handouts also enable you to give your audience more details than you want to talk about in your presentation. You might, for instance, mention the highlights of a sales period or briefly outline the technical features of a new product and then refer your listeners to a handout for further information.[23]

You can use handouts to reduce or eliminate your listeners' need to take notes. If you put key ideas and figures on a handout, listeners' attention will be focused on you instead of on their notebooks—and you'll be sure their notes are accurate. Some speakers use an "electronic blackboard," a plastic write-and-wipe board that can produce handout-sized copies of what you've written on the board.

The biggest problem with handouts is that they can be distracting. The activity that accompanies passing around papers interrupts the flow of your presentation. Once the handout is distributed, you'll have to compete with it for your audience's attention. For this reason, it's better to distribute handouts *after* you've finished speaking. If printed material has to be introduced during your presentation, tell your listeners when to begin referring to it and when to stop: "Let's take a look at the budget on the pink sheet in your folders. . . . Now that we've examined the budget, let me direct your attention to the chart up here."

Presentation Software

Before personal computers became widely accessible, most business speakers had few choices about how to design visuals. They could rely on their own talent and create them by hand—usually with amateurish results—or they could turn the job over to a professional graphic artist who would produce impressive displays—usually at great cost. Now, **presentation software** allows any businessperson with a personal computer and a decent printer to create and deliver text and visuals to an audience at a level of professionalism that used to be possible only from experts.

career tip

Finding Photographs and Videos

Anyone with an Internet connection and Web browser can search among millions of online photos quickly and easily by using the search engine Google (**www.google.com**). Once on Google's home page, type in a description of the photo or drawing you are seeking and click on "Images" right above the search box. To refine your search, click on "Advanced Image Search" and enter the criteria into the on-screen form. Once you activate your search, your screen will display a list of thumbnail photos of the images. Click on any images that you want to view more closely and a larger version will appear.

When you have found an image you want to use in your presentation, you can copy and paste it into PowerPoint or other presentation program, or you can save it for future use.

Be sure to give credit to the source for any photos you use, and honor any restrictions that are posted on the Web site where you find an image.

Advantages of Presentation Software Presentation software helps speakers in many ways by enabling them to generate customized materials on an as-needed basis. Listed below are some of the things you can do with a good software program:

- Deliver an on-screen show with special effects such as smooth transitions between screens, animation, and synchronized timing that reveals each point as you raise it.
- Create visuals in many formats, including slides, overhead transparencies, and screen output.
- Organize a set of speaker's notes for yourself.
- Prepare a variety of handouts for your audience, based on your speaking notes or displays.
- Create "run-time" versions of your displays so that you can distribute copies of your presentation to people who may not have seen you speak.
- Create charts, graphs, and tables.

Microsoft PowerPoint is the dominant program in this field, chosen by over 90 percent of the speakers who use presentation software.[24] According to Microsoft's estimate, over 30 million PowerPoint presentations are made every day.[25] Like all presentation software programs, PowerPoint allows you to create and display information in both outline and slide formats. Figure 11–13 illustrates how presentation software can enhance the display of information by importing and manipulating art from the Internet or other sources.

Computer-assisted designs can often impress audiences in ways that low-tech exhibits can't match. One southern California real-estate development company wanted to convince a slow-growth-oriented city council that its proposed seven-story office building would not overwhelm its surroundings. The developers knew that the traditional architect's rendering would not convince the city council, so they hired a design consultant who used a set of computerized drawing, painting, and animation tools to create a more realistic vision of the completed product. Besides producing a better image, the computerized design proved more flexible. For

career tip

When the Lights Go Down

When you project slides or show video footage, you will probably need to turn off the room lights to help viewers see the images you are presenting. Your own experience will show you that a dim room combined with the hum of electronic equipment can create an atmosphere better suited to napping than to listening attentively. Consider the following ways to minimize putting your audience to sleep:

- *Use the most powerful projector you can get.* High-quality projectors can create an image that is bright enough to overcome normal lighting.
- *Darken only the front part of the room.* When possible, turn off lights nearest the projection screen, leaving the rest of the room lighted. Even if the room doesn't have zone lighting controls, you may be able to adjust window coverings to brighten up the audience area while keeping the screen in shadow.
- *Turn off lights for short periods.* Consider designing a presentation that only requires short periods with dimmed lighting. Unless you are a compelling speaker, your audience will probably pay attention in the darkness for only short periods.

Source: Based on suggestions by Tom Chronster, "Technology Should Not Keep Audiences in the Dark," *Presentations,* May 2002, p. 62.

example, the developers created customized versions of the drawing that showed the name of potential lessees on a sign across the building. As one of the building's planners put it, "I can show that image to Company X and ask, 'How would you like to have your company's name up there?' That's a very strong marketing tool."

Although computer-assisted design can be very effective, it isn't foolproof. Even basic presentation software programs—like their word processing and spreadsheet cousins—take time to learn. If you are using one for the first time, prepare to invest an hour or two of study and practice before turning out a finished product. It's even better to get the help of a friend or co-worker who already is skilled with a design program. Such help can save you a great deal of the time

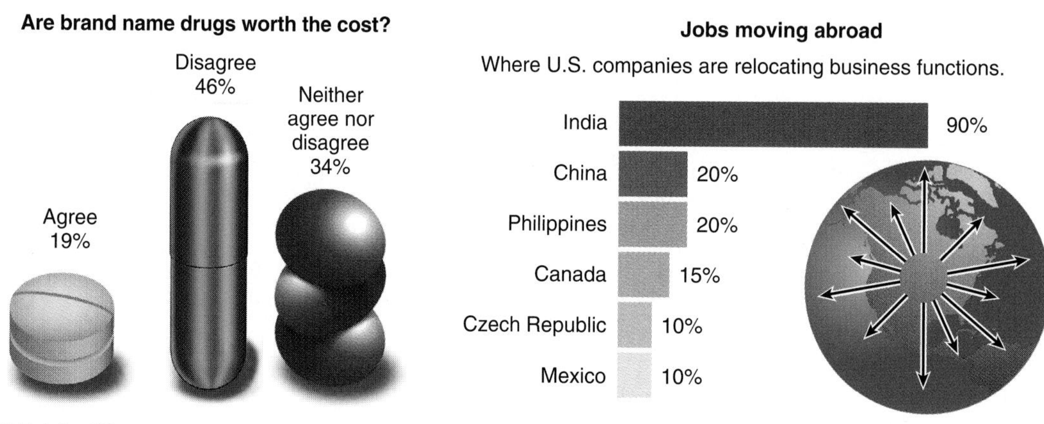

FIGURE 11–13
Spicing Up PowerPoint Slides

Source: In "MARS 2003 OTC/DTC survey," *USA Today*, June 11, 2003, pp. A1, B1.

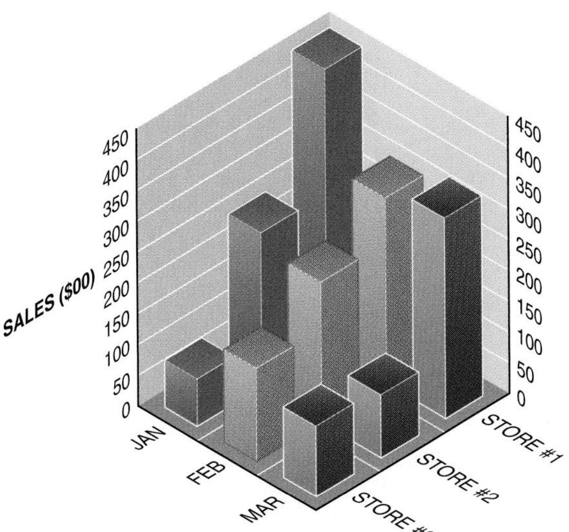

FIGURE 11–14
Displaying Data
Most presentational software programs can display data in a variety of formats. The best exhibits illustrate a point clearly without becoming too complex.

and frustration you would otherwise experience in trial-and-error experimenting or leafing through an instruction book.

Once you have mastered a program, it is important to resist the temptation to overuse it. In most presentations, simplicity is a virtue. Just because it is *possible* to produce an elaborate visual full of detail doesn't mean that this sort of display will communicate your message effectively. For example, the three-dimensional chart in Figure 11–14 is probably as complex as a visual display should be—at least in an oral presentation. If it were any more complex, the figure would be hard to understand in the limited time available for viewing. Detailed visuals may be appropriate for written reports, but in oral talks simplicity is usually the best approach.

Dangers of Presentation Software Every competent speaker should be able to use presentation software when the need arises. But, like any form of technology, PowerPoint and its cousins can cause new problems at the same time they solve old ones.[26] You should avoid several pitfalls of computerized design programs.

Poorly conceived messages Presentation software makes it relatively easy to create charts and graphs, import images, integrate snappy animation, and wrap them all up in a handsome design; but if the structure of your presentation isn't clear, listeners won't understand your message or believe what you say. For this reason, it is essential that you organize your points clearly and back up your claims before you begin transferring your message to software. Resist the temptation to format your ideas with presentation software before you have a structure that follows one of the organizational plans in Chapter 10 and make sure your points are backed up with the kinds of supporting material described earlier in this chapter.

Design over content A common mistake is to spend more time on the design of a presentation than its content. Even the most handsome slides won't make up for weak ideas. As design expert Edward Tufte says:

> *If your numbers are boring, then you've got the wrong numbers. If your words or images are not on point, making them dance in color won't make them relevant. Audience boredom is usually a content failure, not a decoration failure.*[27]

"We have lots of information technology. We just don't have any information."

There is something seductive about the ease with which you can tinker with fonts, backgrounds, and transitions. Before you know it, you will have spent far too much time without much additional return. As one expert put it:

> *We've got highly paid people sitting there formatting slides—spending hours formatting slides—because it's more fun to do that than concentrate on what you're going to say. . . . Millions of executives around the world are sitting there going "Arial? Times Roman? Twenty-four point? Eighteen point?"*[28]

Again, the best way to avoid the seduction of favoring form over content is to create at least a rough outline of your material before you start using your presentation software.

Overly complex presentations Just because you *can* use presentation software to create elaborate computer productions doesn't mean you always *should* use it. A digital display may dazzle your audience, but the spectacle might actually draw attention away from you and your message. It's hardly a success if listeners remember your terrific graphics and elaborate animation, but can't recall the points you made.

Another danger of overly elaborate presentations is the possibility that they will make material more confusing than it would have been if presented in a simpler way. This has been a problem in the U.S. armed forces, where overzealous presenters are known as "PowerPoint Rangers." Secretary of the Army Louis Caldera acknowledged that some military brass have alienated lawmakers by staging overly elaborate presentations. "People are not listening to us, because they are spending so much time trying to understand these incredibly complex slides," he says.[29]

Guidelines for Using Visual Aids

Whether you are using handouts, poster boards, flip charts, transparencies, slides, chalkboard, or computer displays, be sure to follow the basic rules discussed in this section.[30]

Selection As with any part of your presentation, visual exhibits must be chosen with care.

Be sure you have a reason for using a visual aid If your image doesn't explain a point better than words alone, don't use it. Visuals used for their own sake will distract your audience from the point you're trying to make. Douglas Vogel, a professor of management information systems at the University of Arizona, cites an example of how using animation without any purpose can backfire: "If the animation is improperly focused or too clever, people may only remember 'dancing cows' and not 'how milk may be good for you.'"[31]

Match the sophistication of your visuals to the audience Presentations to important audiences—top bosses, key customers, and so on—usually require polished graphics. There are exceptions, however. For example, financial and scientific professionals are usually receptive to a no-frills approach. Amy Ofsthun, product manager of Polaroid's Digital Palette film recorder, explains: "If they see color and exciting visuals, people feel the data is being massaged somehow. They don't trust the results."[32]

For routine talks, you can probably produce perfectly adequate exhibits on your own. Thanks to advances in computer graphics, you may even be spared the trouble of having to create figures from scratch. In any case, you shouldn't mix informal images with more formal ones any more than you would wear tennis shoes with a business suit.

Design Confusing or sloppy exhibits will be counterproductive. The simple guidelines below will help you create clear, neat images.[33]

Make sure the visual is large enough to see The visual that looks so clear on the desktop in front of you might be almost microscopic from where your listeners are seated. Avoid using items, drawings, or photographs that are so small you have to describe them or pass them around. Remember, a distracting or unclear visual is worse than no support at all.

Keep the design of your visuals simple Show only one idea per exhibit and avoid unnecessary details. Use simple typefaces.[34]

Use only a few words Most exhibits are visual images, so you should avoid excessive text. Captions should contain only key words or phrases, not sentences. Omit subtitles. Follow the "Rule of Seven": Each slide should contain no more than seven lines, and each line should have no more than seven words. If an exhibit needs further explanation, supply it verbally. Remember that you are giving an oral presentation, not showing your audience a written report.

Use only horizontal printing Avoid vertical or diagonal wording. If necessary, place captions in margins to allow you to use a horizontal format.

Label all items for clear identification Make sure each exhibit has a descriptive title. Label each axis of a chart, each part of a diagram, and so on.

Presentation The way you present your exhibits is as important as their design.

career tip

Avoiding Computer Catastrophes in Presentations

When you use computers as presentational aids, you can count on an equipment failure sooner or later. The following tips can minimize the chances that hardware or software glitches will scuttle your performance.

- *Set up in advance.* Give yourself lots of time to set up and test your equipment before the presentation is scheduled to begin. The last thing you want your audience to see is you frantically swapping cables and trying to troubleshoot software.
- *Always bring two of everything.* Assume your equipment will fail, because it certainly will at some time. Borrow backups for laptop computers, display panels or projectors, modems, and any other hardware you plan to use.
- *Back up your programs.* Having your work saved on a CD-ROM, flash drive, or some other storage medium can salvage a catastrophe.
- *Have backup technical support available.* Line up an expert who you can call if something doesn't work.
- *Beware of the Web.* Real-time use of the World Wide Web is an invitation to disaster. Connections can be slow, and Web sites can go down without notice. Whenever possible, it's best to store images of sites you will use on your hard drive and use your browser to open those files.
- *Have a contingency plan.* Be prepared for the possibility that your equipment will fail. Have copies of key exhibits prepared as handouts or overhead transparencies. They may not be as glamorous as high-tech displays, but they're far better than nothing.

Don't display a visual until you are ready for it Once you have revealed an exhibit, the audience will try to make sense of it, whether or not you are ready to discuss it. This sort of preview invites confusion and lessens the impact of the point you want to make with the exhibit. In addition, it distracts your listeners from what you are saying now.

Remove a visual after discussing it Leaving a visual on display after its usefulness is over draws away the attention of your audience. If you are using a flip chart, put blank sheets between the visuals. With an overhead projector, turn off the light between exhibits. Erase chalkboard visuals after you have referred to them.

Make sure your visuals will work in the meeting room Double-check the availability of easels, screens, and other equipment you'll need. Be sure that electrical outlets are in the right locations and extension cords are available if you will need them. Check sight lines from all audience seats. Be sure you can easily control lighting levels as necessary.

Practice using your visuals Rehearse setting up and removing visuals smoothly and quickly. Review the comments you'll make with each one. Be sure exhibits are arranged in the right order and lined up properly so that you can avoid the embarrassment of mixed-up charts or upside-down slides.

Self-Assessment Does Your Supporting Material Measure Up?

Use the scale below to answer each item. Then focus your efforts on improving your use of supporting material in areas you identified as needing work.

	Excellent 3	Competent 2	Needs Work 1
1. Each point (claim) contains at least one piece of verbal and/or visual support.	3	2	1
2. Each piece of supporting material makes my claims more:			
a. Clear	3	2	1
b. Interesting	3	2	1
c. Persuasive	3	2	1
3. I used a variety of verbal support (definitions, examples, stories, statistics, and comparisons) to add impact to my presentation.	3	2	1
4. My visuals (charts, graphs, photos, video, etc.) make my points more clear, interesting, and persuasive.	3	2	1
5. I present visuals in a way that contributes to my effectiveness:			
a. I look at my audience, not the at visuals, while speaking.	3	2	1
b. I display visuals only when discussing them.	3	2	1
c. I practiced using all technology (e.g., computers, projectors) to make sure it operates smoothly in the venue where I will speak.	3	2	1
6. I present information honestly and accurately to support my claims.	3	2	1
7. The complexity and sophistication of the materials I cite are appropriate for my audience and topic.	3	2	1
8. I cite the sources of my supporting material when appropriate. *(You don't always cite sources: e.g., for hypothetical examples, some definitions, stories you've created, etc.)*	3	2	1

summary

Supporting material is vital in any presentation. It serves three purposes: to clarify the speaker's ideas, to make the material more interesting, and to offer proof. Definitions, examples, stories (fictional, hypothetical, and factual), statistics, comparisons (figurative and literal), and quotations all serve as verbal support. Speakers create ethical and credible presentations by knowing when and how to cite their sources.

Visual aids are a common and important type of support in most business presentations. They can make a point more quickly and clearly than can words alone, add variety and interest, and boost a speaker's professional image. Visuals serve several functions: They can show how things look, how they work, or how they relate to one another, and they can highlight important information.

Speakers can use several types of visual aids: objects, models, photographs, diagrams, lists and tables, pie charts, bar and column charts, pictograms, graphs, and videos. These visuals can be presented via a number of media: flip charts and posterboard displays, transparencies, photographic slides, computer displays, videoplayers, and handouts.

Presentation software such as PowerPoint allows presenters to develop professional-looking visual exhibits quickly and easily. Given the ease of creating presentation aids, it is important not to overuse special features that result in cluttered and overstimulating, but unclear, aids. Speakers must plan their message carefully, emphasize content over design, and strive for simplicity and clarity.

Whatever the medium, all visuals should follow the same basic rules. They should be easy to understand, purposeful, well suited to the point they illustrate and to the audience, and workable in the presentational setting. Speakers should be familiar with the visuals they use to avoid any unpleasant surprises when the time for delivery comes.

key terms

Test your understanding of these key terms by visiting the Online Learning Center Web site at www.mhhe.com/adler9.

activities

Go to the self-quizzes at the Online Learning Center at www.mhhe.com/adler9 to test your knowledge of chapter concepts.

1. Invitation to Insight

Read a printed version of a speech. You can find sample speeches in your college library or at online sites such as Federal Observer (**http://www.federalobserver.com/speeches.php**) or Newsmax (**http://www.newsmax.com/hottopics/Great_Speeches.shtml**).

Find examples of at least three types of supporting material. For each item, categorize which type of support it is. How well does it follow the guidelines in the text (for example, if it's a citation, does it follow the four-step method?). Then analyze whether the supporting material provides clarity, interest, and/or proof of the thesis. In your analysis, consider the interests and knowledge level of the intended audience. Does this support appeal most to auditory, visual, or tactile learners?

2. Skill Builder

Which types of support introduced in this chapter (definition, statistics, etc.) would you use to add interest, clarity, and proof to the following points? Provide specific examples.

a. Tuition costs are keeping promising students out of college.
b. Textbooks are (are not) overpriced.
c. Timely payment of bills is in the customer's best interest.
d. Companies are helping themselves as well as employees by sponsoring and subsidizing exercise programs during work hours.
e. A liberal arts education can benefit one's career—better in many ways than technical training.

3. Skill Builder

Construct a brief speech about one of the types of supporting material identified in the text. In your mini-speech, present a brief attention-getter, a definition, and a visual aid that illustrates this type of support. Explain potential uses and misuses of this type of support. Close your speech effectively by using one of the types of conclusions discussed in the previous chapter.

4. Skill Builder

Practice your skill at developing visual aids by doing one of the following activities:

a. Develop a chart or graph showing the overall changes in the demographic characteristics (age, sex, and so on) of your student body over the past 10 years.
b. The local chamber of commerce has hired you to compile graphic exhibits that will be used in presentations to encourage people to visit and settle in your area. Design materials reflecting the following information:
i. Average monthly rainfall.
ii. Month-to-month variations in temperature.
iii. Days with sunshine.
If you believe that these figures would *discourage* an audience, choose data that paint an appealing picture of your area.
c. Develop three visual aids that could be used to introduce new students to registration procedures used in your school.

5. Skill Builder

Choose a fact or statistic you can illustrate with visual aids. Develop two different versions of your visual aid that would be effective for two different audiences or occasions (e.g., a group of children, a workshop at a scientific conference, a formal company dinner, a weekly staff meeting).

6. Skill Builder

Collect examples of each type of verbal and visual support described in this chapter. Comment on how effectively each example follows the guidelines in the text. Describe how each one should be adapted for use in an oral presentation.

7. Invitation to Insight

You can get a sense of how visual aids are used, ignored, overused, or misused by attending a presentation of your choice in the community. Identify the visual support the speaker uses and evaluate its effectiveness for the intended audience and occasion. If you had been hired as a consultant, what advice would you give the speaker about the effectiveness of his or her visual exhibits?

resources

In Print

Azarmsa, R. *Powerful Multimedia Presentations*. Belmont, CA: Wadsworth, 2004.

A comprehensive introduction to presentation technology and its applications. This text is enriched by new computer competencies in the field of instruction. The book goes beyond a step-by-step guide to PowerPoint, including sections on planning and organizing an effective presentation, producing effective presentations, using audio and video in presentations, and small and large group presentation techniques.

Ganzel, R. "Destination: Presentation." *Presentations*, February 2000, pp. 48–66.

This article provides a thorough annotated list of how to get various types of information from the

Web for your presentation and is organized by categories: cartoons, clip art, fonts, music, photos, PowerPoint templates, quotes and reference, services, speaking tips, stories, jokes, and anecdotes. Each site is annotated with a brief "What's there" and "What's not" section.

Mayer, Richard E. *Multimedia Learning*. New York: Cambridge University Press, 2001.
Drawing upon 10 years of research, the author provides seven principles for the design of multimedia messages that combine words and pictures together to promote understanding.

Tufte, E. *The Cognitive Style of PowerPoint*. Cheshire, CT: Graphics Press, 2003.
An internationally renowned expert on displaying information explains how "slideware" often reduces the analytical quality of presentations. This brief booklet also offers tips on improving presentations.

Vesper, J., and V. Ruggiero. "Using and Misusing Graphs." In *Contemporary Business Communication: From Thought to Expression*. New York: HarperCollins, 1993.
This chapter emphasizes that effective visual aids must be "judiciously chosen, carefully prepared, and joined to verbal explanations." The authors focus on the thinking process that must precede the choice of visuals.

Zelazny, Gene. *Say It with Charts: The Executive's Guide to Visual Communication*, 4th ed. McGraw-Hill, 2001. Also *Say It with Charts Workbook*. New York: McGraw-Hill, 2004.
These books show you how to create business presentations that best utilize your data and classic presentation principles. Learn to choose the correct type of chart to meet your presentation goal, how to put your ideas and data into charts that work for your audiences, and how to use animation, Web links, video, and more.

Zielinski, D. "The Great Web Copyright Crackdown." *Presentations*, July 2001, pp. 30–40.
Presenters must be careful not to violate copyright laws when using printed paragraphs, images, and music from Internet sites. This article presents information about the Digital Millennium Copyright Act, fair use, and both in-house and external presentations.

On the Web

Supporting Material

The World Wide Web provides access to a range of supporting material undreamed of by earlier generations of researchers. Without a systematic way of locating information, though, the sheer volume of material on the Web can be as much of a curse as a blessing. The Research It! site (**www.itools.com**) provides an array of tools that can help you find needed information quickly and easily. Research It! provides links to dictionaries (with definitions, pronunciation guides, and even rhyming words), several thesauri, tools that will translate a passage from one language to another, and anagram generators. Other tools allow you to search for biographical information by a person's name, quotations by topic, geographical data, and financial data.

Other useful sites for information resources are My Virtual Reference Desk (**www.refdesk.com**) and Information Please (**www.infoplease.com**). Online Newspapers (**www.OnlineNewspapers.com**) indexes 10,000 newspapers around the world and links to their home pages. FindArticles (**www.findarticles.com**) lets you search by key word or subject to articles from over 300 magazines. Quotation Search (**www.quotationspage.com**) provides options for finding quotations in several categories including classic, motivational, and cynical. Use **www.clipart.com** for inexpensive clip art to add visual interest to presentations.

The quality of information on the Web is uneven, and uncritical use can result in including inaccurate material in a presentation. You can evaluate the quality of Web pages you use in your research by taking advantage of several resources designed for this purpose. Evaluating Internet Resources (**www.snc.edu/library/guides/evalnet.htm**) from St. Norbert College Library has links to Web sites that illustrate authority, accuracy, currency, content, objectivity, access, and design. Another source for evaluating Web sites and other informational sources is "How to Critically Analyze Information Sources" at **www.library.cornell.edu/t/help/res_strategy/evaluating/analyze.html**.

Finally, an excellent check sheet to evaluate an informational Web page is at **www.widener.edu/Tools_Resources/Libraries/Wolfgram_Memorial_Library/Evaluate_Web_Pages/659**.

Creating Graphs and Charts

At the Create A Graph Web site (**http://nces.ed.gov/nceskids/graphing**) you can input your own data and then design charts and graphs that can be cut and pasted into your own presentations.

For guidelines on preparing presentation aids go to **http://docme.mc.duke.edu/presentations/Presentation%20Guidelines%20-%20Photos.ppt**.

Tutorials for Microsoft PowerPoint

Microsoft's PowerPoint is the most commonly used software program for creating and presenting computer-generated visual aids in presentations. The program has a multitude of features that make it both powerful and confusing to use. In addition to the tutorial on the CD-ROM that accompanies this book, some useful tutorials for beginning users can be found at

- **www.iupui.edu/~webtrain/tutorials/powerpoint2000_basics.html**
- **www.utexas.edu/its/training/handouts/UTOPIA_PowerpointGS/**
- **www.bcschools.net/staff/PowerPointHelp.htm**
- **www.microsoft.com/office/powerpoint/prodinfo/overview.mspx**

For guidelines on choosing fonts:

- **http://www.presentations.com/presentations/creation/article_display.jsp?vnu_content_id=1000875169**

12 Delivering the Presentation

Chapter Outline

Chapter Objectives

After reading this chapter, you should be able to

1 Choose and use the delivery type best suited for a given presentation.

2 Create and deliver effective extemporaneous and impromptu presentations.

3 Conduct an effective question-and-answer session following suggested guidelines.

4 Apply knowledge about speaker anxiety to speak effectively to others with minimal negative effects.

In an age of instantaneous communication via telephone, computer, and fax, face-to-face presentations might seem like an anachronism. Presentations are enormous consumers of time: Just scheduling a date when everyone can attend can be a major chore. Then the audience members have to travel to the location of the talk—sometimes across the hall, but just as often much farther afield. After the message is delivered, the speaker and audience have to finish up their business and get back to work. With all this effort, even a 10-minute talk to a five-person audience takes at least an hour of working time—much more than it would take to deliver the same message in writing or even over the telephone. As one expert notes, "If it were only about the material, we could simply e-mail our presentations to audiences and have them e-mail any questions back."[1]

Despite their apparent inefficiency, presentations are still an important part of doing business—and with good reason. The potential advantages of speaking to an audience face-to-face are tremendous. You can control the attention of your audience instead of risking the chance that your message will be shuffled aside. You can share your enthusiasm about the message in a way that words on paper or spoken over the telephone can't match. If your listeners have questions or objections, you can address them directly.

To take advantage of these strengths, a presentation has to be well delivered. If you look sloppy, speak in a way that is hard to understand, or seem unenthusiastic, the face-to-face medium changes from an asset to a liability. Instead of leading the audience members to accept your message, poor delivery can cause them to doubt or even reject it. As communication consultant Roger Ailes puts it, "You become the message. People cannot distinguish between the words and who speaks them."[2]

The following pages will offer suggestions that can help you deliver your remarks in a way that makes your message clearer, more interesting, and more persuasive. They describe the various styles of delivery, offer tips for improving your visual and vocal performance, explain how to deal with questions from the audience, and give advice for dealing with the nervousness that often accompanies an important presentation.

Types of Delivery

The word "presentation" may conjure up images of a speaker standing behind a lectern delivering information to a passive audience. While some business and professional presentations follow this model, many of them are far more interactive.

When it comes to presentation style, there are three patterns:[3] *Monologues* are one-way speeches, delivered without interruption. These are most appropriate in large settings and on formal occasions. In smaller groups they can feel artificial and create the impression that the speaker doesn't care much about the audience. *Guided discussions* are more interactive. A speaker presents information and has a preset idea of what material to cover, but listeners are encouraged to speak up with questions and comments. Managing a guided discussion is more challenging, but the potential for more audience buy-in can be worth the effort. *Interactive presentations*, as their name implies, involve the audience even more. The speaker may still stand while listeners sit, and may still use visuals and other aids, but the event feels more like a conversation than a presentation. Interactive presentations are common in sales settings, where the interests of the customer should drive the communication.

When it comes to actually delivering material, speakers have four options, though two of them are so potentially disastrous that only uninformed speakers use them.

Manuscript Presentations

In **manuscript presentations,** speakers read their remarks word-for-word from a prepared statement. Manuscript speaking is common at annual companywide meetings, conventions, and press conferences. Yet few experiences are as boring as the average manuscript presentation.

The most dynamic and personable managers often try to conceal their nervousness at facing a large audience by reading from a script—and they turn into lifeless drones. Since most speakers are not trained at reading aloud, their delivery is halting and jerky. Even worse, a nervous speaker who relies too heavily on a manuscript can make serious mistakes without even knowing it. Management consultant Marilyn Landis describes one such disaster:

> *I remember the president of a large corporation who followed his usual pattern of asking his public relations director to write a speech for him. Due to a collating error, the script contained two copies of page five. You guessed it. The president read page five twice—and didn't even realize it.*[4]

Even when a speaker reads a report flawlessly, the presentation often sounds mechanical and lifeless. To make things worse, the text of a manuscript presentation is often a copy of a written report—usually far too long and detailed for effective oral presentation. "I don't know why we have to sit through people reading a report that's been copied and distributed," one manager complained. "I can read it myself a lot faster."

In legal or legislative testimony, diplomatic speeches, or other situations in which a slight misstatement could have serious consequences, manuscript speaking may be your best means of delivery. Most presentations, however, do not fall into this category. A simple but important rule for most cases, then, is *don't read your presentation*.

Memorized Presentations

If speaking from a script is bad, trying to memorize that script is even worse. You probably have been subjected to a door-to-door salesperson's obviously memorized pitch for magazine subscriptions or carpet cleaning. If so, you know that the biggest problem of a **memorized presentation**—one recited word-for-word from memory—is that it *sounds* memorized.

the neighborhood™ Jerry Van Amerongen

"I think it's safe to say Charlie, himself, was aware of what was proving to be a tedious and uneven presentation..."

It might seem that memorizing a presentation would help with your nervousness, but memorizing almost guarantees that stage fright will become a serious problem. Speakers who spend great amounts of time simply learning the words of a talk are asking for trouble. During the presentation, they must focus on remembering what comes next instead of getting involved in the meaning of their remarks. One expert describes the kinds of problems that can follow from trying to memorize a script:

> *Never memorize! You cannot communicate with your audience if you're struggling to remember each word of a speech. And what happens if you forget?*
>
> *"Studio One" was one of the most popular shows in the golden days of live television. During one memorable broadcast, the scene was the interior of an airplane cabin. The plane was at an altitude of 30,000 feet, flying over the mountains of Tibet. Three men were in the cabin talking when suddenly there was silence. One of the actors had forgotten his lines. There were no retakes, no stopping of the action. That was it. Millions of eager viewers were glued to their black-and-white screens, waiting to see what would happen next. What did the actor do? He got to his feet, in an airplane cabin 30,000 feet over the mountains of Tibet, and voiced this immortal line: "Well, here's where I get off." He left the set and walked into history.*
>
> *If you memorize a speech and forget it anywhere along the line, you'll have to get off that plane at 30,000 feet over Tibet—and there's no parachute. But even if you do find your way back, when you memorize, the material controls you, rather than you controlling the material. Master your material, but don't memorize. Memorizing robs you of being natural.*[5]

Sometimes it's necessary to memorize parts of a presentation since referring to notes at a critical moment can diminish your credibility. A salesperson is usually expected to know the major features of the product—how much horsepower it has, how much it costs, or how many copies per minute it delivers. A personnel manager might be expected to know, without referring to a brochure, the value of the employee's life insurance (if each employee's is the same) and how much the employee contributes to the premium. A co-worker would look foolish at a retirement dinner if she said, "Everybody knows about Charlie's contributions . . ." and then had to pause to refer to her notes. For such situations, you can memorize essential *parts* of a presentation.

Extemporaneous Presentations

An **extemporaneous presentation** is planned and rehearsed, but not word-for-word. If you prepare carefully and practice your presentation several times with a friend, a family member, or even a group of co-workers or subordinates, you have a good chance of delivering an extemporaneous talk that seems spontaneous and even effortless. Virtually every presentation you plan—a sales presentation, a talk at the local high school, a progress report to a management review board, a training lecture, an annual report to employees or the board of directors—should be delivered extemporaneously.

A good extemporaneous presentation should be carefully rehearsed, but it will never be exactly the same twice because you will be speaking *with* the audience, not *at* them. As one speaking coach put it:

> *I tell presenters to strive for dialogue behavior in a monologue setting. Dialogue behavior is two people talking across a kitchen table—it's comfortable and natural, and you don't have to think much about it. Monologue behavior is a presenter talking stiffly to his slides.*[6]

Extemporaneous speakers uses notes for reminders of the order and content of ideas.There is no single best format for these notes. Some speakers prefer abbreviated outlines, while others find that index cards with key words or phrases work best. One hint if you do use note cards: It is a good idea to have them punched and on a ring, so they can't scatter if dropped.

Whatever form you use, your speaking notes should possess the following characteristics.

Notes Should Be Brief Overly detailed notes tempt a speaker to read them. Inexperienced salespeople who rely on a brochure, for instance, often wind up reading to their prospective customers. More experienced salespeople might be able to use the brochure's boldface headings as a guide. If you are using PowerPoint or overhead transparencies, the points on your slides may be all that you need to guide you.

Notes Should Be Legible Your words shouldn't turn into meaningless scribbles when you need them. The writing on your notes should be neat and large enough to be read at a glance. Better yet, use a word processor to print them out in an easy-to-read typeface and size.

career tip

Color-Coded Speaking Notes

Depending on the type of presentation you're giving, you might consider color coding your notes or note cards to help you keep your thoughts organized and your pace interesting. One author suggests using colored ink to signal parts of your speech, such as red for statistics/data, blue for personal stories, etc. This could help your eyes go readily to the items you want in your outline. Another idea is to use color for your organizational elements, such as main points in black, supporting points in red, and transitions in green. Consider colored ink, colored note cards, or colored highlighters to help you best organize your speaking notes for rapid retrieval and ease of use. If you find you are running longer than planned, you can easily spot the items you want to leave out and the items you want to move to. If you see your audience needs a break, you can retrieve your audience involvement notes.

Source: After M. Mobley, "Color Code to Improve Pacing and Flow," *Presentations*, May 2003, p. 34.

Notes Should Be Unobtrusive Most audiences won't be offended if you speak from notes, as long as the notes aren't distracting. A sheet of paper flapping in your hand can become a noisy irritation, as can shuffling several sheets of paper on a lectern. Some speakers avoid such problems by providing their listeners with a guide and then using the guide for their own notes.

Impromptu Presentations

Sooner or later you will be asked to give an **impromptu presentation**—an unexpected, off-the-cuff talk. A customer might stop in your office and ask you to describe the new model you'll have next spring. At a celebration dinner, you may be asked to "say a few words." A manager might ask you to "give us some background on the problem" or to "fill us in on your progress." You may suddenly discover at a weekly meeting that your subordinates are unaware of a process they need to know about in order to understand the project you are about to explain.

Giving an impromptu talk needn't be as threatening as it seems. Most of the time, you will be asked to speak about a subject within your expertise—such as a current project, a problem you've solved, or a technical aspect of your training—which means you have thought about it before. Another reassuring fact is that most listeners won't expect perfection in unrehearsed remarks.

Your impromptu presentations will be most effective if you follow these guidelines.[7]

Anticipate When You May Be Asked to Speak Most impromptu speaking situations won't come as a complete surprise. You may be an "expert" on the subject under discussion or at least one of the people most involved in a situation. Or perhaps your knowledge of the person in charge suggests that impromptu remarks are to be expected. In any case, if you prepare yourself just in case you're asked to speak, your remarks will be better planned and delivered.

Focus on Your Audience and the Situation Think about your audience and the situation in which you'll be speaking. What is on your listeners' minds? What are

Your Impromptu Talk

Practice your ability to speak off-the-cuff by delivering a brief (approximately 1 minute) talk to your group on a topic that has just been presented to you by your instructor, or which you have just drawn out of a hat.

Remember to follow the guidelines for impromptu speaking on these pages as you plan and deliver your remarks. Take a few minutes to organize your thoughts into an identifiable plan: topical, chronological, problem–solution, and so on. Step up with confidence, pause, then begin to present your talk to your classmates. Make sure your introduction and conclusion contain a clear statement of your thesis.

their attitudes? What are the circumstances in which you are speaking? The more you can ground your remarks in the context, the better.

Accept the Invitation with Assurance Try to look confident, even if you're less than delighted about speaking. If you stammer, stall, or look unhappy, your audience will doubt the value of your remarks before you say a word. Once asked, you're going to speak whether or not you want to. You might as well handle the situation well.

Organize Your Thoughts The safest way to avoid rambling is to use the few moments before you speak to sketch an outline—mental if necessary, jotted down if possible. It can follow the introduction-body-conclusion format described in Chapter 10. When you speak, state your thesis in the first moments you are addressing the audience: "I see several problems with that idea," or "From my experience with the Digitech project, I think our cost projections are low." If you aren't sure what your opinion is, present that thesis: "I'm not sure which approach we ought to take. I think we need to look at both of them closely before we decide."

Label each of your main points as you cover it in the body of your remarks: "My first point is that . . ." Then conclude by restating your thesis.

Present Reasons, Logic, or Facts to Support Your Viewpoint As with any presentation, your points will be clearer and more persuasive when you back them up with supporting material: statistics, examples, comparisons, and so forth. Of course, this information won't be as detailed as it would be if you had been able to prepare it in advance, but provide some evidence or explanation to support your points: "As I recall, the Digitech job ran 10 percent over estimate on materials and 15 percent over on labor."

Don't Apologize Nobody expects a set of impromptu remarks to be perfectly polished, so it is a mistake to highlight your lack of knowledge or preparation. Remarks like "You caught me off guard" or "I'm not sure whether this is right" are unnecessary. If you really don't have anything to contribute, say so.

Don't Ramble Many novice speakers make the mistake of delivering their message and then continuing to talk: "So that's my point: I think the potential gains make the risk worthwhile. Sure, we'll be taking a chance, but look what we stand to win. That's why I think it's not just a matter of chance, but a calculated risk, and one that makes sense. We'll never know unless we try, and . . ." The speaker needed only one sentence to conclude: "I think the risk is worth taking."

Guidelines for Delivery

Choosing the best method of delivery will help make your presentations effective, but it is no guarantee of total effectiveness. Your speeches will be better if you also consider the visual and vocal elements of delivery: how you look, what words you use, and how you sound.

Visual Elements

A major part of good delivery is how a speaker looks. You can improve your visual effectiveness by following several guidelines.

Dress Effectively Appearance is important in any setting. How you dress is even more important when you get up to speak, however. You may be able to hide a rumpled suit behind your desk sometimes or get away with wearing clothes more casual than usual office norms dictate the day you move your office furniture—but not when you get up to give your financial report at the annual meeting or present your latest proposal to top management.

Dressing effectively doesn't always mean dressing up. If the occasion calls for casual attire, an overly formal appearance can be just as harmful as underdressing. Automotive consultant Barry Isenberg found that an informal appearance contributed to his success as a leading speaker. While waiting to speak to an audience of hundreds of auto wreckers at a day-long seminar, Isenberg looked on as an attorney dressed impeccably in a three-piece suit gave an organized talk on warranties. Despite the importance of the topic, the audience was obviously bored silly. Isenberg rushed upstairs to his hotel room and changed out of his business suit and into the attire of his listeners—casual pants and an open-neck shirt. When his turn to speak arrived, Isenberg moved out from behind the lectern and adopted a casual speaking style that matched his outfit. Afterward, a number of listeners told Isenberg he was the first speaker who seemed to understand their business.[8]

Step Up to Speak with Confidence and Authority Employees are often surprised to discover that their forceful, personable superiors completely lose their effectiveness when they have to address a group of people—and show this before they say a word. Speakers who fidget with their hands or their clothing while waiting to speak, approach the podium as if they were about to face a firing squad, and then fumble with their notes and the microphone send the nonverbal message "I'm not sure about myself or what I have to say." An audience will discount even the best remarks with such a powerful nonverbal preface.

Your presentation begins the moment you come into the view of your listeners. Act as if you are a person whose remarks are worth listening to.

Get Set before Speaking If you need an easel or projection screen, move it into position before you begin. If a lectern needs repositioning, do it before you begin your talk. The same goes for the other details that come with so many presentations: Adjust the microphone, close the door, reset the air conditioner, rearrange the seating.

Just as important, be sure to position yourself physically before beginning. Usually out of nervousness, some speakers blurt out their opening remarks before they are set in their speaking position. A far better approach is to stand or walk to the

career tip

Stand or Sit?

The decision whether to sit or stand during any presentation will be based upon your goals for that presentation. Certainly, in a large room without amplification, you'll need to stand to be seen and heard. It would seem awkward and unnecessary to stand when presenting to one other person over coffee. There are other times, however, when the decision to sit or stand could go either way.

Consider standing when you want to

- Be perceived as taking charge.
- Be able to breathe and project better.
- See and be seen by the audience and maintain eye contact.
- Stand out from other speakers, who may be seated.

Consider sitting when you want to

- Be seen as building rapport with the group.
- Be considered part of the team.
- Avoid being labeled arrogant or show-stealing.

Source: After J. A. Daly and I. N. Engleberg, *Presentations in Everyday Life*, 2nd ed. (Boston: Houghton Mifflin, 2005), p. 263.

position from which you will talk, get set, wait a brief moment (a "power pause") while you connect with your audience, and then begin speaking.

Begin without Looking at Your Notes Make contact with the audience as you begin speaking. You can't establish a connection if you are reading from notes. You can memorize the precise wording of your opening statement, but it isn't really necessary. Whether you say "I have a new process that will give you more reliable results at a lower cost" or "My new process is more reliable and costs less" isn't critical: The important thing is to make your point while speaking directly to your listeners.

Establish and Maintain Eye Contact A speaker who talks directly to an audience will be seen as more involved and sincere. Whether you're proposing an innovative new product line, reassuring your employees about the effects of recent budget cuts, or trying to convince a group of local citizens that your company is interested in curbing pollution, your impression on the audience can ultimately determine your success.

This kind of immediacy comes in great part from the degree of eye contact between speaker and listeners. Use the moment before you speak to establish a relationship with your audience. Look around the room. Get in touch with the fact that you are talking to real human beings: the people you work with, the potential customers who have real problems and concerns you can help with, and so on. Let them know by your glance that you are interested in them. Be sure your glance covers virtually everyone in the room. Look about randomly: A mechanical right-to-left sweep of the group will make you look like a robot. Many speech consultants recommend taking in the whole room as you speak. If the audience is too large for you to make eye contact with each person, choose a few people in different parts of the room, making eye contact with each one for a few seconds.

Stand and Move Effectively Table 12–1 describes some effective and ineffective ways to stand and move when you are speaking. The best stance for delivering a presentation is relaxed but firm. The speaker's feet are planted firmly on the ground

Table 12–1 Common Interpretations of Speaker's Body Language

Viewed as dictatorial or arrogant:
- Crossed arms
- Pounding fists
- Hands on hips
- Pointing index finger
- Hands behind back
- Hands in "steeple" position
- Hands on lapel or hem of jacket
- Preening gestures

Viewed as insecure or nervous:
- Gripping the lectern
- Chewing on objects, cuticles, fingernails, lips
- Constant throat clearing
- Playing with hair, beard, jewelry
- Rocking back and forth
- Rubbing or picking at clothes or body
- Clenched fists
- Jingling coins or keys in pockets or hands
- Repeatedly putting glasses on and off
- Slouching
- Standing extremely rigidly

Viewed as open and confident:
- Open hands
- Expansive gestures
- Stepping out from behind the lectern
- Walking toward and into the audience
- Animated facial expressions
- Dramatic pauses
- Confident and consistent eye contact

Source: After Dianna Bocher, *Speak with Confidence: Powerful Presentations That Inform, Inspire and Persuade* (New York: McGraw-Hill, 2003).

and spaced at shoulder width. The body faces the audience. The head is upright, turning naturally to look at the audience.

Having good posture doesn't mean standing rooted to the ground. Moving about can add life to your presentation and help release nervous energy. You can approach and refer to your visual aids, walk away from and return to your original position, and approach the audience. Your actions should always be purposeful, though. Nervous pacing might make a speaker feel better, but it will turn listeners into distracted wrecks.

If you're addressing a small group, such as four or five employees or potential customers, it may be more appropriate to sit when you're delivering a presentation. Generally, the same rules apply in such cases. You should sit up straight and lean

career tip

Increasing Credibility with Good Delivery

Illogical as it may seem, listeners are often more persuaded by speakers they find appealing than by the quality of the material being presented. This is especially true when listeners don't have a strong stake in the issue. The following tips can help you deliver your remarks in a way that increases your effectiveness as a speaker.

Look good

One source of attractiveness, of course, is *appearance*. Typically this means being well dressed and well groomed. Of course, the specific look that will serve you best depends on the fashion standards of the people to whom you are speaking.

Compliment the audience

Listeners are also attracted to speakers who are *complimentary*. This doesn't mean you have to lavish your audience with phony flattery. Letting them know that you respect their accomplishments, value their judgment, or like them personally will predispose them toward accepting your viewpoint.

Demonstrate your sincerity

Speakers perceived as believing strongly in their subjects are more persuasive than unenthusiastic ones. The audience reaction is usually "If this person cares so much about the idea, there must be something to it." Sincerity is only impressive if the audience detects it, however; so be sure and share your enthusiasm and passion for your subject with the audience.

Note: For more information, see J. C. McCroskey and J. J. Teven, "Goodwill: A Reexamination of the Construct and Its Measurement," *Communication Monographs* 66 (1999), pp. 90–103.

forward—lounging back in your chair or putting a foot up on the desk indicates indifference or even contempt. Sit naturally; your behavior should be as direct and animated as it would be if you were conversing with these people—which, in a way, you are.

Don't Pack Up Early Gathering your notes or starting for your seat before concluding is a nonverbal statement that you're anxious to get your presentation finished. Even if you are, advertising the fact will only make your audience see the presentation as less valuable. Keep your attention focused on your topic and the audience until you are actually finished.

Pause, then Move Out Confidently Be certain that you drop your pitch to end your remarks so you clearly indicate that you are finished. A raised pitch sounds questioning, unsure, and leaves the audience wondering whether you are finished. When you end your remarks (or finish answering questions and recapping your thesis), pause, then move out smartly. Even if you are unhappy with yourself, don't shuffle off dejectedly or stomp away angrily. Most speakers are their own greatest critics, and there is a good chance the audience rated you more favorably than you did. If you advertise your disappointment, however, you might persuade them that you really were a flop.

Verbal Elements

The words you choose are an important part of your delivery. As you practice your presentation, keep the following points in mind.

Use an Oral-Speaking Style Spoken ideas differ in structure and content from written messages. The difference helps explain why speakers who read from a manuscript sound so stuffy and artificial. When addressing your audience, your speech will sound normal and pleasing if it follows some simple guidelines:

- *Keep most sentences short.* Long, complicated sentences may be fine in a written document, where readers can study them until the meaning is clear, but in an oral presentation your ideas will be easiest to understand if they are phrased in brief statements. Complicated sentences can leave your listeners confused: "Members of field staff, who are isolated from one another and work alone most of the time, need better technology for keeping in touch with one another while in the field as well as with the home office." The ideas are much clearer when delivered in briefer chunks: "Members of the field staff work alone most of the time. This makes it hard for them to keep in touch with one another and with the home office. They need better means of technology to stay in contact."
- *Use personal pronouns freely.* Speech that contains first-person and second-person pronouns sounds more personal and immediate. Instead of saying "People often ask," say "You might ask." Likewise, say "Our sales staff found," not "The sales staff found."
- *Use the active voice.* The active voice sounds more personal and less stuffy than passive use of verbs. Saying "It was decided" isn't as effective as saying "We decided." Do not say "The meeting was attended by 10 people"; say "10 people attended the meeting."
- *Use contractions often.* Unless you need the complete word for emphasis, contractions sound much more natural. Instead of saying "We do not expect many changes," say "We don't expect many changes." Rather than saying "I do not know; I will find out and give you an answer as soon as possible," say "I don't know; I'll find out and give you an answer as soon as possible."
- *Address your listeners by name.* Using direct forms of address makes it clear that you are really speaking to your listeners and not just reading from a set of notes. Personalized statements will help build rapport and keep an audience listening: "Frank, you and your colleagues in the payroll office are probably wondering how these changes will affect you"; "Ms. Diaz, it's a pleasure to have the chance to describe our ideas to you this morning."

Don't Emphasize Mistakes Even the best speakers forget or bungle a line occasionally. The difference between professionals and amateurs is the way they handle such mistakes. The experts simply go on, adjusting their remarks to make the error less noticeable.

Usually, an audience won't even be aware of a mistake. If listeners don't have a copy of your speaking outline, they won't know about the missing parts; even if they notice that you have skipped a section in a brochure you're going over with them or in a prepared outline you've distributed after your speech for their reference, they'll assume you did it on purpose, perhaps to save time. If you lose your place in your notes, a brief pause will be almost unnoticeable—as long as you don't emphasize it by frantically pawing through your notes.

What about obvious mistakes—citing the wrong figures, mispronouncing a name, or trying to use equipment that doesn't work, for example? The best response here is again the least noticeable. "Let me correct that. The totals are for the first quarter of the year, not just for March," you might say and then move on. When equipment fails, adapt and move on: "The chart with those figures seems to be missing. Let me summarize it for you."

Finally, don't emphasize what you *didn't* do (I didn't have time to create a chart like I wanted to"); instead, emphasize what you *did* do ("I researched the sales figures for the past 5 years").

Use Proper Vocabulary, Enunciation, and Pronunciation The language of a board of directors' meeting or a formal press conference is different from that of a factory workers' meeting or an informal gathering of sales representatives at a resort. It is important to choose language that is appropriate to the particular setting.

It is also important to pronounce your words correctly. Few mistakes will erode your credibility or irritate an audience as quickly as will mispronouncing an important term or name: The word is *scenario,* not "screenario," and the author of this book likes to be called "Adler," not "Alder." Enunciation—articulating words clearly and distinctly—is also important. "We are comin' out with a new data processin' system" makes the speaker sound ignorant to many people, even if the ideas are good.

Vocal Elements

How you sound is just as important as what you say and how you look. Speakers' voices are especially effective at communicating their attitudes about themselves, their topics, and their listeners: enthusiasm or disinterest, confidence or nervousness, friendliness or hostility, respect or disdain. The following guidelines are important elements in effective communication.

Speak with Enthusiasm and Sincerity If you don't appear to feel strongly about the importance of your topic, there's little chance the audience will. Yet professionals often seem indifferent when they present ideas they're deeply committed to.[9]

The best way to generate enthusiasm is to think of your presentation as sharing ideas you truly believe in and speak with conviction, in your own style. Consultant Roger Ailes makes this point emphatically:

> *The truth is, no one can manufacture an image for anyone. If you want to improve or enhance yourself in some way, the only thing a consultant can do for you is to advise and guide you. We can point out assets and liabilities in your style and we then offer substitutions and suggestions to aid you. You have to want to improve and work at it. Most importantly, whatever changes you make have to conform to who you really are—at your best. All the grooming suggestions, all the speech coaching, all the knowledge about lighting, staging, and media training—everything popularly associated with "image-making"—won't work if the improvements don't fit comfortably with who you essentially are.*[10]

In the stress of making a presentation, you might forget how important your remarks are. To prevent this, remind yourself of why you are speaking in the moments before you speak. Thinking about what you want to say can put life back into your delivery.

Speak Loudly Enough to Be Heard At the very least, a quiet voice makes it likely that listeners won't hear important information. In addition, listeners often

Self-Assessment Evaluating Your Delivery

Either on campus or using other resources, use a camcorder to capture a rehearsal of a presentation you are planning. If possible, present your remarks to at least one or two listeners, who will represent your real audience.

After your presentation, review the recording and note the effectiveness of your delivery in each of the following areas.

Visual Elements

___ I dressed effectively.
___ I stepped up with confidence and authority.
___ I got set before speaking.
___ I began speaking without looking at notes.
___ I maintained eye contact throughout my presentation.
___ I stood and moved effectively.
___ I didn't pack up before concluding.
___ Upon conclusion, I paused and then moved out confidently.

Verbal Elements

___ I used an oral-speaking style.
___ I didn't emphasize my mistakes.
___ I used proper vocabulary, enunciation, and pronunciation.

Vocal Elements

___ I spoke with enthusiasm and sincerity.
___ I spoke loudly enough to be heard.
___ I avoided disfluencies.
___ I varied the rate, pitch, and volume of my voice.
___ I used pauses effectively.

Your first rehearsal will probably reveal things you want to change about your delivery. After noting areas you want to improve, record and review the presentation again. Repeat this process until you are satisfied with the results.

interpret an overly soft voice as a sign of timidity or lack of conviction. ("She just didn't sound very sure of herself.") Shouting is offensive, too ("Does he think he can force his product down our throats?"), but a speaker ought to project enough to be heard clearly and to sound confident.

Avoid Disfluencies **Disfluencies** are those stammers and stutters ("eh," "um," and so forth) that creep into everyone's language at one time or another. Other "filler words" are "ya know," "like," "so," "OK," and so on. A few disfluencies will be virtually unnoticeable in a presentation; in fact, without them, the talk might seem overly rehearsed and stilted. An excess of jumbles, stumbles, and fillers, however, makes a speaker sound disorganized, nervous, and uncertain.

Vary Your Speech Just as in your best everyday speaking style, the rate, pitch, and volume of your speech in a presentation should vary. Let your genuine enthusiasm for the topic and situation drive your speaking style, just as it does in your everyday conversations. Be sure to slow down and speak slightly louder when you are stating your thesis and your main points, however. Your audience understands such cues to mean "This is important."

Use Pauses Effectively Don't be afraid of silence; it can be used for emphasis, to give your audience time to consider what you've presented, to formulate an answer to a question you've posed, or to indicate the importance of what you've just said. Being comfortable with pauses indicates you're comfortable in the role of speaker; every second does not have to be filled in with words.

Question-and-Answer Sessions

The chance to answer questions on the spot is one of the biggest advantages of oral presentations. Whereas a written report might leave readers confused or unimpressed, your on-the-spot response to questions and concerns can win over an audience.

Audience questions are a part of almost every business and professional talk from sales presentations and training sessions to boardroom meetings. Sometimes question-and-answer sessions are a separate part of the presentation. Other times, they are mingled with the speaker's remarks. In any case, a skillful response to questions is essential.

career tip

Using a Microphone

Sooner or later you are likely to face a speaking situation where you'll need to use a microphone. Microphones are generally one of two types: a stationary one that is attached to a podium or a lavaliere model that clips onto your clothing and requires you to wear a transmitter (about the size of a pack of cigarettes).

When using a stationary microphone, try to keep about 6 to 8 inches between your lips and the mouthpiece to avoid a very nasal or very thin-sounding voice. Keep the microphone about an inch below your lip level to avoid the "popping" sound that can accompany puffs of breath used in sounds like "p" and "t." Maintain a consistent distance for uniform volume. A one-directional microphone has only one spot that picks up sound so even turning your head can prevent your voice from being picked up. A multidirectional mike allows more animated movement, since it can pick up your voice even if you move slightly to one side or the other of the mouthpiece.

With a lavaliere microphone, you have greater range of body motion and can walk around more freely; however, you'll need to plan your dress more carefully. Ideally, choose an outfit with a sturdy lapel or collar to clip the microphone onto. Turtlenecks or collarless tops may not allow the proper distance from lips to microphone; the microphone might flop around on very flimsy fabrics like soft silks or thin knits. When you turn, turn your whole body, not just your head, so that you are always speaking into the microphone. You'll also need to consider the "transmitter bulge." The transmitter might fit easily into pants with front pockets and pleats, in a jacket's inside packet, or clip onto a belt under a loose-fitting jacket. Avoid tight-fitting pants and jackets that won't accommodate the transmitter without an unsightly hump.

Whatever type of microphone you use, test it in advance. If there is someone in charge of the sound system, introduce yourself and ask for any advice with regard to the particular equipment and room. Practice by asking someone to check your volume while sitting in various parts of the room. Move around with a lavaliere microphone to see if any areas of the room produce interference, buzzing, or high-pitched sounds. Be sure your movements don't dislodge the microphone and be certain that you switch it off before and after speaking so that any private conversations remain private.

Source: From Tom Antion, *Great Speaking* 4, no. 6 (April 24, 2002), retrieved from **www.antion.com/ezine/v4n6.txt**; Susan Berkley, "Microphone Tips," *Great Speaking* 4, no. 7 (May 14, 2002), retrieved from **www.antion.com/ezine/v4n7.txt**; and Renee Grant-Williams, "Speak Up!" *Women in Business* 54, no. 2 (March/April 2002), p. 38.

When to Answer Questions

The first issue to consider is whether you should entertain questions at all. Sometimes you have no choice, of course. If the boss interrupts your talk to ask for some facts or figures, you're not likely to rule the question out of order. But there may be cases when time or the risk of being distracted will lead you to say something like "Because we only have 10 minutes on the agenda, I won't have time for questions. If any of you do have questions, see me after my presentation or during the break or lunch."[11] If your presentation does call for questions from the audience, you can pretty much control when they are asked.

During the Presentation Speakers often encourage their listeners to ask questions during a talk. This approach lets you respond to the concerns of your listeners immediately. If people are confused, you can set them straight by expanding on a point; if they have objections, you can respond to them on the spot.

Dealing with your listeners' questions during a talk does have its drawbacks. Some questions are premature, raising points you plan to discuss later in your talk.

career tip

Minimizing Interruptions

A few interruptions can rattle even confident speakers. The following tips can help minimize the chances that deliberate or unintentional interruptions throw you off:

- Post a sign outside the room warning that a presentation is in progress, and close the doors to the room before you begin speaking.
- Program telephones in the room to ring elsewhere, or activate voice mail to prevent them from ringing during your talk.
- Ask that questions and comments be held until the end of your presentation (if you won't be comfortable responding to them during your talk).
- Let the audience know when there will be a break in the presentation.
- Ask your audience to turn off beepers and cell phones for the duration of the presentation.
- Check with service personnel or post notices outside the room to be sure refreshments aren't delivered in the middle of your presentation.
- Be certain that setup for another event isn't about to begin in your room before you are finished. (This is especially important if you are the last speaker in a program.)

Others are irrelevant and waste both your time and your listeners'. If you decide to handle questions during a talk, follow the guidelines below.

Allow for extra time Answering questions sometimes occupies as much time as your planned talk. A 15-minute report can run a half-hour or longer with questions. If your time is limited, keep your remarks brief enough to leave time for the audience to respond.

Promise to answer premature questions later Don't feel obligated to give detailed responses to every question. If you plan to discuss the information requested by a questioner later in your talk, say, "That's a good question; I'll get to that in a moment."

After the Presentation Postponing questions until after your prepared remarks lets you control the way your information is revealed. You don't have to worry about someone distracting you with an irrelevant remark or raising an objection you plan to answer. You also have much better control over the length of your talk, lessening the risk that you'll run out of time before you run out of information.

On the other hand, when you deny listeners the chance to speak up, they may be so preoccupied with questions or concerns that they miss much of what you say. For instance, you might spend half your time talking about the benefits of a product while your listeners keep wondering whether they can afford it. In addition, since most of the information people recall is from the beginning and the end of presentations, you risk having your audience remember the high price you mentioned during the question-and-answer session or the sticky question you couldn't answer rather than the high quality you proved in your presentation.

How to Manage Questions

Whether you handle them during or after a presentation, questions from the audience can be a challenge. Some are confusing. Others are thinly veiled attacks on your position: "How much time have you New York folks spent out here in the Midwest?" Still other questions are off the topic you're discussing: "Your talk about film projectors was very interesting. I wonder, do you ever teach classes on making films?" You can handle questions most effectively by following the suggestions below.

Start the Ball Rolling Sometimes listeners may be reluctant to ask the first question. You can get a question-and-answer session rolling with your own remarks: "One question you might have is . . . ," or "The other day someone asked whether . . ." You can also encourage questions nonverbally by leaning forward as you invite the audience to speak up. You might even raise your hand as you ask for questions.

Anticipate Likely Questions Put yourself in the position of your listeners. What questions are they likely to ask? Is there a chance that they will find parts of your topic hard to understand? Might some points antagonize them? Just as you prepare for an important exam by anticipating the questions that are likely to be asked, you should try to prepare responses to the inquiries you're likely to receive.

Clarify Complicated or Confusing Questions Make sure you understand the question by rephrasing it in your own words: "If I understand you correctly, Tom, you're asking why we can't handle this problem with our present staff. Is that right?" Besides helping you understand what a questioner wants, clarification gives you a few precious moments to frame an answer. Finally, it helps other audience members to understand the question. If the audience is large, rephrase every question to make sure that it has been heard: "The gentleman asked whether we have financing terms for the equipment."

Treat Questioners with Respect There's little to gain by antagonizing or embarrassing even the most hostile questioner. You can keep your dignity and gain the support of other listeners by taking every question seriously or even complimenting the person who asks it: "I don't blame you for thinking the plan is farfetched, Nora. We thought it was strange at first, too, but the more we examined it, the better it looked."

Even when you are certain you are right, you can't win by arguing with audience members. A "yes-but" reply ("Yes, we did exceed the budget, but it wasn't our fault . . .") is likely to make you sound argumentative or defensive and antagonize the questioner. Instead, you can use a "yes-and" response: "Yes, we did exceed the budget, and that bothers us too. And that's why we included an explanation of the problems in our report."[12]

Keep Answers Focused on Your Goal Don't let questions draw you off track. Try to frame answers in ways that promote your goal: "This certainly is different from the way we did things in the old days when you and I started out, Steve. For instance, the computerized system we have now will cut both our costs and our errors. Let me review the figures once more."

You can avoid offending questioners by promising to discuss the matter with them in detail after your presentation or to send them further information: "I'd be happy to show you the electrical plans, Peggy. Let's get together this afternoon and go over them."

Buy Time When Necessary Sometimes you need a few moments to plan an answer to a surprise question. You can buy time in several ways. You can *rephrase the question:* "It sounds like everything about the project looks good to you except the schedule,

ethical challenge

Faking Your Feelings

Every speaker wants to appear confident and enthusiastic. But sometime during the course of your speaking career you are likely to face an audience when you do not feel self-assured or enthusiastic about your topic. How can you reconcile the ethical demand to be honest with the pragmatic reality that business communicators are sometimes asked to present ideas they do not personally like?

Suppose, for instance, that you have been asked to introduce a colleague who you dislike and believe is unqualified for his/her job to a group of new employees or customers. How would you handle this challenge? Or imagine that your supervisor created a proposal for your department to share certain equipment with another department. You do not favor the proposal because you foresee conflicts in completing work on time. Because you are enthusiastic and well-liked in all departments, your supervisor asks you to present the proposal to the other department "with your usual enthusiasm and persuasion." What do you do?

You may choose to use the interviewing skills described in Chapters 6 and 7 of this book to ask experienced communicators how they face these challenges. On the basis of their answers and your own thoughts, develop a policy on how accurately your public demeanor should reflect your private misgivings.

Gene." You can *turn the question around:* "How would you deal with the situation and still go ahead with the project, Mary?" You can also *turn the question outward:* "Chris, you're the best technical person we have. What's the best way to save energy costs?"

Address Your Answer to the Entire Audience Look at the person asking the question while he or she is asking it, but address your answer to everybody. This approach is effective for two reasons: First, it keeps all the audience members involved instead of making them feel like bystanders. Second, it can save you from getting trapped into a debate with hostile questioners. Most critics are likely to keep quiet if you address your response to the entire group. You may not persuade the person who has made a critical remark, but you can use your answer to gain ground with everybody else.

Follow the Last Question with a Summary Since listeners are likely to remember especially well the last words they hear you speak, always follow the question-and-answer session with a brief restatement of your thesis and perhaps a call for your audience to act in a way that accomplishes your purpose for speaking. A typical summary might sound like this:

> *I'm grateful for the chance to answer your questions. Now that we've gone over the cost projections, I think you can see why we're convinced that this proposal can help boost productivity and cut overhead by almost 10 percent overnight. We're ready to make these changes immediately. The sooner we hear from you, the sooner we can get started.*

Speaking with Confidence

If the thought of making a presentation leaves you feeling anxious, you are in good company. According to Irving Wallace and David Wallechinsky's *Book of Lists*, a sample of 3,000 Americans identified "speaking before a group" as their greatest fear, greater even than death.[13] This doesn't mean most people would rather die than give a speech, but it does suggest which event makes them more anxious.

career tip

Confidence-Building Strategies

Sooner or later, even the most confident speakers encounter a situation that generates anxiety. When this happens to you, the following tips can help you keep your feelings under control.

- Before the presentation, walk around or stretch to relieve stress and burn off excess nervous energy. Avoid alcohol and caffeine before speaking.
- Rehearse your presentation in front of friends or colleagues. Make sure your test audience tells you honestly about what works and what doesn't. It's better to learn while there is still time to adjust your approach.
- Before speaking, walk around the room and talk with people who will be listening to your presentation. This will help bridge the speaker–listener gap, and help you think of audience members as real people.
- Remember: A presentation isn't brain surgery. You are sharing what you know with people who want to know it too. Keep the presentation in perspective and you will do better.
- Wear clothing that is familiar and makes you look good. Dressing in a new outfit can contribute to discomfort and feelings like "this isn't the real me."
- During the presentation, seek out friendly faces and establish and maintain eye contact. Once you see that people are on your side, your self-confidence will grow.
- Don't try to be like anyone else. It's fine to observe speakers you admire for pointers, but develop your own approach. Recall how effective you are when you are speaking at your best, and use that as the basis of your speaking style.

Stage fright—or *communication apprehension*, as communication specialists call it—is just as much a problem for businesspeople as it is for the general population. Communispond, a New York communications consulting firm, surveyed 500 executives and found that nearly 80 percent listed stage fright as their greatest problem in speaking before a group, putting it ahead of such items as "handling hostile interrogators."[14] Another survey found that roughly a third of the population in one city suffered from more-than-normal anxiety about speaking to an audience.[15]

When the demands of a job include presentational speaking, career success can be jeopardized by speech anxiety.[16] If you get butterflies in your stomach at the thought of giving a speech, if your hands sweat and your mouth gets dry, if you feel faint or nauseated or have trouble thinking clearly, you might be comforted to know that most people, including famous performers, politicians, and business executives who frequently appear before audiences, experience some degree of nervousness about speaking. Although it is common, communication apprehension doesn't have to present a serious problem.

It is reassuring to know that, however anxious you feel, your apprehension isn't as visible as you might fear. In several studies, communicators have been asked to rate their own level of anxiety.[17] At the same time, other people gave their impression of the speaker's level of nervousness. In every case, the speakers rated themselves as looking much more nervous than the observers thought they were. Even when the anxiety is noticeable, it doesn't result in significantly lower evaluations of the speaker's effectiveness.

These research findings are good news for anxious speakers. It's reassuring to know that, even if you are frightened, your listeners aren't likely to recognize the fact or

Dilbert © Scott Adams/Dist. by United Feature Syndicate, Inc. Reprinted by permission.

find it distracting. And knowing that the audience isn't bothered by your anxiety can actually reduce a major source of nervousness, leading you to feel more confident.

Accept a Moderate Amount of Nervousness

A certain amount of anxiety is not just normal, it's even desirable. One consultant says, "If I had a way to remove all fear of speaking for you, I wouldn't do it. The day you become casual about speaking is the day you risk falling on your face."[18] The threat of botching your presentation can lead to what Edward R. Murrow once called "the sweat of perfection," spurring you to do your best. And the adrenaline rush that comes as you stand up—your body's response to a threatening situation—can make you appear more energetic, enthusiastic, and forceful than would be the case if you were more relaxed and casual.

A proper goal, then, is not to eliminate nervousness but to *control* it. As one experienced speaker put it, "The butterflies never go away; it's just that after a while they begin to fly in formation."

The time of greatest nervousness for most speakers is before they even begin speaking, when they are thinking about an upcoming presentation.[19] Once you get underway, there is a good likelihood that your anxiety will decrease. Keeping this fact in mind ("It will only get better once I start speaking") may even help reduce your prespeech nervousness.

Speak More Often

Like many unfamiliar activities—ice skating, learning to drive a car, and interviewing for a job, to mention a few—the first attempts at speaking before a group can be unnerving. One source of anxiety is lack of skill and experience. In addition, the very newness of the act is frightening.

Since newness generates anxiety, one way to become a more confident speaker is to speak more. As with other skills, your first attempts should involve modest challenges with relatively low stakes. Speech courses and workshops taught in colleges, corporations, and some community organizations provide opportunities for a group of novices to practice before one another and a supportive instructor. Once on the job, it's a good idea to make a number of beginning presentations to small, familiar audiences about noncritical matters. One corporate executive who anticipated having to give a number of important speeches and presentations began calling small meetings of his subordinates more frequently. At these meetings, he presented new information and problems to them as a group and invited them to offer critiques. As a result, he felt much more confident when it was finally time to speak to his "real" audiences.

Rehearse Your Presentation

Many presentational catastrophes come from inadequate rehearsal. Missing note cards, excessive length, clumsy wording, and confusing material can all be remedied if you practice in advance. As you add more and more technological aids to your presentation, the need for complete and careful rehearsal increases dramatically. Projector bulbs can burn out, extension cords can be too short, slides can be upside down or mixed up, and microphones can fail. It's better to find out these facts before you face a real audience.

Computer-assisted presentations can create the ultimate presentational nightmare, as two examples illustrate.

> Multimedia producer Dave Mandala was scheduled to deliver a sophisticated presentation in Hungary. Just to be safe, he shipped himself 12 monitors instead of the 8 he needed. He was horrified to open his metal-framed, cushioned packing cases to find that each one was filled with water.
>
> Craig O'Connor, a telecommuting consultant, used his own equipment to deliver an important talk. Halfway through the presentation, O'Connor's personal calendar program flashed a message onto the two huge projection screens he was using, reminding him of his wife's request to pick up a package of feminine hygiene products on the way home.[20]

Rehearsals can minimize catastrophes like these. They will also ensure that you are familiar with your material by the time you face your audience. As you practice your talk, follow the guidelines below.

Rehearse on Your Feet, before an Audience Mental rehearsal has its place, but you won't know if your ideas sound good or if they fit into the available time until you say them aloud. At least once, and probably more often, you should rehearse in front of real live listeners, not in an empty room. In fact, the more closely the size of your practice audience resembles the number of people you will face in your real presentation, the more confident you will feel.[21] David Green, a curriculum director for Dale Carnegie & Associates, explains: "That's what rehearsal is for—to get your mind off the content and onto connecting with an audience . . ."[22]

Expect Your Talk to Run 20 Percent Longer Presentations almost always run longer in real time than during rehearsals. If you are speaking for 10 minutes, rehearse for about 8. Even if your talk ultimately runs a bit short, nobody will mind.

Rehearse Three to Six Times Rehearsing fewer than three times may leave you feeling shaky about your content and more than six times can make your talk sound canned.

Pay Special Attention to Your Introduction and Conclusion Audiences remember the opening and closing of a talk most clearly. The first and last moments of your presentation have special importance, so make sure you deliver them effectively in a way that makes every word count.

Rehearse in a Real Setting If possible, rehearse in the room where you will actually speak. Make sure that you have all the equipment you will need and that it all works. The checklist in Table 12–2 can help you keep track of the materials you need.

Table 12–2 Speaking Materials Checklist

Equipment	Supplies
Overhead projector	Audio- or videotapes (blank or prerecorded)
Computer (with necessary software)	Pencils, pens
Digital projector, slide projector, or video monitor (with proper connections to computer, DVD, VCR, etc.)	Paper
Projection screen	Name cards
DVD, videotape, and/or audiotape player	Masking tape
Video camera (with connecting cables)	Chalk, marking pens
Prerecorded materials on CD or DVD	Handouts
Extension cord(s)	Attendance list
Flip chart or chalkboard	A "Presentation in Progress" sign
Easel	
Lectern	

Focus on Your Topic and Audience, Not on Yourself

Thinking about your feelings—especially difficult ones like anxiety—is understandable. But obsessing about your nervousness will only make you more anxious. It's far more productive to focus your energy on the message you are delivering and on the audience to whom you are delivering it. If you believe in what you're saying and you have a genuine desire to have your audience understand and accept your message, then your natural enthusiasm will take over and your nervousness will shrink to manageable size.

Think Rationally about Your Presentation

Some speakers feel more apprehensive because of the way they *think* about the speech than because of the act of speaking.[23] Researchers have identified a number of irrational but powerful beliefs that lead to unnecessary apprehension.[24] Among these mistaken beliefs are the following three myths.

Myth: A Presentation Must Be Perfect Whether you're addressing a meeting of potential clients worth millions of dollars to your company or a small group of trainees, your presentation must be clearly organized, well documented, and effectively delivered. Expecting it to be perfect, though, is a surefire prescription for nervousness and depression. "Practice only makes you better," says Otis Williams, Jr., founder of a professional development and training firm in Cincinnati, "but perfection doesn't exist. The goal is to become so comfortable with what you're saying, it'll roll off your tongue with minimum effort."[25] A talk can be effective without being flawless. The same principle holds for other types of speaking errors. Most listeners won't notice if you omit a point or rearrange an idea or two.

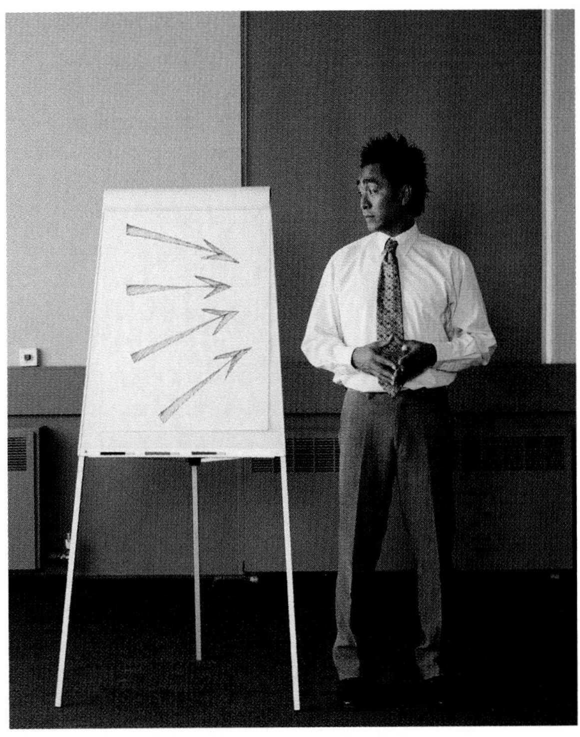

Myth: It Is Possible to Persuade the Entire Audience Even the best products don't sell to everyone, and even the most talented people don't win the full support of their audiences. It is unrealistic to expect one presentation will achieve everything you are seeking. If you think of your remarks as one step in a campaign to achieve your long-term goals, you will feel less pressure. Chapter 14 offers more tips on how to gradually move your audience toward your ultimate goal.

Myth: The Worst Will Probably Happen Some pessimistic speakers make themselves unnecessarily nervous by dwelling on the worst possible outcomes. They imagine themselves tripping on the way to the podium, going blank, or mixing up their ideas. They picture the audience asking unanswerable questions, responding with hostility, or even laughing. Even though such disasters are unlikely, these daydreams take on a life of their own and may create a self-fulfilling prophecy: The fearful thoughts themselves can cause the speaker to bungle a presentation.

Replacing this type of self-defeating thinking with more rational beliefs can result in dramatically increased confidence when you face an audience.[26] One way to overcome the irrational fear of failure is to indulge your catastrophic fantasies. Picture yourself fainting from terror, everyone falling asleep, or the boss firing you on the spot. Then consider the slim likelihood that these worst-case scenarios are likely to happen. Next, consider the possibility that you will encounter minor problems, such as being interrupted or encountering a technology glitch. Consider how you can manage these challenges, and how little they are likely to affect the success of your presentation. Now imagine the best possible outcome, such as receiving a standing ovation or an immediate promotion to the vice presidency. And consider more probable positive outcomes such as keeping the audience's attention and achieving your goal. Realize that catastrophes are unlikely and that, to a great extent, you have the power to determine the outcome of your presentation.

summary

There are four types of presentational delivery: manuscript, memorized, extemporaneous, and impromptu. With rare exceptions, an extemporaneous style is the most effective, as it combines the enthusiasm of spontaneity with the accuracy of rehearsal. A speaker's notes should be brief, legible, and inconspicuous. When an impromptu talk is necessary, it is most effective if the speaker presents a clear thesis; supports it with reasons, logic, or facts; speaks without apologizing; and does not ramble on.

Good delivery involves visual, verbal, and vocal elements. Visually a speaker needs to look enthusiastic and confident by getting set physically and making eye contact before beginning; maintaining eye contact and moving naturally; and ending without rushing away. Verbally, a speaker should use an oral style, avoid calling attention to mistakes, and use appropriate vocabulary and pronunciation. Vocally, a speaker sounds well rehearsed and committed to both the topic and the audience by using enough volume, variety, and pauses without disfluencies.

Question-and-answer sessions are part of almost every presentation. They allow a speaker to respond to an audience more quickly and completely in written documents. A speaker needs to decide whether to invite questions during or after the prepared presentation. Handling questions during a talk permits a speaker to clarify points as they arise, although there is a risk of getting sidetracked. Responding to questions after the talk lets the speaker control the time and the timing of information. Speakers can improve Q&A sessions by asking a question if no one else does, anticipating potential questions, clarifying complex questions, focusing on and addressing the audience with respect, and providing a summary.

Anxiety about speaking is common and a manageable amount of anxiety even contributes to an energetic presentation. Successful speakers keep anxiety within tolerable limits by accepting it as normal, speaking often, rehearsing, being audience-centered (not self-centered), and thinking rationally. Rational thought dispels the myths that the speech needs to be perfect to be effective, that everyone in a single presentation can be persuaded, and that catastrophes are certain.

key terms

Test your understanding of these key terms by visiting the Online Learning Center Web site at www.mhhe.com/adler9.

disfluencies 417
extemporaneous presentation 408
impromptu presentation 409
manuscript presentation 406
memorized presentation 407

activities

Go to the self-quizzes at the Online Learning Center at www.mhhe.com/adler9 to test your knowledge of chapter concepts.

1. Invitation to Insight

With two or more classmates, try the various styles of delivery for yourself. Follow these steps:

a. Begin by choosing a paragraph of text on an appropriate business or professional topic. You can write the copy yourself or select an article from a newspaper, magazine, or some other publication.

b. Read the text to your listeners verbatim. Pay attention to your feelings as you deliver the comments. Do you feel comfortable and enthusiastic? How do your listeners describe your delivery?

c. Try to memorize and then deliver the segment. How difficult is it to recall the remarks? How effective is your delivery?

d. Now deliver the same remarks extemporaneously, rephrasing them in your own words. See whether this approach leaves you more comfortable and your listeners more favorably impressed.

2. Skill Builder

Locate a section of written material from a basic text. Prepare to present the information from this section as an extemporaneous speech. Create a set of speaking notes, written as key phrases rather than as complete sentences. Your notes should be arranged in outline format with an introduction (with an attention-getter, thesis, and preview), a body (organized according to main points and supporting points), and a conclusion. Apply one of the color-coding techniques suggested in the text to the notes. Then use these notes to present the ideas extemporaneously.

3. Invitation to Insight

Scan a current television guide and select a program in which a speaker is making some sort of oral presentation. The subject matter is not important: The show can be educational, religious, political, or news-related.

a. Turn down the volume, and observe the speaker's visual delivery. Notice the effects of dress, posture, gesture, facial expression, and eye contact.

b. What do these aspects of delivery suggest about the speaker's status, enthusiasm, sincerity, and competence?

4. Invitation to Insight

Locate a television or radio program that involves an oral presentation on some subject. The content is not important. Interview shows are fine, but don't choose shows in which the characters are acting roles other than themselves. Use the criteria in the Self-Assessment on page 417 to evaluate the quality of delivery. What lessons can you apply to your speaking from your analysis of this speaker?

5. Skill Builder

Practice using an oral-speaking style. Fill in the empty boxes below with examples of effective oral language. A few examples have been completed for you.

Advice	Poor	Better
Keep most sentences short.	"Members of field staff, who are isolated from one another and work alone most of the time, need better technology for keeping in touch with one another while in the field as well as with the home office."	"Members of the field staff work alone most of the time. This makes it hard for them to keep in touch with one another and with the home office. They need better means of technology to stay in contact."
	"The idea I'd like to explain to you is that, although avoiding and accommodating seem like polite ways of interacting, it can sometimes be preferable to employ an assertive linguistic style."	
	"A substantial body of research indicates that organizing your remarks clearly can make your messages more understandable, keep your audience happy, and boost your image as a speaker."	
Use personal pronouns freely.	"People often ask . . ."	"You might ask . . ."

	"Those who attempt to use this strategy don't always succeed at first."	
	"Students would be well advised to learn strategies of effective communication."	
Use the active voice.	"It was decided that . . ."	"We decided."
	"It has been pointed out that . . ."	
	"Memorization was tried by some of the most apprehensive student speakers in the class."	
Use contractions often.	"We do not expect many changes."	"We don't expect many changes."
	"I will describe the strategies that I have found to be most effective in conducting interviews."	
	"It is important to ponder how often you have been in this situation."	
Address your listeners by name.	"We're pleased to present our ideas this morning."	"Ms. Diaz, it's a pleasure to describe our ideas to you this morning."
	"Members of the audience might like to try this idea."	
	"Last week someone gave a speech about wearing seat belts. Tonight I'll build on that theme."	

6. Invitation to Insight

You can gain useful insights about managing communication apprehension by interviewing several professionals who frequently deliver presentations. Inquire whether they have ever felt anxiety about speaking in front of others. If so, how have they managed their stage fright?

resources

In Print

Baguley, Phil, and Janet Bateman. *Teach Yourself Presenting for Professionals*. Chicago: McGraw-Hill/Contemporary Books, 2003.

Alphabetized contents and a flowchart (to "diagnosis" concerns with presentations) direct you to the pages for specific content including "using your voice" and "handling disasters." The book concludes with a list of useful Web sites for speakers.

Bocher, Dianna. *Speak with Confidence: Powerful Presentations that Inform, Inspire and Persuade*. New York: McGraw-Hill, 2003.

This book organizes 497 presentation tips into easy-to-find and -use chapters. Chapter 3, "Platform Presence," offers ideas to cope with nervousness and includes descriptions of speaker body language that is commonly interpreted in five ways: dictatorial, arrogant, nervous or insecure, open, and emphatic. Chapter 13, "Panache Despite Problems," offers suggestions for equipment failures, stumbling and tripping, forgetting, and handling various audience distractions.

Dwyer, Karen Kangas. *Conquer Your Speech Anxiety*, 2nd ed. Belmont, CA: Thomson Wadsworth, 2005.

The three key parts of this book are understanding speech anxiety, treating speech anxiety, and putting it all together. The first part focuses on definitions and causes, the second and largest part has seven chapters on treatment that include deep breathing, cognitive restructuring, systematic desensitization, visualization, and more. There are plenty of exercises and practical applications.

Lane, Geoffrey. *NuSpeak: Become a Powerful Speaker*. Vancouver, BC: Berkana Books, 1999.

The author emphasizes the importance of speaking in a genuine, authentic style in presentational and other types of business communication.

Patterson, Miles L., and Vicki Ritts. "Social and Communicative Anxiety: A Review and Meta-Analysis." In *Communication Yearbook* 20. Newbury Park, CA: Sage, 1997.

This comprehensive review and analysis of the research on communicative anxiety presents a state-of-the art overview for students interested in exploring what social scientists have learned about the topic.

Richmond, V. P., and J. C. McCroskey. *Communication: Apprehension, Avoidance, and Effectiveness*, 5th ed. Needham Heights, MA: Allyn & Bacon, 1998.

This concise book is one of the best sources of material on communication anxiety. Causes and effects of apprehension about communicating in many contexts, not only the public speaking context, are addressed and the appendix provides multiple self-report instruments for readers to assess their communication apprehension.

Thomas, L. T. *Public Speaking Anxiety: How to Face the Fear*. Fort Worth, TX: Harcourt Brace, 1997.

In just 43 pages the author examines the process of public speaking anxiety, from the thinking that initiates the anxiety to overcoming these often erroneous or exaggerated thoughts. He guides the reader into ways to use nervous excitement to strengthen the preparation and delivery of a speech.

On the Web

Computer Analysis of Verbal Messages

"Diction" is a software program that allows users to determine the tone of a verbal message. Using a powerful language analysis program, Diction searches a passage for five general features including the speaker's sense of certainty; degree of activity; optimistic or pessimistic attitude; use of specific, down-to-earth language; and similarity with the audience's values and communication style. The program includes normative data for all vocal qualities it measures, allowing users to compare their own text to a wide body of works. You can download a demonstration version at **http://www.dictionsoftware.com**.

Speaking Anxiety

Articles to help you understand and work through anxiety are plentiful. These will provide some basic perspectives: "Scared Speechless: Understanding and Conquering Stage Fright" by Tad Simons (**www.3m.com/meetingnetwork/presentations/pmag_scared_speechless.html**); "Top Ten Tips for Reducing Stage Fright" and "About Stage Fright and Performance Anxiety" by Janet Esposito (**www.performanceanxiety.com**); "Getting Over the Jitters Before You Speak" and "How to Relax for Your Talk" by Patricia Fripp (**www.planb.dk**).

13 Informative, Group, and Special-Occasion Presentations

Chapter Outline

Chapter Objectives

After reading this chapter, you should be able to

1 Prepare and deliver the following types of informative presentations: briefing, feasibility report, status report, final report, training session, and explanation.

2 Work with others to plan and deliver a group presentation.

3 Prepare and deliver the following types of special-occasion presentations: welcoming remarks, introducing another speaker, honoring a person or institution, giving a toast, and presenting and accepting an award.

After reading this far, you know how to deliver an effective presentation. The information in Chapters 10 through 12 will serve you well, but specific situations call for specific approaches. This chapter offers guidelines for delivering a variety of presentations: Informative talks (briefings, reports, training, and explanations), group presentations, and remarks you will make on special occasions (welcoming remarks, introductions, giving and accepting awards, honoring special guests, and celebratory toasts).

This chapter will build on the skills you have already learned, helping you gain the extra margin of effectiveness that can make your presentations interesting and effective—even outstanding.

Informative Presentations

Briefings, reports, training, and explanations are certainly informative, but there is also a persuasive element to most, if not all, good informative talks. Unless your audience is already motivated to hear what you have to say—whether management will be giving end-of-year bonuses in December, for example—you'll need to convince them that your remarks are worth listening to. Furthermore, you will almost always be trying to create a good impression about yourself—a persuasive goal. Despite the overlap between informative and persuasive speaking, it's worthwhile to focus on how to proceed when your primary goal is "teaching," not "preaching."

Briefings

Briefings are short talks that give already interested and knowledgeable audience members the specific information they need to do their jobs. Some briefings update listeners on what has happened in the past. For example, nurses and police officers attend briefings before each shift to learn what has been happening since their last watch. Other briefings focus on the future. The executive chef of a restaurant might brief waiters about the details of the day's menu specials, and the account representative handling an advertising account might brief the agency's team about a client's interests and quirks before an important meeting. Although used for many purposes, briefings share the following characteristics:

- *Length*. As their name suggests, most briefings are short—usually no more than 2 or 3 minutes on a given subject.
- *Organization*. Because of their brevity, briefings usually don't require the kinds of attention-grabbing introductions or conclusions described in Chapter 10. They are organized in a simple way, usually topically or chronologically.
- *Content*. Briefings may summarize a position ("As you know, we're committed to answering every phone call within 1 minute"), but they usually don't make complex arguments in its favor. Most briefing attendees already know why they are there, and the main focus should be getting them ready to do the job at hand.
- *Presentational aids*. Some briefings may include simple visual aids ("Here's what our new employee ID badges will look like"), but they rarely contain the kind of detail found in longer and more complex presentations.
- *Language and delivery*. Because of their informal nature, briefings are usually quite conversational. Delivery is more matter-of-fact than dramatic.

Here is a sample briefing for a group of representatives who are preparing to staff a start-up company's exhibit booth at a trade show. Notice that the remarks are concise and well-organized. They briefly state a thesis ("How we handle ourselves will make a huge difference") and then lay out clear instructions for the sales team.

> *This is our first chance to show the public what we've got. The way we handle ourselves the next 3 days can make a huge difference in our initial year. I know you're up to the job. Here are a few last-minute items before we get going.*
>
> *First, about the brochures: They were supposed to show up today via overnight mail, but they haven't arrived yet. Casey will keep checking with the mail room, and*

if they aren't here by 9:00 he will head over to the copy shop across the street and print out 500 fact sheets that we can use until the brochures arrive. So if the brochures are here, we'll use them. If they're not here, we hand out the fact sheets.

It's going to get very busy, especially mid-morning and mid-afternoon. You may not have as much time as you'd like to chat with visitors. At the very least, be sure to do three things. First, be sure each person is signed up for the drawing for our free Caribbean vacation. The information they give us on the sign-up sheets will help us track who visited our booth.

Second, be sure to invite each person to the reception we're giving tomorrow night. Give them one of our printed invitations so they know where and when it is.

Finally—and this is the most important thing—ask them what product they're using and how they like it. If they are happy with their current product, find out what they like about it and show them ways in which they might find ours even easier to use. If they don't like the product they're using, show them the features of ours.

Remember—stay upbeat and never criticize our competitors. Listen to the customers, and show them how our product can meet their needs. Any questions?

Reports

In a **report,** you give your audience an account of what you or someone you represent has learned or done. Reports come in an almost endless variety. Table 13–1 lists some common types. Some are internal, given to audiences within your organization. Others are external, delivered to outsiders such as clients, agencies, or the general public. Some reports are written, and others are oral. Even written reports are often presented orally. Some reports are extremely long and detailed, while others are quite brief. Finally, some reports are formal and others are presented informally.

An organization's culture determines the manner in which you present a report: brief or elaborate, with or without visual aids and question-and-answer sessions, and

Table 13–1 Common Report Types

Progress/Status

- Contractor or architect's report to client
- Quarterly financial report to board of directors
- Monthly marketing report to marketing manager
- Annual report to public

Investigative

- Was a customer's complaint justified?
- Why has our overhead increased 15 percent in the last year?
- Is there gender bias in our hiring and promotions?

Feasibility

- Will staying open 24/7 be profitable?
- Can we afford to offer health insurance to part-time staff?

so on. Learn the conventions for your audience by watching accomplished colleagues and asking experienced (and successful) co-workers.

Status Reports Probably the most common type of informative presentation is the **status report,** sometimes called a *progress report*. In many meetings, you can expect to hear someone ask, "How's the project going?"

The person asking this question usually doesn't want a long-winded blow-by-blow account of everything that has happened since your last report. You will gain the appreciation of your audience and boost your credibility by presenting a brief, clear summary of the situation. The following format will almost always serve you well. Cover each of the points briefly, and expect your listeners to pose questions when they want more information.

1. *Review the project's purpose.*
2. *State the current status of the project.* When relevant, include the people involved (giving credit for their contributions) and the methods you have used.
3. *Identify any obstacles you have encountered and attempts you have made to overcome those obstacles.* If appropriate, ask for assistance.
4. *Describe your next milestone.* Explain what steps you will take, and when they will happen.
5. *Forecast the future of the project.* Focus on your ability to finish the job as planned by the scheduled completion date.

A brief progress report would sound something like this:

> *On February 3, we were told to come up with an improved Web site for the company.* [Reviews the project's purpose.] *Paul and I have been exploring the sites of other companies in the field, and we've developed a list of features that our site should have. We'll be happy to share it with anybody who is interested.* [Describes the current status of the project. In a longer progress report, the speaker might identify the features, and even give examples of them.]
>
> *We know we'll need a Web site designer soon, and we haven't found anybody locally whose work we like.* [Identifies issues and problems. In a longer report, the speaker might list the shortcomings.] *We would welcome any suggestions you might have. If you have some names and contact information, please e-mail them to me so we'll have them in writing.*
>
> *We plan to pick a designer and have sketches ready by the end of next month.* [Describes next milestone.] *If we can do that, we should be able to have the new Web site up by the end of March, right on schedule.* [Forecasts the future of the project.]

Final Reports As its name suggests, a **final report** is delivered upon completion of an undertaking. The length and formality of a final report will depend on the scope of that undertaking. If you are describing a weekend conference to your colleagues it would most likely be quite short and informal. On the other hand, a task force reporting to top management or the general public on a year-long project would most likely deliver a detailed and much more formal report. You can adjust the following guidelines to fit your situation:

1. *Introduce the report.* State your name and your role unless everyone in the audience already knows you. Briefly describe the undertaking you are reporting on.

career tip

Technical Reports

There are two types of technical reports: those given to technical audiences (colleagues in your workplace or at technical conferences) and those given to nontechnical audiences (clients and customers with varying levels of expertise or officials in charge of money or decision making who don't share your level of mastery). Follow these guidelines for both types:

- Use language appropriate for your audience. For a nontechnical audience, use language that is understandable and teach technical terms that are essential to understanding the presentation. Jargon is useful for a technical audience that will understand it; use jargon with absolute precision.
- Use analogies to clarify concepts for a nontechnical audience, being certain to point out limits of an analogy.
- Adapt visual aids to the audience. The nontechnical audience needs visuals that make sense to non-experts; have extra visuals in even simpler formats to use if the audience seems unclear. Knowledgeable audiences appreciate precise data presented in formats common to your field; have extra visuals with more technical data if the audience requires it.
- Watch your audience carefully. If they seem puzzled, try to slow down, reiterate key points, use additional examples, or in a small, interactive group, stop and ask about the puzzled looks. If an audience seems bored or is losing interest, try to become more animated with greater vocal variety and movement.

Note: For more information on technical reports see Laura Gurak, *Oral Presentations for Technical Communication* (Boston: Allyn and Bacon, 2000); and Michael Alley, *The Craft of Scientific Presentations* (New York: Springer-Verlag, 2002).

2. *Provide necessary background.* Tell your listeners what they need to know to understand why the project was undertaken, why you and others became involved, and any other factors that affected your approach.
3. *Describe what happened.* Explain what happened during the undertaking. Aim this discussion at the level of interest appropriate for your audience. For example, if others will be following in your footsteps, give details of challenges and how you dealt with them. If other persons were involved, mention them and offer your thanks.
4. *Describe the results.* Report on the outcomes of the undertaking. Include a discussion of successes and failures. Describe any future events related to your topic.
5. *Tell listeners how to get more information.*

A very abbreviated final report might sound like this:

Hi everybody. My name is Betsy Lane, and I'm the chair of our county's United Way campaign. [Self-introduction.]

As you know, United Way is dedicated to helping people in our community to help themselves develop healthier, more productive lives. We support over 50 agencies that provide a multitude of services: Promoting wellness for all ages and abilities, making sure that all children enter school ready to learn, helping people toward lifetime independence, sustaining safe neighborhoods, and educating young people for responsible adulthood. The need and the opportunities are great, and we set the bar high this year: $3 million. [Provides necessary background.]

This has been an especially challenging year for local nonprofits: The economy has been on the weak side, and there are more deserving causes and people needing support than ever. Rather than letting this situation discourage us, it energized the United Way team. This year we were fueled by the efforts of almost 2,500 volunteers at over 400 organizations, large and small. Every one of them gave generously of their time and talents. [Describes what happened.]

I am delighted to tell you that, as of last Friday, we met our goal. The campaign has raised over $3,125,000 in donations and pledges for the coming year. This means we won't have to say "no" to a single organization. [Describes results.]

There is so much to tell you about this campaign and the work of so many terrific people. We do hope you'll read more about the effort that led to this year's success. Our report will be available in about 3 weeks, and in the meantime you can read the highlights on the United Way Web site. [Tells listeners how to get more information.]

For now, though, let's celebrate!

Feasibility Reports A **feasibility report** evaluates one or more potential action steps and recommends how the organization should proceed. Would a bonus system increase profitability and retain employees? Is job sharing a good idea? Would subsidizing employees who use public transportation solve the parking problem? Feasibility studies help answer questions like these.

Most feasibility reports should contain the following elements.[1] Figure 13–1 illustrates how they would appear in a typical report.

1. *Introduction*. Briefly define the problem and explain its consequences. Explain why it is important to consider the alternatives you will be discussing. Briefly show the audience that you have approached this problem methodically. Consider explaining your conclusions, if the audience won't object strongly. If listeners are likely to object to your recommendation, consider postponing it until later in your presentation.
2. *Criteria*. Introduce the standards you used to evaluate alternative courses of action. For example,

   - Will the course of action really do what's wanted?
   - Can we implement it?
   - Will implementation fit within time constraints?
   - Can we afford it?

   Explaining your criteria is especially important if your recommendations are likely to be controversial. It's hard for anyone to argue with criteria like those above, so getting listeners to accept them before they hear your recommendations can be an effective way of selling your conclusions. (See the criteria satisfaction organizational plan in Chapter 10.)
3. *Methodology*. Describe the process you used to identify and evaluate the plan(s) under consideration. The amount of detail you supply will depend upon the audience and situation. For a relatively minor project, your explanation will probably be brief. For a major feasibility study—especially when it's controversial or when your credibility is in question—you probably will need to describe your approach in detail.
4. *Possible solutions*. Provide a detailed explanation of each solution you considered.

I. Introduction

A. Our company has had a strong year, and we want to give back to the community that has been so good to us. The Community Relations task force has had the job of finding a way to do this that works for both this company and the people we want to support. *(Background and preview of criteria)*

B. Rather than reinvent the wheel, we have researched successful programs and consulted with both our employees and the community to find an approach that is right for our town and our company. *(Preview of approach)*

C. We think we've found an approach that will harness our employees' talents to help the community.

II. Criteria

Our Community Relations task force determined that a good program must . . .

A. Provide genuinely useful outcomes for participating students
   1. Useful workplace skills
   2. Supportive personal relationships between volunteers and students

B. Work for employees
   1. Generate enthusiastic volunteers
   2. Fit into employees' work schedules

C. Fit within company's budget and workload needs
   1. No slippage in deadlines
   2. Minimal overhead cost to company

D. Generate goodwill for the company
   1. Positive coverage in local media
   2. Recognition from schools, community organizations

III. Methodology

We searched for model programs in two ways . . .

A. Identified existing programs and evaluated them according to criteria above
   1. Via Web
   2. In publications of human resources and public information organizations
   3. Via surveys (e-mail and phone) of local schools and youth organizations

B. Solicited feedback for most promising programs from stakeholder groups:
   1. Schools and community groups
   2. Our employees
   3. Key media contacts

IV. Possible Solutions *(listed and evaluated)*

Based on our research, we identified two promising options. Each gives participating employees up to 3 weekly hours of paid "community service" time.

A. Employees participate in any local youth-based activity.
   1. Advantages: Employees choose setting in which they'll volunteer.
   2. Drawbacks: Spreading employees across many settings may reduce impact.

B. The company "adopts" a local school, where employees volunteer.
   1. Advantages: Focused effort maximizes results and publicity for company.
   2. Drawbacks: Potential for imperfect match between school's needs and employee contributions. Doesn't meet the needs of employees who want to volunteer at their children's schools.

V. Recommendation and Conclusion

We recommend adopting a single school. Maximize success of program by

A. Choosing a nearby school for quick, easy access by employee volunteers

B. Working carefully with school staff to engineer a good fit between our volunteers and the school's needs

C. Making sure employees and their supervisors develop a volunteer schedule that doesn't reduce productivity

D. Establishing relationship with local media so our program can be used as a model for other companies

FIGURE 13–1
Feasibility Report Outline

career tip

Adult Learning Styles

Adults in the workplace learn in ways that are different from methods used in educational institutions from primary school through university.

Adults learn best when

- Material is clearly relevant to their personal lives. Show them what personal value the training program will have for them. Encourage learners to explore and explain how they can use the material you present.
- Taking an active role in the training process. Don't just lecture. Give them a chance to experience the principles you are introducing.
- Training is aimed at their level of experience. Go over their heads and you will lose them; approach the topic too simplistically and you will insult and bore them.
- Given some control over the pace of learning. Be prepared to speed up or slow down your coverage in response to feedback from your audience.

Source: Based on information in M. S. Knowles, "Adult Learning," in *The ASTD Training and Development Handbook,* ed. R. L. Craig (New York: McGraw-Hill, 1996), pp. 553–565. For more information about adult learning, see **www.gwu.edu/~tip/knowles.html** and **www.infed.org/lifelonglearning/b-andra.htm**.

5. *Evaluation of the solutions*. Measure the suitability of each solution against the criteria you listed earlier. Offer whatever supporting material is necessary to show how you arrived at your conclusions.
6. *Recommendations*. Describe the solution that best fits the criteria provided earlier. If you have done a good job evaluating solutions using the criteria already introduced, the recommendation should be relatively brief and straightforward.
7. *Conclusion*. Briefly summarize your findings, showing how they can help solve the problem at hand.

Training

Training teaches listeners how to *do* something: operate a piece of equipment or use software, relate effectively with the public, avoid or deal with sexual harassment—the range of training topics is almost endless. Training can be informal, such as the simple advice an experienced employee gives a newcomer about how to transfer a telephone call. At the other end of the spectrum, some training is extensive and highly organized. Corporations including Disney, Anheuser-Busch, Dell Computer, Harley-Davidson, and General Electric have full-blown institutes dedicated to training their employees.[2]

Successful businesses recognize the value of training. One measure of its importance is the amount of time and money that firms invest in training their employees. For example, at McDonald's, every person who takes an order or prepares food has received 80 hours of instruction.[3] On any given day, International Business Machines Corporation is training 22,000 of its employees somewhere in the world. This sort of training doesn't come cheap. The annual cost of this training for IBM is $1.5 billion, not counting the participants' time.[4]

Some training is done by experts. Large organizations have staffers who design and deliver instructional programs. There are also firms and freelancers who create and deliver training on a fee-for-service basis. (See the "On The Web" resources at the end of the chapter for more information about professional trainers.) Despite the existence

of a training industry, the U.S. Bureau of Labor Statistics says that almost 75 percent of all work-related training is delivered informally on the job.[5] This fact suggests that, sooner or later, you will be responsible for designing and delivering training no matter what your job may be. The information here will help you do a good job.

Planning a Training Program A successful training presentation begins long before you face your audience, when you use the guidelines in Chapter 10 (pp. 327–336) to analyze the audience, the occasion, and your own goals and knowledge about the topic. Most training experts agree about the importance of each of the following steps.[6]

Define the training goal Training always aims to change the way your audience acts, so the place to begin is to identify who you want to teach and the results you want to bring about. The more specifically you can identify the target audience and the desired outcome, the more successful your training will be. You can see the difference between vague and specific goals in these examples:

Vague: Train employees to deal more effectively with customer complaints.

Better: Everyone in the Sales and Customer Service departments will know how to use the tactics of listening, asking questions, and agreeing to deal more effectively with customer complaints.

Vague: Train the staff to use our new online purchasing system.

Better: Employees who are authorized to buy new and replacement equipment will know how to use the new online purchasing system to locate vendors, place orders, track shipments, and check their department's purchasing budget.

See the discussion of "Setting Your Goal and Developing the Thesis" in Chapter 10 for more guidelines on defining goals.

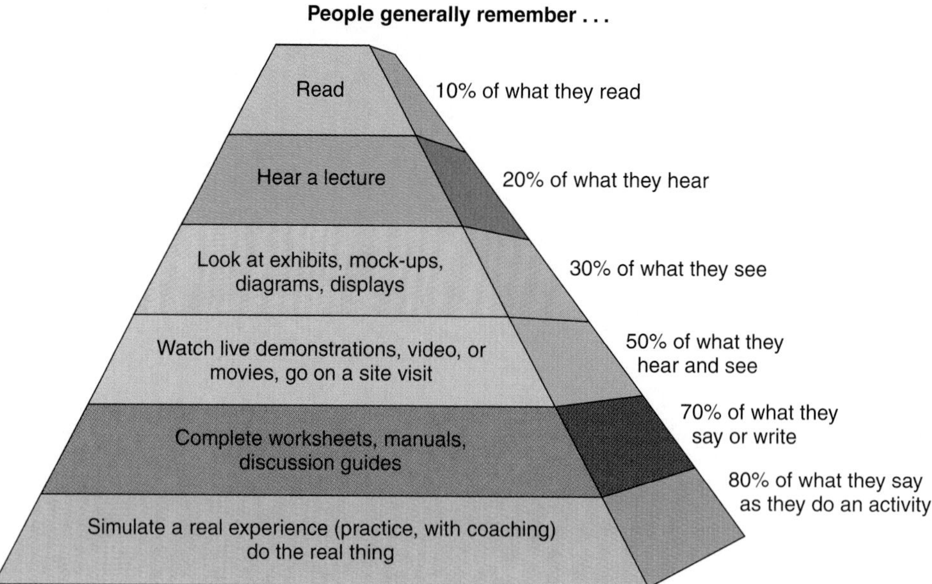

FIGURE 13–2 Average Retention Rates of Various Training Methods
An important learning principle, supported by extensive research, is that people learn best when they are actively involved in the learning process. The "lower down the cone" you go, the more you learn and retain.

Source: Reprinted by permission of NTL® Institute for Behavioral Sciences.

Develop a schedule and list of resources Once you have defined your goals and identified the target audience, you are ready to design the training. This step includes:

- Figuring how much time you will need to plan and publicize the training, and the steps you need to take between now and the time you deliver it.
- Identifying the staffing and physical resources you need, and making sure they are available. Line up the facility, and make sure its furnishings and layout suit your design. Identify the materials participants will need (pens, pencils, folders, name tags; or tents, refreshments, etc.) and the equipment you will use (computer, projection system, lectern, charts, etc.).
- Creating and/or purchasing any necessary training materials.

Involve the audience Lecturing to a passive audience has its place, but it isn't the only way to train an audience. Figure 13–2 lists several ways you can present new information. It shows that listeners who are actively involved in a presentation will understand and remember the material far better than a passive audience.[7] People will learn how to operate a particular machine, fill in a certain form, or perform a specified procedure much better with hands-on experience than they will if they are only told what to do. For example, Lever Corporation trains its representatives to sell industrial cleaning equipment by teaching them to operate the machines themselves.[8]

A variety of other tools involve the audience in a way that boosts both understanding and interest: quizzes, contests, and having trainees teach one another. For example, if you plan to give the audience statistics such as the ethnic makeup of the U.S., first present them with blank charts listing major ethnic groups and have them try to fill in the correct percentages. This way, when you present the information, they will be more eager to hear the statistics and see how accurate or inaccurate their estimates were. The few minutes you take to let an audience fill in the blanks measurably enhances interest in your figures. Similarly, you can create worksheets and surveys that mirror information you'll present. You can also involve the audience by letting them practice the skill you are teaching, having volunteers demonstrate a skill, or pausing for an audience to read a passage silently. You can let the whole audience brainstorm or form small groups to brainstorm and then let each group report back.[9]

Listeners are likely to understand and remember a message when you use more than one approach. You can show a diagram, for example, while you describe it. If you're discussing a physical object, you might display photos of it on slides or even bring in the object itself to show your listeners. If you are illustrating a process, you might decide to play a brief video of it. Talking about a new line of clothing or a new food product isn't nearly as effective as giving your audience a firsthand look or taste, for example. Likewise, telling listeners in a training session how to deal with customer objections isn't nearly as effective as demonstrating the procedure for them or letting them handle a situation themselves.

Organize your presentation Use the tips in this section and see Chapter 10 for methods of organizing the overall presentation. The most reliable format is probably a problem–solution approach, since listeners are most likely to pay attention to the information you provide when they view it as solving a problem that they face.

Delivering the Training When you finally are ready to deliver the training, several tips can help make it most effective.

Link the topic to the audience Sometimes the intrinsic interest of the subject is reason enough to listen; for instance, most people would pay close attention to a session on employee benefits because they know these benefits are worth something to them personally.

What can you do with a subject that isn't intrinsically interesting? One way to boost interest is to show that listening will help the audience avoid punishment. ("Don't try to charge the company for anything you're not entitled to. If you do, you could lose your job.") A more pleasant and effective alternative involves demonstrating the payoffs that come from listening. A financial officer explaining new expense account procedures, for instance, might begin by saying, "We want to make sure you get the company to reimburse you for all expenses you're entitled to. I also don't want you to spend your own money, thinking the company will pay you back, and then find out it won't." Expense reporting might be a tedious subject to many people, but the chance to save money (or to avoid losing money) would interest most listeners.

Start with an overall picture Every presentation needs an introduction. But when the goal is to inform listeners, a clear preview is especially important. Without an overview, your listeners can become so confused by your informational trees that they won't be able to see the conceptual forest. Orient the audience by sketching the highlights of your message in enough detail to help listeners see what they are expected to know and how you will explain it to them:

> *This morning, we're going to learn about the new e-mail system. I'll start by spending a little time explaining how the system works. Then we'll talk about the four ways you can use the system. First I'll show you how you can send messages*

to any person or group of people in the company—instantly. Then we'll talk about how you can get messages others have sent you. After that you will learn how you can put items on the companywide bulletin board. Finally, I'll show you how you can take part in companywide electronic conversations about topics that interest you.

I'll spend about 10 minutes describing each of these steps in detail, and after each description you'll get a chance to try out the system yourself. By the time we break for lunch, you should be able to use the system in a way that will save you time and hassles and keep you better informed about what you need to know to get your job done. You won't be an expert, but you'll know enough to make the system work.

Emphasize the organization of your material You can use a number of devices to help listeners understand the structure of your material:

- *Number items:* "The first advantage of the new plan is . . ." or "A second benefit the plan will give us is . . ."
- *Use signposts:* "We've talked about the benefits of our new health care plan. Now let's talk about who will provide them"; "*Another* important cost to consider is our overhead"; "*Next,* let's look at the production figures"; and "*Finally,* we need to consider changes in customer demand."
- *Use interjections:* "So what we've learned—and this is important—is that it's impossible to control personal use of office telephones."
- *Use repetition and redundancy:* "Under the old system it took 3 weeks—that's 15 working days—to get the monthly sales figures. Now we can get the numbers in just 2 days. That's right, 2 days."
- *Add internal summaries and previews:* "You can see that we've made great progress in switching to the new inventory system. As I've said, the costs were about 10 percent more than we anticipated, but we see that as a one-time expense. I wish I could be as positive about the next item on the agenda—the customer service problems we've been having. Complaints have increased. We do believe we've finally identified the problem, so let me explain it and show you how we plan to deal with it."

Cover only necessary information You will usually be far more knowledgeable about the topic than is the audience to whom you speak. This knowledge is both a blessing and a potential curse. On the one hand, your command of the subject means that you can explain the topic thoroughly. On the other hand, you may be tempted to give listeners more information than they want or need.

If you cover your topic in too much detail, you are likely to bore—or even antagonize—your listeners. One personnel specialist made this mistake when briefing a group of staffers about how to file claims with a new health insurance carrier. Instead of simply explaining what steps to take when they needed care, he launched into a 20-minute explanation of why the company chose the present carrier, how that company processed claims at its home office, and where each copy of the four-part claims form was directed after it was filed. By the time he got to the part of his talk that was truly important to the audience—how to get reimbursed for out-of-pocket expenses—the staffers were so bored and restless that they had a hard time sitting still for the information. Don't make a mistake like this in your

Dilbert © Scott Adams/Dist. by United Feature Syndicate, Inc. Reprinted by permission.

presentations: As you plan your remarks, ask yourself what your listeners need to know, and tell them just that much. If they want more information, they will probably ask for it.

Explanations

Explanations increase listeners' understanding of a subject. An orientation session for new workers falls into this category, as does a meeting in which a new employee-benefits package is introduced or a purchasing policy is explained. When a firm faces a major change in its business fortunes—whether this means growth or cutbacks—wise managers gather their employees and explain how the change will affect each one of them.

Some explanations are aimed at audiences outside the company. A utility company's representative describing the future of electrical rates to the Rotary Club meeting and a community official explaining the effects of new zoning ordinances on local industry are giving explanations. The sample speech that follows this section explains to employees how the company's tax-reduction plan will increase their real income.

The way you structure your explanation will affect how well the audience learns what you are trying to teach them. All the organizing principles in Chapter 10 apply to training sessions. Beyond these basic guidelines, two strategies will help make your ideas easy to follow.

Avoid Jargon Sometimes you will be introducing trainees to specialized terms and language. This may be as simple as introducing new employees to your company jargon for departments ("If you need help with your computer, call IRD") or locations ("This is what we call the Annex"). Some jargon is necessary, but don't use any more than necessary. If you overwhelm your listeners with too much specialized terminology, you will probably bore them and leave them so confused that they'll give up trying to understand the material you are explaining.[10] Don't be a techno-snob: Tell people what they need to know in language they will understand.

Link the Familiar to the Unfamiliar Research has shown that people have the best chance of understanding new material when it bears some relationship to information they already know.[11] Without a familiar reference point, listeners may

Poster Presentations

Most presentations have a clearly defined beginning and ending and are delivered to a fixed group of listeners. Poster sessions are different: They present work to conference attendees who are walking around an exhibit area, choosing the topics that interest them. The presenter usually stands next to the poster, allowing for passersby to engage in one-on-one discussions.

Unlike most presentations where visual aids support the words, in poster sessions a few words support the visuals. At their best, posters are visual representations of ideas, not just papers or slides tacked on a board. Clear titles allow the viewer to locate sections of interest: goals, methods, conclusions.

Practice your skill in this unique form of communication by preparing a brief poster presentation on a topic about which you are familiar. For example, presentations in a typical group might include "How to choose an Internet Service Provider," "How restaurant menus manipulate customers," or "How to choose an internship."

Some guidelines will help you conduct effective poster sessions:

- Prepare a brief (less than 1 minute) explanation of your topic that expands on the information your poster describes. You can deliver this explanation to listeners who ask general questions like "Tell me more about your work."
- Be prepared to speak louder than you usually would to a small audience. Posters are often displayed in noisy, crowded environments without good acoustics.
- Keep your enthusiasm high, remembering that each new person will be hearing your explanation for the first time.
- Be prepared to give interested listeners more information on your work. A handout with more details and/or a Web site or your e-mail address can let them follow up.

Source: Adapted from Catherine Coffin, "Planning and Preparing an Effective Scientific Poster," in *The Health Care Communication Group, Writing, Speaking, & Communication Skills for Health Professionals* (New Haven: Yale University Press, 2001), pp. 118–132. See these pages for a poster presentation checklist and the logistics of developing a poster presentation. Additional resources and slides of effective posters are available at **http://filebox.vt.edu/eng/mech/writing/workbooks/posters.html** and at **www.writing.eng.vt.edu/posters.html**.

have trouble understanding even a clear definition. Two examples illustrate how comparisons and contrasts with familiar information help make new ideas more understandable:

Confusing: Money-market funds are mutual funds that buy corporate and government short-term investments. [In order to understand this definition, the audience needs to be familiar with money-market funds and with corporate and government short-term investments.]

More Familiar: Money-market funds are like a collection of IOUs held by a middleman. The funds take cash from investors and lend it to corporations and the government, usually for between 30 and 90 days. These borrowers pay the fund interest on the loan, and that interest is passed along to the investors. [If the listeners understand IOUs and interest, they can follow this definition.]

Sample Informative Presentation

The following presentation is typical of informative talks given every business day. The personnel specialist in a medium-sized company has gathered a group of staff members together to describe the features of a tax-reduction plan explaining employee benefits. Notice how the speaker uses most of the strategies covered in this chapter to make her ideas clearer and to increase the attention of her audience.

The speaker's goal here is to help listeners decide whether they're interested enough in the benefits plan to attend a much longer meeting on the subject. She wisely chose this approach to avoid going into detail about the plan when some people might not be interested. By giving a short description of how the plan works, she can keep this introductory talk brief and simple.

[The promise of increasing take-home pay is a guaranteed attention-getter.]

I know you're busy, but I don't think you'll mind taking a few minutes away from work this morning. You see, I'm here today to show you a way that you can increase the amount of money you take home each month.

[This opening illustrates the persuasive element that is called for in many informative presentations.]

No, I'm not going to announce an across-the-board raise. But increasing your salary isn't the only way to boost your income. Another way that works just as well is to reduce your taxes. After all, every dollar less you pay in taxes is like having a dollar more in your pocket.

[An overall view of the plan is presented here.]

In the next few minutes, I'll explain the company's Flexible Benefits Plan. It's a perfectly legal option that lets you increase your real income by cutting the amount of taxes you pay, so that your income will grow even without a raise. I know this sounds too good to be true, but it really works! I've already signed up, and figure it will save me almost $2,000 a year. It can probably save you a lot, too.

[A brief transition alerts listeners to the first main point in the body of the presentation: the difference between before- and after-tax dollars.]

Before you can appreciate how the Flexible Benefits Plan works, you have to understand the difference between before-tax and after-tax dollars. [*The speaker shows Exhibit 1 here.*] Before-tax dollars are the amount that shows up every month in the "Gross Amount" box on our paychecks. But we don't get to spend our full salaries. There are several deductions: federal income tax withholding, Social Security (the amount in the "F.I.C.A." box), state tax withholding, and disability insurance premiums (the amount in the "S.D.I." box). What's left in the "Net Amount" box is our pay in after-tax dollars.

[The enlarged display of a familiar paycheck stub clarifies the unfamiliar concepts of before- and after-tax dollars.]

90-2176
1222
7209

PAY One thousand four hundred twenty nine and 60/100 DOLLARS

TIME WK'D	DATE	TO THE ORDER OF	GROSS AMOUNT		FED. W/H	F.I.C.A.	STATE W/H		S.D.I.		CREDIT UNION	NET AMOUNT
	7/31/92	J. Doe	1958.33		293.74	78.33	68.54		88.12			1429.60

DESCRIPTION

G.U. Horton

EXHIBIT 1
Paycheck Stub

[The speaker wisely avoids a complicated discussion of before- and after-tax dollars in different tax brackets.]

Once all those deductions are taken away from our pay, every before-tax dollar shrinks in value to about 73 cents. [*The speaker shows Exhibit 2 here.*] And that's in a low tax bracket. If your income is higher, then the difference between before- and after-tax dollars is even bigger. This means that it takes at least \$136.33 in after-tax dollars to buy something that costs \$100 in before-tax dollars.

[The visual display increases the clarity and impact of the difference between before- and after-tax dollars.]

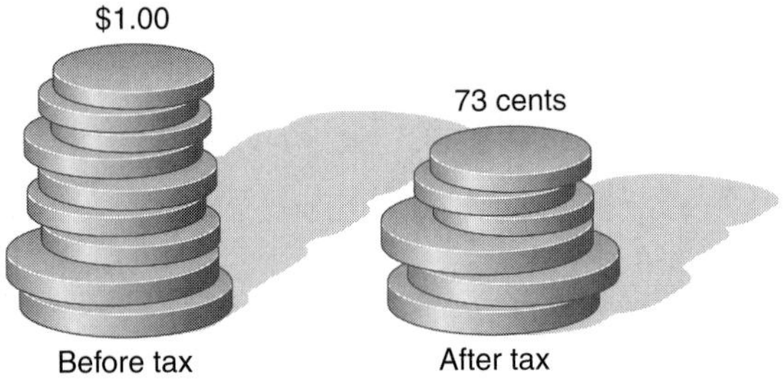

EXHIBIT 2
Value of Before- and After-Tax Dollars

[The transition here makes movement to the second part of the body clear.]

You can probably see now that it's better to buy things in before-tax dollars whenever you can. And that's what the Flexible Benefits Plan lets you do. Let me explain how it works.

[An internal preview orients the audience to the next two points.]

The Flexible Benefits Plan is so great because it allows you to pay for some important items in before-tax dollars. The plan lets you set aside pay in two categories: medical costs and dependent care. Let's cover each of these in detail so you can see which expenses are covered.

[The speaker generates audience involvement by inviting listeners to consider their own expenses in the following areas.]

A look at the chart entitled "Allowable Medical Expenses" shows which items you can use under the Flexible Benefits Plan. [*The speaker points to each item in Exhibit 3 as she discusses it.*] As I cover these expenses, think about how much you spend in each area.

[The chart helps listeners understand which expenses are covered.]

- Health insurance deductibles
- Health insurance co-payments
- Drugs and prescriptions
- Vision care and equipment
- Psychologists and psychiatrists
- Dental care and orthodontia

EXHIBIT 3
Allowable Medical Expenses

[The hypothetical example helps show how the plan works in real life.]

First we'll talk about health-insurance deductibles and co-payments. Under our company's policy, you pay the first $300 of expenses for yourself and each dependent. You also make a $10 co-payment for each visit to a doctor. Let's say that you and one dependent have to pay the $300 deductible each year, and that you made five visits to the doctor. That's a total of $650 per year you could have covered under the plan.

[A citation helps prove that the cost of medicines is considerable.]

Drugs and prescriptions include every kind of medicine you buy, even if you buy it over the counter without a prescription. And, don't forget, the plan covers payments you make for everyone you claim as a dependent: your kids, maybe your spouse, and maybe even an older parent whom you're caring for. Here's an article from *Changing Times* magazine that says that a family of three spends an average of $240 per year on drugs. Maybe you spend even more. Whatever you do spend on medicine can be included in the plan, which means you will pay less for it than if you used after-tax dollars.

[Examples of typical vision-care fees illustrate the potential costs in this area.]

Vision care and equipment include eyeglasses and contact lenses as well as any fees you or your dependents pay to optometrists or ophthalmologists. With a pair of reading glasses costing at least $45 and a new set of contact lenses costing over $80, the money could really mount up.

Psychologists and psychiatrists are also covered, which means that any counseling you receive will cost a lot less.

Dental care and orthodontia are covered, too. If you or your dependents need major dental work, this can mean a lot. And if you're paying for your kids' braces, you can really save a bundle. We did some checking, and the average orthodontic treatment today runs about $3,500 over 3 years—or over $1,000 per year.

[Comparing the unfamiliar benefits plan to the familiar notion of a discount helps make the advantages clear.]

Nobody likes to spend money for medical expenses like these, but paying for them with before-tax dollars under the Flexible Benefits Plan is like getting a discount of 20 percent or more—clearly, a great deal.

[The transition here uses signposting to mark a shift to the second type of expense covered by the plan.]

But medical costs aren't the only expenses you can include in the Flexible Benefits Plan. There's a second way you can boost your take-home pay: by including dependent care in the plan.

[The example of potential savings under the plan is a guaranteed attention-getter for working parents.]

For most people, dependents are children. Any costs of caring for your kids can be paid for in before-tax dollars, meaning you'll pay a lot less. You can include day care services, preschool fees, even in-home care for your child. We did some checking and found that keeping a child in preschool or day care in this area from 8:30 in the morning until 5 P.M. averages about $5,000 per year. By shifting this amount into the Flexible Benefits Plan, the real cost drops by over $1,000. Not bad for filling out a few forms!

[A restatement of the thesis is combined with the introduction of an example to support its claim.]

When you combine the savings on health care and dependents, the potential savings that come from joining the Flexible Benefits Plan are impressive. Let's take a look at a typical example of just how much money the Flexible Benefits Plan can save. Your personal situation probably won't be exactly like this one, but you can still get a feeling for how good the plan is. [*The speaker shows Exhibit 4.*]

[The chart provides a visual outline of the example. Without the exhibit, the dollar amounts would be too confusing to follow.]

	WITHOUT PLAN	WITH PLAN
GROSS SALARY	$23,500	$23,500
SALARY REDUCTIONS		
Health Care	0	650
Prescriptions and Drugs	0	240
Vision Care	0	60
Dental Care	0	180
Dependent Care	0	1,800
	$23,500	$20,570
TAXES		
Federal Income Tax @ 15%	3,525	3,085
State Income Tax @ 3.5%	764	720
FICA and SDI @ 8.15%	1,915	1,676
	$6,204	$5,481
AFTER-TAX EXPENSES		
Health Care	650	0
Prescriptions and Drugs	240	0
Vision Care	60	0
Dental Care	180	0
Dependent Care	1,800	0
Net Pay	$14,366	$15,089
ANNUAL SAVINGS $723		

EXHIBIT 4
Savings with Flexible Benefits Plan

Let's suppose your salary is $23,500 and you have a spouse and one child. Let's say that your health and dependent expenses are pretty much like the ones we've been discussing here today. [*The speaker points to "Salary Reductions" section of chart.*] Your health insurance deductibles and co-payments amount to $650, and you spend $240 over the year on prescriptions and drugs. Let's say that one person in your family needs one set of eyeglasses. You all get dental checkups, and you don't even have cavities! You spend $1,800 on child care—not bad these days.

If we look at the top third of the chart, it might seem that following the plan costs you more. After all, your salary would be $23,500 without the plan but only $20,570 with your expenses deducted from the plan.

[As the speaker points to the "Annual Savings" line on the chart, the audience sees in real dollars the potential advantage of the plan.]

But look what happens once we start to figure taxes. [*The speaker points to "Taxes" section of chart.*] Since your pay with the plan is less, you pay less in taxes. A little subtraction shows that the difference between the $6,204 you'd pay without the plan and the $5,481 you'd pay with it amounts to a savings of $723.

This is just a small example of how much you can save. If your expenses are higher—if you have more medical costs, for example—the advantage is even greater. As your salary goes up and you move into a higher tax bracket, the advantages grow, too. And don't forget that the savings I've been talking about are just for 1 year. As time goes by, your earning power will grow even more.

[In a restatement of the thesis the speaker returns to the main advantage of the plan.]

Now you can see why we're so glad to offer the Flexible Benefits Plan. It can boost your take-home pay even before you get a raise. It costs you nothing.

[Listeners are told what to do next if they are interested in the plan.]

If you're interested in learning more, we encourage you to read the booklet I'll hand out in a moment. It contains a worksheet that will help you estimate how much you stand to save under the plan. If the idea still interests you, please attend the workshop we'll be holding next Friday during the lunch hour in the third-floor meeting room. At that time, we can answer your questions and make an appointment for each of you to sign up at the personnel office. In the meantime, I'll be happy to answer any questions you have now.

Group Presentations

Group presentations are common in the working world. Sometimes the members of a group may be asked (or told) to present their information together. Other times team members choose to speak collectively, realizing that several presenters can be more effective than a single person.

Some group presentations are delivered to internal audiences. For example, a project team may be asked to give a status report to management, computer support staff may introduce a new software package to users, and union representatives may brief members on negotiation progress. Other group presentations are delivered to external audiences: Sales teams make pitches to potential customers. Public officials explain their plans or actions to citizens. Representatives from health care providers explain insurance benefits to employees. School officials inform parents about curriculum changes.

Group presentations can be effective for a variety of reasons. Hearing from several speakers can provide the variety that will keep audience members tuned in. In addition, the skills and perspectives of several people can give a more complete message than any single speaker could provide. For example, a sales pitch to a potential client would probably be strengthened by the contributions of experts in marketing, customer support, and product design. Finally, team presentations can boost audience receptivity by providing a balance of gender, ethnicity, age, and other factors.

Planning a Group Presentation

Group presentations can be more effective than individual ones, but they are often more difficult to create. Planning a group presentation usually takes more time than a solo talk. Decision making requires discussion that isn't necessary when you are on your own, and coordinating each person's role is an extra challenge.

During the planning phase, a smart team will make sure that members work on their own whenever possible and only use meetings to handle business that can profit from shared discussion. As Chapter 9 explained, some tasks are best handled in meetings. Anything that requires the support of every member or can benefit from creative thinking should be discussed collectively. This includes choosing the

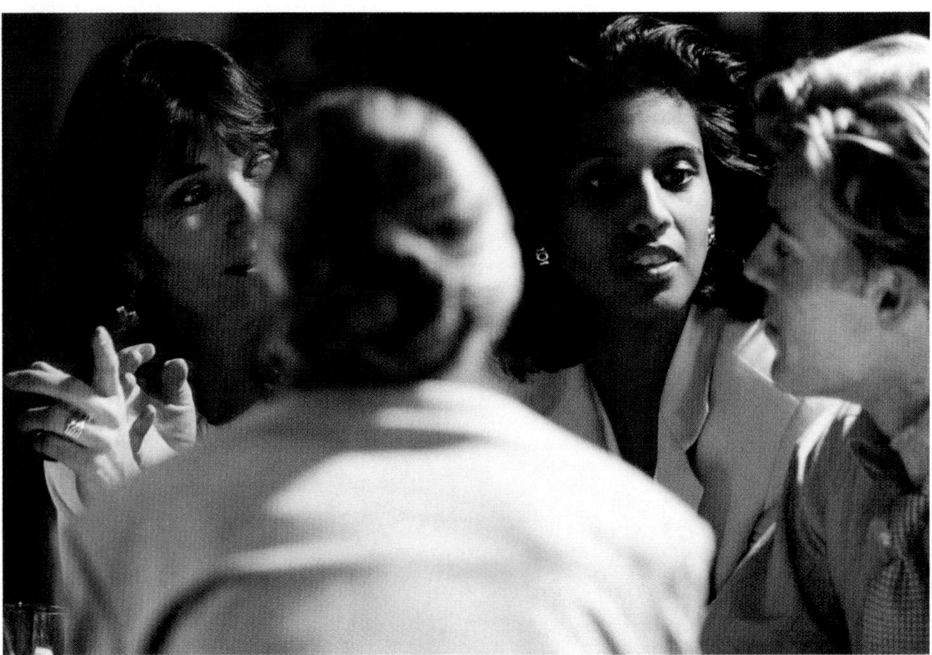

group's topic (if defining it is within your control), determining the group's overall approach, and assigning specific roles.

Once the overall plan is set, members can probably tackle the next stage on their own. Individuals or smaller groups can research and plan their own segments of the talk. There's little advantage to having two or more members dig through the same part of the library or interview the same person to gather information. Some team members can perform specialized jobs, such as making arrangements for the setup of the speaking room and creating visuals for all the presenters to ensure a consistent design.

After members finish their tasks they can meet and assemble their results into a coherent plan. This is probably a good time to start rehearsing the presentation. At this point team members will need to decide logistical questions such as who will set up and operate any equipment used in the presentation and who will serve as timekeeper to keep speakers from talking too long. Running over the allotted time is a common problem for individual speakers, and in group presentations it can create serious problems.

Approaches to Organizing a Group Presentation

There are two ways to decide who will say what in a group presentation: by topic and by task. The approach you take will depend on an analysis of the situation.

Organizing by Topic In some cases, it makes sense to break the presentation into separate segments, with each speaker addressing one or more topics. Organizing by topic is a logical approach when different parts of the material call for special expertise. For instance, a press conference in which county department heads announce new approaches to cost cutting almost demands separate information from each person. Likewise, a sales presentation would profit from having topics like customer support, engineering, and production discussed by representatives from each of those departments.

Organizing by Task Sometimes a presentation doesn't fall neatly into separate topics. In this case, it may make sense to assign speakers separate roles within the discussion of a topic. One role might be "spokesperson," whose job it is to introduce the main points. Other members might take the role of "example givers," offering details to support the spokesperson's claims. For example, a neighborhood association urging the city council to install a new traffic signal at a busy intersection might use a problem–solution plan. One person's job would be to describe the overall problem and the group's solution. After making each of these main points, that speaker would introduce several individuals to back up the points with a range of supporting details. This plan organizes the material clearly and provides an impressive array of speakers who are more likely to convince the council than a single presenter. A rough outline for this approach would look something like this:

1. *Spokesperson describes the problem:* "Lack of a traffic signal encourages speeding traffic, leading to several accidents and near misses. This situation risks lives and exposes the city to liability suits."
2. *Other speakers offer support:* Neighbor 1 cites police reports on the number of speeding tickets issued in the past year. Neighbor 2 describes hospital reports on injuries from accidents at the intersection. Neighbor 3 describes recent near misses. Neighbor 4 (an attorney) explains the city's exposure to lawsuits.
3. *Spokesperson suggests a solution:* "Installation of a new traffic signal will reduce or eliminate the problem in a cost-effective way."
4. *Other speakers offer support:* Person 1 compares the cost of a new signal to the cost of settling lawsuits arising out of future accidents at the intersection. Person 2 shows that funds are available in the city's street improvement fund. Person 3 presents a petition of neighbors requesting traffic control at the intersection (suggesting voter support for the signal).

Planning Introductions, Conclusions and Transitions in Group Presentations

Every presentation needs an effective introduction, conclusion, and transitions connecting main points, but these elements are especially important in group presentations. They help listeners follow the overall plan and prevent confusion that can come when several speakers share the stage.

The following introduction was given by the representative of an architectural firm seeking to make the short list of candidates for a corporate design job. Notice how it gives listeners a clear introduction to who will be speaking and each member's role:

> *Good morning, everybody. Most of you know that I'm Diana Salazar of KBS Associates. My colleagues and I want to thank you for the chance to show how we can work with you on the design and construction of your company's regional service center.*
>
> *Architects like to design beautiful buildings, of course, and we know you like our work or we wouldn't be here today. But beauty alone isn't enough: We create designs that can be constructed on time and on budget. And we are committed to designing buildings that work well for our clients after they're finished. You and your customers*

career tip

Signals in Team Presentations

One advantage of team presentations is that the person not speaking can keep an eye on the audience and signal the speaker on how to keep the presentation moving along effectively. Experienced partners can develop a series of subtle hand signals to manage the flow of information. Here is a sample of some signals developed by one team:

- Speed up/move on: Drum fingers on table slowly and quietly
- Slow down: Hand on table, palm down
- Expand on point: One hand on top of other, palms up
- Minutes remaining: Lay number of fingers on table
- Finish up presentation: Tap finger on opposite wrists

Source: Tom Antion and Judy Shaw, "Tag Team Signals," *Great Speaking* 3, no. 20 (October 24, 2001), retrieved from **http://www.Antion.com**.

are going to use this service center for many years, and it has to meet your needs long after your architects are gone.

This morning we want to give you a picture of how we can work with you to design and build an outstanding service center. You'll meet some of the people who will be involved with this project, and you'll see how KBS has handled some other important jobs over the past few years.

My colleague David Nguyen will begin by showing you samples of some work we've done for other clients: Edutech's corporate headquarters in Dallas, two service centers for the American Automobile Association, and the master plan for the Vista del Sol Center in Austin. David will also be sharing quotes from former clients to give you a feeling for what it would be like to work with KBS Associates. Next, Tom Lee will introduce you to representatives of some of the consultants who will be working with us and you on this job: Bill Whitcroft of Western Engineering, Joy Liebert of Energy Management Systems, and Leo Wang, who would be our liaison with local governing agencies. We are proud of this team, and we want you to get a sense of what it would be like to work with them. Finally, Sabrina Boldt will present some preliminary sketches for the service center, based on the program that the consultants developed with you over the last several months.

In our short time with you this morning, we want you to see that KBS is ready, willing, and able to tailor this project to your specific needs, just as we've done with other clients. So let's begin. David will start by showing you the kind of successful relationships we've built with clients in the last couple of years. David . . .

Like the introduction, transitions are an especially important way to help listeners follow the structure of a group presentation. Clear transitions help smooth the adjustment listeners need to make as they shift their attention from one speaker to another. There are two ways to handle transitions: A single master of ceremonies (probably the person who introduced the presentation) can make them or each speaker can introduce the next person after summarizing his or her own section. Whichever method you choose, make sure the relationship between the preceding and following sections is clear.

Self-Assessment Evaluating Your Group Presentation

Whether you prepare a group presentation in class, at work, or in your community, use this form to evaluate your group's preparation and delivery. Score each item as follows, 1 = needs improvement, 2 = adequate, and 3 = more than adequate, and pay special attention to those you identified as needing improvement:

Planning and Organizing the Group Presentation

Item			
1. Meeting time is used for brainstorming and discussing items that require everyone's participation.			
a. Topic is chosen (if this is the group's prerogative).	1	2	3
b. Overall approach and roles are determined (setup, logistics, research, timekeeper).	1	2	3
2. Group members work independently outside meeting time.	1	2	3
3. Members decide whether to organize by task or by topic.	1	2	3
4. Organizing creates a coherent whole.			
a. Introduction helps orient audience to topic, divisions, and speakers.	1	2	3
b. Transitions create smooth changeovers from one speaker to another and show the audience the relationship of one part to another.	1	2	3
c. Conclusion reviews and summarizes all main points made by all speakers.	1	2	3

Delivering the Group Presentation

Item			
5. Speakers are positioned for quick access and minimal time between speakers.	1	2	3
6. Speakers transition without fumbling, bumping, or disruption.	1	2	3
7. Group members can easily see each person who speaks.	1	2	3
8. Group members give their full attention to the current speaker.	1	2	3
9. Speakers' words reinforce, review, and connect to previous and following speakers' presentations.	1	2	3
10. Speakers do not contradict each other.	1	2	3

The conclusion can be given by the same M.C. or by the final speaker. If you choose the latter approach, be certain that the wrap-up restates the group's overall thesis and main points and doesn't just review the most recent remarks.

Delivering a Group Presentation

The potential for mix-ups and mistakes is especially great in group presentations. The key to minimizing problems is extensive rehearsal. Consider issues like the setup and position of speakers in advance to avoid last-minute bumbling. Will members speak while seated around a table? Will they sit in a row until it is each one's turn? Or will they come up from the audience? Choose the format that helps you make the best possible impression and avoid delays. Waiting for speakers to get from their chairs to the lectern greatly increases lag time, and the larger the room, the greater the distance. Sitting together at a table may provide a better and more cohesive look, as well as minimize delays. If the group does sit around a table, try to angle it so that the members of the team can comfortably see speakers as they present. However you set up the presentation, be sure speakers can rise and sit as necessary without bumping, banging, and clanging into equipment, the table, and each other.

In considering where to position team members when they are not speaking, think about how they will look to the audience. Remember that they will make an impression even when they aren't the principal focus of attention. When it is your turn to speak, be sure to talk to the audience, not your teammates. When you're not speaking, look at the speaker and listen with undivided attention. Even if you are bored because you've heard the remarks so often during rehearsal, or you are nervous about your upcoming turn, act like the ideas are fresh or interesting. Don't review your notes or let your eyes wander from the speaker, or you will encourage the audience to do the same.

Special-Occasion Speaking

In business settings, there are many special speaking occasions and events, some of which you will quite likely be asked to participate in or be given a chance to volunteer for. You may be asked to give a welcome to guests touring your facility, introduce a speaker at a staff meeting or annual banquet, present an award to a retiring employee, or accept an award you've won. Perhaps you'll present a tribute to a member of a civic organization you belong to or bid farewell to a supervisor who was promoted out of your department. Keep in mind that every context is unique; you will want to adjust to the physical, social, chronological, and cultural context of each occasion. The following guidelines will help you feel confident and achieve your goals when delivering special-occasion remarks.

Welcoming a Guest or Group

When you are **welcoming** someone, your remarks often set the tone for the whole event. Warmth and sincerity in words and behavior are important. Whether you are welcoming a special guest for a 2-hour banquet or a group of permanent new employees, try to follow these guidelines:

- Say who you are (if the audience doesn't know) or on whose behalf you are speaking.
- Identify the person or people you are welcoming (unless you are welcoming the entire audience).
- Thank the guest or group for coming (if they had a choice).
- Tell why the occasion is especially important or significant.

As you deliver your remarks, be sure to speak to the person or group you are welcoming. If appropriate, turn to the audience and invite your listeners to participate in the welcome by clearly stating or showing them how you want them to behave. The example below illustrates how this technique can be used with the guidelines to produce effective welcoming remarks:

All of us at Sizetec USA welcome members of our Japanese plant's team to the ribbon cutting of our new facility. We are honored that you took time to travel so far to

ethical challenge

Honoring a Less-than-honorable Person

Imagine your job is to speak briefly to welcome, introduce, toast, or give an award to someone who you know is undeserving of respect. For example, the person about whom you must speak might be manipulative, racist, or lazy. (Feel free to think of a specific person who fits this description, and imagine the circumstances under which you might be required to publicly honor him or her.)

Describe how you would proceed in these circumstances. How could you be true to yourself while dealing with the obligations that often operate in business and professional situations?

be with us today. We have a great deal to learn from one another, and your visit will help all of us make Sizetec an industry leader. This is an exciting day for us, and we extend a warm welcome to you. [Turn to audience.] *Please join me in a round of applause to welcome our Japanese guests.*

Introducing Another Speaker

When handled well, your **introduction of another speaker** will help make his or her remarks a success. Here are some guidelines that will help you deliver an effective introduction. You may choose to switch the order of the information here, but you will almost always need to include it in some way, unless the audience is aware of it already.

- *Briefly preview the topic about which the person will speak.* If the speaker's topic is very familiar, you may only need to mention it. If the audience is unfamiliar with the topic, you may need to include more background information about the topic and explain why it is significant for the group.
- *Give the audience reasons to listen to the person you are introducing.* Share interesting and relevant parts of the speaker's background. Whenever possible, show how his or her remarks will have value for the audience.
- *Enhance the credibility of the person you are introducing.* Share information that will showcase his or her qualifications. Select the most interesting biographical information for your audience to describe the person you are introducing. It is best to give some general information and a few specifics, rather than rattling off long lists: "John has done training with many groups, including the Air Force, IBM, and Baxter Healthcare." Don't be vague ("John has done a lot of training for big groups") but don't burden the audience with too much time-consuming detail either ("John has done training for . . ." followed by a list of 20 companies).

A good introduction requires that you learn about the person you are introducing in advance. If you can, meet in person or interview the speaker over the phone. If possible, obtain a résumé or biographical information in writing ahead of time. The more you know, the better you can make your introduction.

Make sure all the information in your introduction is accurate. Check and practice the pronunciation of names, cities, and companies that you are unsure of. Ask the person how he or she would like to be referred to (title and last name, first and last name, or first name only).

As you plan your introduction, be sensitive to culture and gender differences. For example, members of many cultures prefer to be identified by formal titles (such as "director") that are not commonly used in the United States or Canada. Likewise, the humor that may be appreciated in the United States could easily offend listeners—or the persons being introduced—if they are from cultures with more formal styles of communication. Strive for consistency if you are introducing more than one person. A common faux pas is referring to men as "Mr." or "Dr." while calling women by their first names.

Notice how these points have been incorporated in this informative introduction:

> *For the last 9 months you've heard a great deal about how we will be expanding operations into Mexico. This is a big step for us, and I'm sure everybody has a lot of questions and maybe some concerns.*
>
> *Today I'm pleased to introduce you to Mr. Dante Gutierrez, who will be managing our Mexican operations. Mr. Gutierrez comes to us with a great amount of experience on both sides of the border. After founding and operating one of northern Mexico's foremost import-export firms, Mr. Gutierrez became executive director of Baja California's Asociación de la Industria, a leading business group. He has lived and worked in both Mexico and the U.S. His experience in manufacturing and cross-border trade will be a tremendous help as we expand our operation in Mexico and Central America.*
>
> *Along with his professional credentials, you'll find that Mr. Gutierrez is a great guy. He's friendly and helpful, and very approachable. I'm sure you will find that Mr. Gutierrez is a terrific resource as we learn more about our new market and its customers.*
>
> *Please join me in giving Mr. Gutierrez a warm welcome!*

The following tips will help your introduction be a success:[12]

- Plan your remarks carefully in advance. Don't take an impromptu approach.
- Your introduction should *appear* spontaneous and natural, even though it is planned. Practice your delivery so you won't have to rely on notes.
- When making your introduction, look at the audience, not at the person being introduced.
- Keep the introduction short. You aren't the main attraction. In most cases a 1- or 2-minute introduction will be enough. If the audience already knows the person you are introducing, it can be even shorter.

Honoring a Person or Institution

When you are asked to give a speech of **tribute,** both chronological and topical approaches can be effective. You can follow the person's life or career chronologically and pay tribute to achievements and characteristics along the way, or you might choose some themes or traits from the person's life and organize around those topics. If you do choose to pay tribute along theme lines (bravery and commitment, for example), anecdotes and examples can illustrate your points.

Many of the guidelines for tributes parallel those for introductions: accuracy of names and details and sensitivity to culture, gender, and personal desires. Check your information with the person to whom tribute is being paid if possible or practical; if not, check with an extremely authoritative source. A sample tribute to an accountant who is leaving a firm is presented on page 461. Of course, if the speaker had more time, each of the traits selected could be illustrated with more anecdotes that the audience would be familiar with.

Today is a day of celebration as we pay tribute to Joseph Begay. It is a privilege to speak for the management team here at Contrast Accounts and to honor Joe.

In thinking about Joe's accomplishments here, two words come to mind: commitment and community. Joseph is committed to doing a job well. He commands a tremendous measure of respect and esteem from colleagues in all of our departments. From Betty Murphy in Costs Analysis to Mike Burroughs in Media Relations, Joseph has earned our admiration for his commitment to quality work for our clients. Who else could have persuaded us to redo the entire Simpson account in less than 2 months? Who else could have enticed us with pizzas to get us to stay late and finish? Joe is committed to our clients and to our colleagues. The focal point of his work has been to help us all better understand the needs of members from various departments who populate our company. Joseph has helped us come together to look at specific ways we could meet the needs of diverse departments, and he has provided us with opportunities to give expression to our common frustrations and concerns which revolve around quality products for our clients.

Second only to his commitment is Joe's unique way of building community among us. It is because of Joe that over the past 6 years many of us first discovered our shared interests and commonalities across departments. The collective tasks he assigned to us created a bond and a basis for our common union. He showed us how to let our collective interests rise above our differences and then how to respect and work with our differences. I speak for many of us in saying I have increased admiration and regard for the wisdom and the work of our colleagues and for the intricate web of talents that contribute to Contrast Accounts' success. Through shared endeavors initiated by Joe we realized that we are not interchangeable parts but unique professionals with vision and expertise. Joe helped us all catch a glimpse of what community and connection can mean and how they can be achieved cross-departmentally.

I believe that because of Joe's commitment and creation of community, we are all richer, and Joe, I'd like to have you stand as we pay tribute to you and your endeavors here with a last round of applause.

Giving a Toast

Sooner or later you are likely to be asked to deliver a special type of tribute—a **toast.** Besides honoring the person to whom it refers, a well-crafted toast can boost your visibility and notability in any organization. Remember that toasts usually express appreciation and recognize accomplishments as well as hopes and wishes for the future. Here are some hints to help you choose the right words.

- *Choose the time wisely.* If it is up to you to choose the moment, be sure everyone is present. At a dinner, choose the moment when the group has just been seated or wait until just before dessert. At a stand-around cocktail party or outdoor barbecue, wait until most people have drinks.
- *Be prepared.* Think ahead about the occasion, the attendees, and the person or people you are toasting. Delivering an impromptu toast can be risky. Use some inside information or little-known facts that compliment the person.
- *Look spontaneous.* Even though you have planned your remarks in advance, try to avoid reading notes or sounding memorized.
- *Be brief.* A 30- to 60-second toast is the norm; a 2-minute one is the maximum. If in doubt, say less, not more. End by raising your glass and gently clinking the glass of a person near you and saying, "Cheers," "Salud," or a similar expression.

- *Be visible and audible.* Be sure to stand. If it is an unorganized mill-around affair, look for an elevation: a hillside, a stair (not a chair) to stand on, the step to the stage, the back porch. Be certain you have everyone's attention before speaking and begin loudly enough to be effective.
- *Be inclusive.* Alternate your gaze between the audience and the person or people you are honoring.
- *Be sober.* Beware of your consumption of alcohol beforehand. You may pay the price for a slurred or inappropriate toast for a long time. The beverage need not be alcoholic; club soda and water are also used for toasts.
- *Be appropriate.* If you are debating whether a remark or story would be humorous or offensive, leave it out. If you think something is funny but aren't sure that the humor will be appreciated by the honoree and guests, leave it unsaid.

Go to the Advanced Public Speaking Institute Web site at **http://www.public-speaking.org** and click on "Humor Techniques" or **violet.umf.maine.edu/~donaghue/toasts.html** for more suggestions for toasts.

Presenting an Award

Sometimes persons may know they are recipients of awards, and at other times your announcement may come as a surprise. Depending on the situation, you will choose whether to let the audience (and winner) know who is receiving the award at the beginning of the speech or save that information until the end. For an effective **award presentation,** follow these tips:

- If everyone knows who is receiving the award, mention the person's name early in your remarks. If the audience doesn't know who is receiving the award, you might want to build suspense by withholding his or her name until the end.
- State the name and nature of the award.

- State the criteria for selection.
- Relate the way (or ways) in which the recipient meets the criteria, using specific examples.
- Make the presentation.
- Be sure that the person receiving the award—not you, the presenter—is the center of attention and focus.

As the example below illustrates, this approach can serve as a framework for creating interesting, enthusiastic presentations:

> *"Success isn't measured by where you are, but by how far you've come from where you started." These words exemplify the spirit of the Most Improved Player award. Each year, players have the privilege and difficult task of voting for the player they believe is the most improved. The winner of this award must have demonstrated to her teammates spirit and commitment and must have shown improvement and refinement in skills. This is not an easy task. Always spurring others on and never giving up even when we were down 14–7 against the Bulldogs, this year's winner went from being unable to stop a goal to stopping six goals in our last championship game. So, Mary Lee, it is with gratitude and delight that I present to you from your teammates the Most Improved Player award.*

Accepting an Award

When you accept an award, a few brief remarks are usually all that's necessary. Recalling the long-winded speeches at the annual Academy Awards ceremony will help you appreciate the sentiment behind Marlene Dietrich's advice to Mikhail Baryshnikov when she sent him to accept her award from the Council of Fashion Designers: "Take the thing, look at it, thank them, and go."[13] This approach is probably too extreme, but brevity is certainly an important element of most acceptances. So, too, is gratitude. The following plan can help you organize your sincere gratitude in an effective way:[14]

1. Express your sincere gratitude (and surprise, if appropriate).
2. Acknowledge and show appreciation to contributors.
3. Describe how the reward will make a difference.
4. Say thank you again.

The following thank-you remarks, given by the head of a volunteer committee that had staged a profitable fund-raiser, illustrate how this simple approach can be sincere, easy, and effective:

> *You have really surprised me today. When I said I'd help plan the auction, the last thing on my mind was an award. Raising scholarship money was our goal, and breaking last year's fund-raising record was the only reward I'd hoped for. Getting this special thank-you is more than I had ever expected, and I am deeply honored.*
>
> *I'm also a little embarrassed to be singled out like this. We couldn't have broken that record without a tremendous amount of hard work by everybody. Chris and her committee rounded up an incredible bunch of auction items. Ben and his gang provided food and entertainment that we'll be talking about for years. Darnelle's publicity team brought in the donors. And Leo's talents as an auctioneer squeezed every last dollar out of those items. With wonderful people like this, how could we have gone wrong?*

I'm going to put this plaque in my office, right above my desk. Whenever I'm feeling tired and discouraged about human nature, it will remind me how generous and hard working people can be for a good cause. It will also remind me how lucky I am to know you all and to have worked with you.

So thanks again for this wonderful award. You're a great bunch of people, and I can hardly wait until we do it all again next year!

summary

Speakers in business and professional contexts frequently make informative, group, and special-occasion presentations.

Informative presentations include briefings, reports (status, feasibility, and final), training sessions, and explanations. Briefings are very short and give the minimum information needed. Status reports review the project's purpose, describe its current state, any obstacles and efforts to overcome them, the next milestone, and the future of the project. Final reports require introductions, background information, a description of events, results, and directions to get more information. A feasibility report includes an introduction, criteria, methodology, possible solutions, an evaluation of solutions, recommendations, and a conclusion. Training sessions necessitate careful planning by defining the training goal, scheduling the needed time and resources, choosing the best training method, and organizing all training elements. Effective trainers link information to the audience, create an overall picture, emphasize their organizational plan, and cover only the required information. Pragmatic explanations avoid jargon and carefully link the familiar to the unfamiliar.

Group presentations require special planning that often proves more difficult than planning a solo presentation. Group presentations are usually organized either by topic or by task. Careful analysis of the topic and situation often reveals the best approach. Group presentations need effective introductions and conclusions, and especially well-planned transitions to connect main points and avoid confusion that can happen with more than one speaker. Attention to nonverbal communication at all times can help each speaker enhance the presentation's flow and create unity and cohesion.

Business contexts often require various special-occasion presentations. These include speeches of welcome and introductions as well as toasts, honoring persons or institutions, and presenting and accepting awards. Effective business communicators are familiar with each of these basic presentations.

key terms

Test your understanding of these key terms by visiting the Online Learning Center Web site at www.mhhe.com/adler9.

award presentation 462
briefing 434
explanation 445
feasibility report 438
final report 436
report 435
speech of introduction 459
status report 436
toast 461
training 440
tribute 460
welcoming remarks 458

activities

Go to the self-quizzes at the Online Learning Center at www.mhhe.com/adler9 to test your knowledge of chapter concepts.

1. Skill Builder

Construct an outline for the key points in each of these presentations:

a. A briefing for employees about a new procedure for entering their vacation requests.
b. A status report for your instructor on your work in this class so far this semester.
c. A feasibility report on a specific change you'd recommend for the university bookstore or cafeteria.
d. A final report to your classmates on a project you have completed on your own in another class: a service-learning project, team project, civic or community service project.

2. Skill Builder

Create an approach that will involve the audience in each of the following trainings. Use ideas from this chapter and the Web sites listed on pages 446–467. Demonstrate your technique in class.

a. How to handle phone customer complaints nondefensively.
b. How to use digital photos to update your Web site.
c. How to use a particular campus system (computer or phone registration, student job placement) or fill out a widely used form (financial, graduation, or internship application).

3. Skill Builder

Define a specific training goal and a method to link the information to the audience for the following training sessions.

a. Listening skills for student service employees.
b. A "Dress for Success" seminar for older persons returning to the workforce.
c. Training volunteer students to lead campus tours for visiting high school students.
d. Using APA style to cite sources in term papers for nontraditional students.
e. Understanding diversity in our state (or company) for all new employees.

4. Invitation to Insight

Increase your understanding of adult learning styles by conducting one of the following exercises.

a. Interview a professional who conducts trainings in the workplace. Ask your interviewee to describe successful strategies for motivation, direct involvement, and retention.
b. Attend a workplace training or explanation session. Analyze the presenter's use of goals, motivation, direct involvement of the learners, and techniques to enhance retention.

5. Skill Builder

With a small group of your classmates, plan a group presentation in which you (a) review the meaning of a communication concept you've learned about in this class, (b) provide examples to illustrate the concept, and (c) explain how students can apply this concept in their own lives.

Decide whether you will organize your presentation by topic or by task. Assign speaking roles, and plan your introduction, transitions, and conclusion. Agree on a set of unobtrusive signals you can use to regulate teammates' delivery. Conduct at least one dress rehearsal of your presentation. When you are ready, videotape the presentation.

Watch your video. Evaluate your presentation, using the Self-Assessment form found on page 457. Discuss your evaluation with your teammates.

6. Skill Builder

Prepare the following special-occasion speeches.

a. Welcome. Prepare a speech of welcome for a guest from the community who is visiting your class to better understand your college's opportunities.

b. Introduction. Create an introduction for a guest from a prominent community business who is invited to speak to your class about job interview strategies.

c. Speech to honor. Construct and present a speech (3 minutes) that honors one of your classmates or a person or institution in your community whom you believe deserves recognition.

d. Award. Create an award for a classmate (best team member, best speaker, most improved speaker) that reflects some achievement or activity during the semester.

e. Celebration dinner. Your work team has just met a very important project deadline and your work received rave reviews from your supervisor.

resources

In Print

Antion, T. S. *Wake 'em Up: How to Use Humor and Other Professional Techniques to Create Alarmingly Good Business Presentations*. Landover Hills, MD: Anchor, 1996.

This book offers ways to make presentations more interesting and entertaining. It includes sections on room setups, appropriate humor (with many cautions about inappropriateness), sales presentations, copyright issues, audiovisuals, and international speaking.

Biech, Elaine. *Training for Dummies*. Hoboken, NJ: Wiley Publishing, Inc., 2005.

In addition to sections on how adults learn, the training cycle, designing, preparing, and delivering training, this book includes trends in training (such as e-training); practical ways to increase participation, add humor, and follow up; and ideas for part-time trainers.

Daly, John A., and Anita L. Vangelisti. "Skillfully Instructing Learners: How Communicators Effectively Convey Messages." In *Handbook of Communication and Social Interaction Skills*, eds. John O. Greene and Brant R. Burleson. Mahwah, NJ: Lawrence Erlbaum, 2003.

The authors provide a summary of research on informative communication, covering topics including gaining attention, creating a climate that encourages learning, and enhancing understanding.

Mottet, Timothy P., Virigina P. Richmond, and James C. McCroskey. *Handbook of Instructional Communication: Rhetorical and Relational Perspectives*. New York: Allyn & Bacon, 2005.

This scholarly book summarizes research on strategies for teaching and training. Chapters discuss how instructors influence students, how students influence instructors, and resistance of learners.

Stolovitch, Harold. *Telling Ain't Training* (2002) and *Beyond Telling Ain't Training Fieldbook* (2005). Alexandria, VA: ASTD Press.

Telling an audience is not the same as training them. These two resources make it abundantly clear that trainers need to do more than talk. In an interactive style, the author shows you how to prepare different types of engaging training for adult audiences.

On the Web

Successful Presentations

The Virtual Presentation Assistant (**www.ku.edu/~coms/virtual_assistant/vpa/vpa.htm**) provides tools for developing presentations, assistance in numerous aspects of speaking, and links to various other public-speaking Web sites. For a refresher in business presentations, visit **www.presentingsolutions.com/effectivepresentations.html**. Although it is a commercially maintained site specializing in presentation equipment, this Web page contains news, trends, and tips from the business presentation world.

Training and Development

Training and development is a big business, and several organizations are dedicated to helping professionals perform these jobs effectively. Among the best are

- American Society for Training and Development (**www.astd.org**). This is the leading organization in training and development. The Web site offers information about research, developments in the field, publications, and other advice.
- International Society for Performance Improvement (**www.ispi.org**). This organization serves human performance technologists and designers, and it offers many resources for practitioners in this field.
- *Training* magazine (**www.trainingmag.com**). This magazine offers reports, products, and services for training professionals. Much of this information will be useful for anyone who offers on-the-job instruction.
- Workshops by Thiagi (**http://thiagi.com/index.html**). An experienced trainer provides training games and tips, a free subscription to "Play for Performance," an online newsletter and archives, links to "freebies and goodies" (useful techniques and ideas for trainers), numerous handouts and articles, and links to other useful sites.
- Fun Team Building (**www.funteambuilding.com**). This site contains "Top Ten Tips for Outstanding Trainers" and more resources.

Copyrights and Permissions

When you prepare a presentation and want to use items from other sources, you should know when permission and/or fees are required of you. Check the U.S. Copyright Office site (**www.copyright.gov**) for information about copyrights and Web sites. Other sites with copyright and Fair Use information include the Stanford University site (**http://fairuse.stanford.edu**) and Copyright Web site (**www.benedict.com**). For Intellectual property information, go to **http://www.eff.org/IP**. CETUS, Consortium for Educational Technology for University Systems, provides information and sample documents to ask for permission (**http://www.cetus.org/fairindex.html**).

14 Persuasive Presentations

Chapter Outline

Chapter Objectives

After reading this chapter, you should be able to

1 Identify real-world situations that involve motivational speeches, goodwill speeches, proposals, and sales presentations.

2 Design a persuasive appeal that is ethical as well as effective.

3 Apply the persuasive strategies discussed in these pages to a presentation you are designing.

4 Choose the most persuasive organizational plan for your topic, audience, and situation.

Types of Persuasive Presentations

Unlike purely informative presentations that don't advocate a position, persuasive presentations aim to change the way an audience thinks, feels, or acts. The most common types of persuasive presentations are motivational and goodwill speeches, proposals, and sales presentations.

Consider these examples to see how common persuasion is on the job:

- Two partners are convinced that they have a winning idea for a new restaurant. They meet with a commercial loan officer from a local bank to seek financing for their project.
- Faced with a wave of injuries, the foreman of a construction crew convinces his team members that they need to observe safety practices more carefully.
- A local real-estate brokerage has merged with a nationwide chain. Ever since the news became public, rumors have swept the office about how the changes will affect pay, policies, and even job security. The owner has called a companywide meeting to reassure employees that the change will benefit them.
- As part of a community-relations program, the electric company has started a community speakers' bureau. The bureau's director is speaking to a group of employees to recruit them as volunteers for the service.
- A group of employees has grown increasingly disgruntled with the boss's policy on vacation scheduling. They have chosen a three-person delegation to present their grievances.

At one time or another, everyone in an organization needs to influence the thinking or actions of others. When an issue is especially important, though, the persuasion frequently takes place in a presentation. Even when you have made your case in writing, a good presentation is often essential. Business consultant James Lukaszewski explains:

> *We live in a "tell me" world. The last time you presented a plan to your boss to accomplish something—you know—that beautiful 2-inch-thick, tabbed notebook with 150 pages, 31 tabs, and 5,000 well-chosen words? Was it actually read? Or did your boss simply put his hand on it, look you in the eye, and say, "Show me what's in here and tell me how it's going to help us achieve our objectives."*[1]

Motivational Speeches

A **motivational speech** attempts to generate enthusiasm for the topic being presented. At their worst, motivational speeches can combine the most oppressive elements of a bad sermon and a high school pep rally. On the other hand, when delivered effectively and at the proper time, such presentations can produce good results. For example, the organizers of a fund-raising event need to generate enthusiasm to recruit and motivate volunteers. Likewise, a manager trying to persuade her subordinates to fill out lengthy reports or work extra hard to cut costs will only succeed if she can sell her ideas to a potentially skeptical workforce.

Goodwill Speeches

As its name implies, a **goodwill speech** aims to create a favorable image of the speaker's cause in the minds of the audience. Representatives of organizations frequently speak to audiences to promote interest or support for their organizations. A corporate recruiter addressing graduating seniors and a bank economist explaining economic forecasts are making speeches of goodwill. So is the company's representative addressing the press after an oil spill.

These goodwill speeches may seem informative, but they also try to change the attitudes or behavior of their listeners. The corporate recruiter is trying to encourage some students to apply for jobs with his company; the economist is trying to build the image of her institution as a leading business bank; and the utility company representative is trying to soften negative reactions.

Proposals

In a **proposal** you advocate that your audience take specific action. Some proposals are aimed at external audiences. Other proposals are focused on internal audiences. You might, for example, try to persuade management to support a ride-sharing program or reimburse employees for educational costs, or you might try to convince your boss to give you more staffing support or a raise in pay. (See the Career Tip on page 471 for advice on requesting a raise.)

Whatever the topic and audience, the most straightforward approach for a proposal is the problem–solution approach described in Chapter 10. While the particulars will vary, each section of this two-part approach is likely to include information listed here:

1. *Introduce the problem*
   a. Demonstrate the nature of the problem in terms the audience will understand.

career tip

How to Request a Raise

Asking for a raise is a kind of proposal, even though you typically will present your arguments informally to your boss. Here are tips that can increase your chances for success:

The best time to seek a raise

- When you or your department have been recognized for doing a good job.
- After you have volunteered to take on additional responsibilities (and have handled them successfully).
- If the organization can't easily replace you or do without your services.
- After you have contributed directly to the company's profitability and success (and you can demonstrate this connection).
- When the organization is in strong financial shape.
- When your relationship with your boss is good.

What to ask for

- Research the compensation range for jobs like yours in the industry. Check with professional associations in your field or Web-based salary surveys such as **www.jobstar.org**. Demonstrate that your request is reasonable by providing comparative figures.
- Consider asking for noncash benefits. For many people, pay isn't the only kind of compensation. For example, you might also seek more vacation time, a more flexible schedule, discounts on company products, or use of a company vehicle.

Don'ts

- Don't get emotional. Losing your temper is unlikely to be persuasive, and it can damage your long-term relationship with your boss.
- Don't confuse effort with contribution. Working hard is admirable, but effort alone probably won't be enough to earn you a raise. Show your boss that the *results* you produce justify better compensation.
- Don't rely on longevity ("I've been here for 8 years") or personal need ("My rent just went up 20 percent"). It's better to demonstrate that you *deserve* a raise.

Evaluate your chances of a raise with the *Fortune* magazine quiz "Do You Deserve A Raise?" at **http://www.fortune.com/fortune/quizzes/careers/raise_quiz.html.**

Source: Based on information in Anne Fisher, "How to Get the Raise You Deserve," *Fortune* 138 (September 7, 1998), p. 169; Robin Ryan, "How to Ask for a Raise—And Get It," *Money* 26 (December 1997), p. 28; and Jane Thomas, "How to Request a Raise," *Women in Business* 51 (January–February 1999), p. 23.

b. Show undesirable consequences of the problem.
c. Highlight ethical dimensions of the situation if the current situation is morally wrong.
d. Provide causal analysis of the situation. (How did this problem develop?)

2. *Provide a solution (with supporting evidence)*
   a. Describe the positive consequences of your proposal.
   b. Show how your proposal will avoid bad consequences.
   c. Highlight the ethical reasons for your approach. Show why it's the right thing to do.
   d. Address the feasibility of your proposal. Show that it can be done: cost, time, motivation, etc. Include an operational timeline to strengthen the proposal.

Here, in outline form, is how the problem–solution plan would look in the body of a presentation proposing an employee wellness program:

I. Health-related problems are hurting our company [*Problem*]
  A. Health costs are increasing
    1. Insurance premiums are increasing
    2. Out-of-pocket expenses for employees are growing
  B. Productivity is declining due to employee health problems
    1. Absenteeism is growing
    2. Workers who stay on the job are less productive
    3. Some employees are leaving us due to health problems

II. A wellness program could reduce the impact of these problems [*Solution*]
  A. Elements of a program
    1. Nutrition education
    2. Exercise education
    3. Substance-abuse counseling
  B. Benefits
    1. Healthier employees
    2. More-productive employees
    3. Lower health costs (insurance and out of pocket)

When circumstances warrant, you might consider organizing your proposal by using one of the other persuasive strategies originally discussed in Chapter 10 and revisited later in this chapter: criteria satisfaction, comparative advantages, or motivated sequence.

Sales Presentations

In a **sales presentation,** one party presents remarks aimed at persuading another to purchase a product or service. Unlike the communication in retail settings, sales presentations are planned in advance. Sales presentations range from platform speeches in front of large audiences to less formal sit-down talks with small groups of decision makers.

Whatever their size, sales presentations will adhere to the guidelines that follow.

Establish Client Relationships before Your Presentation Whenever possible, establish relationships with your audience before you make your presentation. Getting to know the people you hope to persuade will give you valuable information on what they want, and suggest how you can satisfy their needs. Just as important, pre-existing relationships will make your listeners more comfortable with you.

Just before speaking, try to talk informally with the people to whom you'll present. This sort of conversation can help build rapport, and it can also give you ideas about how to fine tune your remarks to address what's on their minds.

Put Your Clients' Needs First Your clients don't want to hear about you or what you have to offer. They want to hear how to solve their problems. Don't focus on your products, company, services, or needs, but on the buyer's problems and concerns. What isn't working well for the client right now? What does he or she want to happen? Once you know what's missing, you can find out how your product or service can fill that need. As business expert and educator Robert Kiyosaki puts it,

"True selling means being *passionate* about your company's product or service and *compassionate* with the wants, dreams, needs of your fellow human beings." He adds that "manipulation, deception, pressure, false sincerity, and phony smiles is *not* selling. *Selling is communication*. True selling is caring, listening, solving problems and serving your fellow human being."[2]

Listen to Your Clients Unlike most other presentations, sales-oriented talks call for greater audience involvement. One study of salespeople found that the difference between top and average performers was the willingness to listen. The prospective buyers of top performers spoke between 30 and 70 percent of the time.[3] Rather than viewing questions and comments as interruptions, welcome them as a chance for you to learn what the client wants. Once you hear what's on your listeners' minds, you have the chance to speak directly to their concerns. Remain flexible: If you are interrupted, address the concerns. Then review your last points before moving on. Trainer Kevin Hogan captures this approach: "The great salespeople ask questions and have great listening skills. Poor salespeople get locked into script mode. They focus on the product they have to sell rather than the client who has a need."[4]

Emphasize Benefits, Not Features **Features** are qualities of a product or service that make it desirable and distinguish it from the competition. Salespeople can get understandably excited about features, and they are often tempted to promote these features to prospective customers. But it really isn't features that will impress customers—it's the **benefits** that will flow from those features. So you must "sell the benefit, not the feature."[5]

Here is an example of the difference between some features and benefits of a Web-based customer service product. It's obviously important to describe the features, but the benefits are what will motivate customers to sign on.

Feature	Benefit
100% Web-based	You don't have to host the product on your server or maintain it.
"Knowledge base" gives customers answers to frequently asked questions (FAQs)	Your telephone support costs are substantially reduced.
	Your support personnel are relieved from the drudgery of repeatedly answering the same questions.
	Your staff can add new solutions with a single mouse click.
Fully customizable	Lets you create the content, look, and feel just right for your business.

Use an Effective Closing Strategy In closing, a presenter must be upbeat and optimistic. Clear and realistic goals from the outset help you determine how best to close. An effective close summarizes the primary benefits and the ways in which the benefits meet or exceed clients' needs. It then calls for action. The action might be any action that moves the sale along: agreement to a test or trial run, agreement to another meeting, agreement to attend a demonstration or arrange for your presentation to higher-level decision makers. Think long term. As consultant Hans Stennek states, "I've never been a believer in closing because my objective is not to close the sale but to open a relationship."[6]

Ethical Persuasion

Since persuasion often conjures up images of unscrupulous hucksters peddling worthless products to gullible consumers, it is important to begin our discussion with a definition of persuasion as an ethical and honorable form of communication. **Persuasion** is the act of motivating an audience, through communication, to voluntarily change a particular belief, attitude, or behavior.[7] This definition helps distinguish persuasion from other ways of influencing an audience.

To understand the nature of persuasion, imagine that the city council has announced its intention to turn a local athletic field and playground into a parking lot. The area's residents are understandably upset. Faced with this situation, the residents have four choices. First, they could accept the decision and do nothing to change it. This alternative is neither persuasive nor satisfying.

A second alternative would be to use *coercion*—forcing the council against its will to reverse its decision. The group could try to coerce a change by invading and disrupting a council meeting, demanding that the council promise to keep the park or face more demonstrations. Threatening to mount a recall campaign against any members who insist on supporting the parking lot would be another coercive approach. Although threats and force can change behavior, they usually aren't the best approach. The recipient of the threats can counterattack, leading to an escalating cycle of hostility. Threatened parties often dig in their heels and resist changing to save face or as a matter of principle, responding, "I'll be damned if I'll change just because you threaten me." Coercion also makes the instigator look bad.

Dilbert: © Scott Adams/Distributed by United Feature Syndicate, Inc. Reprinted by permission.

A different approach to getting someone to change his or her mind involves *manipulation*—tricking the other party into thinking or acting in the desired way. A deceptive approach to the park-versus-parking lot problem might be to present the council with a petition against the lot containing forged signatures that inflate the petition's size or to gain public sympathy by exaggerating the adverse effects of the project on certain groups—children, the elderly, and small-business owners, for example.

It is reassuring to know that, besides being ethical, honesty is also the best effective policy when it comes to changing the mind of an audience. Social judgment theory (explored in detail later in this chapter) reveals that a "boomerang effect" often occurs when receivers learn that they have been the target of manipulative communication. Faced with this discovery, they will often change their attitudes in the direction opposite that advocated by a speaker.[8] In other cases, speakers are viewed as more credible when they openly admit that they are trying to persuade an audience.

A final way to achieve change is persuasion—communication that convinces the other person to act voluntarily in the desired way. The citizens' group could organize an appeal showing that the community sees keeping the park as more important than increasing the amount of available parking. It could describe the benefits of the park, bringing in local residents to testify about its importance to the community. What you'll learn in the following pages is how to make the best possible case for your position so that others will voluntarily choose to accept it.

Manipulation, persuasion, and coercion don't fall into three distinct categories. Rather, they blend into one another, like colors of the spectrum:

Coercion Persuasion Manipulation

ethical challenge

Principled Persuasion

Contrast an ethical persuasive approach to each of the following situations with coercive and manipulative alternatives:

1. A boss tries to get volunteers to work weekend hours.
2. A union representative encourages new employees to join the union.
3. An insurance agent tries to persuade a young couple to buy life and income protection policies.
4. The representative for a waste disposal company tries to persuade residents of a town that locating a regional recycling center nearby would be good for the community.
5. A sales representative needs one more sale to meet his monthly quota and knows that a competitor's product better meets this client's needs.

Consider the example of the city park: Speakers could remind the council that unhappy voters might remember the decision to close the park and choose other candidates in the next election. Approaches like this seem to have a coercive element even if they give the other party a choice of whether to comply. The boundary between persuasion and manipulation is also fuzzy. If speakers compliment council members on their past concern for the environment and responsiveness to the voters before trying to persuade them to cancel the parking facility, are the speakers being persuasive or deceitful? If they stage an emotional but accurate series of pleas by children who will be forced to play in the street if the lot is built, are they being manipulative or merely smart?

The point where one method of gaining compliance stops and another begins will vary from situation to situation. Perhaps the best measures of whether a particular message is genuinely persuasive are (1) whether the recipient feels truly free to make a choice and (2) whether the originator would feel comfortable if he or she were the recipient of the message instead of its sender.

Persuasive Strategies

Over 2,500 years ago, the Greek philosopher Aristotle crafted a study of persuasion called *The Rhetoric.*[9] In that work, Aristotle identified three approaches that can maximize a speaker's influence. He labeled them *ethos,* which today is usually termed "credibility"; *logos,* or logic; and *pathos,* which includes what could be called "emotionally resonant psychological appeals."

Revisiting and updating Aristotle's strategies provides a wealth of guidelines for effective persuasion. The following pages will review each of these strategies.

Maximize Your Credibility

Winston Churchill once said that, when it comes to public speaking, what matters most is who you are, then how you say what you want to say, and, finally, what you say. Even without taking this assertion literally, it is true that credibility is a powerful factor in persuasion. **Credibility** is the persuasive force that comes from the audience's belief in and respect for the speaker. When your audience has little time or inclination to examine your evidence and reasoning in detail, it will rely almost exclusively on your credibility to decide whether to accept your claims.[10] Research shows that you can enhance your credibility in a variety of ways.[11]

Demonstrate Your Competence Listeners will be most influenced by a speaker who they believe is qualified on the subject. You are more likely to believe career advice from a self-made millionaire than from your neighbor who has been fired from four jobs in 3 years. Similarly, the department staff is more likely to accept the direction of a new manager who seems knowledgeable about the specific work of that department. Management is more likely to agree to take a risk on a new manufacturing material if the product manager seems to know the market very well. These are all examples of trusting someone's competence.

There are three ways to boost your competence. The first is by demonstrating your *knowledge of the subject*. For example, the product manager might help to establish her credibility by citing statistics ("Our market research showed that 85 percent of the potential market is more concerned with maintenance costs than the initial cost of the product. A study published in the trade journal last month demonstrated that maintenance costs are often 80 percent of the cost of the equipment"). She could also remember facts ("Dorwald Associates tried something like this, although only in government markets, and it was pretty successful") and recent appropriate examples ("I was checking the records last week, and I realized that we could afford to replace the machines every 5 years on what we'd save on maintenance if we used plastic instead of metal").

A second way to demonstrate competence is by making your *credentials* known. These credentials could be academic degrees, awards and honors, or successful experiences ("I helped set up Hinkley's very profitable system a few years ago, and I think the same approach we took there could help us now"). To avoid the appearance of egotism, it can be best to have others talk about your credentials ("Clara has a degree in accounting, so her ideas have special value here").

A third way to show your competence is through *demonstration of your ability*. This means speaking effectively during your presentation, of course. But with an audience who already knows you, the reputation you have acquired over time will be even more powerful. If you have a reputation for being talented and hardworking, listeners will be disposed to accept what you have to say. If they regard you as incompetent, you will have a hard time persuading them to accept the ideas in your presentation.

Earn the Trust of Your Audience The most important ingredient of trustworthiness is *honesty*. If listeners suspect you aren't telling the truth, even the most impressive credentials or grasp of the subject will mean little. For instance, a union leader gets little support from union members if they think that he's made a private agreement with management. If your motives will ever be suspect, confess them before others can raise doubts ("I know the compensation plan in this proposal will benefit me, but I hope you can see how it will boost productivity and cut turnover"). Of course, you should never say *anything* that can be considered dishonest.

Impartiality is a second element of trustworthiness. We are more likely to accept the beliefs of impartial speakers than of those who have a vested interest in persuading us. If you have a vested interest in the position you are presenting (e.g., asking for a pay raise or a desired assignment), you can boost your credibility by citing impartial third parties who support your position. With the pay raise, for example, you might cite salary surveys showing that the compensation you are seeking is in

line with industry standards. If you are asking for a plum assignment, you could get the people with whom you would be working to endorse your request.

Emphasize Your Similarity to the Audience Audiences are most willing to accept the ideas of a speaker whose attitudes and behaviors are similar to their own. This persuasive ability exists even when the similarities are not directly related to the subject at hand. Thus, a subordinate may get a better hearing from the boss when both are golfers, have children of the same age, come from the same part of the country, or dress similarly. Customer-service representatives for farm machinery generally wear casual clothing and open-necked shirts to fit in with the people they visit. Many sales representatives begin conversations with prospects by mentioning a common interest—gardening, baseball, or a recent event that affects the customer's business.

Similarity in areas related to the speaker's topic is even more persuasive. This fact has led to the strategy of establishing *common ground* between speaker and listeners early in a presentation. A speaker who shows that he and the audience have similar beliefs will create goodwill that can make listeners willing to consider more controversial ideas later on. Notice, for example, how a business owner seeking a zoning variance based her appeal to the local architectural review board:

> *Like you, I'm a strong believer in preserving the character of our town. As a businesswoman and a long-time resident, I realize beauty and lack of crowding are our greatest assets. Without them, our home would become just another overgrown collection of shopping malls and condominiums.*
>
> *Also, like you, I believe that change isn't always bad. Thanks to your efforts, our downtown is a more interesting and beautiful place now than it was even a few years ago. I think we share the philosophy that we ought to preserve what is worth saving and improve the town in whatever ways we can. I appreciate the chance to show you how this project will make the kind of positive change we all seek.*

This speaker's chances of gaining acceptance for her proposal were increased by her demonstrated support for the principles the board promotes. Of course, the board has to believe that the speaker is sincere. If they suspect she is just telling them what they want to hear, her credibility will shrink, not grow.

Use Logical Arguments

An organized presentation isn't necessarily a logical one. Many arguments that sound logical at first are actually flawed by errors in reasoning, or **fallacies.**[12] Fallacious reasoning isn't always intentional: The person making the case might not be aware that his or her thinking is flawed. Whether or not they are deliberate, fallacies can weaken your case by casting doubt on the merits of your position. The following pages describe the most common fallacies (by both their English and Latin names), so you can avoid using them.[13]

career tip

Logic vs. Emotion: Which Is Better?

Some presentations are based on highly reasoned arguments backed up by plenty of fact-based supporting material. Others appeal more to the listeners' emotions. What support they offer may have more entertainment value than logical force. Well-told jokes or dramatic stories may not pass a careful analysis, although they can capture the attention of some audiences.

Which type of support—logical or emotional—is better? According to the *elaboration likelihood model of persuasion*, the answer depends on your audience. Listeners who are highly involved in a subject and care deeply about it are most likely to look for strong arguments backed up by a wealth of supporting material. By contrast, listeners who are less involved with the subject are more easily persuaded by an engaging speaker who delivers easy-to-digest stories and examples. They also rely more heavily on the credibility and likability of a speaker than the content of his or her arguments.

Fortunately, choosing logic vs. emotion isn't an either–or matter: Most presentations will contain elements of each approach. Still, understanding your audience can help you decide which approach has the best chance of success in a given situation.

Note: For a more detailed discussion of the elaboration likelihood model, see Em Griffin, *A First Look at Communication Theory*, 5th ed. (New York: McGraw-Hill, 2003).

Personal Attack (*Ad Hominem*) An *ad hominem* fallacy attacks the integrity of a person in order to weaken the argument he or she is making. Some ad hominem arguments are easy to spot: Calling someone an "idiot" isn't very persuasive. Other *ad hominem* arguments aren't so obvious, though.

Reduction to the Absurd (*Reductio Ad Absurdum*) A *reductio ad absurdum* fallacy attacks an argument by extending it to such extreme lengths that it looks ridiculous. "If we allow developers to build homes in one section of this area, soon we will have no open spaces left." Or, "If we have our after-hours customer service handled by an offshore company, pretty soon we won't have any employees here at home." Far-fetched projections like these call for a closer look: Developing one area doesn't necessarily mean that other areas have to be developed, and hiring some employees from overseas won't necessarily lead to widespread layoffs at home. Either of these policies might be unwise, but the *ad absurdum* reasoning doesn't prove it.

Either-Or An either–or fallacy sets up false alternatives, suggesting that if the inferior one must be rejected, then the other must be accepted. "If you believe that the arts in this community are important, you'll contribute to our fund-raising campaign." This sort of argument ignores the fact that it's possible to support the arts in other ways besides donating to a particular cause.

False Cause (*Post Hoc Ergo Propter Hoc*) A *post hoc* fallacy mistakenly assumes that one event causes another because they occur sequentially. Post hoc fallacies aren't always easy to detect without careful research. For example, a critic might blame the policy of letting some employees work from home for a drop in productivity, noting that output began to drop shortly after telecommuting was introduced. A casual link in this case *may* exist, but there might be other reasons for the decline: A change in the nature of work, for example.

career tip

Standing in Your Audience's Shoes

Many persuasive attempts fail because communicators fail to understand how their appeals look to the people they are trying to reach. You can overcome this sort of blindness by imagining yourself to be a member of your prospective audience. What would you know? What would your attitudes be toward the topic? Your level of interest? How would you regard the speaker? By walking a mile in your listeners' shoes, you can learn how to construct messages that focus on them, and not on yourself.

Bandwagon Appeal (*Argumentum Ad Populum*) An *argumentum ad populum* fallacy is based on the often dubious notion that, just because many people favor an idea, you should too. Sometimes, of course, the mass appeal of an idea can be a sign of its merit. If leading companies have adopted a product, then there's a good chance it will work for yours. But in other cases widespread acceptance of an idea is no guarantee of its validity. The majority of employees in your company might invest the bulk of their retirement plan dollars in the company's stock, but almost every financial advisor will tell you that this is a dangerous idea. The lesson here is simple to comprehend but often difficult to follow: Don't just follow the crowd; consider the facts carefully and make up your own mind.

Use Psychological Appeals

Logical arguments and your own credibility are both strong assets when you're trying to persuade others. In addition, though, a number of strategies for presenting your arguments will boost the odds that you can achieve your goal.

Appeal to the Needs of Your Audience Perhaps the key to effective selling is identifying the prospect's needs and showing how the product can satisfy them. One organization's success at implementing this principle was featured in *Fortune* magazine:

> *[At Lanier] a salesman does not merely sell hardware. He goes into an office, asks to see how the paperwork is handled, makes himself an overnight expert about the business involved, then prepares a plan for increasing its productivity by using a specific Lanier machine. When he gives a demonstration, he programs the machine to churn out that prospect's actual paperwork.*[14]

Even if the audience is not interested in or is unsympathetic to an idea, there is usually some way to link a proposal to the listeners' needs or values. A representative of an oil company speaking to residents of a coastal town where offshore drilling is being proposed could defend the move by showing how the local economy would benefit and how drilling platforms increase the abundance of marine life in the oceans, which in turn improves fishing.

Whenever possible, base your appeal on several needs. Listeners who are not reached by one appeal can still be persuaded by another. If you were trying to persuade your fellow workers to use public transportation instead of driving their own cars to work, you could identify several needs and show how your proposal would satisfy each one:

Need	Satisfaction
Save money	Getting out of your car, even for a few days each week, means you'll spend less on gas, parking, wear, and auto maintenance.
More time	On the bus or train, you can read and/or work instead of having to drive yourself.
Less stress	You won't have to deal with the aggravation of traffic congestion and annoying drivers.

Make Your Goal Realistic Presentational speaking is like most other aspects of life: You usually don't get everything you want. Even the best presentation can't accomplish miracles. Asking audience members to accept an idea that they strongly oppose can backfire. Social scientists have refined this commonsense principle into *social judgment theory*.[15]

This theory helps speakers decide how to craft their arguments by identifying the range of possible opinions listeners might have about a speaker's arguments. (See Figure 14–1.) A listener's preexisting position is termed an **anchor.** All the arguments a persuader might use to change the listener's mind cluster around this anchor point in three zones. The first area is the listener's **latitude of acceptance.** As its name implies, this zone contains positions the listener would accept with little or no persuasion. By contrast, the **latitude of rejection** contains arguments that the listener opposes. Between these areas lies the **latitude of noncommitment,** containing arguments that the listener neither accepts nor rejects.

Social judgment theory teaches a very practical lesson about how much to ask from your audience. Arguments in the listeners' latitude of noncommitment may not impress them, and those in the latitude of rejection will just strengthen their opposition. The best chance for success comes when your plea is at the outer edge of the audience's latitude of acceptance. Communication scholar Em Griffin offers a perfect example of this principle:

> *A striking story of social judgment theory in action comes from a university development director I know who was making a call on a rich alumnus. He anticipated that the prospective donor would give as much as $10,000. He made his pitch and asked what the wealthy businessman would do. The man protested that it had been a lean year and that times were tough—he couldn't possibly contribute more than $20,000.*

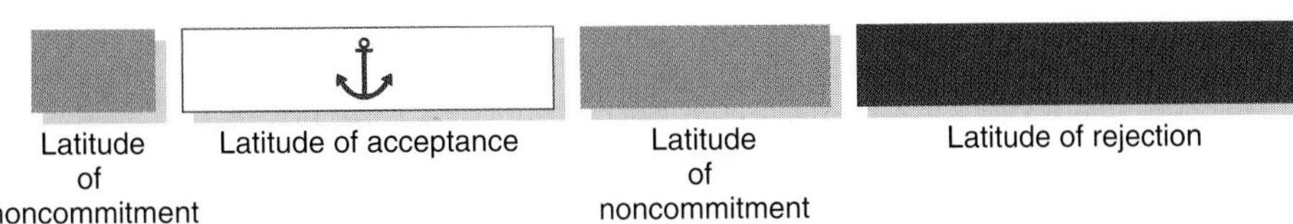

FIGURE 14–1 Range of Responses to a Persuasive Appeal

The fund-raiser figured that he had seriously underestimated the giver's latitude of acceptance and that $20,000 was on the low end of that range. Without missing a beat he replied, "Trevor, do you really think that's enough?" The alumnus wrote a check for $25,000.[16]

Social judgment theory teaches that persuasion isn't a one-shot affair. In many cases your persuasive campaign will consist of many messages delivered over time, each one aimed at expanding your listeners' latitude of acceptance. An oil company representative defending his company's proposal to start offshore drilling shouldn't expect his arguments about promoting business growth and increasing marine life to turn opponents into enthusiastic supporters. Rather than asking for their endorsement, his goal might simply be to have them recognize that offshore drilling is "not all that bad." Similarly, a sales representative trying to sell furnishings for a new office building should not expect to make a $2 million sale on her first call; she might try only to make an appointment to present her proposal to a planning committee.

A human resources assistant at a medium-sized company used the lessons of social judgment theory to choose a realistic goal in her campaign to persuade the corporation to set up a day care center for the preschool-aged children of employees. Rather than ask her boss to authorize funds for the center—a goal she knew was unrealistic—she requested approval to conduct a feasibility study in which she would explore the ways that similar companies provided for child care. If the boss responded favorably to the center after seeing the results of this survey, she would present a full-blown proposal. If he still had doubts, her backup proposal was to suggest that the company subsidize tuition at a nearby child care center—a plan closer to the boss's anchor point.

Focus Appeals on Critical Audience Segments Sometimes one or two listeners have the power to approve or reject your appeal. In cases such as this, it is important to identify the interests, needs, attitudes, and prejudices of the key decision makers and then focus your appeal toward them. For instance, if the office-furnishings sales representative finds that most of the members of the planning committee vote with the president, her presentation to the committee will be aimed at his apparent needs and interests. If she finds that the president doesn't meet with the planning committee, she might try to get an appointment to speak with the president.

Defer Thesis with Hostile Audience Usually, you state your thesis during the introduction of a presentation, but this rule may not be effective with skeptical or hostile listeners. If a manager seeking acceptance of changes in staffing thinks that the audience will respond favorably to her thesis ("Increased business has led us to open up several new positions, and we'd like you to apply for them"), she'll put the idea in the introduction of the speech. If she believes the thesis will not be received enthusiastically ("Employee contributions to health care premiums will have to increase") or if she believes an audience that hears the news too early will be too upset to accept—or even hear—the rationale behind the decision, she will present the thesis later in the speech.

A presentation with a deferred thesis still needs an introduction to capture the attention of the audience, demonstrate the importance of the topic, and orient the listeners to what will follow. In talks with a deferred thesis, the part of the introduction containing the preview carries the extra burden of setting up the thesis without stating it directly:

> *It's no secret that increasing health care costs, combined with an industrywide slump, have hurt the company. Today I want to tell you how management has tried to cope with these problems in a way that will protect our jobs as much as possible.*

After the preview, the body of the presentation leads the audience members, step by step, to the point at which they are ready to understand and accept the speaker's thesis:

> *Given the problems we've faced, management's choice has been to either lay off personnel, cut wages, or ask all of us to help pay for our own health care. We hope you agree that our decision to ask us to chip in on health costs is the best one under the circumstances and that you'll realize we still consider you valuable members of our team.*

Present Ample Evidence to Support Claims Chapter 11 outlined the types of support that can help you prove your claims: examples, stories, statistics, comparisons, and quotations. When your goal is to persuade an audience, the generous use of support is especially important.

Research demonstrates that when an audience hears persuasive evidence backing up a persuasive claim, the chances increase that the influence of the message will last long after the presentation has concluded.[17] Furthermore, evidence supporting a claim makes listeners less likely to accept opposing viewpoints that they may hear after you have finished speaking.

The best evidence comes from credible sources. If your credibility on the subject is not high, be sure to cite others whose expertise and impartiality your listeners respect. For example, a prospective customer would expect a sales representative to praise a product he or she is trying to sell. But if the salesperson cites others who know the product and who don't have an interest in its sale, the message ("This product is excellent") becomes more persuasive. In this case, the testimony of other customers or of an independent testing service such as Consumers Union would be excellent evidence.

Consider Citing Opposing Ideas Research indicates that it is generally better to mention and then refute ideas that oppose yours than to ignore them.[18] There are three situations when it is especially important to forewarn listeners about opposing ideas.

When the audience disagrees with your position With hostile listeners, it's wise to compare their position and yours, showing the desirability of your thesis. If management has previously opposed products similar to the one you are about to propose, for instance, you'll need to bring up the managers' objections ("It's too risky, the capital outlay is too big, and the sales force can't sell it") and show how your proposal will meet their objections ("We can minimize the risk and the initial costs by limiting the first production run; if we put extra emphasis on advertising and show the salespeople how other companies have sold similar products very successfully in the last few years, they'll be more enthusiastic and more effective"). Similarly, if you're trying to sell an out-of-the-way plant location to a company that is planning to build its new plant in a more central location, you might show that transportation is as cheap and available in your location as in the central one or that savings on real estate taxes and labor will allow the company to pay higher transportation costs. If you don't mention arguments that are already on their minds, your listeners may consider you uninformed.

When the audience knows both sides of the issue Well-informed listeners, even if they haven't made up their minds about an issue, will find a one-sided appeal less persuasive than a presentation that considers opposing arguments. Discussing these ideas shows that you are not trying to avoid them. Even if you refute the competition, considering it at all is more evenhanded than focusing exclusively on your plan and never acknowledging that alternatives exist.

An account executive at a full-service stock brokerage showed that he respected the knowledge and judgment of his listeners at an investment seminar when he discussed the alternatives to using the services of his firm:

> *I know that most of you are familiar enough with the financial marketplace to be asking yourself "Why don't I save money and use a discount brokerage?" And that's a fair question. After all, discount firms charge you a much smaller commission for each transaction than full-service houses like mine. I'd like to suggest that the answer to the question of which kind of brokerage to use lies in the old saying "You get what you pay for." If you use a discount firm, you'll get limited service. Now, that may be all you want and all you need. But if you're looking for a source of financial support and attention, you'll get it at a full-service brokerage. Let me explain.*

When the audience will soon hear your viewpoint criticized or another one promoted You will be better off defusing the opponents' thesis by bringing up and refuting their arguments than by letting them attack your position and build up theirs in its place. For example, a union organizer speaking to a group of plant workers might anticipate an argument from management this way:

> *The company representative will tell you that after we organized the Oregon plant, the people were out of work, on strike, for 4 months the next year. That's true. What the company probably won't tell you is that the people got strike pay from the union. The company also won't tell you that the people there were losing money every year before that because their wages weren't keeping up with inflation, and the strike got them guaranteed cost-of-living raises, plus life, health, and disability benefits and improved safety conditions.*

Adapt to the Cultural Style of Your Audience

The cultural background of your listeners may affect the way they respond to various types of persuasive appeals.[19] The intensity of emotional appeals is a good example. The traditional Euro-American ideal is to communicate without becoming too excited. By contrast, cultures in Latin America and the Middle East are generally more expressive, and their members respond more favorably to displays of emotion. An approach that would seem logical and calm to an audience in Seattle or Toronto might seem cold and lifeless to a group in Mexico City or

Istanbul. Conversely, a Mexican or Turk speaker might seem overly excitable to a group in the United States or Canada.

The types of supporting material that are regarded as most persuasive also differ from one culture to another. Euro-American culture places a high value on data that can be observed and counted. Statistical data and eyewitness testimony are considered strong evidence. Communicators from other backgrounds are less impressed by these sorts of proofs. Arab speakers commonly rely on religious and national identification. They are more likely to use elaborate language, which would be considered flowery by other cultural standards. In some parts of Africa, for example, the words of a witness would be regarded with suspicion because members of that culture believe that people who speak out about a topic have a particular agenda in mind.

As Chapter 10 suggested, acceptable ways of organizing a message also vary. U.S. presenters are used to straightforward messages that introduce a thesis early in the presentation, develop it in the body, and summarize it in the conclusion. Japanese presenters rely less on a strong, direct close. Instead, they stress harmony with the audience, relying on this climate to generate acceptance of an idea.

Differences like these make it important to know the cultural preferences of your audience. Just because listeners come from a particular country or belong to a particular ethnic group doesn't mean they can be stereotyped, especially in a shrinking world where communication and travel blur national boundaries. Nonetheless, being sensitive to the attitudes of your listeners can help you avoid delivering a message that antagonizes, rather than persuades, them.

Organizing Persuasive Messages

Credibility may be important, but the way you structure your message also plays a major role in determining how successful you will be at persuading an audience. Chapter 10 discussed several patterns for organizing the body of a presentation. Here we recap the use of problem–solution, comparative advantages, criteria satisfaction, and motivated sequence patterns as they apply to persuasive situations. As Table 14–1

Table 14–1 Considerations for Choosing a Persuasive Organizational Pattern

Organizational Plan	Considerations
Problem-solution	Most basic persuasive pattern. Most helpful when audience needs convincing that a problem exists.
Comparative advantages	Use when audience is considering alternatives to your proposal. Show how your plan is superior to others. Defer thesis if audience will object to idea before hearing your reasoning.
Criteria satisfaction	Use when audience is not likely to consider alternative plans. Choose criteria important to your audience, and show how your plan meets them. If audience may be hostile to your plan, introduce criteria before discussing the plan.
Motivated sequence	Use when problem and solution are easy to visualize. Effective when seeking immediate audience reaction.

shows, there is no single best plan. The one you choose will depend on the topic and your audience's attitude toward it.

Problem–Solution

As its name suggests, a **problem–solution** plan first persuades the audience that something is wrong with the present situation and then suggests how to remedy the situation. This plan works especially well when your audience does not feel a strong need to change from the status quo. Since listeners have to recognize that a problem exists before they will be interested in a solution, showing them that the present situation is not satisfactory is essential before you present your idea. For example:

Problem	Solution
Many employees are arriving late due to increasing congestion.	Offer flexible working hours.
Cost of travel is skyrocketing.	Increase capability to hold some meetings via videoconference.

A problem–solution pattern might also be used to show how updating a computer system will solve problems with inventory monitoring, why a potential customer needs a personal financial advisor, or why a department needs additional staff.

If your listeners already recognize that a problem exists, you may not need to spend much time proving the obvious. In such circumstances, you might touch on the problem in the introduction to your talk and devote the entire body to suggesting a solution. If you are competing against other ideas, however, a comparative advantages plan may be a better organizational strategy.

Comparative Advantages

A **comparative advantages** approach puts several alternatives side by side and shows why yours is the best. This strategy is especially useful when the audience is considering an idea that competes with the one you're advocating. Under this circumstance, ignoring alternative plans is a bad idea. A head-on comparison that supports your case is a far more effective plan. The manager of a health club used a comparative advantages approach to encourage new members:

Introduction: When you decide to join a health club, you have several choices in the area. You might be tempted by the special introductory rates at some other clubs in town, but a feature-by-feature look shows that Millennium is your best choice.

Body:

I. The club is open longer every day than any other club in town.

II. The club has more exercise machines than any other in town.

III. The club has a wider variety of activities than any other in town: aerobics classes, swimming, saunas, massage, racquetball, and a snack bar.

IV. The club's staff are all licensed fitness counselors—a claim that no other club in town can make.

Conclusion: When it comes to value for your dollar, Millennium is your best health-club choice.

In the preceding example, the speaker made her thesis clear at the beginning of her presentation. A comparative advantages approach also works well when you choose to defer your thesis. In this instance, you can build a case showing how your proposal is superior to the alternatives and then present your thesis as a conclusion. An insurance agent used this strategy to convince an audience to buy coverage:

Introduction: How should you spend your discretionary income?

Body: There are several alternatives.

I. You can spend it all on recreation, but that won't buy financial security for your family if anything happens to you.

II. You can make investments to plan for the future, but there is always the risk of losing that money.

III. More expensive housing is an option, but it risks placing you even more in debt.

IV. Insurance guarantees your family an income if you die or are disabled.

Conclusion: At least some of your disposable income ought to be devoted to insurance. [*Deferred thesis*]

In this situation, deferring the thesis was a smart idea. If the speaker had started by praising the virtues of buying insurance, most listeners would have tuned out. Since very few people relish the thought of spending their discretionary income on something as intangible as more insurance coverage, they'd probably reject the idea unless they were led to the conclusion that it is the best choice.

Criteria Satisfaction

A **criteria satisfaction** strategy sets up criteria for a plan that the audience will accept and then shows how your idea or product meets them.

> "When you look for a long-distance phone carrier, you want one that has low rates. You also want one that has a strong signal and allows you to make calls when you're away from home."

After establishing your criteria, you show how the product, service, or idea you are presenting will meet the criteria.

> "Let me show you how TeleCall offers you low rates from anywhere, with quality that meets or beats the big carriers."

on your feet

Public Service Announcement

Public service announcements (PSAs) are short pieces aimed at persuading audiences to support nonprofit organizations, issues, or causes.

Develop your persuasive skills by creating and presenting to your group a 30-second or 1-minute PSA that supports the good cause of your choice. This may be an on-campus service (e.g., counseling, job placement, health services, fitness center) or a community cause (United Way, open space, recycling, child care).

Organize your PSA using the motivated sequence approach described on this page and pages 345–353 in Chapter 10. Create an outline that follows this plan, labeling each step (attention, need, satisfaction, visualization, action).

It can be even more effective to invite the audience to supply the criteria. If you have researched your audience, you should know in advance what they are likely to want, and your appeal will be even more effective:

> "I'd like you to tell me, What are the things that you want in a long-distance phone carrier?"

Once your listeners have identified what will satisfy them, you can show how your product or service will meet their needs. Organize criteria in the order of importance to the client, not to you.

Unlike a comparative advantages approach, a criteria satisfaction plan does not consider alternative ideas. For this reason, it is a good approach when your audience isn't likely to think of alternative plans.

Motivated Sequence

As you read in Chapter 10, the **motivated sequence** approach has five steps:

1. Attention
2. Need
3. Visualization
4. Satisfaction
5. Action

The need and satisfaction steps are similar to those in a problem–solution approach, but the visualization and action steps add a new element. The visualization step allows listeners to picture how your solution could work for them. An event planner proposing to organize a wedding or a business meeting might show clients photos of similar occasions she planned or describe in vivid detail the way she proposes to create a memorable occasion for this client. As its name implies, the action step calls for the listeners to go beyond just agreeing with the presenter to take a step toward adopting his or her plan. Salespeople sometimes call this step "closing," because it cements the deal.

Self-Assessment Persuasive Strategies

Rate your presentation on the following items using this scale: 3 = accomplished excellently, 2 = accomplished competently, 1 = needs improvement.

	3	2	1
1. I maximized my credibility by			
a. Demonstrating my competence through knowledge of the topic and sharing my credentials.	3	2	1
b. Earning the trust of my audience via honesty and impartiality	3	2	1
2. I structured my arguments logically by			
a. Using the most effective organizational plan for my goal and audience (problem-solution, criteria satisfaction, comparative advantages, motivated sequence).	3	2	1
b. Avoiding the use of logical fallacies (*ad hominem, post hoc*, etc.).	3	2	1
3. I used appropriate psychological strategies such as			
a. Appealing to the needs of my audience.	3	2	1
b. Structuring a realistic goal.	3	2	1
c. Focusing my appeals on my critical audience segment.	3	2	1
d. Deferring my thesis with a hostile audience.	3	2	1
e. Presenting ample evidence to support my claims.	3	2	1
f. Citing opposing ideas when appropriate.	3	2	1
g. Adapting to the cultural style of my audience.	3	2	1
4. I took an ethical approach by relying on genuine persuasion, not coercion or manipulation.	3	2	1

Sample Sales Presentation

The following presentation (outlined in Figure 14–2) demonstrates most of the persuasive principles covered in this chapter as well as the general guidelines about speaking to an audience introduced in Chapters 10 through 13. The purpose and approach are based on a sound audience analysis. As you will see, the talk has a clear thesis and a clear, logical organizational structure. A variety of verbal and visual supports add interest, clarity, and proof.

The speaker's company, Ablex Technologies, manufactures sophisticated electronic components. One of its best customers is BioMedical Instruments (BMI), which produces a wide variety of sophisticated medical diagnostic instruments. The company's biggest contracts with BMI are for kidney-dialysis and blood-analyzer parts, which total almost $1 million per year.

Under a much smaller and older contract, Ablex also supplies BMI with parts for an X-ray unit. BMI doesn't make the unit anymore but is committed to furnishing

FIGURE 14–2
Outline of Sample Presentation

```
Thesis: The proposed forecasting and purchasing agreement will allow
both BMI and Ablex to better supply X-ray parts in a timely, affordable,
and trouble-free manner.

Introduction
      I. Our basically positive relationship with BMI has only one
         problem: the X-ray parts.
     II. While a problem does exist,there is a solution
            A. The problem involves erratic orders for X-ray parts.
            B. Our solution has several benefits.

Body
      I. Supplying X-ray parts has been a continuing headache.
            A. Orders for X-ray parts are irregular and unpredictable.
               [line graph]
            B. These irregular orders make it tough to ship orders to
               BMI in a timely way. [example]
     II. Fortunately, there is a solution to the X-ray problem.
            A. Here's an outline of our plan.
            B. The plan has several advantages.
                  1. Orders can be delivered more quickly.
                     [comparison chart]
                  2. Order is more flexible. [examples]
                  3. Time can be saved in ordering and follow-up.
                     [example]
                  4. The unit cost is less than under current plan.
                     [column chart, comparison chart]

Conclusion: By now you can see that there's a solution to the X-ray
  problem.
      I. The plan has advantages for everyone involved.
     II. We look forward to putting it into action soon.
```

current users with replacement parts until the machines drop out of use, and Ablex is obliged to supply BMI. Producing these X-ray parts is usually a problem: Orders are small and sporadic, leading to delays and headaches for everyone concerned. The speaker is presenting a plan that offers a better way to handle replenishment of the X-ray parts.

The audience is Mary Ann Hirsch, the buyer at BMI, and two production engineers. Although the purchasing director and the chief project engineer are not at the presentation, they will rely on the information gathered by their subordinates and, ultimately, will be the ones to approve or reject this idea—so in a way, they're part of the audience, too.

[Introduction emphasizes the positive aspects of the relationship with the customer. Brief sketch of the problem establishes common ground. "We're in this together, and it's no good for either of us."]

We've been involved in a long, positive relationship with BMI. The only troubles we've ever encountered have come from the X-ray parts. Even though they are only a small part of our business with you, they seem to involve the greatest headaches for you and us. The timing of these orders is impossible for you to predict, which makes it hard for us to get parts from our suppliers and deliver the product to you quickly. This leads to all sorts of problems: unhappy customers who have to wait for the equipment they ordered and time spent by people at both of our companies keeping in touch.

[Preview lists the main advantages of the plan that will be proposed.]

We think there's a better way to handle the X-ray problem. It'll reduce frustration, cut costs, and let all of us spend our time on more productive parts of our jobs. But before we talk about this new plan, let me review why the present arrangement for handling X-ray orders is such a headache.

[Transition leads to the "problem" section of the presentation.]

The main problem we face is irregular orders. A look at the order history for the last year shows that there's no pattern—and no way to predict when customers will order replacement parts for their X-ray units. [*The speaker shows Exhibit 1 here.*]

[Visual exhibit clearly demonstrates the unpredictable nature of customer orders.]

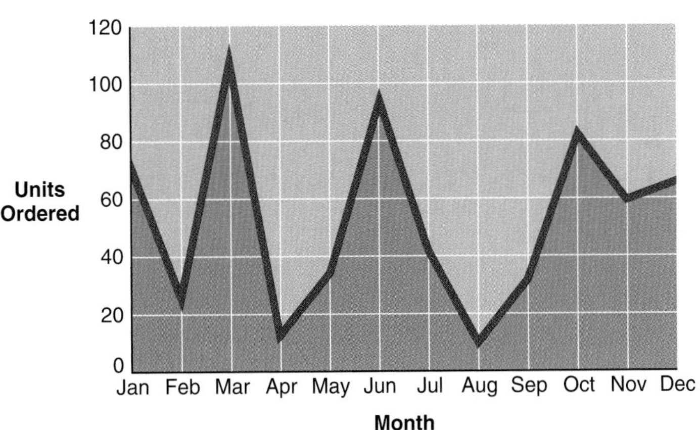

EXHIBIT 1
X-Ray Ordering Pattern

[Example shows the problems flowing from irregular orders.]

This unpredictable pattern makes it tough for us to serve you quickly. We have to order parts from our suppliers, which often can take a long time. For instance, in the February 17 order, it took 6 weeks for our suppliers to get us the parts we needed to manufacture the X-ray components you needed. Once we had the parts, it took us the usual 4 weeks to assemble them. As you said at the time, this delay kept your customer waiting almost 3 months for the components needed to get their equipment up and running, and that's poison for customer relations.

[Example highlights amount of time wasted.]

Delays like this aren't just bad for your relationship with customers, they also waste time—yours and ours. Mary Ann, do you remember how many phone calls and letters it took to keep track of that February order? In fact, every year we spend more time on these X-ray orders that involve a few thousand dollars than we do on the dialysis and blood-analyzer parts that involve around a million dollars annually. That's just not a good use of time.

[Transition leads to the second consequence of irregular orders: wasted time. "Solution" part of the presentation then introduced.]

So we clearly have a situation that's bad for everybody. Fortunately, we believe there's a better way—better for you, us, and your customers. The plan involves your giving us an annual purchasing forecast for X-ray parts. Instead of waiting for your customers to place individual orders, you'd estimate the total sales likely to occur in a year. Then we would acquire enough parts from our suppliers to assemble those items so that we could have them ready quickly as your customers place orders.

[Advantages of solution are previewed in the chart.]

This simple plan has several advantages. They're summarized on this chart, but let me explain them in a little more detail. [*The speaker shows Exhibit 2 here.*]

- Quicker delivery
- Flexible ordering
- Fewer problems
- Lower cost

EXHIBIT 2
Advantages of Annual Forecasting for X-Ray Parts

[Strongest advantage to listeners is introduced first to get positive impression early.]

The first advantage is that advance purchasing will speed up delivery of your orders. Instead of waiting for our suppliers to ship parts, we can begin to assemble your order as soon as you send it. You can get an idea of the time savings by looking at how much time this plan would have saved on the order you placed in February. [*The speaker shows Exhibit 3.*]

[Bar chart graphically demonstrates time saved.]

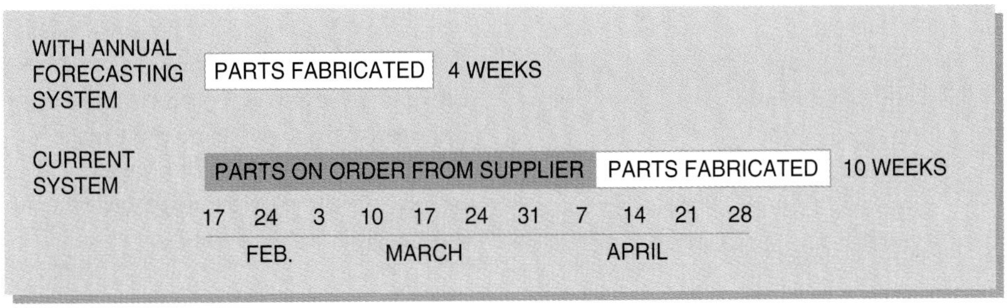

EXHIBIT 3
Annual Forecasting Speeds Delivery Time

[Transition leads to the second advantage of the plan: flexibility. Hypothetical example helps audience visualize this advantage.]

Besides being quick, the plan is flexible. If you wind up receiving more orders than you anticipated when you made your original forecast, you can update the plan every 6 months. That means we'll never run out of parts for the X-ray units. Suppose you projected 1,400 units in your original forecast. If you've already ordered 1,000 six months later, you could update your forecast at that point to 2,000 units and we'd have the parts on hand when you needed them.

[Transition leads to anticipation of a possible listener objection: What if orders decrease? Credible authority is cited to support this point.]

This semiannual revision of the forecast takes care of increases in orders, but you might be wondering about the opposite situation—what would happen if orders are less than you expected. The plan anticipates that possibility, too. We're willing to extend the date by which you're obliged to use your annual estimate of parts to 18 months. In other words, with this plan you'd have 18 months to use the parts you expected to use in 12. That's pretty safe, since Ted Forester [BMI's vice president of sales and marketing] predicts that the existing X-ray machines will be in use for at least the next 6 or 7 years before they're replaced with newer models.

[Internal review reminds listeners of previously introduced advantages and leads to identification of a third benefit: less wasted time.]

Flexibility and speed are two good advantages, but there are other benefits of the plan as well. It can save time for both you and us. You know how much time we spend on the phone every time there's a surprise X-ray order, and I imagine you have to deal with impatient customers, too. Talking about delays is certainly no fun, and with this annual purchasing plan it won't be necessary since we can guarantee delivery within 3 weeks of receiving your order. Think of the aggravation that will avoid!

[Second most important advantage is introduced last, where it is likely to be remembered by listeners.]

By now, you can see why we're excited about this plan. But there's one final benefit as well: The plan will save you money. When we order our parts in larger quantities, the unit price is less than the one we face with smaller orders. We're willing to pass along the savings to you, which means that you'll be paying less under this plan than you are now. Notice how ordering a year's supply of parts drops the unit price considerably. [*The speaker shows Exhibit 4.*]

[Chart visually highlights cost savings.]

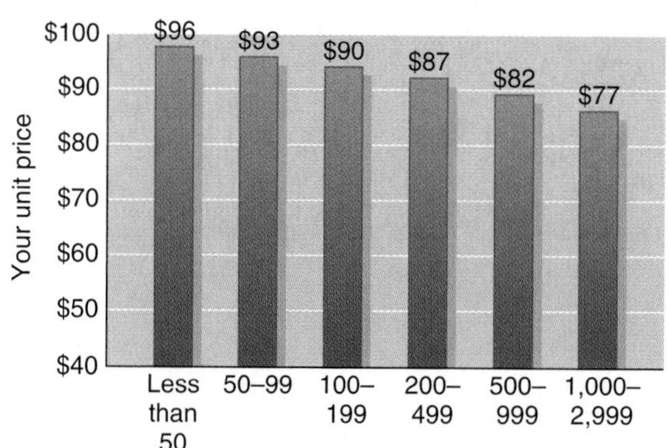

EXHIBIT 4
Annual Forecasting Reduces Unit Price

You can see that this plan is a real money saver. Compare the savings you could have realized on last year's order of 597 units if this plan had been in effect. [*The speaker shows Exhibit 5.*]

597 units at higher unit price	$55,506
597 units at volume unit price	45,969
First year savings	$ 9,537

EXHIBIT 5
One Year's Saving with Annual Forecasting Plan

[Conclusion reviews the plan's advantages and makes appeal to adopt it.]

So that's the plan. It's simple. It's risk-free. It's convenient. It's flexible. And along with all these advantages, it can cut your costs. We're prepared to start working with you immediately to put this plan into action. If we start soon, we'll never have to deal with X-ray headaches again. Then we can put our energy into the larger, more satisfying projects that are more rewarding for both of us.

summary

Many business occasions call for persuasive presentations such as motivational and goodwill speeches. Other times a proposal or sales presentation is needed. Proposals advocate a specific action and consist of two parts: the problem and the solution (with evidence). Sales presentations are most successful in the long term when they establish client relationships, consider client needs, listen to and welcome clients' participation, focus on benefits not features, and use effective closings.

Ethical persuasion differs from manipulation and coercion although all are best thought of on a continuum rather than as absolutely distinct. Coercion implies pressure or force and manipulation connotes trickery. In contrast, ethical persuasion encourages listeners to make free choices after hearing sound reasoning and accurate information.

Speakers heighten their credibility by demonstrating competence, trustworthiness, and similarity to the audience. Speakers earn the trust of their audience through honesty and impartiality. Successful speakers avoid fallacies or errors in reasoning such as personal attacks, reduction to the absurd, either–or, false cause, and bandwagon appeals.

Finally, the persuasiveness of the message is directly linked to the messages organizational plan. The audience, topic, and goal will determine which persuasive organizational plan will be the most effective: problem–solution, comparative advantage, criteria satisfaction, or motivated sequence.

key terms

Test your understanding of these key terms by visiting the Online Learning Center Web site at www.mhhe.com/adler9.

activities

Go to the self-quizzes at the Online Learning Center at www.mhhe.com/adler9 to test your knowledge of chapter concepts.

1. Invitation to Insight

Attend a professional persuasive presentation. Based on the descriptions in this text of various types of persuasive presentations, would you consider the presentation successful? Which of the speaker's strategies did you find effective? Which strategies did you find to be ineffective? Did the presentation illustrate ethical persuasion? How did the speaker establish credibility? Explain your answers and provide examples.

2. Skill Builder

Choose a product or service that you are familiar with, or choose one of these: off-site archiving of computer files; cell phone pricing plan with unlimited long distance; deli delivery service for employees; company-supported memberships at a health club.

a. Identify an audience to whom you could sell this product.
b. Create a chart with two columns: features and benefits. List and differentiate between the features and benefits of the product.

3. Skill Builder

Browse through the editorial or opinion columns section of your local newspaper. Locate two or three logical fallacies. Revise the statements so they illustrate accurate facts and sound logic.

4. Skill Builder

Select two topics about which you are qualified to deliver a persuasive presentation (e.g., if you have worked as a babysitter, you could explain why it's important to read out loud to children; if you own a cat, you could encourage the audience to have their pets neutered; if you cycle you might encourage cyclists to wear helmets). How would you make your audience aware of your credibility in your speech?

5. Skill Builder

What organizational plan would be best suited to the message in each of the following situations?

a. Showing a customer why leasing a car is a better choice than buying one.
b. Convincing a charitable foundation to grant money to your job-training program for disadvantaged teenagers.

c. Demonstrating the features of an expensive computer system.
d. Persuading the loan officer at a local bank to lend you money for your proposed business venture.
e. Encouraging local businesspeople to join a service club to which you belong.

6. Invitation to Insight

Read a persuasive article in a magazine or newspaper. Try to determine which organizational pattern the article follows. Why do you think the author chose this pattern? Is it effective for the intended audience?

resources

In Print

Bates, Suzanne. *Speak Like a CEO*. New York: McGraw-Hill, 2005.

This guide to persuasive communication is useful for presenters at every stage of their careers. It describes the characteristics of effective business communicators and offers guidelines on a variety of topics including how to handle question-and-answer sessions and deal with the mass media.

Daley, Kevin, and Laura Daley-Caravella. *Talk Your Way to the Top*. New York: McGraw-Hill, 2004.

Communicators who aspire to advancing in their careers will find useful guidelines in this practical book. Persuasive guidelines include how to sell ideas, how to deliver bad news, and how to move a group to action.

Inch, Edward S., and Barbara Warnick. *Critical Thinking and Communication: The Use of Reason in Argument*, 5th ed. Boston: Allyn & Bacon, 2005.

The authors show how constructing and countering arguments is important in interpersonal and public speaking settings. They provide examples of effective reasoning in everyday life with examples from law, education, and business contexts. The book includes insights into the role of ethics and culture in constructing and understanding arguments.

Larson, Carl U. *Persuasion: Reception and Responsibility*, 11th ed. Belmont, CA: Wadsworth, 2007.

This text contains many resources for aspiring persuaders: a discussion of ethical issues (Chapter 2), perspectives from the humanities (Chapter 3) and social sciences (Chapter 4), and cultural perspectives (Chapter 9).

Stiff, James B., and Paul A. Mongeau. *Persuasive Communication*, 2nd ed. New York: The Guilford Press, 2003.

This text examines the fundamentals of persuasion research and the components of persuasive transactions such as source credibility, rational and emotional appeals, and receiver characteristics and settings. The authors blend classic theory and current research examples.

On the Web

Successful Presentations

The Virtual Presentation Assistant at **www.ku.edu/~coms/virtual_assistant/vpa/vpa.htm** provides tools for developing presentations, assistance in numerous aspects of speaking, and links to various other public speaking Web sites. For a refresher in business presentations, visit **www.presentingsolutions.com/effectivepresentations.html**. Although it is a commercially maintained site specializing in presentation equipment, this Web page contains news, trends, and tips from the business presentation world.

Evaluating Online Evidence

For help in critically analyzing information on the Web, go to **www.widener.edu/Tools_Resources/Libraries/Wolfgram_Memorial_Library/Evaluate_Web_Pages/659/?vobId=1816**. Another Web site that offers tips for critically analyzing various information sources, including Web sites, is maintained by Cornell University and can be found at **http://www.library.cornell.edu/okuref/research/skill26.htm**. This site lists questions to ask during an initial appraisal of the source and for a more in-depth content analysis. Finally, the site hosted by Mankato, **http://krypton.mnsu.edu/~verkom/w3pgs/text.htm#eval** takes you step-by-step through

Web site evaluations and provides links to several Web review tools.

Argument and Persuasion Resources

The Humboldt State University Web site (**www.humboldt.edu/~speech**) provides multiple links to Internet resources helpful in constructing and evaluating persuasive messages, including resources for critical thinking, argument, logic, and several guides to fallacies with examples and exercises, plus links to public address archives and rhetoric resources from other universities.

Logical Fallacies

Find out more about how fallacies interfere with effective reasoning by referring to Stephen's Guide to Logical Fallacies (**www.intrepidsoftware.com/fallacy/toc.php**) or The Nizkor Project (**www.nizkor.org/features/fallacies**). For additional guides, go to **www.csun.edu/~dgw61315/fallacies.html** and **www.drury.edu/ess/Logic/Informal/Overview.html**.

appendix

Business Writing

Entire books and academic courses are devoted to the study of business writing. This appendix is no substitute for a thorough study of this important topic. It does, however, provide some guidelines about creating the most common types of written business messages. Many organizations have their own styles, which may vary in one or more ways from these basic rules. When you are writing on behalf of an organization, you will want to learn and follow its conventions.

Fundamental Considerations

Just as your style of dress and grooming creates a first impression when you meet others in person, the appearance of your written messages makes a powerful statement to readers, who are likely to consider them a reflection of your other qualities. Besides creating a good impression of yourself, well-designed and well-executed business writing makes your message easier to understand. Likewise, a shabby report, letter, or memo has the same effect as stained clothes, bad breath, mumbling, or rambling on disjointedly.

Formatting

The appearance of your written message can shape the reaction it creates as much as the content. One consultant put it this way: "In memos and reports, intonation and body language aren't available to you. That's what formatting is for—to substitute for them."[1]

The first decision when formatting a business document is whether to write it in longhand or type it. The culture of an organization usually offers clues about when handwritten notes are acceptable, so pay attention to how the successful people around you communicate.

Two occasions when handwritten notes are definitely appropriate—even preferable—are for personal messages of congratulations or condolence. In addition, it may be acceptable to jot a quick note to a colleague or boss in longhand. In virtually every other situation, though, use a word processing program and the best-quality printer you can find. High-quality print is easier to read and creates a more businesslike impression than a handwritten or poorly printed one.

Most organizations prefer black type. Be certain that the printer you are using produces sharp, uniform letters that are dark enough to read and that all of the lines print square with the paper. Reprint any pages that are out of alignment.

Documents should be laid out on the page so that they are easy to read and understand. Margins should be at least an inch all around. Center the copy on the page so it is not crammed toward the top, bottom, or one side. A left-aligned document with a ragged right edge is easier to read than a justified document that has a straight right margin.

For most documents, choose a type size between 9 and 12 points. On shorter pieces of correspondence, you might use 12-point fonts and increase the margins to create a better-looking layout. On longer documents, resist the temptation to squeeze everything on one page by using print smaller than 9 point or margins less than 1 inch. Rewriting more concisely or using two pages makes a better impression than cramming.

The typeface you use also sends a message. The most common typefaces used in business are Times Roman (called a serif typeface because its "feet" make the letters appear to flow together and is easy to read) and Helvetica or Arial (sans serif typefaces with no "feet"). Sans serif typefaces work well for titles and headings, as they are sharp and clear. In business documents, avoid shadow, script, outline, or radically different typefaces, as they can be difficult to read and may call more attention to the medium than the message.

Paper

The traditional dimensions for business correspondence in the United States and Canada are 8½ by 11 inches, although some memo forms are smaller, and legal documents are usually printed on 8½- by 14-inch paper. White is the standard color for business paper, although neutral colors like light gray or tan are sometimes used, especially for company letterhead stationery. In certain organizations, memos are sent on colored paper to make them easily identifiable: red borders to get attention and green for those requiring a response.[2] Know what is expected in your organization. It is best to avoid brightly colored paper, since it is hard to read or make copies of. Slick or highly textured paper may result in blurred ink.

High-quality paper makes your messages look better and ensures that they will stand up under the reading, routing, filing, photocopying, faxing, and other punishments many documents receive. Paper quality is measured in weight: The higher the weight, the higher the quality. For reports and memos most offices use 16- to 20-pound paper. Stationery and résumés create the best effect when they are printed on at least 24-pound paper. The cotton content of paper is also a measure of its quality. Stock of at least 25 percent cotton has a better look and feel than the noncotton variety. Color, weight, and design of second pages and envelopes should match.

Spelling and Grammar

The content of your correspondence should match its high-quality appearance. Even a single error can stand out to readers, drawing their attention away from all the effective aspects of your message. A glaring mistake in an otherwise perfect document can have the same effect as a piece of food stuck between the teeth of an impeccably dressed and groomed person.

Some spelling errors can be caught with spell-check programs, but this technology will not correct all mistakes. Spell-checks may not catch *principle* instead of *principal* or *it's* where *its* is correct. You must still proofread. Spell-checking is also no help with most names. You will have to be sure that the letter to Ms. MacGregor doesn't leave your desk addressed to Ms. McGregor.

Grammar is just as important as spelling. Incorrect constructions can make you look ignorant or sloppy, leaving the reader to speculate about whether you may be as incompetent in other areas as you are in writing. Many word processing programs have a grammar-checking capability, but they are not foolproof. Careful reading can improve both grammar and syntax.

Writing Well

How well you write is as important as how your documents look. Here are some guidelines for effective business writing.

Adapt to Your Audience

Put yourself in the shoes of the person or people who will read your message, and write in a way that addresses their concerns, knowledge, and interests. Ask yourself questions such as "What do they want or need to know? How much detail is necessary? Why should they care about my topic? What will motivate them to do what I'm asking?"

Once you have identified what your readers care about, write in a way that demonstrates your concern. When responding to a complaint, don't say, "The long wait you experienced was due to a temporary staffing shortage." (The reader isn't likely to care about your staffing problems.) Instead, say, "You are absolutely right: Customers shouldn't have to wait for service." Make the receiver's needs the subject of your first sentences. Instead of writing "We received your request for a refund and will begin working on it" write "You should receive your refund within 4 days."

Organize Carefully

Business writing must first and foremost be organized. As when you are planning an oral presentation, start by listing all of the items you need to cover. Then group the items into logical categories. Finally, arrange the categories into a clear organizational pattern according to your purpose. One general rule is to list items from most to least important. Another is to consider what the reader needs to know first in order to understand what comes next. The organizational patterns in Chapter 10 can also be used in many written messages.

Writing experts recommend putting good news first whenever possible: "Your order will be shipped today." If you are delivering bad news, try to begin by expressing agreement, appreciation, or explanation: "I was very pleased with the quality of your crew's work on the recent job. The only question I have is about the $250 listed as 'extra charges.' . . ."

Your message will be clearest if you build coherence into each paragraph as well as into the overall design. Use parallel structure, repeat key words, and use transitions as demonstrated in Chapter 10.

Be Concise

Time is precious for most businesspeople. Author William Strunk said: "Vigorous writing is concise. A sentence should contain no unnecessary words, a paragraph no unnecessary sentences, for the same reason that a drawing should have no unnecessary lines and a machine no unnecessary parts." There are several ways to tighten up your writing:

- *Omit needless words and phrases.* If one word will do, use it and eliminate the others. Some phrases are too cumbersome for business writing. For instance, "at the present time" can more succinctly be stated "now." Other common phrases can be shortened:[3]

Lengthy Phrase	Shortened Version
The question as to whether	Whether
Enclosed please find	Enclosed
In the month of May	In May
We are in receipt of	We received
Please do not hesitate to call	Please call
Please be advised that I will arrive at 8:00.	I will arrive at 8:00.
A distance of 3 feet	3 feet

- *Eliminate "who is" and "that are."*[4] The sentence "Jeannette, who is the paralegal, declined to comment on the case" could be stated more simply: "The paralegal Jeannette declined comment on the case," or "Jeanette, the paralegal, . . ."
- *Don't overuse intensifiers* ("really," "very," "so") *and superlatives* ("fantastic," "best"). Avoid excessive and unnecessary adverbs ("absolutely," "positively").
- *Avoid "fumblers."* Phrases like "what I mean is" and "what I'm trying to get at is" imply "I don't think I'm being clear" or "I don't think you can understand what I mean from what I wrote."[5]

Be Clear

Whenever possible, use precise terms, describe in details, and quantify facts rather than give opinion or evaluations. Use concrete statements rather than abstract ones and avoid jargon, slang, clichés, and idioms.

- *Use precise terms that give specific details.* "We will contact you soon" leaves the reader asking, Who will contact me? How will contact be made? Letter, phone, in person? When will I be contacted? Next week? Next month? Instead, write "Our sales manager, Nahid Ravi, will phone you by June 6th."
- *Avoid slang and pop culture terms.* Author Patricia O'Conner tells the story of a Microsoft techie who used the phrase "I'll run some cycles on that." She didn't know what he meant and only after several conversations with colleagues did she discover that he probably meant that he'd think about it.[6]
- *Avoid jargon.* When writing for external audiences, avoid jargon and acronyms that may not be understood. Certain writers, like human resource personnel, may be particularly guilty of corporate-speak or what O'Conner calls "jargonistas" as they try to make a corporate message palatable to those negatively affected by it. She defines jargon as "language used by windbags and full of largely meaningless, pseudotechnical terms that are supposed to lend the speaker an aura of expertise."[7] But when writing for internal audiences, carefully

evaluate your use of jargon and acronyms: If you are certain all readers understand them, they may save time.

- *Back up your writing with facts.* Eliminate phrases such as "I believe" and "We think." If what you say is true, state the fact. If not, leave opinion out. Words such as "good" or "slow" evaluate without telling the reader the facts. Relative words such as "big" or "small," "expensive" or "cheap" give the reader no data on which that word choice was made. It can be advantageous to use both evaluative and factual words: "This office space is economical. The lease is only $4,000 per month."

Evaluative or Relative Words	Facts and Figures
This is an *excellent buy.*	Construction costs are $85 per square foot.
This new printer is *expensive.*	It costs $875.
We need a *large* office space.	We need at least 8,000 square feet.
Many customers made returns *recently.*	Five customers made returns today.
This printer is *wonderful.*	It prints 18 sheets per minute and uses refillable cartridges.

- *Use the active voice.* The passive voice exists when the person who is performing the action is the object of a preposition or the direct object in a sentence. "The memo was sent by the director" is passive. "The director sent a memo" uses active voice. Active voice creates more lively and direct writing.
- *Avoid bias.* Avoid language and visuals that reinforce stereotypes of sex, disability, ethnicity, or age. Respectful unbiased language can promote goodwill, portray you and your company in a positive light, and avoid legal complications.

  You can avoid gender bias several ways. Use "woman" rather than "girl" for an adult female. Write without assuming gender or marital status. Avoid "vice presidents and their wives" and use "vice presidents and guests." Use titles that describe the job, not the gender.

Avoid	Better
Workman	Worker or employee
Fireman; policeman	Firefighter; police officer
Waiter or waitress	Server or waitstaff

Avoid using masculine pronouns (he, his, him) when referring to both men and women. When possible, use a plural subject so that you can use plural pronouns (they, them, their). For example, instead of saying, "A financial planner should give his clients his best advice," write "Financial planners should give their clients their best advice." If it is appropriate to be directive, using the second-person form of address ("you") is another way to write with a gender-neutral style: "You need to give your clients your best advice." Another technique (depending on your audience) is to reword the sentence to eliminate the pronoun: "A financial planner must give the client the best advice, even when doing so may lead to reduced compensation." If none of these techniques will work, use both pronouns: "A financial planner must give his or her clients the best advice." Use this method as a last resort, since sentences like this are awkward and call attention to your usage.

- *Use names and titles consistently*. If you are referring to everyone in a group by first and last name, don't add a title (Mrs. or Dr.) to only one person. If you are referring to everyone with a title and a last name, don't refer to lower-ranking, female, or minority participants by first name. Stay fair and consistent. Use "Ms." to refer to all women, unless you are certain there is a personal preference for Mrs. or Miss.
- *Refer to the age, race, or different ability of an individual only if it is necessary*. If you need to refer to ethnicity or race, use the term preferred by the group or the individual (see Chapter 2's discussion of ethnicities and disabilities). Always refer to a person before a condition. Use "persons with HIV," not "HIV patients or victims." Use "persons who use wheelchairs" not "crippled persons" or "persons *confined* to wheelchairs." Don't label groups of people by a condition (epileptics, amputees). Use the additional guidelines for avoiding bias in your writing found at **www.apastyle.org/disabilities.html**.
- *Avoid terms that call attention to the success or competence of someone in a way that implies their achievement is unusual*. Do not say: "He is quite computer-literate for a 60-year-old" or "She is a well-qualified woman."

Build Goodwill

The best way to build goodwill is to demonstrate that you have the reader's best interests in mind.

- *Emphasize positive concepts rather than negative ones*. State what can be done rather than what can't be or hasn't been done. When writing to your boss to say that you cannot work next Tuesday, be certain to state that you are available any other day of the week. If you will be unavailable for phone calls from October 22–24, state in your memo that you will be available at 8:00 A.M. on July 25.
- *Adopt a helpful and respectful approach*. Blaming others and using "you" statements often create defensiveness. "You didn't turn in your time sheet before the June 1 deadline" is an accusatory "you" statement that blames the reader. You minimize the chance of a defensive reaction by saying the same thing just as clearly and less aggressively: "Since we received your time sheet on June 4, your check will be processed with others submitted that week and will be ready June 15."

Use Business Writing Resources

Many Web sites provide help with general writing skills and business writing issues. Four premier online writing workshops are hosted by Purdue University (**http://owl.english.purdue.edu**), University of Texas (**www.utexas.edu/cola/uwc**), Colorado State University (**http://writing.colostate.edu/index.cfm**), and University of Kansas (**www.writing.ku.edu**). Grammar, punctuation, sentence, and paragraph help are just a click away—along with excellent advice, tutorials, exercises, and links to additional resources. For additional business writing tips, go to **www.techpubs.com/resources.html** and **www.grammarbook.com**.

Two excellent resources for business writers are M. E. Guffey, *Business Communication: Process and Product*, 5th ed. (Cincinnati: South-Western College Publishing, 2006); and K. O. Locker, *Business and Administrative Communication with CD, PowerWeb, and BComm Skill Booster*, 6th ed. (Boston: McGraw-Hill/Irwin, 2002).

Routine Business Correspondence: Memos, Letters, E-Mail

Most routine business writing falls into three categories: memos, letters, and e-mail. Each type of document has its own writing conventions.

Memos

Memos are the form to use when you are sending important messages within your organization. It isn't necessary to create a formal memo for every message. When you need to send a quick note to an officemate, jotting a few words on a memo form, Post-it Note, or scratch paper may be appropriate. If your message is an important one, if it will affect the way you are judged in the organization, and if it will be filed for future reference, you should invest the time to carefully draft and format your memo.

Style and Format Most memos should be short and to the point, although they should never be so brusque as to seem rude. Memos don't contain a salutation or complimentary close, and it isn't necessary to begin or conclude with the kind of niceties ("It was good to see you yesterday") you might use when writing a letter.

Most organizations have standardized formats for memos. The document in Figure A–1 illustrates a common one. Most word processing programs have memo templates. Because they are used for internal messages, memos are usually not sent on the kind of top-quality paper that is used for letters. The paper used may be regular 8½- by 11-inch paper or half-size sheets measuring 5½ by 8½ inches. The paper size is usually standardized within the organization.

The body of a memo should resemble a letter in appearance: single-spaced, with blank lines separating paragraphs. Ideally the memo will be no longer than one page, since lengthier ones may not get the kind of full reading you want.

Elements Every memo should contain the same basic elements:

1. Heading
2. Date
3. Addressee
4. Sender
5. Subject

Heading Memos are usually identified by the heading MEMO or MEMORANDUM, in capital letters centered at the top of the page.

FIGURE A–1
Memo Format

MEMORANDUM

DATE: April 6, 2007
TO: Distribution*
FROM: K. Osgood
Director of Support Services
SUBJECT: Voice mail training

The new voice mail system is scheduled for installation on May 11. To have a smooth transition from our present phone system, all employees should receive training before installation day.

The following dates and times are available for training. All training will be conducted in the second-floor conference room. Please arrange to have everyone in your department attend one session.

Only 15 employees can be accommodated at each meeting, so please write or call Jane Finney at extension 327 to reserve spaces. Personnel who have not reserved times by April 19 will be scheduled into available slots.

Date	Time
April 27	9:00–10:30
	11:00–12:30
	1:00–2:30
April 28	8:30–10:00
	10:30–12:00
	1:00–2:30
May 4	9:00–10:30
	11:00–12:30
	1:00–2:30
May 8	1:00–2:30
	3:00–4:30

* Department heads
K. Fernandez
E. Washington

c: H. Wylie, Key Communications Corp.

Date The date should indicate when the memo was sent, not when it was written. If the information in the memo changes before the memo is sent, adjust the content and the date.

Addressee In a memo, it is usually not necessary to use a courtesy title like "Mr." or "Dr." with the addressee's name. You should include a courtesy title only if you would use the title when speaking to the addressee in person. In many organizations the accepted form is simply the addressee's first initial and last name (e.g., "J. Banducci").

If the memo is being sent to an entire group of people (e.g., department heads, sales representatives), simply indicate the category on the addressee line. If the memo is going to a large number of people who do not fit into an easy category, put the words "See distribution list," or simply "Distribution" with an asterisk, on the addressee line. Then list the names of all the addressees below the body of the memo.

Sender Use the same format for your name as you do for the addressee's name, usually minus any courtesy titles ("Mr.," "Ms."). If the recipient does not know you, or if it would be helpful to add the weight of your position in the organization, include your department and/or your personal title ("Monica Bayless, Accounts Receivable Supervisor"). A memo doesn't contain a signature line, but you may write your initials next to your name on the "FROM" line after the message is printed out.

Subject The "SUBJECT" line helps the receiver identify the nature of your message quickly and makes it easier to file the memo. Try to keep the subject line brief. Instead of saying "Results of the survey you requested on customer satisfaction," simply put "Results of customer satisfaction survey."

Letters

Whereas memos are used for internal correspondence, letters are the right format when you are sending printed correspondence to people outside your organization.

Standard Elements Figure A–2 illustrates the standard elements in a business letter. Using the proper format isn't just a social nicety: Each element serves a purpose.

The standard elements of a business letter include:

1. Heading
2. Date
3. Inside address
4. Salutation
5. Body
6. Complimentary close
7. Signature block

Heading The heading of a letter shows its source: the organization's name, address, and phone number. Most organizations have printed letterhead that contains the heading. For personal correspondence, position this information (excluding your name) about 2 inches from the top of the first page. A word processing program allows you to create a simple, yet professional, letterhead by using a distinctive typeface and size.

Dateline Insert the date the letter was written 13 lines from the top or 1 blank line beneath the bottom of the letterhead. Spell out the month and include the number of the day and all four digits of the year. In the United States and Canada, the most common dateline format is month-day-year (January 15, 2006), although in the military and some other organizations the day-month-year (3 February 2006) format is used (with no comma separating the month and year). For international correspondence, check the accepted format for the recipient's region.

Inside address The inside address identifies the recipient of the letter and is separated from the date by one blank line. The amount of space separating the inside address from the date may be adjusted to suit the length of the letter.

A courtesy title should precede the recipient's name. For men, "Mr." is correct unless the addressee merits a professional title such as "Doctor" or "Captain." For

Heading	8719 Weldon Drive Raleigh, NC 28328 (919) 555-9812
Date	January 12, 2007
Inside address	Claims Department Triton Health Insurance Co. P.O. Box 27212 Chicago, IL 60601
Attention line	Attention: Mr. Newsome
Salutation	Dear Mr. Newsome:
Subject line	Subject: Policy No. 27-445-8976-1
Body	Thank you for helping to clarify my questions about the delay in paying my claim for physical therapy arising from my recent tennis injury. As you requested in our phone conversation today, I am enclosing the following information: 1. A copy of the most recent statement from my physical therapist. 2. A letter from the personnel director at Carlton Industries verifying that I was a full-time employee at the time of my injury. It has been four months since I first filed my claim for these services. As you can imagine, I am anxious to be reimbursed for the expenses, as provided in my policy. If you need any further information, please write or phone me immediately.
Complimentary close	Sincerely,
Signature block	Geoffrey Hsu
Enclosure line	Enclosures (2)
Copy line	Copy: Personnel Office, Carlton Industries

FIGURE A–2
Modified-Block Letter Format

women who do not use a professional title, "Ms." is generally the safest form of address. If, however, you know that the addressee prefers to be identified as "Mrs." or "Miss," you should use that title.

It is always best to address your letter to a specific person. You can usually identify the name of the person you are seeking by checking the organization's Web site or telephoning the organization and saying, "I will be sending some correspondence to the volunteer coordinator. Can you give me that person's name?" If you do not know the name of a specific person, it is acceptable to address the letter to the department or to a job title (e.g., "Director, Department of Human Resources").

If the addressee's organizational title is short, it can be included on the same line as his or her name: "Ms. Miranda Cortez, General Manager." If the recipient has a longer title, or if the title includes a department, this information can be displayed on a single line below the name.

Immediately following the addressee's name and title, separate lines should contain the name of his or her company, the street address or post office box number, and the city and state or province with proper zip or postal code. If you are writing internationally, the addressee's country should follow in capital letters and occupy its own line.

Salutation The way you address the recipient is governed by your relationship with that person. If you have not met, or if the relationship is a formal one, use his or her title and surname: "Dear Mr. Cooper." If you are on a first-name basis with the recipient, it is probably appropriate to use that form of address in your salutation: "Dear Marianne."

If you need to write a letter without knowing the name of the recipient, you may use "Ladies and Gentlemen" or "Dear Sir or Madam." "Dear Business Manager" and "Dear Customer Service Representative" may also be used but these forms of address sound impersonal and are more often used in mass mailings. It might be possible to forego the salutation if the title on the inside address will assure delivery to the correct person.

Body The body of your letter will usually occupy the greatest amount of space. It should be single-spaced, with a blank line separating it from the preceding and following parts of the letter. You should also separate each paragraph of the letter by a blank line.

Within the body, use formatting to help the reader: indented and/or bulleted lists, italics, and bold. Be certain these are consistent with your organization's style sheet and with the message you want to convey.

Complimentary close The complimentary close is a single word or phrase, separated from the body by a blank line. Your choice of close provides a way to create just the desired tone. "Very truly yours" or "Sincerely yours" seem outdated. "Sincerely" and "Cordially" are widely accepted closings. "Best regards" is a less formal closing.

Signature block Place the signature block four lines below the complimentary close. Include your name and title (either on the same line as your name or immediately below). If your name might leave doubt about your gender, you may include a title in the signature block. If you prefer a specific title (Ms.), include it here.

Additional Elements In some letters you may have to include additional information that is not part of the standard elements. There are special ways of formatting this information that allow you to convey specific messages without cluttering up the body of the letter. It is unlikely that you will ever send a letter containing all of these elements, but sooner or later each of them will find its way into your correspondence.

Addressee notation This line should be printed above the heading, separated by two blank lines. It is used to indicate any special handling the letter should receive. Common notifications include "URGENT," "CONFIDENTIAL," and "PERSONAL." The entire addressee notification should be in capital letters to emphasize its importance.

Attention line The attention line is a means of directing your letter to a specific department or position title when you do not know the name of the person for whom your message is intended. It can also be used to personalize a letter when you only know the last name of the recipient. Common attention lines take these forms:

ATTENTION: CREDIT DEPARTMENT

ATTENTION: Food Services Director

ATTENTION: Ms. James

The attention line may be placed within the inside address, just below the name of the company, or it may be placed two lines below the inside address. In either case, the form you use on the mailing envelope should match the form you use in the letter itself.

Subject line The subject line provides a clear indication of the topic of a letter, which is especially important when you are writing to an office that receives a high volume of mail. The subject line will increase the chances that your message will get the right sort of attention and that it will be easy to file and locate.

There are two possible positions for the subject line: It may be positioned just below the salutation, separated by a blank line. Alternatively, it can be set above the salutation, in the position that an addressee notation might go in another type of correspondence.

Reference initials When the person who processes the letter is someone other than its signer, that person's initials are usually included below the signature block. If the writer's name is included in the signature block, only the preparer's initials need appear as a reference. If the letter is written on behalf of a company and does not bear the signature of an individual sender, then the initials of both the writer (in capitals) and the preparer (in lowercase letters) should be included. Either of the following forms is acceptable:

SWA:gh SWA/gh

Enclosure line An enclosure line indicates that materials accompany the letter itself. This serves as a useful check to make sure that anything that was supposed to be included in the mailing is, indeed, enclosed. It also provides a permanent record about any enclosed material.

The enclosure notation appears at the bottom of the letter, a line or two below the signature block and reference initials, if any. The notation may simply state "Enclosures" if the specific contents are described in the body of the letter. Or it may specify either the number of enclosures ("Enclosures: 2") or their actual contents ("Enclosure: Rate schedule").

Copy line A copy notation lets the addressee know who else will be receiving the letter. The notation should be set flush with the left margin, below any reference initials and enclosure notations. The following forms are commonly used to indicate a copy notation:

cc: Rebecca Haynes   pc: Rebecca Haynes
c: Rebecca Haynes   copy to Rebecca Haynes

Mailing line If the letter is sent by a means other than first-class mail (e.g., certified mail, special delivery, fax), it may be desirable to indicate this fact. The notation may be placed in either of two locations: at the top of the letter, just above the inside address; or below the signature block and any other notations described in this section.

Postscript A postscript (p.s.) is traditionally an afterthought that occurs to the sender after the body is written but before the letter is sent. When taken in this sense, postscripts should be avoided: If a message is important enough to dignify with a letter, you should compose it thoughtfully.

A second use for postscripts is to emphasize or separate an idea from the body of the letter. You might, for example, append personal congratulations for an accomplishment or thanks for a favor to the body of a businesslike message. Because of their "by the way" nature, postscripts are more appropriate when the sender and addressee have a familiar relationship than in a letter to a stranger.

Second-page header If a letter is longer than one page, a heading at the left margin top of the second and following sheets will help make your correspondence easy to identify. Subsequent pages should contain the name of the addressee, the page number, and the date. Each of these elements may be on a separate line:

Mr. Eldon Press
July 22, 2006
Page 2

They may be combined on a single line set flush with the left margin:

Mr. Eldon Press, July 22, 2006, Page 2

Or they may be separated by tabs and centered on the page:

Mr. Eldon Press   2   July 22, 2006

Letter Formats Most business letters follow one of two formats: the block format (see Figure A–3) and the modified-block format (see Figure A–2). The main differences between these styles are the placement of elements and the way they are indented. Either format is acceptable for a business letter, although some organizations may have a standard style that should be followed in any correspondence written on company letterhead.

In the block format, each element and paragraph is set flush with the left margin. In the modified-block format, the date, complimentary close, and signature block appear just to the right of the center of the page. In this format the first line of each paragraph in the body may also be indented five spaces, although this feature is not required.

Envelopes The envelope that contains your letter will be the first thing the receiver sees, so it should look just as professional as the correspondence contained

1225 Chicago Ave.
Evanston, IL 60208

March 14, 2006

Ms. Mary Lou Nelson
Manager of Human Resources
Continental Industries, Inc.
2900 Rosemont Blvd.
Rosemont, IL 60018

Dear Ms. Nelson:

Come to the point. Reveal your purpose and interest. Identify the position and your source of information. Introduce your themes.

I am applying for the Web developer position that was advertised with Northwestern University Career Services this week. The position seems to fit very well with my education, experience, and career interests.

Outline your strongest qualifications that match the position requirements based on the themes you selected. As much as possible, provide evidence of your related experiences and accomplishments. Make reference to your enclosed résumé.

Your position requires skills in various types of programming and software used in Web development. My academic program in computer studies emphasized C, C++, Visual Basic, Assembler, Java, and SQL. In addition, I have extensive experience in using several software packages in Web development, including Adobe Illustrator, Photoshop, After Effects and Dreamweaver. My experience as a department computer consultant gave me exposure to both PC (Windows 3.1, 95, 98, NT) and Macintosh platforms as well as Novell and NT LANs. Additionally, I worked as a summer intern in computing operations for a major city newspaper where I gained knowledge of enterprise systems and e-commerce operations. My enclosed résumé provides more details on my qualifications.

I am confident that I can perform the job effectively. Furthermore, I am genuinely interested in the position and in working for Continental Industries, Inc. Your firm has an excellent reputation and comes highly recommended to me.

Suggest an action plan. Request an interview, and indicate that you will call during a specific time period to discuss interview possibilities.

Please consider my request for a personal interview to discuss further my qualifications and to learn more about this opportunity. I shall call you next week to see whether a meeting can be arranged. Should you need to reach me, please feel free to contact me at 847/683-4388 or m-lopez@northwestern.edu.

Express appreciation to the reader for his or her time and consideration.

Thank you for your consideration. I look forward to talking with you.

Sincerely,

Maria Lopez

Maria Lopez

FIGURE A–3
Job Application Letter in Block Format

Source: From *Job Choices: Diversity Edition 2003* (Bethlehem, PA: National Association of Colleges and Employers), p. 54. Retrieved from **www.naceweb.org**.

Jennifer Grasso
752 Crossfield St.
Denver, CO 80221

Mr. Gregory Larsen
Capitol Service Corp.
111 Dearborn St.
Orlando, FL 32805

FIGURE A–4
Envelope Format

inside (see Figure A–4). In addition, a clearly addressed envelope minimizes the chances that your message will be lost on its way to the addressee.

The address on the envelope should match the content and style of the inside address on the letter it contains. Since the postal service routes mail by reading from the bottom of the address upward, your letter should start with the most specific information and add increasingly more general information on each succeeding line:

1. Name of the addressee.
2. Department or group.
3. Name of the organization.
4. Name of the building or mail-stop number.
5. Street address and suite number or post office box number.
6. City, state or province, and zip code or postal code.
7. Country (if the letter is being mailed overseas).

In North America, most envelopes for business correspondence are "No. 10" size, which measures 9½ by 4¼ inches—just the right size to contain an 8½- by 11-inch piece of stationery folded in thirds. If your correspondence is too bulky to fit easily in such an envelope, don't try to cram it in. Instead, mail it in a larger envelope. The address on a larger piece of correspondence will look most professional if you print out and attach a mailing label. If you use an envelope without the organization's return address printed on it, use a printer for your return address.

While the recipient isn't likely to notice that a letter is properly folded, a poorly folded one can create an unwelcome impression. For standard 8½ by 11 stationery, fold the sheet (or sheets) in thirds. Begin by folding the bottom third upward and creasing it neatly. Then fold the top third downward, leaving a quarter inch or so of space between the top of the page and the first crease. Finally, insert the letter with the open end at the top and the loose flap facing out. When enclosing sheets in a large envelope, place the letter facing the rear of the envelope so that it is immediately visible when opened.

E-Mail

Since the first message was sent via the Internet in 1972, e-mail has become a common and indispensable tool. Since you are likely to use this channel more than any other form of written communication, it is important to use it well.

Overall Considerations Because e-mail is a relatively new type of business communication, the rules for using it are still developing. You will be wise to pay close attention to your company's policies on e-mail use. When deciding whether and how to use e-mail as a channel for your business communication, keep these points in mind:

- *Treat every e-mail as a public, permanent document.* E-mail only appears to be as casual and transitory as conversation. A misaddressed message can lead to embarrassment and humiliation. Despite what you might assume, e-mail is not private: It has the potential to be forwarded (purposely or accidently) without your permission or knowledge. E-mail is written communication, and as such it can survive as a permanent record. Even if you delete a message, it can remain available to employers, other businesses, and courts for years. In fact, e-mail has the same weight as a letter or memo sent on company letterhead.[8]
- *Don't use company e-mail for personal business.* Use your own personal e-mail account for private correspondence, chatting with friends, and other nonbusiness exchanges. One expert advised thinking of e-mails as "giant, moving billboards, exposing our every thought to the cyberworld."[9] Your personal e-mails most likely would not be the best advertising for your company.
- *Be cautious about using e-mail for delicate topics.* Don't use e-mail to avoid personal discussions that would better be handled by phone or in person. E-mail is not an appropriate forum for reprimands, negative appraisals, firings, and resignations. E-mail has the potential to be misunderstood, so avoid using it in a hurry or to convey sarcasm or humor if the receiver is likely to misunderstand. Stop, think, and wait to send an e-mail if you are angry or frustrated. The short note you wrote in anger to one person may be forwarded to many colleagues. Once a message is sent, it is irretrievable and the impact on your career could be disastrous if your message was not well thought out. Never send information you are not sure is accurate (e.g., canceled meetings, changed deadlines, budget figures).
- *Don't use e-mail to impose on others.* Just because you can send e-mail messages quickly doesn't mean you should. Avoid the temptation to send unnecessary messages to others or forward ones that the recipient won't appreciate. Most businesspeople are already overwhelmed with e-mail.

Many people see e-mail as a way to flatten hierarchies in business and keep people higher up informed of your work. It can be a way to reach important people, expedite projects, and reduce time otherwise spent in meetings. Despite these advantages, it is often safer to follow the regular chain of command. Pay attention to your corporate culture and your communication goals. Sending an e-mail to your CEO suggesting a new procedure for your division without first checking with your immediate supervisor could spell disaster for your career.

The Netiquette home page (**www.albion.com/netiquette/index.html**) offers a complete guide to e-mail etiquette. This site presents the opportunity to read the basics, take a quiz, and receive e-mail updates. Net User Guidelines and Netiquette (**www.fau.edu/netiquette/net**) also has practical information for users of e-mail, newsgroups, and other Internet applications. Job Web (**www.jobweb.com/Resources/Library/Samples/Email_Etiquette_A_209_01.htm**) provides more information on using e-mail professionally.

Format The form of your message is just as important as its content. These guidelines will help you create e-mail that accomplishes its goals.

- *Be mindful about using special formatting*. If you and the recipient are in the same e-mail system, you have more leeway in formatting your messages. If you are not in the same system, avoid colored backgrounds and different typefaces, as they are often hard to read or may not translate into different systems. The same is true of bold, italics, and other formatting styles: If the recipient is not in the same system as you, these items may be lost or they may turn into meaningless symbols.
- *Include relevant parts of the original message in your replies*. Your recipients may not remember what they wrote to you about or what question they asked you, so it is important to include parts of the original message along with your response. Include only that part of the message that is relevant and that you are responding to. Quoted material is usually marked with <> signs; many programs automatically do this. If the part you must quote is long, put it at the end of your message.
- *Use separate messages for separate topics*. If it is necessary to discuss several topics, consider separate messages, each with its own subject header. This makes it easier for the recipient to keep track of and respond to each one. If you send an unavoidably long message such as a newsletter, an index at the beginning can help readers scan and find information quickly.[10] If the message is lengthy, consider a phone conversation or an in-person chat instead.
- *Be careful when adding attachments*. Attachments (e.g., photos, spreadsheets, word processing files) should be used only with a great deal of thought. An attachment may be preferable for a lengthy document; before you attach, consider the receivers. If they use the same e-mail system as you, then attachments should download and open easily. However, external recipients may be fearful of viruses and choose not to download attachments. Recipients may be traveling or checking e-mail from a handheld device that can't download documents. Downloading graphics takes a lot of time and space. Given these drawbacks, you might ask the recipients if they need to and want to receive the larger document and verify how they would like to receive it: attachment, fax, or hard copy. When you do use an attachment for necessary and lengthy reports, let the recipient know where to look for the essentials either by highlighting or stating in the body of your message: "See figures on page 4 and summary on page 8."[11]

Elements Like a traditional memo, every business e-mail should have four parts: address, subject line, salutation, close.

Address Most programs have the capacity to designate "cc" and "bcc" addressees. CC is variously regarded as "carbon copy," "computer copy," or "courtesy copy." In any case "cc" tells the recipient of the message who will be receiving copies. The designation "bcc" signifies a blind copy: The person to whom the message is addressed won't know you have sent this copy. Use "cc" when others need and expect copies and when you want the recipient to know that you are sending them. In reply to a customer's complaint, you might want that customer to see that you are sending your response regarding safety to all technicians who were part of the problem. Consider a blind copy if you want the primary recipient to read your message and not know there are copies to others. For example, if the technicians would be upset with your announcing the problem to the boss, you might send a "bcc" of the above message to your boss with your notation, "This is how I resolved the complaint I mentioned last week." Additionally, when you are sending a message to multiple recipients, consider using the blind cc capacity so that others don't need to scroll through the whole list of recipient names.

Subject line The subject line should be clear and concise. For example, "Don't forget about the survey" is not as useful as "Survey deadline tomorrow!" Never leave the subject line blank. Be cautious about forwarding messages unnecessarily, but if you do decide it is necessary to forward something, update the subject line so that others don't need to read "RE: RE: RE:" or "FW: FW: FW." Clean up the message as well; no one wants to open a message and see scores of addresses and > symbols.

It helps the new reader if you clean up the format, but it is never acceptable to change someone's message when you forward to a third party. Unless a particular type of message forwarding is routine and expected at your company (e.g., all requests for leave are forwarded to HR), ask the sender's permission to forward a message.

Salutation Without a salutation an e-mail can sound harsh. As one expert pointed out, "Blunt is not businesslike."[12] "Dear Mr. Nakayama" or "Dear Gina" starts on a cordial note. Bulk or broadcast messages or those to groups can begin with "Good morning," or "Dear Computer Policy Committee Members."

Close Wrap up your message with a brief, appropriate close such as "Regards," "Cordially," or "Thank you." There is no consensus about the advisability of including a complete signature block listing your name, company, phone, fax, Web site, and address at the end of the message, but most professionals recommended including it.[13] This information allows others to reach you easily, regardless of where they are picking up your message. Cute quotations and graphics in your signature are not advisable for business, unless it is your company slogan or a tag line indicating the work you do.

Style "Keep it short" is the most important stylistic guideline in crafting a useful e-mail message. Whenever possible, limit your e-mail to two or three paragraphs—one screenful of text. Use bullets to make information more readable and accessible. Don't ramble: Keep your messages clear and as brief as possible. Tell the reader the details and end with the action requested or required.

Although e-mail seems like an informal medium, capitalization, grammar, and spelling are important. For better or worse, your messages create an image of you and your company in the reader's mind. With friends outside work, shortcuts ("wanna", "sorta"), emoticons, and chat acronyms (LOL "laughing out loud") may seem fine, but in business they can create problems, especially with strangers. Most e-mail systems have a spelling/grammar checking function, which you should use. However, be sure to supplement these tools to make sure you have chosen the right word (e.g., "its" versus "it's"). For important or longer messages, consider writing the message first in your word processor if its spelling/grammar functions are more powerful. Single-space your message with a double space between paragraphs. Don't type in all capital letters since this creates the effect of shouting; all lowercase is unprofessional and inappropropriate. Profanity, off-color remarks, and gossip never belong in company e-mail.

Managing the volume of e-mail Managing the volume of e-mail is a feat. In the year 2000, the average corporate user received 31 messages per day and spent 2 hours managing it. Experts predict that the volume of e-mail will continue to grow.[14] Here are some suggestions for managing e-mail.[15]

- *Develop shortcuts*. You and a core group of co-workers can agree on some e-mail shortcuts such as using the subject line only for short messages and responses with the notation "EOM" (end of message). This eliminates the need for the receiver to open the message. In response to a notice of meeting, you could respond with a subject line "Will attend. EOM." You might also create a folder that automatically deletes messages after a month. Use it to temporarily store messages you don't think you'll need, but want to keep for a bit.
- *Send e-mail on a "need to know" basis*. Does everyone need to see your report? Or your reply to the supervisor? Be careful about "reply to all" when you only want to reply to sender. Bombarding receivers with what they regard as junk e-mail may cause them to disregard important messages when you send them.
- *Avoid the unnecessary replies*. Endless, unnecessary replies clog systems: "Thanks," "OK," "Got it," "Great," "Appreciate it," "Any time." Let the other person have the last word. Indicate in your message that no response is necessary; FYI (For Your Information) in the subject line signals the recipient that this is informational only and no response is requested.
- *Use filters*. If your e-mail software has the capability, use filters to identify mail by sender and/or subject line and automatically put it in a folder for your easier access. (See your e-mail program's documentation for details.) Filters can also identify junk e-mail (spam) and isolate it in a folder labeled as such.
- *Discourage unwanted messages*. Let others know if they are sending you unwanted e-mail. Ask to be removed from the joke list or simply say, "Thanks for thinking of me, but it won't be necessary for you to send me your subcommittee meeting minutes each week. I'd appreciate a summary of your work each quarter."

Writing for Employment

Chapter 7 describes several paths to seeking employment. At some point most job seekers will send a job application letter and a résumé. The résumé remains a mainstay of the employment process and now Internet options can enhance both the résumé process and product.

Résumés

A résumé is a marketing document—an advertisement in which you sell yourself to potential employers. A résumé summarizes your background and qualifications for employment. Résumés serve as a screening device, helping prospective employers decide which candidates' applications are worth further consideration.

A résumé won't get you hired, but it can put you on the short list of candidates to be considered or cause you to be dropped from the running. As you read in Chapter 7, in competitive hiring situations, screening candidates is a process of elimination as much as selection. The people doing the hiring have more applications than they can handle, so they naturally look for ways of narrowing down the candidates to a manageable number. A good résumé can keep you in the running. A résumé can also be useful for presenting yourself to potential employers who might hire you for a job that hasn't been announced or even been created yet.

Besides listing your qualifications, a résumé offers tangible clues about the type of person that you are. Are you organized and thorough? How well can you present your ideas? Is your work accurate? After you have left the interview, your résumé will remain behind as a reminder of the way you tackle a job and of the kind of employee that you are likely to be.

The most effective résumés are tailored to the interests and needs of a particular position and employer. This may not be practical, however, if you are applying to several firms at the same time. At the very least, your résumé should reflect the requirements of a field. For example, a medical technician should stress laboratory skills when applying for a job in a lab; but when a job opening is in a clinic, the same technician should emphasize experience that involves working with people. A résumé that encourages job offers focuses on the employer's needs and how you can help the employer.

Appearance Like every important business document, your résumé should be impeccable. Any mistakes or sloppiness here could cost you the job by raising doubts in an employer's mind. Because the design of résumés can be complicated, many candidates hire professional services to create them. Remember, the purpose of the résumé is to get an interview. It must be well organized so that vital information is readily accessible.

Whether you create the résumé yourself or have it professionally done, the final product should reflect the professional image you want to create. It should meet these criteria:

- Be neat and error-free. No whiteout or hand corrections.
- Contain plenty of white space to avoid crowding.
- Be printed on heavyweight paper, either white or a light, neutral color.
- Be reproduced clearly on a high-quality printer or copy machine.

Résumés use the word "I" sparingly and avoid abbreviations. Begin sentences with positive verbs (created, developed, analyzed). The words "fired" and "unemployed" do not belong on your résumé.[16] Be certain that information in your résumé is accurate.

Although you want to make yourself stand out from the crowd, be cautious about using unusual kinds of paper or fonts. A novel approach may capture the fancy of a prospective boss, or it may be a turn-off. The more you know about the field and the organization itself, the better your decisions will be about the best approach. In companies and positions looking for creativity, some novel ideas may work. A third-place winner of an Enterprise Rent-A-Car creative résumé contest had submitted a pizza box résumé to a pizza corporation and her photo on a milk carton (to alert the company of its "missing" worker) to another.[17] Other creative résumés included a shoe (now that I've got my foot in the door), a game board, and a Popsicle-stick house. You may be remembered with a creative and unusual résumé, but these gimmicks won't work in most traditional employment situations. The résumé is a business document and needs to look professional.

Your résumé should almost never exceed two pages in length, and one is usually better. Employers are often unimpressed with longer résumés, which are hard to read and can seem padded, especially when they come from people with comparatively little job experience. A long résumé may even prompt your disqualification early in the selection process. One magazine editor admitted that while screening 150 applicants he got tired of lifting the first pages to see the second page, so he threw out all the résumés that were longer than one sheet. Later, when his boss asked him how he was progressing, he was able to say, "Very well! I've already eliminated half of them."

Elements While résumés can be organized in more than one way, they will almost always contain the same basic information. Résumés are not autobiographies: The purpose is to get an interview, not tell your life history. Personal information like age, height, weight, religion, race, marital status, and children does not belong in a résumé.

Name and contact information This usually includes your name, address, phone numbers, e-mail address, and Web site. Make sure that the information allows an interested employer to reach you easily. If you are currently employed, this can be difficult and delicate. Career specialists recommend that you proceed "carefully and cautiously" and set up boundaries to keep your job search out of your current employment.[18] Listing a personal e-mail address and home or cell phone number is preferable to listing a current employer's. Be certain to check these frequently and respond speedily. Be certain your e-mail address is not offensive or does not create an impression you wouldn't want. "Devilgirl" or "Lazyboy" does not convey the impression of a serious job candidate. You might set up a separate e-mail account expressly for seeking employment. If you will not be at your school or other current address long, you will want to list both a permanent home address and a school address. Indicate how long (i.e., "until May 31") an address will be valid.

Job or career objective Most employers agree that a statement of professional objective should be included in a résumé. An effective statement consists of two parts: The first should announce your general goal and mention some important demonstrated skills—talents that will qualify you for the job. The second part should detail one or more specific areas in which you want to work. For example:

> "A position in public relations using proven skills in writing, researching, and motivating. Special interests in radio and television programming."
>
> "Entry-level position in design and development of microprocessor circuitry. Eventual advancement to position as project leader or technical manager."

Education Employers are usually interested in learning about your post–high school education and training, degrees earned, major and minor fields of study, and dates of attendance and/or graduation. If you attended college, it is unnecessary to include high school. Begin with your most recent education and work backward. If the information is helpful and space permits, list notable courses you have taken. If your grade-point average is impressive, include it. Finally, note any honors or awards you have earned. If they are numerous, list them in a separate "Awards and Honors" section.

Experience Every employer wants to know what kinds of work you have performed. By using the general title "Work Experience" instead of the more limited "Employment History," you can highlight a summer internship, delete a dishwashing job, group minor or similar jobs together, and include volunteer work or club activities that taught you marketable skills.

Employers are more interested in the duties you performed than in job titles. They search for the answers to two questions: What can you do? What are your attributes as an employee? You can provide answers to these questions by accompanying your job title, name of employer, and city with a list of the duties you performed. There is no need to use complete sentences—phrases will do. Be sure to use very concrete language, including technical terminology, to describe the work you performed. Place this section either before or following the section on education, depending on which will be most important to an employer. For an extensive list of words that might help you accurately describe the transferable skills you have, see **http://owl.english.purdue.edu/handouts/pw/p_skillinv.html**.

Special interests and aptitudes Most employers want to know about special abilities that will make you a more valuable employee. These include community-service activities (cite offices you have held), languages you can write or speak, special equipment you can operate, relevant hobbies, and so on. The key here is to include only information that the employer will find useful and that casts you in a favorable light.

Memberships If you belong to any organizations in your field, list them under "Memberships." Include any offices or significant committee appointments you have held. Membership in service and civic groups is usually less important, so include it only if you have held a major office.

Certifications If you are certified or licensed in any occupational field, create a category in which to display that fact, even if it has only one entry. For instance, if you are a Microsoft Certified Systems Engineer, list your MCSE certification. If your Notary Public or CPR certification could benefit an employer, include it.

Types of résumés There are three common approaches to organizing a résumé: chronological, functional, and hybrid (also called modified chronological or combination). Each has its own advantages, and the one you choose will probably depend on the specific job description you are applying for and your past accomplishments.

Chronological approach The chronological approach emphasizes your education and work experience and is most effective when such experience clearly relates to the job you are seeking, when you have worked within the field. Within the categories "Education," "Work Experience," and "Related Experience" (if you have such a section) list entries in reverse order, beginning with your most recent experience. Under each position, describe your responsibilities and accomplishments, emphasizing ways in which they prepared you for the job you are now seeking. If you are a recent graduate, you may want to list your education first. (See Figure A–5.) Only cite your grades if they are especially strong.

Functional approach The functional approach features the skills you bring to the job (organizer, researcher, manager, etc.) and as Figure A–6 illustrates, it provides

FIGURE A–5
Chronological Résumé Featuring Education and Work Experience

Source: From **http://www.jobweb.com/Resources/Library/Samples/Four_Sample_Resumes_68_01.htm.**

MEG A. HERTZ

Current Address	**Permanent Address**	**E-mail Address and URL**
12 Gates Lane	34 Apple Court	hertzm@ucolo.edu
Boulder, CO 23849	Glendale, CA 19058	http://www.ucolo.edu/
(614) 555-6145	(714) 555-7145	cac/hertzm

OBJECTIVE
A position in software development.

EDUCATION
B.S. in Computer Science, expected May 2004
University of Colorado, Boulder, CO
Cumulative G.P.A. 3.66

WORK EXPERIENCE

Freelance Computer Consultant, September 1997–present

Create World Wide Web home pages and customize computer systems for clients in the Boulder, CO, area.

Intern, June-August 1997
Microsoft Corp., Redmond, WA
Worked as software design engineer intern on SNA Server 3.0. Implemented name-space providers (Windows 95/NT DLLs written in C) for a variety of network protocols, including TCP/IP, Netware IPX, Lanman, Banyan VINES, and AppleTalk.

Undergraduate Research Assistant, September 1996-May 1997
University of Colorado Laboratory for Computer Science
Worked with Professor Daniel S. Patel in the parallel and distributed operating group. Ported UNIX applications to XOK, a prototype exokernal implementation for the Intel x86.

Lab Attendant, September 1995-May 1996
Center for Academic Computing, University of Colorado
Maintain computer hardware and assist users on Windows 95 and Macintosh operating systems and various software packages.

Crew Leader, Summers 1993 and 1994
Mimi's Muffins, Glendale, CA
Supervised crew and managed bakery's daily operations.

COMPUTER SKILLS

Languages and Software
C, C++, Java, LaTeX, HTML, Word, WordPerfect.

Operating Systems
UNIX (Linux, Ultrix SunOS), Windows 95, Macintosh.

examples of the most significant experiences that demonstrate these abilities. This approach is especially appropriate in the following instances:

- When you are first entering the job market or reentering it after an absence.
- When you have held a variety of apparently unrelated jobs.
- When you are changing careers or specialties.

- When your work history has been interrupted.
- When your past job titles don't clearly show how you are qualified for the position you are seeking.

When you write a functional résumé, follow the "Skills" category immediately with a chronological "Work History" and a scaled-down "Education" section that lists only institutions, degrees, and dates. Either of the latter two categories may come first, depending on whether you gained most of your skills and experience in school or on the job.

Whatever format you choose, experts agree that strong résumés possess the same qualities:

- *They focus on the employer's needs.* If you understand what qualities (perseverance, innovation, ability to learn quickly) and skills (e.g., mastery of software, selling) an employer needs, you can focus your résumé to show how you fit the job.
- *They are concise.* A long-winded résumé sends the wrong message in a business environment where time is money and clarity is essential. Use simple, brief statements to describe yourself, and avoid verbose language.
- *They are honest.* Outright lies are obvious grounds for disqualification, of course. But getting caught exaggerating your qualifications will raise serious doubts about your honesty in other areas. As one expert put it, "Be aggressive, be bold, but be honest."[19]

For a checklist to critique your résumé go to **http://www.quintcareers.com/resume_critique_worksheet.html**.

Reference list Create a reference list separate from your résumé and bring it to an interview. Don't list references on a résumé and unless it is specifically requested, don't mail your reference list along with your résumé. This list can include three to five persons who know your work and character, and are not relatives. Be certain that you contact each potential reference and ask permission to use his or her name. Give each reference a copy of your résumé and keep each informed of the places and positions you are applying for. You might remind a college professor of the term project you completed or remind a past employer of an accomplishment you'd like mentioned. You can also be sure you have current contact information and the preferred contact information (home or work, cell phone or e-mail). After each person's listing, include the person's relationship to you (past or present employer, colleague, supervisor, manager). Use the same paper and print that you used for your résumé.

Electronic Résumés

Electronic résumés are an increasingly widespread alternative to the paper-and-ink variety. Since many employers look for—and sometimes even require—applicants to submit information electronically, it is important to know how this part of the hiring system operates.

Types of Electronic Résumés The most common types of electronic résumés are e-mail attachments, scannable format, and Web-based documents.[20]

E-mail résumés Submitting an e-mail résumé involves attaching a computer file of the résumé to an e-mail message and sending it to one or more prospective employers. The résumé is typically created in a word processing format, but in other cases it might consist of a Web page (HTML) file, or in some cases even an audio or video format. The most important consideration when crafting a résumé you plan to submit as an e-mail attachment is to be sure the recipient will be able to open and read it after downloading. On occasion, you may be asked to submit a résumé within an e-mail message. In that case, use the plain text format described in Table A–1.

Online résumés and job banks If you have your own Web site, you can post your résumé there; but there is another alternative. Web-based job banks are services where job seekers can post information about themselves for potential employers to review. Résumés posted on some job banks are open to anyone who wants to see them, while other banks allow you to store a résumé and send it to employers you select. More information on résumé banks is available at **http://jobstar.org/internet/res-main.htm**.

There are several advantages of Web-based résumés. Literally thousands of employers worldwide can access your materials as quickly as you post them. You can update and change your résumé readily. You can include portfolios with accessible graphics and sound that demonstrate your experience and showcase your expertise in displaying your work on the Internet.[21]

Despite these advantages, online résumés have their unique set of drawbacks. Once your résumé is posted on the Web, you may have no control over who sees it and where it is transferred. Many currently employed job seekers have been chagrined to learn that their current boss has found their postings in job banks. Check the privacy policies of sites before posting, but be aware that those policies may change. The bottom line is that privacy is not assured once a résumé is posted. Be sure to date your résumé in case it becomes a permanent irretrievable fixture in cyberspace. For résumés posted online, you may choose to protect at least some of your privacy by listing only an e-mail address for contact. Before posting a résumé for a specific employer, check the employer's existence and legitimacy. You may want to leave out your current employer, listing only the type of position or the industry you are currently employed in so unscrupulous headhunters don't contact you at your present job. For more information on confidentiality and privacy online, go to **http://featuredreports.monster.com/privacy/intro** or **http://infoweek.techengine.com/candidates/Allen_Career_Counsel/page03.asp**.

Scannable Résumés A scannable résumé (shown in Figure A–7) is a paper résumé that is formatted so that prospective employers can enter its contents into a database. The use of scannable résumés has grown from the fact that human resource personnel are unable to review all of the materials they receive from job applicants, so they use OCR (optical character recognition) software to enter the content of résumés into their databases. Once the content is digitized, employers can sort it according to a variety of criteria including applicants' employment experience and skills.

Employers program their software to search scanned résumés for key words, so be sure to identify and include terms commonly used in the field where you are seeking work. For example, industrial engineers might include "Kaizen" and "time studies" while a pharmacist might list "compounding." Include any industry-related jargon and acronyms that the scanning software may be programmed to recognize. For example, OCP (Oracle Certified Professional) and CCNA (Cisco Certified Networking Associate) are recognized in the Information Technology sector. For examples of skill key words (by job categories) and personal trait key words, see **www.eresumes.com/eresumes.html**. Use the *Occupational Outlook Handbook* (**www.bls.gov/oco**) and other

FIGURE A–6
Functional Résumé Focusing on Demonstrated Skills

Source: From **www.quintcareers.com/resume_sample_1.html**.

Amy Matthews

Harvard University
Box C-23123
Cambridge, MA 02138
617-555-0392
amatthews@harvard.edu

OBJECTIVE

To contribute my education and health management skills in a position with a growing and dynamic firm.

EDUCATION

BACHELOR OF SCIENCE
Harvard University, Cambridge, Massachusetts, May 2003
Major: Health Sciences
Minor: Management

RELEVANT COURSES

- Human Anatomy & Physiology I
- Human Anatomy & Physiology II
- Health Policy
- Organizational Analysis and Health Care
- Health Care Management
- Human Resource Management

Health Management Skills

- Served as Assistant to the Director of the Stacey G. Houndly Breast Cancer Foundation.
- Functioned as Public Health Representative for the Cambridge Area Public Health Administration.
- Coordinated Harvard University Public Health Awareness Week, 1996, 1997.

Communications Skills

- Served as a phone-a-thon caller on several occasions, soliciting donations from Harvard alumni and parents for Harvard University.
- Volunteered for a political campaign, distributing literature door to door, fielding questions and making phone calls to local constituents.

Management Skills

- Handled all back-office management functions, including employee relations and accounting.
- Oversaw client relations, order processing and routine upkeep of the business.
- Coordinated efforts between customer needs and group personnel.
- Designed all market research analysis and projects for our client.
- Delegated suggestions and duties to other team members.
- Presented market research results to client with suggestions of implementation.

Leadership Skills

- Participated in Youth Leadership Boston, a group dedicated to developing leadership skills through diverse programming.
- Served as formal/social coordinator for my sorority program council.
- Elected Vice President of Risk Management for Panhellenic, a group that oversees and coordinates educational programming for Harvard's Greek system.

Systems Abilities

- Microsoft Office
- HTML/Web Publishing
- WordPerfect
- PageMaker

AMY MATTHEWS

Harvard University
Box C-23123
Cambridge, MA 02138
Phone: 617-555-1849
E-mail: amatthews@harvard.edu

OBJECTIVE

Health management position utilizing my education and skills with a growing firm.

QUALIFICATIONS SUMMARY

Several years experience and education in health management, leading to the development of communications, client relations, order processing, interpersonal, accounting, marketing, health policy, leadership, and management skills.

SYSTEMS SKILLS

Microsoft Office, HTML/Web publishing, WordPerfect, PageMaker.

EDUCATION

B.S., Harvard University, Cambridge, Massachusetts
--Major: Health Sciences
--Minor: Management

RELEVANT COURSES

Human Anatomy & Physiology I
Human Anatomy & Physiology II
Health Policy
Organizational Analysis and Health Care
Health Care Management
Human Resource Management

HEALTH MANAGEMENT EXPERIENCE

-Assistant to the Director, Stacey G. Houndly Breast Center Foundation.
-Public Health Representative, Cambridge Area Public Health Administration.
-Coordinator, Harvard University Public Health Awareness Week, 1996, 1997.

COMMUNICATIONS EXPERIENCE

-Solicited donations from Harvard alumni and parents for Harvard University while serving as a phone-a-thon caller on several occasions.
-Honed interpersonal communications while volunteering for a political campaign through distributing literature door-to-door, fielding questions, and making phone calls to local constituents.

MANAGEMENT EXPERIENCE

-Knowledge of all back-office functions, including employee relations and routine accounting.
-Dealt with client relations, order processing, and routine upkeep of the business.
-Managed customer relations by coordinating efforts between customer needs and group personnel.
-Designed market reseach analysis and projects for client.
-Presented market research results to client with suggestions for implementation of results.

LEADERSHIP

-Participated in Youth Leadership Boston, a group dedicated to the development of leadership skills through various programming activities.
-Served as Formal/Social Coordinator for my sorority program council.
-Elected Vice President of Risk Management for Panhellenic, which is a group that governs over and coordinates education progamming for Harvard's Greek system.

REFERENCES

Available upon request.

FIGURE A–7 Scannable Résumé

Source: From **www.quintcareers.com/scannable_resume_sample.html**.

Table A-1 Formats for Electronic Résumés

File Format	Extension (in Microsoft Windows)	Common Programs Used to Create	Advantages	Disadvantages	Means of Transmission	Additional Hints
ASCII plain text file	.txt	Microsoft Notepad, Apple Simple Text	All computers can read. Preferred by many job boards.	There is no formatting, so document looks very plain.	E-mail attachment	Use space bar rather than tab key for spacing. Avoid columns. Use no bold, italic, or underline. Use key words.
Rich text format	.rtf	Microsoft Word, WordPerfect (Save as “rich text format”)	Greater formatting options.	Not all software programs can read this format.	E-mail attachment	Be certain the recipient’s e-mail system can receive this type of file.
HTML (Hypertext Markup Language)	.htm or .html	FrontPage, Express, Composer	Can provide links to several pages. Can demonstrate creativity or technical expertise.	You must attract employers to your Web page. A poor-quality one may be worse than none at all.	Usually posted on World Wide Web. Can be saved as independent file, attachable to e-mail. Can be opened with Web browser.	Include the word “Résumé” in the title so search engines can categorize it properly. Incorporate traditional résumé techniques with Web page design.

Source: After Rebecca Smith, “eResumes 101: Choosing Your Best Electronic Résumé Format,” retrieved June 5, 2001, from **http://www.eresumes.com/tut_eresume.html**; and S. J. Gerson and S. M. Gerson, *Technical Writing: Process and Product,* 3rd ed. (Upper Saddle River, NJ: Prentice Hall, 2000), pp. 167–169.

career resources online for lists of key words specific to your career field. Note any key words used in the job description. Since length and details don't faze a computer, scannable résumés may be longer than paper ones, giving you the best chance of including everything that might impress a prospective employer.

A résumé has the best chance of being scanned accurately if you follow these guidelines:[22]

- Create and save the document in ASCII plain text formatting. (For more information on ASCII format, see the Boston College Career Center's Web site at **www.bc.edu/offices/careers/skills/resumes/convert**.
- Be sure only your name is on the top line. An address on the same line will confuse the software.
- Send only a high-quality laser printed copy, not a photocopy. The scanning device is better able to get all of your information from a high-quality printer.
- Use only simple fonts in standard sizes and only white paper. The scanner is unable to recognize large fonts, patterned paper, script, graphics, boxes, and vertical or horizontal lines.
- Do not fold or staple the résumé.
- Be certain your name is on each page.

It is prudent to keep an updated scannable copy of your résumé handy. If you are sending a résumé, call ahead and ask whether the résumé will be scanned. If it will, consider sending two résumés, the scannable version and one for human eyes (be sure to indicate which is which).[23] Or you might send the scannable résumé and take the (better-looking) one-paged résumé to the interview. For additional information about scannable résumés, go to **www.quintcareers.com/scannable_resumes.html** and **www.eresume.com**. Many employers post specific guidelines for scannable résumés submitted to them; be certain to check whether the specific employer you are targeting does this. (See **http://www.quintcareers.com/scannable_guidelines.html** for a sample of one employer's specific guidelines.)

Strategies for Electronic Résumés Résumé preparation and delivery are changing, but a basic principle holds: Adapt to your audience. Customize the content and method of transmission of your résumé for individual companies, positions, and, when possible, the people who will read it.

Compared to paper résumés, electronic ones have both advantages and drawbacks. When you send a paper résumé, the recipient sees exactly what you created, although receiving and forwarding it to others may take time. With electronic résumés, there is a greater risk that your reader may not be able to view the document for technical reasons or may not want to open the file because of the additional time it takes and the potential for a virus. Furthermore, some companies automatically delete unsolicited e-mails with attachments, so find out before you attach.

When you do submit a résumé electronically, follow these guidelines:[24]

- Don't bombard employers with résumés for positions that don't exist or for which you are not qualified.
- Be sure to include a cover letter that tells the employer what position you are applying for.

- Although plain text files and e-mail limit your formatting, you can still use bullets to make your cover letter more readable by using plus signs (+) or asterisks (*).

Formatting Electronic Résumé Materials To make sure potential employers can read your electronic résumé, you need to understand the three most commonly used file formats for these documents: plain text, rich text, and hypertext. Each of these file formats is coded in ASCII (American Standard Code for Information Interchange), although the terms "ASCII" and "plain text" are often used interchangeably. As Table A–1 outlines, each has advantages and disadvantages and readily recognizable features.

Additional Information on Electronic Résumés The Purdue Online Writing Lab (**http://owl.english.purdue.edu/handouts/pw/index.html**) offers several tutorials on job searches, résumés, and cover letters. See also *Tips for Formatting Text-based Resumes* at **www.studentpress.org/acpjobs/resumetips.html#sample**.

If you still need convincing about the importance of proofreading your résumé, visit Resumania (**www.resumania.com/arcindex.html**) for a laughable collection of unintentional mistakes made on résumés.

Job Application Letters

Whenever you send your résumé to a prospective employer, accompany it with a job application letter (also called a cover letter) that is personalized for the particular job you are applying for and the organization to which you are applying. A cover letter according to one expert is "an introduction, a sales pitch and a proposal for further action all in one."[25] You want your cover letter to result in an interview so use it to demonstrate your fit for the job. Show interest, enthusiasm, qualifications, and professionalism.

Cover letters should be sent to a specific individual. If you do not know the appropriate person, call the company and ask for the individual's name, being certain that you get the spelling and title correct.

As Figure A–3 illustrates, cover letters include the following information:

- The first lines should let the reader know what position you are applying for, how you know of the position, and any connection you have to the company. If you are responding to an advertisement, mention the job title, number, and publication. You might be writing at the suggestion of a mutual acquaintance or as a result of your research.
- An introduction (or reintroduction) of yourself if the reader doesn't know (or remember) who you are.
- A brief description of one or two of your most impressive accomplishments that are relevant to the job at hand. Remember: Don't just say you can help the organization. Offer some objective evidence that backs up your claim. Show knowledge of the company through personal experience or positive news articles.
- A statement regarding the next step you hope to take—usually a request for an interview. Detail any information about limits on your availability, but keep these to an absolute minimum.
- A final, cordial expression of appreciation to the reader for considering you.

For sample cover letters, go to **www.jobweb.com/Resources/Library/Samples**.

Follow-up Letters

Always follow up an interview by sending a thank-you letter to the interviewer(s). Besides showing your good manners, a follow-up letter is an opportunity to remind the interviewer of your uniqueness and the strengths you will bring to the company.

Your follow-up letter should thank the interviewer for the opportunity to meet and the chance to have learned more about the position and the company. Also offer thanks for the chance to have met any other people to whom you were introduced. Use the letter to assert why you believe you are well qualified for the job, and how you can serve the company's needs. Address any concerns the interviewer may have had, and add information about yourself that you did not have an opportunity to state during the interview. Be certain the letter concludes on a positive note and expresses goodwill. Be absolutely positive that you have spelled every name you use correctly and that your letter is free of any other mistakes. Errors are likely to raise doubts about the quality of work that you might do after you are hired.

Thank-you letters are also appropriate for someone who has referred you to an employer, given a recommendation (phone or written) for you, or given job-search information to you.

Other types of follow-up letters include an inquiry when you had no response after an interview and ones accepting or declining a job offer. Go to **http://owl.english.purdue.edu/handouts/pw/p_letemploy.html** for further guidelines for follow-up letters.

Reports

Reports are a part of business life. They vary in size and frequency from two-paragraph weekly memos on the number of new hires to an occasional 20-page report complete with graphs, analysis, and recommendations on the feasibility of some new office space. The readers' needs and the corporate culture will determine the size, format, and frequency of reports.

Types of Reports

Reports, like presentations, may be informative or persuasive. Some reports present information, some may propose solutions to problems, and others analyze a problem and propose a course of action. Common reports include trip, progress, incident, feasibility, and minutes of meetings.

Trip Trip reports often justify the money organizations spend on them. Know why the report is being written and for whom. Is it for your manager to justify the type of workshop you attended or for accounting to withstand an audit? Usually trip reports answer these questions: Where did you go? With whom? Why? When? What did you learn? Whom did you meet? State the name of the conference or meeting, city and location, and your purpose for attending.

In the body of your narrative, emphasize two or three key points. If your job is to report to all employees, select information employees need and will find interesting on safety, legal issues, or changes in policy. If your conference covered new products or new prices for old products, you may want to detail those. If your report goes only to your supervisor, you may want to include a section on needs or ideas for change that you learned on the trip.

Progress Progress reports (also called periodic operating reports) occur at fixed intervals: weekly sales reports, monthly customer complaints, yearly safety reports. These reports may be largely statistical, but most will require some description of regular events and any unusual events (special sales, emergency closures, power outages). Answer the question, What is our status? If appropriate, indicate any hurdles you have overcome or have yet to overcome and then describe the next objective.

Incident Incident reports (also called situational reports) report on nonroutine occurrences such as accidents or special events. They may be required in the form of memos. Some organizations have special forms for these reports with very precise requirements for legal or human resource concerns. Before beginning an incident report be sure you know who is asking for the report and the level of detail required. Always ask if you aren't sure. When describing the incident, use precise facts such as numbers, dates, times, and quotations. Rather than report, "An employee fell on a staircase," write "Jane Winthrop, an employee in the Claims Department, reported that she fell on the north staircase inside the building at 4:00 P.M., Tuesday, June 26, 2006."

Feasibility Reports Feasibility reports address the questions of whether projects are possible, practical, advantageous, safe, or advisable. They use data to analyze the advantages and disadvantages of a particular project or to determine whether something can or should be done.

Begin by knowing what the main question is: How can we improve employee accessibility to supplies without loss of supplies? How can we improve training on new equipment in a timely manner to minimize repairs caused by improper use of new equipment? Then describe the problem or need, the criteria for comparing solutions, the possible solutions, and how well each solution meets the criteria. Tables, graphs, and other visuals are effective ways to add to this analysis section. Be certain you understand whether your assignment is to report information only or to draw conclusions and make recommendations. If the latter is part of your assignment, you'll want a section in which you give your recommendations.

Minutes of Meetings Minutes are a record of a group's meeting. They are especially useful when the events of a meeting will be of interest to people who were not present. Minutes are also helpful when a group needs to determine what happened at an earlier point in time.

Minutes should have a heading that indicates the name of the organization, the name of the group that met (Parking Task Force or Quality Assessment Team), "Minutes of (date)," and the place and time of the meeting. List the meeting facilitator and members present. If people other than regular members are present, indicate their position after their names (Salvadora Rojas, advisor; Arthur Urlin, guest). Minutes will usually include these sections: Agenda, Announcements, Old Business, New Business, and Action Items. Use numbers or bullets to identify separate items; under old and new business, use bullets or boldfaced headings to organize topics. Under Action Items, identify who is responsible for completing an item and the completion date.

Lab Reports For information on lab reports and other types of scientific writing, visit The Writing Center at Rensselaer (**www.rpi.edu/web/writingcenter/labs.html**) or the University of Wisconsin (**www.wisc.edu/writing/Handbook/ScienceReport.html**) or Virginia Tech (**www.writing.eng.vt.edu/index.html**).

Report Elements

Not every report should include all of the following elements. The amount of information covered, its nature, the conventions of the organization, and the needs of your readers will help you decide which parts to include.

Title Page Every report needs a descriptive title. If the document is a long one, the first page should include the title; "Submitted by . . ." or "Prepared by . . .," with the author(s) name; and "Submitted to . . ." or "Prepared for . . .," with the name of the intended audience or person requesting the report. The last item on the page is the date of submission.

Letter of Transmittal If the report is presented to persons inside the company, use a memo (instead of letter) of transmittal. The letter or memo will include a short history of the report (who assigned or authorized it and why), a brief summary of significant findings, conclusions, expression of thanks and acknowledgment of assistance from others, and clear instructions regarding how the reader is to respond. It is also appropriate to offer to answer questions and indicate how best to contact you.

Table of Contents If the report is a long one with several sections, a table of contents will help readers locate material. Show the major sections of the report and page each begins on.

Abstract or Executive Summary This section provides readers with a quick overview of the report's key sections. In most cases the summary should be no longer than one page or 10 percent of the full report.

Exhibits and Appendixes Many reports include tables, charts, graphs, and other visuals that illustrate points made in the body of the document. If there are several, a list of each exhibit and page number helps readers locate them. Depending on the accepted style in your field, these items can either be listed as exhibits within the body of the report or in appendixes at the back of the document.

Bibliography or References Depending on the accepted practices in your occupation and the formality of the report, you might include only sources you cited or those you cited plus others you used but didn't cite. Some reports will include not only those sources cited and used but also additional sources of information.

Tips for Reports

Regardless of the report's contents and size, the following guidelines will help you produce a top-quality document on schedule.

Understand the Purpose Begin by knowing the purpose of the report. A specific goal statement for reports should follow the same format for presentations explained in Chapter 10:

> "After reviewing this report, the Operations Manager will have a clear idea of how the cost of electricity has changed over the past 3 years, and how costs are likely to change in the next 2 years."

"After reading this report, my boss will see that giving traveling staff laptop computers will increase their productivity enough to pay for the equipment."

You can define the purpose of a report by asking yourself what it will be used for, who will read it, and what amount of detail is required. A routine one-paged expense report isn't the place to present your ideas for reforming the company's accounting policy. By contrast, if you have been asked to analyze a problem of high employee turnover, simply presenting data without including your analysis of causes and proposing solutions would make the report incomplete. If you have any doubts about the purpose of the report, ask the person or people who have requested it for clarification.

Create a Schedule for a Longer Report Once you understand the purpose of the report, list all of the tasks necessary to complete the report and devise a workable schedule. Allot time for researching (Internet, library visits, studies, surveys, interviews), outlining, writing a draft, getting any preliminary approvals needed, creating exhibits, and editing and writing the final copy.

Organize for Comprehension Determine what organizational pattern will help readers understand your report. The organizational patterns discussed in Chapter 10 can be used for written reports, also. Chronological patterns are often used for progress reports. Topical patterns work for reports that need to cover several areas. For example, a report on a possible location for a new factory might be organized by topics such as natural resources, transportation, workforce availability, and tax base. Another common pattern for reports is by importance. A report on the growing loss of quality personnel might focus on the most important features first and move to less important ones. Create an outline to work from; it will help you clarify the organizational pattern.

Format for Readability Break your report into logical divisions and indicate these with formatting: boldface, boxes, horizontal lines, headings, bullets, numbers, and white space. All of these can help the reader see what goes together and which are the important features. If it is permissible in your organization, use the templates for reports that are included in most word processing programs.

Document Carefully The purpose of documentation is to give credit to your sources and allow the reader to identify and find the source if more information is needed. Citing your sources avoids plagiarism. In longer reports to scientific and academic organizations, use MLA or APA style. In business, use the style of documentation that is accepted within your organization or industry. Study the resources from the University of Minnesota (**http://writing.umn.edu/tww/plagiarism/index.htm**) and Georgetown University (**www.georgetown.edu/honor/plagiarism.html**) to better understand what plagiarism is and how to avoid it.

glossary

Note: The number in parentheses at the end of each definition refers to the chapter in which the term is first discussed.

A

action-oriented listening style A listening style in which the listener's primary concern is understanding and organizing facts to accomplish a task or get a job done. *See also* Content-oriented listening style, People-oriented listening style, Time-oriented listening style. (3)

agenda A list of topics to be covered in a meeting. Agendas also usually note the meeting's time, length, and location and the members who will attend. Complete agendas also provide background information and outcome goals. (9)

anchor A listener's preexisting position on an issue being advocated. (14)

audition interview A type of interview in which a prospective employer asks the candidate to demonstrate (rather than describe) his/her ability to perform a job-related task. (7)

authoritarian leadership style A leadership style in which the designated leader uses legitimate, coercive, and reward power to control members. (8)

authority rule A group decision-making method in which a designated leader makes a final decision, either with or without consulting group members. (8)

award presentation A type of presentation in which the speaker describes an award and explains the reasons the recipient is receiving it. (13)

B

bar chart A chart consisting of horizontal or vertical bars that depict the values of several items in comparative terms. (11)

behavioral interview An employment interview in which the candidate is asked to give concrete examples of past behaviors that show how he or she behaved in certain situations. (7)

benefits As used in a sales presentation, advantages that the target audience will gain from the features of a product or service. (14)

biased language Any statement that seems to be objective but actually conceals the speaker's emotional attitude. (4)

bona fide occupational qualification (BFOQ) A job requirement that is deemed reasonably necessary for the performance of a particular job. In employment interviewing, only questions exploring BFOQs are lawful. (7)

brainstorming An approach to idea generation that encourages free thinking and minimizes conformity. (8)

briefing An informative presentation that succinctly informs listeners about a specific task at hand. (13)

C

career research interview An informational interview to help a candidate define and achieve career goals. (7)

cause–effect pattern An organizational arrangement which shows that events happened or will happen as a result of certain circumstances. (10)

channel The method or medium used to deliver a message (e.g., face-to-face communication, written memos, or the telephone). (1)

chronological pattern An organizational arrangement that presents points according to their sequence in time. (10)

claim A statement asserting a fact or belief. (10)

closed questions Questions that restrict the interviewee's responses, usually to yes or no, a number or item from preselected items, or an either-or response. (6)

co-culture A group that has a clear identity within the encompassing culture. (2)

coercive power The ability to influence others that arises because one can impose punishment or unpleasant consequences. (8)

cohesiveness The degree to which group members feel part of and want to remain with the group. (8)

collectivist culture A culture with strong social frameworks in which members of a group (such as an organization) are socialized to care for one another and for the group. (2)

column chart A visual exhibit consisting of vertical columns that depict the quantity of one or more items at different times; used to show changes in quantity over time. (11)

communication climate A metaphor used to describe the quality of relationships in an organization. (5)

communication networks Regular patterns or paths along which information flows in an organization. *See also* Formal communication networks, Informal communication networks. (1)

comparative advantages organizational plan An organizational strategy that puts several alternatives side by side and shows why one is the best. (10, 14)

comparisons A type of support in which the speaker shows how one idea is similar to another; may be figurative or literal. (11)

compromise An orientation toward negotiation which assumes that each side needs to lose at least some of what it was seeking. (5)

computer conferencing A form of technology that allows individuals to work on a single document via computer, making changes that can be viewed by other participants. (1)

confirming messages Messages that express value toward other persons. (5)

conflict phase The second of Aubrey Fisher's four group problem-solving phases; characterized by members' taking strong stands that result in conflict within the group. (8)

connection power The ability to influence that arises because of one's connections and associations inside and outside the organization. (8)

consensus A decision-making method in which the group as a whole makes a decision that each member is willing to support. (8)

content messages The dimension of messages that focus upon the topic under discussion. *See also* Relational messages. (1)

content-oriented listening style A listening style in which the listener hears details and analyzes and evaluates what is said. *See also* Action-oriented listening style, People-oriented listening style, Time-oriented listening style. (3)

context The environment of physical, social, chronological, and cultural variables that surrounds any process of communication. (1)

contingency approaches to leadership Leadership theories which assert that the most effective leadership style is flexible, changing as needed with the context. (8)

counterfeit questions Utterances that appear to be questions but are actually statements, forms of advice, traps, or attacks on the speaker. (3)

credibility The persuasive force that comes from the audience's belief in and respect for the speaker. (14)

criteria satisfaction organizational plan An organizational strategy that sets up standards (criteria) that the audience accepts and then shows how the speaker's idea or product meets the criteria. (10, 14)

critical incident questions Interview questions that ask the interviewee about a specific situation rather than a hypothetical one. (6)

culture The set of values, beliefs, norms, customs, rules, and codes that leads people to define themselves as a distinct group, giving them a sense of commonality. (2)

D

decoding The process of attaching meaning to words, symbols, or behaviors. (1)

definition A form of support that explains the meaning of terms that are unfamiliar to an audience or are used in a specialized or uncommon way. (11)

democratic leadership style A leadership style in which the designated leader encourages members to share decision making. (8)

descriptive statements Statements that describe the speaker's perspective instead of evaluating the sender's behavior or motives. *See also* "I" language, "You" language. (5)

designated leader A leader whose title indicates a leadership role, either by appointment or by group selection. (8)

diagnostic interview An interview in which professionals (e.g., doctors and lawyers) gather information on their patients' or clients' needs. (7)

direct question (in a group) A question addressed (by name) to a particular individual. (9)

direct questions (in an interview) Straightforward questions that ask exactly what the interviewer wants to know. (6)

disconfirming messages Messages that show a lack of valuing for other persons. (5)

disfluencies Vocal disruptions such as stammers (uh, um) or filler words (ya know, like, OK) that distract audiences and interfere with understanding. (12)

downward communication Communication that flows from superiors to subordinates. (1)

E

e-mail *See* Electronic mail.

electronic mail (e-mail) A communication system whereby messages are exchanged via computer networks. (1)

emergence phase The third of Aubrey Fisher's four group problem-solving phases; characterized by an end to conflict and emergence of harmony within the group. (8)

emergent leader A leader chosen by the group, either officially or informally. (8)

emotional intelligence Aptitude and skills needed for interacting well with others. Refers to interpersonal communication skills rather than cognitive or intellectual abilities. (5)

employment interview An interview designed to judge the qualifications and desirability of a candidate for a job. (7)

encoding The intentional process of creating a message. (1)

equivocal terms Words with more than one meaning. Equivocation can lead to unintentional misunderstandings. In contrast, *strategic ambiguity* is often used in business to promote harmony and soften the blow of unpleasant messages. (4)

ethnocentrism The inclination to see all events from the perspective of one's own culture and to evaluate one's own culture as superior and other persons or cultures as inferior. (2)

examples Brief illustrations that back up or explain a claim. (11)

exit interview An interview designed to discover why an employee is leaving an organization. (7)

expert opinion A decision-making method in which a single person perceived as an expert makes a decision for the group. (8)

expert power The ability to influence that arises because of one's knowledge, ability, and expertise in a particular area. (8)

explanation An informative presentation that increases listeners' understanding of a subject. (13)

extemporaneous presentation A type of delivery in which the major ideas are planned and rehearsed but the speech is given spontaneously from notes. (12)

F

factual questions Questions that ask for verifiable, factual information rather than opinion. (6)

fallacy An error in the logic of an argument. (14)

feasibility report A type of presentation that evaluates potential action steps and makes recommendations about how to proceed. (13)

features Qualities of a product or service that make it desirable and distinguish it from the competition. (14)

feedback The recognizable response of a receiver to a sender's message. (1)

feminine style of speech Culturally influenced style of speaking motivated by a concern for creating connections, establishing goodwill, showing support, and building community. *See also* Masculine style of speech, Rapport talk. (4)

final report Report delivered upon completion of an undertaking. (13)

flip chart A large pad of paper, attached to an easel, that is used to create and/or display visuals. (11)

formal communication networks Officially designated paths of communication designed by management to indicate who should communicate with whom. (1)

forming stage A phase in problem-solving groups characterized by tentative statements and getting-acquainted types of communication. Also termed *orientation phase*. (8)

functional roles Types of behavior that are necessary if a group is to do its job effectively. *See also* Relational roles, Task roles. (8)

G

genderlects Distinct and different styles of speaking that characterize masculine and feminine speech. (4)

general goal A broad indication of the purpose of a speech, generally to inform, persuade, or entertain. (10)

goodwill speech A speech with the primary aim of creating a favorable image of the speaker's cause in the minds of the audience. (14)

graph A visual display that shows the correlation between two quantities. (11)

groupthink A condition in which group members are unwilling to critically examine ideas because of their desire to maintain harmony. (8)

H

handout Document(s) distributed during or after a presentation. (11)

hidden agenda A group member's personal goal that is not made public. (8)

high-context culture A culture that relies heavily on subtle, often nonverbal cues to convey meaning and maintain social harmony. (2)

high-level abstractions Terms that cover a broad range of possible objects or events without describing them in much detail. (4)

highly structured interview An interview that consists of a standardized list of questions, sometimes in precise order and wording, as in research interviews. (6)

horizontal (lateral) communication Communication in which messages flow between members of an organization who have equal power or responsibility. (1)

hostile work environment Verbal or nonverbal behavior that has the intention or effect of interfering with someone's work or creating an environment that is intimidating, offensive, or hostile. (4)

hypothetical questions Questions that ask an interviewee how he or she might respond under certain circumstances. (6)

I

"I" language Language in which the communicator describes his or her feelings, needs, and behaviors without accusing others. (5)

immediacy Verbal and nonverbal behaviors that indicate closeness and liking. (4)

impromptu presentation A type of delivery in which the speaker has little or no preparation time before presenting his or her remarks. (12)

indirect questions Questions that get at information the interviewer wants to know without asking for it directly. (6)

individualistic culture A culture whose members are inclined to put their own interests and those of their immediate families ahead of social concerns. (2)

informal communication networks Patterns of interaction that are based on proximity, friendships, and shared interests. (1)

information power The ability to influence that arises because of one's access to otherwise obscure information. (8)

instant messaging (IM) An Internet-based tool that allows the exchange of typed messages between two or more people in real time. (1)

interview A two-party, somewhat structured conversation in which at least one person has a specific purpose. (6)

intranet An infrastructure that allows people within an organization to exchange information in digital form. (1)

investigative interview An interview designed to discover the causes of an incident or problem. (7)

J

jargon Specialized terminology used by members of a particular group. The word is used in a derogatory sense when applied to language that is overly obscure. (4)

L

laissez-faire leadership style A leadership style in which the leader gives up power and transforms a group into a leaderless collection of equals. (8)

lateral communication *See* Horizontal communication.

latitude of acceptance The range of positions or arguments a person would accept with little or no persuasion. (14)

latitude of noncommitment The range of positions or arguments a person neither accepts nor rejects. (14)

latitude of rejection The range of positions or arguments a person opposes. (14)

leading questions Questions that direct the interviewee to answer in a certain way, often by indicating the answer the interviewer wants to hear. (6)

life-cycle theory of leadership An approach to understanding leadership that suggests that a leader's attention to tasks and relationships should vary depending on the organizational maturity of subordinates. (8)

long-term orientation Cultural orientation that defers gratification in pursuit of long-range goals. *See also* Short-term orientation. (2)

lose–lose orientation An approach to negotiation in which one party's perceived loss leads to an outcome with negative consequences for the other parties. (5)

low-context culture A culture that uses language primarily to express thoughts, feelings, and ideas as clearly and logically as possible. (2)

low-level abstractions Highly specific statements that refer directly to objects or events that can be observed. (4)

M

majority vote A decision-making method in which a vote is taken and the item with the most votes is the one accepted. (8)

manuscript presentation A type of delivery in which the speaker reads word-for-word from prepared remarks. (12)

masculine style of speech Culturally influenced style of speaking that focuses less on feelings and relationships and more on information, facts, knowledge, and competence. *See also* Feminine style of speech, Report talk. (4)

memorized presentation A type of delivery in which the speech is memorized and recited word-for-word from memory. (12)

message Any symbol or behavior from which others create meaning or which triggers a response. (1)

minority decision A decision-making method in which a few members make a decision for the whole group. (8)

moderately structured interview A flexible interview in which major topics, their order, questions, and probes are planned but not rigidly adhered to. (6)

monochronic time orientation Cultural orientation in efficiency in accomplishing tasks is generally a higher priority than addressing personal relationships. *See also* Polychronic time orientation. (2, 4)

motion In a meeting conducted according to parliamentary procedure, a specific proposal for action that must be seconded in order to be discussed by the group. (9)

motivated sequence organizational plan An organizational strategy that presents a topic in terms of five sequential concepts: attention, need, satisfaction, visualization, and action. (10, 14)

motivational speech A speech aimed primarily at generating enthusiasm for the topic being presented. (14)

N

negotiation Discussion of specific proposals for the purpose of finding a mutually acceptable agreement or settlement. (5)

networking The process of meeting people and maintaining contacts to get career information, advice, and job leads. (1)

noise Any factor that interferes with a message. Such factors are also called *barriers* or *interference*. (1)

nominal group technique (NGT) A five-phase method for giving group members' ideas equal chance at consideration. (9)

nonstructured interview An interview that consists of a topical agenda but no planned, specific questions. (6)

nonverbal communication Communication that consists of messages sent by nonlinguistic means, whether visually, physically, or vocally. (4)

norming stage A phase in problem-solving groups characterized by an end to conflict and emergence of harmony within the group. Also termed *emergence phase*. (8)

norms Informal rules about what behavior is appropriate in a group. Explicit norms are made clear by speaking about them or writing them out. Implicit norms are not openly discussed but are known and understood by group members. (8)

O

online meeting A type of virtual meeting in which computer users create a chat room and exchange typed messages in real time. (9)

open questions Questions that invite a broad, detailed response. *See also* Closed questions. (6)

opinion questions Questions that seek the respondent's judgment about a topic. (6)

organizational chart A drawing or model that shows the levels of authority and reporting relationships in an organization. (1)

organizational culture A relatively stable picture of an organization that is shared by its members. (2)

orientation phase The first of Aubrey Fisher's four problem-solving phases of groups; characterized by tentative statements and getting-acquainted types of communication. (8)

overhead question A question directed at all members of a group, inviting a response from any member. (9)

P

panel interview An interview conducted by a group of questioners with whom the candidate will work, who are commonly from different levels within an organization. (7)

paralanguage Nonlinguistic vocal qualities such as rate, pitch, volume, and pauses. (4)

paraphrasing Listening to another and restating what has been said in your own words. Both feelings and factual content can be paraphrased. (3)

parliamentary procedure An established set of rules that govern the process of conducting meetings. Codified in *Robert's Rules of Order*. (9)

people-oriented listening style A style of listening in which the listener is most concerned with creating and maintaining positive interpersonal relationships. *See also* Action-oriented listening style, Content-oriented listening style, Time-oriented listening style. (3)

performance appraisal interview An interview, usually conducted by a superior, in which the quality of a subordinate's work is discussed. (7)

performing stage A phase in problem-solving groups characterized by members' active endorsement of group decisions. Also termed *reinforcement phase*. (8)

persuasion The act of motivating an audience, through communication, to voluntarily change a particular belief. (14)

pictogram A visual support that employs an artistic or pictorial variation of a bar, column, or pie chart. (11)

pie chart A round chart that is divided into segments to illustrate percentages of a whole. (11)

polychronic time orientation Cultural orientation in which personal relationships are generally a higher priority than efficient use of time. *See also* Monochronic time orientation. (2, 4)

power distance A measure of a culture's acceptance (high or low) of differences in authority. (2)

presentation software Computer software programs (e.g., Microsoft PowerPoint) that create displays used in presentations. Such programs typically include capabilities for creating special audio, visual, and transition effects, speaker notes, and handouts. (11)

primary questions Interview questions that introduce a new topic or a new area within a topic. *See also* Secondary questions. (6)

problem-oriented messages Messages that aim at meeting the needs of both the sender and the other party. (5)

problem–solution pattern (organizational plan) An organizational arrangement in which the speaker first convinces the audience that a problem exists and then presents a plan to solve it. (10, 14)

proposal A type of presentation that advocates for a particular position or action. (14)

Q

quid pro quo sexual harassment A form of sexual harassment that implies a job benefit is tied to an employee submitting to unwelcome sexual advances. (4)

quotation A form of support that uses the words of others who are authoritative or articulate to make a point more effectively than the speaker could on his or her own. (11)

R

rapport talk Language that creates connections, establishes goodwill, and builds community; more typically used by women. (4)

receiver Any person who perceives a message and attaches meaning to it, whether the message was intended for that person or not. (1)

referent power The ability to influence because one is respected or liked by the group. (8)

reflective-thinking sequence A seven-step problem-solving approach developed by John Dewey. (8)

reinforcement phase The fourth of Aubrey Fisher's four group problem-solving phases; characterized by members' active endorsement of group decisions. (8)

relational messages The dimension of messages that focus on how communicators feel about one another. *See also* Content messages. (1)

relational roles Functional roles that help facilitate smooth interaction among members. (8)

relative words Terms that only have meaning in relationship to other (unspecified) terms. (4)

relay question In groups, a question asked by one member which the leader then addresses to the entire group. (9)

relevancy challenge A request that asks a group member to explain how his or her seemingly off-track idea relates to the group task. (9)

report An informative presentation that describes the state of an operation. (13)

report talk Language that conveys information, facts, knowledge, and competence; more typically used by men. (4)

research interview An interview designed to gather data on which to base a decision. (7)

reverse question In groups, a question asked of the leader which the leader refers back to the person who asked it. (9)

reward power The ability to influence that arises because one can induce desirable consequences or rewards. (8)

rhetorical question A question with an obvious answer, which does not call for an overt response. (10)

risky shift A type of harmful conformity in which groups take positions that are more extreme (on the side of either caution or risk) than the positions of individual members. (8)

S

sales presentation A type of presentation aimed at persuading others to purchase a product or service. (14)

scannable résumé A résumé prepared in plain text format with clear key words and phrases to be "read" and evaluated by software to screen potential job candidates. (7)

secondary questions Interview questions that seek additional information about a topic that is under discussion. *See also* Primary questions. (6)

self-directed work teams Groups that manage their own behavior to accomplish a task. (8)

self-monitoring The process of paying close attention to one's own behavior and using these observations to shape the way one behaves. (4)

sender Any person who sends a message, whether intentionally or unintentionally. (1)

short-term orientation Cultural orientation that seeks quick payoffs for effort rather than deferred gratification in pursuit of long-range goals. *See also* Long-term orientation. (2)

sincere questions Requests for information that are genuinely meant to help the listener understand. *See also* Counterfeit questions. (3)

slides Color transparencies that are projected onto a screen. (11)

social orientation Cultural orientation that places a greater priority on personal relationships than on accomplishing tasks. *See also* Task orientation. (2)

spatial pattern An organizational arrangement that presents material according to its physical location. (10)

specific goal A concrete statement of what response a speaker is seeking as the result of his or her remarks. (10)

speech of introduction A type of presentation that prepares the audience to listen to another speaker by emphasizing the upcoming speaker's qualifications or importance of the topic. (13)

statistics Numbers used to represent an idea. (11)

status report A type of informative presentation that reviews the purpose, progress, obstacles, and milestones of a project. Also called a *progress report*. (13)

stories Detailed descriptions of incidents that illustrate a point; may be factual or hypothetical. (11)

storming stage A phase in problem-solving groups characterized by members' taking strong stands that result in conflict within the group. Also termed *conflict stage*. (8)

stress interview An employment interview in which the candidate is subjected to the pressures typically encountered on the job. (7)

style approach to leadership An approach to studying leadership based on the assumption that the designated leader's style of communication affects the group's effectiveness. (8)

supporting A type of listening in which the listener responds with reassurance or comfort.

supporting material Material that backs up claims in a presentation. (11)

survey interview An interview conducted with a number of people to gather information for conclusions, interpretations, or future action. (7)

T

task orientation Cultural orientation that places a greater priority on accomplishing tasks than on managing personal relationships. *See also* Social orientation. (2)

task roles Functional roles that are needed to accomplish a group's mission. (8)

team A group that is especially cohesive and effective because of clear and inspiring goals, a results-driven structure, competent members, unified commitment, a collaborative climate, standards of excellence, external support and recognition, and principled leadership. (8)

teleconferencing A technology that allows participants in two or more locations to see and speak with each other. (1, 9)

theory X Theory of human motivation that assumes employees are inherently lazy and will avoid work if they can.

Organizations that operate on Theory X typically have close supervision of workers and comprehensive systems of controls. *See also* Theory Y. (2)

theory Y Theory of human motivation that assumes employees, under optimal conditions, are self-motivated, anxious to accept greater responsibility, and capable of self-control and self-direction. *See also* Theory X. (2)

thesis statement A single sentence that summarizes the central idea of a presentation. (10)

time-oriented listening style A listening style in which the listener thinks most about efficiency and prefers a fast pace. Such listeners often appear impatient. *See also* Action-oriented listening style, Content-oriented listening style, People-oriented listening style. (3)

toast A type of tribute that expresses appreciation and/or honors the accomplishments of an individual or group. (13)

topical pattern An organizational arrangement in which ideas are grouped around logical themes or divisions of the subject. (10)

training An informative presentation that teaches listeners how to perform a task. (13)

trait approach to leadership A leadership theory based on the belief that all leaders possess common traits that make them effective. (8)

transition A statement used between parts of a presentation to help listeners understand the relationship of the parts to one another and to the thesis. (10)

transparency A clear sheet used with an overhead projector to cast an image on a screen. (11)

triangle of meaning A model illustrating the indirect relationship between an object, idea, process, or other referent and the word (or other symbol) used to represent it. (4)

tribute A type of special-occasion presentation that honors a person's or group's achievements or characteristics. (13)

trigger words Terms that have such strong emotional associations that they set off an intense emotional reaction in certain listeners. (4)

U

uncertainty avoidance A measure of how accepting a culture is of a lack of predictability. (2)

upward communication Communication that flows from subordinates to superiors. (1)

V

videoconferencing The holding of a meeting or conference by means of audio and visual transmissions that enable two or more geographically separated persons to see, hear, and talk to each other. (1, 9)

virtual team A team which conducts most or all of its work via electronic channels. (8)

voice mail A technology that allows telephone callers to record messages in their own voices for the receiver to hear later. (1)

W

welcoming remarks A type of special-occasion presentation in which the speaker welcomes an individual or group, indicating the significance of the visit and setting the tone for the occasion. (13)

win–lose orientation An approach to negotiation that assumes that any gain by one party is only possible at the expense of the other party. (5)

win–win orientation A collaborative approach to negotiation which assumes that solutions can be reached that meet the needs of all parties. (5)

work group A small, interdependent collection of people with a common identity who interact with one another, usually face-to-face over time, to reach a goal. (8)

Y

"you" language Language that often begins with the word *you* and accuses or evaluates the other person. (5)

notes

Chapter 1

1. *Job Outlook 2005* (Bethlehem, PA: National Association of Colleges and Employers), retrieved October 3, 2005, from **www.jobweb.com/joboutlook/2005outlook/3a.htm**.
2. I. N. Engleberg and D. R. Wynn, "DACUM: A National Database Justifying the Study of Speech Communication," presented at the Eastern Communication Association Convention, Washington, DC, April 1994.
3. "Industry Report 1999," *Training* 36 (1999), pp. 37–81. See also R. H. Krapels and B. D. Davis, "Communication Training in Two Companies," *Business Communication Quarterly*, September 2000, pp. 104–10.
4. B. W. Bowman, "What Helps or Harms Promotability?" *Harvard Business Review* 42 (January–February 1964), p. 14.
5. D. Whetten and K. S. Cameron, *Developing Management Skills: Managing Conflict* (New York: HarperCollins, 1993), pp. 8–11.
6. T. W. Harrell and M. S. Harrell, "Stanford MBA Careers: A 20 Year Longitudinal Study," Graduate School of Business Research Paper No. 723, Stanford, CA, 1984.
7. D. A. Nellermoe, T. R. Weirich, and A. Reinstein, "Using Practitioners' Viewpoints to Improve Accounting Students' Communications Skills," *Business Communication Quarterly* 62 (1999), pp. 41–60.
8. See, for example, A. L. Darling and D. P. Dannels, "Practicing Engineers Talk about the Importance of Talk: A Report on the Role of Oral Communication in the Workplace," *Communication Education* 52 (2003), pp. 1–16.
9. Bob Calandra, "Toward a Silver-Tongued Scientist," *The Scientist* 16 (September 16, 2002), p. 42.
10. *Santa Barbara News-Press*, August 22, 1999, p. J1.
11. J. Richman, "The News Journal of the Life Scientist," *The Scientist* 16 (September 16, 2002), p. 42.
12. M. S. Peterson, "Personnel Interviewers' Perceptions of the Importance and Adequacy of Applicants' Communication Skills," *Communication Education* 46 (1997), pp. 287–91.
13. "Harper's Index," *Harper's*, December 1994, p. 13.
14. Joint Commission on Accreditation of Healthcare Organizations, "Sentinel Event Statistics," accessed August 7, 2006, from **http://www.jointcommission.org/SentinelEvents/Statistics**.
15. W. Levinson, D. Roter, and J. P. Mullooly, "Physician-Patient Communication: The Relationship with Malpractice Claims Among Primary Care Physicians and Surgeons," *Journal of American Medical Association* 277 (1997), pp. 553–59.
16. *Making the Grade: What American Workers Think Should Be Done to Improve Education* (Rutgers, NJ: John J. Heldrich Center for Workforce Development), accessed February 2, 2001, from **www.heldrich.rutgers.edu/worktrends.cfm**.
17. G. Goldhaber, *Organizational Communication*, 6th ed. (Dubuque, IA: Wm. C. Brown, 1993), p. 143.
18. *Management Education at Risk: Report of the Management Education Task Force to the AACSB International Board of Directors*, August 2002, p. 19. Retrieved July 11, 2003, from the Association to Advance Collegiate Schools of Business Web site at **http://www.aacsb.edu/members/metf/default.asp**.
19. A. S. Bednar and R. J. Olney, "Communication Needs of Recent Graduates," *Bulletin of the Association for Business Communication*, December 1987, pp. 22–23.
20. S. Ginsberg, "So Many Messages and So Little Time," *Business Outlook*, May 5, 1997, p. C1.
21. See, for example, A. Petofi, "The Graphic Revolution in Computers," in *Careers Tomorrow: The Outlook for Work in a Changing World*, ed. E. Cornish (Bethesda, MD: World Future Society, 1988), pp. 62–66.
22. M. Collins and D. Oberman, "What's the Job Outlook?" *Journal of Career Planning & Employment*, Winter 1994, pp. 57–58.
23. J. L. Winsor, D. B. Curtis, and R. D. Stephens, "National Preferences in Business and Communication Education: An Update," *Journal of the Association for Communication Administration* 3 (1997), pp. 170–79. See also M. S. Peterson, "Personnel Interviewers' Perceptions of the Importance and Adequacy of Applicants' Communication Skills," *Communication Education* 46 (1997), pp. 287–91.
24. *Job Outlook '99* (Bethlehem, PA: National Association of Colleges and Employers, 1999).
25. F. S. Endicott, *The Endicott Report: Trends in the Employment of College and University Graduates in Business and Industry 1980* (Evanston, IL: Placement Center, Northwestern University, 1979).
26. Cited in V. V. Weldon, "The Power of Changing the Context," *Vital Speeches of the Day* 60 (1994), pp. 217–19.
27. For a discussion of content and relational messages, see R. Adler and N. Towne, *Looking Out/Looking In*, 11th ed. (Belmont, CA: Wadsworth, 2005), pp. 27–28.
28. A. C. Michalos, *A Pragmatic Approach to Business Ethics* (Thousand Oaks, CA: Sage, 1995).
29. D. M. Driscoll, et al., "Who Says Ethics Are Nice?" *Across the Board* 34 (June 1997), pp. 47–50.

30. M. D. Montgomery and C. Ramus, "Corporate Social Responsibility Reputation Effects on MBA Job Choice," *Graduate School of Business Research Paper #1805*, May 2003, Stanford, CA. Retrieved September 26, 2005, from **https://gsbapps.stanford.edu/researchpapers/library/RP1805.pdf**.
31. C. R. Roberts, "He Argues for Ethics," *Tacoma News Tribune*, May 16, 2005. Retrieved October 1, 2005, from **http://elibrary.bigchalk.com**.
32. Gene R. Laczniak, "Framework for Analyzing Marketing Ethics," *Journal of Macromarketing* 3 (1983), pp. 7–18, adapted by M. Schminke and M. L. Ambrose, "Asymmetric Perceptions of Ethical Frameworks of Men and Women in Business and Nonbusiness Settings," *Journal of Business Ethics* 16 (1997), pp. 119–29.
33. You can grow professionally by greater study of traditional ethics (the first two guidelines) as found in the works of Immanuel Kant, John Stuart Mill, and others. Footnote: Patricia J. O'Connor and Susan H. Godar, "How Not to Make Ethical Decisions: Guidelines from Management Textbooks," *Teaching Business Ethics* 3: (1999), pp. 69–86. See also D. B. Tinsley, "Ethics Can be Guaged by Three Key Rules," in *Business Ethics 05/06*, 17th ed., J. E. Richardson, ed. (Dubuque: McGraw-Hill/Dushkin, 2005), pp. 11–12.
34. For a discussion of the characteristics of networks, see P. R. Monge, "The Network Level of Analysis," in *Handbook of Communication Science*, eds. C. R. Berger and S. H. Chafee (Newbury Park, CA: Sage, 1987), pp. 239–70.
35. For a review of research on formal networks, see F. M. Jablin, "Formal Organization Structure," in *Handbook of Organizational Communication*, eds. F. Jablin, L. Putnam, K. Roberts, and L. Porter (Newbury Park, CA: Sage, 1987), pp. 389–419.
36. "Managers' Shoptalk," *Working Woman*, February 1985, p. 22.
37. D. Katz and R. Kahn, *The Social Psychology of Organizations*, 2nd ed. (New York: Wiley, 1978), p. 239.
38. T. J. Peters and R. H. Waterman, Jr., *In Search of Excellence: Lessons from America's Best-Run Companies* (New York: Harper & Row 1982), p. 267.
39. S. Silverstein, "Corporate Communications Gap Keeps Executives, Lower Ranks in the Dark," *Los Angeles Times*, January 10, 1999, p. C5.
40. See, for example, J. W. Kassing, "Investigating the Relationship between Superior-Subordinate Relationship Quality and Employee Dissent," *Communication Research Reports* 17 (2000), pp. 58–70.
41. L. Schuster, "Wal-Mart Chief's Enthusiastic Approach Infects Employees, Keeps Retailer Growing," *The Wall Street Journal*, April 20, 1982, p. 21.
42. F. Rice, "Champions of Communication," *Fortune*, June 3, 1991, pp. 111–20.
43. Adapted from Katz and Kahn, *The Social Psychology of Organizations*, p. 245.
44. J. W. Kassing, op. cit.
45. W. G. Bennis, *An Invented Life: Reflections on Leadership and Change* (Reading, MA: Addison-Wesley, 1993).
46. L. P. Stewart, A. D. Stewart, S. A. Friedley, and P. J. Cooper, *Communication between the Sexes: Sex Differences and Sex-Role Stereotypes*, 2nd ed. (Scottsdale, AZ: Gorsuch Scarisbrick, 1990), p. 226.
47. F. Dansereau and S. E. Markham, "Superior-Subordinate Communication: Multiple Levels of Analysis," in *Handbook of Organizational Communication*, eds. F. M. Jablin, L. L. Putnam, K. H. Roberts, and L. W. Porter (Newbury Park, CA: Sage, 1987).
48. T. Petzinger, Jr., "Two Executives Cook Up Way to Make Pillsbury Listen," *The Wall Street Journal*, September 27, 1996, p. B1.
49. J. E. Spillan, M. Mino, and M. S. Rowles, "Sharing Organizational Messages Through Effective Lateral Communication," *Qualitative Research Reports in Communication* (Fall 2002), pp. 96–104.
50. G. Goldhaber, *Organizational Communication*, 6th ed. (Dubuque, IA: Wm. C. Brown, 1993), pp. 163–64.
51. D. O. Wilson, "Diagonal Communication Links within Organizations," *Journal of Business Communication* 29 (Spring 1992), pp. 129–43.
52. K. Mieszkowski, "Change—Barbara Waugh," *Fast Company* 20 (December 1998), p. 146.
53. Adapted from Goldhaber, *Organizational Communication*, pp. 174–75.
54. T. W. Ferguson, "Who's Mentoring Whom?" *Forbes*, May 19, 1997, p. 252.
55. See, for example, P. G. Doloff, "Beyond the Org Chart," *Across the Board*, February 1999, pp. 43–47.
56. J. E. Lukaszewski, "You Can Become a Verbal Visionary," *Executive Speeches* 12 (August–September 1997), pp. 23–30.
57. "Did You Hear It Through the Grapevine?" *Training & Development*, October 1994, p. 20.
58. See R. Cross and A. Parker, *The Hidden Power of Social Networks: Understanding How Work Really Gets Done in Organizations* (Boston: Harvard Business School Press, 2004), p. 11.
59. T. E. Deal and A. A. Kennedy, *Corporate Cultures: The Rites and Rituals of Corporate Life* (Reading, MA: Addison-Wesley, 1982), p. 86.
60. D. Krackhardt and J. R. Hanson, "Informal Networks: The Company Behind the Chart," *Harvard Business Review* 71 (1993), pp. 104–11.
61. R. M. Kanter, "The New Managerial Work," *Harvard Business Review* 67 (1989), pp. 85–92.
62. J. B. Bush, Jr., and A. L. Frohman, "Communication in a 'Network' Organization," *Organizational Dynamics* 20 (Autumn 1991), pp. 23–36.

63. E. M. Eisenberg and H. L. Goodall, Jr., *Organizational Communication: Balancing Creativity and Constraint* (New York: St. Martin's, 1993), p. 9.
64. T. J. Murray, "How to Stay Lean and Mean," *Business Month*, August 1987, pp. 29–32.
65. M. Jackson, "Study Shows Workplace Goofing Off Often Pays Off for the Employer," *Santa Barbara News-Press*, January 7, 1998, p. B8.
66. K. Roane, "Nuances of Networking: A Savvy Approach for the Next Century," retrieved October 1, 2005, from **http://www.susanroane.com/articles/nuance.html**.
67. For more advice on networking, see R. E. Kelley interviewed by A. M. Webber, "Are You a Star at Work?" *Fast Company Career Guide* (New York: Fast Company Media Group, 2000), pp. 46–50.
68. T. H. Feely, "Testing a Communication Network Model of Employee Turnover Based on Centrality," *Journal of Applied Communication Research* (2000), pp. 262–77. See also "Network Inside Your Organization," *Fast Company Career Guide* (New York: Fast Company Media Group, 2000), p. 13.
69. P. S. Dodds, R. Muhamad, and D. J. Watts., "An Experimental Study of Search in Global Social Networks," *Science* 301 (2003), pp. 827–29.
70. K. S. Lyness and D. E. Thompson, "Climbing the Corporate Ladder: Do Female and Male Executives Follow the Same Route?" *Journal of Applied Psychology* 85 (2000), pp. 86–101. See also K. Miller, *Organizational Communication: Approaches and Processes*, 4th ed. (Belmont CA: Wadsworth, 2006) pp. 265–67.
71. K. E. Kram, "Phases of the Mentoring Relationship," *Academy of Management Journal* 12 (1983), pp. 608–25.
72. L. Gardenswartz and A. Rowe, "Starting a Mentoring Program?" *Managing Diversity* 6 (January 1997), pp. 1–2. See also *Mentoring Process*, retrieved January 25, 2006, from **www.advancingwomen.com/wk_mentprocess.html**.
73. See, for example, L. M. Flaherty, K. J. Pearce, and R. B. Rubin, "Internet and Face-to-Face Communication: Not Functional Alternatives," *Communication Quarterly* 46 (1998), pp. 250–68; V. C. Sheer and L. Chen, "Improving Media Richness Theory: A Study of Interaction Goals, Message Valence, and Task Complexity in Manager-Subordinate Communication," *Management Communication Quarterly* 18 (2004), pp. 76–93.; and E. Vaast, "O Brother, Where Are Thou?: From Communities to Networks of Practice Through Intranet Use," *Management Communication Quarterly* 18 (2004), pp. 5–44.
74. R. L. Daft and R. H. Lengel, "Information Richness: A New Approach to Managerial Behavior and Organizational Design," *Research in Organizational Behavior*, eds. L. L. Cummings and B. M. Staw (Homewood, IL: JAI Press, 1984), pp. 191–233.
75. See, for example, J. M. Kayany, C. E. Wotring, and E. J. Forrest, "Relational Control and Interactive Media Choice in Technology-Mediated Communication Situations," *Human Communication Research* 22 (1996), pp. 399–421.
76. A. Bryant, "Fare Rage," *Newsweek*, October 23, 2000, p. 46.
77. R. T. Herschel and P. H. Andrews, "Ethical Implications of Technological Advances on Business Communication," *Journal of Business Communication* 34 (1997), pp. 160–70.
78. " 'We Never Talk Anymore:' Survey Reveals Few Executives Use Telephone or Meet in Person at Work," retrieved February 9, 2006, from **http://www.officeteam.com/PressRoom;jsessionid=CwZX1nzn5DxDdnY3LYsphbxRPS4JQ22ftzKJXHcyMT0d4Gp8H4S0**.
79. M. Taylor, "Intranets—A New Technology Changes All the Rules," *Telecommunications* (Americas Edition) 31 (January 1997), pp. 39–40.
80. L. Garton and B. Wellman, "Social Impacts of Electronic Mail in Organizations: A Review of the Research Literature," *Communication Yearbook* 18 (Newbury Park, CA: Sage, 1995), pp. 434–53. See also M. Parks and L. Roberts, "Making MOOsic: The Development of Personal Relationships On-line and a Comparison to Their Off-line Counterparts," presented at the annual conference of the Western Speech Communication Association, Monterey, CA, February 1997.
81. "Are You Connected?" *Training & Development*, November 1994, p. 18.
82. A. Overholt, "Intel's Got (Too Much) Mail," *Fast Company*, March 2001, p. 44.
83. A. Harmon, "Clique of Instant Messagers Expands into the Workplace," *The New York Times*, March 11, 2003, p. C1.
84. M. Marriott, "The Blossoming of Internet Chat," *The New York Times* online, accessed February 2, 2001, from **http://www.nytimes.com/library/tech/98/07/circuits/articles/02chat.html**.
85. C. Biggs, "Instant Messaging," *Enterprise Systems Journal* 16 (January 2001), p. 42.
86. Harmon, op. cit.
87. "Startup Looking to Push the Envelope in Internet Communications," *Investors Business Daily*, January 23, 2006, p. A6.
88. Lengel and Daft, "The Selection of Communication Media," p. 229.
89. J. Montague, "When E-Mail Just Won't Do," *Hospitals & Health Networks* 70 (October 20, 1996), pp. 10–11.
90. See, for example, L. A. Baxter, "'Talking Things Through' and 'Putting It in Writing': Two Codes of Communication in an Academic Institution," *Journal of Applied Communication Research* 21 (1993), pp. 313–23.

91. J. J. Mitchell, "Why Can't We All Get Along? E-mail vs. Voice Mail Culture Should Provide a Clue," *San Jose Mercury News*, July 21, 1996, p. 6E. For a discussion of the importance of personal contact in an increasingly technological world, see S. R. Herndon, "Theory and Practice: Implications for the Implementation of Communication Technology in Organizations," *Journal of Business Communication* 34 (1997), pp. 121–29.

Chapter 2

1. J. F. Kikoski and C. K. Kikoski, *Reflexive Communication in the Culturally Diverse Workplace* (Westport, CT: Quorum, 1996), p. 3.
2. "Tripling of Hispanic and Asian Populations in 50 Years; Non-Hispanic Whites May Drop to Half of Total Population," U.S. Census Bureau publication CB04-44. Retrieved October 13, 2005, from **http://www.census.gov/Press-Release/www/releases/archives/population/001720.html**.
3. *2004 American Community Survey* (Washington, DC, United States Census Bureau). Retrieved November 2, 2005, from **http://factfinder.census.gov**.
4. *Directory of Foreign Firms Operating in the U.S.*, 18th ed. (Millis, MA: Uniworld Business Publications, 2005).
5. Fidelity Investments, *Fidelity's Targeted International Equity Funds* (Boston: Fidelity Distributors, 1996), pp. 2–4.
6. U.S. Census Bureau, *Population Profile of the United States: 2000*. Retrieved October 15, 2005, from **http://www.census.gov/hhes/www/laborfor/laborforce.html**.
7. Kiplinger Letter 79 (December 27, 2002).
8. "Employment at U.S.-Based Global Companies," *Workforce Management*, July 2005, pp. 36–46.
9. *Directory of Foreign Firms*, op cit.
10. V. Manson, *Globalizing Employee Ownership Plans for Multinational Corporations: Multinational Companies and Employee Ownership* (Oakland, CA: National Center for Employee Ownership, 1996).
11. K. H. Hammonds, "Fast Forward," *Fast Company* 44 (March 2001), p. 113.
12. DuPont advertisement, reprinted in L. E. Boone, D. L. Kurtz, and J. R. Block, *Contemporary Business Communication*, 2nd ed. (Englewood Cliffs, NJ: Prentice Hall, 1996), p. 637.
13. L. Copeland, "Making the Most of Cultural Differences at the Workplace," *Personnel*, June 1988, p. 53.
14. N. Bartrum, "Diversity for All," *Association Management*, July 2003, p. 58.
15. C. H. Deutsch, "Want to Sail to Top? Go Overseas," *Albuquerque Tribune*, August 4, 1988, p. B7.
16. M. W. Lustig and J. Koester, *Intercultural Competence: Interpersonal Communication Across Cultures*, 4th ed. (Boston: Allyn & Bacon, 2003), p. 27.
17. E. Hall, *The Silent Language* (Greenwich, CT: Fawcett, 1959), p. 169.
18. J. A. Barker, *Future Edge: Discovering the New Paradigms of Success* (New York: William Morrow, 1992), p. 124.
19. Ibid., p. 125.
20. Boone, Kurtz, and Block, *Contemporary Business Communication*, p. 603.
21. C. J. Williams, "Not All Ways Wal-Mart as Chain Takes on Germany," *Los Angeles Times*, August 15, 1999, p. C1.
22. K. M. Glover, "Do's and Taboos," *Business America* 111 (August 13, 1990), p. 5.
23. F. H. Katayama, "How to Act Once You Get There," *Fortune's Pacific Rim Guide*, 1989, p. 87.
24. T. Padgett and C. S. Lee, "Go South, Young Yanquis," *Newsweek*, September 19, 1994, p. 48.
25. F. Trompenaars, *Riding the Waves of Culture* (Burr Ridge, IL: Irwin, 1994), p. 122.
26. Ibid., p. 123.
27. M. Park and M. Kim, "Communication Practices in Korea," *Communication Quarterly* 40 (1992), pp. 398–404.
28. M. Miller, "A Clash of Corporate Cultures," *Los Angeles Times*, August 15, 1992, pp. A1, A8.
29. E. Hall, *Beyond Culture* (New York: Doubleday, 1959).
30. K. Melymuka, "Tips for Teams," *Computerworld* 31 (April 28, 1997), p. 72.
31. M. Morris, *Saying and Meaning in Puerto Rico: Some Problems in the Ethnology of Discourse* (Oxford: Pergamon, 1981).
32. D. Locke, *Increasing Multicultural Understanding: A Comprehensive Model* (Newbury Park, CA: Sage, 1992), p. 140.
33. G. Thurmon, "Oral Rhetorical Practice in African American Culture," in *Our Voices: Essays in Culture, Ethnicity, and Communication: An Intercultural Anthology*, eds. A. Gonzalez, M. Houston, and V. Chen (Los Angeles: Roxbury, 1994), p. 82.
34. G. Hofstede, *Cultures and Organizations: Software of the Mind* (New York: McGraw-Hill, 1997).
35. See, for example, M. Nishishiba and L. D. Ritchie, "The Concept of Trustworthiness: A Cross-Cultural Comparison between Japanese and U.S. Business People," *Journal of Applied Communication Research* 28 (2000), pp. 347–67.
36. D. Taub, "Global Recruiting: Richard Ferry Helped Take Korn/Ferry International from Two-Man Office to World's No. 1 Executive Search Firm," *Los Angeles Business Journal*, December 16, 1996, p. 1.
37. "Formula for Success," *Financial World*, December 8, 1992, p. 40.
38. Hofstede, *Cultures and Organizations*, pp. 189–210.

39. R. L. Birdwhistell, *Kinesics and Context* (Philadelphia: University of Philadelphia Press, 1970), pp. 30–31.
40. See B. J. Hall, *Among Cultures* (Fort Worth: Harcourt College Publishers, 2002), p. 239, for a discussion of Greek and Israeli conflict styles.
41. Lustig and Koester, *Intercultural Competence*, p. 267.
42. E. C. Condon, "Cross-Cultural Interferences Affecting Teacher–Pupil Communication in American Schools," *International and Intercultural Communication Annual* 3 (1976), pp. 108–120.
43. L. A. Samovar and R. E. Porter, *Communication between Cultures*, 5th ed. (Belmont, CA: Wadsworth, 2004) p. 199.
44. K. G. Stone, "Disability Act Everyone's Responsibility in America," *Albuquerque Journal*, February 19, 1995, p. H2.
45. D. O. Braithwaite and D. Labrecque, "Responding to the Americans with Disabilities Act: Contributions of Interpersonal Communication Research and Training," *Journal of Applied Communication Research* 22 (1994), pp. 285–94. See also D. O. Braithwaite, "'Just How Much Did That Wheelchair Cost?': Management of Privacy Boundaries by Persons with Disabilities," *Western Journal of Speech Communication* 55 (1991), pp. 254–75.
46. "Communicating with People with Disabilities," *Business First* 11 (October 9, 1995), p. 14B. See also A. L. Colvert and J. Smith, "What Is Reasonable? Workplace Communication and People Who Are Disabled," in *Handbook of Communication and People with Disabilities: Research and Application*, eds. D. O. Braithwaite and T. L. Thompson (Mahwah, NJ: Erlbaum, 2000).
47. See J. Skelly, "The Rise of International Ethics," *Business Ethics*, March–April 1995, pp. 2–5. Reprinted in J. E. Richardson, ed., *Business Ethics 97–98* (Guilford, CT: Dushkin/McGraw-Hill, 1997), pp. 164–68.
48. P. F. Buller, J. J. Kohls, and K. S. Anderson, "A Model for Addressing Cross-Cultural Ethical Conflicts," *Business & Society* 36 (June 1997), pp. 169–93.
49. See T. Donaldson, "Values in Tension: Ethics Away from Home," *Harvard Business Review*, September–October 1996, pp. 48–62.
50. Ibid.
51. J. F. Kiboski, "Effective Communication in the Performance Appraisal Interview: Face-to-Face Communication for Public Managers in the Culturally Diverse Workplace," *Public Personnel Management* 28, no. 2 (Summer 1999), pp. 301–23.
52. M. Marby, "Pin a Label on a Manager—and Watch What Happens," *Newsweek*, May 14, 1990, p. 43.
53. Copeland, "Making the Most of Cultural Differences," p. 60.
54. T. Weiss, "Reading Culture: Professional Communication as Translation," *Journal of Business & Technical Communication* 11 (1997), pp. 321–38.
55. L. M. Millhous, "The Experience of Culture in Multicultural Groups," *Small Group Research* 30 (1999), pp. 280–308.
56. J. C. Pearson, L. Turner, and W. Todd-Mancillas, *Gender and Communication*, 3rd ed. (Madison, WI: Brown & Benchmark, 1995), pp. 153–57.
57. M. Houston, "When Black Women Talk with White Women: Why Dialogues Are Difficult," in *Our Voices*, eds. Gonzalez, Houston, and Chen, p. 137.
58. J. N. Martin and T. K. Nakayama, *Intercultural Communication in Contexts* (Boston: McGraw-Hill, 2004), pp. 420–21.
59. C. M. Kelly, *The Destructive Achiever: Power and Ethics in the American Corporation* (Reading, MA: Addison-Wesley, 1988), p. 159.
60. E. Cose, *The Rage of a Privileged Class: Why Are Middle-Class Blacks So Angry? Why Should America Care?* (New York: HarperCollins, 1993), p. 9.
61. S. F. Gale, "The Bookstore Battle," *Workforce Management Online*, August 2003. Retrieved October 30, 2005, from **http://www.workforce.com/archive/feature/23/49/48/index.php?ht=bookstore%20battle%20bookstore%20battle**.
62. T. E. Deal and A. A. Kennedy, *Corporate Cultures: The Rites and Rituals of Corporate Life* (Reading, MA: Addison-Wesley, 1982), pp. 16–17.
63. E. C. Ravlin and C. L. Adkins, "A Work Values Approach to Corporate Culture: A Field Test of the Value of Congruence Process and Its Relationship to Individual Outcomes," *Journal of Applied Psychology* 74 (June 1989), pp. 424–33.
64. J. Kotter and J. Heskett, *Corporate Culture and Performance* (New York: Free Press, 1992), p. 7.
65. J. Keyton, *Communication and Organizational Culture* (Thousand Oaks, CA: Sage, 2005).
66. J. W. Gilsdorf, "Organizational Rules on Communicating: How Employees Are—and Are Not—Learning the Ropes," *Journal of Business Communication* 39 (April 1998), pp. 173–201.
67. R. D. Ireland, "Corporate Culture Best Conveyed by Mid-level Managers," *Baylor Business Review* 10 (Spring 1992), pp. 18–19.
68. Gilsdorf, op. cit.
69. *Workforce Week*, May 25–29, 2003; retrieved May 27, 2003, from **http://www.workforce.com/section/09/article/23/44/64.html#values#values**.
70. R. S. Hansen, "Uncovering a Company's Corporate Culture Is a Critical Task for Job-Seekers," retrieved November 26, 2001, from **http://www.quintcareers.com/employer_corporate_culture.html**.
71. D. McGregor, *The Human Side of Enterprise* (New York: McGraw-Hill, 1960.)
72. See M. W. Kramer and J. A. Hess, "Communication Rules for the Display of Emotions in Organizational

Settings," *Management Communication Quarterly* 16 (2002), pp. 66–80.

73. M. H. Brown, "Defining Stories in Organizations: Characteristics and Functions," in *Communication Yearbook 13,* ed. J. A. Anderson (Newbury Park, CA: Sage, 1990), pp. 162–90. See also J. Meyer, "Tell Me a Story: Eliciting Organizational Values from Narratives," *Communication Quarterly* 43 (1995), pp. 210–24.
74. J. K. Barge, "Memorable Messages and Newcomer Socialization," *Western Journal of Communication* 68 (2004), pp. 233–56.
75. E. Gustkey, "A Team of Cut-Ups," *Los Angeles Times,* June 21, 1996, pp. C1, C7.
76. T. J. Peters and R. H. Waterman, *In Search of Excellence: Lessons from America's Best-Run Companies* (New York: Harper & Row, 1982), p. 240. See also J. M. Byer and H. M. Trice, "How an Organization's Rites Reveal Its Culture," *Organizational Dynamics,* Spring 1987, p.15.
77. B. Filipczak, "Corporate Body Language," *Training* 33 (November 1996), p. 8.
78. The following sections are adapted from T. E. Deal and A. A. Kennedy, *Corporate Cultures: The Rites and Rituals of Corporate Life* (Reading, MA: Addison-Wesley, 1982), pp. 129–33.

Chapter 3

1. P. Senge, A. Kleiner, C. Roberts, R. Ross, G. Roth, and B. Smith, *The Dance of Change: The Challenges of Sustaining Momentum in Learning Organizations* (New York: Doubleday/Currency, 1999).
2. J. Stewart, K. E. Zediker, and S. Witteborn, *Together: Communication Interpersonally: A Social Construction Approach,* 6th ed. (Los Angeles: Roxbury, 2005), p. 173. See also L.W. Black, "Building Connection While Thinking Together: By-products of Employee Training in Dialogue," *Western Journal of Communication* 69 (2005), pp. 273–92.
3. S. Covey, *The Seven Habits of Highly Effective People* (New York: Simon & Schuster, 1989).
4. T. Peters, "Leadership Is Confusing as Hell," *Fast Company,* March 2001. Online at **http://www.fastcompany.com/online/44/rules.html**.
5. J. Franzen, "The Listener," *New Yorker,* October 6, 2003, p. 85.
6. K. K. Murphy, *Effective Listening: Hearing What People Say and Making It Work for You* (New York: Bantam, 1987), p. 74.
7. J. L. Winsor, D. B. Curtis, and R. D. Stephens, "National Preferences in Business and Communication Education: An Update," *Journal of the Association for Communication Administration* 3 (1997), pp. 170–79.
8. V. Marchant, "Listen Up!" *Time,* June 28, 1999, p. 74. See also K.W. Hawkins and B. P. Fillion, "Perceived Communication Skill Needs for Work Groups," *Communication Research Reports* 2 (1999), pp. 167–74.
9. T. Rankin, "The Measurement of the Ability to Understand Spoken Language," *Dissertation Abstracts* 12 (1952), pp. 847–48.
10. J. D. Weinrauch and J. R. Swanda, Jr., "Examining the Significance of Listening: An Exploratory Study of Contemporary Management," *Journal of Business Communication* 13 (February 1975), pp. 25–32.
11. J. P. Kotter, "What Effective General Managers Really Do," *Harvard Business Review* 60 (1982), pp. 156–67; and R. G. Nichols and L. A. Stevens, "Listening to People," *Harvard Business Review* 68 (1990), pp. 95–102.
12. H. Mintzberg, "The Manager's Job: Folklore and Fact," *Harvard Business Review* 53 (July–August 1975), pp. 49–61.
13. S. L. Becker and L. R.V. Ekdom, "That Forgotten Basic Skill: Oral Communication," *Association for Communication Administration Bulletin* 33 (1980), pp. 12–15.
14. V. DiSalvo, D. C. Larsen, and W. J. Seiler, "Communication Skills Needed by Persons in Business Organizations," *Communication Education* 25 (1976), pp. 269–75.
15. R. Bommelje, *The Listening Leader* (e-mail newsletter), received July 22, 2002, from **rick@listeningleader.com (www.listeningleader.com)**.
16. *U.S. News & World Report,* May 26, 1980, p. 65.
17. H. MacGregor, "Hindu Sues for Wrongly Being Served a Beef Burrito," *Los Angeles Times* (Ventura County Edition), January 24, 1998, p. B1.
18. D. H. Sweet, "Successful Job Hunters Are All Ears," *Managing Your Career* (New York: Dow Jones, 1993).
19. A. J. Sutcliffe, *First-Job Survival Guide* (NY: Henry Holt, 1997).
20. B. D. Sypher, R. N. Bostrom, and J. H. Siebert, "Listening, Communication Abilities, and Success at Work," *Journal of Business Communication* 26 (1989), pp. 293–303.
21. S. D. Johnson and C. Bechler, "Examining the Relationship between Listening Effectiveness and Leadership Emergence," *Small Group Research* 29 (1998), pp. 452–71.
22. E. R. Alexander, L. E. Penley, and I. E. Jerigan, "The Relationship of Basic Decoding Skills to Managerial Effectiveness," *Management Communication Quarterly* 6 (1992), pp. 58–73.
23. L. O. Cooper, D. R. Seibold, and R. Suchner, "Listening in Organizations: An Analysis of Error Structures in Models of Listening Competency," *Communication Research Reports* 14 (1997), pp. 312–20.
24. Ibid.
25. V. Alonzo, "5 Steps to Bigger Sales," *Incentive* 174, no. 10 (October 2000), pp. 117–19.

26. "General Interactional Skills," National Breast Cancer Centre, accessed March 10, 2003, from **http://www.nbcc.org.au/pages/subsections/skills.htm**.
27. USMLE Web site, accessed July 28, 2003 (**http://www.usmle.org/news/cse/harris.asp**).
28. Ibid.; and R. K. Sobel, "The Art of Listening," *U.S. News & World Report,* June 9, 2003, p. 58.
29. J. Brownell, "Listening in the Service Industries," in *Listening in Everyday Life: A Personal and Professional Approach,* eds. D. Borisoff and M. Purdy (Lanham, MD: University Press of America, 1991), pp. 229, 256.
30. P. LaBarre, "Leader-Feargal Quinn," *Fast Company* 52 (November 2001), p. 88. Accessed July 28, 2003, from **http://www.fastcompany.com/magazine/52/quinn.html**.
31. B. H. Spitzberg, "The Dark Side of Incompetence," in *The Dark Side of Interpersonal Communication* (Hillsdale, NJ: Erlbaum, 1994), pp. 27–28.
32. R. G. Nichols, "Listening Is a 10-Part Skill," *Nation's Business* 75 (September 1987), p. 40.
33. R. G. Nichols, *Are You Listening?* (New York: McGraw-Hill, 1957), pp. 1–17.
34. See, for example, S. Golan, "A Factor Analysis of Barriers to Effective Listening," *Journal of Business Communication* 27 (1990), pp. 25–36; and J. E. Hulbert, "Barriers to Effective Listening," *Bulletin for the Association for Business Communication* 52 (1989), pp. 3–5.
35. Peter Senge quoted in "Listening Quotations," January 20, 2003. Received from **webmaster@listen.org** (International Listening Association).
36. "McDonald's Listens—Finally!" *Listening Leader,* March 9, 1998. Online at **http://www.listencoach.com**.
37. A. Vangelisti, M. L. Knapp, and J. A. Daly, "Conversational Narcissism," *Communication Monographs 57* (1990), pp. 251–74.
38. T. Peters, *Thriving on Chaos: Handbook for a Management Revolution* (New York: Knopf, 1987), p. 117.
39. P. F. Drucker, "Management Communications," in *Management—Tasks, Responsibilities, Practices* (New York: Harper & Row, 1974).
40. *Industrial Marketing,* April 1982, p. 108.
41. D. Borisoff and M. Purdy, eds., *Listening in Everyday Life: A Personal and Professional Approach* (Lanham, MD: University Press of America, 1991), p. xiii.
42. E. Cooper, "Are You in the Listening Zone?" *On Wall Street* 11, no. 7 (July 2001).
43. S. Peterson, "Managing Your Communication: The Year 2000 and Beyond," in *Vital Speeches of the Day,* January 1, 1995.
44. Ibid., p. 77.
45. T. D. Thomlison, "Intercultural Listening," in *Listening in Everyday Life: A Personal and Professional Approach,* eds. D. Borisoff and M. Purdy (Lanham, MD: University Press of America, 1991), p. 119.
46. M. Houston, "When Black Women Talk with White Women: Why Dialogues Are Difficult," *Our Voices: Essays in Culture, Ethnicity, and Communication: An Intercultural Anthology,* eds. A. Gonzalez, M. Houston, and V. Chen (Los Angeles: Roxbury, 1994), pp. 133–39.
47. Thomlison, "Intercultural Listening," p. 117.
48. M. L. Lusting and J. Koester, *Intercultural Competence: Interpersonal Communication across Cultures,* 3rd ed. (New York: Longman, 1999), p. 250.
49. L. D. Mare, "Ma and Japan," *Southern Speech Communication Journal* 55 (Spring 1990), pp. 319–28.
50. J. C. Pearson, R. L. West, and L. H. Turner, *Gender and Communication,* 3rd ed. (Madison, WI: Brown & Benchmark, 1995), pp. 35–36.
51. D. Tannen, *You Just Don't Understand: Women and Men in Conversation* (New York: Morrow, 1990), p. 142.
52. C. A. Rategan, "He Said, She Said," *Current Health* 2 (September 1993), p. 6.
53. M. Booth-Butterfield, "She Hears . . . He Hears: What They Hear and Why," *Personnel Journal,* May 1984, pp. 36–42.
54. D. Tannen, *Talking from 9 to 5* (New York: Morrow, 1994), p. 284.
55. L. Iacocca and W. Novak, *Iacocca: An Autobiography* (New York: Bantam, 1984), p. 74.
56. D. J. McNerney, "Improve Your Communication Skills," *HR Focus* 71 (1994), p. 22. See also J. Procter, "You Haven't Heard a Word I Said: Getting Managers to Listen," *IEEE Transactions on Professional Communication* 37 (1994).
57. A. D. Wolvin and C. G. Coakley, "A Survey of the Status of Listening Training in Some Fortune 500 Companies," *Communication Education* 40 (1991), pp. 152–65.
58. L. L. Barker and K. W. Watson, *Listen Up* (New York: St. Martin's Press, 2000).
59. K. W. Watson, L. L. Barker, and J. B. Weaver, *The Listening Styles Profiles* (New Orleans: SPECTRA, 1995).
60. Covey, *The Seven Habits,* p. 252.
61. Tyena Dollinger, "Listen Using the 20/80 Rule," *Listening Leader* newsletter, March 29, 2004.
62. C. M. Anson and L. L. Forsberg, "Moving Beyond the Academic Community," *Written Communication* 7 (1990), p. 7.
63. D. Carnoy, "Rick Pitino," *Success* 45 (October 1998), pp. 68–71.
64. D. Borisoff and D. A. Victor, *Conflict Management: A Communication Skills Approach* (Englewood Cliffs, NJ: Prentice Hall, 1989), p. 45.
65. Michael J. Marquardt, *Leading with Questions: How Leaders Find the Right Solutions by Knowing What to Ask,* (Hoboken, NJ: Jossey-Bass, 2005), p. 92.
66. Covey, *The Seven Habits,* p. 235.

67. K. A. Kiewra, N. F. DuBois, D. Christian, and A. McShane, "Note-Taking Functions and Techniques," *Journal of Educational Psychology* 83 (June 1991), pp. 240–46.

Chapter 4

1. B. Keysar and A. S. Henly, "Speakers' Overestimation of Their Effectiveness," *Psychological Science* 13 (2002).
2. C. K. Ogden and I. A. Richards, *The Meaning of Meaning* (New York: Harcourt Brace, 1923).
3. R. Bello, "Determinants of Equivocation," *Communication Research* 27 (2000), pp. 161–94.
4. M. Meyer and C. Fleming, "Silicon Screenings: The Marriage of Hollywood and Silicon Valley Gets Off to a Rocky Start," *Newsweek*, August 15, 1994, p. 63.
5. M. Miller, "A Clash of Corporate Cultures," *Los Angeles Times*, August 15, 1992, pp. A1, A8.
6. J. S. Armstrong, "Unintelligible Management Research and Academic Prestige," *Interfaces* 10 (1980), pp. 80–86.
7. D. Legard, "IT Vendors Worst for Jargon, Deloitte Says," IDG News Service, June 17, 2003, at **http://www.idg.net/idgns/2003/06/17/ITVendorsWorstForJargonDeloitte.shtml**.
8. "Up in Smoke," *Accountant's Journal* 66 (April 1987), p. 10.
9. T. Simmons, "Are You a Buzzword Abuser?" *Presentations*, April 2003, pp. 31–34.
10. T. Terez, "Eager for a Paradigm Shift? Not So Fast!" *Workforce*, February 2002, p. 26.
11. T. Weiss, "Translation in a Borderless World," *Technical Communication Quarterly* 4 (1995), pp. 407–25.
12. See, for example, J. B. Bavelas, A. Black, N. Chovil, and J. Mullett, *Equivocal Communication* (Newbury Park, CA: Sage, 1990); and E. M. Eisenberg and H. L. Goodall, Jr., *Organizational Communication: Balancing Creativity and Constraint*, 2nd ed. (New York: St. Martin's, 1997), pp. 23–36.
13. A. Schneider, "Why You Can't Trust Letters of Recommendation," *The Chronicle of Higher Education* online, June 30, 2000, at **http://chronicle.com**; and C. Conrad and M. S. Poole, *Strategic Organizational Communication in a Global Economy*, 6th ed. (Belmont, CA: Thomson Wadsworth, 2005), p. 265.
14. "Litigation-Proof Letters of Recommendation," accessed February 16, 2001, at **http://www.wildcowpublishing.com/other/letter.html**.
15. R. Rubin, "Doctor-Patient Language Gap Isn't Healthy," *USA Today*, May 1, 2003, p. 9D.
16. Conrad and Poole, op. cit.
17. J. J. Bradac, J. M. Wiemann, and K. Schaefer, "The Language of Control in Interpersonal Communication," in *Strategic Interpersonal Communication*, eds. J. A. Daly and J. M. Wiemann (Hillsdale, NJ: Erlbaum, 1994), pp. 102–4. See also S. H. Ng and J. J. Bradac, *Power in Language: Verbal Communication and Social Influence* (Newbury Park, CA: Sage 1993), p. 27.
18. L. A. Hosman, "The Evaluative Consequences of Hedges, Hesitations, and Intensifiers: Powerful and Powerless Speech Styles," *Human Communication Research* 15 (1989), pp. 383–406.
19. J. Bradac and A. Mulac, "Attributional Consequences of Powerful and Powerless Speech Styles in a Crisis-Intervention Context," *Journal of Language and Social Psychology* 3 (1984), pp. 1–19.
20. J. J. Bradac, "The Language of Lovers, Flovers [sic], and Friends: Communicating in Social and Personal Relationships," *Journal of Language and Social Psychology* 2 (1983), pp. 141–62.
21. D. Geddes, "Sex Roles in Management: The Impact of Varying Power of Speech Style on Union Members' Perception of Satisfaction and Effectiveness," *Journal of Psychology* 126 (1992), pp. 589–607.
22. D. Tannen, *You Just Don't Understand: Women and Men in Conversation* (New York: Morrow, 1990), p. 47. For a detailed summary of masculine and feminine language, see D. Canary and T. Emmers-Sommer, *Sex and Gender Differences in Personal Relationships* (New York: Guilford, 1997); D. Tannen, *Talking from 9 to 5: How Women's and Men's Conversational Styles Affect Who Gets Heard, Who Gets Credit, and What Gets Done at Work* (New York: Morrow, 1994); and J. T. Wood, *Gendered Lives: Communication, Gender, and Culture*, 4th ed. (Belmont, CA: Wadsworth, 2001).
23. D. Tannen, *Talking from 9 to 5*, pp. 45–46.
24. See, for example, D. Geddes, "Sex Roles in Management: The Impact of Varying Power of Speech Style on Union Members' Perception of Satisfaction and Effectiveness," *Journal of Psychology* 126 (1992), pp. 589–607.
25. For a discussion of the principle "You can't not communicate nonverbally," see T. Clevenger, Jr., "Can One Not Communicate? A Conflict of Models," *Communication Studies* 42 (1991), pp. 340–53.
26. L. McCoy, "First Impressions," *Canadian Banker* 10 (September/October 1996), pp. 32–36.
27. J. B. Stiff, J. L. Hale, R. Garlick, and R. G. Rogan, "Effect of Cue Incongruence and Social Normative Influences on Individual Judgments of Honesty and Deceit," *Southern Speech Communication Journal* 55 (1990), pp. 206–29.
28. H. S. Friedman, "Paradoxes of Nonverbal Detection, Expression, and Responding: Points to PONDER," in *Interpersonal Sensitivity: Theory and Measurement*, eds. J. A. Hall and F. J. Bernieri (Mahwah, NJ: Erlbaum, 2001), pp. 351–62.
29. P. Ekman, "Cross-Cultural Studies of Facial Expression," in *Darwin and Facial Expression*, ed. P. Ekman (New York: Academic Press, 1973).

30. N. Sussman and H. Rosenfeld, "Influence of Culture, Language and Sex on Conversational Distance," *Journal of Personality and Social Psychology* 42 (1982), pp. 67–74.
31. William C. Taylor, "The Leader of the Future," *Fast Company* 25 (June 1999), p. 130.
32. See, for example, J. K. Burgoon, T. Birk, and M. Pfau, "Nonverbal Behaviors, Persuasion, and Credibility," *Human Communication Research* 17 (1990), pp. 140–69.
33. See J. D. Rothwell, *In Mixed Company*, 3rd ed. (Ft. Worth, TX: Harcourt Brace Jovanovich, 1998), pp. 246–48.
34. S. Roan, "Overweight and Under Pressure," *Los Angeles Times*, December 18, 1990, pp. E1, E4.
35. "Philip Condit, CEO, Boeing/McDonnell Douglas: A True Listening Leader," *Listening Leader*, November 24, 1997, **http://www.listencoach.com/SiteFrameSet.html**.
36. J. Matthews, "In Offices across America, Attire Is Changing," *Washington Post*, January 31, 1994, p. 26.
37. K. H. Hammonds, "All the Right Moves: Meanwhile, Back at the Office," *Fast Company* 72 (July 2003), p. 70. Retrieved December 5, 2005, from **http://www.fastcompany.com/magazine/72/backattheoffice.html**.
38. J. H. Laabs, "Mixing Business with Passion," accessed January 22, 2001, from **http://www.workforce.com/archive/article/000/77/84.xci?topicname5business_issues_and_trends**.
39. I. Amiel, "A Nationwide Survey on Business Casual Conducted by a Team of AICI Professionals," Association of Image Consultants International, accessed February 14, 2001, from **http://www.aici.org/dec99p5.html**.
40. Ibid.
41. Dana May Casperson quoted in M. Marchetti, "Barbarians at the Buffet," *Successful Meetings*, May 2003, p. 57.
42. W. Wells and B. Siegel, "Stereotyped Somatypes," *Psychological Reports* 8 (1961), pp. 1175–78.
43. V. Reitman, "Learning to Grin—and Bear It," *Los Angeles Times*, February 22, 1999, p. A1.
44. B. Hunter, "Are You Ready to Face '60 Minutes'?" *Industry Week*, March 8, 1982, p. 74.
45. "Memos," *Industry Week*, January 11, 1982, p. 11.
46. A. Mehrabian, *Silent Messages*, 2nd ed. (Belmont, CA: Wadsworth, 1981).
47. D. Borisoff and L. Merrill, *The Power to Communicate: Gender Differences as Barriers*, 2nd ed. (Prospect Heights, IL: Waveland, 1992), p. 48.
48. E. Hall, *The Hidden Dimension* (New York: Doubleday, 1969), pp. 113–25.
49. M. L. Knapp and J. A. Hall, *Nonverbal Behavior in Human Interaction*, 3rd ed. (Ft. Worth, TX: Harcourt Brace Jovanovich, 1992), pp. 127–30.
50. Ibid., p. 129.
51. Mehrabian, *Silent Messages*, p. 51.
52. D. Ogilvy, *Principles of Management* (New York: Ogilvy & Mather, 1968), p. 2.
53. W. Griffitt, "Environmental Effects of Interpersonal Affective Behavior: Ambient Effective Temperature and Attraction," *Journal of Personality and Social Psychology* 15 (1970), pp. 240–44.
54. T. Allen, "Meeting the Technical Information Needs of Research and Development Projects," M.I.T. Industrial Liaison Program Report No. 13-314, Cambridge, MA, November 1969.
55. F. Steele, *Physical Settings and Organizational Development* (Reading, MA: Addison-Wesley, 1973).
56. Ibid., p. 65.
57. P. Manning, *Office Design: A Study of Environment* (Liverpool: Pilkington Research Unit, 1965), p. 474.
58. Research summarized in P. A. Andersen and L. L. Bowman, "Positions of Power: Nonverbal Influence in Organizational Communication," *The Nonverbal Communication Reader* (Prospect Heights, IL: Waveland, 1990), pp. 404–5.
59. Steele, *Physical Settings and Organizational Development*, p. 38.
60. J. E. McGrath and J. R. Kelly, *Time and Human Interaction* (New York: Guilford, 1989). See also D. I. Ballard and D. R. Seibold, "Time Orientation and Temporal Variation across Work Groups: Implications for Group and Organizational Communication," *Western Journal of Communication* 64 (2000), pp. 218–42.
61. R. J. Schoenberg, *The Art of Being a Boss* (New York: New American Library, 1978), p. 36.
62. "Are You Really Ready to Change Jobs?" in "Fall Job Market," advertising supplement to the *Washington Post*, September 28, 1986, p. 22.
63. "Coaching Football—Italian Style," *Thousand Oaks (CA) News Chronicle*, January 4, 1990, pp. 1, 20.
64. Research summarized in D. E. Hamachek, *Encounters with the Self*, 2nd ed. (Fort Worth: Holt, Rinehart and Winston, 1987), p. 8. See also J. A. Daly, A. L. Vangelisti, and S. M. Daughton, "The Nature and Correlates of Conversational Sensitivity," in *Interpersonal Communication: Readings in Theory and Research*, ed. M. V. Redmond (Fort Worth: Harcourt Brace, 1995).
65. D. A. Dunning and J. Kruger, "Unskilled and Unaware of It: How Difficulties in Recognizing One's Own Incompetence Lead to Inflated Self-Assessments," *Journal of Personality and Social Psychology* 77 (1999), pp. 1121–34.
66. A. Mehrabian, *Nonverbal Communication* (Chicago: Aldine/Atherton, 1972).
67. Research summarized by V. P. Richmond and J. C. McCroskey, *Nonverbal Behavior in Interpersonal Relations*, 5th ed. (Boston: Allyn & Bacon, 2004).
68. H. S. Friedman, R. E. Riggio, and D. F. Casella, "Nonverbal Skill, Personal Charisma, and Initial

Attraction," *Personality & Social Psychology Bulletin* 14 (1988), pp. 203–11.

69. D. Goleman, *Emotional Intelligence: Why It Can Matter More Than I.Q.* (New York: Bantam, 1995), p. 115.
70. E. S. Sullins, "Emotional Contagion Revisited: Effects of Social Comparison and Expressive Style on Mood Convergence," *Personality and Social Psychology Bulletin* 17 (1991), pp. 166–74.
71. See E. Griffin, "Expectancy Violations Theory," in *A First Look at Communication Theory*, 6th ed. (New York: McGraw-Hill, 2006).
72. L. Jansma, "Sexual Harassment Research: Integration, Reformulation, and Implications for Mitigation Efforts," in *Communication Yearbook 23* (Thousand Oaks, CA: Sage, 2000).
73. From **http://www.de.psu.edu/harassment/legal**.
74. From **http://www.eeoc.gov/stats/harass.html**.
75. U.S. EEOC Press Release, "EEOC and Ford Sign Multi-million Dollar Settlement of Sexual Harassment Case," **http://www.eeoc.gov/press/9-7-99.html**, accessed July 29, 2003.
76. MSPB, 1995, xi, cited in M. A. Newman et al., "Sexual Harassment in the Federal Workplace," *Public Administration Review* 63, no. 4 (July/August 2003).
77. New Mexico Commission on the Status of Women, *Dealing with Sexual Harassment*. (2002). Retrieved December 6, 2005, from **www.state.nm.us/womenscommission/Publications/sexhbrochre.pdf**, p. 5.

Chapter 5

1. D. B. Curtis, J. L. Winsor, and R. D. Stephens, "National Preferences in Business and Communication Education," *Communication Education* 38 (1989), pp. 6–14.
2. L. Goodspeed, "'People Skills' Stressed over Experience for Tech CEOs," *Boston Business Journal* 19 (April 23, 1999), p. 46.
3. R. H. Hersh, "Intentions and Perceptions: A National Survey of Public Attitudes toward Liberal Arts Education," *Change* 29 (1997), pp. 16–23. For more information on the importance of communication skills for managers, see D. St. John, "Forget the Global Communication Climate for a Minute: How's the Weather inside Your Own Organization?" *Communication World* 12 (March 1996), p. 24.
4. See, for example, R. Bellinger, "It Takes More than Tech," *Electronic Engineering Times*, August 30, 1999, pp. 91–96; and J. M. Napolitano, "Learning to Really Communicate," *Journal of Property Management*, March/April 2000, p. 12.
5. L. Iacocca and W. Novak, *Iacocca: An Autobiography* (New York: Bantam, 1984), p. 58.
6. D. Goleman, *Emotional Intelligence: Why It Can Matter More than I.Q.* (New York: Bantam, 1995). See also H. Weisinger, *Emotional Intelligence at Work: The Untapped Edge for Success* (San Francisco: Jossey-Bass, 1997); and D. Goleman, *Working with Emotional Intelligence* (New York: Bantam, 2000).
7. Goleman, *Working with Emotional Intelligence*, p. 211.
8. R. L. Dilenschneider, "Social Intelligence," *Executive Excellence* 14 (March 1997), p. 8.
9. R. M. Guzley, "Organizational Climate and Communication Climate: Predictors of Commitment to the Organization," *Management Communication Quarterly* 5 (1992), pp. 379–402. See also D. T. Bastien, R. D. McPhee, and K. A. Bolton, "A Study and Extended Theory of the Structuration of Climate," *Communication Monographs* 62 (1995), pp. 87–109; and T. J. Houghton, "A Study of Communication among Supervisors: The Influence of Supervisor/Supervisee Verbal Aggressiveness on Communication Climate and Organizational Commitment," *Dissertation Abstracts International* 61(2001), p. 3826.
10. Pamela Shockley-Zalabak, *Fundamentals of Organizational Communication: Knowledge, Sensitivity, Skills, Values*, 3rd ed. (New York: Longman, 1995), pp. 249–52.
11. R. Fisher and S. Brown, *Getting Together: Building Relationships as We Negotiate* (Boston: Houghton Mifflin, 1988).
12. "Nineteen Eighty-Nine Turkeys of the Year," *San Jose Mercury News*, November 23, 1989, p. 1D.
13. K. Patterson, *Crucial Skills* 3, no. 28 (July 20, 2005). This is an e-newsletter from and copyright by VitalSmarts, L. C., **www.vitalsmarts.com**.
14. K. Patterson, "Creating a Culture of Accountability," *Crucial Skills* 3, no. 39. This is an e-newsletter from and copyright by VitalSmarts, L. C., **www.vitalsmarts.com**, 2005.
15. See also G. Howerton, "Rewards with a Personal Touch," accessed January 19, 2001, at **http://www.workforce.com/archive/article/001/17/96.xci**.
16. C. Carson and W. R. Cupach, "Facing Corrections in the Workplace: The Influence of Perceived Face Threat on the Consequences of Managerial Reproaches," *Journal of Applied Communication Research* 28 (2000), pp. 215–34.
17. R. Korobkin and C. Guthrie, "Psychological Barriers to Litigation Settlement and Experimental Approach," *Michigan Law Review* 107 (1994), pp. 107–92.
18. K. Anderson, "Handling Criticism with Honesty and Grace," *Public Management* 82 (May 2000), pp. 30–34.
19. J. Slaton, "Hoteliers Say Hiring Is Their Toughest Job," *New Orleans City Business*, November 25, 1996.
20. S. Berglos, "Harmony Is Death: Let Conflict Reign," *Inc.*, May 1995, pp. 56–58.
21. L. Coser, *The Functions of Social Conflict* (New York: Free Press, 1956).
22. For a detailed account of these conflict types, see W. W. Wilmot and J. L. Hocker, *Interpersonal Conflict*, 7th ed. (New York: McGraw-Hill, 2007), pp. 62–75, 138–65.

23. J. P. Folger, M. S. Poole, and R. K. Sturtman, *Working through Conflict: Strategies for Relationships, Groups, and Organizations*. 5th ed. (Boston: Allyn & Bacon, 2004).
24. For more detailed descriptions of the approaches to conflict discussed in the text, see Wilmot and Hocker, op. cit., pp. 138–65.
25. D. Starkey, "Finding Common Ground," *Sacramento Business Journal*, February 20, 1998, pp. 12–13.
26. D. Tannen, *Talking from 9 to 5* (New York: Morrow, 1994), p. 91.
27. M. H. McCormack, *What They Don't Teach You at Harvard Business School* (New York: Bantam, 1984), pp. 152–53.
28. T. O'Neill, "Here's the Church, Here's the (Fake) Steeple," *Cincinnati Enquirer*, January 20, 1996, pp. B1, B6.
29. C. Pavitt and B. Kemp, "Contextual and Relational Factors in Interpersonal Negotiation Strategy Choice," *Communication Quarterly* 47 (1999), pp. 133–50. See also S. D. Friedman, P. Christensen, and J. DeGroot, "Work and Life: The End of the Zero-Sum Game," *Harvard Business Review*, November–December 1998, pp. 119–29.
30. R. J. Burke, "Methods of Resolving Superior-Subordinate Conflict: The Constructive Use of Subordinate Differences and Disagreements," *Organizational Behavior and Human Performance* 5 (1970), pp. 393–411.
31. R. Fisher and W. Ury, *Getting to Yes: Negotiating Agreement without Giving In* (Boston: Houghton Mifflin, 1981), pp. 41–57.

Chapter 6

1. C. J. Stewart and W. B. Cash, Jr., *Interviewing: Principles and Practices*, 11th ed. (New York: McGraw-Hill, 2006), p. 1.
2. Ibid.
3. M. H. McCormack, *What They Don't Teach You at Harvard Business School* (New York: Bantam, 1984), p. 87.
4. D. Harper, "Strictly for Salesmen," in a review of G. Gard, "Championship Selling," *Industrial Distribution*, May 1987, p. 122.
5. L. B. Andrews, "Mind Control in the Courtroom," *Psychology Today* 16 (March 1982), p. 70.
6. K. O. Locker, *Business and Administrative Communication* (New York: Irwin/McGraw-Hill, 2003), p. 371.
7. W. G. Kirkwood and S. M. Ralston, "Inviting Meaningful Applicant Performances in Employment Interviews," *Journal of Business Communication* 36 (1999), pp. 55–76.
8. D. Deaver, in Shirley J. Shepherd, "How to Get That Job in 60 Minutes or Less," *Working Woman*, March 1986, p. 118.
9. Adapted from G. L. Wilson and H. L. Goodall, Jr., *Interviewing in Context* (New York: McGraw-Hill, 1991), p. 291.

Chapter 7

1. S. Walton and J. Huey, *Made in America* (New York: Bantam, 1993), pp. 104–5.
2. M. Hopkins, "The Anti-Hero's Guide to the New Economy," *Inc.*, January 1998, pp. 37–48.
3. M. Granovetter, *Getting a Job: A Study of Contacts and Careers*, 2nd ed. (Chicago: University of Chicago Press, 1995).
4. R. N. Bolles, *What Color Is Your Parachute? A Practical Manual for Job-Hunters and Career-Changers 2005 edition*. (Berkeley, CA: Ten Speed Press, 2005), pp. 27–42.
5. W. Baker, *Achieving Success through Social Capital* (San Francisco: Josey-Bass, 2000), p. 10.
6. G. Crispin and M. Mehler, "Impact of the Internet on Source of Hires," at **http://www.careerxroads.com/news/IMPACTOFTHEINTERNET.doc**.
7. M. S. Granovetter, "The Strength of Weak Ties," *American Journal of Sociology* 78 (1973), pp. 1360–80.
8. E. M. Rogers, *Diffusion of Innovations*, 3rd ed. (New York: Free Press, 1983), p. 297.
9. K. Dobbs, "Knowing How to Keep the Best and Brightest," *Workforce*, April 2001, pp. 57–60.
10. M. S. Peterson, "Personnel Interviewers' Perceptions of the Importance and Adequacy of Applicants' Communication Skills," *Communication Education* 46 (1997), pp. 287–91.
11. H. D. Tschirgi, "What Do Recruiters Really Look For in Candidates?" *Journal of College Placement*, December 1972–January 1973, pp. 75–79.
12. For an assessment of interview effectiveness, see W. G. Kirkwood and S. M. Ralston, "Inviting Meaningful Applicant Performance in Employment Interviews," *Journal of Business Communication* 66 (1999), pp. 55–76.
13. "The Hidden Hurdle: Executive Recruiters Say Firms Tend to Hire 'Our Kind of Person,'" *The Wall Street Journal*, May 12, 1979, p. 1.
14. Bolles, *What Color Is Your Parachute?* p. 38.
15. R. N. Bolles, *What Color Is Your Parachute? A Practical Manual for Job-Hunters and Career-Changers* (Berkeley, CA: Ten Speed Press, 1997), p. 173.
16. S. Murphy, "The Second Interview," *Santa Barbara News Press*, December 19, 1999, p. E1.
17. "Ace Your Audition Interview," retrieved April 28, 2001, from **http://www.wetfeet.com/asp/article.asp?aid562**.
18. J. Trotsky, "Oh, Will You BEHAVE?" *Computerworld*, January 8, 2001, pp. 42–43.
19. P. Farmery, "Recruiters Offer a New View of the Job Interview," *Job Choices: Diversity Edition* (Bethlehem,

PA: National Association of Colleges and Employers, 2000), pp. 61–64.

20. J. Ayres, T. Keereetaweep, P. Chen, and P. A. Edwards, "Communication Apprehension and Employment Interviews," *Communication Education* 47 (1998), pp. 1–17.
21. D. B. Goodall and H. L. Goodall, Jr., "The Employment Interview: A Selective Review of the Literature with Implications for Communications Research," *Communication Quarterly* 30 (Spring 1982), pp. 116–22.
22. R. W. Eder and G. R. Ferris, eds., *The Employment Interview: Theory, Research, and Practice* (Newbury Park, CA: Sage, 1989).
23. H. A. Medley, *Sweaty Palms: The Neglected Art of Being Interviewed* (Belmont, CA: Wadsworth, 1978), p. 1.
24. Medley, *Sweaty Palms*, p. 19.
25. C. Caggiano, "'What Were You In For?' and Other Great Job-Interview Questions of Our Time," *Inc.*, October 1998, p. 14.
26. C. L. Cooper, "No More Stupid Questions," *Psychology Today* 26 (May–June 1993), pp. 14–15.
27. G. Martz, *How to Survive without Your Parents' Money* (New York: Villiard, 1996), p. 57.
28. Bolles, *What Color is Your Parachute?* pp. 238–39.
29. S. M. Ralston and W. Kirkwood, "The Trouble with Applicant Impression Management," *Journal of Business and Technical Communication* 13 (1999), pp. 190–207. See also S. M. Ralston, "The 'Veil of Ignorance': Exploring Ethical Issues in the Employment Interview," *Business Communication Quarterly* 63 (2000), pp. 50–52.
30. P. Rosenfeld, "Impression Management, Fairness and the Employment Interview," *Journal of Business Ethics* 16 (June 1997), pp. 801–8.
31. R. H. Beatty, *The Interview Kit*, 3rd ed. (Hoboken, NJ: John Wiley & Sons, Inc., 2003), pp. 49–50.
32. S. Silverstein and N. R. Brooks, "And Be Sure to Mention Your Favorite Subject: You," *Los Angeles Times*, March 1, 1993, p. D3.
33. Quoted in C. Kleiman, "Passion Play," *The Salt Lake Tribune and the Deseret News*, February 16, 2003, p. F1.
34. Medley, *Sweaty Palms*, p. 164.
35. M. B. Dickson, *Supervising Employees with Disabilities: Beyond ADA Compliance* (Menlo Park, CA: Crisp, 1993), p. 107.
36. M. Z. Sincoff and R. S. Goyer, *Interviewing* (New York: Macmillan, 1984), p. 80. See also T. Washington, "Advice on Answering Illegal Interview Questions: Reply Candidly or Tactfully Decline," *The Wall Street Journal Career Journal*, retrieved April 24, 2001, from **http://www.careerjournal.com/emailfriend/sendmail1.asp?txtTargetPage5http%3A//www.careerjournal.com/jobhunting/interviewing/19971231-washington.html**.
37. J. K. Springston and J. Keyton, "So Tell Me, Are You Married? When the Interviewee Knows You're Asking an Illegal Question," *Proceedings of the 1988 Annual National Conference of the Council of Employee Responsibilities and Rights* 2 (1988), pp. 177–86.
38. J. Woo, "Job Interviews Pose Risk to Employers," *The Wall Street Journal*, March 11, 1992, pp. B1, B5.
39. E. McShulskis, "Be Aware of Illegal Interview Questions," *HR Magazine* 42 (June 1997), pp. 22–23.
40. R. Fry, *Your First Interview*, 4th ed. (Franklin Lakes, NJ: Career Press, 2002), pp. 157–58.
41. R. Townsend, *Further Up the Organization* (New York: Knopf, 1984), p. 153.
42. D. Fandray, "The New Thinking in Performance Appraisals," *Workforce* 80, no. 5 (May 2001), pp. 36–40.
43. K. Blanchard, "Rating Managers on Performance Reviews," *Today's Office* 22 (August 1987), pp. 6–11.
44. C. W. Downs, G. P. Smeyak, and E. Martin, *Professional Interviewing* (New York: Harper & Row, 1980), p. 167.
45. K. Blanchard, "Rating Managers on Performance Reviews," p. 7.
46. C. O. Longenecker, "Truth or Consequences: Politics and Performance Appraisals," *Business Horizons* 27 (November–December 1989), pp. 169–82.
47. D. Dauten, "Worker Appraisals Are Like Having the Cat Spayed," *Albuquerque Business Outlook Journal*, March 26, 2001, p. 13.
48. G. L. Wilson and H. L. Goodall, *Interviewing in Context* (New York: McGraw-Hill, 1991), p. 181.
49. L. Iacocca and W. Novak, *Iacocca: An Autobiography* (New York: Bantam, 1984).
50. J. L. Pearce and L. W. Porter, "Responses to Formal Performance Appraisal Feedback," *Journal of Applied Psychology* 71 (1986), pp. 211–18.

Chapter 8

1. R. Reich, *Tales of a New America* (New York: Time Books, 1987), p. 126.
2. D. J. Devine, L. D. Clayton, J. L. Phillips, B. B. Dunford, and S. B. Melner, "Teams in Organizations: Prevalence, Characteristics, and Effectiveness," *Small Group Research* 30 (1999), pp. 678–711.
3. M. V. Redmond, "A Plan for the Successful Use of Teams in Design Education," *Journal of Architectural Education* 17 (May 1986), pp. 27–49.
4. "Professional Occupations in Multimedia," *California Occupational Guide*, No. 2006 (Sacramento, CA: California State Employment Division, 1995), p. 4. See also *A Labor Market Analysis of the Interactive Digital Media Industry: Opportunities in Multimedia* (San Francisco: Reagan & Associates, 1997), pp. 15–29.
5. D. L. Welles, Jr., and S. H. Hartley, "Teamwork and Cooperative Learning: An Educational Perspective for Business," *Quality Management Journal*, July 1994, p. 30; and A. Radding, "Skills They'd Kill For," *ComputerWorld* 31 (June 2, 1997), pp. 93–95.

6. C. Lazzareschi, "Being Part of the Team at Work," *Los Angeles Times*, September 12, 1994, pt. 2, p. 13.
7. For a more detailed discussion of the advantages and drawbacks of working in groups, see J. D. Rothwell, *In Mixed Company: Small Group Communication*, 6th ed. (Belmont, CA: Wadsworth, 2007), pp. 70–74.
8. G. M. Blair, "Groups that Work," retrieved August 26, 2003, from **http://www.rotman.utoronto.ca/~baum/mgt2003/gmbart0.htm**.
9. D. J. Rachman and M. H. Mescon, *Profile Kit for Business Today*, 4th ed. (New York: Random House, 1990), profile 2.
10. See, for example, J. R. Katzenbach and D. K. Smith, "The Discipline of Teams," *Harvard Business Review* 86 (March–April 1993), pp. 111–20.
11. T. J. Peters and R. H. Waterman, Jr., *In Search of Excellence: Lessons from America's Best Run Companies* (New York: Harper & Row, 1982), p. 32.
12. E. Bormann, *Small Group Communication: Theory and Practice* (New York: Harper & Row, 1990).
13. J. Gribas, "Organizational Sports Metaphors: Reconsidering Gender Bias in the Team Concept," *Communication Research Reports* 16 (1999), pp. 55–64.
14. R. E. Parker, "Distinguishing Characteristics of Virtual Groups," in *Small Group Communication: Theory & Practice*, eds. R. Y. Hirokawa et al. (Los Angeles: Roxbury, 2003).
15. K. Melymuka, "Tips for Teams," *ComputerWorld* 31 (April 28, 1997), p. 72.
16. "Virtual Teams: Reaching across Space, Time and Organizations with Technology," *HR Magazine* 42 (July 1997), pp. 133–34.
17. S. L. Herndon, "Theory and Practice: Implications for the Implementation of Communication Technology in Organizations," *Journal of Business Communication* 34 (January 1997), pp. 121–29.
18. P. Mohta, "Virtual Networking via the Internet," *Computer Technology Review*, Winter 1996, pp. 12–13.
19. J. Blau, "Global Networking Poses Management Challenge/Risk," *Research-Technology Management* 40 (January/February 1997), pp. 4–5.
20. Rothwell, *In Mixed Company*, pp. 137–38.
21. K. Lewin, R. Lippitt, and R. K. White, "Patterns of Aggressive Behavior in Experimentally Created Social Climates," *Journal of Social Psychology* 10 (1939), pp. 271–99.
22. R. Foels, J. E. Driskell, B. Mullen, and E. Salas, "The Effects of Democratic Leadership on Group Member Satisfaction," *Small Group Research* 20 (2000), pp. 676–701.
23. L. L. Rosenbaum and W. B. Rosenbaum, "Morale and Productivity Consequences of Group Leadership Style, Stress, and Type of Task," *Journal of Applied Psychology* 55 (1971), pp. 343–58.
24. R. R. Blake and J. S. Mouton, *The New Managerial Grid* (Houston, TX: Gulf, 1985).
25. F. E. Fiedler, *A Theory of Leadership Effectiveness* (New York: McGraw-Hill, 1967).
26. P. Hersey and K. Blanchard, *Management of Organizational Behavior*, 4th ed. (Englewood Cliffs, NJ: Prentice Hall, 1982); and K. Blanchard, "Selecting a Leadership Style That Works," *Today's Office* 23 (September 1988), p. 14.
27. Bormann, *Small Group Communication*. For a succinct description of Bormann's findings, see Rothwell, *In Mixed Company*, pp. 131–33.
28. R. Fisher and A. Sharp, *Getting It Done: How to Lead When You're Not in Charge* (New York: Harper Business, 1998).
29. R. S. Wellins, W. C. Byham, and J. M. Wilson, *Empowered Teams: Creating Self-Directed Work Groups That Improve Quality, Productivity, and Participation* (San Francisco: Jossey-Bass, 1991), p. 3.
30. P. A. Chansler, P. M. Swamidass, and C. Canmann, "Self-Managing Teams: An Empirical Study of Group Cohesiveness in 'Natural Work Groups' at a Harley-Davidson Motor Company Plant," *Small Group Research* 34 (2003), pp. 101–20.
31. The discussion of the first five types of power is adapted from the work of J. R. P. French and B. Raven, "The Bases of Social Power," in *Studies in Social Power*, ed. D. Cartwright (Ann Arbor: University of Michigan, Institute for Social Research, 1959). Information power was introduced by B. Raven and W. Kruglanski, "Conflict and Power," in *The Structure of Conflict*, ed. P. G. Swingle (New York: Academic Press, 1975), pp. 177–219. Connection power was introduced by Hersey and Blanchard, *Management of Organizational Behavior*, p. 179.
32. A. T. Pescosolido, "Informal Leaders and the Development of Group Efficacy," *Small Group Research* 32 (2001), pp. 74–93.
33. S. T. Loh, "You Say the Boss Is How Old?" *Los Angeles Times*, March 1, 1993, pt. 2, pp. 9–10.
34. M. Zey, ed., *Decision Making: Alternatives to Rational Choice Models* (Newbury Park, CA: Sage, 1992).
35. See R. Y. Hirokawa, "Group Communication and Problem-Solving Effectiveness: An Investigation of Group Phases," *Human Communication Research* 9 (1983), pp. 291–305; Edward R. Marby and Richard E. Barnes, *The Dynamics of Small Group Communication* (Englewood Cliffs, NJ: Prentice Hall, 1980), p. 78; Norman R. F. Maier and Robert A. Maier, "An Experimental Test of the Effects of 'Developmental' vs. 'Free' Discussions on the Quality of Group Decisions," *Journal of Applied Psychology* 41 (1957), pp. 320–23; and Ovid L. Bayless, "An Alternative Model for Problem-Solving Discussion," *Journal of Communication* 17 (1967), pp. 188–97.

36. For a contemporary version of the reflective-thinking model, see D. Gouran, R. Hirokawa, K. Julian, and G. Leatham, "The Evolution and Current Status of the Functional Perspective on Communication Decision-Making and Problem-Solving Groups," in *Communication Yearbook* 16, ed. S. Deetz (Newbury Park, CA: Sage, 1993).
37. M. E. Mayer, "Behaviors Leading to More Effective Decisions in Small Groups Embedded in Organizations," *Communication Reports* 11 (1998) pp. 123–32.
38. See, for example, Zey, ed., *Decision Making*.
39. B. A. Fisher, "Decision Emergence: Phases in Group Decision Making," *Speech Monographs* 37 (1970), pp. 53–66. See also M. S. Poole and J. Roth, "Decision Development in Small Groups, IV: A Typology of Group Decision Paths," *Human Communication Research* 15 (1989), pp. 232–56.
40. B.W. Tuckman, "Developmental Sequence in Small Groups," *Psychological Bulletin* 63 (June 1965), pp. 384–99. The terms *forming, storming, norming,* and *performing* originate from this article.
41. T. Kuhn, "Do Conflict Management Styles Affect Group Decision Making?" *Human Communication Research* 26 (2000), pp. 558–90.
42. G. Buzaglo and S. A. Wheelan, "Facilitating Work Team Effectiveness," *Small Group Research* 30 (1999), pp. 108–29.
43. M. S. Poole and J. Roth, "Decision Development in Small Groups, V: Test of a Contingency Model," *Human Communication Research* 15 (1989), pp. 549–89. See also E. M. Eisenberg and H. L. Goodall, Jr., *Organizational Communication: Balancing Creativity and Constraint*, 2nd ed. (New York: St. Martin's, 1996), pp. 267–68.
44. For a discussion of relational roles, see J. Keyton, "Relational Communication in Groups," in *Handbook of Group Communication Theory and Research*, ed. L. R. Frey (Thousand Oaks, CA: Sage, 1999).
45. E. Matson, "The Seven Sins of Deadly Meetings," *Fast Times* 2 (April 1996), pp. 122–25.
46. See, for example, M. E. Mayer, "Behaviors Leading to More Effective Decisions in Small Groups Embedded in Organizations," *Communication Reports* 11 (1998), pp. 123–32.
47. Joel A. C. Baum, "Running an Effective Team Meeting," *HomePage for Game Theory and Competitive Strategy MGT 2056–Fall 2003*, retrieved August 26, 2003, from **http://www.rotman.utoronto.ca/~baum/mgt2003/meetings.html**.
48. B. Day, "The Art of Conducting International Business," *Advertising Age*, October 6, 1990, p. 48.
49. "A Purpose and a Place," *News for a Change*, May 2001, p. 5 (publication of Association for Quality and Participation at **www.aqp.org**).
50. Ibid.
51. For a discussion of how norms develop, see C. M. Anderson, B. L. Riddle, and M. M. Martin, "Socialization Processes in Groups," in *Handbook of Group Communication Theory and Research*, ed. L. R. Frey (Thousand Oaks, CA: Sage, 1999).
52. Eisenberg and Goodall, *Organizational Communication*, p. 264.
53. L. Browning, "Reasons for Success at Motorola," paper presented at the conference of the International Communication Association, Miami, May 1992.
54. See, for example, P. W. Mulvey, L. Bowes-Sperry, and H. J. Klein, "The Effects of Perceived Loafing and Defensive Impression Management on Group Effectiveness," *Small Group Research* 29 (1998), pp. 394–415.
55. J. G. Oetzel, T. E. Burtis, M. I. Chew Sanchez, and F. G. Perez, "Investigating the Role of Communication in Culturally Diverse Work Groups: A Review and Synthesis," *Communication Yearbook* 25 (Mahwah, NJ: Lawrence Erlbaum, 2001).
56. Some sequences of escalating penalties for nonconformity have been described in the literature. See, for example, J. R. Wenberg and W. Wilmot, *The Personal Communication Process* (New York: Wiley, 1973); and T. D. Daniels and B. K. Spiker, *Perspectives on Organizational Communication*, 4th ed. (Dubuque, IA: Wm. C. Brown, 1997), p. 237.
57. Melymuka, "Tips for Teams," p. 72.
58. I. L. Janis, *Victims of Groupthink* (Boston: Houghton Mifflin, 1972), p. 9.
59. K. L. Gammage, A. V. Carron, and P. A. Estabrooks, "Team Cohesion and Individual Productivity," *Small Group Research* 32 (2001), pp. 3–18.
60. Adapted from E. G. Bormann, *Discussion and Group Methods*, 2nd ed. (New York: Harper & Row, 1975), pp. 176–95. See also P. Adler and P. Adler, "Intense Loyalty in Organizations: A Case Study of College Athletics," *Administrative Science Quarterly* 33 (1988), pp. 401–18.
61. Janis, *Victims of Groupthink*, p. 9.
62. D. G. Myers and H. Lamm, "The Group Polarization Phenomenon," *Psychological Bulletin*, July 1976, pp. 602–27. For a more detailed discussion of how the risky shift operates, see A. BarNir, "Can Group- and Issue-Related Factors Predict Choice Shift?" *Small Group Research* 29 (1998), pp. 308–38.
63. S. P. Robbins, *Organizational Behavior: Concepts, Controversies, and Applications*, 4th ed. (Englewood Cliffs, NJ: Prentice Hall, 1990), p. 289.
64. A. Osborn, *Applied Imagination* (New York: Scribner's, 1959). See also F. Hurt, "Better Brainstorming," *Training & Development*, November 1994, pp. 57–59.
65. K. H. Mettkee, ed., *Creativity Fringes*, cited at **http://appreciativeinquiry.case.edu**.
66. W. H. Cooper, R. B. Gallupe, S. Pollard, and J. Cadsby, "Some Liberating Effects of Electronic Brainstorming," *Small Group Research* 29 (1999), pp. 147–78.

Chapter 9

1. D. Coleman, "The Electronic Rorschach," *Psychology Today* 17 (February 1983), pp. 35–43.
2. "Meetings in America: A Study of Trends, Costs, and Attitudes Toward Business Travel and Teleconferencing, and Their Impact on Productivity" (Greenwich, CT: Infocom, 1998). Accessed March 20, 2006, from **http://e-meetings.mci.com/meetingsinamerica/uswhitepaper.php**. See also C. D. Cole, "Meetings That Make Sense," *Psychology Today* 23 (May 1989), pp. 14–15.
3. L. Tuck, "Meeting Madness," *Presentations*, May 1995, p. 20.
4. M. Barr, "Virtual Meetings," *Indiana Business Magazine* 43 (May 1999), pp. 42–47.
5. P. Sandwich, "Better Meetings for Better Communication," *Training & Development* 46 (January 1992), pp. 29–31.
6. S. M. Smith, "Managing Your Meeting from the 'Bottom Line Payoff,'" in *Innovative Meeting Management*, eds. R. A. Swanson and B. O. Knaps (Austin, TX: Minnesota Mining and Manufacturing, 1997), p. 53.
7. S. G. Rogelberg, D. J. Leach and J. L. Burnfield, "'Not Another Meeting!' Are Meeting Time Demands Related to Employee Well-Being?" *Journal of Applied Psychology* 91 (January 2006), pp. 83–96.
8. E. Matson, "The Seven Sins of Deadly Meetings," *Fast Company* 2 (April 1996), pp. 122–25.
9. F. Williams, *Executive Communication Power: Basic Skills for Management Success* (Englewood Cliffs, NJ: Prentice Hall, 1983), p. 65.
10. L. Tuck, "What's in the Cards?" *Presentations*, January 1996, pp. 23–28.
11. J. Hill, "In-House Webconferencing Aids Company with Many Franchises," *Presentations*, November 2002, p. 15.
12. Adapted from S. D. Collins, *Communication in a Virtual Organization* (Cincinnati: Thomson, 2003), pp. 48–49; and *The Listening Leaders Newsletter*, December 8, 2004, accessed from the International Listening Leadership Institute at **www.ListeningLeaders.com**.
13. For a more detailed analysis of the pros and cons of virtual meetings, see J. F. Coates and J. Jarratt, "Managing Effectively in the Emerging Electronic Communications Environment," in *Making Connections: Readings in Relational Communication*, eds. K. M. Galvin and P. Cooper (Los Angeles: Roxbury, 1996); and J. D. Rothwell, *In Mixed Company*, 2nd ed. (Ft. Worth, TX: Harcourt Brace, 1998), pp. 235–37.
14. L. Tuck, "Brave New Meetings," *Presentations*, September 1996, pp. 28–36.
15. F. Stone, "We've Got to Stop Meeting Like This," *Getting Results . . . for the Hands-on Manager* 42 (February 1997), p. 5.
16. From *Six Secrets to Improve Your Future Business Meetings* (Austin, TX: 3M Visual Systems); 3M Corporation, "Decide If a Meeting Is Needed," accessed at **http://www.3m.com/meetingnetwork/readingroom/aa_ae_me_meeting_needed.html**; S. De Wine, *The Consultant's Craft: Improving Organizational Communication* (New York: St. Martin's, 1994), p. 162; and S. M. Lippincott, *Meetings: Do's, Don'ts, and Donuts*, 2nd ed. (Pittsburgh, PA: Lighthouse Point Press), 1999.
17. See, for example, J. M. Cook, "Tips for Planning an Effective Meeting," *Presentations*, August 1997, p. 26.
18. C. Allard, "Trust and Teamwork: More than Just Buzzwords," *En Route*, August 1992, p. 41.
19. 3M Meeting Network, "Building Great Agendas," retrieved August 28, 2003, from **http://www.3m.com/meetingnetwork/readingroom/meetingguide_building.html**.
20. Ibid.
21. Cathy Olofson, "The Ritz Puts on Stand-Up Meetings," *Fast Company* 17 (September 1998), p. 62. Retrieved August 28, 2003, from **http://www.fastcompany.com/magazine/17/minm.html**.
22. C. O. Steele, "Make Your Meetings More Productive," *Black Enterprise* 24 (March 1994), p. 76.
23. De Wine, *The Consultant's Craft*, p. 165.
24. *Leading Meetings*, vol. 1 (Great Neck, NY: Xerox Learning Systems), pp. 15–17.
25. D. Tannen, *Talking from 9 to 5: How Women's and Men's Conversational Styles Affect Who Gets Heard, Who Gets Credit, and What Gets Done at Work* (New York: Morrow, 1994), p. 290. For an overview of the subject, see J. A. Bonito and A. B. Hollingshead, "Participation in Small Groups," *Communication Yearbook 20* (Newbury Park, CA: Sage, 1997).
26. For a detailed description of the nominal group technique, see S. A. Beebe and J. T. Masterson, *Communicating in Small Groups: Principles and Practices*, 5th ed. (New York: Longman, 1997), pp. 227–31.
27. *Leading Meetings*, vol. 1, p. 50.
28. 3M Management Institute, "Meeting Quality: A Chicken-Egg Question?" *Meeting Management News* 4 (June 1992), pp. 2–3.
29. Allard, "Trust and Teamwork," p. 41.
30. *Leading Meetings*, vol. 2, pp. 41–45.

Chapter 10

1. D. Z. Meilach, "Even the Odds with Visual Presentations," *Presentations*, November 1994, p. 51.
2. L. Tuck, "Profiling the Presentation Professional," *Presentation Products*, November 1992, pp. 35–42.
3. J. M. Lannon, *Technical Communication*, 9th ed. (New York: Longman, 2003), p. 639.

4. J. P. Wright, *On a Clear Day You Can See General Motors* (New York: Avon, 1979), p. 96.
5. H. M. Boettinger, *Moving Mountains, or The Art of Letting Others See Things Your Way* (New York: Collier, 1969), p. 6.
6. "The Conference Board," *Across the Board* 24 (September 1987), p. 7.
7. E-mail from Suzanne Frey, Manager, Publications and Public Relations, Toastmasters International (**sfrey@ toastmasters.org**), June 5, 2003.
8. D. R. Seibold, S. Kudsi, and M. Rude, "Does Communication Training Make a Difference? Evidence for the Effectiveness of a Presentation Skills Program," *Journal of Applied Communication Research* 21 (May 1993), pp. 111–29.
9. R. L. Spiro and B. A. Weitz, "Adaptive Selling: Conceptualization, Measurement, and Nomological Validity," *Journal of Marketing Research* 24 (1990), pp. 61–69.
10. L. Iacocca and W. Novak, *Iacocca: An Autobiography* (New York: Bantam, 1984), p. 117.
11. J. T. Molloy, *Molloy's Live for Success* (New York: Bantam, 1985), p. 16.
12. Personal correspondence from Steven Vasilion, September 24, 1997.
13. M. Frank, *How to Have a Successful Meeting in Half the Time* (New York: Simon & Schuster, 1989).
14. Cited in *This Just In*, March 19, 1995 (**archie@netcom.com**).
15. B. E. Bradley, *Fundamentals of Speech Communication: The Credibility of Ideas*, 6th ed. (Dubuque, IA: Wm. C. Brown, 1991), pp. 58–61.
16. Meilach, "Even the Odds," p. 3.
17. "The Gray Flannel Sideshow," *Presentations*, November 1993, p. 50.
18. H. L. Marsh, "Summary Membership Remarks," speech delivered at a meeting of the New York Chapter of the Institute of Internal Auditors, New York, May 13, 1983.
19. S. Linver and J. Mengert, *Speak and Get Results: The Complete Guide to Speeches and Presentations That Work in Any Business Situation*, rev. ed. (New York: Fireside, 1994), p. 14.
20. For a discussion of research supporting the value of organization see S. E. Lucas, *The Art of Public Speaking*, 7th ed. (New York: McGraw-Hill, 2001), pp. 192–93. Also, see J. A. Daly and I. N. Engleberg, *Presentations in Everyday Life: Strategies for Effective Speaking* (Boston: Houghton Mifflin, 2001), pp. 129–30.
21. Adapted from C. L. Bovée and J. T. Thill, *Business Communication Today*, 2nd ed. (New York: Random House, 1989), pp. 89–90. Student examples of moving from what audiences know to what they don't know are found in J. A. DeVito, *The Elements of Public Speaking*, 7th ed. (New York: Longman, 2000), pp. 364–65.
22. "President Discusses Strengthening Social Security in Florida," Tampa Convention Center, Tampa, Florida, February 4, 2005. Accessed March 31, 2006, from **http://www.whitehouse.gov/news/releases/2005/02/20050204-13.html**.
23. For a discussion of nonlinear organizing patterns, see C. Jaffe, *Public Speaking: Concepts and Skills for a Diverse Society*, 3rd ed. (Belmont, CA: Wadsworth, 2001), pp. 174–77; and M. W. Lustig and J. Koester, *Intercultural Competence: Interpersonal Communication across Cultures*, 4th ed. (New York: Allyn & Bacon, 2003), pp. 243–52.
24. "Presentation Planning: Draw a Logic Tree," *Meeting Management News*, April 1993, pp. 1–2.
25. S. Hybels and R. L. Weaver II, *Communicating Effectively*, 6th ed. (Boston: McGraw-Hill, 2001), pp. 447–49; and M. Osborn and S. Osborn, *Public Speaking*, 5th ed. (Boston, Houghton Mifflin, 2000), pp. 378–80.
26. The uppermost limit of items people can usually recall from their short-term memory is seven. For oral presentations, however, limiting the number of main points to five increases the odds that listeners will retain them. For a summary of research supporting this conclusion, see G. Rodman, *The New Public Speaker* (Ft. Worth, TX: Harcourt Brace Jovanovich, 1996), chap. 8.
27. D. Zielinski, "Perfect Practice," *Presentations*, May 2003. Retrieved March 6, 2006, from **http://www.presentations.com/presentations/delivery/article_display.jsp?vnu_content_id=1902958**.
28. R. Moran, "Tips on Making Speeches to International Audiences," *International Management* 44 (1989), p. 74.
29. Story adapted from P. Preston, *Communication for Managers* (Englewood Cliffs, NJ: Prentice Hall, 1979), p. 24.
30. "Errors Are Common in Credit Reports, Small Study Suggests," *The Wall Street Journal*, May 27, 1991, p. B7.
31. Quoted in J. W. Robinson, *Winning Them Over* (Rocklin, CA: Prima, 1987), p. 279.
32. D. M. Roderick, "A Most Ingenious Paradox," speech delivered at the National Press Club, Washington, DC, and reprinted in *Executive Speaker* 5 (January 1984), p. 4.
33. *Executive Speechwriter Newsletter* 8 (1993), p. 3.
34. "How to Close a Speech," retrieved June 9, 2003, from **http://www.public-speaking.org/public-speaking-closings-article.htm**.

Chapter 11

1. L. Poole, "A Tour of the Mac Desktop," *Mac World* 1 (February 1984), p. 16.
2. C. Spangenberg, "Basic Values and the Techniques of Persuasion," *Litigation*, Summer 1977, p. 64.
3. H. Anderson, "Day Care: Big Hit at the Office," *Los Angeles Times*, May 21, 1989, pp. 30–33.
4. J. Lawlor, "Offbeat Perks Can Perk Up Workers," *USA Today*, August 17, 1992, p. 2B.

5. J. Applegate, "Best, Worst Small-Business Names of 1994," *Los Angeles Times*, April 12, 1994, p. D3.
6. Ibid.
7. A. Simmons, *The Story Factor: Inspiration, Influence, and Persuasion through the Art of Storytelling* (New York: Basic Books, 2001), p. 3.
8. Adapted from J. A. Daly and I. N. Englebert, *Presentations in Everyday Life* (Boston: Houghton Mifflin, 2001), p. 311.
9. A. Rooney, "Sales vs. Service," *Executive Speechwriter Newsletter* 14 (May 1989), p. 5.
10. J. Slan, *Using Stories and Humor—Grab Your Audience!* (Boston: Allyn & Bacon, 1998), p. 12.
11. J. E. Lukaszewski, "You Can Become a Verbal Visionary," *Executive Speeches* 12 (August/September 1997), pp. 23–30.
12. L. L. Lindsey and K. A. Yun, "Examining the Persuasive Effect of Statistical Messages: A Test of Mediating Relationships, *Communication Studies* 54 (2003), pp. 306–21.
13. "Making Time and Money Real," *Executive Communication Report* 3 (March 1987), developed by *Small Business Report*, 203 Calle del Oaks Mount, Monterey, CA 93940.
14. T. G. Labrecque, "A Radical Approach to Banking Reform: Legalize Competition," speech delivered at the University of Richmond Business School, February 12, 1987, and reprinted in *Executive Speaker* 8 (August 1987), p. 5.
15. S. J. Diamond, "Some Airlines' Ads Mislead without Lying," *Los Angeles Times*, June 13, 1991, p. E1.
16. J. Surowiecki, "Cloak-and-Dagger, Inc.," *New Yorker*, February 19 and 26, 2001, p. 70.
17. D. B. Yoffie and M. Kwak, "Judo Strategy: 10 Techniques for Beating a Stronger Opponent," *Business Strategy Review* 13 (Spring 2002), pp. 20–30.
18. J. Flaherty, "Recipe for a Business Best Seller: Analogies about Anything but Business," *The New York Times*, September 5, 2001, p. C14.
19. "Miners Deserve Better," *Los Angeles Times*, January 5, 2006, p. B12.
20. The quotes in this section were accessed March 22, 2006, from **http://www.woopidoo.com/business_quotes**.
21. "Paper Work Is Avoidable (If You Call the Shots)," *The Wall Street Journal*, June 17, 1977, p. 24.
22. D. R. Vogel, G. W. Dickson, and J. A. Lehman, "Driving the Audience Action Response," *Computer Graphics World* 5 (August 1986), pp. 25–28. See also D. R. Vogel, G. W. Dickson, and J. A. Lehman, *Persuasion and the Role of Visual Presentation Support: The UM/3M Study* (Austin, TX: 3M Corporation, 1986), pp. 1–20.
23. For more suggestions on how to use handouts, see R. W. Pike, "Handouts: A Little Charity to Your Audience Goes a Long Way," *Presentations*, May 1994, pp. 31–35.
24. T. Simons, "MultiMedia or Bust?" *Presentations*, February 2000, pp. 40–50.
25. I. Parker, "Absolute PowerPoint," *New Yorker*, May 28, 2001, pp. 76–87.
26. For a discussion of PowerPoint's limitations, see R. Ganzel, "Power Pointless," *Presentations*, February 2000, pp. 54–57.
27. E. R. Tufte, *The Cognitive Style of PowerPoint* (Cheshire, CT: Graphics Press, 2003), p. 22.
28. Parker, op. cit., p. 86. See also T. Simons, "Does PowerPoint Make You Stupid?" *Presentations*, March 2004, pp. 25–31.
29. G. Jaffe, "What's Your Point, Lieutenant? Just Cut to the Pie Charts," *The Wall Street Journal*, April 26, 2000, p. A1.
30. For more information on using visual aids effectively, see S. M. Kosslyn and C. Chabris, "The Mind Is Not a Camera, The Brain Is Not a VCR: Some Psychological Guidelines for Designing Charts and Graphs," *Aldus Magazine*, September/October 1993, pp. 33–36.
31. L. Tuck, "Improving Your Image with LCD Panels," *Presentations*, January 1994, p. 32.
32. L. Pearson, "The Medium Speaks," *Presentation Products*, June 1993, pp. 55–56.
33. See, for example, L. Tuck, "Using Type Intelligently," *Presentations*, April 1994, pp. 30–32; and S. Hinkin, "Not Just Another Pretty Face: 10 Tips for the Most Effective Use of Type," *Presentations*, January 1995, pp. 34–36.
34. J. Terberg, "Font Choices Play a Crucial Role in Presentation Design," *Presentations*, April 2005. Retrieved March 14, 2006, from **http://www.presentations.com/presentations/creation/article_display.jsp?vnu_content_id=1000875169**.

Chapter 12

1. David Green, curriculum director with Dale Carnegie & Associates in San Diego, quoted in D. Zielinski, "Perfect Practice," *Presentations*, May 2003. Retrieved from **www.presentations.com/presentations/delivery/article_display.jsp?vnu_content_id=1902958**.
2. R. Ailes, "You Are the Message," *Executive Communications*, January 1988, p. 1.
3. K. O. Locker, *Business and Administrative Communication*, 5th ed. (Boston: McGraw-Hill/Irwin, 2000), pp. 485–87.
4. M. Landis (Houser), "Taking the Butterflies Out of Speechmaking," *Creative Living* 9 (Spring 1980), p. 19.
5. M. Frank, *How to Get Your Point Across in Thirty Seconds or Less* (New York: Simon & Schuster, 1986), p. 64.
6. D. Zielinski, "Perfect Practice," *Presentations*, May 2003. Accessed March 25, 2006, from **http://www.presentations.com/presentations/delivery/article_display.jsp?vnu_content_id=1902958**.

7. Adapted from L. Fletcher, *How to Design and Deliver a Speech*, 4th ed. (New York: Harper & Row, 1990), pp. 347–51.
8. J. Grossman, "Resurrecting Auto Graveyards," *Inc.*, March 1983, pp. 73–80.
9. W. L. Haynes, "Public Speaking Pedagogy in the Media Age," *Communication Education* 38 (1990), pp. 89–102.
10. Ailes, "You Are the Message," p. 5.
11. P. J. Stella, "Are There Any Questions?" *Presentations*, November 1994, p. 12.
12. K. E. Cleveland, *Agree for Maximum Impact* (Victoria, BC: Pertinent Information, Inc.). Retrieved July 2, 2003, from **www.pertinent.com/articles/persuasion/kenrickP2.asp**.
13. I. Wallace and D. Wallechinsky, *Book of Lists* (New York: Bantam, 1977), p. 469.
14. "The Speaker May Look Calm but Survey Confirms Jitters," *Los Angeles Times*, September 13, 1981, pt. 5, p. 13.
15. M. B. Stein, J. R. Walker, Jr., and D. R. Forde, "Public-Speaking Fears in a Community Sample: Prevalence, Impact on Functioning, and Diagnostic Classification," *Archives of General Psychiatry* 53 (1996), pp. 169–74. See also "Addressing Fears," *Psychology Today* 29 (June 1996), p. 11.
16. A. K. Watson, "Taking the Sweat Out of Communication Anxiety," *Personnel Journal* 74 (1995), pp. 111–17.
17. See, for example, R. R. Behnke, C. R. Sawyer, and P. E. King, "The Communication of Public Speaking Anxiety," *Communication Education* 36 (April 1987), pp. 138–39; J. Burgoon, M. Pfau, T. Birk, and V. Manusov, "Nonverbal Communication Performance and Perceptions Associated with Reticence," *Communication Education* 36 (April 1987), pp. 119–30; and K. L. McEwan and G. Devins, "Increased Arousal in Emotional Anxiety Noticed by Others," *Journal of Abnormal Psychology* 92 (November 1983), pp. 417–21.
18. J. C. Humes, *Talk Your Way to the Top* (New York: McGraw-Hill, 1980), p. 135.
19. C. R. Sawyer and R. R. Hehnke, "State Anxiety Patterns for Public Speaking and the Behavior Inhibition System," *Communication Reports* 12 (1999), pp. 33–41.
20. D. Pogue, "Panic on the Podium," *Mac World*, January 1995, pp. 97–98.
21. T. E. Smith and A. Bainbridge, "Get Real: Does Practicing Speeches Before an Audience Improve Performance?" *Communication Quarterly* 54 (2006), pp. 111–25.
22. Zielinski, "Perfect Practice."
23. J. A. Daly, A. L. Vangelisti, and D. J. Weber, "Speech Anxiety Affects How People Prepare Speeches: A Protocol Analysis of the Preparation Processes of Speakers," *Communication Monographs* 62 (1995).
24. See, for example, A. Ellis, *A New Guide to Rational Living* (North Hollywood, CA: Wilshire Books, 1977); and A. Beck, *Cognitive Therapy and the Emotional Disorders* (New York: International Universities Press, 1976).
25. D. Baskerville, "Public Speaking Rule: #1 Have No Fear," *Black Enterprise* 24 (May 1994), pp. 76–81.
26. J. Ayres, T. Hopf, and E. Peterson, "A Test of Communication-Orientation Motivation (COM) Therapy," *Communication Reports* 13 (2000), pp. 35–44.

Chapter 13

1. Based on guidelines at **http://www.personal.psu.edu/faculty/p/m/pmk8/202D/feasibility-structure**.
2. J. C. Meister, *Corporate Universities*, revised ed. (New York: McGraw-Hill, 1998).
3. R. E. Wilkes, "Mortgage Megatrends," speech delivered at a meeting of the Austin Association of Professional Mortgage Women, Austin, TX, September 15, 1987, and reprinted in *Executive Speaker* 9 (1988), p. 9.
4. E. Graham, "High-Tech Training," *The Wall Street Journal*, February 9, 1990, p. R16.
5. M. Lowenstein and J. Spletzer, *Informal Training: A Review of Existing Data and Some New Evidence*, Report NLS 94–20 (Washington, DC: U.S. Bureau of Labor Statistics, 1994). Retrieved April 14, 2003, from **http://www.bls.gov/ore/pdf/nL940050.pdf**.
6. M. Molenda, J. A. Pershing, and C. M. Reigluth, "Designing Instructional Systems," in *The ASTD Training and Development Handbook*, ed. R. L. Craig (New York: McGraw-Hill), 1996, pp. 266–93.
7. K. Blanchard, "Managers Must Learn to Teach," *Today's Office* 22 (October 1987), pp. 8–9.
8. "How Lever's 'Hands-On' Demos Ignited Rep Enthusiasm," *Business Marketing Digest* 18 (Third Quarter 1993), pp. 29–32.
9. D. Bocher, "Chapter 11: Speak with Confidence," in *Powerful Presentations That Inform, Inspire and Persuade* (New York: McGraw-Hill, 2003).
10. J. Robinson, "Six Tips for Talking Technical When Your Audience Isn't," *Presentations* 11 (September 1997), p. 30.
11. Research summarized in T. H. Leahey and R. J. Harris, *Human Learning*, 2nd ed. (Englewood Cliffs, NJ: Prentice-Hall, 1989), p. 203.
12. Adapted from J. A. Daly and I. N. Eisenberg, *Presentations in Everyday Life* (Boston: Houghton Mifflin, 2001), p. 344.
13. C. Osgood, *Osgood on Speaking: How to Think on Your Feet without Falling on Your Face* (New York: Morrow, 1988), p. 39.
14. Adapted from G. C. Gard, "Accepting an Award: How to Be Gracious and Effective in 30 Seconds," *Toastmaster*, November 1988, p. 20.

Chapter 14

1. J. E. Lukaszewski, "You Can Become a Verbal Visionary," *Executive Speeches* 12 (August/September 1997), pp. 23–30.
2. R. Kiyosaki in the forward to B. Singer, *$ales Dogs* (New York: Warner Books, 2001).
3. A. Fisher, "Willy Loman Couldn't Cut It," *Fortune* (November 11, 1996), p. 210.
4. Kevin Hogan quoted in V. Alonzo, "5 Steps to Bigger Sales," *Incentive* 174 (October 2000), pp. 117–19.
5. *Specialty Speeches* (Mission Viejo, CA: Toastmasters International, 1992), p. 10.
6. Quoted in N. Rackham, *Spin Selling* (New York: McGraw-Hill, 1988), p. 51.
7. Adapted from R. B. Adler and G. Rodman, *Understanding Human Communication,* 8th ed. (New York: Oxford University Press, 2003), pp. 404–7.
8. M. Burgoon and M. D. Miller, "Communication and Influence," *Human Communication: Theory and Research,* eds. G. L. Dahnke and G. W. Clatterbuck (Belmont, CA: Wadsworth, 1990), pp. 233–34.
9. Aristotle, *The Rhetoric: A Theory of Civic Discourse.* Translated, with introduction, notes, and appendixes by George A. Kennedy (New York: Oxford University Press, 1991).
10. R. E. Petty and J. T. Cacioppo, "Involvement and Persuasion: Tradition versus Integration," *Psychological Bulletin* 107 (1990), pp. 367–74.
11. For a detailed review of credibility, see R. H. Gass and J. S. Seiter, *Persuasion, Social Influence and Compliance-Gaining* (Boston: Allyn & Bacon, 1999); and S. E. Lucas, *The Art of Public Speaking,* 7th ed. (New York: McGraw-Hill, 2001), pp. 400–5.
12. This discussion of fallacies is adapted from R. B. Adler and G. Rodman, *Understanding Human Communication,* 9th ed. (New York: Oxford University Press, 2006), pp. 441–42.
13. J. Sprague and D. Stuart, *The Speaker's Handbook,* 3rd ed. (Ft. Worth: Harcourt Brace Jovanovich, 1992). p. 172.
14. "At Lanier a Better Mousetrap Isn't Quite Enough," *Fortune* (February 26, 1979), pp. 74, 76.
15. D. J. O'Keefe, "Social Judgment Theory," in *Persuasion: Theory and Research* (Newbury Park, CA: Sage, 1990). See also "Social Judgment Theory" in E. M. Griffin, *A First Look at Communication Theory,* 7th ed. (New York: McGraw-Hill, 2006).
16. Griffin, *A First Look,* p. 194.
17. M. Burgoon and J. K. Burgoon, "Message Strategies in Influence Attempts," in *Communication and Behavior,* ed. G. J. Hanneman and W. J. McEwen (Reading, MA.: Addison-Wesley, 1975), p. 153.
18. M. Allen, "Determining the Persuasiveness of Message Sidedness: A Prudent Note about Utilizing Research Summaries," *Western Journal of Communication* 57 (1993), pp. 98–103. See also M. Allen et al., "Testing a Model of Message Sidedness: Three Replications," *Communication Monographs* 57 (1990), pp. 275–91.
19. For more information on cultural differences in styles of persuasion, see M. L. Lustig and J. Koester, *Intercultural Competence: Interpersonal Communication across Cultures,* 5th ed. (Boston: Pearson Education, 2006), pp. 239–48; and D. A. Lieberman, *Public Speaking in the Multicultural Environment* (Englewood Cliffs, NJ: Prentice Hall, 1994), p. 16.

Appendix

1. B. Lewis, "Make Sure You Actually Communicate Rather than Simply Offer Information," *InfoWorld,* November 22, 1999, p. 80.
2. S. Fung, "What Color Is Your Memo?" *Across the Board,* July/August 1999, p. 62.
3. J. Evers, *The Economy of Plain English* (Nanuet, NY: James L. Evers Associates) and "Five Phrases to Eliminate from Your Business Writing," *Manager's Intelligence Report,* September 2000, p. 1.
4. Michael Bugeja, "Say What You Mean," *Successful Meetings,* October 2000, p. 135.
5. "Trim the Fat from Your Business Writing with These Ideas," *Manager's Intelligence Report,* January 2000, p. 4.
6. J. Laabs, "Make It Your Business to Write Clearly," *Workforce,* September 2000, p. 134.
7. Patricia O'Conner, as quoted in ibid.
8. P. Lucrezio, "Companies Must Develop, Enforce E-Mail Usage Policies," *Capital District Business Review,* February 2, 2000, p. 37.
9. L. Baldrige and G. O'Brien, "Netiquette," *Kinko's Impress,* 2000, pp. 20–21.
10. E. O. Brownell, "Dress Your E-Mail for Success," retrieved May 31, 2001, from **http://powerpointers.com/showarticle.asp?articleid5378**.
11. A. Overholt, "Intel's Got (Too Much) Mail," *Fast Company,* March 2001, p. 56. Retrieved May 27, 2001, from **http://www.fastcompany.com/online/44/intel.html**.
12. A. Humphries, "E-mail for Careerists: Care Enough to Send the Very Best," September 29, 2000; retrieved May 28, 2001, from **http://www.cnn.com/2000/CAREER/corporateclass/09/29/email.protocol/index.html**.
13. K. C. Ivey, "E-Mail Eriquette," retrieved May 12, 2001, from **http://www.eeicommunications.com/eye/utw/98may.html**; and Baldrige and O'Brien, "Netiquette."
14. A. Nucifora, "High E-Mail Volume Points up Etiquette Needs," *Long Island Business News,* April 7, 2000, p. 48A.
15. Overholt, "Intel's Got (Too Much) Mail."
16. *The Job Hunters Guide,* prepared by the Bureau of Economic Research and Analysis, New Mexico Department of Labor, March 2000, pp. 10–13.

17. C. D. Bass, "Unusual Résumé May Net That Job," *Albuquerque Journal*, June 18, 2000, p. I-1.
18. "Looking for a Job While You're Employed," *Planning Job Choices: 2000*, National Association of Colleges and Employers, p. 21.
19. W. S. Enelow, "What Do Employers Really Want in a Résumé?" retrieved June 22, 2001, from **http://www.jobweb.com/catapult/enelow-r.html**.
20. R. Smith, "eRésumés 101: Choosing Your Best Electronic Résumé Format," retrieved June 5, 2001, from **http://www.eresumes.com/tut_eresume.html**.
21. S. J. Gerson and S. M. Gerson, *Technical Writing: Process and Product*, 3rd ed. (Upper Saddle River, NJ: Prentice Hall, 2000), pp. 167–69.
22. Yana Parker, "Guide for a Scanner-Friendly Resume," retrieved on June 11, 2001, from **http://www.damngood.com/jobseekers/ScanGuide.html**.
23. Ibid.
24. K. Hansen, "Common Sense Steps Can Prevent Employer Backlash against Online Résumés," includes some citing of S. Armour, *USA Today*, July 15, 1999. Retrieved June 13, 2001, from **http://www.quintcareers.com/online_resume_guide.html**.
25. M. Tullier, "The Art and Science of Writing Cover Letters: The Best Way to Make a First Impression," retrieved June 22, 2001, from **http://resume.monster.com/coverletter/coverletters**.

credits

Text

Chapter 1: (Table 1–1) Reprinted from "Job Outlook 2005", with permission of the National Association of Colleges and Employers, copyright holder; (Ethical Challenge, p. 12) Adapted from the quiz "How Ethical Are You?", *Business Ethics 03/04*, 15th ed., John E. Richardson, ed., Guilford, CT: McGraw-Hill/Dushkin, 2003, p. 200; (Career Tip, p. 15) From *Getting Praised, Raised and Recognized* by Muriel Solomon. Reprinted with permission of Prentice Hall Direct, an imprint of Pearson Education Co.; (Fig. 1–3) Reprinted from *Organizational Dynamics* 30, No. 2., R. Cross et al., "Knowing What We Know: Supporting Knowledge Creation and Sharing in Social Networks", pp. 100–120, Copyright © 2001, with permission from Elsevier; (On Your Feet, p. 24) Adapted from Marie Wallace, "The Elevator Speech—It's There for You," retrieved September 22, 2005 from Law Library Resource Exchange, **www.llrx.com**; (Career Tip, p. 29) Based on Frank Thorsberg, "Ten Tips for Proper IM Manners," AOL Computer Center, August 12, 2002, and Kate Lorenz, "Six Rules for IM-ing at Work," September 29, 2005.

Chapter 2: (Fig. 2–1) From "The Changing American Pie, 1999 and 2025." Population Research Bureau, Washington, DC, 2000. **www.prb.org**. Reprinted by permission; (Figs. 2–2 and 2–3) From Fons Trompenaars, *Riding the Waves of Culture* (McGraw-Hill/Irwin, 1994). Reproduced with permission of The McGraw-Hill Companies, Inc.; (Table 2–2) From *Intercultural Communication: A Reader*, 8th ed., by Samovar/ Porter. © 1997. Reprinted with permission of Wadsworth, a division of Thomson Learning: **www.thomsonrights.com**. Fax 800-730-2215 and Richard Porter; (Table 2–3) Adapted from *Cultures and Organizations: Software of the Mind* by G. Hofstede, New York: McGraw-Hill, 1997; (Table 2–4) Adapted from M. P. Orbe and T. M. Harris, *Interracial Communication: Theory into Practice* (Belmont, CA: Wadsworth, 2001), p. 65. Reprinted by permission of Mark P. Orbe; (Self-Assessment) From P. C. Earley and E. Mosakowski, "Cultural Intelligence," *Harvard Business Review*, October 2004, p. 143. Reprinted by permission; (Fig. 2–4) Conceptualized by Chris Maxwell and Ann M. Greenhalgh, Undergraduate Leadership Program, The Wharton School, University of Pennsylvania. Adapted from *Module 6: Intercultural Communication for Business*, by O'Rourke/Yarbrough. © 2005. Reprinted with permission of South-Western, a division of Thomson Learning: **www.thomsonrights.com**. Fax 800-730-2215; (Table 2–5) Reprinted from *Managing Cultural Differences*, 2nd ed., by Philip R. Harris and Robert T. Moran, pp. 245–247, Copyright © 1987, with permission from Elsevier; (Ethical Challenge, p. 63) From *Bottom Line/Business* 1 (September 1995). Courtesy of Texas Instruments.

Chapter 3: (Fig. 3–1) From *Perspectives on Listening* by A. D. Wolvin and C. G. Coakley. Copyright © 1993 by A. D. Wolvin and C. G. Coakley. Reproduced with permission of Greenwood Publishing Group, Inc., Westport, CT; (Self-Assessment) From *Listen Up* by L. Barker and K. Watson, Copyright © 2000 by the author and reprinted by permission of St. Martin's Press, LLC; (Career Tip, p. 89) From *Listen Up* by L. Barker and K. Watson, Copyright © 2000 by the author and reprinted by permission of St. Martin's Press, LLC.

Chapter 4: (Fig. 4–1) Adapted from *The Meaning of Meaning* by C. K. Ogden and I. A. Richards, New York: Harcourt Brace, 1923, p. 11. Reprinted by permission; (Table 4–1) From Steven Altman, Enzo Valenzi, and Richard M. Hodgetts, *Organizational Behavior: Theory and Practice*. Reprinted by permission of Steven Altman; (Table 4–3) Reprinted by permission of the College of Business Administration, Business Communication, University of Northern Iowa: Cedar Falls; (Self-Assessment) Adapted from V. P. Richmond, J. C. McCroskey, and A. D. Johnson, "Development of the Nonverbal Immediacy Scale (NIS): Measures of Self- and Other-Reported Nonverbal Immediacy." Copyright 2003 from *Communication Quarterly*. Reproduced by permission of Taylor & Francis Group, LLC., **http://taylorandfrancis.com**.

Chapter 5: (Table 5–1) Adapted from J. M. H. Fritz, "How Do I Dislike Thee? Let Me Count the Ways: Constructing Impressions of Troublesome Others at Work," *Management Communication Quarterly* 15 (2003), pp. 410–438. Copyright © 2003 by Management Communication Quarterly. Reprinted by permission of Sage Publications; (Table 5–3) Adapted from Hendrie Weisinger, *The Critical Edge: How to Criticize Up and Down Your Organization and Make It Pay Off*. Little Brown & Co. Copyright © 1989 by Hendrie Weisinger, Ph.D. Permission granted by Inkwell Management, New York, NY; (Career Tip, p. 147) "The Art of Apology" by Patrick J. Kiger. Reprinted with permission, *Workforce* (October 2004). Copyright

Crain Communications, Inc. **www.workforce.com**; (Table 5–4) From "Toward Multi-Dimensional Values in Teaching: The Example of Conflict Behavior," by Kenneth W. Thomas, *Academy of Management Review*. Copyright 1987 by Academy of Management. Reproduced with permission of Academy of Management in the format Texbook via Copyright Clearance Center; (Career Tip, p. 156) From Robert Bacal, *The Complete Idiot's Guide to Dealing with Difficult Employees* (Indianapolis: Alpha Books, 2000); and Robert M. Bramson, *Coping with Difficult People* (New York: Anchor/Doubleday, 1981); (Career Tip, p. 161) Steven Covey, "Seven Methods of Influence," *Incentive* 17 (October 1996), p. 22.

Chapter 6: (Table 6–2) From Gerald L. Wilson and H. Lloyd Goodall, Jr., *Interviewing in Context*, New York: McGraw-Hill, 1991. Reprinted by permission of Gerald L. Wilson.

Chapter 7: (Table 7–1) Adapted from C. J. Stewart and W. B. Cash, Jr., *Interviewing: Principles and Practices*, 4th ed., Copyright © 1995, The McGraw-Hill Companies, Inc. Reproduced with permission; (Table 7–2) From Victor R. Lindquist, *The Northwestern Endicott Report 1988*. Used with permission of Northwestern University; (Self-Assessment) Adapted from Ron and Caryl Krannich, *Interview for Success: A Practical Guide to Increasing Job Interviews, Offers, and Salaries*, 8th ed. Manassas Park, VA: Impact Publications, 2003, pp. 12–17; (Career Tip, p. 233) From J. Flesher, "How to Clean Up Your Digital Dirt Before It Trashes Your Job Search." *Career Journal*, January 17, 2006.

Chapter 8: (Table 8–1) Adapted from J. D. Rothwell, *In Mixed Company*, 5th ed. (Belmont, CA: Wadsworth, 2004), p. 76; and A. P. Hare, "Roles, Relationships, and Groups in Organizations: Some Conclusions and Recommendations," *Small Group Research* 34 (April 2003), pp. 123–154; (Career Tip, p. 259) Kathleen Melymuka, "Tips for Teams," *Computerworld* 31, April 28, 1997, p. 72. J. Dan Rothwell, *In Mixed Company: Communicating in Small Groups and Teams*, 6th ed., Belmont, CA: Wadsworth, 2007, pp. 386–387; (Fig. 8–1) From *Leadership Dilemmas—Grid Solutions* by Robert R. Blake and Anne Adams McCanse (formerly the *Managerial Grid* by Robert R. Blake and Jane S. Mouton). Houston: Gulf Publishing Company, p. 29. Copyright 1991 by Scientific Methods, Inc. Reproduced by permission of Grid International Inc.; (Career Tip, p. 263) Reprinted by permission of Waveland Press, Inc. from M. Z. Hackman and C. E. Johnson, *Leadership: A Communication Perspective*, Long Grove, IL: Waveland Press, Inc., 2004. All rights reserved; (Table 8–2) From Ed Kur, "The Faces Model of High Performing Team Development", *Management Development Review* 9 (6), 1996, pp. 32–41. Adapted by permission of Emerald Group Publishing Limited; (Figure 8–2) From Gloria J. Galanes, Katherine Adams, and John K. Brilhart, *Effective Group Discussion*, 11th ed., Copyright © 2004, The McGraw-Hill Companies, Inc. Reproduced with permission; (Table 8–3) From Kenneth D. Benne and Paul Sheats, "Functional Roles of Group Members," *Journal of Social Issues* 4 (1948), pp. 41–49. Used with permission of Blackwell Publishers, Ltd.; (Table 8–4) Research summarized in S. A. Wheelan et al., "Member Perceptions of Internal Group Dynamics and Productivity," *Small Group Research* 29 (1998), pp. 371-393; (Table 8–5) From Joel A. C. Baum, "Avoiding Common Team Problems," HomePage for Game Theory and Competitive Strategy MGT 2056—Fall 2003, **http://www.rotman.utoronto.ca/~baum/mgt2003/avoid.html**, retrieved August 26, 2003.

Chapter 9: (Career Tip, p. 300) Adapted from S. M. Lippincott, *Meetings: Do's, Don'ts and Donuts*, 2nd ed. (Pittsburgh, PA: Lighthouse Point Press, 1999); (Fig. 9–2) From John E. Tropman, "The Agenda Bell." Copyright © John E. Tropman. Used with permission; (Career Tip, p. 307) Adapted from Ana M. Keep, *Moving Meetings* (New York: Irwin, 1994).

Chapter 10: (Career Tip, p. 332) Adapted from LaTresa Pearson, "Think Globally, Present Locally," *Presentations*, April 1996, pp. 20–27, 68; and Kathy Schmidt, "How to Speak So You're Open to Interpretation," *Presentations*, December 1999, p. 126; (Fig. 10–1) From G. L. Morrisey, T. L. Sechrest, and W. B. Warman, *Loud and Clear*, 4th ed., p. 146-7. Copyright © 1997 by Perseus Books Publishing, L.L.C. Reprinted by permission of Basic Books, a member of Perseus Books, L.L.C.

Chapter 11: (Fig. 11–7) U. S. Bureau of Labor Statistics; (Fig. 11–8) Source for projections: CIBC World Markets; (Career Tip, p. 394) Based on suggestions by Tom Chronster, "Technology Should Not Keep Audiences in the Dark," *Presentations*, May 2002, p. 62; (Fig. 11–13) In "MARS 2003 OTC/DTC survey," *USA Today*, June 11, 2003, pp. A1;

Chapter 12: (Career Tip, p. 409) Adapted from M. Mobley, "Color Code to Improve Pacing and Flow," *Presentations*, May 2003, p. 34; (Career Tip, p. 412) Adapted from J. A. Daly and I. N. Enleberg, *Presentations in Everyday Life*, 2nd ed. (Boston: Houghton Mifflin, 2005), p. 263; (Table 12–1) From D. Bocher, *Speak with Confidence: Powerful Presentations That Inform, Inspire and Persuade*. Copyright © 2003 The McGraw-Hill Companies, Inc. Used with permission; (Career Tip, p. 419) From Tom Antion, *Great Speaking* 4, no. 6 (April 24, 2002), retrieved from **http://www.antion.com/ezine/v4n6.txt**; Susan Berkley, "Microphone Tips," *Great Speaking* 4, no. 7 (May 14, 2002), retrieved from **http://www.antion.com/ezine/v4n7.txt**; and Renee Grant-Williams, "Speak Up!" *Women in Business* 54, no. 2 (March/April 2002), p. 38.

Chapter 13: (Fig. 13–2) From National Training Labs Institute. Reprinted by permission of NTL® Institute for Applied Behavioral Sciences; (Career Tip, p. 456) Tom Antion and Judy Shaw, "Tag Team Signals," *Great Speaking* 3, no. 20 (October 24, 2001).

Chapter 14: (Career Tip, p. 471) Based on information in Anne Fisher, "How to Get the Raise You Deserve," *Fortune* 138 (September 7, 1998), p. 169; Robin Ryan, "How to Ask for a Raise—And Get It," *Money* 26 (December 1997), p. 28; and Jane Thomas, "How to Request a Raise," *Women in Business* 51 (January–February 1999), p. 23.

Appendix: (Fig. A–3) From *Job Choices: Diversity Edition 2003* (Bethlehem, PA: National Association of Colleges and Employers), p. 54. Retrieved from **www.naceweb.org**; (Fig. A–5) From **http://www.jobweb.com**; (Figs. A–6 and A–7) From **www.quintcareers.com.**

(Table A–1) From Rebecca Smith, "eResumes 101: Choosing Your Best Electronic Résumé Format," retrieved June 5 2001, from **http://www.eresumes.com/tut_eresume.html**; and S. J. Gerson and S. M. Gerson, *Technical Writing: Process and Product*, 3rd ed. (Upper Saddle River, NJ: Prentice Hall, 2000), pp. 167–169.

Photos

(p. 5) © Royalty-Free/Corbis; **(p. 10)** © Kevin Radford / SuperStock; **(p. 20)** © PhotoDisc/Punchstock; **(p. 39)** © David McGlynn/TaxiGetty Images; **(p. 45)** © Helen King/CORBIS; **(p. 50)** © Dale O'Dell/CORBIS; **(p. 54)** © Thinkstock/Punchstock; **(p. 66)** © Bill Varie/Workbookstock; **(p. 75)** © Powerstock / SuperStock; **(p. 80)** © PhotoDisc/Punchstock; **(p. 88)** © Camelot/Amana Images/Getty Images; **(p. 99)** © Antonio Mo/Taxi/Getty Images; **(p. 116)** Jon Feingersh/ Masterfile; **(p. 127)** © Powerstock / SuperStock; **(p. 137)** © Roy Botterell/Taxi/Getty Images; **(p. 143)** © PhotoDisc/Getty Images; **(p. 148)** © Anton Vengo / SuperStock; **(p. 159)** © Jonnie Miles / SuperStock; **(p. 173)** © Zia Soleil/Iconica/Getty Images; **(p. 185)** © Jiang Jing/ Superstock; **(p. 189)** © age fotostock / SuperStock; **(p. 201)** © Brand X Pictures/Punchstock; **(p. 215)** © John Lund/The Image Bank/Getty Images; **(p. 232)** © Jean-Yves Bruel/Masterfile; **(p. 253)** © Ken Davies/Masterfile; **(p. 255)** © Paul Vozdic/Iconica/Getty Images; **(p. 260)** © WireImageStock/Masterfile; **(p. 283)** © Noel Hendrickson/Masterfile; **(p. 293)** © Powerstock / SuperStock; **(p. 297)** © Digital Vision/Getty Images; **(p. 306)** © Goodshoot/Punchstock; **(p. 325)** © Deborah Davis/Photographer's Choice/Getty Images; **(p. 329)** © Digital Vision/Punchstock; **(p. 343)** © James Baigrie /The Image Bank/Getty Images; **(p. 351)** © Tom Collicott/Masterfile; **(p. 371)** © Creatas/Punchstock; **(p. 379)** © Linda Lewis/StockFood Creative/Getty Images; **(p. 405)** © Colin Anderson/Blend Images/Getty Images; **(p. 408)** © Comstock/ Punchstock; **(p. 418)** © PhotoDisc/Getty Images; **(p. 427)** © Max Oppenheim/The Image Bank/Getty Images; **(p. 433)** © Jon Smyth/SuperStock; **(p. 441)** © Zia Soleil/Iconica/Getty Images; **(p. 454)** © PhotoDisc/Punchstock; **(p. 462)** © Infocus International/The Image Bank/Getty Images; **(p. 469)** © Digital Vision/Punchstock; **(p. 475)** © Masterfile; **(p. 478)** © Karen Beard/The Image Bank/Getty Images; **(p. 484)** © White Packert/Photonica/Getty Images

index

C

E

F

I

Q

R

S

T

X

Y

Z